SCARCE AND VALUABLE TRACTS

ON

COMMERCE.

SELECT COLLECTION

OF

SCARCE AND VALUABLE TRACTS

ON

COMMERCE,

FROM THE ORIGINALS OF

EVELYN, DEFOE, RICHARDSON, TUCKER, TEMPLE, AND OTHERS.

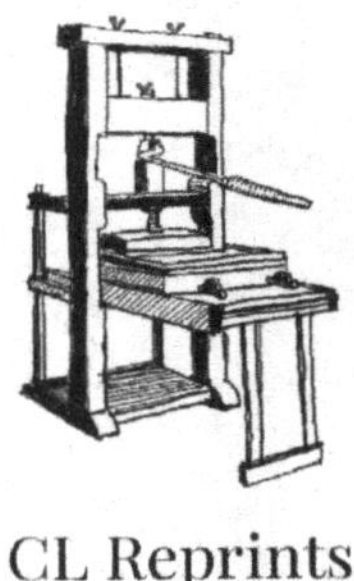

CL Reprints

CL Press | Fraser Institute

Published by CL PRESS
A Project of the Fraser Institute
1770 Burrard Street, 4th Floor
Vancouver, BC V6J 3G7 Canada
www.clpress.net

Scarce and Valuable Tracts on

Commerce

By J.R. McCulloch

Scarce and Valuable Tracts on Commerce
was originally published in 1859 by Lord Overstone.

First printed: February 2024

ISBN: 978-1-957698-14-4

Foreword by CL Press, 2024

The present volume was edited by a man with a calling to expound and promote the teachings of political economy. John Ramsay McCulloch (1789–1864) understood the truths and conclusions of political economy to run along classical-liberal lines, in the tradition of Adam Smith. For more than 40 years McCulloch promoted use of the word *liberal* in its original political sense, which is to say its Smithian sense.

Part of McCulloch's calling was to recover the early developments of liberal political economy. He avidly collected books, especially on economic topics. His collection of 8,000 books was perhaps the best collection of the kind of his time.

McCulloch was again a proselytizer, laboring to republish the old literature he found "scarce and valuable." The present volume reprints one of six volumes compiled by McCulloch, volumes consisting of writings from the 17th, 18th, and early 19th centuries. McCulloch wanted people to know of such works, some going back more than 200 years before his own time, works that helped to develop political economy. Financial assistance from Lord Overstone helped McCulloch to edit and publish the six volumes:

1. *Early English Tracts on Commerce* (1856)   –& CL Press 2024
2. *Scarce and Valuable Tracts on Money* (1856)
3. *Scarce and Valuable Tracts on Paper Currency and Banking* (1857)
4. *Scarce and Valuable Tracts on the National Debt and the Sinking Fund* (1857)
5. *Scarce and Valuable Tracts on Commerce* (1859)   –& CL Press 2024
6. *Scarce and Valuable Economical Tracts* (1859)   –& CL Press 2024

The bolded titles are now reprinted by CL Press.

All six of the volumes were republished in 1995 by the publisher Pickering & Chatto, titled *Classical Writings on Economics*, Volumes 1–6. The first volume contains a new general introduction by Denis Patrick O'Brien, who had earlier published *J. R. McCulloch: A Study in*

Classical Economics (1970). O'Brien also edited McCulloch's collected works and Overstone's correspondence.

O'Brien's 1995 general introduction helps with the authorship of the items. We now list the contents of three volumes newly reprinted by CL Press. In the following listing we modernize spellings and abridge the titles for the sake of conciseness:

Early English Tracts on Commerce (1856)

Contents:

1. A DISCOURSE OF TRADE (1621) by **Thomas Mun**
2. A DISCOURSE OF FOREIGN TRADE (1641) by **Lewes Roberts**
3. ENGLAND'S TREASURE BY FOREIGN TRADE (1664) by **Thomas Mun**
4. ENGLAND'S INTEREST AND IMPROVEMENT (1673) by **Samuel Fortrey**
5. ENGLAND'S GREATEST HAPPINESS; OR, A DIALOGUE BETWEEN *CONTENT* AND *COMPLAINT* (1677), *authorship unknown*
6. *BRITANNIA LANGUENS*, OR A DISCOURSE OF TRADE (1680) by *authorship unknown, possibly* **William Petty**
7. DISCOURSE UPON TRADE (1691) by **Dudley North** (the first part perhaps written by **Roger North**)
8. CONSIDERATIONS ON THE EAST-INDIA TRADE (1701), by (probably) **Henry Martyn**

Scarce and Valuable Tracts on Commerce (1859)

Contents:

1. OBSERVATIONS TOUCHING TRADE AND COMMERCE WITH OTHER NATIONS (*circa* 1610) perhaps by **Walter Raleigh**, perhaps by **John Keymore**
2. NAVIGATION AND COMMERCE, THEIR ORIGINAL AND PROGRESS (1674) by **John Evelyn**
3. EXTRACTS FROM A PLAN OF THE ENGLISH COMMERCE (1730) by **Daniel Defoe**

Scarce and Valuable Economical Tracts (1859)

Contents:

9. A Dissertation on the Poor Laws (1776) by **Joseph Townsend**
10. Thoughts and Details on Scarcity (written 1795, pub. 1800) by **Edmund Burke**
11. An Inquiry into the Prohibition of the Use of Grain in the Distilleries (1808) by **Archibald Bell**

In her entry on McCulloch in the *Oxford Dictionary of National Biography*, Phyllis Deane wrote: "It is now apparent that for most of the half-century preceding his death [in 1864] this hard-working, largely self-educated Scot did more than any other economist of this day to introduce the new science of political economy to an interested public." The volumes now reprinted by CL Press show the enduring value of McCulloch's service to those interested in the history of economic thought and the historical arc of liberalism.

₊ This volume has been printed by Lord Overstone for distribution among his friends: it has been edited by J. R. McCulloch, Esq.

With Lord Overstone's compliments

PREFACE.

THE contents of this volume are alike various and interesting.

1. The first article " Observations touching Trade and Commerce with the Hollanders, &c.," is said to have been presented to James I, by Sir Walter Raleigh, to whom it is usually ascribed. It is doubtful, however, whether he was really its author. Oldys, in his Life of Raleigh, appears disposed to believe, that it was the work of a Mr. John Kymer, who published " Observations on the Dutch Fishery," in, or about, the year 1601. But whatever doubts may exist in regard to its paternity, it certainly dates as far back as the reign of James; and is interesting, from its being one of the earliest, as well as the best known of the Tracts in which the extravagant and often repeated statements were put forth in regard to the magnitude of the herring fishery carried on by the Dutch. It tells us, for example, that about 20,000 ships and vessels, and 400,000 hands were employed in the fishery on our coasts, of which by far the largest portion belonged to Holland! And though the extreme exaggeration of this statement be too obvious to require notice, it was long considered as of undoubted authority, and was invariably quoted to conciliate the pub-

lic support to the many projects that were formerly prevalent, for improving the fisheries. But it would not be fair to judge the tract by this single specimen. It contains some judicious observations in regard to the circumstances which had contributed to the growth of the trade and wealth for which Holland was then so famous.

2. The next tract, written by John Evelyn, S.R.S., author of the Sylva and other publications, appeared in 1674. It contains a short sketch of the rise and progress of Navigation and Commerce, followed by a vindication of his Britannic Majesty's claim to the "dominion of the sea." Though brief and superficial, the first is the most valuable portion of the work. The latter, however, is curious, inasmuch as it shows the nature and extent of the claims to the exclusive navigation and fishery of the surrounding portions of the ocean that we were accustomed to put forward, and the sort of arguments by which it was sought to justify the wars to which they sometimes led. The claims, indeed, were not of a description that could be conceded by any really independent state; and the reasoning in their defence, though supported by a great display of learning, is as flimsy as can be easily imagined.* It is useless, however, to insist on this point, for Evelyn himself admits, in a letter to Pepys, the secretary to the Admiralty (19th September, 1682), that he had written this portion

---

* See especially the *Mare Clausum*, of the famous John Selden, folio, London, 1635. This work, written in answer to the *Mare Liberum* of Grotius, was translated into English by Marchmont Nedham, and published with Appendixes, in folio, in 1652.

of his work to recommend himself by bolstering up our pretensions which he proceeds to show were entirely unfounded!* And, no doubt, he was entitled, after this acknowledgment, to tell Pepys that "wise men" should be very suspicious of all histories, unless it can be demonstrated that their authors had no interest of their own, or their superiors, or public cry, to support. So much for the straightforwardness and honesty of this model courtier of the reign of Charles II.†

3. This article consists of extracts from a "Plan of the English Commerce," published in 1728, of which Defoe is known to have been the author. Though desultory it is well written. In the extracts we have laid before the reader, the influence of trade and industry in promoting the well-being of all classes, is forcibly illustrated. It says little for the public taste, that Defoe's work should have been almost entirely neglected‡, while the very inferior work of Gee, published nearly at the same time, enjoyed a large share of popularity§. Defoe truly represented the trade of the kingdom as thriving; whereas, according to Gee, it was in a declining and, in some respects, ruinous condition. But it has been often re-

---

* Memoirs of the Life and Writings of Evelyn, Vol. ii, p. 260 Ed. 1818.

† We have corrected several obvious blunders in the text of this work, and have subjoined a few notes.

‡ The second edition is merely the first with a new title page and an Appendix.

§ The work of Gee, "The Trade and Navigation of Great Britain Considered," was first published in 1730. A sixth edition was published at Glasgow in 1755.

marked that, when conscious of the contrary, people are rather well pleased to be reckoned unprosperous.

4. We come next to the remarkable " Essay on the Causes of the Decline of Foreign Trade," originally published in quarto in 1744. It is singular, that notwithstanding its great ability and popularity, we have no certain information in regard to its author. It is one of the few works that have been distinguished by being referred to by Adam Smith, who ascribes it without any hesitation to Sir Matthew Decker, M.P., one of the most eminent merchants of the time. But it is doubtful whether Smith had sufficient grounds for this conclusion. A pamphlet entitled " Serious Considerations on the several High Duties which the Nation labours under," published in 1748, was directly ascribed to Decker by Massie and others, who replied to it, and by the public generally. And supposing, of which indeed there seems to be little doubt, that the pamphlet was justly attributed to Decker, he could hardly be the author of the Essay; for though published nearly at the same time, and containing each a novel plan of taxation, these plans are as different as possible; that of the pamphlet being a proposal to replace all taxes by a tax on houses, and that of the Essay to replace them by a license duty, to be laid on the consumers of luxuries in proportion to their supposed incomes. It may also be stated, that Decker died in March 1749, and that the second edition of the Essay, from which this reprint has been made, published in 1750, purports to be revised by the author. And further, a well-informed contemporary, Mr. Francis Fauquier, author of a tract on Ways

and Means, published in 1757, states distinctly that the Essay now before the reader was written by a Mr. Richardson; and in this instance we are inclined to prefer his authority to that even of Adam Smith.

But to whomsoever we may be indebted for this Essay, it is one of no common merit. The hypothesis, indeed, on which it is founded, that trade was then in a declining state, is wholly erroneous. But the measures proposed by the author to obviate this imaginary evil and to extend and improve trade, are at once liberal and judicious. He is an intelligent and uncompromising enemy of all sorts of monopolies, restrictions, and prohibitions. There are, indeed, but few works, in which the injurious influence of the protective system, and the advantages of freedom are so clearly and ably set forth.

5. There is, luckily, no difficulty in regard to the author of the " Essay on the Advantages and Disadvantages which respectively attend France and Great Britain in regard to Trade, with Proposals, &c." It is the work of Josiah Tucker, A.M. (afterwards D.D.), Dean of Gloucester, and was published about 1750. It is well written; and is interesting from the valuable information it embodies respecting the condition of the countries to which it especially refers. Though too ready to invoke the aid of the legislature, and too much disposed to place confidence in police regulations, Tucker's ideas are in the main enlightened and liberal. And most part of his proposals, such as that for a legislative union with Ireland, for the adoption of the warehousing system, the abolition of exclusive companies, the introduction of

canals, &c., have been adopted. Tucker was among the first to discern the true nature of the war with America; and he had the boldness to proclaim that it would be good policy to emancipate the colonies. But the Tract now reprinted, though one of the earliest, is probably the best of his numerous publications.*

We have substituted for the Appendix in Tucker's Tract, which consists of an extract from the "Essay on the Causes of the Decline of Foreign Trade," a letter of Smollett on the state of France in 1765. It is interesting from its foreshadowing that tremendous Revolution of which that kingdom was at no very distant period destined to be the theatre.

6. This article consists of "Proposals made by His Highness the Prince of Orange to the States General of Holland for Redressing and Amending the Trade of the Republic."

The commerce and navigation of Holland appear to have attained to a maximum about 1670, after which æra they became first stationary and then gradually declined, the decline becoming more apparent after the Treaty of Utrecht in 1713. From this time down to the middle of the century the state of trade attracted much attention, and several inquiries were made into the causes of its falling off, and the methods by which they might be countervailed. But these having had little or no effect, the

---

* The Bishop of Gloucester, Warburton, said of Tucker that trade was his religion, and religion his trade. Had he been inclined to retaliate, Tucker might have said that controversy was the bishop's religion, and religion his trade.

subject was taken up by Government, and the Stadtholder, William IV, having obtained the advice and assistance of the most intelligent and eminent merchants, they prepared a Dissertation or Statement, in which they set forth what, in their estimation, had been the principal causes of the extraordinary growth of trade and industry in Holland and of their subsequent decline, and what were the means most likely to restore them to their former flourishing condition. This Dissertation, having been submitted to the States General, was ordered to be printed; and in the same year, 1751, it was translated into English and published in London in the form now laid before the reader.

This paper is one of the most valuable and important of the class to which it belongs. Several of its suggestions were adopted, and had the anticipated effect. But owing to the pressure of the very heavy load of taxes, which had grown out of her long struggle with Spain and her subsequent contests with France and England, and still more, perhaps, to the growth of trade and navigation in the surrounding States, Holland has not been able to recover any portion of her old commercial preponderance. She is still, however, despite the many vicissitudes she has undergone, the wealthiest and most industrious country of Europe. And her present, no less than her former, state affords the most striking example to be met with of the capacity of industry and economy to overcome all sorts of difficulties.

It is singular that this excellent dissertation does not seem to have attracted any attention in this country. It has long been extremely scarce.

7. In 1756, a prize, given by Lord Viscount Townshend to the University of Cambridge, was adjudged to Mr. William Bell, M.A., for a "Dissertation on the Causes which principally contribute to render Nations Populous, and on the Effects of their Populousness on their Trade." This Dissertation, though the best, probably, of those submitted to the decision of the judges, had but slender claims to the distinction by which it was honoured. It is confused and contradictory; and consists of little more than worn out homilies in praise of virtue, simplicity, agriculture, and so forth, with tirades against luxury and "the elegancies of life," and attempts to show the mischievous and dangerous nature of commerce. It appears to have made little impression. But it was not to be expected that such a publication should emanate from one of the Universities without being noticed; and it was both speedily and completely answered in the Tract now reprinted, "A Vindication of Commerce and the Arts, &c.," by I. B., M.D., London, 1758.

The I. B. is pseudonymous, the author being a Mr. William Temple, a clothier, of Trowbridge.* His refutation of Bell leaves nothing to be desired; and he displays throughout much knowledge and acuteness, and expresses himself clearly and forcibly.

8. The last of the reprints in this volume, is entitled " New and Old Principles of Trade Compared," London, 1788. The new principles referred to are those of Smith,

---

* See letter of Dean Tucker to Lord Kames, in Woodhouselee's Life of the latter, III., 161.

the " Wealth of Nations " having been published in 1776. The comparison is fairly made, and the superior advantageousness of the new principles is shown in a very satisfactory manner.

It would be useless, even if our space permitted, to add to this collection. The great principles of sound commercial policy were now fully explained and laid before the public, and while they have not since been questioned by any writer of authority, the widest experience has fully confirmed their truth.

CONTENTS.

OBSERVATIONS

TOUCHING

TRADE and COMMERCE

With the

HOLLANDER, and other Nations.

Presented to King JAMES,
By Sir Walter RALEIGH, Knt.

Wherein is proved,

That our Sea and Land Commodities serve to inrich and strengthen other Countries against our own.

From **RALEIGH'S** *Miscellaneous Works,*

London, 1751.

ACCORDING *to my duty, I am imboldened to put your Majesty in mind, that about fourteen or fifteen years past, I presented you a book of extraordinary importance for the honour and profit of your Majesty and posterity; and doubting that it hath been laid aside, and not considered of, I am encouraged (under your Majesty's pardon) to present unto you one more, consisting of five propositions: Neither are they grounded upon vain or idle grounds, but upon the fruition of those wonderful blessings wherewith God hath endued your Majesty's sea and land; by which means you may not only inrich and fill your coffers, but also increase such might and strength, (as shall appear, if it may stand with your Majesty's good liking to put the same in execution in the true and right form:) so that there is no doubt but it will make you in short time a Prince of such power, so great, as shall make all the Princes your neighbours, as well glad of your friendship, as fearful to offend you. That this is so, I humbly desire that your Majesty will vouchsafe to peruse this advertisement with that care and judgment which God hath given you.*

Most humbly praying your Majesty, that whereas I presented these five propositions together, as in their own natures, jointly depending one of another, and so linked together, as the distraction of any one will be an apparent maim and disabling to the rest; that your Majesty would be pleased that they may not be separated, but all handled together jointly and severally, by Commissioners, with as much speed and secrecy as can be, and made fit to be reported to your Majesty, whereby I may be the better able to perform to your Highness that which I have promised,

and

and will perform upon my life, if I be not prevented by some that may seek to hinder the honour and profit of your Majesty for their own private ends.

The true ground, course and form, herein mentioned, shall appear how other countries make themselves powerful and rich in all kinds, by merchandize, manufactory, and fulness of trade, having no commodities in their own country growing to do it withal.

And herein likewise shall appear, how easy it is to draw the wealth and strength of other countries to your kingdom, and what royal, rich, and plentiful means God hath given this land to do it (which cannot be denied) for support of traffick, and continual employment of your people, for replenishing of your Majesty's coffers.

And if I were not fully assured to improve your native commodities, with other traffick, three millions of pounds more yearly than now they are, and to bring not only to your Majesty's coffers, within the space of two or three years, near two millions of pounds, but to increase your revenues many thousands yearly, and to please and greatly profit your people, I would not have undertaken so great a work: All which will grow by advancement of all kind of merchandizing to the uttermost, thereby to bring manufactory into the kingdom, and to set on work all sorts of people in the realm, as other nations do, which raise their greatness by the abundance of your native commodities, whilst we are parling and disputing whether it be good for us or not.

OBSER-

OBSERVATIONS

TOUCHING

TRADE and COMMERCE, &c.

May it please your most Excellent Majesty,

I HAVE diligently, in my travels, observed how the countries herein mentioned do grow potent with abundance of all things to serve themselves and other nations, where nothing groweth; and that their never dryed fountains of wealth, by which they raise their estate to such an admirable height, as that they are at this day even a wonder to the world, proceedeth from your Majesty's seas and lands.

I thus moved, began to dive into the depth of their policies and circumventing practices, whereby they drain, and still covet to exhaust, the wealth and coin of this kingdom, and so with our own commodities to weaken us, and finally beat us quite out of trading in other countries. I found that they more fully obtained these their purposes by their convenient privileges, and settled constitutions, than *England* with all the laws, and superabundance of home-bred commodities which God hath vouchsafed your sea and land: And these, and other mentioned in this book, are the urgent causes that provoked me in my love and bounden duty to your Majesty and my country, to address my former books to your princely hands and consideration.

By which privileges they draw multitudes of merchants to trade with them, and many other nations to inhabit amongst them, which makes them populous, and there they make store-houses of all foreign commodities,

5

wherewith

wherewith, upon every occasion of scarcity and dearth, they are able to furnish foreign countries with plenty of those commodities, which before in time of plenty they engrossed and brought home from the same places ; which doth greatly augment power, treasure to their state, besides the common good in setting their poor and people on work.

To which privileges they add smallness of custom, and liberty of trade, which maketh them flourish, and their country so plentiful of all kind of coin and commodities, where little or nothing groweth, and their merchants so flourish, that when a loss cometh they scarce feel it.

To bring this to pass they have many advantages of us ; the one is, by their fashioned ships called boyers, hoy-barks, hoys, and others that are made to hold great bulk of merchandise, and to sail with a few men for profit. For example, though an *English* ship of two hundred tons, and a *Holland* ship, or any other of the petty states of the same burden be at *Dantzick*, or any other place beyond the seas, or in *England*, they do serve the merchant better cheap by one hundred pounds in his freight than we can, by reason he hath but nine or ten mariners, and we near thirty ; thus he saveth twenty men's meat and wages in a voyage ; and so in all other their ships according to their burden, by which means they are freighted wheresoever they come, to great profit, whilst our ships lie still and decay, or go to *Newcastle* for coals.

Of this their smallness of custom inwards and outwards, we have daily experience ; for if two *English* ships, or two of any other nations be at *Bourdeaux*, both laden with wine of three hundred tons apiece, the one bound for *Holland*, or any other petty states, the other for *England*, the merchant shall pay about nine hundred pounds custom here, and other duties, when the other in *Holland*, or any other petty states, shall be cleared for less than fifty pounds, and so in all other wares and merchandizes ac-

cordingly,

cordingly, which draws all nations to traffick with them; and although it seems but small duties which they receive, yet the multitudes of all kind of commodities and coin that is brought in by themselves and others, and carried out by themselves and others, is so great, that they receive more custom and duties to the state, by the greatness of their commerce in one year, than *England* doth in two years; for the one hundredth part of commodities are not spent in *Holland,* but vended into other countries, which maketh all the country merchants to buy and sell, and increase ships and mariners to transport them.

My travels and meaning is not to diminish (neither hath been) your Majesty's revenues, but exceedingly to increase them, as shall appear, and yet please the people, as in other parts they do.

Notwithstanding their excises bring them in great revenues, yet whosoever will adventure to *Bourdeaux* but for six tons of wine, shall be free of excise in his own house all the year long; and this is done of purpose to animate and increase merchants in their country.

And if it happen that a trade be stopped by any foreign nation, which they heretofore usually had, or hear of any good trading which they never had, they will hinder others, and seek either by favour, money, or force, to open the gap of traffick for advancement of trade amongst themselves, and employment of their people.

And when there is a new course or trade erected, they give free custom inwards and outwards, for the better maintenance of navigation, and encouragement of the people to that business.

Thus they and others glean the wealth and strength from us to themselves; and these reasons following procure them this advantage of us.

1. The merchant staplers which maketh all things in abundance, by reason of their store-houses continually replenished with all kind of commodities.

 2. The

2. The liberty of free traffick for strangers to buy and sell in *Holland*, and other countries and states, as if they were free-born, maketh great intercourse.

3. The small duties levied upon merchants, draws all nations to trade with them.

4. Their fashioned ships continually freighted before ours, by reason of their few mariners and great bulk, serving the merchant cheap.

5. Their forwardness to further all manner of trading.

6. Their wonderful employment of their busses for fishing, and the great returns they make.

7. Their giving free custom inwards and outwards, for any new-erected trade, by means whereof they have gotten already almost the sole trade into their hands.

All nations may buy and sell freely in *France*, and there is free custom outwards twice or thrice in a year, at which time our merchants themselves do make their great sales of *English* commodities, and do buy and lade their great bulk of *French* commodities to serve for the whole year; and in *Rochel* in *France*, and in *Britain*, free custom all the year long, except some small toll, which makes great traffick, and maketh them flourish.

In *Denmark*, to incourage and inrich the merchants, and to increase ships and mariners, there is free custom all the year long for their own merchants, except one month between *Bartholomew-tide* and *Michaelmas*.

The *Hans-towns* have advantage of us, as *Holland* and other petty states have, and in most things imitate them, which makes them exceeding rich and plentiful of all kind of commodities and coin, and so strong in ships and mariners, that some of their towns have near one thousand sail of ships.

The merchandises of *France*, *Portugal*, *Spain*, *Italy*, *Turkey*, *East* and *West-Indies*, are transported most by the *Hollanders*, and other petty states, into the east and north-east kingdoms of *Pomerland*, *Spruceland*, *Poland*,

Denmark,

Denmark, *Sweedland*, *Leifland*, and *Germany*, and the merchandises brought from the last-mentioned kingdoms, being wonderful many, are likewise by the *Hollanders* and other petty states most transported into the southern and western dominions, and yet the situation of *England* lieth far better for a store-house to serve the south-east and north-east regions than theirs doth, and hath far better means to do it, if we will bend our course for it.

No sooner a dearth of fish, wine, or corn here, and other merchandise, but forthwith the *Embdeners*, *Hamburghers*, and *Hollanders*, out of their store-houses, lade fifty or one hundred ships, or more, dispersing themselves round about this kingdom, and carry away great store of coin and wealth for little commodity, in those times of dearth; by which means they suck our commonwealth of her riches, cut down our merchants, and decay our navigation; not with their natural commodities, which grow in their own countries, but the merchandises of other countries and kingdoms.

Therefore it is far more easy to serve ourselves, hold up our merchants, and increase our ships and mariners, and strengthen the kingdom; and not only keep our money in our own realm, which other nations still rob us of, but bring in theirs who carry ours away, and make the bank of coin and store-house to serve other nations as well, and far better cheap than they.

Amsterdam is never without seven hundred thousand quarters of corn, besides the plenty they daily vend, and none of this groweth in their own country: A dearth in *England*, *France*, *Spain*, *Italy*, *Portugal*, and other places, is truly observed to inrich *Holland* seven years after, and likewise the petty states.

For example, the last dearth, six years past, the *Hamburghers*, *Embdeners*, and *Hollanders*, out of their storehouses, furnished this kingdom; and from *Southampton*, *Exeter*, and *Bristol*, in a year and a half, they carried

away

away near two hundred thousand pounds from these parts only: Then what great quantity of coin was transported round about your kingdom from every port-town, and from your city of *London*, and other cities, cannot be esteemed so little as two millions, to the great decay of your kingdom, and impoverishing your people; discredit to the company of merchants, and dishonour to the land, that any nation that have no corn in their own country growing, should serve this famous kingdom, which God hath so enabled within itself.

They have a continual trade into this kingdom with five or six hundred ships yearly, with merchandises of other countries and kingdoms, and store them up in storehouses here until the prices rise to their minds; and we trade not with fifty ships into their country in a year, and the said number are about this realm every eastern wind, for the most part to lade coals and other merchandise.

Unless there be a scarcity, or dearth, or high prices, all merchants do forbear that place where great impositions are laid upon the merchandise, and those places slenderly shipped, ill served, and at dear rates, and oftentimes in scarcity, and want employment for the people; and those petty states finding truly by experience, that small duties imposed upon merchandise draw all traffick unto them, and free liberty for strangers to buy and sell doth make continual mart; therefore whatever excises or impositions are laid upon the common people, yet they still ease, uphold and maintain the merchants by all possible means, of purpose to draw the wealth and strength of Christendom to themselves; whereby it appeareth, though the duties be but small, yet the customs for going out and coming in do so abound, that they increase their revenues greatly, and make profit, plenty and employment of all sorts, by sea and land, to serve themselves and other nations, as is admirable to behold: And likewise the great commerce, which groweth by the same means, enableth

the

the common people to bear their burden laid upon them, and yet they grow rich by reason of the great commerce and trade, occasioned by their convenient privileges and commodious constitutions.

There was an intercourse of traffick in *Genoa*, and there was the flower of commerce, as appeareth by their antient records, and their sumptuous buildings; for all nations traded with merchandise to them, and there was the store-house of all *Italy*, and other places; but after they had set a great custom of 16 *per cent.* all nations left trading with them, which made them give themselves wholly to usury, and at this day we have not three ships go there in a year: But to the contrary, the Duke of *Florence* builded *Leghorn*, and set small custom upon merchandise, and gave them great and pleasing privileges, which hath made a rich and strong city, with a flourishing state.

Furthermore, touching some particulars needful to be considered of the mighty huge fishing that ever could be heard of in the world, is upon the coasts of *England*, *Scotland* and *Ireland*; but the great fishery is in the *Low-Countries*, and other petty states, wherewith they serve themselves and all Christendom, as shall appear.

In four towns in the east kingdoms within the *Sound*, *Quinsbrough*, *Elbing*, *Statten*, and *Dantzick*, there are carried and vended in a year, between thirty and forty thousand lasts of herrings, sold but at fifteen or sixteen pounds the last, is about six hundred and twenty thousand pounds, and we none.

Besides, *Denmark*, *Norway*, *Sweden*, *Leifland*, *Rie*, *Nevill*, the *Narve*, and other port-towns within the *Sound*, there is carried and vended above ten thousand lasts of *herrings*, sold at fifteen or sixteen pounds the last, is one hundred and seventy thousand pounds more yearly; in such request are our herrings there, that they are oftentimes sold for twenty, twenty-four, thirty, and thirty-six

pounds

pounds the last, and we send not one barrel into all those east countries.

The *Hollanders* sent into *Russia* near fifteen hundred lasts of herrings, sold about thirty shillings the barrel, amounteth to twenty-seven thousand pounds, and we but about twenty or thirty lasts.

To *Stoade, Hamborough, Bremen* and *Emden,* upon the river of *Elve, Weser,* and *Embs,* are carried and vended, of fish and herrings, about six thousand lasts, sold about fifteen or sixteen pounds the last, is one hundred thousand pounds, and we none.

Cleaveland, Gulickland, up the river of *Rhine,* to *Cullen, Francfort* on the *Main,* and so over all *Germany,* is carried and vended, fish and herrings, near twenty-two thousand last, sold at twenty pounds the last, is four hundred and twenty thousand pounds, and we none.

Up the river of *Maiz, Leigh, Maestrich, Venlow, Zutphen, Deventer, Campen, Swoole,* and all over *Lukeland,* is carried and vended seven thousand lasts of herrings, sold at twenty pounds the last, is one hundred and forty thousand pounds, and we none.

To *Guelderland, Artois, Hainault, Brabant, Flanders,* up the river of *Antwerp,* all over the Archduke's countries, are carried and vended between eight or nine thousand lasts, sold at eighteen pounds the last, is one hundred and seventy-one thousand pounds, and we none.

The *Hollanders,* and others, carried of all sorts of herrings to *Roan* only in one year, besides all other parts of *France,* fifty thousand lasts of herrings, sold at twenty pounds the last, is ten hundred thousand pounds, and we not one hundred lasts thither; they are sold oftentimes there for twenty, and four and twenty, and thirty pounds the last.

Between *Christmas* and *Lent,* the duties for fish and herrings came to fifteen thousand crowns at *Roan* only, that year the Queen deceased; Sir *Thomas Parry* was

agent

agent there then, and *S. Savors* his man, knows it to be true, who handled the business for pulling down the impositions. Then what great sums of money came to all in the port-towns to inrich the *French* king's coffers, and to all the kings and states throughout Christendom, to inrich their coffers; besides the great quantity vended to the Streights, and the multitude spent in the *Low-Countries,* where there is likewise sold for many a hundred thousand pounds more yearly, is necessary to be remembered; and the stream to be turned to the good of this kingdom; to whose sea-coasts God only hath sent and given these great blessings, and multitude of riches for us to take, howsoever it hath been neglected, to the hurt of this kingdom, that any nation should carry away out of this kingdom yearly great mass of money for fish taken in our seas, and sold again by them to us which must needs be a great dishonour to our nation, and hindrance to this realm.

From any port-town of any kingdom within Christendom, the bridge-master, or wharf-master, for twenty shillings a year, will deliver a true note of the number of lasts of herrings brought to their wharfs, and their prices commonly they are sold at; but the number brought to *Dantzick, Cullen, Rotterdam,* and *Enchuisen,* is so great, as it will cost three, four, or five pounds for a true note.

The abundance of corn groweth in the east kingdoms, but the great store-houses for grain to serve Christendom, and the heathen countries in the time of dearth, is in the *Low-Countries,* wherewith, upon every occasion of scarcity and dearth they do inrich themselves seven years after, employ their people, and get great freights for their ships in other countries, and we not one in that course.

The mighty vineyards and store of salt is in *France* and *Spain;* but the great vintage and staple of salt is in the *Low-Countries,* and they send near one thousand sail of ships with salt and wine only into the east kingdoms yearly, besides other places, and we not one in that course.

The

The exceeding groves of wood are in the east kingdoms, but the huge piles of wainscot, clapboard, fir-deal, masts, and timber, is in the *Low-Countries*, where none grow, wherewith they serve themselves and other parts, and this kingdom with those commodities; they have five or six hundred great long ships continually using that trade, and we none in that course.

The wool, cloth, lead, tin, and divers other commodities, are in *England*; but by means of our wool and cloth going out rough, undress'd, and undy'd, there is an exceeding manufactory and drapery in the *Low-Countries*, wherewith they serve themselves and other nations, and advance greatly the employment of their people at home, and traffick abroad, and put down ours in foreign parts, where our merchants trade unto, with our own commodities.

We send into the east kingdoms, yearly, but one hundred ships, and our trade chiefly dependeth upon three towns, *Elbing*, *Kingsborough*, and *Dantzick*, for making our sails, and buying their commodities sent into this realm at dear rates, which this kingdom bears the burden of.

The *Low-Countries* send into the east kingdoms yearly, about three thousand ships, trading into every city and port-town, taking the advantage, and vending their commodities to exceeding profit, and buying and lading their ships with plenty of those commodities, which they have from every of those towns 20 *per cent.* cheaper than we, by reason of the difference of the coin, and their fish yields ready money, which greatly advanceth their traffick, and decayeth ours.

They send into *France*, *Spain*, *Portugal*, *Italy*, from the east kingdoms that passeth through the *Sound*, and through your narrow seas, yearly, of the east country commodities, about two thousand ships, and we none in that course.

They

They trade into all cities, and port-towns in *France*, and we chiefly to five or six.

They traffick into every city and port-town round about this land, with five or six hundred ships yearly, and we chiefly but to three towns in their country, and but with forty ships.

Notwithstanding the *Low-Countries* have as many ships and vessels as eleven kingdoms of Christendom have, let *England* be one, and build every year near one thousand ships, and not a timber-tree growing in their own country, and that also all their home-bred commodities that grow in their land in a year, less than one hundred good ships are able to carry them away at one time; yet they handle the matter so for setting them all on work, that their traffick with the *Hans-towns* exceeds in shipping all *Christendom*.

We have all things of our own in super-abundance to increase traffick, and timber to build ships, and commodities of our own to lade about one thousand ships and vessels at one time (besides the great fishing) and as fast as they have made their voyages might relade again, and so year after year all the year long to continue; yet our ships and mariners decline, and traffick and merchants daily decay.

The main bulk and mass of herrings from whence they raise so many millions yearly, that inrich other kingdoms, kings and states coffers, and likewise their own people, proceedeth from your seas and lands, and the return of the commodities and coin they bring home in exchange of fish, and other commodities, are so huge, as would require a large discourse apart; all the amends they make us is, they beat us out of trade in all parts with our own commodities.

For instance, we had a great trade in *Russia* seventy years, and about fourteen years past we sent store of goodly ships to trade in those parts, and three years past

we

we set out but four, and this last year two or three; but to the contrary, the *Hollanders* about twenty years since traded thither with two ships only, yet now they are increased to about thirty or forty, and one of their ships is as great as two of ours, and at the same time (in their troubles there) that we decreased, they increased; and the chief commodities they carry with them thither, is *English* cloth, herrings taken in our seas, *English* lead and pewter made of our tin, besides other commodities; all which we may do better than they. And although it be a cheap country, and the trade very gainful, yet we have almost brought it to nought, by disorderly trading, joint stock, and the merchants banding themselves one against another.

And so likewise we used to have eight or nine great ships to go continually a fishing to *Wardhouse*, and this year but one, and so, *pro rata*, they outgo us in all kind of fishing and merchandizing in all countries, by reason they spare no cost, nor deny no privileges that may encourage advancement of trade and manufactory.

Now if it please, and with your Majesty's good liking stand, to take notice of these things, which I conceive to be fit for your Majesty's consideration, which in all humbleness (as duty bindeth me) I do tender unto your Majesty, for the unfeigned zeal I bear to the advancement of your honour and profit, and the general good of your subjects; it being apparent, that no three kingdoms in Christendom can compare with your Majesty for support of traffick, and continual employment of your people within themselves, having so many great means, both by sea and land, to inrich your coffers, multiply your navy, inlarge your traffick, make your kingdoms powerful, and your people rich; yet, through idleness, they are poor, wanting employment, many of your land and coast-towns much ruinated, and your kingdom in need of coin, your shipping, traffick, and mariners decayed, whilst your Majesty's neighbour princes, without these means, abound in

wealth,

wealth, inlarge their towns, increase their shipping, traffick, and mariners, and find out such employment for their people, that they are all advantageous to their commonwealth, only by ordaining commodious constitutions in merchandizing, and fulness of trade and manufactory.

God hath bless'd your Majesty with incomparable benefits; as with copper, lead, iron, tin, allum, copperas, saffron, fells, and divers other native commodities, to the number of about one hundred, and other manufactories vendible, to the number of about one thousand, (as shall appear) besides corn, whereof great quantity of beer is made, and most transported by strangers; as also wool, whereof much is shipped forth unwrought into cloth or stuffs, and cloth transported undress'd and undy'd, which doth employ and maintain near fifty thousand people in foreign parts, your Majesty's people wanting the employment in *England*, many of them being enforced to live in great want, and seek it beyond the seas.

Coals, which do employ hundreds of strangers ships yearly to transport them out of this kingdom, whilst we do not employ twenty ships in that course.

Iron ordnance, which is a jewel of great value, far more than it is accounted, by reason that no other country could ever attain unto it, although they have assayed with great charge.

Your Majesty hath timber of your own for building of ships, and commodities plenty to lade them, which commodities other nations want, yet your Majesty's people decline in shipping, traffick, and mariners.

These inconveniences happen by three causes especially.

1. The unprofitable course of merchandising.

2. The want of course of full manufactory of our home-bred commodities.

3. The undervaluing of our coins, contrary to the rules of other nations.

 For

For instance. The merchant adventurers by over-trading upon credit, or with money taken up upon exchange, whereby they lose usually ten or twelve, and sometimes fifteen or sixteen *per cent.* are enforced to make sale of their cloths at under rates, or keep their credit, whereby cloth, being the jewel of the land, is undervalued, and the merchant in short time eaten out.

The merchants of *Ipswich*, whose trade for *Elbing* is chiefly for fine cloths, all dy'd and dress'd within our land, do, for the most part, buy their fine cloths upon time; and by reason they go so much upon credit, they are enforced (not being able to stand upon their markets) to sell, giving fifteen or eighteen months day of payment for their cloths, and having sold them, they then presently sell their bills so taken for cloth, allowing after the rate of fourteen or fifteen, and sometimes twenty *per cent.* which money they employ forthwith in wares at excessive prices, and lose as much more that way, by that time their wares be sold at home : Thus by over-running themselves upon credit, they disable themselves and others, inhancing the prices of foreign commodities, and pulling down the rates of our own.

The west-country merchants that trade with cloths into *France* or *Spain*, do usually employ their servants (young men of small experience) who by cunning combining of the *French* and *Spanish* merchants, are so entrapped, that when all customs and charges be accounted, their masters shall hardly receive their principal monies. As for returns out of *France*, their silver and gold is so highly rated, that our merchants cannot bring it home, but to great loss; therefore the *French* merchants set higher rates upon their commodities, which we must either buy dear, or let our monies lie dead there a long time, until we can conveniently employ the same.

The northern merchants of *York, Hull,* and *Newcastle,* trade only in white kerseys and coloured dozens; and

every

every merchant, be his adventure never so small, doth, for the most part, send over an unexperienced youth, unfit for merchandising, which bringeth to the stranger great advantage, but to his master and commonwealth great hindrance; for they, before their goods be landed, go to the stranger, and buy such quantities of iron, flax, corn, and other commodities, as they are bound to lade their ships withal, which ships they engage themselves to relade within three weeks, or a month, and do give the price the merchant stranger asketh, because he gives them credit, and lets them ship away their iron, flax, and other commodities, before they have sold their kerseys, and other commodities, by which means extraordinary dear commodities are returned into this realm, and the servant also enforced to sell his cloths under-foot, and oftentimes to loss, to keep his credit, and to make payment for the goods before shipped home, having some twenty days or a month's respite to sell the cloths, and to give the merchant satisfaction for his iron, flax, and other wares; by which extremities our home-bred commodities are abased.

Touching Manufactory.

There have been about fourscore thousand undress'd and undy'd cloths yearly transported.

It is therefore evident, that the kingdom hath been yearly deprived of about four hundred thousand pounds within these five and fifty years, which is near twenty millions that would have been gained by the labour of poor workmen in that time, with the merchants gains for bringing in dying stuffs, and return of cloths dress'd and dy'd, with other benefits to the realm, besides exceeding enlarging of traffick, and increase of ships and mariners.

There would have been gained in that time about three millions, by increase of custom upon commodities returned for cloths dress'd and dy'd, and for dying stuffs, which

would

would have more plentifully been brought in and used for the same.

There hath been also transported in that time yearly by bays, *Northern* and *Devonshire* kerseys, white, about fifty thousand cloths, counting three kerseys to a cloth, whereby hath been lost about five millions by those sorts of cloths in that time, which would have come to poor workmen for their labour, with the customs for dying stuffs, and the people's profit for bringing them in, with returns of other commodities, and freights for shipping.

Bays are transported white into *Amsterdam*, and there being dress'd and dy'd, are shipped into *Spain*, *Portugal*, and other kingdoms, where they are sold in the name of *Flemish* Bays, setting their own town-seal upon them ; so that we lose the very name of our home-bred commodities, and other countries get the reputation and profit thereof. Lamentable it is, that this land should be deprived of so many above-mentioned millions, and that our native commodities of cloth, ordained by God for the natural subjects, being so royal and rich in itself, should be driven to so small advantage of reputation and profit to your Majesty and people, and so much improved and intercepted by strangers, considering that God hath enabled, and given your Majesty power to advance dressing and dying, and transporting of all your cloths within a year or two; I speak it knowingly, to show how it may be done- laudably, lawfully, and approved to be honourable, feasable, and profitable.

All the companies of your land transport their cloths dress'd and dy'd, to the good of your kingdom, except the merchant adventurers, whereby the *Eastland* and *Turkey* merchants, with other companies, do increase your Majesty's customs, by bringing in, and spending dying stuffs, and setting your people on work, by dressing before they transport them ; and they might increase far more custom to your Majesty, and make much more profit to them-

selves

selves and this realm, and set many thousands of poor people more on work for dressing and dying, and likewise employ more ships and mariners, for bringing in dying stuffs, were it not for the merchant adventurers, who transport their cloths white, rough, undress'd and undy'd, into the *Low-Countries*, where they sell them to the strangers, who afterwards dress, dye, and stretch them to such *unreasonable lengths*, contrary to our law, that they prevent and forestall our markets, and cross the just prohibitions of our state and realm, by their agents and factors lying in divers places with our own cloths, to the great decay of this kingdom in general, and discredit of our cloths in particular.

If the accompt were truly known, it would be found that they make not clear profit only by cloth transported rough, undress'd, and undy'd, sixty thousand pounds a year: but it is most apparent your Majesty in your customs, your merchants in their sales and prices, your subjects in their labours, for lack of not dressing and dying, your ships and mariners, in not bringing in of dying stuffs, and spending of allum, is hindered yearly near a million of pounds; so that trade is driven to the great hindrance of your Majesty and people by permitting your native commodities to pass rough, undress'd, and undy'd, by the merchant adventurer.

Touching Fishing.

The great sea business of fishing doth employ near twenty thousand ships and vessels, and four hundred thousand people are employed yearly upon your coast of *England, Scotland,* and *Ireland,* with sixty ships of war, which may prove dangerous.

The *Hollanders* only have about three thousand ships to fish withal, and fifty thousand people are employed yearly by them upon your Majesty's coasts of *England, Scotland,* and *Ireland.*

 Thesc

These three thousand fishing ships and vessels of the *Hollanders* do employ near nine thousand other ships and vessels, and one hundred and fifty thousand persons more by sea and land to make provision to dress and transport the fish they take, and return commodities, whereby they are enabled, and do build yearly one thousand ships and vessels, having not one timber-tree growing in their own country, nor home-bred commodities to lade one hundred ships, and yet they have twenty thousand ships and vessels, and all employed.

King *Henry* the Seventh, desirous to make his kingdoms powerful and rich, by increase of ships and mariners, and employment of his people, sent unto his sea-coast towns, moving them to set up the great and rich fishing, with promise to give them needful privileges, and to furnish them with loans of money, if need were, to encourage them; yet his people were slack. Now since I have traced this business, and made mine endeavours known unto your Majesty, your noblemen, able merchants, and others, (who having set down under their hands for more assurance) promised to disburse large sums of money for the building up of this great and rich large sea-city, which will increase more strength to your land, give more comfort, and do more good to all your cities and towns, than all the companies of your kingdom, having fit and needful privileges, for the upholding and strengthning of so weighty and needful a business.

For example, twenty busses built and put into a sea-coast town where there is not one ship before, there must be to carry, recarry, transport, and make provision for one buss, three ships; likewise every ship setting on work thirty several trades and occupations, and four hundred thousand persons by sea and land, insomuch as three hundred persons are not able to make one fleet of nets in four months for one buss, which is no small employment.

Thus by twenty busses are set on work, near eight
                              thousand

thousand persons by sea and land, and an increase of above one thousand mariners, and a fleet of eighty sail of ships to belong to one town, where none were before to take the wealth out of the sea, to inrich and strengthen the land, only by raising of twenty busses.

Then what good one thousand or two thousand will do, I leave to your Majesty's consideration.

It is worthy to be noted, how necessary fishermen are to the commonwealth, and how needful to be advanced and cherished, &c.

1. For taking God's blessing out of the sea to inrich the realm, which otherwise we lose.

2. For setting the people on work.

3. For making plenty and cheapness in the realm.

4. For increasing of shipping, to make the land powerful.

5. For a continual nursery for breeding and increasing our mariners.

6. For making employment of all sorts of people, as blind, lame, and others, by sea and land, from ten or twelve years and upwards.

7. For inriching your Majesty's coffers, by merchandises returned from other countries for fish and herrings.

8. For the increase and enabling of merchants, which now droop and daily decay.

Touching the Coin.

For the most part, all monarchies and free states, both heathen and christian, as *Turky, Barbary, France, Poland,* and others, do hold for a rule of never-failing profit, to keep their coin at higher rates within their own territories, than it is in other kingdoms.

The Causes.

1. To preserve the coin within their own territories.

2. To bring unto themselves the coin of foreign princes.

3. To

8. To enforce merchant strangers to take their commodities at high rates, which this kingdom bears the burden of.

For Instance.

The King of *Barbary* perceiving the trade of Christian merchants to increase in his kingdom, and that the returns out of his kingdoms were most in gold, whereby it was much enhanced, raised his ducat (being then current for three ounces) to four, five, and six ounces; nevertheless it was no more worth in *England*, being so raised, than when it went for three ounces.

This ducat, current for three ounces in *Barbary*, was then worth in *England* seven shillings and sixpence; and no more worth, being raised to six ounces; since which time (adding to it a small piece of gold) he hath raised it to eight, and lastly, to ten ounces; yet at this day it is worth but ten shillings and one penny, notwithstanding your Majesty's late raising of your gold.

Having thus raised his gold, he then devised to have plenty of silver brought into his kingdom, raised the royal of eight, being but two ounces, to three and three pence half-penny, which caused great plenty of silver to be brought in, and to continue in his kingdom.

FRANCE.

The *English Jacobus* goeth for three and twenty shillings in merchandising.

The *French* crown for seven shillings and sixpence.

Also the king hath raised his silver four souce in the crown.

NORTH-HOLLAND.

The double *Jacobus* goeth for three and twenty shillings *sterling*.

The *English* shilling is there eleven stivers, which is two shillings over in the pound.

 POLAND.

POLAND.

The king of *Poland* raised his *Hungary* ducat from fifty-six to seventy-seven and an half *Polish* groshes, and the rix-dollar from thirty-six to forty-seven and an half groshes; the rix-dollar, worth in *Poland* forty-seven and an half groshes, is, by account, valued at six shillings and fourpence *sterling*, and here in *England* is worth but four shillings and sevenpence; the *Hungary* ducat, seventy-seven, is worth, by account, in *Poland* ten shillings and four pence, and in *England* is worth but seven shillings and tenpence; the *Jacobus* of *England*, here current for twenty-two shillings, in *Poland* twenty-four shillings, at the rate of seven shillings and tenpence for the *Hungary* ducat.

Now to turn the stream and riches raised by your Majesty's native commodities into the natural channel, from whence it hath been a long time diverted; may it please your Majesty to consider these points following.

1. Whether it be not fit that a state-merchant be settled within your dominions, which may both dispose more profitably of the riches thereof, and encounter policies of merchant strangers, who now go beyond us in all kind of profitable merchandising?

2. Whether it be not necessary, that your native commodities should receive their full manufactory by your subjects within your dominions?

3. Whether it be not fit the coals should yield your Majesty and subjects a better value, by permitting them to pass out of the land, and that they be in your subjects shipping only transported?

4. Whether it be not fit your Majesty presently raise your coin to as high rates as it is in the parts beyond the seas?

 5. Whether

5. Whether it be not necessary that the great sea-business of fishing be forthwith set forward?

If it please your Majesty to approve of these considerations, and accordingly to put them in a right course of execution, I assure myself (by God's help) in short time your Majesty's customs, and the continual comings into your coffers, will be exceedingly increased, your ships and mariners trebled, your land and waste towns (which are now run out of gates) better replenished, and your people employed, to the great inriching and honour of your kingdom, with the applause, and to the comfort of all your loyal subjects.

May it please your Majesty,

I have the rather undergone the pains to look into their policies, because I have heard them profess they hoped to get the whole trade and shipping of Christendom into their own hands, as well for transportation, as other-wise, for the command and mastery of the seas; to which end I find that they do daily increase their traffick, augmenting their shipping, multiplying their mariners strength and wealth in all kinds, whereat I have grieved the more, when I consider'd how God hath endued this kingdom, above any three kingdoms in Christendom, with divers varieties of home-bred commodities, which others have not, and cannot want, and endowed us with sundry other means to continue and maintain trade of merchandising and fishing beyond them all, whereby we might prevent the deceivers, ingross the commodities of the in-grossers, inrich ourselves, and increase our navigation, shipping, and mariners, so as it would make all nations to vail the bonnet to *England*, if we would not be still wanting to ourselves in employment of our people.

Which people being divided into three parts, two parts of them are mere spenders and consumers of a commonwealth, therefore I aim at these points following.

To

To allure and encourage the people for their private gain, to be all workers and erecters of a commonwealth.

To inrich and fill your Majesty's coffers by a continual coming in, and making your people wealthy, by means of their great and profitable trading and employment.

To vend our home-bred commodities to far more reputation, and much more profit to the king, the merchant, and the kingdom.

To return the merchandises of other countries at far cheaper rates than now they are, to the great good of the realm in general.

To make the land powerful by increasing of ships and mariners.

To make your people's takings in general to be much more every day than now they are, which, by God's help, will grow continually more and more, by the great concourse and commerce that will come by settled constitutions and convenient privileges, as in other parts they do by this their great freedom of trade.

All this, and much more, is done in other countries, where nothing groweth; so that of nothing they make great things.

Then how much more mighty things might we make, where so great abundance and variety of home-bred commodities and rich materials grow for your people to work upon, and other plentiful means to do that withal, which other nations neither have, nor cannot want, but of necessity must be furnished from hence? And now, whereas our merchandising is wild, utterly confused, and out of frame, as at large appeareth, a state-merchant will roundly and effectually bring all the premises to pass, fill your havens with ships, those ships with mariners, your kingdom full of merchants, their houses full of outlandish commodities, and your coffers full of coin, as in other places they do, and your people shall have just cause to hold in happy memory, that your Majesty was the begin-

ncr

ner of so profitable, praise worthy, and renowned a work, being the true philosopher's stone to make your Majesty a rich and potent king, and your subjects happy people, only by settling of a state-merchant, whereby your people may have fulness of trade and manufactory, and yet hold both honourable and profitable government, without breaking of companies.

And for that in the settling of so weighty a business, many things of great consequence must necessarily fall into consideration, I humbly pray, that your Majesty may be pleased (for the bringing of this great service to light) to give me leave to nominate the commissioners, and your Majesty to give them power to call before them such men as they shall think fit to confer with upon oath, or otherwise, as occasion shall offer; that the said commissioners, with all speed, for the better advancement of this honourable and profitable work, may prepare and report the same unto your Majesty.

Your Majesty's most loyal and true-hearted subject,

W. RALEIGH.

NAVIGATION

AND

Commerce,

THEIR

ORIGINAL

AND

PROGRESS.

Containing

A succinct Account of Traffick in General; its Benefits and Improvements: Of Discoveries, Wars and Conflicts at Sea, from the Original of Navigation to this Day; with special Regard to the ENGLISH Nation; Their several Voyages and Expeditions, to the Beginning of our late Differences with HOLLAND; In which His Majesties Title to the DOMINION of the SEA is Asserted, against the Novel, and later Pretenders.

By *J. EVELYN*, Esq; *S.R.S.*

Cicero ad *Attic.* L. 10. Ep. 8.

Qui MARE *teneat, eum necesse* RERUM *Potiri.*

LONDON,

Printed by *T. R.* for *Benj. Tooke*, at the Sign of the *Ship* in St. *Pauls Churchyard*, 1674.

TO

The King.

SIR,

THAT *I take the boldness to inscribe Your Majesties name on the front of this little History, is to pay* a tribute, *the most due, and the most becoming my relation to your Majesties service of any that I could devise; since Your Majesty has been pleas'd among so many noble and illustrious persons, to name me of the* Councel *of Your* Commerce, *and* Plantations : *And if it may afford Your Majesty some diversion, to behold, as in a* table, *the course, and importance of what Your Majesty is the most absolute* arbiter *of any Potentate on earth, and excite in Your loyal subjects a courage, and an industry becoming the advantages which* God *and* Nature *have put into their hands, I shall have reach'd my humble ambition, and Your Majesty will not reprove these expressions of it in*

SIR,

Your *Majestie's* Most

Dutiful, Most Obedient,

and ever Loyal

Subject and Servant,

J. EVELYN.

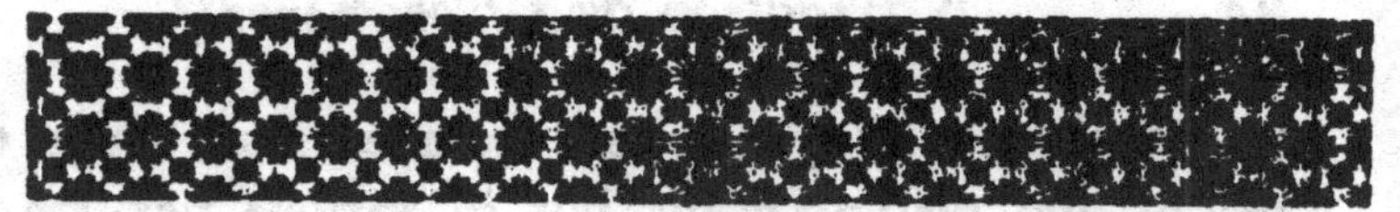

NAVIGATION

AND

COMMERCE,

THEIR

Original and Progress.

1. **W**HOSOEVER shall with serious attention contemplate the divine fabrick of this inferiour orb, the various, and admirable furniture which fills, and adorns it; the constitution of the elements about it, and, above all, the nature of man (for whom they were created) he must needs acknowledge, that there is nothing more agreable to reason, than that they were all of them ordain'd for mutual use and communication.

2. The earth, and every prospect of her superficies, presents us with a thousand objects of utility and delight, in which consists the perfection of all sublunary things: And, though, through her rugged and dissever'd parts, rocks, seas, and remoter islands, she seem at first, to check our addresses; yet, when we ag'en behold in what ample baies, creeks, trending-shores, inviting harbours and stations, she appears spreading her arms upon the bordures of the ocean; whiles the rivers, who repay their tributes to it, glide

not

not in direct, and præcipitate courses from their conceil'd, and distant heads, but in various flexures and meanders (as well to temper the rapidity of their streams, as to water and refresh the fruitful plains) methinks she seems, from the very beginning, to have been dispos'd for trafick and commerce, and even courts us to visit her most solitary recesses.

3. This meditation sometimes affecting my thoughts, did exceedingly confirm, and not a little surprize me; when reflecting on the situation of the *Mediterranean Sea* (so aptly contriv'd for intercourse to so vast a part of the world) I concluded; that if the *Hollanders* themselves (who, of all the inhabitants in it, are the best skill'd in making canales and trenches, and to derive waters) had joyn'd in consultation, how the scatter'd parts of the earth might be rendred most accessible, and easie for commerce; they could not have contriv'd, where to have made the inlet with so much advantage, as God and nature have done it for us; since by means of this sea, we have admission to no less than three parts of the habitable world, and there seems nothing left (in this regard) to humane industry, which could render it more consummate; so impious was the saying of *Alphonsus* (not worthy the name of prince) that had he been of counsel with the Creator when he made the universe, he could have fram'd it better.

Rhoderigo de Toledo, lib, 1. c. 6.

4. If we cast our eyes on the plains and the mountains; behold them naturally furnish'd with goodly trees; of which some there are, which grow as it were, spontaneously into vessels and canoes, wanting nothing but the launching, to render them useful; but, when the art of man, or of God rather (for it was he, who first instructed him to build) conspires, and that he but sets his divine genius on work, the same earth furnishes materials, to equip, and perfect the most beautiful,

useful,

useful, and stupendious creature (so let us be permitted to call her) the whole world has to shew: And if the winds, and elements prove auspicious (which was the third instance of our contemplation) this enormous machine (as if inspir'd with life too) is ready for every motion, and to brave all encounters and adventures, undertakes to fathom the world itself; to visit strange, and distant lands; to people, cultivate, and civilize uninhabited, and barbarous regions, and to proclaim to the universe, the wonders of the architect, the skill of the pilot, and, above all, the benefits of commerce.

5. So great, and unspeakable were the blessings which mankind received by his yet infant adventures; that it is no wonder, to see how every nation contended, who should surpass each other in the art of navigation, and apply the means of commerce to promote and derive it to themselves; God Almighty (as we have shew'd) in the constitution of the world, prompting us to awaken our industry for the supply of our necessities: For man only being oblig'd to live politickly, and in society, for mutual assistance, found it would not be accomplish'd without labour and industry; nature, which ordains all things necessary for other creatures, in the place where she produces them, did not so for man, but ennobling him with a superior faculty, supply'd him with all things his needs could require. Wheresoever therefore men are born (unless wanting to themselves) they have it in their power, to exalt themselves, even in these regards, above the other creatures; and the lillies which spin not, and are yet so splendidly clad, are not in this respect, so happy as an industrious and prudent man; because they have neither knowledge, or sense of their being and perfections: And, though few things indeed are necessary for the animal life; yet, has it no prerogative by that alone, above the more rational, which man

onely

onely enjoys, and for whom the world was made; seeing
the variety of blessings that were ordained to serve him,
proclaims his dominion, and the vastness of his nature;
nor, had the great Creator himself been so glorified,
without an intellectual being, that could contemplate,
and make use of them. We are therefore rather to
admire that stupendious mixture of plenty and want,
which we find disseminated throughout the creation;
what St. *Paul* affirms of the members of the little
world, being so applicable to those of the greater, and
no one place, or country able to say, I have no need of
another, considered not onely as to consummate perfections, but even divers things, if not absolutely necessary,
at least, convenient.

6. To demonstrate this in a most conspicuous instance, we need look no farther than *Holland*, of which
fertile (shall we say) or inchanted spot, 'tis hard to
decide, whether its wants, or abundance are reaily
greater, than any other countries under heaven; since,
by the quality, and other circumstances of situation
(though otherwise productive enough) it affords neither
grain, wine, oyle, timber, mettal, stone, wool, hemp, pitch,
nor, almost, any other commodity of use; and yet we
find, there is hardly a *nation* in the world, which enjoyes
all these things in greater affluence: And all this, from
commerce alone, and the effects of industry, to which
not onely the neighbouring parts of *Europe* contribute,
but the *Indies*, and *Antipodes :* so as the whole world
(as vast as it appears to others) seems but a *farm,*
scarce another *province* to them; and indeed it is that
alone, which has built, and peopl'd goodly cities, where
nothing but rushes grew; cultivated an heavy *genius*
with all the politer arts ; enlarg'd, and secur'd their
boundaries, and made them a name in the world, who,
within less than an age, were hardly consider'd in it.

7. What fame and riches the *Venetians* acquir'd,

whilst

whilst they were true to their *spouse*, the Sea (and in acknowledgment whereof, they still repeat and celebrate the nuptials) histories are loud of: but, this, no longer continu'd than whilst they had regard to their *fleets*, and their *trafick*, the proper business, and the most genuine to their situation. From hence, they founded a glorious city, fixt upon a few muddy, and scatter'd islands; and thence, distributed over *Europe*, the product of the eastern world, 'till changing this industry into ambition, and applying it to the inlarging of their territories in *Italy*, they lost their interests, and acquists in the *Mediterranean*, which were infinitely more considerable. Nor in this recension of the advantages of commerce, is her neighbour *Genoa* to be forgotten, whose narrow dominions (not exceeding some private lordships in *England*) have grown to a considerable state; and from a barren rock, to a proud city, emulous for wealth and magnificence, with the stateliest *emporiums* of the world.

8. The Easterlings, and *Anseatick Towns* (famous for early traffick) had perhaps never been heard of, but for courting this mistress; no more than those vaster tracts of *Sweden, Norway, Muscovy,* &c. which the late industry of our own people, has rendred considerable. The *Danes,* 'tis confess'd, had long signaliz'd themselves by their importunate descents on this island, and universal piracies; whilst negligent of our advantages at sea, we often became obnoxious to them; but, when once we set up our moving fortresses, and grew numerous in shipping, we liv'd in profound tranquillity, grew opulent, and formidable to our enemies.

9. It was Commerce, and Navigation (the daughter of Peace, and good Intelligence) that gave reputation to the most noble of our native staples, Wool, exceedingly improv'd by forreigners; especially, since the reigns of *Edward* the *Second,* and *Third*; and has been the

principal

principal occasion, of instituting, and establishing our
merchant-adventurers, and other worthy fraternites; to
mention onely the esteem of our *horses, corn, tin, lead,
iron, saffron, fullers-earth, hides, wax, fish*, and other
natural and artificial commodities, most of which are
indigene, and domestick, others imported, and brought
from forraign countries.   Thus, *Asia* refreshes us with
spices, recreates us with perfumes, cures us with drougs,
and adorns us with jewels: *Africa* sends us ivory and
gold; *America*, silver, sugar and cotton : *France, Spain*
and *Italy*, give us wine, oyl and silk : *Russia*, warms us
in furrs; *Swethen*, supplies us with copper; *Denmark*
and the northern tracts, with masts, and materials for
shipping, without which, all this were nothing. It is
commerce, and navigation that breeds, and accomplishes
that most honourable and useful race of men (the pillars
of all magnificence) to skill in the exportation of superfluities, importation of necessaries; to settle staples,
with regard to the publick stock; what 'tis fit to keep
at home, and what to send abroad : to be vigilant over
the course of exchange; to employ hands for regulated
salaries : and, by their dexterity, to moderate all this,
by a true, and solid interest of state, which, without this
mystery, cannot long subsist, as not alwaies admitting
permanent, and immutable rules : In a word, the sea
(which covers half the patrimony of man, renders the
whole world a stranger to it self, and the inhabitants,
for whom 'twas made, as rude as *canibals*) makes them
but one family by the miracles of commerce ; and
yet we have said nothing of the most illustrious
product of it ; that it has taught us religion, instructed
us in polity, cultivated our manners, and furnish'd us
with all the delicacies of virtuous and happy living.

10. Whether the first authors of traffick were the
Tyrians, Trojans, Lydians ; those of *Carthage ;* or (as
Josephus will) the mercurial spirits soon after the Flood,

See Mr. Coke.

Antiq. l. 1.

to repair, and supply the ruines of that universal over-throw, we are not solicitous: that it entered with the earliest, and best daies of the restored world, we shall prove hereafter, by the timely applications of industrious men, to inlarge, and improve their condition. The *Romans* indeed, were not of a good while, favourable to merchandizing; for, the *Patricians, Senators* and great men might not be owners in particular, of any consider-able vessel, besides small barks and pleasure-boats, and the most illustrious nations have esteem'd the gain by traffick and commerce incompatible with *nobless*: not, for being enemies to trade; but, because they esteem'd it an ignoble way of gain, *Quæstus omnis indecorus patribus visus,* saies *Livy,* and were all for conquest and the sword; for, otherwise, they so encourag'd this industry, that the *Latins* (whom for a long time, they held under such servitude, that they might not devise their estates when they dyed) if any one of them came to be able to build an handsome ship, fit for burthen and traffick, he was *Libertate donatus,* and obtained his freedom, with power to make his testament, and capable of bearing office: And one would wonder that traffick being so profitable, *Lycurgus* (that great law-giver amongst the *Lacedemo-nians*) should prohibit it; some believe it was for its being so obnoxious to corruption, and the luxury intro-duc'd amongst the people by commerce with strangers; the lying and deceit, purjury and theft, in buying, selling, and making bargains; for which reason *Plato* design'd the towns of his common-wealth to be built far distant from the sea; and our *Saviour* scourg'd the mony-changers out of the Temple; so difficult a thing it is for those who deal much, to preserve their hands clean: But, 'tis said, *Plato* changed his mind; and we all know, that as the *Romans* themselves grew wiser, so they dignified it, and took off that ill-understood reproach, as the *Orator* has himself told us,

Lib. 21. c. 63.

Latini multis modis conse-quuntur Civi-tatem Roma-nam; *Ut, si Navem ædifi-caverint duo-rum Millium Modiorum ca-pacem,* &c. Ulpian. *Instit.* Tit. *Latinis,* N. 6.

when (condemning the pedlary, and sordid* vices of retailers) he acknowledges, that where staple, and useful commodities can be brought in to supply the needs of whole countries, 'tis a commendable service, *videturque jure optimo, posse laudari*; nay, shew'd by their own example, that for the greatest men to turn merchants, did less taint their blood, than their sloth and effeminacy; and upon this account, the wisest of the heathens (for such were *Thales, Solon, Hippocrates,* and even *Plato* himself) have honour'd merchandize; and, of later times, many kings and princes; and then indeed, does traffick rise to its ascendent, when 'tis dignified by their example, and defended by their power: This, the Dukes of *Florence,* and other potentates have long since understood; and, now at last, the *French* King: Witness the repair of his ports, building of ships, cutting new channels, instituting companies, planting of colonies, and universal encouragement of manufactures by cherishing, and ennobling of sedulous and industrious persons: But, more yet than all this, or rather all this in more perfection; His *Majesty* (our glorious monarch) by whose influences alone (after all the combinations of his late powerful enemies) such a trade has been reviv'd, and carried on, and such a fleet, and strength at sea to protect it, as never this nation had a greater, nor any other of the past ages has approach'd; witness, you three mighty neighbours, at once, taught to submit to him! For the blessings of navigation, and visiting distant climes, does not stop at traffick only; but (since 'tis no less perfection to keep, than obtain a good) it enables us likewise with means to defend, what our honest industry has gotten; and, if necessity, and justice require; with inlarging our dominions too: vindicating our rights, repelling injuries, protecting the oppress'd, and with all the offices of humanity, and good nature; in a word, justice, and the right of nations, are

the

the objects of commerce: It maintains society, disposes to action, and communicates the graces, and riches which God has variously imparted: From all which con-siderations, 'tis evident; that a spirit of commerce, and strength at sea to protect it, are the most certain marks of the greatness of empire, deduced from an undeniable *sorites*; that whoever commauds the ocean, commands the trade of the world, and whoever commands the trade of the world, commands the riches of the world, and whoever is master of that, commands the world it-self; so as had the *Spaniard* treble his wealth, he could neither be rich, nor safe with his prodigious sloth; since, whilst he has been sitting still; we, and other nations have driven the trade of the *East Indies*, with his treasure of the *West*, and, uniting, as it were, extreams, made the *Poles* to kiss: They are not therefore small matters, you see, which men so much contend about, when they strive to improve commerce, and, by degrees, promote the art of navigation, and set their empire in the deep, from whence they have found to flow such notable advantages. *Instances* of this we might add in abundance; and that it is not the *vastness* of *terri-tory*, but the convenience of *situation*; nor the *multi-tude* of men, but their *address* and *industry* which *improve* a nation. *Cosmo di Medicis* would often say; that the *prince* who had not the *sea* to friend, was but half a *prince:* and, this, *Charles* the *Fifth* had well con-sidered, when he gave it for a *maxime* to his son *Philip*, that if ever he would sit *quiet* at *home*, and advance his *affairs* abroad, he should be sure to keep up his *reputa-tion* on the *waters*. The *truth* is, this great *Emperour* had neglected his *interest* at *sea*, and it laid the *founda-tion* of the *rebellion* of his *Low Country Subjects*, against his successor: To pretend to *universal monarchy* without *fleets*, was long since looked on, as a politick *chymæra*, and was wittily insinuated to *Antigonus* by *Patroclus*,

Athenæus De-
nosoph. l. 8.

18

when

when (being a *commander* under *Ptolomy Lagus's* son) he sent him a *present* of *fish* and green *figgs*, intimating, that unless he had the *sea* in his power, he had as good sit at home, and trifle: It was but labour in vain: And this was the sense of another as great a *captain*, when reckoning up the infinite *prerogatives* which the *sea* afforded; *Xenophon* seems to *despise* the advantages of the *land* in comparison: Truly the *Romans* themselves, were longer in struggling for a little *earth* in *Italy* only, than in subduing the whole *world*, after once their *eagles* had taken flight towards the *sea*, and urg'd their fortune on the deep. When once they had subdu'd *Agrigentum*, *Carthage* was no longer impregnable; and after they had pass'd *Gades* and the *Herculean Streight*, nothing was too hard for them, they went whither they would, and *cruiz'd* as far as *Thule*.

11. We shall not adventure to divine, who the hardy person was who first resolv'd to trust himself to a plank within an inch of death, to compel the woods to descend into the waters, and to back the most impetuous, and unconstant element; though probably, and for many reasons, somebody long before the *Deluge; Isti sunt potentes: 6. Gen. 4. Grotius* on the place will have the *navigationis repertores, piratæ,* such as in succeeding ages were *Jupiter Cretensis, Minos,* &c. Since it is not imaginable, the world, that must needs be so populous, and was so curious, should have continu'd so many ages without adventures by sea: But, the first vessel which we read of, was made by divine instinct and direction, and whilst the *prototype* lasted (which histories tell us was many hundred years) doubtless they built many strong, and goodly ships: But, as all things are in continual flux and vicissitude; so the art in time impair'd, and men began anew to contrive for their safety or necessity in rafts, and hollow trees; nay, paper, reeds, twigs, and leather (for of such were the rude beginnings

of

of the finish'd pieces we now admire) till advancing the art, by making use of more durable materials, they then began to build like ship-wrights, when *Pyrrhon* the *Lydian* invented the bending of planks by fire, and made boats of several contignations; nor contented with the same model, the *Platenses, Mysians, Trojans* and other nations, contended for the various shapes. Thus to *Sesostris* is ascribed the long ship fitted for expedition: *Hippus* the *Tyrrian* devis'd *carricks* and *onerary* vessels of prodigious bulk, for traffick or offence: *Athenæus* speaks of some that for their enormous structure had been taken for mountains, and floating islands; such was that of *Hiero* described by the *Deipnosophist,* a mooving palace adorn'd with gardens of the choicest fruit, and trees for shade: *Hippagines* is said to have transported the first horses in larger boats; others ascribe it to *Darius,* when he retir'd into *Thrace;* though we think them rather of antienter date; for what else means the ferrying over King *David's* goods and carriages, mention'd in the second of *Samuel?* Thus far the keel; for to the divers parts of vessels, for better speed, and government, several were the pretenders. The *Thasii* added decks; *Pisæus* the *rostrum* or *beakhead; Tiphys* the rudder; *Epalamius* compleated the anker, which was at first but of one flook: But, before all these, was the use of oars, which from the *bireme,* invented by the *Erythræi,* came at last to no less than fourty *ordines,* or banks (for so many had *Ptolomy Philopater's* gally) which, how to reconcile with possible (though that famous vessel were built for pomp, and ostentation only, and therefore with a double prow) together with those monstrous ships of war set forth by *Demetrius,* which had in them 4000 rowers, let the curious consult the most learned *Palmerius,* in his *Diatriba* upon a fragment of *Memnon :* And for portentous and costly vessels, the late *Vendosme* built by

Oneraria Cerealis Siracusia, &c.

2 *Sam.* 19.

Biremis Pistrix, Vallata Turrita, &c. *Plutarch* in *Demet. Athenæus,* lib. c. 9.

• *Phoc.* 717.

                                              Lewis

Lewis the XIIIth. of *France;* the *Swedish Magaleza,* the *Venetian Bucentoro;* not to omit those *carricks* which the *Spaniard* emploies yearly to his *Indies.* But, neither did all these helps suffice, 'till they added wings too: they attribute indeed the invention of masts, and cross yards to those of *Creete;* but to *Theseus, Icarus,* and *Dedalus* the application of sails, which 'tis said, *Proteüs* first skill'd to manage, and shift with that dexterity, as he was fain'd to turn himself into all shapes; and it was doubtless, no little wonder, to see that a piece of cloth (or, as *Pliny,* wittily, a despicable seed, for so he calls that of hemp, of which sails were made) should be contriv'd to stir such a bulk, and carry it with that incredible celerity, from one extream of the earth to the other: Of that esteem was this ingenious invention, that, besides *Prometheus,* and the rest we nam'd, whole countries challeng'd it, and the *Rhodians, Iönians, Corinthians,* those of *Tyrus, Ægypt, Ægineta, Boetia* with innumerable other, vaunt themselves masters of the science, nor is there any end of their names. It were a thing impossible, to investigate by whom the several riggings of vessels, and compleat equipment were brought into use: The skill of *pilotage* has aids from the *mathematics* and *astronomy;* and that of governing ships in fight is another, and a different talent. These, and many more, were the daughters of *Time, Necessity,* and *Accident;* so as even to our daies, there is ever something adding, or still wanting to the complement of this incomparable art. Of the *magnet* we shall speak hereafter, nor are we to despair in the perfecting of longitudes, *Dies, diem docet,* and whilst many pass, Science shall still be improv'd: We shall onely observe, concerning men of war, fleets, and *Armada's* for battel, that *Minos,* was reported to be the author, which shews that manner of desperate combat on the waters, to be neer as antient as men themselves,

Vegetius, Pollux, Laz. Baji-stus, Cresentius, Fournier, &c.

since

since the *Deluge* : indeed, to this prince do some attri-   *Diodorus,* l. 6.
bute the first knowledge of navigation, and that he   *Strabo,* l. 10.
disputed the Empire of the seas with *Neptune* himself,
who, for his power on the watry element, was esteem'd
a God: But, however these particulars may be uncertain,
we are able to make proof, that the first fregats were
built by the *English*, and generally, the best, and most
commodious vessels for all sort of uses in the world ;
and, as the ships, so those who man them, acknowledg'd
for the most expert, and couragious in it. But,

12. From the building of ships, we pass to the most
celebrious expeditions that have been made in them.
The *Gentiles* (who doubtless took *Saturn* for *Noah*, and
his sons, for other of the deities) magnifie sundry of
their adventures by sea : And, if from the immediate
offspring of that ancient patriarch, *Shem* and *Japhet*, the
Asiatick Iles, and those at remoter distance in the
Mediterranean and *European* seas, were peopl'd (whilst
the continent, and less dissever'd *Africk*, was left to
Cham) we have a certain *Epoche*, for the earliest expeditions, and shall less need to insist on those of the
Mythical, and *Heroic* Age ; the exploits of *Osiris*,
Hercules, Cadmus ; the Wandrings of *Ulysses*, and the
leaders that expugn'd *Troy*. To touch but a few of these ;
Bacchus, whose dominion lay about the gulph of *Persia*,
made of the first adventures, when from him (after the
rape of *Ariadne*) the *Tyrrian* pirates learn'd the art of
navigation, or rather to become more skillful rovers ; if
at least, they were not of the first for antiquity in this
art ; since the *Phœnicians* (whether expell'd by *Joshua*,
or transported by their curiosity) having spread their
name in the *Mediterranean*, were admir'd as Gods for
their boldness on the waters, and esteem'd among the
first that navigated, according to that of the Poet,

Prima ratem ventis credere docta Tyrus.   *Tibullus.*

17   That

That *Cadmus* sail'd into *Greece*, peopl'd those iles in the *Ægæan*, taught them letters, and sciences, as he had learn'd them from the *Hebrews*, we have undoubted testimony : Some affirm that the *Phœnicians* circl'd the world long since, and *Herodotus* has something to that purpose, where in his *Melpomene*, he speaks of those whom king *Necus* caus'd to embark from the *Red* Sea, and that ten years after return'd home by the Columns of *Hercules* through the Streights : However, that they penetrated far beyond the *Western* Ocean, and the shores of *Africk*, the expedition of *Hanno* in a Navy of LX. ships makes out by grave writers; so their coming as far as our *Britain*, the pillars which they fixt at *Gades*, and *Tingis*, to which some report they crept in early daies : And as towards the *west*, so *eastward*, taking colonies from *Elana* and the *Persian* Gulph. As to what they might be for merchants, illustrious is the proof out of *Isaiah*, where *Tyrus* is call'd the *Crowning City*, whose *Merchants* are princes, and whose *Traſickers* the honourable of the earth; when under the pretence of transporting commodities into *Greece*, they carried away *Io*, daughter of *Inachus*, which the *Cretans* requited, when shortly after, their amorous God, sail'd away with the fair *Europa* in the *White-Bull*; for so was the vessel call'd, which gave occasion to the fable, and serves to prove, how antient the giving names, and * badges is. Indeed so expert were those of *Crete* in sea-affairs, and so numerous in *shipping*, as by the suffrage of ancient times, there were none durst contend with them for *sovereignty*: let us hear the *Tragædian*,

> *O maria vasti* Creta *dominatrix freti,*
> *Cujus per cmne littus innumeræ rates*
> *Tenuere pontum :* quicquid Assyria *tenus*
> *Tellure* Nereus *pervium rostris secat.*

18. The *Colchick* exploit in the famous *Argo* (so call'd from her nimble sailing) was perform'd by above 50 gallants, of which nine were chief under *Jason*, and *Glaucus* his experienc'd pilot: But, whether they went to those countries about the *Euxine* shores in hopes of golden mines (shadow'd by the Fleece) or in expectation of the *Philosophers Stone* (said to be in possession of king *Æta*) we leave to the *Romancers*: There is in *Homer* a list of *Hero's*, and ships under their command, mention'd to be set out by the Παναχαίοι, or *States General* of those provinces, reported to have been no less than a thousand;

Non anni domuére decem, non mille Carinæ.   *Iliad. 2.*

And that this number is not fictitious; not onely the wondrous exactness of the poet in describing the commanders by name, but the number of ships under each flag, as the learned Mr. *Stanley* shows us beyond exception in his excellent notes upon *Æschylus* and we propose the instance, because it is so very remarkable for its antiquity.

14. But, to quit these dark, and less certain memorials, and mingle that of commerce with martial undertakings: The first for whom we have divine, and infallible record, is of the greatest, and the wisest prince, that ever sway'd a scepter: For, though it appear, the *Phœnicians* had us'd the sea before, and, perhaps, were the * first *Merchants* in the world since the Deluge; yet, it was *Solomon* doubtless, who open'd the passages to the *South*, when animated by his directions, and now leaving-off their rafts, and improving their adventures in ships, and stouter vessels, they essay'd to penetrate the farthest *Indies*, and visit an unknown *Hemisphere*: or if haply, they preceded him; yet, were now glad to joyn with this glorious monarch; because of those advantagious ports his father had taken from the

* Πρῶτοι δε εμπορίης ἁλιδίνετο ἐμνήσαντον. *Dionys.* Περιηγ.

Idumeans, which might otherwise interrupt their expeditions. What a mass of gold, and other precious things (the peculiar treasure of princes) this fleet of his brought home, the succeeding story relates; and there is farther notice of mariners, whose trading was for *spices* and *curiosities;* and the voyage to *Tarshish* (which by some is intrepreted the Ocean, as indeed it signifies in the *Chaldæan* language, but doubtless, means *Tartessus* in *Spain*) is again repeated. *Jehoshaphat,* after *Solomon,* neglected not these prosperous beginings, though, not with equal success; for the ships were broken at *Esion-Geber:* We shall onely remark, upon the account of commerce, that *Solomon* had no less than two fleets destin'd for trafick, of which, one went to *Ophir* (perhaps *Sophara, Taproban,* or *Ceilon*) in the *East-Indies,* and the other to *Tarsis,* that is (*Tartessus*) *Cales* (*Cadiz*) which being then, and long after esteem'd for the utmost confine of the world, had its name from the *Phœnicians,* as well as divers other places, and ports of *Europe* (even as far as *Italy, France,* and *Britany* it self) which both they, and we observe to this day in no obscure footsteps: and that *Spain* abounded in plenty of *gold* too (whatever some superficial searchers think) we learn from *Strabo, Diodorus, Mela, Pliny,* and several grave authors, whose attestation may be of good weight; the *Tyrians,* and *Phœnicians* frequently sailing into those parts. But, though we had yet no print of this from the Sacred Volumes, it is not to be devis'd, how the isles of the *Gentiles,* and other places of inaccessible distance could be planted and furnish'd, without those early intercourses by sea, which, by degrees (as in part is shew'd) accomplish'd the dominions of warlike men, and states, and encourag'd some to stupendious attempts.

15. To proceed to instances of unquestionable credit,

we have those of the *Persians*, and *Greeks* both before, and since the *Peloponnesiack* war: And, indeed the *Greeks* were the first of the *heathens* that joyn'd learning with arms, that did both do and write what was worthy to be remembred; and that small parcel of ground, whose greatness was then onely valu'd by the vertue of the inhabitants, planted *Trebezond* in the East, and divers other cities in *Asia* the Less, the protection of whose liberties was the first cause of war between them and the *Persians*: As to exploits, the *Athenians*, and smaller islands of the *Ægean*, exceedingly amplified their bounds with their naval-power; so as *Thucydides* enumerates their annual descents upon *Peloponnesus*, during that quarrel: but the exploits of *Alcibiades*, both when so ungratefully exil'd from his country, and after he was again restor'd to it, were celebrated in story, as well as those of *Conon*, *Justin.* l. 5. under whom, we first hear of a Treasurer of the Navy, for the better paying of the seamen, even in those early daies: But, these conflicts did many of them concern the *Persian* by *Tissaphernes* under *Darius*, *Artaxerxes*, and others: The differences also with the *Megarenses*, where *Pisistratus* obtain'd the victory, and the exploits of *Themistocles*; but, especially that decretory battle in which *Xerxes's* fleet of 1500 men of war was vanquish'd by less than 400, which gave the absolute dominion of the sea to one city, and so inrich'd it, that the *Lacedemonians* (envious at her prosperity) maintain'd a war against it, to the almost ruine of both, see the effects of avarice! But this was indeed before the *Peloponnesian* war, between the LXXX and LXXXIV *Olympiad*, and first commenc'd against strangers, and then the *Lacedemonians*, *Corcyreans*, and other their neighbours for the space of seven years continuance, till by the courage, and good conduct of *Lysander*, a peace was at last concluded,

                                     with

with the destruction of *Athens,* as it usually happens to the first who give the occasion, and are the agressors. She was yet set-up once again, by that gallant exile whom we nam'd, under the banner of *Artaxerxes;* but so to the desolation of poor *Greece* (weakn'd by her many conflicts) that King *Philip,* and his son *Alexander,* soon took their advantage, to make themselves, first masters at sea, and then of the world; for they are infallible consequents. And here we might speak something of *Corinth,* a city (if ever any) emulous of the highest praises for traffick, and exploits at sea; but we involve her amongst the *Grecians,* and pass over to the opposite shore; where, upon division of the *Macedonian* empire, we find the *Carthaginians* (a people originally from *Tyrus*) of the earliest fame for commerce, and so well appointed for the sea, as gave terrour to *Rome* her self: Nor do we forget the *Syracusans,* renown'd for their many glorious actions at sea, which continu'd to the very *Punick* war, the most obstinate that history has recorded.

16. It was 492 years from the foundation of the city, before they had atchieved any thing considerable on the waters; when finding the wonted progress of their victories obstructed by those of *Carthage* (then lords at sea) they fell in earnest to the building of ships of war, and devising engines of offence, which before they hardly thought of. Their first expedition by sea, was under *Appius Claudius,* against the *Sicilians,* which made those of *Africa* look about them, and gave rise to the *Punick* war under *Cajus Duillius,* and his colleague, with an hundred rostrated vessels, and 75 gallies: but, the most memorable for number, was, when the two admirals *Regulus,* and *L. Manlius,* with above an hundred thousand men (in ships that had every one 300 at the oar) were encounter'd with a yet more prodigious force, in the battle at *Heraclea,* unfortunate to the *Car-*

thaginians :

thaginians: But, neither did it so determine: For, when *Hannibal* (returning out of *Spain*) invaded *Italy*; the *Romans* found no better expedient to divert him, than by dispatching *Scipio*, with a fleet into *Africa*. The third, and last contest (after a little repose) determin'd not till the utter ruine, and subversion of that emulous neighbour. These several conflicts with this hostile city (which lasted near twenty years) are admirably describ'd by *Polybius*; especially that of *M. Regulus*, who, with that unequal power, fought three battles in one day; and, in another, *Æmilius* (with about the same number of ships) took, and sunk above an hundred more, and slew near 40000 of the enemy, though by the terrible and unfortunate wrack, which afterwards surpriz'd him, such another victory had undone them. They made war, after this, with the *Achaians*, *Balearians*, *Cilicians*, *Sertorians*, and those of *Crete*; indeed, wheresoever they found resistance, diffident yet at first, of this unaccustom'd manner of combate, and which for sometime, caus'd them to lay it by; but, they quickly resum'd it, and overcoming all difficulties, then onely might be said to speed conquerours of the world, when they had conquer'd the sea, and subdu'd the waters.

17. The *piratick*-war of *Pompey* we find celebrated by *Tully*, *pro lege Manilia*: he invaded the *Cyclades*; won *Corcyra*, got *Athens*, *Pontus*, and *Bithynia*, and cleared the seas with that wonderful diligence, that in forty daies time, he left not a rover in all the *Mediterranean*, though grown to that power, and number, as to give terrour to the common-wealth. We forbear to speak of *Sextus* his unfortunate son, vanquish'd by the treachery of his *Libertus* † *Menodorus*, and pass to the great *Augustus*, who in many sea-conflicts signaliz'd his courage; especially, in that decretory battail at *Actium*, where the contest was *de summa rerum*, and the world

Florus, Plutarch.

†Call'd also *Menas* by *Horace Epod.*

by sea, first subdu'd to the Empire of a single person.
What discoveries this mighty prince made, did as far
exceed his prædecessours, as the frozen *North* and horrid
coasts of *Cimbria,* the milder clime of our *Britain,* which
was yet in those daies esteem'd another world, and her
boundaries, as much unknown, as those of *Virginia* to
us: 'Twas called *Alter Orbis*; and grave authors,[*] who
speak of the unpassableness of the *ocean,* mention the
worlds that lay beyond it: *Morinorum gentem ultimam
esse mortalium,* says *Ptolomy*; and the prince of poets,

——*Extremique hominum Morini.*

For it appears no late fancy, that all was not discover'd
long before *Columbus*; though those who took the hea-
vens for a kind of hollow arch, covering onely what
was then detected, little dream'd of *Antipodes*: 'Tis
famous yet what the prophetick *tragædian* has offer'd
at,[*] and a thing beyond dispute, that the antients had
the same notions of our country, as we of *America*:
But to leave these enquiries at present (till we come
more particularly to speak of our country in the following *series*) we shall onely, as to the *Romans*, give
the curious a tast, what care these wise people had of
their naval preparations, when once (as we have shew'd)
they found the importance of it, and after how prudent
a method they dispos'd it.

18. *Augustus* had in his military establishment one
squadron of men of war at *Ravenna,* as a constant
guard of the *Adriatic*; and another riding at *Misenum,*
to scowr the *Tyrrhen*-Sea, together with a *brigade* of
24
foot

* Especially
*Clem. Ro-
manus.* See
also *Claudius,*
*Servius, Jose-
phus, Dio,
Eutropius,
Scaliger,* &c.

*Sen.*in *Med.*

Sueton in*Auq.*
c. 49.

---

* Venient annis sæcula seris,

Quibus Oceanus vincula rerum

Laxet, et ingens pateat tellus,

Tethysque novos detegat orbes;

Nec sit terris ultima Thule.

Medea, Act II, lin. 375.

foot souldiers at either port, to clap on board upon any sudden occasion. The *Misenian* fleet lay conveniently for *France, Spain, Morocco, Africk, Ægypt, Sardinia,* and *Sicily*; that at *Ravenna,* for *Epirus, Macedon, Achaia, Propontis, Pontus*; the *Levantine* parts, *Creete, Rhodes,* and *Cyprus,* &c. So as by the number of their vessels, and arms, they made a bridge (as it were) to all their provinces, and vast dominions at what distance soever: And many of these particulars we could farther illustrate by medals, and noble inscriptions, to be gather'd out of good records, did we need the ostentation of any farther researches. We shall only observe, that they had their *Præfectus Classis,* who inspected all this. *Marine* laws and customes they also had: Whence was it else that the corn-fleet was still from *Alexandria* to make *Puteoli,* as it were by coquet bound? So the ships of that port: see *Acts* 28. 11, 12, 13. Whence else was it that onely the same corn-fleet, as being of so absolute necessity for the sustenance of the *Imperial* city, had the priviledge to come into harbour with top and top-gallant; unless the rest did *supparum dimere,* or strike sail to the ports of the Empire? So early was the claim to the flag, and the ceremonies of naval honour stated. Yet higher: Their Rostrate-crowns; and that pretty insolence by act of senate allow'd to *C. Duillius* after having won the *Romans* their first victory at sea, that he should, all his life after, be brought to the publick entertainments in the Town-hall, with a pipe playing before him; and *flambeaux* on each side; that *column,* too, whose fragments yet preserv'd, exhibit with the memory of that illustrious action, perhaps the ancientest piece of *Latin* now extant, at least in the originals. All these allegations do abundantly testifie with what transports of joy that aspiring people receiv'd the accession of power by sea. They also had their *Decuriæ Fabrorum Ravennatium,* master ship-wrights of the dock at *Ravenna*; and,

Vegetius.

Notitia Imperii.

MIL. CL. P. RAV *Miles Classis Prætoriæ Ravennatis.* PRÆTOR. MAR. ET. CL. M. R. *Militiæ Ravennatis.*

See *Tully de Senect.*

Gruter's Inscriptions.

we

we find fire-ships mention'd in *Frontinus ;** stink-pots,
nay snake-pots, and false colours; for such, we read,
were us'd by *Cassius, Scipio, Annibal, M. Portius,
Iphicrates, Pisistratus,* and others: and, if the *Trajan*
port at *Ostia* were now extant, we might see such a
pattern of a mole,* lantern, magazine for ships, and accommodation for merchants goods, as was never before
in the world, and would put to shame all modern
industry of that nature; to shew the care they had,
and the prodigious expences they made, for this so
important, and necessary a work: But these things
hapning in her early and best daies, the fervour quickly
abated; for from the death of *Augustus,* and some few
of the succeeding Emperours (as in that † decline, by

the conduct of *Belizarius, Artabanes,* and some of the
later captains) the *Romans,* as powerful by land as they
were, performed not much at sea; those glorious actions were the consequents of a frugal and vigilant
people; but, when softness, and prodigality took off
their minds from the great, and nobler enterprizes of
their ancestors, and the defence of their country was
discompos'd by factions among themselves, the *Goths,
Vandales, Lombards,* and *Saracens* broke in upon them,
to the utter ruine, and subversion of that renowned
Empire.

19. But the business of *navigation,* and *commerce*
(which could not long be eclips'd so soon as a magnanimous prince appear'd,) was again reviv'd under
Charles the Great; about whose time, it were not
hard to find out the original of almost all the naval
officers, and *Thalassarchia* or Admiralty, to this day continuing; as appears in both the *Notitiæ Imperii Occi-
dentalis et Orientalis,* wherein there occur divers notable particulars concerning them, even till the loss of

---

* The breakwater at Civita Vecchia is the work of Trajan,
and does honour to his illustrious name.

Constantinople, and the Imperial seat itself: But, to trace this great article from its source, and shew the progress it has made in the ages past, we have but to look over the *catalogue* which *Eusebius* has given us, adjusted to the *epoche* in which they had successive dominion of the *sea*; namely, the *Lydians* whom (as appearing the most conspicuous) he sets in the *van*: Then the *Pelasgi, Thraces, Rhodians, Phrygians, Phœnicians*, the *Ægyptians, Milesians*, those of *Caria, Lesbia*, the *Phocenses, Naxii, Eretrienses, Æginetæ* and others too long to recite: Let us look back to the *Ægyptians*, who we read, were so addicted to traffick, as they essayed to joyn the *Mediterranean* with the *Red* Sea, and thereby open a passage to the commerce of *Arabia, Æthiopia*, and the shoars of *India*: Which attempt (unsuccessful as it prov'd) did not yet impeach the *Alexandrian* staple, from whence *Rome* of old, the *Genoezes, Venetians*, and others of later date, have inricht themselves: for the *Eastern* scale being in *Cæsars* time at *Coptos*, and afterwards, remov'd to *Alexandria*; when the *Arabs* and *Goths* overran the world (and the *Indian* trade interrupted) was convey'd to *Trebezond* upon the *Euxine*, and from thence by *caravan* to *Aleppo*, thence again recover'd to the *Red*-Sea, and *Alexandria* by the *Sultan*, who then possessed *Cairo*, where it was long monopoliz'd by the *Venetians*, of whom we give a more particular account. What immense treasure the *Romans* received out of *Asia*, and *Syria*; out of *Africa* from *Ægypt*, and by the *Nile*; the *Persian* Gulph, and from *India*, we are told out of *Strabo* †. This merchandize was first convey'd over-land from *Berenice*, by *Philadelphus* (to avoid the perils of navigating the *Red*-Sea) to *Coptos* on the *Nilus*; and thence (with the stream) to *Alexandria*, though many ships adventur'd to pass from *Musiris* (or the *Berenice* above-mention'd) even to the very *Indies*; by which means there came

In *Chron.*

† *Lib.* 17.

yearly to *Rome*, no less than 1000 tuns of gold,* besides other precious commodities.   But, when the Empire fell to decay, the *Venetians* (as we noted) took their advantage, till then a few scatter'd cotages of poor fisher-men, and others, fugitives from the *Gothic* inundation, and setling by degrees upon a cluster of divers muddy, and almost, inaccessible islands : See what commerce can effect ! But, these industrious people essay'd another way, namely, from the *Ganges* through *Bactria*, and the river *Oxus*, and so to the *Caspian* Lake, *Astracan* and the *Volga*; thence to the *Euxine* by the *Tanaïs*, and so to *Venice*; truly an immense circle, and which soon wearied them out, when even of later times, the negoce of *India* was supplied from *Tripoly*, and *Alexandretta* (cities of *Syria*) and from *Aleppo* by *caravan*, to which scale merchants came from *Armenia, Arabia, Ægypt Persia*, and generally, from all the *Oriental* countries. From *Aleppo* again they return'd to *Bir* on the *Euphrates*; thence all down the stream to *Balsara*, and the Gulph : To this *Balsara* is yet brought all sorts of *Indian* commodities, as far as *Æthiopia*, and the islands of that ocean; where being charg'd on smaller vessels, they are tow'd up against the *Euphrates* to *Hit* and *Bir*, or against the *Tigris* to *Bagdat* and *Mosul*; in which passage, being now and then interrupted by the thievish *Arabs* (especially at the frontiers) intelligence is familiarly convey'd by the inter-nunce of *pidgeons* trained up for the purpose, that is, carried in open cages from the *dove*-houses, and freed, with their letters of advice

28   (contriv'd

---

* This is an entirely erroneous statement. Neither gold nor silver came in antiquity from the East to Rome. On the contrary, in those days as at present, the exportation of the precious metals from Europe to the East was carried on to a great extent, and was loudly complained of. *Minimaque computatione millies centena millia sestertium annis omnibus, India et Seres, peninsulaque illa (Arabia) imperio nostro adimunt.* Plin. Hist. Nat. lib. xii, cap. 18.

(contriv'd in narrow scrowls about their bodies, and under the wing) which they bring with wonderful expedition: as they likewise practice it from *Scanderoon* to *Aleppo* upon the coming in of ships, and other occasions. These were the later intercourses from *Venice* to, and from the *Oriental* parts, till in the year 1497, that the famous *Vasco de Gama* (that fortunate *Portugueze*, and whom we may truly call the *Restorer* of *Navigation*) found out a nearer way, by going farther about: For *Henry*, the third son of *John* the First of *Portugal*, hearing that *Bethen-Court*, a *Norman*, had detected certain islands in the *Atlantick* Ocean some years before; sent two ships in search of the *Africa* shoars southwards: ten years after this, *Gonsalvo Zarco* and *Tristan Vaz* made discovery of *Madera, and certain *Genoezes* had sail'd as far as the *Sierra Lione*, within eight degrees of the *Æquator*; after which, there was little advance till the reign of *Alphonsus* the Second, in whose time, the *Portuguezes* coasted as far as the promontory of *St. Katharine* under the second degree of southern latitude: But, *John* the Second sending men by the old way of *Alexandria*, and the *Midland*-Sea to *Goa*, *Peter Covilham*, an active spirit amongst them, hearing of a famous Cape, which extending itself far into the sea, and that being doubl'd, did open a passage into the *East*, brought news of it to King *Emanuel* (then reigning) who thereupon, employ'd the two brothers *Vasco* (whom we nam'd) and *Paulo*, with four vessels, and 160 men, with that success, as to discover a passage to the *Indies* by *Long-Sea*, to the almost utter ruine of *Venice*; and, in a short time after, to the total interruption of that tedious circle by *land, rivers*, and *lakes*, which we have been describing; nor are we to forget *Alvarez, Almeida*, and others: And in this manner, for divers years (at least till the reign of *John* the Third) did the *Portugals* and *Spaniards* carry the trade of the world, from the rest of the world, till the *Hollanders*

29 (being

1497.

1410.

1419 or 1420.

* *Detected before by one* Machin an Englishman. (This is doubtful.)

(being prohibited all intercourse with the ports belonging to the *catholick* kings) attempted the same discovery, and in short time, so out-did the former; that, by the year 1595, they had establish'd a company for the *East Indies*, and within a while after, another for the *West*, which has subdu'd the best part of *Brazile*, and in the year 1628, fought, and took the *Spanish* plate-fleet, to their immense inrichment: but, in what manner they have setled themselves and factories in those parts, and by what arts maintain'd it, will require a fuller discovery.

1595.

1624.

1628.

20. We not long since mention'd the *Goths* and *Vandals*, and who almost has taken notice of the ancient port of *Wisbuy*, formerly a receptacle of ships, and famous *emporium* in those parts? when even the laws, and ordinances of *Wisbuy*, took place like those of *Oleron*, from *Muscovy*, to the Streights of *Gibraltar*; and though both *Olaus Magnus*, *Herberstan*, and others have exceedingly celebrated this city, and haven; yet we cannot learn, how it came to be deserted, unless by the luxury, and dissentions of the inhabitants; by none (that we can find) recorded: But, that it was once in so flourishing a state, testifie the yet remaining heaps, the columns of *marble, jasper,* and *porphyrie*: the gates of brass and iron, exquisitely wrought, and other footsteps of august foundations. *Albertus* the *Swedish* King, endeavour'd by great privileges, to have it establish'd again, and restor'd to its ancient splendour, but it did not succeed: Nevertheless, the laws we mention'd (written in the old *Theutonick* language, and without date) obtain'd amongst the *Germans, Danes, Flemmings*, and almost all the *Northern* people: We mention the instance to shew, that as some places have set up, and thriven by their industry; so others, have lost what they once possess'd; and that this vicissitude is unavoidable, *Tyrus*, and *Carthage*, and *Corinth*, and *Syracuse* (that in their turns contended with all the world for *navigation* and *commerce*) are pregnant

examples. The famous *Brundusium* (whence the great *Pompey* fled from the fortune of *Cæsar*) is now quite choak'd up: *Joppa* is no more, and *Tingis*, which of old deriv'd its name from *commerce*, and was a renown'd *emporium* near three hundred years before *Carthage* was a city, was lately the desolate *Tanger*; though now again, by the influence of our glorious monarch, raising its aged head with fresh vigour: But, what's become of hundreds we might name; *Spina* near *Ravenna*, *Luna* in *Etruria*, *Lesbus*, and even *Athens* her self?* When nearer home, and at our own doors, *Stavernen* in *Friezland*, anciently a famous port, now desolate, *Antwerp* (lately the staple for the spice and riches of the *East*, and that sold more in one month, than *Venice* did in four and twenty) lies abandon'd: The stately *Genoa* (which once employ'd twice twenty thousand hands in the silken manufacture)† is now, with her elder sister *Venice*, ebbing apace; *Venice*, I say, the belov'd of the sea, seems now forlorne, compar'd to what she was, and from how a small a principle she had spread!

Strabo. Dionys. Halicarnas. See *Isaiah*, c. 23.

21. The *Bretons* and *Normans* (especially against the *Saracens*) those of *Province*, *Marselles*, *Narbon*, &c. had long since been famous at sea, we say, long since; for the ancient *Gaules* had great commerce with those of *Carthage* (as appears out of *Polybius* and *Livy*) but the *French* in general, have of later daies, and since the reign of *Charles* the Eighth, performed little considerable: *Francis* the First (that magnificent prince, who had made the famous *Andrea d' Oria* his admiral)‡ built

Phil. Comines.

31

indeed

---

* For interesting notices of these towns, and especially of Spina, Luna, and those that are least known, see the names in Smith's Dictionary of Greek and Roman Geography.

† An extreme exaggeration.

‡ Doria did not continue for any very considerable period to command the fleets of Francis; by far the greatest portion of his long and glorious career was passed in the service of the great rival of the latter, the Emperor Charles V.

indeed no less than fifty gallies for the *Italick* war, and had some conflicts with our king his neighbour; but *Henry* the Fourth, seem'd wholly negligent of sea affairs, as relying upon the generosity of Queen *Eliza-beth*, in whose daies, neither he, nor any other poten-tate about her, durst pretend to shipping, or such fleets as might give jealousie to their allies; which, had this incomparable princess, or, rather, her peaceful succes-sor, as well observ'd with the *Hollanders* in point of *commerce* and *trade* too, the ages to come, as well as present, had been doubly oblig'd to their memory: But the scene is now chang'd, as well with them as with *France*; since Cardinal *de Richlieu*, in the reign of *Lewis* the Thirteenth, instituting a colledge, and frater-nity of *merchants* about thirty years since; and by opening, enlarging, and improving their ports and ma-gazines, has put the present *Monarch* into such a condi-tion, as has exceedingly advanc'd his *commerce*, and given principle to no inconsiderable navy; and if *Claudius Sesellius* the *Bishop* of *Marselles's* prophecies succeed (who writ about the time of *Lewis* the Twelfth) the *Northern* world is like to have an *importunate neighbour* within few years to come, from his growing power, even upon the *ocean*.

22. The *Danes*, and more *Northern* people were for-midable (especially to this island) under the conduct of their brave *Canute*, *Ubbon* the *Frizian*, and other cap-tains; making frequent descents upon us in mighty *fleets*, encounter'd by the *Saxons*: But, all these living more by *brigandize*, and *piracy*, than by *traffick*, gave place to the *Spaniard*, and *Portugals*, whose successful expeditions, and discoveries, have rendered them deser-vedly more worthy for these last six, or seven hundred years, than any we have hitherto mention'd, for their shedding of blood, and invasions. Nor with less glory, and timely application of themselves to sea-affairs, did the formerly-mention'd *Genoezes*, and others of the

Ligurian coast, signalize their courage, as well as their dexterity in traffick; especially, against the *Saracens*; since which, they did exceedingly flourish; till the Dukes of *Tuscany*, by better policy, and the direction of Count *Dudley* (pretended Duke of *Northumberland*) raising its neighbour *Ligorn* from a despicable, and neglected place, to a free and well defended port, did well nigh ruin it; for, by this means, the greatest *merchants* for repute in the world (namely those of *Genoa*) are become the greatest, and sordidst *usurers* in it; as having otherwise little means to employ the *riches*, which they formerly got, by a more honest, and natural way of *trade*: But, as the opening of *Marselles* may in time endanger that of *Ligorn*, whilst the *French* King is courting all the world with *naturalization*, and other popular immunities; other princes are instructed how to render themselves considerable, who are blest with any advantagious post upon the bordures of the *ocean*; and, of this, *Gotenberg* (not to mention *Villa-Franca*, and some other ports) is now a worthy instance; which, till of late, was hardly known beyond its wooden *suburbs*, though it must be acknowledg'd, that both the *Danes* and *Sweeds* had perform'd notable exploits; the *former* from *Harold* the Third, by the conduct of *Ubbon* the *Frisian* (not to insist on their heavy impositions on this *island*) and the *latter* from *Gustavus* the *first*, who serv'd himself of *gallies* even upon the *Northern* seas, built for him by the *Venetians*, and set out that enormous ship, we mention'd, which carryed 1800 men: What *conquests* the late great *Adolphus* made, who went into *Prusia* with an *armada* of 200 *ships*, is known to the amazement of *Europe*.

23. We have more than once shew'd, from how humble a rise *Venice* had exalted her head, and spread the fame of her conquests, as well as navigation, over *Asia, Ægypt, Syria, Pontus, Greece* and other countries, bordering upon the *ocean*: she war'd against the *Is-*

trians,

trians, vanquish'd the *Saracens*.   In the *Holy-land*;
they won *Smyrna*, devasted all the *Phœnician* shoars,
especially under *Dominico Michaele*, who with 200
vessels, having rais'd the siege of *Joppa*, took *Chius*,
Samos, Lesbos; to omit their successes against the *Genoëzes* emulous of their growth, but never to forget
the former, and of late, strenuous resistance against
the *Turk*; especially in that signal battle of *Lepanto*,
and what their famous General *Capello* did at *Tunis*,
and *Algiers* of later time, and the building, furniture,
and oeconomy of their *arsenal*, and *magazines* celebrated throughout the world; when (before the lucky
Portuguezes had doubl'd the cape of *Bon-Esperanza*)
the sweet of the *Levantine* commerce (transfer'd from
this port onely) invited men to build not ships alone,
but houses, and palaces in the very bosom of *Neptune*,
with a stupendious expence, and almost miraculous: The
government of their *maritime-affairs*, care of their
forrests, victualling, courage and industry of their
greatest *noble-men*, who are frequently made *captains* of
single *gallies*, and sometimes arriving to be chief *admirals*, come near a *dictatorship*; are things worthy of
praise; and of the name they have obtain'd.   *Genoa*
(whom we mention'd) had signaliz'd it self against the
Saracens, the *Republic* of *Pisa*, and even *Venice* it self,
especially under *Paganino Doria* in the *year* 1352, near
the *Bosphorus* streight;* and with the *island* of *Tenidos*
had been hir'd by the young *Andronicus* to come into
his assistance: From the time of *Cosmo di Medicis*,
and *Sylvio Piccolomini* their *admiral*, the *Florentines*
gave proof of their *valour* in *Africa*, and of their care
for *sea* affairs, the *arsenal* at *Pisa* gives a commendable
instance.

24. The *Rhodians* (to whom some attribute even the
invention of *navigation*, and whose constitutions were
34   universally

---
* Thracian Bosphorus.

universally receiv'd) obtain'd a mighty repute at *sea*; and the couragious exploits of the *Maltezes*, and other military orders against the common enemy, the *Turk*, are renown'd over the world; witness, *ten thousand* which they slew, and half as many that they took in the *year* 1308, with *hundred thousands* of those *miscreants* destroy'd by them since their removal to *Malta*; especially when joyn'd with the gallies of *Venice* and *Genoa*, in the *years* 1601, 1625, 1638, and other slaughters innumerable. We name the *Turk*, and they give us cause to remember them, by what the *Christian Pale* has too often felt, when more by their numbers, than their courage, they took from it *Cyprus*, *Rhodes*, and the never to be forgotten *Candia*; besides, their conquests and incursions, on the rest of *Europe* and *Asia*: they are not, 'tis confess'd, of any name for much commerce, but for the disturbance of it, which calls aloud upon the *Christian* world to put a timely period to their insolence, before it be incorrigible, and to pursue the bold, and brave exploits of our *Blakes*, *Lawsons*, and *Sprags* against the *Moores* and *Barbares*, and by example of our heroic prince, to restore that security to trade, which can onely make it re-flourish.

25. The *Æthiopians*, *Persians*, *Indians*, and *Chinezes* (for those of *Tartary*, present, or ancient *Scyths*, come hardly into this account) may be reckon'd among the nations of traffic; especially, the last named, as who are by some thought to have had knowledge of the *magnet* before the *Europeans*: nay, so addicted were they to *sailing*, that they invented *veliferous chariots*, and to sail upon the land: It was long since that they had intercourse with those of *Madagascar*, and came sometimes as far as the *Red-Sea* with their wares; and for *vessels*, have to this day about *Nankin*, *jonks* of such prodigious size, as seem like *cities*, rather than *ships*, built full of houses, and replenish'd with whole families:

 In

In short, there is hardly a nation so rude, but, who, in some degree, cultivate *navigation*, and are charm'd with the advantages of *commerce :* But, it would cost an immense volume, to discourse at large of these things in particular, and to mention onely, the brave men, who have in all ages signaliz'd themselves at sea for their arms, or, more peaceful arts; to count the names of the famous captains, and adventurers of later times, whose expeditions have been war-like, and for invasion, and many for discoveries and commerce. Here, then we contract our sails, and shall direct our course nearer home, from whence we have been so long diverted.

26. The first, that presents it self to our second consideration, are the *Spaniards,* and *Castilians,* who (upon the success of their neighbours the *Portugals*) making use of that fortunate stranger *Columbus,* prompted by a magnanimous genius, and a little philosophy, discover'd to us a new world: This great man, being furnish'd out by *Ferdinand* and *Isabella* of *Castile,* in four voyages, which he made from the year 1492, to *An.* 1502, detected the *Antillias, Cuba, Jamaïca, &c.* with some of the *Terra firma;* though to let pass *Zeno* (a noble *Venetian,* reported to have discover'd the northeast part of *America* above an hundred years before) there be, who tell us, that a certain obscure mariner (*Alphonso Zanches* by name, a pilot of *Huelva*) had the first sight of this goodly prospect, eight years before this glorious *Genoëze* (for *Columbus* was of that city) or any the pretenders: This poor sea-man, hurried upon those unknown coasts by tempests (which continu'd for almost a full month) was carried as far as St *Domingo* in *Hispaniola :* How he return'd is not said; but, that from the observations of this adventurer, *Christopher* receiv'd the first notices of what he afterwards improv'd, being at that time in the *Maderas,* where *Zanches* arriving, died not long after, and bequeath'd

1492.

1390.

him

him all his *charts* and *papers.**   There are likewise who affirm, that some mean *Biscayers* (loosing themselves in pursuit of *whale*-fishing) had fall'n upon some of the *American* islands, above an hundred years, before either of the former; but, since of this we have no authentic proofs; certain it is, that *Columbus*, taking his conjectures from the spiring of certain winds from the *western* points, by strong impulse, concluded, that there must needs be some continent towards those quarters: Upon this confidence, he offers first, his service to *John* King of *Portugal*, and then, to our *Henry* the *Seventh of England*, by both which princes rejected for a *romantic* dream, he repairs to the court of *Spain*, where, partly by his importunity, and much by the favour of *Isabella*, he was with great difficulty set-out at last, when to equip him, the *Royal Lady* was fain to pawn some of her *jewels* : But it was well repaid, when for the value of 17000 crowns, he not long after, return'd her almost as many tuns of *treasure*, and, within eight or nine years, to the Kings sole use, above 1500000 of *silver*, and 360 tuns of *gold* : See the reward of faith, and of things not seen ! These fortunate beginnings were pursu'd by *Americus Vesputius* (a *Florentine*, and a stranger too) who being sent by *Emanuel* of *Portugal* to the *Molucca* islands (five years after) hapning to be driven upon the same ` coast, carried away the name, though not the honour from all the former, though, there be, who upon good proof affirm, that *John Chabot* a *Venetian*, and his son *Sebastian* (born with us at *Bristol*) had discover'd *Florida*, and the shoars of *Vir-*

1497.

37

ginia,

---

* There does not appear to be the smallest foundation either for this or the other statements in regard to the discovery of America prior to Columbus. See the Introductory Discourse to the excellent account given by Navarrete of the four Voyages of Columbus, French Trans. tom. i, pp. 109—124.

ginia, with that whole tract as far as *New-found-Land,* before the bold *Genoëze;* nay, that *Thorn,* and *Eliot* (both countrymen of ours) detected this *New-World* before *Columbus* ever set foot upon it; for we will say nothing of the famous *Owen Gwynedd,* whose adventures are of yet greater antiquity, and might serve to give reputation to that noble enterprize, if we had a mind to be contentious for it. But,

27. That indeed the most shining exploits of this age of *discoveries,* were chiefly due to the several *hero's* of this island, we have but to call over the names of *Drake, Hawkins, Cavendish, Frobisher, Davis, Hudson, Raleigh,* and others of no less merit: For impossible it was, that the *English* should not share in dangers with the most renowned, in so glorious an enterprize; our *Drake* being the first of any mortal, to whom God vouchsafed the stupendious atchievment of encompassing, not this *New-World* alone, but *New* and *Old* together: Both of them twice embrac'd by this *demigod;* for *Magellan* being slain at the *Manillas,* was interrupted in his intended course, and left the exploit to *Sebastian del Cano* his collegue.

28. This voyage of *Drake* was first to *Nombre de Dios;* where coming to a sight of the South-Seas, with tears of joy in his eyes, his mind was never in repose, till he had gotten into it, as in five years after he accomplish'd it, when passing through the *Magellan* Streight towards the other *Indies,* and doubling the famous promontory, he circum-navigated the whole earth, and taking from the *Spaniard* St. *Jago, Domingo, Cartagena,* and other signal places, crown'd in the name of his mistress the Queen, at *Nova Albion,* he return'd to his country, and to a crown of immortal honour. This gallant man was leader ·to *Cavendish,* another country-man of ours, of no less resolution; for these brave persons scorning any longer to creep

by

by shoars, and be oblig'd to uncertain constellations; plow'd up unfathomable abysses, without ken of earth or heaven, and really accomplish'd actions, beyond all that the *poets* of old, or any former record (fruitful in *wonders*) could invent or relate.

29. And now every *nation*, stimulated by these adventures, daily added new-things to the accomplishment of the art: Things, I say, unknown to former ages: And herein were the *Portugals* very prosperous, one of whose princes brought first into use the *astrolabe* and tables of *declination*, with other *arithmetical*, and *astronomical* rules, applicable to *navigation*; besides, what several others had from time to time invented: But, neither were these to be compar'd to the *nautic box*, and feats of the *magnet*; before which the science was so imperfect, and mariners so terrified at long voyages; that there were laws to prohibit sailing upon the *Mediterranean*, during the *winter* season; and, however great things have been reported of *Plato's Atlantic*, the discoveries of *Hanno*, *Eudoxius*, and others of old time, from the *Persian Gulph*, as far as *Cadiz*; it was still with sneaking by the shoar, in continual sight of land; or by chance, which indeed has been a fruitful mother in these, and most other discoveries; that men might learn humility, and not sacrifice to their own uncertain reasonings. In that memorable expedition of the *French* to invade our country, there was hardly a *pilot* to be found, who durst adventure twenty leagues into the *main*; and those who had been the most assur'd, did hardly reach within many degrees of the *Æquinoctial*. The *Azores* were first stumbl'd-upon by a roming pirat, surpriz'd by storm:* all the *Asiatic Indian* seas, and some of

1305.

Africa,

---

* The particulars in regard to the discovery of the Azores are not well known. Most probably it took place about the middle of the 15th century.

Africa, lay almost as much in the dark, as the *Hyper-boreans*, and horrid *North*. And though this defect was encounter'd more than two ages past, by that ever to be renown'd *Italian Flavio* of *Amalphi* (for we pass what is reported of the ancient *Arabs*, *Paulus Venetus*, and others) yet, was it near fourscore years after, ere it came so far *north* as these countries of ours, to which his needles continually pointed: But, it was now when the fullness of time was come, that by this means, the Western *Indies* should be no longer a secret, and what have been the incomparable advantages, which this despicable *stone* has produc'd (the property whereof is ever to have its poles, converted to the poles of the world, and its axes directed parallel to the axes of the world) is argument of admiration: But, that by vertue of this dull *pibble*, such a continent of land, such myriads of people, such inexhaustible treasures, and so many wonders should be brought to light, plainly astonishes, and may instruct the proudest of us all, not to contemn small-things; since so it oftentimes pleases the Almighty to humble the loftiness of men, and to choose the base things of the world, to confound the things that are mighty. And less than this we could not say, concerning that inestimable *jewel*, by whose aid and direction, the commerce, and traffick of the world has receiv'd such advantages.

80. We have now dispatch'd the *Portugals* and the *Spaniards*: there remain the *English* and the *Holland-ers*, who courting the good graces of the same mistris, the *trade* of the *world*, divide the *world* between them: Deservedly then we celebrate the industry of the *Bata-vians*: They must really be look'd upon as a *wonderful people*; nor do we diminish our selves whilst we magnifie any worthy actions of theirs; since it cannot but redound to our glory, who have been the occasion of it; and, that as oft as they have forgotten it, we have been able to chastize them for it: It is, I say, a

miracle,

miracle, that a people (who have no principle of *trade* among themselves) should in so short a space, become such masters of it: Their growth ('tis confess'd) is admirable; and if it prove as solid, and permanent, as it has been speedy, *Rome* must her-self submit to the comparison: But, we know, who has calculated her *nativity*, and that *violent* things are not alwaies lasting. We will yet give them their due; they are *gyants* for stature, fierce in beard and countenance, full of goodly towns; strong in *munition*, numerous in *shipping*; in a word *high* and *mighty-states*, and all this the product of *commerce* and *navigation*; but by what just arts equally, and in all parts improv'd, we may hereafter enquire, as well as to whose kindness they have been the most obliged, and the most ingrateful: We omit to speak here of their discoveries, and plantations, which the curious may find in the journals of *Heemskerk*, *Oliver Vander-Nordt*, *Spilbergen*, *Le Maire* (who went six degrees farther *south* than *Magellan* himself, and found a shorter passage into those seas) to these we may add *L'Ermite*, the late compilers of their *atlases*, and others, which many volumes would hardly comprehend, and because they are generally known; *Tacitus*, and other famous authors have celebrated their early exploits at *sea*, and of later times, *Fredric Barbarossa* did bravely against the *Saracens* at *Pelusium* in *Ægypt*: The *Frisians* greatly infested the *Danes*, and those of *Flanders*, especially under *William* the son of *John* count of *Holland*, and in the time of *Philip* the good duke of *Burgundy*: They were the first that wore the *broome*, when, *Anno* 1488, they had clear'd the *Levantine* seas, subdu'd the *Genoëzes*, and vanquish'd the *French* about an hundred years after: How they plagu'd the *Spaniard* and *Portugals*, from the year 1572 to almost this day, there is no body ignorant of; and for that of their discoveries, *Qua vero ignota littora, quasve desinentis*

Marginal notes:
1219.

Bentivoglio hist. Flan.

V. Pont. *Heuterus Austr.* l. 13.

Dec. 1. l. 1.

desinentis mundi oras scrutata non est Belgarum *nauticæ?* was justly due to them from *Strada;* and the truth is, they have merited of fame for many vertues, and shew'd from what small, and despicable rudiments, great things have emerged; and that traffick alone, which at the first raised, has hitherto supported this grandure against a most puissant *Monarch,* for almost an age intire: But, their admission of forreigners, increase of hands, encouraging manufactures, free, and open ports, low customes, tolleration of religions, natural frugality, and indefatigable industry could indeed, portend no less. We conclude then with *England,* which though last in order, was not the last in our design; when upon reflection on our late differences with our neighbours of *Holland,* we thought it not unsuitable to præface something concerning the progress of that commerce, which has been the subject of so many conflicts between us.

81. To the little which has been hitherto said of the great things which our nation has perform'd by *sea* in the later ages, we might super-add the gallantry, and brave adventures of former; since from no obscure authors we learn, the *Britains* to have accompanied the *Cimbrians* and *Gauls,* in their memorable expedition into *Greece,* long before the incarnation of our *Lord,* and whilst they were yet strangers to the *Roman* world; not to insist on the *Cassiterides,* known to the *Phœnicians,* and with so much judgment, vindicated by a learned author, in that his excellent and useful *Institution:* In all events, we resort to the greatest captain, and, without dispute, the purest of ancient writers: The description which *Cæsar* makes of the supplies this island afforded the *Gauls* (and, which made him think it worth his while to bring-over his legions hither) will inform us, that the structure of their *vessels* was not altogether of *twigs,* and *oxes-hides;* and the *Veneti,*

Camdenus. Strabo, l. 3.

W. Howel Instit. Hist. *Bocharti Canaan,* l. 1. c. 39. & l. 3. c. 9.

De Bello Gall lib. 3.

it

it seems, had then a navy of no less than 200 sail, built of goodly *oak*, tall, and so bravely equipped for war, and to endure the sea, as that great general acknowledg'd the *Romans* themselves had nothing approach'd it: which we mention, because divers grave authors believe the *British* vessels (sent sometime as auxiliaries) were thought to be like them: And the slender experience which the *Gauls* (or, in truth any other neighbour of theirs) had of the opposite shoars, when the *Britains* were thus instructed both for defence, and commerce (and, at that time permitted certain merchants onely to frequent their coasts) is a fair præscription, how early she intituled her self to the *dominion* of the seas; which, if at any time interrupted by barbarous surprize, or invasion (as in the ages following it seem'd to be) yet, neither did that continue any longer, than till the prevalent force was established, which soon asserting the title, as *lords*, and in right of *England*, maintain'd her prærogative from time immemorial: I know not why therefore, a solitary writer, or two, should go about to deprive this nation of more than twelve hundred years at once; because an heroick Prince has had the misfortune to have his mighty actions reported by some weak, and less-accurate pens: Yet, such, as the times wherein they liv'd, could furnish; especially too, since this has been the fate of as brave men, as any whom history has recorded: But, by this pretence, some there are, who would take from us, the renowned *Arthur*, who is reported to have led his squadrons as far as *Ise-Land*, and brought the *Northern*-people under his flag, planting the confines of the *British*-Ocean, as far as the *Russian* tracts; and this (together with all the *Northern*, and *Eastern* Isles) to be *de jure*, appendices unto this kingdom, we may find in the *Leges Edwardi* confirm'd by the *Norman* Conquerour; for so it had indeed been left to the famous *Edgar* (to mention onely

See 'ΑΡΧΑΙ-ΟΝΟΜΙΑ, *sive, de Priscis Anglorum Legibus*, written by *Lambard*, and publish'd by Mr. *Wheelock*.

Egbert,

Egbert, Alfred, Ethelfred, &c. princes, all of them, signally meritorious for their care of the *sea*) who soon finding by experience what benefit, and protection his country receiv'd by the extraordinary vigilancy on the coasts, and the vindicating of his dominions on the waters, cover'd them at once, with no less than four thousand sail; nor, it seems, without cause (the time consider'd) since we lay so expos'd to a barbarous enemy. *Alfred* (whom we mention'd) found it so in his daies; a sober, and well-consulted prince; and therefore provided himself of the same expedient against the troublesome *Danes,* whom he not seldome humbl'd: But, this *maxime,* as often as neglected, did as certainly expose the *nation* to prey, and contempt, as not long after it, to the *Norman* power, and may so again to a greater, when through a fatal supineness, we shall either remit of our wonted vigilancy and due provisions, or suffer our up-start neighbours to incroach upon us; so true is that saying, *By what means any thing is acquir'd by the same 'tis preserv'd.*   Did this island wisely consider the happiness of not needing many fronteirs to protect her from hourly alarms, or inland fortresses to check the suddain, and rude incursions, to which all *continents* are obnoxious; she would not think her bounty to her *prince* a burthen; who by maintaining a glorious, and formidable navy at sea, not onely renders her inhabitants secure at home, without multiplying of governours, and guarnisons (which are ever jealous to a free, and loyal people) but, unless wanting to themselves, repairs their layings-out, with immense advantages; and by securing, and improving that *trade,* and *commerce,* which onely can render a nation flourishing, and, which has hitherto given us the ascendent over the rest of the world: so true is another *axiom, Qui* mare *tenet, eum necesse rerum potiri;* but, without which, 'tis in vain to talk of sovereignty.

Nimis multa extare documenta Britanniæ *esse Dominos, qui essent maris. Grot. Hist.* l. 13.

Cic. ad Atic. l. 10. Ep. 8.

44

32. By

32. By these politicks King *John* was enabl'd to pass the seas into *Ireland* with a fleet of 500 sail; imperiously commanding whatever *vessels* they should meet withal about the eight circumfluent seas, to arrest them, and bring them to understand their duty: But, our third *Edward* (to whom the house of *Burgundy* ow'd so much) equipp'd above a thousand tall ships upon another occasion; with an handful whereof, he defeated a prodigious navy of the *French*, and *Spaniards*, that were gotten together; and we have seen a perfect, and undoubted list of no fewer than 700 men of war, which this prince brought before *Calais*, though he made use of but 200 of them, to vanquish a fleet consisting of more than double the number with the loss of thirty thousand *French;* which had such an influence on his neighbours, that, whereas, till then, there had been some remisness in the nation, and a declension of sea-affairs; the bravest, and greatest men in the land, began greedily to embrace maritime employments; and the title of * *Admiral,* introduc'd in his prædecessors time, was now held in highest esteem.

33. We mention'd the house of *Burgundy*, and it had reason to remember us, and our *wool*, which was the fairest flower of that *ducal coronet*, and as some good *antiquaries* remark, really gave institution to their *Golden Fleece*: However it were, this wise prince, representing to the *Flemings* their miserable posture (at that time obnoxious to the *French*, as of late they have likewise been) and, inhibiting the importation of forraign cloths: the serene and quiet condition of this happy island, invited them over to settle here, erect their manufactures amongst us, and joyn their art to our nature.

34. We pass by the exploits, and glorious atchievments perform'd by our kings against the *Saracens* in the *Holy-War*, which charg'd the sheilds of the ancient

** Thalassiarcha. See Vossius de Vitiis Sermonis Lat. l. 2. It's deriv'd from Emir, or A-mir Præfectus in Arab.*

nobless,

nobless, and, of which, all *Asia* resounded: here our *Edwards, Henries,* and *Richards* did memorable things; in particular, *Richard* the *Second* took of the *French,* almost an hundred ships at once, of which some were vessels of great burthen, richly fraite: and an earl of *Arundel* (bearing this princes name) beat, took, and destroy'd 226 ships deep laden with 13000 tuns of wine, coming from *La Rochelle,* after an obstinate encounter, and many brave exploits: To these we might add, the gallant preparations of *Henry* the *Fifth,* and of several more, had we a design, or any need to accumulate instances of our puissance, and successes at sea, so thick sown in forreign, as well as domestic histories: But, he that would be instructed for a more ample discourse, may take notice of the league made between *Charles* the *Great,* and our *Mercian Offa* (now more than 700 years since) as he may find it in an epistle of *Albinus,* or the learned *Alcuin* ('tis all one) and consult our country-men *Walsingham, Malmesbury,* and other writers; where he will see in what high repute this nation has been, both for its numerous shipping, and the flourishing commerce it maintain'd in most known-parts of the world; and, which we may farther confirm, by the several authentic statutes, and immunities yet extant, not omitting the *policy of keeping the sea,* facetiously, yet solidly, set forth in the good *old prologue,* intituled, *The Process of the Libel,* written more than 200 years past, not unworthy our deepest reflexions: And verily, it were a madness in us to neglect the care of those causes, from whence (as by a *series* of them will yet appear) the effects of all our temporal blessings spring, and, by vertue whereof, they can only be maintain'd.

85. *Henry* the *Seventh,* and his magnificent successor, were both of them powerful at sea; though the too weak-faith of the former, depriv'd him of the most glo-

rious

rious accession, that was ever offer'd to mortal-man: This, he endeavour'd to have repair'd, by the famous *Cabot*, whom he afterwards employ'd to seek adventures; and, though the success were not equal, it was yet highly laudable, and (as we have shew'd) not altogether without fruit.

86. *Henry* the *Eight* his son, had divers conflicts with the *French*,† triumphing sometimes in sails of cloth of gold, and cordage of silk : But, that which indeed repair'd the remisness of the one, and profusion of the other, and gave a demonstration of how absolute concern, traffic, and strength at sea are to this island, was the care which Queen *Elizabeth* took, when by her address alone, she not onely secur'd her kingdoms from the formidable power of *Spain;* but, reap'd the harvest too, of that opulent monarch, and brought his *Indies* into her .own exchequer; whilst that mighty prince, had onely the trouble to conquer the New-World, and prepare the treasure for her : And this she did, by her influence on *navigation*, and by the courage and conduct of those renowned *hero's*, who made her reign so famous.

† Lord Cherbury *Hist.* Hen. 8. *See also that rare piece of* Hans Holbein's *in his Majesties* Gallrey *at* White-Hall

87. This glorious *Princess* had 130 sail of fair ships, when she sent over for the island voyages, of which 60 were stout men-of-war; and with these (besides many other exploits) she defended *Holland*, defied *Parma*, and aw'd the whole power of *Spain:* With an handful of these (comparatively) she defeated the Invincible *Armada* in LXXXVIII, encounter'd, and took *gallions*, and other vessels of prodigious strength and bulk; and, what havock was made at *Cadiz* (in 1596) by yet a smaller number, her enemies to this day feel: *Grotius*, speaking of this action, tells us, that the wealth gotten there by the Earl of *Essex*, was never any where parallel'd with the like naval success; and, that if these beginnings had been pursu'd (as with ease they might,

1588.

Annal. l. 5.

                                         had

had the brave mans counsel been follow'd) it had
prov'd one of the most glorious enterprises that history
has recorded : however, besides the immense spoil, and
treasure they took, and the marks they left of their
fortitude (to the loss of 1200 great guns of the enemies,
irreparable in those daies) the *Spaniard* was not so re-
doubted abroad, as they left him miserably weakn'd at
home : To these, we may number the *trophies* won by
particular adventurers : Sir *Francis Drake*, having with
four ships onely, taken from the *Spaniard* a million,
and 189200 *ducats* in one expedition; and in a single bottom 25000 *pezos* of the most refined gold ; and after (in
1585 and 1586) with a squadron of five and twenty sail,
terrifying the whole ocean, he sack'd St. *Jago, Domingo,*
and *Cartagena* (as before mention'd) and, carried away
with him, besides other incredible booty, 240 pieces of
artillery, which was a prodigious spoil in those early
daies, and, when those instruments of destruction were
not in such plenty as now they are.　What shall we say
of *John Oxenham,* one of the *Argo-nauts* with *Drake?*
who, in a slender bark, near *Nombre de Dios* (having
drawn-up his vessel to land, and cover'd it with a few
boughs) marched with his small crue over unknown
paths, till arriv'd at a certain river, and there building
a *pinnace,* with the timber which they fell'd upon the
spot, he boldly launches into the *South Sea*, and, at the
Island of *Pearls,* took from the *Spaniard* 60000*l.*
weight of massie-gold, and 200000 in silver ! though
lost in his return with it, by the perfidy of his asso-
ciates;* such an exploit is hardly to be parallel'd in any
story. Sir *Richard Grenvill,* in another voyage to *Cadiz,*
with but 180 souldiers (of which 90 were sick and
useless) in the ship *Revenge,* maintain'd a conflict for

48

24 hours

---

* He was taken by the Spaniards and executed as a pirate.

·24 hours, against 50 *Spanish gallions*, and slew above 7000 men, sinking four of their best vessels : Than this, what have we more ——! What, can be greater! In sum, so universal was the reputation of our country-men in those daies, for their strenuous exploits at sea ; that even those who took all occasions to depress, and extenuate them, are forc'd *here* to acknowledge, and that from the pen of an author whose word goes far, * *That the* Greeks *and* Romans, *who of old, made good all their mighty actions by naval victories, were at this time, equal'd by the fortitude and courage of the* English.

38. 'Twas in her daies, they discover'd far into the *north-east*, and *north-west*, *Cathaian*, and *China* passages, by the indefatigable diligence of *Willoughby*, *Burroughs*, *Chanceler*, *Button*, *Baffin*, *Frobisher*, *James*, *Middleton*, *Gilbert*, *Cumberland*, and others, worthy to be consign'd to fame : In her brother's the Sixt *Edwards* reign, the formerly mention'd *Chabot*, had six times attempted the north-west tracks to the *Indies*; and, long before these, a bold Prince of ours, essay'd to pass the *Moluccas* by the same course; entred the streights of *Anian*, and is, by some, intituled to the first discovery of the *Canaries*. The *Summer*-Islands, and the goodly continent of *Virginia*, were first detected, and then planted by the *English*; among whom we may not pass by the industry of Captain *John Smith*, and other late adventurers, whose great exploits (as *romantic* as they appear) were the steady effects of their courage and good fortune: We have said yet nothing of *Pool*, who began the *whale*-fishing, nor of Captain *Bennet*, who discover'd *Cherry*-Island : *Pet* and *Jack-man** that passed the *Waigatz*, *Scythian Ices*, and

49

the

* Graiorum, Romanorum-que gloriæ,qui res olim suas navales per acies asseruerunt, non dubie tunc Anglorum & fortuna, & Virtuerespondit. Grot. Hist. l. L

---

* These were but indifferent navigators, mostly keeping close to the shore and in shallow water. Barrow's Voyages to the Arctic Regions, p. 99.

the river *Ob*, as far as *Nova Zembla:* Of *John Davis*, who had penetrated to 86 degrees of latitude, and almost set his foot upon the *Northern-Pole:* Here let us also remember Captain *Gillan*, to the lasting honour of his Highness, Prince *Rupert*, and the rest of those illustrious adventurers; nor forget to celebrate the heroic inclination of his sacred Majesty, our great Charles, under whose *auspices*, Sir *John Narborough* has lately pass'd, and re-pass'd the *Magellan* Streight; by which that modest, and industrious man, has not onely performed what was never done before; but has also made way for a prospect of immense improvement. Finally,

39. It was Queen *Elizabeth* who began, and establish'd the trade of *Muscovy, Turky, Barbary*, and even that of the *East-Indies* too, however of late interrupted by ungrateful neighbours: Nor less was she vigilant at *land*, than at *sea*; mustering at once no fewer than one hundred and twenty thousand fighting-men of her own vassals, not by uncertain computation; but, effectually fit for war: And indeed, but for the extraordinary vertue of this brave *virago*, not *England* alone, but even *France* and *Holland* had truckl'd under the weight of *Spain*, whose ambition was then upon its highest pinnacle: In one word, *navigation* and *commerce* were in her days in so prosperous a condition, that they seem to have ever since subsisted but upon the reputation of it; and the success of our country-men in their attempts at sea was so far superiour to other nations, as by the suffrage of the most learned strangers (and to shew it was universal) they could not but acknowledge, *Omnibus hodie gentibus navigandi industria, & peritia, superiores esse* Anglos, *& post* Anglos, Hollandos; for we do not fear to give even our greatest enemies their dues, when they deserve it.

Keckerman.

40. We now arrive to King *James*, and *Charles* the

First

First (princes of immortal memory) And for the former; there was in his time built (besides many others) those two gallant ships, the *Trades Increase*, and the *Prince*; the one for encouragement of *commerce*, and the other a *man* of *war*; and, though upon different accounts, and at different times, they both unhappily miscarried; yet, they serv'd to testifie, that neither *defence*, nor *trade* were neglected; since, as to that of the first, Sir *Walter Raleigh* doubts not to affirm; that the *shipping* of this nation, with a squadron of the *navy royal*, was in this princes time, able, in despight of *Europe*, to command the ocean, much more, to bring the *Nether-Lands* to due obedience: But, says he, as I shall never think him a lover of his country, or prince, who shall perswade his Majesty from cultivating their amity; so would I counsel them to remember, and consider it: That seeing their intercourse lies so much through the *British* seas, that there is no part of *France*, from *Calais* to *Flushing*, capable of succouring them; that, frequently, out-wards by western winds, and ordinarily, home-wards, both from the *Indies*, *Straites*, and *Spain*, all southerly-winds (the breezes of our climat) thrust them of necessity into his Majesties harbours; how much his Majesties favour does import them: For, if (as themselves confess) they subsist by *commerce* onely; the disturbance of that (and, which *England* alone can disturb) will also disturb their subsistence: I omit the rest: Because I can never doubt either their gratitude, or their prudence. But, this brave man was it seems, no prophet, to fore see how soon they would forget themselves: They began in his days to be hardly warm in comparison, and indeed it is not (as observes the same person) much beyond a century, that either the *French*, *Spanish*, or *Hollander*, had any proper fleets belonging to them as kingdoms, or states; the *Venetians*, *Genoezes* and *Portugals*, being then

 (as

(as we have noted) the only competitors both for strength, and traffick; the *Dutch* little considerable; since within these fifty years, the *Spanish* and *Portugals* employ'd many more ships at sea than the *Hollander* (their fishing-busses expected) who, 'til furnish'd with our artillery, were very contemptible, as might be made out by undeniable evidence: Insomuch that the formerly mention'd *Raleigh* affirms, one lusty ship of his Majesties, would have made forty *Hollanders strike sail*, and come to an anchor: They did not then (says he) dispute *de Mari Libero*. But will you know in a word from him, what it was that has exalted them to this monstrous pitch? It was the employing their own people in the fishery upon our coasts; by which they infinitely inrich'd themselves; 2. Their entertaining of auxilliaries in their difficult land-services; by which they preserv'd their own vassals: 3. The fidelity of the house of *Nassaw*; from which they had a wise, and experienc'd general: 4. The frequent excursions of the Duke of *Parma* into *France*, hindring the prosecution of his growing successes: 5. The imbargo of their ships in *Spain*, and interdicting them free-trade with that nation, which first set them upon their *Indian* adventures: 6. And, above all, the kindness of Queen *Elizabeth*: But, the case is (it seems) much alter'd since that worthy knight made his observations and took his leave of the Prince of *Orange* at *Antwerp*; when (after *Leicesters* return) he pray'd him to say to her Majesty, *Sub umbra alarum tuarum protegimur*; for that they had wither'd in the bud, without her assistance.

41. We have yet but only mention'd the inherent right of the crown of *England* to the *dominion* of the seas; because the legality and the reason of it have been asserted by so many able and famous pens, from which we learn, that it doth of justice appertain to the kings of Great *Britain*, not only as far as protection extends

Seldenus.

                          (though

(though there were no other argument to favour us)
but, of sacred, and immemorial royalty: But, 'tis pretended by those great names, who have of late disputed
this subject, and endeavoured to depose our princes of
this empire *jure naturæ & gentium:* That the sea is
*fluxile elementum, & quod nunquam idem, possideri non
posse;* that 'tis always in succession, and, that one can
never anchor on the same billow; that water is as free
as the air; and that the sea terminates empires which
have no bounds; and therefore, that no empire can terminate that which acknowledges none; and, though all
this were nothing; that his Majesties father, had tamely
lost it to the late usurpers, which is an insolent scoff of
Morisotus's, triumphing ore a fetter'd Lion; whilst for
all this, to patch up a wretched pretence, he descends
to take hold of a certain obsolete, and fœudatarie
complement, sometime since passing between the two
kings; as if a ceremonious acknowledgment for a province or two in *France* (which is an usual deference
among princes upon certain tenures) gave sufficient
title, and investiture to all that the kings of *England*
possess in the world besides. But in this sort do the
partizans of aspiring monarchs manage their egregious
flatteries. Whilst to silence all the world, we can shew
its prescription so far beyond the present race of kings,
that even the name of their *Pharamond* was not known,
when our *empire* on the *sea* set limits to the coasts of
Gauls, and said, *Hitherto shall ye come*——Nor, to that
alone, but even as far as *Spain* it self: For, what pretence
could those princes have to this dominion, whose very
monarchy is but of yesterday, in respect to the goodly
extent, which now they call *France?* and especially
when the only maritime provinces were shread into so
many fragments and cantons, under their petty princes;
for so were *Narbon, Bretagne, Aquitaine* and even *Normandy* it self (portions belonging then to our kings)

nor

*Grotius, Mori-
sotus, Cleirac,
Is. Pontanus.
Palatius, &c.*

Orbis Marit.

Mela.

nor had they 'till of later days, so much as the office of admiral belonging to the sea, that is, till their expedition into the *Holy-Land,* when yet they were fain to make use of the *Genoezes* to transport them as we have it confess'd by their own authors. As to their other arguments, we need not spend much breath to dilute those pitiful cavels of the instability, and fluctuation of the waves &c. which could not be there, without a channel and a bottom to contain them, as if we contended for the drops of the sea, and not for its situation, and the bed of those waters; and since rivers and streams have the same reason on their side to exempt them from being in common, and at every mans disposure.

And these things I have only touch'd, to repress the pruriency of some late flatterers, who not only injure a truth as resplendent as the sun; but the justice of a great prince, whom by these false colours, they would provoke to unrighteous disputes; whilst we pretend to nothing but what carries with it, the strongest eviction, (proof) a thing of this nature is capable of.

42. Needless it would be to amuse the reader with recounting to him at large, how in the ancient division of things, the sea, having been assign'd over with the land, there sprung up from the same original, a *private dominion;* but undoubtedly, when God gave to man the soveraignty of the ocean, by intitl'ing him to the fish, which were produc'd in the bowels of it (that is, to the *thing it self,* by its use, and enjoyment) by the same grant, he passed over to him, and consign'd to his disposure, the distribution of it, and introduction of a separate, and peculiar jurisdiction: There is nothing more perspicuous than our case, and as to his Majesties claim (the reasons for it rightly consider'd) from so many royal predecessours, and so long a tract of years, who for security of navigation, and commerce between their neighbours and allies, were at such vast expences,

to

to equip, and set forth great ships, and navies; and that, upon the intreaty, and solicitation of those, who recurr'd to their protection; and might themselves justifie the prescribing rules and boundaries to such as should pass the seas, and receive such recognitions, and emoluments, as were peculiar, and within their circle, both for their honour, and maintenance.

The deduction shall be very short, considering how vast an ocean of matter lies before us; but it shall be full.

43. *Cæsar*, ere he had invaded *Britain*, summoning the *Gallic* merchants to inform him of the shores, and situation of our ports, could it seems learn nothing from them; for, says he, not a man of them frequented that rivage without licence; and when *Claudius* had sub-du'd the more southern parts of the nation, the *British Sea*, following the fate of the whole island, came with the same privileges to be annex'd to the empire, and did never loose them, through all the revolutions which happen'd; but that as soon as the prevalent power came to be settl'd, they immediately asserted their do-minion on the sea. That of very wide extent this nation had peculiars of its own, the consternation of the *Calidonians* evince; when in the time of *Domitian*, *Agricola* sailing round the island, they were in such perplexity to see him in their chambers, for so they called those northern streams. But not longer to insist on these early beginnings, and what the *Romans* did; when the frame of that empire was chang'd, about the time of the great *Constantine*, the *comites* of the *Saxon* shore (substitutes to him who commanded the west) had their jurisdiction over all the sea, from the borders of that shoar, and west part of *Denmark*, to the western *Gallia*, all along the other side.

44. There are who put some stress here, upon ancient inscriptions, especially that mention'd by

De Bello
Lib. 4.

Tacit. in
Agric.

Gruter,

Gruter, of a *præfect* of a *British* fleet ; and on the
ornaments, and ensigns of dominion, found in several
medals, and antiquities to be met withal in the
collections of learned men ; vindicating the peculiar we
contend for, and continu'd from *Edward* the Third in
several fair stamps, nor are they to be rejected : It
suffices us, that whatever the Government were, still
the dominion of the sea return'd with that of the land
to the nation ; as when the *Britains* rejected the *Roman*
yoak, which how extended, when it came under the
power of the *English Saxon* kings, and *Danes*, is known
to all the world, as well as with what mighty navies,
Edgar, *Canutus*, and others, asserted, and protected it,
under no lower style, than that of *King*, *Supream Lord
and Governour* of the *Ocean*, lying round about *Britain* ;
for so runs the settlement of certain revenues, given
by King *Edgar*, to the *cathedral* of *Worcester*, says
Mr. *Selden.*

Zosimus l. 60
An. 43o. See
Claud. in
Land. Stil.
l. 2.

45. Since the *Norman* Conquest, the governours
the several provinces, or *sheriffs*, exercised jurisdiction on
the sea, as far as their countys extended. *Henry* the *Third*
constituted Captain Guardians; and our first *Edward* distributed this guard to three admirals; so did the second
of that name; and the form of our ancient commissions to the several admiralties, mention the dominion
of our kings upon the sea; nor did any other nation
whatsoever contest it, as having little, or nothing on
the opposite shoars; whilst 'tis evident, the *English*
monarchs possess'd their right in its intire latitude, for
more than a thousand years, under one intire empire,
and an un-interrupted enjoyment of the sea, as an
appendant.

46. To this we might add the *pass-ports* sued for by
forreigners from the reign of *Henry* the *Fourth*, and so
down to Queen *Elizabeth*, who during her war with
Spain sometimes gave leave to the *Swedes*, *Danes*, and

                    Ansiatic

Asiatic towns, and sometimes prohibited them, petitioning for passes, to sail through her seas; nay, more, she caus'd to be taken, and brought into her harbours, laden-ships of those nations transgressing her orders, as far as the Streights of *Lisbon*, which she could never have justify'd, had she not been acknowledged *Soveraign* of the Seas, through which they were to pass: And though her successour King *James*, appointed certain limits on the *English* coast, by imaginary lines drawn from point to point, round the island, in which he sometimes extended them far into the sea; it was not to circumscribe a jurisdiction (a thing which he most industriously caution'd his *Ministers* never to yield, so much as in discourse) beyond which he did not pretend; but in relation only to acts of hostility, between the two great antagonists, the *Spaniard* and the *Hollander*, declaring himself both lord, and moderator of the *British* seas from his royal predecessors.

Rot. pat. 2 Jac. part 32.

47. In several commissions given to sea commanders, by *Edward* the *Third*, the words are, Our progenitors, the kings of *England*, have before these times, been lords of the *British* seas on every side; and in a certain bill, prefer'd in parliament to the same prince, 'tis said, that the *English* were ever in the ages past so renown'd for navies, and sea-affairs, that the countries about them, usually esteem'd, and call'd them Soveraigns of the Sea; And from the same *Parliamentary* testimony in the reign of *Henry* the *Fifth* we learn, that the estates in that august assembly, did with one consent affirm it as a thing unquestionable, that the Kings of *England* were Lords of the sea, and that *that* sea was all which flow'd between the stream on both sides, and made no doubt, but a tribute might be impos'd, by authority of Parliament upon all strangers passing through them, as we shall find *Richard* the *Second* to have done long before.

Rot. Scot. 10. Ed. Membran. 16.

Rot. pat. 46. Ed. 3. N. 2.

Rot. pat. 8. Hen. 5. Mem. 3. Art. 6.

48. In the reign of *Edward* the *Second*, *Robert* Earl of

Rot. pat. 14. Ed. 2. p. 2. M 26. in dorso.

of *Flanders*, complaining of injuries done his subjects at sea, alledges, that the King of *England* is bound in right to do him justice, for that he was Lord of the Sea : But there cannot in the world be a more pregnant instance for the vindication of this dominion, and the silencing all objections, than the famous complaint against the *Genoeze Grimbaldi*, who during the war between the *French* and those of *Flanders*, infesting the seas, and disturbing commerce, occasion'd all the nations of *Europe*, bordering on the sea, to have recourse, and appeal to the Kings of *England* ; whom from time to time, and by right immemorial, they acknowledged to be in peaceable possession of the soveraign lordship and dominion of the seas of *England*, and islands of the same ; this libel, or complaint was exhibited in the time of *Edward* the *First*, almost three hundred years since, and is still extant in the *archives* of the Tower.

49. And thus we have seen how the sea is not only a distinct province, capable of propriety, limits, and other just circumstances of peculiar dominion, as a bound, not bounding his Majesties empire, but as bounded by it in another respect; and that this was never violated so much as by *syllogism*, 'till some mercenary pens were set on work against *Spain*, through whose tender sides, at that time, and with great artifice, the *Barnevelt* faction endeavour'd to transfix us ; soon it was perceiv'd, and as soon encounter'd; in the mean time, that one would smile to find their mighty champion then fairly acknowledg upon another occasion, and when it seems he resolved to speak out. *Anglia Regina Oceani Imperium*—That the Queen of *England*, was *Dominatrix* of the Sea—*So great is the truth, and will prevail :* In a word, if the *premier occupant*, be a legal and just plea to the right of other possessions, the Kings and Queens of *England*, descending from, or succeeding to them who first asserted the title, are still

1509. Treaty with *Spain*, concerning trade to the *Indies*.

Grot. Annal. l. 2. 1570.

invested

invested with it: Sure we are, this argument was held good, and illustrated by the first and best foundation of empire, when the State of *Venice* (claiming the *Adriatic* by no other) held that famous controversie with (the Emperor) *Ferdinand* in *Friuli* (in 1563) by their advocates *Rapicio* and *Chizzola*,* commissioners being mutually chosen to determine it.† And how far antiquity is on our side, the *Greeks, Romans, Tyrians, Phænicians*, and others have abundantly declar'd, and with what caution they interdicted strangers here with us, till the *Claudian* expedition annex'd it, with the dominion of all *Britain*, to that glorious empire; which to protect against the piratical *Saxons* (then not seldom infesting our coasts) the *Comites Maritimi Tractus* were by the *præfect* establish'd, as we have already shew'd: And so it continu'd for near five hundred years after, when the *Saxons* taking greater advantage of the *Roman* remissness (distracted as they grew by intestine troubles) made their descents upon us, and with the fortune of conquest, carried that likewise of the sea.

50. We have but mention'd King *Edgar*, whose survey is so famous in story, when with more than four thousand vessels, he destin'd a *quaternion* to every sea, which annually circl'd this isle, and as a monument of their submission, was sometime row'd in his royal gally by the hands of eight kings. This signal action becoming the reverse of a *medal*, was by a like device illustrated in the *rose-noble*, in which we have represented the figure of a king invested with his *regalia*, standing in the middle of a ship, as in his proper, and most resplendent throne; for the *same* reason likewise (as some interpret)

---

* The former appeared for the Emperor, the latter for Venice.

† See an account of this controversy appended to Nedham's translation of Selden's *Mare Clausum*, folio, London, 1652.

interpret) did *Henry* the *Eight*, add the *portchœe* to his current mony, as a character of his peculiar title to this *dition* (dominion), exclusive to all others.

51. We have spoken of the *Danes*, and *Normans*, and their successive claim, and of the *Custodes Maritimi*, more antient than that of admiral, as now constituted, which indeed began with the *Edwards*, when the *French*, at war with *Flanders*, but pretending to usurp that dignity, were fain to abolish their new office, and acknowledging they had no right, pay the damages of the depredations they made, as appears by that famous record in the Tower, mention'd by Sir *John Barroughs** in which the title of our kings is asserted from immemorial prescription; nay, when at this time, he had not all the opposite shoar to friend.

52. The constitution of our *Cinque-Ports* give another noble testimony to this claim, and the addition of two more admirals by our *Third Edward*, guarding as many seas, as there were superiour officers of this denomination, not omitting the title of *Lords of both Shoars*, anciently us'd from hence to *Henry* the *Fifth*; nay, when *Edward* renounc'd his claim to *Normandy* (as at the treaty of *Chartres*) the *French* themselves acknowledg'd this right, and therefore neither *here*, nor at the Court of *Delegates* in *France*, did they claim any pretence to the islands, or interfluent seas. But what need we a more pregnant instance, than that universal deference to the laws of *Oleron* (an island of *Aquitania* then belonging to this Crown) published after the *Rhodian* had been long antiquated, which obtain'd over all the Christian world. And to this we might add the *Dane-Gelt* (in plain *English*, a ship-mony tax) impos'd as well on strangers as denisens that practic'd commerce upon our coasts and seas east and north, where the

1166.

                great

---

* See his Treatise, "His Majesties Propriety and Dominion of the British Seas asserted." London, 1672.

great *intercursus* was; nor expir'd it here, but continu'd customary, as appears by innumerable records, for enabling the King to protect the seas, and to obstruct, or open them as he saw convenient, with title to all royal fishes, wracks, and goods found floating in *alto-mari*, as we can prove by several commissions, and instruments, and confirm by precedents, not of our *municipal* constitutions alone, but, such as have been binding, and accepted for such, of the nations about us; witness that famous accord made between our *Edward* the *First*, and the *French* King *Phillip* the *Fair*, calling him to account for the piracies we have mention'd. And

58. To this we might produce the spontaneous submission of the *Flemings* in open Parliament, in *Edward* the *Seconds* reign, and the *honour*, or rather *duty* of the *flag*, which King *John* with his peers, had many ages since, challeng'd, upon the custom ordain'd at *Hastings*, decreed to take place universally, not barely as a civility, but as a right of importance for the making out, and confirmation of our title to the dominion we have been vindicating; and that this has been claim'd and pay'd *cum debitâ reverentiâ* (to use the express words of those old commissions, which had been long since given by *William* and *Maurice* Princes of *Orange*) to all the sea commanders in those days; we have for almost this whole later *century*, seen the matter of fact testified not only by continual claims, orders, commissions and instructions; but by searching divers authentick journals, which have noted the particulars in a thousand instances: Nor has this been paid to whole fleets only, bearing the royal pavillion; but to single vessels, and those of the smaller craft (as they are stil'd) wearing his Majesties cognizance, to whom this homage has been done, even by the greatest navies, meeting them in any of the *British* seas in their utmost latitudes. Nor has this been so much as question'd,

1200.
M.S.Common.
de Rebus *Ad-*
mir. fol. 28.

O. C. 1672.
See his letter
of 23 *Septem.*
to the Am-
bass. at *Lon-
don.*

till that arch rebel for ends of his own, would once have betray'd it; and that the late *demagogue De Witt,* with no less insolence, would have perverted his countrymen, by entring into an injurious disquisition in justifica-tion of the wrong he would have made us swallow; but his Majesty was not so to be hector'd out of his right as appears by the honourable provision he has made to secure it, in the late treaty with the *Dutch* and what all the world has paid us, which puts it out of dispute: In the mean time it was necessary, and no way improper to the scope of this treatise, that after what has been so newly pretended, to the prejudice of the title we have asserted, some thing should be said to abate the confidence of impertinent men, and to let the world know, that our princes (to whom God, and na-ture has imparted such prerogatives) will not be baffl'd out of them, by the sentences, and sophisms of lawyers, much less by sycophants, and such as carry not the least shadow of reason: But it would fill many volumes to exemplifie the forms of our ancient commissions from time to time, investing our admirals, with the exercise of this soveraign power; as well as that of safe conducts, writts of seisure, and arrests; the copies of grants, and permission to fish (of which in the next period) ob-tain'd of our kings, by petition &c. to be found at large in our books, parliament rolls, and other authentick pieces too long for this tract: But, if any will be con-tentious, because they are some of them of ancient date, we have, and shall yet shew instances sufficient, and *ex abundanti* for this last age, to which our *antago-nists* have from time to time submitted, not only in the wide, and ample sea, or at our own coasts, but in the very ports, and harbours of strangers, where they looked for protection; that all the world may blush at the weak and unreasonable contentions, which would invalidate this claim, if at least there be in the world any such thing as right, prescription, deference, or

other

other evidence, which amongst sober men, is agreed to be *law*, for the clearing of a title.   To sum up all then, if right of prescription, succession of inheritance, continual claim, matter of fact, consent of history, and confessions even from the mouths, and pens of adversaries, be of any moment to the gaining of a cause; we may bespeak our nation, as he did King *James* upon another occasion, and as justly transfer it to his glorious successor—*Queis dat jura mari* &c.

Gret. Sylva. l. 2.

And with this I should conclude, did not the fishery, which is another irrefragable proof of his Majesties dominion, require a little survey, before we shut up this discourse.

54. How far this royal jurisdiction has extended, may best be gather'd out of the Reverend *Camden*, speaking of King *James* the *Sixth* of *Scotland*, and of Queen *Elizabeth* of *England* who first discovering the *Whale*-fishing, had consequently, title to those seas, as far as *Green-land* northward; and what it was to the south, the proclamation of our *Third Edward* (yet extant) abundantly makes appear : This confirm'd by the *Fourth* of that name, guards, and convoys, were appointed to preserve the rights inviolable ; as was likewise continued by the three succeeding *Henrys, Fifth, Sixth, and Seventh*, and their descendents, who impos'd a certain tribute upon all forreiners, in recognition of their indulgence to them.* Witness the *French*, the Dukes of *Bretagne*, of *Burgundy* (especially *Philip*) and those of *Flanders*, who never presum'd to cast a net without

Elis. & Britan.

1489.

63 permission,

---

* This statement appears to be liable to much doubt. In the *Intercursus Magnus*, or Commercial Treaty, between Henry VII and Philip, Sovereign of the Netherlands, agreed to in 1496, it is stipulated, Art. 3, that—

"The fishers, on both sides, may freely fish on the seas without any safe conduct asked ; and when driven into each other's ports by tempest or other necessity, they shall be safe there, and have free liberty to depart, paying the customary dues."

permission, and a formal instrument first obtained, the originals whereof, are yet to be seen, and may be collected out of both the *French*, and *Burgundian* stories; and, as it doth indeed to this day appear by his Majesties neighbourly civility, granted to the *French* king for the provision of his own table, and to the town of *Bruges* in *Flanders*, by a late concession; the number and size of boats, and other circumstances being limited, upon transgression whereof, the offenders have been imprison'd, and otherwise mulcted.

55. And, as the *French*, so the *Spaniard* did always sue to our princes for the like priviledg and kindness: King *Phillip* the *Second* (as nearly related as he was to Queen *Mary* his wife) finding a proviso in an act of parliament, that no forreiner should fish in those seas without permission, paid into the *Exchequer* no less than an annual rent of one thousand pounds, for leave to fish upon the north of *Ireland*, for the supply of his dominions in *Flanders*: Now for the *Dutch*.

56. That famous record *Pro hominibus Hollandiæ* (so the title runs) points to us as far as our first *Edward*, not only how obsequious then they were in acknowledging the kings dominion on the sea, but his protection, and permission to fish on the environs of it;* and his successor *Edward* the *Third*, as he gave leave to the Counts of *Holland* (who always petition'd for it) so he prescribed laws, and orders concerning the burden of the vessels to be employ'd about it: The like did *Henry*

64

the

---

* This proclamation or letter is printed in Rymer's Fœdera (vol. i. part iii. and iv., p. 148, ed. 1745), but it hardly bears out what is said respecting it in the text. It is addressed by the King, Edward I, to the magistrates of Yarmouth, and directs them to intimate to all persons employed in His Majesty's service, that they are not to molest the foreigners fishing on our shores, but that, on the contrary, they are to give them every assistance. Not a word is said in regard to licenses to fish, or payments due, or to be made by the foreigners.

the *Sixth* to the *French*, and others; with the season, place, and method to be observ'd, which are all of main importance in the cause: And this was so religiously inspected in former times, that *Edward* the *Fourth*, constituted a *triumvirat* power to guard both the seas, and the fishery against all pretenders whatsoever, as had *Richard* the *Second* long before him, who impos'd a tribute on every individual ship that passed through the northern admiralty, for the maintenance of that sea-guard, amounting to six-pence a tun, upon every fishing vessel weekly, as appears by a most authentick record, and the opinion of the most eminent judges, at that early day; who upon consideration, that none but a soverein power could impose such a payment, gave it in as their opinion, that this right and dominion, was a branch of the royal patrimony, and inseparable: Nay, that wise prince *Henry* the *Seventh*, thought it so infinitely considerable, that (upon deeply weighing the great advantages) he was (for) setting up a trade, or staple of fish, in preference (say some) to that of wool itself, and all other commerce of his dominions; which being long before the *Low-Countries* had a name for merchants, they had still perhaps, neglected, if some *renegado's* of our own (*Violet*, and *Stephens* by name) had not encourag'd the *Dutch* of *Enchuysen* (with other mal-contented persons of the craft, deserting their country, and their loyalty) to molest his Majesties streams, upon the accompt of these men; since which, they, and others, have continu'd their presumptions even to insolence:

57. Neither was less the care of King *James* to vindicate this incomparable prerogative, than any of his vigilant predecessors, who, having deriv'd that accession of the *Shetland* Islands by marriage with a daughter of *Denmark*, publish'd his proclamations immediately after his coming into *England*: For it must be acknowledg'd that Queen *Elizabeth* did not so nicely and warily look

1606.
1468.
1609.

after

after this jealous article, as had been wish'd; diverted by her extraordinary pitty, and abundant indulgence to the distressed States. But, this Prince roundly asserts his patrimony, upon many prudent reasons of state, and especially, for encouragement of the maritime towns, fallen much to decay, and plainly succumbing under the injurious dealing of such as took the fish from before their dores; and renew'd his commands, that none should for the future, presume so much as to hover about, much less abide on our coasts, without permission first obtain'd under the Great Seal of *England*, and upon which the *Hollanders* petition'd for leave, and acknowledged the limits appointed them, as formerly they had done: Let us hear the historian describe it and blush.

"The *Hollanders* (says he) taking infinite plenty of "*herring* upon this coast, and thereby making a most "gainful trade, were first to procure leave (by ancient "custom) out of *Scarborow*-Castle; for the *English* "permit them to fish; reserving indeed the honour to "themselves, but, *resigning the benefit* to strangers, to "their incredible inriching &c. What could be said more to our purpose, or to our reproach? This was that which King *James* endeavour'd to bring into a better method, when taking notice of the daily incroachment of our neighbours he enjoyn'd his ambassador (who was then Sir *Dudley Carleton*) to expostulate with the States, as may be seen in that sharp letter of Mr. *Secretarie* (*Naunton*) dated the twenty first of *December* 1618, in which he tells them, "That unless they sought leave "from his Majesty, and acknowledg his right, as other "princes had done, and did; it might well come to pass, "that they who would needs bear all the world before "them by their *Mare Liberum*, might soon endanger their "having neither *terram, nec solum, nec rempublicam* "*liberam*: I do only recite the passage as I find it pub-

lish'd

lish'd, and take notice how prophetick it had lately like
to have been.

58. This happy prince taking umbrage at the war
between the *Hollander* and the *Spaniard*, did fix limits
by commission, and survey, nearer than which (though
as moderator, he offer'd equal protection to both) no
enemy to another state, might commit any hostile act, *Seldenus l.*
and producing his reasons for it, asserted his right so *c. 22.*
to do; not as if those boundaries circumscrib'd his
dominions, but, as being sufficient for the vindication
of his due in that great article. And their not observing this, incited King *Charles* the *First* of blessed
memory, to animadvert upon it, when in the year 1639, *1639.*
our good friends behaved themselves with so little
respect, in that memorable conflict with the *Spaniard*;
and when approaching too near our shoars, they were
check'd for their irreverence in his Majesties Imperial
Chambers; indeed, for the *first* (but seeming) affront,
that this nation did ever receive upon it.

59. And now it will not be amiss, nor inconsistent
with our title, to let the world see, the immense advantages of the trade which has been driven upon the sole
account of the fishery; by the prodigious emolument
which it has (to our cost and reproach) afforded our
more industrious neighbours, the foundation of whose
greatness has been laid in the bottom of our seas;
which has yielded them more treasure than the mines
of *Potosi*, or both *Indies* to *Spain*.

Who would believe that this people raise yearly by
the *herring*, and other fisheries, a million of pound
sterling, and that *Holland*, and *Zealand* alone (whose
utmost verge doth hardly exceed many *English* shires)
should from a few despicable boats, be able to set forth
above twenty thousand vessels of all sorts, fit for the
rude seas, and of which more than 7000, are yearly
employed upon this occasion?   'Tis evident, that by

                              this

this particular trade, they are able to breed above fourty thousand fisher-men, and one hundred and sixteen thousand mariners (as the *census* has been accurately calculated) and the gain of it is so universal, that there's hardly a beggar in their country, nor an hand, which doth not earn it's bread. This is literally true, and the consideration of it seem'd so important, that even in the days of *Charles* the *Fifth*, that great monarch is reported to have sometimes visited the tomb of *Bueckels* (where he had been above two hundred years interr'd) in solemn recognition of his merit, for having, as 'tis said, been the inventor of pickling and curing *herring :* In a word, so immense is the advantage which this article alone brings the state, that a very favourable rent, still in arrear to his Majesties *Exchequer,* for permission to fish (as should be prescribed, and appointed them) amounts to more than half a million of pounds, and the custom only at home of what they take, with the tenth fish for waftage, to near five hundred thousand pounds more; but the quantities which they sell abroad, to a sum almost not to be reckon'd: Then let it be computed, the hands employ'd for spinning of *yarn,* weaving of nets, and making other necessaries for the salting, curing, packing, and barelling, building of vessels, and fitting them out to sea : It is certain the shipping (which is more than all *Europe* can assemble besides) sea-men, commerce, towns, harbours, power, publick-wealth, and affluence of all other things, is sprung from this source ; and, that in barter for fish (without exportation of coin) they receive from *Spain, Italy, Germany,* &c. oil, wine, fruit, corn, hony, wax, allum, salt, wool, flax, hemp, pitch, tarr, sopeashes, iron, copper, steel, claw-boards, timber, masts, dollars, armour, glass, mill-stones, plate, tapestry, munition, and all things that a country (which has no one material of these of proper growth) can need to render

it

it consummately happy. The *Indies* and farthest regions of the earth, participate of this industry; and to our shame be it spoken, we blush not to buy our own fish of them, and purchase that of strangers, which God, and nature has made our own, inriching others to our destruction, by a detestable sloath; whilst to encourage us, we have timber, victuals, havens, men, and all that at our dores, which these people adventure for in remoter seas, and at excessive charges; And thus the prize is put into our hands, whilst we have not the hearts to use it; nor do we produce any reasons, why we are thus uncoucern'd, that ever I could find, were solid; some objections indeed are presented, but they appear'd to me so dilute, and insignificant, that 'tis not possible to compose ones indignation at the hearing of them, and see a kingdom growing every day thinner of people, and fuller of indigence, without some extraordinary emotion: To see with what numerous, and insulting fleets, our neighbours have been often prepar'd to dispute our title to these advantages, by the benefit and supply of that which we neglect, and condemn as unpracticable: If this be not enough to raise in us some worthy resentments: Let the confession of the *Dutch* themselves incite us to it; who (in a proclamation, publish'd near fifty years since) have stil'd their *Fishing Trade*, the *Golden Mines* of their provinces, and stimulated an industrious and emulous people with all the topicks of eucouragement: Were this alone well consider'd, and briskly pursu'd, there would need no great magick to reduce our bold supplanters to a more neighbourly temper: The subjects of this nation have no more to do, than apply themselves to the fishery, to recover at once their losses, and as infallibly advance the prosperity of the kingdom, as 'tis evident it has enabled our late antagonists to humble *Spain*, and from little of themselves, to grapple with the most

See Mr. L'*Estrange's* late Discourse of the Fishery.

1624.

 puissant

puissant Monarch of *Europe*, and bring him to the ground: For my part, I do not see how we can be able to answer this prodigious sloath of ours any longer; and especially, since 'tis evident, it will cost us but a laudable industry; and (in regard of our situation, and very many advantages above them) much less trouble and charge: Or suppose a considerable part of our forrein less-needfull expences were diverted to this work, what were the dis-advantages? We talk much of *France* (and perhaps with reason) but are we so safe from our dear friend, upon this composure, as never to apprehend any future unkindness? For my own part, I wish it with my soul: But of this I am sure, we may prevent, or encounter open defiance; but whilst we are thus undermin'd, we suffer a continual hostility; since the effects of it ruin our commerce, and by consequence the nation: Nor speak I here of our neighbours the *Hollanders* only; but of those of *Hamborough, Lubec, Embden,* and other interloopers, who grow exceedingly opulent, whilst we sit still, and perish, whose advantages for taking, curing, and vending of herrings, and employ of hands (were the expedients mention'd put in practice, or the ruinous numbers of our men, daily flocking to the *American* plantations, and from whence so few return, prudently stated, and acts of naturalization promoted) are so infinitely superiour to theirs; But, so our cursed negligence, will yet have it, not for want of all royal encouragement, but a fatality, plainly insuperable.

60. We have said little yet of our *American* fishery, and the loss we make of a vast treasure on the coasts of *Virginia, Green-land, Bermudas,* &c. sacrificing infinite wealth both at home, and abroad to the *Spaniards, French,* those of *Portugal,* and *Biscay.* 'Tis well known that *Green-land,* was first detected by the *English,* about the latter end of Queen *Elizabeths* reign, and afterwards the royal standard erected there,

in

in token of dominion, by the name of King *James's New-land*, his Majesty asserting his just rights, by many acts of state, as more particularly on the tenth of *January* 1613, when he signified his pleasure by Sir *Noel Carew* then in *Holland*, in vindication of his title both to the *island* fishery, and all other emoluments whatsoever *jure dominii*, as first discoverer, and to prohibite strangers interposing, and fishing in his seas without permission: For this effect, commissioners were establish'd at *London* to grant licences, yearly renewable, for such as would fish on the *English coast* and at *Edenbrough*, on the northern, and by proclamation, interdicting all un-licenced practises; the Duke of *Lennox* (as Admiral of *Scotland*) being order'd to assert the right of·the assize-herring, which was paid.

61. The following years, what interruptions happen'd, upon our neighbours declining to come to an adjustment for the indulgences they had found, is universally known, 'till the year 1635, when to prevent some incroachments, and disorders of those who fished under his protection, the late King *Charles* of blessed memory issu'd out his proclamations, and gave instructions to his ministers abroad, signifying that no strangers should presume to fish in the *British* seas without his Majesties licence; and that those who desired them, might be protected, he thought fit to equip, and set forth such a fleet, as became his care, and vigilancy for the good and safety of his people, and the honour of the nation: This was the year, and the occasion of building several considerable ships, and amongst others, that famous vessel, the *Royal Soveraiyn*, which to this day, bears our triumphant *Edgar* for its badge and cognizance, and to mind the world of his undoubted right to the dominion of the seas, which he had by this time asserted and secur'd beyond danger of dispute, had not a deluded people (as to their own

71   highest

1613.

1609.

1616.

1617.

1635.

See Mr. Secretary *Cook's* letter *April* 16, 1635, to his Majestie s Resident at the *Hague*.

highest concern, glory, and interest) and the fatality of
the times, disturb'd the project of an easie tax as an
imaginary invasion of their liberties, which that blessed
Prince, design'd only to protect them : It is fresh in
memory what were the opinions of Attourny *Noy*, many
learned civilians, and near a jury of grave judges upon
this conjuncture; and the instances of King *Ethelred's*
having levy'd it many hundred years before, shew'd it
to be no such innovation; nor could there be a more
pressing occasion than when all our neighbours around
us were (as now) in a state of hostility : but I list not
here to interrupt my reader upon this chapter, which
has already suffer'd so many sore digladiations and contests; only as to matter of fact, and as concern'd the
navigation, and improvement of commerce, I touch it
briefly, and pass to what follow'd, which was the setting
out no less than sixty tall ships, first under the Earl of
Lindsey, and afterwards *Northumberland*, by the account of whose accurate journal, it appears, how readily
our neighbour fisher-men (though under convoy of
fleets superiour to ours in number) sued for, and took
licences to the value of *fifteen hundred pounds, fifteen
shillings and two pence*, as I have perus'd the particulars :
I do only mention the licences, which were also taken,
and accepted at land, and they not a few, distributed by
Sir *William Boswell* at the *Hague* it self, upon which his
Majestie's minister then at *Bruxelles*, advertis'd the
Infanta that the *Dunkerkers* should take care not to
molest such of the *Hollanders* (though at that time in
actual hostility with them) as had his Majestie's permission, and accordingly, the *Cardinal* did grant them
passes, which they took without scruple; so as we find
it was not for nothing, that they came under protection,
but receiv'd a real benefit; Nor was this a novel imposi-
tion, but familiar, and customary, as appears by the
many precedents which we have recited; to which we

may add, that of the *Scotch* fishery, under King *James* the first: 1424. 21. *Act.* of the first *Parliament,* having already spoken of what concern'd our own princes, especially what *Richard* the *Second* impos'd, *Henry* I.V.VI.VII. Queens *Mary,* &c. with that of *Edward* the *First Pro Hominibus Hollandiæ &c,* which protection is yet extant, and granted frequently by treaties, as a priviledg only during the subsistance of such treaties, and no farther, totally rescinding and abolishing the pretences grounded by some upon the *intercursus magnus* made with the Dukes of *Burgundy:* So as to summ up all that has been produc'd to fortifie our domestick evidences, we have many Acts of Parliament, we have the several successours of our Princes granting licences to strangers: we have the assiduous instances made by King *James,* by his ambassadours, and secretaries of state; We have the acknowledgments actually, and already paid, and accounted for to the *exchequer,* and have seen the occasion of the late interruptions of it, and the invalidity of mens pretences: And if these be not evidences sufficient to subvert the sophisms of a few mercenary pens, and dismount the confidence of unreasonable people, it is because there is so little vigour in our resolutions at home, and so little justice in the world abroad: Nor has this been arrogated by the monarchs of this nation, but a right establish'd upon just reason; namely, that they might be enabl'd to clear the seas of rovers, and pirates, and protect such as follow'd their lawful affairs: And for this effect, the Kings of *England,* did not only take care to defend their own subjects, but to convoy, and secure all strangers, sometimes (as we have seen) by proclamation, sometimes by fleets, and men of war, where they fish'd by agreement, upon treaty, or leave obtain'd, yet restraining them to certain limits, retaining the dominion of the neighbouring seas, as in the reign of *Henry* the

1495.

Fourth, where we find an accord made between him and the *French* King, that the subjects of either nation might fish in one part of the seas, and not in another; the possession of all privileges of this nature ever accompanying the royal licence, and strangers having either special indulgences, or being under protection of special officers, appointed in former times for the safe guarding of the fishery, who were so impower'd by patent, and had certain dues appointed for that attendance, which they levied upon all forreiners, with the express direction (in the reign of *Henry* the *Seventh*) that the acknowledgment was to be so levied, notwithstanding any letter of safe-conduct, which stranger fishermen might pretend from any king, prince or government whatsoever: So as by all the arguments of right, claim, and prescription, the title is firm; all other pretences of right or possession interrupted, arrogated and precarious, or else extinguish'd by infractions of treaties, never since revived by any subsequent act:

62. We might here mention the toll paid the King of *Denmark* at the *Sundt,* and the respect which strangers shew to his castle of *Cronnenburg,* according to a treaty made between him and the *Dutch;* and to the *Swedish* king, whom they acknowledg sovereign of the *Baltick,* and northern tracts to an immense extent, where he receives tribute, as well as those of *Denmark,* and *Poland* by impositions at *Dantzick* and the *Pillau,* where they only enjoy for it a cold and hungry passage, whilst with us, we give them not only passage, harbours, and protection through a dangerous sea, but an emolument accompanying it, which inriches our neighbours with one of the most inestimable treasures, and advantagious commerce under heaven: To this we also might add what has obtain'd the *suffrages* not only of our own countrymen of the long robe and others, but of almost all the dis-interested learned per-

sons

sons who have discuss'd this subject; universally agreeing, that as to a peculiar, and restrictive right, fisheries may, and ought to be appropriated, and that as well in the high-seas (as the *lawyers* term them) as in lakes, and rivers, and narrower confinements, and as the *republick* of *Genoa* does at this day, let to farm their fishery for *thunnies* in their neighbouring seas; and the contract between Queen *Elizabeth* and *Denmark* about the like liberty upon the coast of *Norway*, and the prohibitions made, and the licences given by that crown at this present, do abundantly evince; namely that the *Dane* is, and hath of long time been, in possession upon the coasts we have mention'd, of as much as we asser't to be due to his Majesty in the *British* seas.

$$Extracts\ from$$

A
PLAN

OF THE

English COMMERCE,

BEING A

COMPLEAT PROSPECT

OF THE

TRADE of this NATION, as well the
HOME TRADE as the FOREIGN.

Humbly offered to the Consideration of the KING *and* PARLIAMENT.

The SECOND EDITION.

LONDON:

Printed for CHARLES RIVINGTON, at the *Bible* and
Crown in St. *Paul's Church-Yard*, 1730.

PLAN

OF THE

ENGLISH COMMERCE,

&c.

---

* * * Are we a rich, a populous, a powerful nation, and in some respects the greatest in all those particulars in the world, and do we not boast of being so? 'Tis evident it was all deriv'd from trade. *Our merchants are princes*, greater and richer, and more powerful than some sovereign princes; and in a word, as is said of *Tyre*, we have *made the kings of the earth rich with our merchandise*, that is, with our trade.

If usefulness gives an addition to the character, either of men or things, as without doubt it does; trading-men will have the preference in almost all the disputes you can bring: There is not a nation in the known world, but have tasted the benefit, and owe their prosperity to the useful improvements of commerce: Even the self-vain gentry, that would decry trade as a universal mechanism, are they not every where depending upon it for their most necessary supplies? If they do not all *sell*, they are all forc'd to *buy*, and so are a kind of traders themselves, at least they recognize the usefulness of commerce, as what they are not able to live comfortably without.

Nay,

Nay, in many parts of *Britain*, they are really traders, both buyers and sellers; *for example*, where the landlords are obliged to take their rents in kind, as the clergy do their tithes; here they are (in a word) general traders; they sell their barley to the malt-makers, their wheat to the millers and bakers, their oates to the corn-factors, their sheep and bullocks are sold at the markets to the butchers, or at fairs to the graziers; they are sheep-shearers, and sell their wool to the stapler or clothier; and when they kill a bullock, or a calf, or a sheep, for their family-use, they are beholding to the felmonger, and the tanner, to buy the raw hides and skins; when they sell their timber, they are oblig'd to turn mechanicks, and sell the bark to the tanners, the timber to the ship-wright and the carpenters, the brushwood and bavins to the baker and the brick-maker.

In a word, useful trade supports the gentleman; and without these mechanicks he could not dispose the produce of his estate, or make any rent of his land; and rather than not dispose of it, such is his necessity, that we see he will stoop to buy and sell for himself, and trade and deal like a meer mechanick.

But this is not all, if they would look a little nearer, they would see themselves not by practice only degenerated into trading men, but even their fortunes, nay, their very blood mingled with the mechanicks, *as they call them;* the necessity of their circumstances frequently reconciles the best of the nobility to these mixtures; and then the same necessity opens their eyes to the absurdity of the distinctions which they had been so wedded to before.

It is with the utmost disgrace to their understanding, that those people would distinguish themselves in the manner they do, when they may certainly see every day prosperous circumstances advance those mechanicks, *as they will have them called*, into the arms, and into the

4

rank

rank of the gentry; and declining fortunes reduce the best families to a level with the mechanick.

The rising tradesman swells into the gentry, and the declining gentry sink into trade. A merchant, or perhaps a man of a meaner employ thrives by his honest industry, frugality, and a long series of diligent application to business, and being grown immensely rich, he marries his daughters to gentlemen of the first quality, perhaps a coronet; then he leaves the bulk of his estate to his heir, and he gets into the rank of the peerage; does the next age make any scruple of their blood, being thus mix'd with the antient race? Do we not just now see two dukes descended by the female side, from the late Sir *Josiah Child*, and the immediate heir a peer of *Ireland?* Many examples of the like kind might be given.

On the other hand, the declining gentry, in the ebb of their fortunes, frequently push their sons into trade, and they again, by their application, often restore the fortunes of their families: Thus tradesmen become gentlemen, by gentlemen becoming tradesmen. I could give examples of this too, but they are too recent for our naming.

They that learn thus to despise trading people as such, must either be intirely ignorant of the world, or perfectly uncapable of the just impressions of these things; they must forget, sure, that the gentry are always willing to submit to the raising their families, by what they call *city fortunes;* and how useful trade has always been, and still is in the world on that account; while others who call themselves gentlemen, by way of distinction, became unworthy by the scandal of their morals, to match with the meanest citizen, if she be a woman of modesty and virtue.

But to go on in generals, which is proper to the head I am talking of; trade is the universal fund of wealth throughout the world; the gold of *Africa* and *Brazil*, the silver of *Mexico* and *Peru* had but for trade remained

 undisturbed

undisturbed in the mines, and in the sands of the rivers of *Guinea* and *Chili :* The diamonds of *Golconda,* and of *Borneo* had been glittering in the dirt, and remain'd un-polish'd to this day, if diligence had not found them out; if navigation had not assisted the discovery, and if trade had not spread and dispers'd them over the whole globe.

Even *Solomon* had wanted gold to adorn the Temple, unless he had been supply'd by miracles; if he had not turn'd merchant-adventurer, and sent his fleets to fetch it from the *East Indies,* that is to say, from *Achin,* on the Island of *Sumatra,* which is supposed to be the *Ophir* which his factors procur'd it at.

So effectually has trade rais'd the wealth of the world, that 'tis remarkable, and worth the most curious observation, that throughout the known world, nations, and kingdoms, and governments are rich or poor, as they have, or have not, a share of the whole commerce of the world, or more or less, some concern in it.

The *Turks,* who are enemies to trade, and who discourage industry and improvement, 'tis plain they dispeople the world, rather than improve and cultivate it: View their condition; they are miserably poor! distressedly poor! they are idle, indolent and starving, their governments have some wealth, because they are tyrannical, and take what they please from the poor people, throughout a vast extent of dominion; so that if it be but a little in a place, it amounts to a very great sum in the whole, the people and nations which are tributary to them, being so many; but those people and nations are poor and wretched to the last degree, and all for want of trade.

As to trade, excepting what the *Europeans* and the *Jews* drive among them, it is so little, that it hardly deserves the name of commerce; they have neither produce of the land, or labour of the people; neither merchandise or art, nothing is encouraged among them;

6

ignorance

ignorance boasts indeed of the rich return we bring from them, such as drugs, hair, silk, &c. But we know it is not of *Turky,* or the growth of *Turky,* but is either the product of *Armenia* and *Georgia,* the Provinces of *Guilan* and *Indostan,* part of *Persia* on the shoar of the *Caspian* Sea, quite out of the *Turk's* dominions, and even there they are the product of the old Christians labour, the original inhabitants of those provinces: the *Mahometans,* have little or no hand in it; they abhor business and labour, and despise industry, and they starve accordingly; or those goods are the produce of the islands in the *Levant* and the *Archipelague,* where the *cotton-yarn,* the *grogram* or *goats-hair* yarn, the white or *beladine silks,* &c. are the manufacture of the poor *Greeks* inhabitants of those islands, and who by their labour in cultivation, cause the earth to produce the silk and the wool, and by their labours in manufacturing, spin and make it up into yarn, and into form, as we have it from them. Now, *see the consequence;* as the *Mahometans* I say have little trade, so they have little wealth, the produce of their lands yields little, and that little sells for such a little value, that one would pity so vast a body of people labour-ing, as it were, for nothing: All the fruitful rich countries of *Natolia* and the *Lesser Asia,* from the *Ægean* to the *Euxine Sea,* once the most rich, populous, and fertile provinces of the world, with all the *Morea,* the *Achaia,* (the *Peloponnesus* of the antients) and the fruitful plains of *Thessaly, Macedonia,* and *Thrace,* from the *Ionian Sea,* to the banks of the *Danube;* what do they now produce? The great city of *Constantinople* is supplied with corn indeed, but how? (N.B. This is the reason of mention-ing it) when produc'd, sold to the merchant, shipt on board the vessels which carry it by sea, the freight paid, and all charges of loading and unloading; yet their barley has been bought in the market at *Constantinople* for 3*d. per* bushel.

If this were some ages ago, if it were not known to be so very frequently, and if there were not some merchants now living in *London*, who are persons of undoubted credit, who assure me they have bought it so: I say if it were only, that it had been so some ages ago, it had been nothing extraordinary, for all know it has been thus in *England*; but this has been so at *Constantinople* within these ten or twelve years, and I doubt not it might be prov'd is often so still in the same place, when plentiful years of corn happen; what the poor husbandman must have for his plowing, sowing, harvesting, threshing, and carrying it out, is hard to imagine; or what the landlord has for the land: But I suppose the Grand-Seignior is general landlord, and has his tax from the whole country, instead of rent.

Now, whence is all this poverty of a country? 'tis evident 'tis want of trade, and nothing else: And we go back for an example of it to our own country, when the product of the land, and the labour of the people were as low here, when good wheat was worth about 4*d. per* bushel, a fat sheep about 3*s.* 4*d.* and a fat ox about 18 to 24*s.* and when was this?   But when we had no trade, and because we had no trade; neither is the present difference owing to anything else, but to the increase of commerce, as well here as in other parts of the world; and 'tis evident the rate of provisions, and the value of lands in all parts of the world are high or low, great or small, as the people have or have not trade to support it.

Trade encourages manufacture, prompts invention, employs people, increases labour, and pays wages: As the people are employ'd, they are paid, and by that pay are fed, cloathed, kept in heart, and kept together; that is, kept at home, kept from wandering into foreign countries to seek business, for where the employment is, the people will be.

This keeping the people together, is indeed the sum of

the

the whole matter, for as they are kept together, they multiply together; and the numbers, which by the way is the wealth and strength of the nation, increase.

As the numbers of people increase, the consumption of provisions increases; as the consumption increases, the rate or value will rise at market; and as the rate of provisions rises, the rents of land rise: So the gentlemen are with the first to feel the benefit of trade, by the addition to their estates.

And here it would not have been improper to have made a transition to our *English* history, and to have enquir'd how punctually the course of things have obey'd the laws of nature in this very particular; how as trade has increased; so by equal advances, provisions have been consum'd, lands cultivated, rents raised, and the estates of the gentry and nobility been improv'd: I mean as to periods of time, as well as to the proportion of value; which enquiry would have been an unanswerable proof of the fact; but I am confin'd here to generals, and must only lay it down as a proposition.

As the consumption of provisions increase, more lands are cultivated; waste grounds are inclosed, woods are grubb'd up, forrests and common lands are till'd, and improv'd; by this more farmers are brought together, more farm-houses and cottages are built, and more trades are called upon to supply the necessary demands of husbandry: In a word, as land is employ'd, the people increase of course, and thus trade sets all the wheels of improvement in motion; for from the original of business to this day it appears, that the prosperity of a nation rises and falls, just as trade is supported or decay'd.

As trade prospers, manufactures increase; as the demand is greater or smaller, so also is the quantity made; and so the wages of the poor, the rate of provisions, and the rents and value of the lands rise or fall, as I said before.

And here the very power and strength of the nation

is concern'd also, for as the value of the lands rises or falls, the taxes rise and fall in proportion; all our taxes upon land are a kind of pound rate; and bring in more or less, as the stated rents of the land are more or less in value; and let any one calculate, by the rate of lands in *England*, as they went in the times of *Edward* IV. or even in King *Henry* VII. time, when trade began, as it were, just to live in *England*; and tell us how much they think a land tax would then have brought in : For example,

If a tax of four shillings in the pound now brings in above two millions, I suppose it would have been thought very well then, if it had brought in three hundred thousand pound, all the rest is an increase occasion'd by trade, and by nothing else; trade has increas'd the people, and people have increas'd trade; for multitudes of people, if they can be put in a condition to maintain themselves, must increase trade; they must have food, that employs land; they must have clothes, that employs the manufacture; they must have houses, that employs handicrafts; they must have household stuff, that employs a long variety of trades : so that in a word trade employs people, and people employ trade.

I once saw a calculation of trade for the planting a new town in the south parts of *England*, where, for the encouragement of people to come and settle, the lords of the manors (for the place lay in three manors,) agreed to give a certain quantity of lands to fifty farmers, who would undertake to bring each two hundred pound stock with them, and settle there.

To every such farmer, they allotted two hundred acres of good land, rent-free for twenty years; and if the farmer brought three hundred pound stock, he had three hundred acres; besides the land, the said lords agreed to find timber, and all other materials for the building, to every farmer a house, and out of their own pockets to build to each house a barn and stables; and thus, with

other

other encouragements, fifty families of substantial farmers were brought to live in a kind of circle within themselves, with every one a good farm to manage, and sufficient quantity of land rent-free; the land was good in it self, tho' never cultivated before, so that being clear'd and inclos'd, and gradually plow'd or improv'd, it soon return'd them a profitable increase.

The land was so laid out in a large circle, that all the farm-houses being built at the extremities of the respective farms, towards the center, left a handsome large square piece of land which the lords reserv'd for the building a town; and as the farm-houses were so regularly plac'd, as to front all inwards, they left ten spaces like streets before their doors, of which five of the farm-houses, with their out-houses, made one side, and the other remained to build into a street as occasion should present.

At the same time they publish'd, that whoever would come and build on that vacant ground, should have a certain proportion'd measure of land allow'd him, according to the size of the house he would build, should have timber given him gratis, out of the woods belonging to the estate, sufficient for his building; and to every house, land also added for a garden and orchard, no rent to be paid for ten years, and then a moderate rent for twenty years more; and then a certain rent (not at last immoderate) for the time to come.

When the farmers were settled, for there is the substance and reason of the thing, and in this it is exactly to my purpose; immediately comes a butcher, and he runs up a little shed for the present, till he could build a house, and sets up a shop, to kill and sell meat for the farmers.

N. B. As these farmers had every one two hundred pounds stock to begin, so they are supposed to be all men of families, that had wives and children,

and

and every one had at least one or two, and some three servants.

Nor could one butcher be sufficient to furnish meat to fifty families, but they were oblig'd to send to neighbouring towns for provision, till the first butcher having encouragement, two or three more came afterwards, and set up also.

After the example of the butcher, in the next place came a baker, and he erects an oven to supply them with bread.

Fifty families of farmers must necessarily find work for a smith or farrier to shoe their horses, and at least two wheel-wrights to make and repair their carts, waggons, plows, harrows, &c. and these with the necessary iron-work for so much building, called in a couple of black-smiths, whereof one being a man of substance, made himself a kind of iron-monger, laying in a stock of all sorts of wrought iron and brass for building and furniture, which on such an occasion they could not be without.

This collection of tradesmen naturally requir'd a shoe-maker or two to set up, who soon found trade enough to supply the growing numbers of people with shoes and boots; and likewise a good honest country cobler or two could not fail of employment to repair them; and (to add the other trades working in leather), they could not be without a collar-maker or two, for harness, pannels, saddles, and all the necessary things relating to a team.

Add to these a turner, an earthern-ware seller, a glover, a rope-maker, three or four barbers, (perhaps a *midwife*) and several such trades as the nature of things required.

But to go back to the building part, three master carpenters would be the least that could be employ'd in building houses, and these would require at first five or six pair of sawyers at least, with journeymen; that is to

say,

say, workmen; two or three bricklayers, with their servants and labourers, and perhaps hard by a brick and tile-maker.

To supply these, one of the carpenters, a man of substance, builds himself a wind-mil, and another builds a second, and they both find work enough (as the town encreased) to keep them constantly employ'd.

The town going thus forward, and standing in the great post road, comes an honest victualler, and he sets up an ale-house; and soon after, he is follow'd by five or six more; as the first encreasing in stock, sees room for it, he enlarges his building, and makes his little ale-house out into a good inn, and a second follows him, and then a third, and in process of time, the number of public-houses encrease to eleven or twelve in all; whereof as above, three are very handsome inns, and perhaps sell wine as well as strong drink.

By this time the lords of the manors begin to think it proper to build their new tenants a church, for which they lay out a handsome piece of ground in the center of the town, and a large burying-ground added to it; and obtaining licence from the bishop, they consecrate the building; and being joint patrons, present in turn, getting a law to erect it into a parish, and to ascertain the tithe and maintenance of the incumbent, as in like cases.

Hitherto nature acted it all, but this part indeed, the piety of the patrons supplies; our business is (in both) to observe the ordinary course of things, the concourse of tradesmen follow the concourse of people, as naturally as warmth attends the approach of the sun; the settlement of the farmers gives a summons to the tradesmen that supply them with necessaries, and lets them know, that there they may find business and employment: The necessity of meat and drink, brings the butcher, baker and victualler to settle with them, as naturally as sutlers follow an army.

 But

But to proceed; fame spreads the news of a town newly erected, and a number of families brought together; a grocer goes to see if there is no room for him, and finding no supplies of his kind, he takes a piece of ground in one of the principal streets, and marks himself out a place for his house; but first, as before, runs up a booth or shed, stores it with goods, and opens a shop, and two or three chandler shops do the same in remoter parts, buying their goods perhaps of him.

An apothecary does the like next door to him, and a mercer next to him; then a haberdasher of hats, a draper and a milliner; and thus the town is inhabited and furnish'd by degrees with all sorts of necessary people and things; till after some time, the lords of the manors, to carry on the improvement, get a patent for a market once a week, and a fair perhaps twice a year, or oftner, as there is occasion.

In these advanc'd circumstances, other trades fall in; as 1*st*, more ale-houses; 2*d*, a common brewer; 3*d*, a cooper for casks of all sorts; a pewterer, two or three lawyers, (or attorneys, rather) for drawing writings, making bonds, bargains and agreements between man and man, and one of these in time gets himself made a justice of peace, and so there is an immediate magistrate among them.

In the mean time other trades fill up the streets; a malt-house, perhaps two or three are erected, that the inhabitants may brew their own beer if they please; a surgeon in case of disaster, for by this time the town begins to grow populous.

The good women also being diligent, and good housewives, they spin, and in consequence of that, there must be a linen weaver, and a woollen-weaver, a flax and hemp-dresser, and in a word, whatever depends upon their thrift.

Thus far the nature and consequence of things agree with what is advanced above: Thus towns and families,

nay

nay nations and countries are planted and peopled, and made flourishing and populous by their commerce.

Let us now cast up the account, and according to antient custom number the people, the list by the poll will stand thus.

50 farmers, with their wives and two children each, one with another, which I take to be the least that can be supposed. - - -	200
Two men servants and one maid to each farmer, no farmer with 200 acres of land could be supposed to make shift with less. - -	150
The several families of tradesmen necessarily brought together on such an occasion, I cast up at 143 families, at 5 to each house. - - - - - - -	715
Add to these hired servants which would fall in from other countries; nurses, midwives, hostlers, apprentices, &c. In all - -	335
	1400

Here are fifty farmers, who with their servants make up but three hundred and fifty people in all; but necessarily draw one thousand one hundred people more to them. Thus people make trade, trade builds towns and cities, and produces every thing that is good and great in a nation; and wherever fifty farmers were thus to settle, I insist, that at least one thousand people must of course throng to them, and live about them.

There are numbers of examples to be given of it, the *Venetian* Republic began thus; a despicable croud of people flying from the fury of the *Barbarians* which over-run the *Roman* empire, took shelter in a few inaccessible islands of the *Adriatic* Gulph.

Here they had safety indeed, and life; but nothing else. But falling into trade, applying themselves to the sea, to navigation and commerce; how soon did they

raise

raise themselves in the world, spreading themselves into the *Archipelague*, and into the *Levant;* conquering the great and rich Islands of *Candia* and *Cyprus*, *Negropont* and *Scio*, possess'd the *Morea*, *Dalmatia* and *Epirus*, and gradually rais'd their dominion to such a degree, as was superior to many kingdoms.

Their city we see raised to a prodigious splendor and magnificence, and their rich merchants rank'd among the antient nobility, and all this by trade: Their fleets of men of war have oftentimes engag'd and beaten the *Turkish* navy, driven them into port, and dar'd them at the mouth of the *Dardanelli;* and all this power is rais'd by trade.

I might from this example lead you to the *Hans*, the great confederacy of commerce, the greatest in the world; who meerly by the acquir'd greatness of their trade, became so rich, and so powerful, that they were many years the terror of the north; whoever hired their men of war, were sure to conquer their enemies at sea, and several times they beat whole fleets of the *Danes*, and at last brought the King of *Denmark* to make a dishonourable peace with them; till the kings of the neighbouring countries grew justly jealous of them, and oblig'd all the cities within their jurisdiction to withdraw from their alliance, and to renounce their confederacy.

The *Dutch*, I mean the States-General of the United Provinces, when they broke off from the obedience of *Spain*, and as it may be rightly said, cast off the *Spanish* yoke, were a poor, mean, frighted generation, driven to the refuge of the water, by the terrible power of King *Philip*, and reduc'd to such distress, that, but for the assistance of Queen *Elizabeth*, they had been ruin'd and destroy'd; yet pushing into trade, and having recourse to the sea, they built themselves upon their marine power; and the success of their navigation rais'd them to that pitch of naval greatness which we now see them at, in

                                            which

which they are superior to all the world, *Great Britain* excepted, of whom I shall speak by themselves.

As it has been with nations, so it has been with cities and towns; such has been the case of the cities of *Hamburgh*, *Dantzick*, *Lubec*, *Frankfort*, *Nuremberg*, *Rochelle*, *Marseilles*, *Genoa*, *Leghorn*, *Geneva*, and many other cities that might be nam'd, who have been rais'd to a pitch of opulence and wealth, equal to some principalities, by their meer situation for, and success in their *commerce* : I on the other hand might name several cities, which being depriv'd of their trade, have sunk again in proportion, as their trade has been taken away; such as the city of *Antwerp*, the towns of *Dunkirk*, *Southampton*, *Ipswich*, and many more.

As their trade has been cut off, their merchants have removed, the inhabitants decreased, and the shells of the towns remain without the kernel, the houses without the people, and the people without the wealth.

When the *Dutch* cut off the free navigation of the *Scheld* from the city of *Antwerp*, how did it decline? the *English* staple remov'd to *Hamburgh*, the fishing trade to *Amsterdam*, and the merchants followed; and what is that city now compar'd to what it formerly was?

When the King of *France* was oblig'd by the late war to demolish the works, and ruin the harbour of *Dunkirk*, so that the navigation received a blow; how did the town sensibly decay? from eighteen thousand families, which once inhabited that place, 'tis said, not two thirds remain; all the people depending upon the naval affairs, are gone with the royal arsenal; all the magazines of naval-stores, either for the king or the merchant, employ'd and carried off; and the trade that attended that part sunk with it; few ships now belong to it, few merchants now reside in it, and in a few years more, the empty houses being unrepaired, may publish its decay in a more visible manner, and show the wounds receiv'd by the loss

 of

of their trade, as is the case at *Southampton*, at *Ipswick*, &c. in a visible manner.

I need not travel over the globe, to give you examples in remoter places, where the great emporiums, the greatest trading cities in the world, have sunk into ruin by the stop of their commerce, such as *Tripoli*, *Sinope*, and *Trapezond* in the *Euxine* or *Black Sea*, whose trade is cut off, by the *Turks* stopping the navigation of the *Bosphorus*, and cutting off the trade they carried on with *Europe*; or such as *Suez*, and *Alexandria*, ports antiently of prodigious concourse, both of ships and merchants; but emptied of both, by the *Europeans* finding the way to the *East Indies* by the Cape of *Good-hope*; or such as the famous cities of *Tyre* and *Corinth*, who having been the envy of the world for wealth, and that wealth obtain'd by their commerce, were overturn'd; the first by the *Grecians*, the last by the *Romans*, purely for the avaritious part; and who, their merchants being destroy'd, and their trade overthrown, never recover'd their figure any more than their fortunes in the world.

In a word, it appears by innumerable examples, that trade is the life of the world's prosperity, and all the wealth that has been extraordinary, whether of nations or cities, has been raised by it.

The nature of the thing indeed implies it; as the industry of mankind is set on work, their hopes and views are rais'd, and their ambition fir'd: The view and prospect of gain inspires the world with the keenest vigor, puts new life into their souls; and when they see the success and prosperity of trading nations, it rouses them up to the like application.

Let us view the differing face of the nations, (and of the people who inhabit them) where they have no trade; how miserable is the scene of life? The countries look desolate, the people sad and dejected, poor and disconsolate, heavy and indolent; not for want of will to labour, but for want of something to labour profitably at; the rich are slothful, because they are rich and proud, the poor, because they are poor and despair; for it will ever be true

That poverty makes sloth, and sloth makes poor.

We say of some nations, the people are lazy, but we should say only, they are poor; poverty is the fountain of all manner of idleness; they have in short nothing to do, no employment in which they can get their bread by their labour; their work gets no wages for want of trade, and their trade no increase for want of labour; diligence promotes trade, and trade encourages diligence; labour feeds trade, and trade feeds the labourer.

There is hardly that country to be nam'd in the world, where there is no room for improvement by industry and application; nay, we find an industrious people often thriving and wealthy, under the weighty discouragements of a barren soil, an inhospitable climate, a tempestuous sea, a remote situation, having yet something or other for trade to work upon.

The people of *Norway* and *Russia* having nothing but mountains and woods, and the most barren inclement air and soil in the world; yet rather than not trade, and rather than not labour, they cut down their trees, and send them abroad to build cities, and build navies in other countries, and have hardly any of their own.

If their woods grow remote from the sea or water carriage, industry dictates to them to cut them down and burn them; and to trade, if it be but with the very sap and juices of the trees: Hence they send us tar, pitch, rosin, turpentine; and we see as it were a whole wood brought away in cask; ten, twenty thousand last of tar brought from *Russia* at a time, every last being ten to twelve barrels.

If *Greenland* and *Spitsbergen* are unsufferably cold;

if

if nature, not being able to support the violence of it, leaves those places uninhabited ; the diligent trader not being to be discouraged by difficulties, flies directly thither ; there among a thousand dangers, surrounded with mountains of ice, terrible, and horrors enough to chill the very soul to describe them, *hunts* the great *Leviathan* of the seas, and loads his ships with the fat (blubber) of a thousand whales.

I might instance in the severities of the torrid, as well as frigid zone, and shew the hardships undergone in places scorch'd with the violence of the heat ; and which are every way as terrible in their kind, as those of excessive cold ; such are the diseases and terrors of the long calms, where the sea stagnates and corrupts for want of motion ; and by the strength of the scorching sun stinks and poisons the distrest mariners, who are rendered unactive, and disabled by scurvies, raging and mad with calentures and fevers, and drop into death in such a manner, that at last the living are lost, for want of the dead, that is, for want of hands to work the ship.

Yet nothing discourages the diligent seaman, or the adventrous merchant in pursuit of trade, and pushing on discoveries, planting colonies, and settling commerce, even to all parts of the world.

Now as I said before, that the nations who want trade look dejected and sad, so, on the contrary, let the curious traveller observe, as he passes thro' the world, the trading manufacturing nations have a quite different aspect ; their labour, however hard and heavy, is perform'd chearfully ; a general sprightliness and vigour appears among them ; their countenances are blith, and they are merrier at their labour, than others are at their play ; their hearts are warm, as their hands are quick ; they are all spirit and life, and it may be seen in their faces ; or which is more, it is seen in their labour ; as they live better than the poor of the same class in other countries, so they work harder: And here the same *antithesis* is observable as before, tho' in its contrary extreme; for as I said there, that poverty makes sloth, and sloth makes poor: So here,

Labour makes gain, and gain gives strength to labour.

As they labour harder, so they get more for their work than other nations, and this gives them spirit for their labour. And this is the immediate effect of trade, for the poor of the trading and manufacturing countries are employ'd on better terms, and have better wages for their work, than the poor of those countries where there is less trade.

We are told, that in *Russia* and *Muscovy*, when for want of commerce, labour was not assisted by art; they had no other way to cut out a large plank, but by felling a great tree, and then with a multitude of hands and axes hew away all the sides of the timber, till they reduc'd the middle to one large plank; and that yet, when it was done, they would sell this plank as cheap, as the *Swedes* or *Prussians* did the like, who cut three or four, or more planks of the like size from one tree by the help of saws and saw-mills: The consequence must be, that the miserable *Russian* labour'd ten times as much as the other did, for the same money.

We are told frequently, when such and such great works or buildings were finished, men work'd for a penny a day here in *England*; and perhaps they did so; but as I said before, speaking of the cheapness of provisions, that it was before we had any trade among us; so it must be as to wages, for as trade raises wages, so wages raise provisions; and this is the reason, why, as all foreigners grant that our poor in *England* work harder than they do in any other nation; so it must be own'd, they eat and drink better in proportion; and this is, because they have better wages.

I might examine this article of wages, and carry it

 thro'

thro' almost every branch of business in *England*; and it would appear, that the *English* poor earn more money than the same class of men or women can do at the same kind of work, in any other nation.

Nor will it be deny'd, but that they do more work also: So then, if they do more work, and have better wages too, they must needs live better, and fare better; and it is true also, that they cannot support their labour without it.

And here I may grant, that a *French* man shall do more work than an *English* man, if they shall be oblig'd to live on the same diet; that is to say, the foreigner shall starve with the *English* man for a wager, and will be sure to win: He will live and work, when the *English* man shall sink and dye; but let them live both the same way, the *English* man shall beggar the *French* man, for tho' the *French* man were to spend all his wages, the *English* man will out-work him.

It is true again, the *French* man's diligence is the greatest, he shall work more hours than the *English* man; but the *English* man shall do as much business in the fewer hours, as the foreigner who sits longer at it.

To conclude this head, I would not seem to be partial in favour of our own country; but it must be added, that their work is better perform'd also; and I appeal for the truth of it, to their several performances, of which I could give examples, and which all the markets in the world are at this time witnesses to; but this begins to be particular, I shall speak at large to the several examples of it in their proper places.

It is sufficient to the purpose here to observe as above, that the diligent trading manufacturing world work chearfully, live comfortably; they sing at their labour, work by their choice, eat and drink well, and their work goes on pleasantly, and with success: Whereas the unemploy'd world groan out their souls in anguish and sorrow, not by

their

their work, but for want of it; and sink, as I may justly say, under the weight of their idleness and sloth; what little work they do, is done with reluctance and grief, because the small wages they have for it, gives them no comfort when it is done.

Travelling in the north part of *Britain*, I observed, that, in the time of their harvest, they had always an overseer to keep the reapers to their work, and a bag-pipe to encourage them while they were at work: And one of our company observing that we had no such merry doings at our harvests in *England*; another answer'd him, 'twas true, nor was there any need of it, for that the *English* work'd merrily enough without musick; adding, our workmen have good victuals and good drink: Let's enquire how these poor people feed, said he; and so we did, when we found that the best of their provision was a cake of oat bread, which they call a bannock, and a draught of water only; and twice in the day, the farmer or steward gave them every one a dram of *Glasgow* brandy, as they call'd it; that is to say, good malt spirits.

Upon the whole, it was evident, the poor men had need enough of music to encourage them at their labour; nor would the music do neither, without the overseer or steward being in the field too, to see that they stood to their work.

In *England* we see the farmers in harvest time, providing good beef and mutton, pyes, puddings, and other provisions to a strange profusion, feasting their workmen, rather than feeding them; and giving them good wages besides: But let any man see the difference of the work, these need no music, the feast is better than the fiddle, and the pudding does more than the bag-pipe; *in short*, they work with a vigor and spirit, not to be seen in other countries.

I could give like examples among the manufacturers; the spirit and courage of the workmen, is seen in

the

the goodness and substance of their manufacture; of which, this must be said, our manufacture may not be so cheap as the same kinds made in other countries; but bring them to the scale and try their substance, you will find the *English* man's work, according to his wages, outweigh the other; as his beer is strong, so is his work; and as he gives more strength of sinews to his strokes in the loom, his work is firmer and faster, and carries a greater substance with it, than the same kinds of goods, and of the same denomination made in foreign parts.

I remember in our former contests about commerce, great noise was made of the *French* imitating our woollen manufacture, and making them to such perfection, as to out-do us in foreign markets; from whence it was inferr'd, that they would in time supplant our trade, and carry away the business from us: The reason that was given, was, that their poor could work so much cheaper than ours, that their goods would be sold cheaper than the *English*, and consequently they would have the first and best of the market always from us; and had this been fully and fairly made out; had they brought sufficient evidence of the facts suggested, the inference had been good. Now to prove how finely the *French* perform'd, and how good their cloths were; patterns were shew'd here of their several cloths, as finish'd for the *Turky* trade, by the great manufactory, as they call it, in *Languedoc*; for it was this part that was brought for the support of the argument; and it is true, that the patterns were extraordinary, the cloth well dress'd, the colours well dy'd; nay, to perfection; and to a superficial eye, they rather went beyond the *English*, than come short of them.

But when they came to be look'd well into by clothiers and workmen who understood it, and whose business it was; the deficiency soon discover'd it self; their cloths appear'd to be slight, thin, without substance and proportion, and unfit to do service in wearing; in a word, they

were

were no way equal in goodness to the *English* manufacture of the same kind. This was farther prov'd by the
Armenian merchants at *Aleppo,* at *Smyrna,* and other
places in *Turky,* where the said goods were usually sold;
where upon bringing the *English* and *French* cloths to
the scale, there was no comparison between them; but
the *English* always out weigh'd them forty to fifty pound
per bale, and sometimes much more; the consequence of
which was,

1. That those *Armenian* merchants would very seldom
buy the *French cloths,* so long as there were any of the
English cloths left at the market.

2. That when they did buy them, they always had
them at a much cheaper rate.

This is an evident proof of the *English* manner of performing; and it will hold in many other cases, perhaps
in all manufacturing cases: The strong labour of the
English workmen in all their manual operations is very
remarkable in the works themselves: And I say, it is
evident in many other manufactures, besides that of
broad-cloths; *in a word,* our workmen, by the meer vigour
and strength of their spirits, supported by their strong feeding, and by their better wages than in any other nation,
are not used to work slight and superficially, but strong
and substantial in every thing they do; and as they have
better wages for it than other nations give, and perform
their work accordingly, so their goods make it evident, for
that they fetch a better price at market, than any goods
of the same species, made in any other country.

It is the same thing in their several manufactures of
brass and iron, and other hard-ware works; but especially,
in their building of ships, in which it is evident the
Dutch and *French, Swedes* and *Danes,* build cheaper; but
the *English* build stronger and firmer; and an *English*
ship will always endure more severity, load heavier, and
reign (*as the seamen call it*) longer, than any foreign built

ship

ship whatever; the examples are seen every year, particularly in the coal trade, the loading of which is very heavy, and the ships swim deep in the water, by the eagerness of the masters, to carry large burthens; and yet it is frequently known, that a *New-Castle* or *Ipswich built colier*, shall reign, (as I say the seamen call it) forty to fifty years, and come to a good end at last; that is, be broken up; not founder at sea, or break her back upon the sands, as ships weaker built, often, nay generally do.

The firm building, as well as beautiful moulds of our men of war confirm this also, in which they out-last, as well as out-shine, the strongest and finest built ships of most other nations, if not of all nations in *Europe*, except only those castle-built clumsy things called *galeons*, which are built so strong, that is, so thick, that they are scarce fit for any thing.

The comparison is still to my purpose in every part, (*viz.*) that trade invigorates the world, gives employment to the people, raises pay for their labour, and encreases that pay as their labour encreases, and as their performance excels; and it appears that what is said of *England* is no compliment to our own country, but a real, historical truth; for that 'tis undeniable, that the labour of the poor is no where rated so high as in *England*: There is no nation in the world where the poor have equal wages for their work as in *England*, in proportion to the rate of money, and to the rate of provisions.

By this means the labouring poor are kept in heart, kept strong, and made able for the business they are employ'd in; and the contrary, is the reason why the *French*, the *Italians*, and most other nations, rather make their manufacture (of any kind) gay than good, fine than strong. I allow them to be as exquisite in art, nay, I may allow them to be more apt to invent and contrive, and perhaps finish some things with more ornament: But for

strength

strength of hand in their works, where strength is essential to the value of the work, there our people out-do them all.

I could carry this on thro' many particulars, and it would lead me into some very useful speculations, but they would be remote from my purpose; I bring it back therefore to the single point which I am upon; namely, the great advantage of commerce to the world, and to particular nations.

When we had no trade, we had no ships, no populous cities, no numbers of people, no wealth compar'd to what we see now; provisions bore no price, lands yielded no rent; and why? The reason is plain and short; 'tis sum'd up in a word, *labour* brought in *no wages.*

N.B. Observe by the word, no, or none, is not meant litterally and strictly *none at all;* but comparatively none compar'd to what is seen now.

The people were divided into master and servant; not landlord and tenant, but the lord and the vassal; the tenant paid no rent, but held his lands in vassalage; that is, for services to be performed; such and such tenants plow'd his land; such and such fenc'd his park; such and such lands were let out to furnish the lord's kitchen with poultry, such with eggs, some with one thing, some with another; and thus the lord liv'd, as the *Scots* call it, in the middle of his geer.

The under people to these tenants held by villenage; that is, the labourers, those we now call husbandmen and cottagers, these did the drudgery, were grooms to look after his horses, drive his teams, fell his woods, fence, hedge, ditch, thresh, and in a word, do all servile labours; and for this they had their bread; that is, they had a poor cottage, scarce so good as a tolerable modern hogstye to live in, they drank at the pump, and eat at the kitchen door, beggar-like: As for the rest, the lord of the manor was their king; nay, if I had said their God, 1 had not

 err'd

err'd, so much as some may think; for they worship'd him with such a blind subjection, that at his command they would rebel against their king, and take up the bow and arrow against whomsoever he commanded them.

This was the case, even in this flourishing nation of *England*, till trade came in to make the difference; and give me leave to assume so much, I insist upon it, that trade alone made the difference; and the climax is very remarkable.

Before the people fell into trade, what was the case as to wealth? You see how it stood with the people; but what was the case of the trade.

1. We had no manufacture: we had wool indeed, and tin, and lead, those were funds, and brought in some substance; but who had it? Truly, the church and the gentry; the religious houses and the barons had the lands and the sheep, and consequently the wool: And we find that in King *Edward* III's time, the clergy and the religious houses gave the king a fifth part of all their wool for carrying on his wars against *France*: This wool was sent abroad to the *Flemings*, and this money was the wealth of the nation.

2. This money went all abroad again generally speaking, for those ruinous wars, which for many ages the Kings of *England* carried on, sometimes in *France*, sometimes in the *Holy Land*, sometimes in *Flanders*, sometimes in *Brittany*, and the like in other places; so that still the people were impoverish'd, I mean the gentry and clergy; for this wealth was theirs, and they paid all the taxes: As for the labouring poor, they scarcely knew what money was.

3. As to trade, it was carry'd on by the *Esterlings*; that is to say, the *Hans* Towns, and by the *Flemings*; and they carry'd away your wool, lead, tin, and whatever else you had, and supply'd you again with cloths, spice, (wine there was none, or but little to be had) and in a word,

with

with hemp, flax, pitch, tar, iron, and whatever else was to be had from abroad; and these run away with all the little wealth which the king and the wars left among you; they brought you ships, they coin'd your money, and they in short grew rich by you, and you look'd on and starv'd.

At last, by the prudence of King *Henry* VII. you fell to trade among yourselves; and gradually getting ground of the world, you made yourselves masters ,of your own manufactures, about the middle of Queen *Elizabeth's* reign; and what she did to encourage it, I shall shew in its place. And now what follow'd? The consequences were most gloriously seen in a few years, as follows.

1. Your people turn'd merchants abroad, as well as manufacturers at home: they tasted the sweets of commerce, and being encourag'd by the gain, soon supplanted their supplanters, built their own ships, sent out their own goods, brought home their own returns, cashier'd the *Esterlings*, forbid the wool going abroad, and thereby ruin'd the *Flemings*; and thus they set up for themselves.

2. As to the country, the revolution of trade, brought a revolution in the very nature of things; the poor began to work, not for cottages and liveries, but for money, and to live, as we say, at their own hands: The women and children learnt to spin and get money for it, a thing entirely new to them, and what they had never seen before. The men left the hedge and the ditch, and were set at work by the manufacturers to be wool-combers, weavers, fullers, clothworkers, carriers, and innumerable happy labours they perform'd, which they knew nothing of before; nay the *Flemings* came over (for money) and taught them how to perform those things at first, *I say at first*, for the people soon became able to send home their masters, and teach one another; then the villains and vassals were taken apprentices to the manufacturers, till coming to be masters, the name, nay the very things themselves call'd vassalage and villanage grew out of use.

The vassals got money by trade, and the villains by labour; and the lords found the sweets of it too, for they soon buy off the services, and bring the lords to take money. Thus the cottagers growing rich, bought their little cotts with right of commonage for their lives, renewable so and so, as they could agree, and this was called coppy-hold. On the other hand, the vassals and feu-holders, as they are call'd to this day in the *north*, growing rich, lump'd it with the lords, and for a sum of money bought off their slavish tenures, and got their leases turn'd into free-holds; and to finish the great fabrick, the farmers of lands were now enabled to take them at a rent certain, and the gentry got a revenue in money, which they understood nothing of before.

I might enlarge here upon the differing effects of luxury and frugality, which became more than ordinarily visible upon this change of affairs; namely, that as the frugal manufacturers, encourag'd by their success, doubled their industry and good husbandry, they lay'd up money, and grew rich; and the luxurious and purse proud gentry, tickl'd with the happy encrease of their revenues, and the rising value of their rents, grew vain, gay, luxurious and expensive: So the first encreas'd daily, and the latter, with all their new encreas'd and advanc'd revenues, yet grew poor and necessitous, till the former began to buy them out; and have so bought them out, that, whereas in those days, the lands were all in the hands of the *barons*; that is to say, the nobility, and even the knights and esquires who had lands, and were call'd the gentry, held them by servile tenures, as above: Now we see the nobility and the ancient gentry have almost every where sold their estates, and the commonalty and tradesmen have bought them: So that now the gentry are richer than the nobility, and the tradesmen are richer than them all.

I have given this sketch of the growing wealth of the

world

world by trade, as in *England*; that is, I have placed the scene as in *England*, because being talking to the *English* nation, it will be understood with the more ease. But the subject is general, and the thing is not of private interpretation: It will hold in its degree, in all the trading nations of *Europe*, as well as here; tho' perhaps in none more eminently, the trade here having made so visible a change in the face of the nation, and in the circumstances of the people, that the like is not to be shewn of any other nation, in so very remarkable a degree; so that if I had been writing in any other country or language, I should certainly have singled out *England* for an example.

I may, however, refer to other nations for evidence in their proportion, for in all the manufacturing countries in *Europe* the case is the same in degree; as trade has encreas'd, the miseries of the people have abated, the poor being employ'd by manufacture, by navigation, and the ordinary labours which trade furnishes for their hands; they have accordingly liv'd better, their poverty has been less, and they have been able to feed, who before might be said only to starve; and in those countries 'tis observable, that where trade is most effectually extended, and has the greatest influence, there the poor live best, their wages are highest; and where wages are highest, the consumption of provisions encreases most; where the consumption of provision is most encreas'd, the rate of provision is highest; and where provisions are dearest, the rents of lands are advanc'd most.

Again, *for the climax does not end here*; where the rents of lands are advanc'd, the taxes and payments to the governour are the larger; and where the larger taxes are levy'd, the revenue being encreased, that prince or governour is the richer; and where nations grow richer, they in proportion grow more powerful.

Thus trade is the foundation of wealth, and wealth of

power :

power: In former days the poverty of the northern nations added to their multitude, made them formidable; as the people encreas'd, the country not being able to maintain them, the old ones drove the young ones out, as bees cast their swarms, to seek place to dwell in, and by the force of their arms, to make room for themselves in warmer climates, and move in a more fruitful soil. Thus the *Alani*, the *Gauls*, the *Hunns*, invaded *Italy*; the *Goths* overrun *Spain*; the *Vandals*, *Spain* and the northern parts of *Africa*; the *Thracians*, *Natolia* and *Macedonia*, and the like.

But in our times, the case alters universally, the art of war is so well study'd, and so equally known in all places, that 'tis the longest purse that conquers now, not the longest sword. If there is any country whose people are less martial, less enterprising, and less able for the field; yet, if they have but more money than their neighbours, they shall soon be superior to them in strength, for money is power, and they that have the *gelt*, (as the *Dutch* call it) may have armies of the best troops in *Europe*, and generals of the greatest experience to fight for them at the shortest warning imaginable; thus upon sudden quarrels, princes and states do not now go home and raise armies, and list men, but they go home and raise money; and that being done, they look abroad to hire armies and hire men, and even to entertain generals; so that they need never bring any new raised troops into the field, but old *veteran* experienc'd soldiers, such as *Swiss*, *Germans*, &c. well officer'd, and led on by the greatest generals in the world; so that war is made in a trice, and decisive battles are fought now in shorter time than troops in former times could be brought into the field.

Thus the *Venetians* have had their Generals *Shuylenbergh*, *Coningsmark*, *Baden*, &c. to lead their troops; the *Spaniards* had their Marquis *de Lede*; the *Muscovites*

their

their Duke of *Croy*, their Generals *Gordon*, *Konningseck*, &c. and armies of *Danes*, *Prussians*, *Lunenbergers*, *Saxons*, *Hessians*, and *Bavarians*, and other *Germans*, besides *Swiss* and *Grisons*, are to be hired for money, alternately to fight, for now one side, then another; I say, *alternately*, as the persons direct them whose money they take; without regard to parties or interests; either of politicks or religion, tho' whether for or against the party or religion they profess; to day for Papist, to morrow for Protestant; be it for God or for *Baal*, as they're hired, they go

> *And always fight according as they're paid.*

Thus money raises armies, and trade raises money; and so it may be truly said of trade, that it makes princes powerful, nations valiant, and the most effeminate people that can't fight for themselves, if they have but money, and can hire other people to fight for them, they become as formidable as any of their neighbours.

Seeing trade then is the fund of wealth and power, we cannot wonder that we see the wisest princes and states anxious and concerned for the encrease of the commerce and trade of their subjects, and of the growth of the country; anxious to propagate the sale of such goods as are the manufacture of their own subjects, and that employs their own people; especially, of such as keep the money of their dominions at home, and on the contrary, for prohibiting the importation from abroad, of such things as are the product of other countries, and of the labour of other people, as which carry money back in return, and not merchandize in exchange.

Nor can we wonder that we see such princes and states endeavouring to set up such manufactures in their own countries, which they see are succesfully and profitably carried .on by their neighbours, and to endeavour to procure the materials proper for setting up those manu-

factures

factures by all just aud possible methods from other countries.

* * * * *

This also confirms what has been said above, namely, that as the trading, middling sort of people in *England* are rich ; so the labouring, manufacturing people under them are infinitely richer than the same class of people in any other nation iu the world.

As they are richer, so they live better, fare better, wear better, and spend more money, than they do in other countries; and I make no doubt 'tis the same in some other places in their proportion, as well as here; at least, in free nations, where the people are not affraid to own their circumstances, and to appear in good condition when they are in good condition : In short, the tradesmen in *England* live in better figure than most of the meaner gentry ; and I may add than some of the superior rank in foreign countries; nay, not to magnifie things here, and lessen them abroad, it is very evident that we have tradesmen or shop-keepers, of very ordinary employments in *London*, such as *cheesemongers, grocers, chandlers, brasiers, upholsterers*, and the like, who are able to spend more money in their families, and do actually spend more than most gentlemen of from 300 to 500 pounds a year, and that with this remarkable addition, that the tradesman shall spend it, and grow rich, and encrease under the weight of the expence; whereas the gentleman spends to the extent of his revenue, and lays up nothing.

How many shop-keepers, ware-house-keepers, and wholesale traders, (to go a step higher) have we seen in *London*, such as drapers, iron-mongers, salters, haberdashers, *Blackwell-hall*, and other factors, &c. who shall spend 500 pound a year in their housekeeping, and other incidents and lay up 500 pound a year more, while a gentleman of a thousand pound a year estate, can hardly

bring

bring both ends together at the close of the year, and not live in a much better figure than the tradesman, and not at all in better credit?

How do our merchants in *London, Bristol, Liverpole, Yarmouth, Hull,* and other trading sea-ports, appear in their families, with the splendor of the best gentlemen, and even grow rich, tho' with the luxury and expence of a count of the Empire! so true it is, that *an estate is* but *a pond,* but *trade is a spring.*

But to look at the meaner people (for among them, generally, the wealth of which I am now speaking is lodg'd, because their number is so exceeding great) those, it is evident, are in *England* supported after a different manner from the people of equal rank in trade among other nations; let any man that has seen how the trading people, and the labouring poor live abroad, make the comparison, it is too evident to be disputed.

It is upon these two classes of people, the manufacturers and the shopkeepers, that I build the hypothesis which I have taken upon me to offer to the publick, 'tis upon the gain they make either by their labour, or their industry in trade, and upon their inconceivable numbers, that the home consumption of our own produce, and of the produce of foreign nations imported here, is so exceeding great, and that our trade is raised up to such a prodigy of magnitude, as I shall shew it is.

I need not describe it at large, a few words will give a sketch of it, and a great volume will not line it out compleatly: They eat well, and they drink well; for their eating, (*viz.*) of flesh-meat, such as beef, mutton, bacon, &c. in proportion to their circumstances, 'tis to a fault, nay, even to profusion; as to their drink, 'tis generally stout strong beer, not to take notice of the quantity, which is sometimes a little too much, or good table beer for their ordinary diet; for the rest, we see their houses and lodgings tolerably furnished, at least stuff'd well with useful

and

and necessary household goods: Even those we call poor people, journey-men, working and pains-taking people do thus; they lye warm, live in plenty, work hard, and (need) know no want.

These are the people that carry off the gross of your consumption; 'tis for these your markets are kept open late on *Saturday* nights; because they usually receive their week's wages late: 'Tis by these the number of alehouses subsist, so many brewers get estates, and such a vast revenue of excise is raised; by these the vast quantity of meal and malt is consumed: And, in a word, these are the life of our whole commerce, and all by their multitude: Their numbers are not hundreds or thousands, or hundreds of thousands, but millions; 'tis by their multitude, I say, that all the wheels of trade are set on foot, the manufacture and produce of the land and sea, finished, cur'd and fitted for the markets abroad; 'tis by the largeness of their gettings, that they are supported, and by the largeness of their number the whole country is supported; by their wages they are able to live plentifully, and it is by their expensive, generous, free way of living, that the home consumption is rais'd to such a bulk, as well of our own, as of foreign production: If their wages were low and despicable, so would be their living; if they got little, they could spend but little, and trade would presently feel it; as their gain is more or less, the wealth and strength of the whole kingdom would rise or fall: For as I said above, upon their wages it all depends; the price of provisions depends on the consumption of the quantity; upon the rate of provisions the rent of lands, upon the rent of lands the value of taxes, and upon the value of taxes, the strength and power of the whole body: So that these are originally the first spring of all the motion.

In like manner it affects foreign trade; if the poors wages abate, the consumption of quantity also, as above,

would

would abate; if the quantity abates, the foreign importation would abate, the brandy, the oyl, the fruit, the sugar, the tobacco: For if the poor have not the money, they can't spare it for superfluities, as those foreign articles generally are, but must preserve it for necessity; upon their necessity depends the consumption of the ordinary food, which is the home produce; and upon their superfluity depends the consumption of their extraordinaries, which is the foreign importation.

Even the wine, the spice, the coffee and the tea, after the gentry have taken the nice and fine species off, are beholding to the mean, middling and trading people to carry off the coarser part, and the bulk of the quantity goes off that way too: So that these are the people that are the life of trade.

The silk manufactures are indeed a branch, the chief part of which the gentry may be said to support, and to help out trade in: As to the linen, they take indeed the finest hollands, cambricks, muslins, &c. But the middling tradesmen break in upon them, and follow them so at the heels, that 'tis to be questioned, whether, as the humour runs now, the tradesmen by the help of numbers do not out go them, even there also; not to mention the vast quantity of linens of other kind, which they consume every day, imported from *Ireland, France, Russia, Poland* and *Germany*.

Having thus mention'd the substance of our trade, and the support of it, it remains to examine a little the magnitude of these several branches, as well of exportation, as of importation, in order to make this discourse be according to my title, a true *Plan of the English Commerce*; and here it is necessary to make some little provisos, against the too forward expectation of the reader, as to numbers and calculations, in which it may be impossible to go the length which may be unreasonably expected.

There are many things in our commerce, as well
 abroad

abroad as . at home, in which no exact calculation can be made; and yet perhaps our estimates and conjectures may not be so remote as some may imagine, or so, as that no probable prospect, no rational view of the commerce may be made from them : *For example,*

It is not possible to make any calculation of the number of shop-keepers in *Great Britain*, or of the number of spinners, or of the quantity of wool, or of the bulk of the woollen manufacture ; and yet, from what has been, and shall be said, I doubt not, we shall form just and rational *ideas* in our thoughts, of the greatness of our manufacture, and of our home trade; and so of many other things which we cannot otherwise judge of, than by such general estimates.

The world must be left in the dark, concerning many useful parts of knowledge, if we were to take no measures, and form no ideas of things from the lights that are given ; tho' t should be true, that those lights do not amount to demonstrations; and especially, in matters of this kind, where the foundations are subject to various changes, and where the whole is rather matter of observation, than real intelligence of fact.

We may make an estimate of many branches of trade, without being able to determine the dimensions of either the subject on which those branches are founded, or of the particular parts themselves : We may make just estimates of the returns of treasure from the *Spanish West-Indies*, without enquiring into the fund of that treasure, (*viz.*) how many mines there are discovered, in which the silver is found, or how much every mine that is discover'd produces ; and thus we may entertain a true notion of the magnitude of woollen manufacture, and of the great advantage of it to this nation, without being able to know, to what value the return of it amounts in a year : We may give an account of its being able to consume the whole quantity of the growth of our wool in *England,*

and of much from *Ireland;* and we may bring this in evidence of the magnitude of the whole trade, without being able to cast up how much that wool amounts to, *and so of the rest.*

We may venture to say in publick, that we are a most powerful nation in shipping, having the greatest number of ships and seamen, of any nation in · the world, without being able to give a particular account how many ships we have, or how many seamen we employ.

Upon the same foundation, 'tis reasonable to say, we may judge of the magnitude of our commerce in general, by the several circumstances of the particular branches; *for example*, the encrease of the consumption of such and such goods imported, which are absolutely requisite for such or such a manufacture, is a just measure, by which to conclude the encrease of that manufacture: In other cases we may have plainer rules to judge from, and to make our estimates by; and yet, even those rules are not such, as that we can ascertain those estimates upon that foot, because of several incidents in trade, which cannot be accounted for, any more than they can be avoided.

We may judge of the consumption of wines in *England*, because they are all imported from abroad, and we can have an exact account of the annual importation from the Custom-house books: but we cannot positively ascertain the consumption from that importation, because, tho' all that are enter'd at the Custom-house, are imported and consum'd, yet all that are consum'd may not be enter'd at the Custom-house; clan·destine trade, and smuggling has a great stroke in it; and the like of foreign brandy: *Of both which hereafter.*

Thus again, we may judge of the consumption of spirits, by the quantity of malt distill'd, and the spirits of the first extraction gaug'd by the excise-man; but clan-

 destine

destine concealments have so great a share in that trade, that we can never say our calculations are exact.

Upon the whole, if our calculations and guesses are rational and probable, we hope in these cases it may be allow'd to be sufficient, because it is as far as any man can go. The commerce of *England*, is an immense and almost incredible thiug, and as we must content our selves with being in some cases in a difficulty as to numbers and figures; but in all such cases, we expect the reader will be content with the utmost possible inquiry, and the utmost possible discovery that we are able to make, and with such reasons as may be drawn from what appears, to judge of what cannot be fully discover'd. * * *

AN ESSAY

On the *Causes* of the *Decline* of the

FOREIGN TRADE,

CONSEQUENTLY

Of the *Value* of the *Lands* of *Britain*,

AND

On the MEANS *to Restore both.*

The SECOND EDITION,
With Additions.

---

*Trade has always been the best support of all Nations,
and the principal Care of the wisest.*
Ld. *Chesterfield's* Speech, *Dublin, Oct.* 8, 1745.

LONDON:

Printed for JOHN BROTHERTON at the *Bible*
in *Cornhill.*

MDCCL.

THE
PREFACE.

THE merchant, the manufacturer, and the sailor, who at first view appear to have the greatest interest in trade, will, upon examination, be found not to be so deeply concerned in its well or ill being as the land-holder, whose interest seems more remote, and who (with sorrow it must be said) too often by his indifference gives occasion to suspect, that he thinks he hath no concern in it at all.

The former are not fix'd to a country ; their effects are all moveables, vendible in many parts of the world ; if they are oppress'd in one place, they can soon pack up and fly to another where greater freedoms invite them ; they may indeed be bound by leases of lands or houses, but parchment chains seldom prevent despairing fugitives : Therefore the number of people in any country, as well as their well-being, depends intirely on trade.

The land-holder hath an immoveable property, valuable only to some few of his neighbours or countrymen, the produce of which if trade carries not off, nor brings in people to consume, but on the contrary by its decay drives the consumers away, his tenants must decay, break, fly, his lands be untenanted ; he may indeed sell at one price or another, but when the bulk of his neighbours are in as bad a situation as himself, and all rents declining, the value of untenanted farms and empty houses must be very low.

The

The traders are indeed the first pinched, but then they have the first warning to avoid the calamity, which coming but by degrees to the ultimate, the land-holders, they are the longer lulled in a deceitful security.

Who then is the most concerned in point of interest with regard to trade, he whose property is in moveables, who hath the first warning, and the greatest choice of purchasers; or he whose property is immoveable, who feels not the danger until it is far advanced, hath the least choice of purchasers, and those declining ones too, like himself?

As men naturally pursue their own interest, this indifference in our land-holders is monstrous. Is it pride which makes them think the subject beneath them? All foreign Courts are now studying it attentively. Is it the fear that the subject is too intricate? A little attention will make it as easy to them as to foreigners. Is it their places that engross all their time? What they think they get by these, they may doubly lose in their lands. Is it their pleasures they now make their chief business? Alas! they are paying very dear for them, and deservedly too, if that is the case. These causes may affect some few, but the general one I take to be the craft, covetousness, or false notions of interest in our ancestors, who thought to lay the burden of taxes as remote as possible from their lands by laying them on trade, and to buttress that up by prohibitions; both which have had quite contrary effects, and their children's feet are catched in the traps their forefathers laid for others; which cynical spirit, it is to be feared, is not yet quite worn out.

To remove all false prejudices with regard to trade, from our land-holders, to point out to them their true interest, to clear a plain easy subject from the imputation of intricacy, to remove those destructive distinctions without any difference of landed and trading interests, or to sum up all, to prove the strong connexion in point of

interest

interest, between land and trade, is the occasion of publishing this essay.

An attempt is here made to shew the symptoms of our decay, the difficulties and discouragements our trade at present labours under, by which only foreigners can rival us, the prodigious artificial value we thereby put upon our goods to the hindrance of their sale abroad; the fictitious value they make in the rents the land-holder now receives, compared with the real, true, intrinsic value, a free-trade would make; the great natural advantages our country is bless'd with superior to any nation in *Europe*, the means proper to preserve these by unburdening our trade, which will employ our poor, increase the stock of people, and increase our riches; all which must terminate in increasing the value of lands.

As of all the methods of raising taxes on the people, the easiest and most equal must naturally raise the most money and the fewest murmurs; a proposal is here offered to the consideration of the publick, for one tax on the voluntary consumers of luxuries, to supply all our present, positive, and involuntary taxes, without their ill consequences, more easy, more equal, speedier raised, productive of more money, which will at the same time restore trade and increase the value of our lands.

The consideration of our numerous monopolies naturally led to an enquiry into the nature of a free-port trade, as well as the strong prejudices now subsisting against it; and tho' a difference in opinion will herein be found with several great men who have wrote on this subject, yet it is not intended to cast any reflexion on their memories, or lessen that esteem which their past endeavours for their country's good justly intitles them to; but only to set the subject in that general light they seem not to have viewed it in, and put it to the strongest trial it is capable of.

Perhaps it may seem strange that no bounty should be

proposed

proposed as a means to restore trade; but if a free-port will gain us all those trades we are naturally capable of, it will appear to be itself the greatest bounty, and in endeavouring to force nature, the expence is certain, but the success doubtful.

As an impartial search after truth was the author's sole motive for writing upon this subject, so he desires the reader to be assured that he has not published any thing but what appears to him as such; and as an earnest of his sincerity he declares, that whatever mistakes are proved to be committed, no person shall be more willing to retract, or more grateful for the favour of better information, and which he will not fail to own whenever this essay shall be found to deserve another edition. If the several proposals here offered for the restoring of our trade, and therewith the value of our lands, shall appear to be founded on reason and the nature of commerce, he flatters himself that there is virtue and publick spirit enough left in the nation to carry them into execution; which, whether done or not, signifies no more to him than to any other person whatever, except the desire of a portion of that heart-felt joy which those obtain, whose labours are blessed with their country's good.

THE bookseller desiring a second edition, the opportunity of correcting the mistakes in the first, was a sufficient inducement to comply with his request; as to such errors which may still have escaped, the former promise of acknowledging is now renewed.

Considerable alterations have happened in the finances, by the late war; additional taxes and great deficiencies: What the true general produce will be, a year or two of peace cannot shew, therefore the same calculations are continued, as were in the former impression.

Our late superiority at sea has so checked the *French*, that until they get their hands at liberty our trade may

seem

seem to flourish for a little time: But increased causes must have increased effects; above thirty millions of new debts and above a million of additional taxes must be felt. Time will shew whether such advantages as might have been made by a sea war, can on the present footing be maintained by the peace.

During a confined knowledge of trade, the clamours of oppressive taxes, overloading debts, a threatening public-bankruptcy, will have weight, and distress every Admini-stration. But if a general-knowledge was obtained of the extensive nature of a free-trade, the increase of the revenue with a liquidation of the national debt, would (I think) appear extreme easy; and a general prosperity stop the mouths of all gainsayers.

THE
CONTENTS.

PART I.

Dutch

Contents.

PART II.

     PART

Contents.

PART III.

Objection.

Contents.

Will

Contents.

AN

AN
ESSAY

On the *Causes* and *Decline* of the

FOREIGN TRADE.

THE foreign trade of *Britain* may be defined to be its exports and imports of commodities to and from other countries, with the navigation and intercourse of exchanges thereby caused.

The general measures of the trade of *Europe* at present are gold and silver, which, tho' they are sometimes commodities, yet are the ultimate objects of trade ; and the more or less of these metals a nation retains, it is denominated rich or poor.

Those nations that have no mines of gold and silver, have no means to get them but by foreign trade, and, according to the degree of those metals they retain, the prices of their commodities, the numbers of their people, and therewith the value of their lands rise and fall in proportion.

Therefore if the exports of *Britain* exceed its imports, foreigners must pay us the balance in treasure, and the nation grow rich.

But if the imports of *Britain* exceed its exports, we must pay foreigners the balance in treasure, and the nation grow poor.

The imports cannot exceed the exports in any country where the trade is free, especially if the country abounds with home commodities, because these not being raised to

                    artificial

artificial prices by taxes, must be so cheap to the inhabitants, that foreign commodities could not answer the charges of transporting for the consumption of such a country, unless the people exported so much of their best commodities as to want, or content themselves with a supply of inferior ones from other nations; so that the chief imports of a free-port trade in a fruitful country, can't be for the consumption of the people, until they make room for them with advantage to themselves, but must be either materials to be manufactured, which will afterwards be re-exported in goods improved by the people's labour at least twice, it may be ten times their first cost, increasing thereby a nation's treasure in proportion; or else goods to lay up in storehouses, for it being the interest of merchants to buy any commodities that offer in cheap times to sell again when the markets are advanced, part of such imports, tho' they be luxuries, as most of our *India* goods are, and purchased with treasure, do become at some time or other advantageous exports, and besides paying for what is consumed at home, do bring in plenty of treasure, as was the case of our *East-India* trade formerly: Of which *Holland* is at present an example, tho' it affords neither corn, naval stores, or materials of manufacture to subsist the eighth part of its people; tho' it consumes great quantities of *French* wines and brandies, yet because its trade is almost free, its merchants bring the balance in its favour with almost all countries.

The barometer of trade between any two nations is the course of the exchange, the nation over-balanced having always its money undervalued.

The barometer of the general trade of a nation is its Mint, if plenty of treasure is brought in, and little carried out, part of it will be continually coining, and much new money will appear, the certain symptom of a flourishing trade.

14

But

But if much treasure be brought in, yet more be carried out, the Mint must lie idle, little new money will appear, the sure sign of a decaying trade.

That the foreign trade of *Britain* declines, will appear by the following symptoms.

The many petitions to Parliament complaining of the decay of the woollen manufacture.

The starving condition the poor are reduced to in the clothing countries.

The low price of wool.

The long credit shop-keepers take.

The great numbers of bankrupts.

The exchange being against us this *Feb.* 8, 1740, to places where formerly it was for us, *viz. Hamburgh, Holland, Venice,* and *Genoa.*

The exchange being more against us with *France,* than in the times of open trade, tho' its goods are loaded with such high duties as amount almost to a prohibition.

The exchange being less for us with *Portugal* than it was during Queen *Ann*'s war, tho' we had troops and subsidies to pay there.

The great exportation of *bullion.*

The Mint's lying idle, little or no new coin appearing.

The present scarcity of money, especially silver.

The great arrears of rent the tenants are in all over *England,* which the landlords every where complain of.

The great numbers of farms thrown upon the landlords hands.

The vast increase of the poor's rates.

These symptoms of the decline of our foreign trade being so very plain, the causes are the things to be found out, and then the remedy may be easy. It is a maxim in philosophy, Take away the cause and the effect will cease; but we have troubled our heads so little of late days with this good maxim, that our remedies of high taxes, prohibitions, and penal laws, have been applied to stop effects,

                                                                          while

while the causes have never been thought on, and since
they have not had any success, or ever can in our present
circumstances, and would appear needless were the causes
understood and removed: I shall attempt to show what
are,

I. *The causes of the decline of our foreign trade.*

II. *The reasons why the decline of foreign trade sinks the
value of lands.*

III. *Offer some means to restore both.*

PART I.

THE *causes of the decline of our foreign trade will
appear to be,*

I. *Our present taxes, some of which are unequal, and
all of them fraught with oppressive consequences.*

II. *Monopolies, whereby the many are oppressed for
the gain of a few.*

III. *Ill-judged laws.*

IV. *Our large national debt.*

I. *Our present taxes,* consisting of 1st, the *Stamp duties;*
2dly, the *Window-tax;* 3dly, the *Coal-tax;* 4thly, the
Land-tax; 5thly, the *Salt-duty;* 6thly, the *Excises* on
Sope, Candles, Leather, &c. 7thly, and lastly, the *Customs,
the oppressive consequences* of which I shall endeavour to
shew.

First, the *Stamp-duty.*

This seems to be a hardship on the oppressed, for if
knaves defraud honest people of their property, these last
are deterred from endeavouring to recover it by this
excessive tax on law, and a poor man suing for 20*l.* pays
the same Stamp-duties as a rich man who sues for 20000*l.*

                                        which

which greatly prevents the poor, and oftentimes the rich from recovering their just rights.

Perhaps the stamps on bonds, deeds, &c. at a very moderate rate, may be necessary to prevent forgeries; and those on cards and dice tend to discourage gaming : But on law-proceedings the Stamp-duty is certainly a great grievance.

Secondly, The *Window-tax.*

This is an old tax new-modelled, with what equality is to be considered : The rates are according to the numbers of windows, but these are no just foundations for taxing. Mechanicks work-houses, inns, lodging-houses, &c. may have as many windows as a nobleman's seat, and the possessors pay equal sums upon very unequal fortunes: Some old houses have many windows, some modern ones in the *Italian* taste but few; here the sums are unequal let the fortunes be what they will. Again, the idle may shut out the light, the industrious can't work without, the former favour and the latter tax themselves, for what? for working. Well may we pray *Lighten our darkness.*

Thirdly, The *Coal-tax.*

Gee, on Trade, says, that *coals brought to* London *pay about* 10*s. per chaldron duty.*

Ditto, *Water-born to other parts of the kingdom,* 5*s.*

Ditto, *Exported to foreigners,* 8*s.*

This favours foreigners more than our own people, more especially the inhabitants of *London* and its neighbourhood, who pay about 7*s.* more duty *per* chaldron than foreigners, so that we hereby encourage them to underwork the *Londoners* more immediately in iron-wares, and something likewise in all manufactures where *coals* are used. A tax on a commodity of such general use to the poor as well as the rich, must, like our *excises,* add to the dearness of the poor's living, raise the wages of their labour, and the price of manufactured goods, which likewise insensibly affects the rich : But who can express the

hardships

hardships and miseries of the poor when hard winters (such as that in *January* 1739–40) raise the price of *coals* excessively, and yet a heavy tax on them still adding to the oppression?

Fourthly, The *Land-tax*.

This being now at 4*s.* in the pound, is paid by some to the full, but by many not to above 2*s.* in the pound, and that without any reason, but because the estates happen to be in different counties, which were variously affected to a new king when the present assessment was made, whereby some members of the community being ever since put undeservedly in a worse condition than others, are a dead weight against even our most necessary enlarged expences; wrong policy, that increases dissension always in times of difficulty. The tediousness of the coming in of this tax, which is generally two years, is a great disadvantage; in times of safety creates annual expensive loans; but in times of the greatest danger leaves us quite in distress: 'Tis the highest impropriety to call that the aid of the present year which is to be paid in the two next ensuing. This tax has besides been attended with a very bad consequence to the nation, in having made a distinction where there is no difference, *viz.* of *landed* and *trading interests*. Country gentlemen, finding the *Land-tax* a heavy burden on them, thought to ease themselves by loading the trader, whom they look'd upon with a jealous eye, thinking his situation easier, whereby that trade which had raised the value of their estates, and which only could support the increased value, being deprived of their protection, and cramp'd with duties without mercy on all occasions, has indeed been brought sufficiently low, and is bringing down with it the rents of their lands; and they may see the fatal error when it is perhaps too late, trade being like a coy dame, difficult to be brought back when slighted.

Mr. *Locke* in his *Considerations of the Consequences of*

the

the lowering of Interest, and raising the Value of Money, asserts it to be an undoubted truth, *That hé* (i.e. the land-holder) *is more concerned in trade, and ought to take a greater care that it be well managed, than even the merchant himself; for he will certainly find that when a decay has carried away one part of our money out of the kingdom, and the other is kept in the merchants or tradesmens hands, that no laws he can make, nor any little arts of shifting property among ourselves, will bring it back to him again; but his rents will fall, and his income every day lessen, till general industry and frugality, joined to a well-ordered trade, shall restore to the kingdom the riches and wealth it had formerly.*

Fifthly, The *Salt-tax.*

This is collected with the greatest expence of any, in proportion to its amount, consequently is more grievous to 'the subject, and less beneficial to the Government: Is attended with more pernicious consequences than any single tax, for it has an universal influence on all manufactures, by laying great hardships on the working poor, whose chief food is bacon and salted flesh, and who in many places are forced to lay in a stock of salted provisions for the winter: The same with respect to the farmers all over the kingdom: Is prejudicial also to our navigation, by enhancing the expense of victualling of ships, which raises the freights on *English* bottoms, to the great advantage of foreigners; or forces the merchant to victual abroad, to the great damage of our lands: prevents even the very improvement of our lands, salt being the best manure, and on account of its easy carriage the cheapest. But the greatest prejudice of all is, its preventing the improvement of our herring-fishery, that great nursery of seamen, by enhancing its expences to the great profit of the *Dutch:* for tho' we allow a bounty on exported fish, yet the home-consumption, which would be a vast help to promote the fishery, being taxed, has made the trade languish, and little is done either for the home or foreign demand: And notwithstanding that this article of cured herrings is so necessary for the support of the working poor, yet are they loaded with so heavy a duty, as makes them too chargeable a morsel for the poor to encourage the fishery.

The *States-General,* in their proclamation dated at the *Hague,* 19 *July,* 1624, call the great fishing, and catching herrings, *the chiefest trade and principal gold-mine of the* United Provinces, *whereby many thousands of housholds, families, handicrafts, trades and occupations, are set on work, well maintained, and prosper, especially the sailing and navigation, as well within as without these countries, is kept in great estimation.*

Should so beneficial a trade that well maintains handicrafts, trades, &c. and keeps in great estimation a navigation, should such a trade as this, I say, be obstructed for the sake of a paltry tax, that produces but about 150,000*l.* *per annum* neat to the Government: Have we lost all our senses, and shall we leave the *Dutch* unrivall'd for ever in a trade, which they declare to be a principal gold mine, and yet is the neglected produce of our own *coasts?*

Sixthly, The *Excises.*

Tho' the *excises* on *sope, candles, leather,* &c. by their manner of raising are so disagreeable to the nation in general, that any invective against them at this time would be needless, having been so largely treated on already by our greatest political authors: And as the intent of this essay is only to set things in that single point of view which relates to trade, I shall consider them no otherwise than as taxes on commodities, but attempt to shew the augmentative faculty of all such taxes, and the great prejudice they do to trade; for whatever raises the necessaries of life raises labour, and of course the price of every thing that is produced by labour. And it will be

made

made appear hereafter by a calculation of the oppressive consequences of the *excises,* &c. that they almost treble themselves to the people for what they raise to the Government; and it is to be feared it would appear much more, if we could go to the bottom of the oppression, for if it be considered that tradesmen in a country, by their mutual dependence on each other, are like wheels in a machine, in which if one is touched the others are affected. Amidst so many trading movers to what degree the oppression is increas'd is impossible to know, nor must we be startled at the largeness of such calculations as being too great for us to pay, for being circulated chiefly among ourselves, and going out by dribblets we hardly perceive them; but yet are surprised to find wages and necessaries grow dearer and dearer, because few use themselves to consider the immensity of such collected advances in small sums; but if we compare the difference of the prices of necessaries between *England* and *France,* we shall find that difference plainly accounting for the vast amount of the consequences of our taxes; nor can it be a trifle that makes such a fruitful country as *England* is, so dear, and its trade decline so fast; for our working people being forced to purchase the necessaries of life dear, must work dear to live, until their willing working hands are quite tied up by foreigners, who live less taxed, and of course work cheaper, so that they must and do undersell us at all markets for manufactured goods where they come in competition with us, and in time must stop all such exports. And I appeal to the experience of every honest man conversant in trade, whether it does not decline year after year, more especially our woollen trade, which has been estimated to be as necessary to us as bread is to the life of man, for our dearer goods must lie unsold or be sold with loss, which must stop or break our merchants; they our clothiers and weavers; these last their journeymen, who must either starve, turn beggars, thieves, or fly to our

enemies

enemies and help them to ruin us the faster, which has happened too much of late years. Oppress trade, and the generality of the common people become miserable and burdensom to the rich; every little accidental slackening of trade increases that wretched number, as the following case will fully illustrate.

A poor man either by hard weather, the dead time of the year in his particular trade, (for all trades have such times) sickness, or various other accidents cannot work, but having saved ten good shillings is determined to allow himself only bare necessaries, which, if untaxed, might cost about 4*d. per* day; his money then will hold thirty days.

But if necessaries are advanced by the consequences of our taxes 2*d. per* day on his consumption, in that case 6*d. per* day is only equal to the above 4*d.* for his maintenance, and he can then hold out but twenty days, and is forced the earlier by ten days (in which possibly he might get employment) to starve, beg, or steal.

Absolute starving, we must hope, seldom or never happens amongst so humane a people as the *English*, but want of necessaries may so impair a poor man's health that he may never recover it, and then an useful subject, part of the riches of the nation, is lost.

Begging but ten days learns the poor man an idle way of life that few ever get rid of, and then instead of an useful subject he becomes a burdensom, and oftentimes a villanous one.

Stealing, whereby he becomes the bane of society, and not contented with injuring his neighbour in his property, is prompted sometimes to take away his life; and in both cases exposes himself to be cut off by the hand of justice. Every way a loss to the nation.

In all these cases the poor man may have a large family of children, adding misery to misery.

Encourage but trade by knocking off one of those

fetters,

fetters, its *excise*, and the children of the poor will be trained up to labour, become useful industrious subjects, live comfortably as journeymen, or perhaps as masters, and contribute their assistance to add more power to the nation, and help to ease the rich of their taxes; for the greater number of individuals there are in a country capable of paying, the less the tax will be on each of them if equally laid. It is the interest of the rich to let the poor be able to get money for their assistance, for by preventing them, they bring the greater weight on their own shoulders; for these oppressions do not stop with the poor, but extend like a plague to the rich and the noble, whose fortunes insensibly moulder away by them; are the chief causes of the present declining condition of their tenants, that great increase of the poor's tax the nation now labours under, which in some places has lately been at above 8*s.* in the pound, and must by degrees inevitably sink the value of their estates, until one ruin involves all.

Several authors have thought *excises* and *land-taxes* to be the most equal methods of raising supplies, but, if strictly attended to, they will appear far otherwise; any thing positive and involuntary cannot avoid oppression, which humanity should always make the first consideration in raising money from the people, and good policy the second, in order to prevent evasion and fraud, the children of oppression.

A working bachelor pays the excise, &c. on his own shoes only.

A working married-man does the same for himself, the same for his wife, the same for his five sons, the same for his five daughters; twelve in family.

A landed bachelor of 1000*l. per annum*, when the *land-tax* is at 2*s.* pays 100*l.*

A landed married-man of the same estate does the same, having a wife and ten children.

Will

Will any one say in these cases that the *excise* on *leather*, and the *land-tax*, are equal taxations? In the first case, is not the oppression increased twelve articles to one; and in the second, at least four to one? For the landed married-man, with such a family, cannot, should not live more comfortably on his whole estate, than the bachelor can do on the quarter of his; and how are the landed gentlemen that are married oppress'd, who are now in both cases?

And here it may not be improper to examine the inconveniences of a *poll-tax*, such as the *States of Holland* issued an ordonnance on the 28th of *March*, 1742, for establishing : In the preamble to which it is said, *That the safety of the country, and its inhabitants, requiring a greater number of troops to be kept up than ordinary, their noble and high mightinesses have been obliged to search for the most proper means to provide for the expenses of that augmentation, and they have not found any more fitting than the establishment of a* poll-tax, *proportioned to the abilities of every one.   The first class is of those who earn, spend, or possess an income of*

600 florins, out of which they shall pay 6 florins to this tax.

700	*ditto*	8 *florins*	4000 *florins*	75 *florins*	
800	*ditto*	12 *ditto*	4500 *ditto*	90 *ditto*	
1000	*ditto*	15 *ditto*	5000 *ditto*	120 *ditto*	
1200	*ditto*	18 *ditto*	6000 *ditto*	140 *ditto*	
1500	*ditto*	25 *ditto*	7000 *ditto*	160 *ditto*	
2000	*ditto*	32 *ditto*	8000 *ditto*	180 *ditto*	
2500	*ditto*	40 *ditto*	9000 *ditto*	200 *ditto*	
3000	*ditto*	50 *ditto*	10000 *ditto*	250 *ditto*	
3500	*ditto*	60 *ditto*	12000 *ditto*	300 *ditto*	

and so on, increasing on the foot of 50 florins for every 2000 *florins income.*

24

With

With due respect to their noble and high mightinesses, I shall beg leave to repeat what I have just before asserted, *viz.* that any thing positive and involuntary cannot avoid oppression, &c. and add a few remarks on this *poll-tax* to support that assertion.

1st, *It is unequal, consequently unjust and oppressive.*

By this tax a married man of 600 florins income with six, eight or ten children, whose family is so numerous that his income is scarce sufficient to maintain them, and who at the year's end has hardly one florin left, is to pay the same as a bachelor who hath only himself to maintain, and perhaps lays up sixty florins a year: What injustice and oppression is here?   Six florins are exacted from one man, who has not conveniently, cannot have one to spare, and no more from another who can spare sixty; and yet this is not the worst view this tax is capable of being put in, for, suppose the bachelor's 600 florins income to arise from the interest of his stocks in *Holland* or *England,* and the married man's by his labour; here is a farther shocking piece of injustice, whereby industry and idleness are put on the same footing.

2dly, *It injures trade, consequently impoverishes a country.*

By raising the prices of labour and goods; for a man who earns by his trade 600 florins a year, and whose numerous family consumes the whole, if six florins are exacted from him, he must raise them by advancing the prices of his labour or his goods; else he cannot live, and the dearer goods grow, the less vendible they are, consequently the less trade this man will have; so that this tax increases his expences, and at the same time lessens his income; if this is not oppression, I know not what is.

All taxes on necessaries or trade do the same.

3dly, *It tends to corrupt the manners of the people, consequently to make them tumultuous and less governable.*

For being to pay in proportion to what they earn, spend, or possess, the just value whereof is impossible to be known but by themselves, and to force them to a declaration, an oath is always imposed, which makes a struggle between interest and conscience, an extreme wise law, whereby an honest man is put on a worse footing than a perjured knave: He that forswears himself pays less than his due and saves his money, but he that is conscientious pays to the full; which latter suspecting others to evade, is peaked at paying more than his neighbours, and wonders why a false oath should not sit as easy on him as on so many others; whereby the most solemn pledge of truth among men becomes frequently violated, is despis'd, diregarded, and interest rides triumphant over conscience, which latter being to men as a dike to keep out the torrent of vice, if once a thorough breach is made, a deluge of iniquity ensues, whereby all good principles are drowned: And the more vicious men grow, the readier they are to oppose authority.

Seventhly and lastly, The *customs*.

Customs are duties collected in sea-port or frontier-towns, by authority of state, on goods coming in or going out of a country.

All authors agree that low customs are one of the causes of the great trade of *Holland*.

If low customs cause great trade, it follows that high customs cause little trade; which is comparatively our case now.

If the lower the customs the greater the trade, no customs or free-ports must carry trade to its utmost height; which case might be ours.

If low customs have such good effects in *Holland*, which hath the most natural disadvantages of any country; a free-port must have the greatest and best effect in *Britain*, whose natural advantages are beyond those of any country in *Europe*, as will be proved hereafter.

26

That

That the above observations are founded in truth will appear, by shewing how customs, especially high ones, obstruct the trade of these nations.

First, *they prevent our country's being an universal storehouse.*

Because our duties being so great an additional disbursement to the first cost of the goods, no merchant will let so much of his capital lie dead for duties here, when he can have it all circulating in commodities in other countries; nor can such goods be re-exported, because the officers fees in and out, which always remain, and the interest of the money lying dead for duties paid (tho' they be mostly drawn back) are so great a charge (the natural interest of money being much higher with us than in *Holland*) that the goods cannot come near so cheap from us to any foreign market, as from a free-port where nothing is paid in or out; therefore they prevent our country's having the best choice of goods at the cheapest prices, to tempt our customers: The great duties on *India* goods discourage foreigners buying at our sales, who pay an extraordinary charge of commission on that advanced price, and are forced to lie some months out of their money for the draw-back; besides, the strict rule of declaring goods at the *Custom-House*, makes publick to every one each transaction of trade, and thereby prevents shipping for foreign ports such goods as are there prohibited, which deprives us of several beneficial branches of trade that are carried on from *Holland*, or free-ports, to the great advantage of foreigners.

Secondly, *they prevent the increase of our navigation;*

By enhancing the expences of building and navigating our ships.

Boards, hemp, flax, sail-cloth, and iron, paying duties, those materials must be dear, and several necessaries of life paying some customs (and some excises) the ship-builders

labour

labour must be dear; also the provision and stores put on board the ships.

The *English* sailor paying, on his own and family's necessaries, customs, (and excises) must have, and hath higher wages than most other countries give.

So that a *British* vessel built and rigged with dear materials, by dear labour, supplied with dear stores, and navigated by sailors at dear wages, must have dear freights, bring in all foreign necessaries and materials for manufacture dear, and carry out all our own products and manufactures dear to foreign markets, much to the disadvantage of their sale.

This shews the reason why we could never rival the *Dutch, Hamburghers*, &c. in the *Greenland* trade, the navigation of the *Baltick*, or the herring-fishery, which being trades carried on for small profits, our dear navigation effectually excludes us from making any increase those ways.

By not having an universal storehouse, our ships, like empty houses, lie by idle in our harbours, waiting months for freights, the interest of the money they cost eating out their profits ; or else are obliged to lose their time, and be at great expences in going from one port to another to endeavour to get a cargo.

Thirdly, *they prevent the increase of sailors, the true strength of this nation.*

This is a consequence of the two last remarks ; for no trade breeds so many or so good sailors as the free-port and carrying trades, the employment being the greatest, and the experience the largest, as the voyages are the most various and extensive, for 'tis no less than the trade of the whole world.

As customs are inconsistent with such a trade, of course they debar us of that increase of sailors which must be necessary to carry it on, and who would protect us from, or carry vengeance to those enemies that durst insult us.

The

The customs upon foreign salt, a commodity so necessary to our fishery, is likewise a great prevention to the increase of sailors; the numbers employed in *Holland* by their fishery are prodigious, I fear ours bear no comparison.

The *British* sailor being forced by customs and excises to live dear, must have dear wages, which excludes him from employment wherever foreigners can be legally had, to the great discouragement of our sailors, and prevents their increase.

All this is not only destructive to our riches, but also to our security, it being difficult in time of war to man our navy, not improperly called our floating castles, and occasions that hard custom of pressing, which puts a free-born *British* sailor on the footing of a *Turkish* slave: The *Grand Signior* cannot do a more absolute act, than to order a man to be dragged away from his family, and against his will run his head before the mouth of a cannon; and if such acts should be frequent in *Turkey* upon any one set of useful men, would it not drive them away to other countries, and thin their numbers yearly? and would not the remaining few double or treble their wages? which is the case of our sailors in time of war, to the great detriment of our trade and manufactures.

Fourthly, *they lessen the capitals of our merchants.*

By keeping a great part of their stocks by them idle to pay the duties of the goods they import, which is, in effect, making them not only advance their money for the service of the state, but likewise run the risk in the credit they give of ever being reimbursed, and is diverting a stream of riches that should water trade; for it often happens that when our merchants are short of cash, and they have both customs and manufacturers to pay, so much money goes for the first, that nothing is left for the latter, which causes a circulation of disappointments seldom known in *Holland* on that account; and the *Dutch* merchants can carry on the same trade with much less stock

than

than ours, sell cheaper, extend their commerce farther, and of course give better encouragement to their working people, whereby they cause them to be more industrious than ours.

The following case will shew the difficulties and discouragements our merchants labour under more than the *Dutch* our great rivals in trade.

Suppose a merchant in *Roterdam* to ship corn for *Bourdeaux*, and the neat produce to amount to the value of 2000*l*. *sterling*; if he orders it to be invested in wines, and shipp'd for *Holland*, he will not pay for duties 40*l*.

Suppose a merchant in *London* to ship corn for *Oporto*, and the neat produce to amount to the value of 2000*l*. *sterling*; if he orders it to be invested in wines, and shipp'd for *England*, he will pay for duties above 2000*l*.

Therefore the *Dutch* merchant's prime cost and duties of his cargo will be, £2040

The *English*, *ditto*, 4000

1960*l*. of the *English* merchant's disburse more than the *Dutch* merchant's in the amount of the duties, is imprisoned until the people he trusts pay him, which may be a year or a year and a half; whereas if the *Dutch* merchant's capital be equal, he has had 1960*l*. to employ in buying up goods to freight another adventure, may be of woollens, giving quick employment to the navigation and manufactures of his country.

Suppose the retailers they trust break about the year's end, and make a composition amounting to 25 *per cent.* on the prime cost and duties of the wines:

The *Dutch* merchant's loss will be, £1530

The *English*, *ditto*, 3000

This also makes our merchants risk in trade greater, and their losses heavier than in *Holland*.

Fifthly, *they encourage and force the consumption of foreign superfluities.*

The dearer outlandish luxuries are, the more are they

esteemed

esteemed by our people of taste; 'tis the expence that makes the elegancy, therefore duties on them only further their sale, as Mr. *Locke* clearly proves in his *Considerations,* &c. *For it being vanity, not use, that makes the expensive fashions of your people, the emulation is, who shall have the finest, that is, the dearest things, not the most convenient or useful? How many things do we value and buy, because they come at dear rates from* Japan *and* China, *which, if they were our own manufacture or product to be had common, and for a little money, would be contemned and neglected? Have not several of our own commodities, offered to sale at reasonable rates, been despised, and the very same eagerly bought and bragged of when sold for* French *at a double price? You must not therefore think that the raising their price will lessen the vent of fashionable foreign commodities amongst you, so long as men have any way to purchase them, but rather increase it.*

But besides encouraging, our customs force the consumption here of most foreign superfluities that are imported; for tho' the duties be mostly drawn back on some articles, yet the interest of the money lying dead for duties and fees in and out, hinder in some degree their re-exportation, and in many articles the duties are only in part drawn back, so that what remains is such an additional load as prevents such goods being saleable at any other market, consequently forces us to consume all such superfluities. This makes a people luxurious, who can do nothing with foreign superfluities but riot and indulge; whereas the *Dutch* having the object of gain always before their eyes, by the advance of foreign markets for those superfluities they have in their storehouses, are check'd from indulging in what appears to them common, and of no great value for the present, but may be attended with great profit hereafter; which accounts for the *Dutch* frugality, so justly celebrated by all authors.

It is the excessive consumption, not the trade of

foreign

foreign superfluities that should be discouraged, and which is best done by taxing the consumers, letting the goods as objects of trade go quite free, whereas our high duties on them do just the reverse, for they encourage the consumption and destroy the trade, to the immense loss of the nation.

Sixthly, *they encourage smuggling.*

Where the avoiding high customs makes the profit great, no risk, no danger can prevent mens attempting it; it is throwing out a bait to a greedy fish, he will snap at it tho' ruin ensues; this prejudices and discourages the fair trader, either tempts, or forces him to turn smuggler, and associate himself with those many examples of depravity we have at this time among our people, living in a state of war with the Government, in defiance of laws, whereby an universal corruption of manners and contempt of authority must ensue, if not early prevented: Besides, it being chiefly the articles of luxury that are smuggled, as brandy, tea, *French* wine, laces, silks, &c. it spreads their consumption among the lower class of people, who are tempted to imitate at a less expence the luxuries of their superiors; and the same smugglers that bring us these superfluities, carry off vast quantities of raw wool, to the great prejudice of our manufactures, and the nation in general.

Seventhly, *they ruin manufactures, more especially the woollen.*

Customs prevent the bartering away our manufactures for foreign goods, not only for our own consumption, but also for exportation, which might enlarge the vent of our goods ten times more than it now is; for if a merchant now exports woollen goods, and would barter them for wines, the duties on them would amount to more than the cost of his woollen goods; so that he must have a double capital for such an adventure, or let it quite alone, whereby the sales of great quantities of woollen goods are lost to the nation.

As

As customs enhance the expences of our navigation, the freights must be raised accordingly, whereby the prices of the sope, oil, and dye-stuffs used in manufacturing our wool, are advanced to the maker, and the freights on the cloths or stuffs exported being also raised, are additional clogs upon the sales of our woollen goods.

Customs prevent the carrying and fishing trades, the great nurseries of seamen, whereby our sailors being few, and their expences raised by taxes, they have the highest wages of most people in *Europe,* which is another additional advance on the freights, to the prejudice of our woollen trade as above.

Customs taking away so great a part of our merchants stocks, they are thereby deprived of driving that great trade, and purchasing those quantities of woollen goods they would otherwise do; besides, our merchants risk in trade being greater than in *Holland,* and their losses heavier by our customs, their bankruptcies must be more frequent; this sensibly affects our manufacturers, who are generally considerable creditors; for broken merchants may be well compared to nine-pins, one of which seldom falls without beating down many others.

Customs recommend foreign manufactures of fine goods, by making them expensive, which vanity on that account soon renders fashionable, whilst our own are despised, tho' superior in goodness, and are a great discouragement to our manufactures.

Customs are the cause of the smuggling of wool, because the gain being great by running tea, brandy, and *French* goods, on account of the high duties, hath raised the contraband trade to a great height, and the smugglers cannot make their returns in any commodity of so quick and certain a vent, or that gives so good a profit as our wool, for the *French* being less taxed than we, can work cheaper, and their own wool being coarse, *English* and *Irish* wools are so much in demand, that they will give

great

great prices for them, for which reason they receive vast quantities, to the ruin of our manufactures.

Customs on ashes, bay-salt, cotton, copper, coals, drugs, foreign sope, flax, fruit, furs, hemp, iron, leather, linens, oil, paper, rice, tobacco, tallow, threads, tapes, silk, and sugar, being necessaries of life, or materials of manufacture, must necessarily make all our commodities dear, not only to our own people, but to foreigners likewise, (tho' our workmen should have no excises to pay) and such discouragements give opportunity to foreigners to send their manufactures cheaper to foreign markets, and smuggle them in defiance of all laws into our own country, to the ruin of our manufacturers; for all the above customs are as much taxes on our woollen manufacture, as if they were laid on the wool itself, or more; for the workman must raise the money on the woollen goods he makes, to pay the duties of what he uses of the above articles, with the advances, in all the hands they pass through before they come to him. 'Tis by these, that we ourselves drive away our own manufactures, and prevent our ever getting more; and foreigners could not rival the people of so fruitful a country as *Britain*, if we did not furnish them with the means by our high taxes and restraints, that are always prejudicial to trade, tho' designed to amend it, and never effect the thing intended tho' fortified with the most rigorous penal laws, of which Mr. *Locke* gives an instance in his *Considerations*, &c. p. 116, *'Tis death in* Spain *to export money; and yet they who furnish all the world with gold and silver, have least of it among themselves; trade fetches it away from that lazy and indigent people, notwithstanding all their artificial and forced contrivances to keep it there; it follows trade against the rigour of their laws, and their want of foreign commodities makes it openly be carried out at noon-day.*

This seems to be a parallel of the state we are coming to, and which some foreigner may by and by make.

'Tis

'Tis felony in *England* to export wool, and yet they who furnish all the world with wool, have least of the manufacturing of it among themselves; the smuggling trade fetches it away from that excised and custom-loaded people, notwithstanding all their artificial and forced contrivances to keep it there: It follows the smuggling trade against the rigour of their laws, and their want of taking off the taxes on their manufacturers, makes it openly be carried out at noon-day.

By this we see that neither death or banishment can force trade to an unnatural channel, and it may be compared in one respect to water which cannot be compress'd within its natural dimensions, the more force is exerted the sooner is the vessel broke that contained it, and the water let loose never to return. The great *De Wit*, in his *Memoirs, Ratisbon* Edit. p. 77, asserts, *that the navigation, the fishery, the trade, and manufactures, which are the four pillars of the State, should not be weakened or encumbered by any taxes, for 'tis they that give subsistence to the most part of the inhabitants, and which draw in all sorts of strangers, unless the necessity was so great that the country was threatened with an intire destruction, and these fundamentals should be attacked upon the hopes that these taxes would not last long; at least haste should be made as soon as the storm was over, to take them off; again, this distinction should be made that manufactures should not or cannot be taxed at all, because they are not fixed to the country, and we must fetch from foreign countries the stuffs and materials to work them up.*

Eighthly, *they send away our specie.*

Britain having no mines of gold or silver, has no other means of getting or preserving its treasure but by foreign trade. As customs confine our trade to mere importation for our own necessaries or vanities, and at the same time ruin our manufactures; what we want in exports to balance the imports must be paid in specie, making the

balance

balance of trade every year more and more against us ; for
as we raise the prices of our goods so high by taxes that
foreigners won't take them, and yet continue to import
their superfluities, which we now chiefly and in time must
intirely pay for with our gold and silver, as appears by the
bills of entry in every week, we are beginning to do ; and
our high duties encouraging smugglers who have seldom
a settled habitation, or any stock of our manufactures by
them, they carry out vast quantities of specie to purchase
their cargoes : Such large draughts make our mint lie idle,
we see but little new coined gold, and hardly any silver ;
we find our money disappear, and grow scarcer and
scarcer every year ; our trade declines, and our people
starve.

To shew how *excises*, *customs*, and *salt-duties*, increase
the expences of the people and consequently ruin our
trade, the following account may not be improper.

First, the *duties* themselves.

The net produce of the taxes following, was before the
war computed to be one year with another as under :

Excises,	about	£2,800,000
Customs,	about	1,700,000
Salt,	about	150,000
		4,650,000
The charges of raising these duties are about		
ten *per cent.*		465,000
		5,115,000

Secondly, the *advanced price of those goods* the above
duties are laid on.

Woful experience teaches us that every small duty laid
on commodities, raises the prices of them considerably to
the consumer, beyond the gross duty.

By the fees given to officers, the tyrants of traders.

By tradesmens loss of time in attending upon excisemen
or at custom-houses : A trader's time is his bread.

By taking away a quarter part of our traders stock for
duties, and forcing them to take as great profit on ¼ of their
stocks laid out in goods, in order to live, as they wou'd on
the whole if duty-free.

By tradesmens profits on the duty and advances in all

the

Brought over £5,115,000

the hands all taxed goods come through to the consumer; as for example:

Suppose there should be no other tax but that on leather, let us see how many advances that would make on the price of our shoes.

The grazier lays (1) on the beast he fats his advanced price of shoes; he sells to the butcher, who takes (2) his profit on the grazier's advanced price of the beast, and raises (3) on the hide his advanced price of shoes; he sells to the tanner whose journeymen raise (4) their wages on account of their advanced price of shoes; the tanner pays (5) the tax of 2*d. per* pound on leather; takes (6) his profit on the before-mentioned five advances, and raises (7) on the tann'd hide his advanced price of shoes; he sells to the leather-cutter, who takes (8) his profit on the before-mentioned seven advances, and raises (9) on the hide he cuts his advanced price of shoes; he sells to the shoemaker, whose journeymen raise (10) their wages on account of their advanced price of shoes; the shoemaker takes (11) his profit on the before-mentioned ten advances, and raises (12) on the shoes he makes, the advanced price of the shoes he wears; he sells to the consumer with all these *twelve advances* highly magnified beyond the bare duty.

So much for the tax on leather only: But the grazier, butcher, tanner, leather-cutter, and shoemaker use sope, that sope like leather is taxed, and like that leather tax must be raised; but that caused twelve advances on our shoes, true, place therefore twelve advances more on shoes for the sope-tax. These tradesmen use candles, twelve advances more for the tax on them; and the same for every other tax on necessaries.

All which duly considered, might be computed at above *cent. per cent.* on the gross produce of the duties, but though the large duties cause some farther advance on all the goods they are laid on, charged with profit upon profit through every hand they pass; yet as they keep not pace with the small duties, and all calculations appear fairest when moderate, I choose to abate in the advances, and to set them only at fifty *per cent.*   2,557,500
——————

The amount of the advanced price of the goods the above duties are laid on.   7,672,500
——————

Let us see how this 7,672,500*l.* circulates through the people, advances the prices of our goods, consequently ruins our trade.

37

First,

First, This dearness of all necessaries which raises the first cost of goods, must advance the price of all labour.

The *Spectator*, No. 200, computes that the people without property, who work for their daily-bread, do consume ⅔ of our *customs* and *excises*, therefore they pay ⅔ of them and their consequences; as these people live but from hand to month, whatever is laid on them they must therefore shift off or they can't live; and since these various taxes have been projected, they must earn enough when they do work to pay the taxes, the advanced price of taxed goods, and the advanced prices of all other necessaries, *viz.* meat, bread, clothing, or whatever they can use, not only for the consumption of the days they are employed, but for those also that they are not; therefore they are the cause of raising the wages of the working people ⅔ of 7,672,500*l.* the amount of the advanced price of the goods the above duties are laid on, which makes

         5,115,000

Secondly, This dearness of all necessaries forces the master-tradesmen to raise on their customers the taxes and advances on their consumption.

The above *Spectator* allows ⅓ consumption of our *customs* and *excises* to the people with property, but as these may be divided into two classes, *viz.* in trade, and out of trade, and the proportion consumed by each, not being ascertained by any author, I shall compute them at half and half. Therefore the master-tradesmen or people, with property in trade *viz.* merchants, manufacturers, mechanicks, farmers, wholesale dealers, and retailing shop-keepers, must each lay on the goods they sell, the advanced price of the taxed goods they consume; whether food, clothing, or utensils: Their ⅙ consumption of 7,672,500*l.* the amount of the advanced price of the goods the above duties are laid on, makes

         1,278,750
         ————
         6,393,750

Thirdly, Tradesmens paying advanced prices on their goods must have advanced profits, for whether they lay out their stocks of money in goods that bear their natural value only, or goods that bear double that value by taxes, still a living profit must be obtained on the stocks they employ.

For the wages of the manufacturer, the mechanick, the labourer, and the expences of the master-tradesmen, being of necessity raised, the first cost of goods must be so too; and considering the various tradesmens hands that goods pass through from the workman or labourer to the consumer, charged with profit upon profit by each of them, (which in the little *trades* must be very great, otherwise their returns being small they could not live) the advance thereby occasioned may, at a moderate rate, be computed at 50 *per cent.*

         to

Brought over   £6,393,750

to the consumer on the above two articles, which raise the first cost of goods, and makes   3,196,875

9,590,625

People with property out of trade, their ⅙ consumption of 7,672,500*l* the amount of the advanced price of the goods the above duties are laid on, makes   1,278,750

Total advance, £10,869,375

This is part of the amount of the consequences of raising 4,650,000*l.* for the government by our present manner of taxing goods.

Our other taxes are, the *land-tax,* the gross produce, at about 4*s.* in the pound is about   1,960,000

The *stamps, windows, post-office,* &c. their computed gross produce about   500,000

The *poor's tax* is computed, on a midling rate, to equal the *land-tax,* but must be much more when trade is reduced, and the price of provisions high, however to reckon it at no more than the *land-tax* or   1,960,000

General amount of all our taxes, and part of their consequences, before the war.   £15,289,375

Let us see now the amount of our taxes, with regard to our expences : The *British Merchant,* (I. p. 165) computes our people at seven millions, and their expences at 7*l. per* head ; but as necessaries are grown dearer since the year 1713, when he wrote, and the number of people increas'd, I shall compute the people at eight millions, and their expences at 8*l. per* head, which makes our total expence annually   £64,000,000

Of which 64 millions the people pay for the taxes, and their consequences as above.   15,289,375

Which being substracted, their expenses, if untaxed, would be only.   £48,710,625

15,289,375*l.* charged on 48,710,625*l.* is a tax of above 31 *per cent.* on the expences of the people, which must add a prodigious artificial value to our goods, consequently render them less saleable, and ruin our trade.

If it is asked, whether foreigners, for what goods they take of us, do not pay on that consumption a great portion of our taxes ?

The answer is, that it must be admitted they do; but if that was originally intended and expected to continue

the

the same as at the first laying on of our taxes, it will be the strongest argument against them; for as our taxes on necessaries are proved to be so burdensom and extensive by raising the prices of our goods, foreigners take less of them yearly, and when the demand is reduced, the people having less work, find less money to pay, and yet have their taxes proportionably increas'd on them as they lose their trade; for, as the Government abates neither expences or taxes, and if one method of taxing fails another is tried; what foreigners cease to pay, we must; or in other words, the less trade and money, the more taxes; and the more our taxes are, the less and less trade and money we know we must expect. Is not this like adding to a horse's burden, and diminishing his meat? and must we wonder if he sinks under his load? Perhaps figures may explain this still clearer, by stating a similar account thro' 30 years.

Suppose that in the year 1710 all our taxes, and part of their consequences, were as they are now, *viz.* 15,289,375*l.* that foreigners paid then $\frac{1}{7}$ of them, and our own people $\frac{6}{7}$; that foreigners going to cheaper markets since, have ceased taking goods from us yearly in proportion to one *per cent.* only on their former $\frac{1}{7}$ part of our taxes and their consequences, the account every five years will stand thus :

	Foreigners paid of our taxes, &c.	Our own people paid.
Anno 1710	£2,184,196	£13,105,179
1715	2,074,987	13,214,388
1720	1,965,778	13,323,597
1725	1,856,569	13,432,806
1730	1,747,360	13,542,015
1735	1,638,151	13,651,224
1740	1,528,942	13,760,433

By this it plainly appears, in what manner our present taxes drive away our trade, and burden our people, who have by this account 655,254*l.* more to pay in 1740, than they had in 1710, with $\frac{1}{10}$ less trade to pay it with.

                                                                    To

To conclude this head. Two of our greatest authors clearly foresaw at the laying on our numerous excises, customs, &c. that these unhappy consequences must necessarily follow, and their arguments are a full proof of what has been already advanced.

Mr. *Locke*, in his *Considerations*, &c. says, *That for raising three millions on commodities, and bringing so much into the* exchequer, *there must go a great deal more than three millions out of the subjects pockets; for a tax of that nature cannot be levied by officers to watch every little rivulet of trade without a great charge, especially at first trial; but supposing no more charge in raising it than of a* land-tax, *and that there are only three millions to be paid 'tis evident that to do this out of commodities, they must to the consumer be raised ¼ in their price, so that every thing to him that uses it must be a quarter dearer. Let us see now who, at the long-run, must pay this quarter, and where it will light; 'tis plain the merchant and broker neither will nor can, for if he pays a quarter more for commodities than he did, he will sell them at a price proportionably raised; the poor labourer and handicraftsman cannot, for he just lives from hand to mouth already, and all his food, clothing, and utensils, costing a quarter more than they did before, either his wages must rise with the price of things to make him live, or else, not being able to maintain himself and family by his labour, he comes to the parish.*

And afterwards he proves, that in the home-consumption the whole burden falls on land at last.

Dr. *Davenant*, in his *Essays on Trade* (vol. 3, p. 30), asserts, that *as to manufactures, high excises in time of peace are utterly destructive to that principal part of* England's *wealth; for if malt, coals, salt, leather, and other things bear a great price, the wages of servants, workmen, and artificers, will consequently rise, for the income must bear some proportion to the expence; and if such as set the poor to work find wages for labour, or*

41

manufactures

manufactures advance upon them, they must rise in the price of their commodity, or they cannot live; all which would signify little, if nothing but our own dealings among one another were thereby affected, but it has a consequence far more pernicious in relation to our foreign trade, for 'tis the exportation of our own product that must make England rich.

And in page 31. *But the consequence of such duties, in times of peace, will fall most heavily upon our woollen manufactures, of which most have more value from the workmanship than the material; and if the price of this workmanship be enhanced, it will in a short course of time put a necessity upon those we deal with of setting up manufactures of their own, such as they can, or of buying goods of the like kind and use from nations that can afford them cheaper.*

II. *Of monopolies, whereby the many are oppressed for the gain of a few.*

Besides the misfortunes arising from our taxes, we have some monopolies very destructive to a trading nation, and inconsistent with a free one; which encourage idleness, villany, and extravagant demands for wages or goods, whereby the many are deprived of their rights, without having committed any crime to forfeit them, and for the benefit of a few only; a country that suffers them cannot send its goods so cheap to a foreign market as its neighbours, for never yet was a monopolized trade extended to the degree of a free one; therefore any country abounding in monopolies must decline in trade.

To apply this to *Britain*, which hath more monopolies than are generally thought on.

First monopoly. *Britain against its other dominions.*

The trade of exporting woollens, and some other sorts of goods, with the trade to some particular countries given

to

to companies, we monopolize to ourselves; and in our abundant wisdom pay all the charges of Government; our fellow subjects in *Scotland* pay but a trifle to the general support, in *Ireland* and the plantations nothing at all; these trade under the protection of fleets that cost them not a farthing : Our generous wise land-wars, to maintain the balance and liberties of *Europe* at the risk of our own, cost them not a doit; all that we endeavour is to starve them without expence, and ourselves with; for that is the case, we drive one part of our people out of trade by monopolies, and the other by taxes. We bleed ourselves almost to death, and think to recruit our spirits by devouring three millions of starved *Irish* and *Americans*, and by excess of cunning make the ruin general.

Second monopoly. *Companies with exclusive charters,* viz. East-India, South-Sea, *and* Turkey *Companies.*

These companies prevent the increasing the vent of our manufactures abroad, consequently they starve our poor, as will appear by the following reasons.

1. By being all of them confined to *London*, the prices of the woollens they export are enhanced by long land-carriages up to town, with the additional charges of commission, warehouse-rent, porterage, *&c.* much to the prejudice of their sale; and what materials of manufacture they import are dispers'd over many parts of the kingdom by the like expensive conveyance, to the great disadvantage of the nation in general.

2. The *Turkey* Company, whose trade is almost dwindled away, can prevent dispatching their ships for one year, if they please, to raise the price of silk at home for their own advantage, though the nation thereby loses one whole year's vent and consumption of its woollen goods in *Turkey*, which it's said hath happened formerly; and if an iniquitous rise is given to silk here, we cannot manufacture it with such advantage as our neighbours. The reader will be pleased to consider the fine situation our poor em-

ployed in the woollen and silk manufactures must be in at
such a time.

3. It is not the interest of the *East-India* Company to
increase the quantities of the woollens they export, but
rather to contract them (which I suppose was the reason
for obliging them by their charter to export woollens to
a certain value) for at all markets where there are any
demands for goods, the smallness of the quantities naturally enhances the price; and if the company can gain as
much on 5000 cloths as on 10000, is it not their interest
to prefer the lesser quantity on account of the less disbursement and risk? tho' it's plain the nation would lose
the sale of one half of the manufactures capable of being
vended; whereas private traders pushing against one
another, study to increase the vent of their goods by
selling at moderate profits, making the quantities answer
to themselves and their country.

4. The large charges the *East-India* and *South-Sea*
Companies are forced to be at for the salaries of the
directors, governors, supercargoes, &c. besides what may
slip thro' their fingers sometimes, must make these companies neglect all trades that will not yield extraordinary
profits to defray them, which trades private merchants
would be glad of, and turn to good account for themselves
and their country, were they not debarred by exclusive
charters.

5. The *East-India* and *South-Sea* Companies buying
at home by directors, and selling abroad by servants, who
may have an eye to their own or friends interest, and the
foundation of all being the company's money, they cannot
naturally be supposed to be so industrious as those who
trade only on their own stocks; therefore companies can
never extend trade like private dealers, but must decay
where interlopers are admitted, of which our *African*
Company is a strong instance.

6. What confirms the whole is the prohibition of the

East-

East-India Company against their servants carrying out cloth, which would be needless, did they not know that their servants can undersell them, for the Company wants not money to supply all the cloth that can be vended with the usual profit. In the year 1741, a seizure was made in one of the out-ports of a large quantity of cloth designed for *India*, belonging to one of the Company's servants, when at the same time, by the decay of our woollen trade, the poor's rates were at 8*s.* in the pound in some of our clothing towns; from whence this absurdity arose, that whilst our clothiers were starving, the exportation of cloth was a contraband trade.

It is impossible to make any inquiry into our Companies, without taking notice of their past villanies, which, as they have been made sufficiently publick, few can be ignorant of; therefore the bare mention of them is enough, such as the fatal *South-Sea* scheme, that ruined thousands of families. What need to mention former directors receiving salaries from Companies, and, tho' contrary to law, being notwithstanding concerned in the *Ostend* trade to *India*, whereby they were cutting the throats of their benefactors; the selling goods by false samples, and buying them for their private accounts; carrying on private trade contrary to treaty, and bribing officers to wink at them with the Company's money, and charged to account by the genteel name of presents, subjecting thereby the Company's effects to seizures, and their country to perpetual jars. The rapaciousness of governors abroad, who by engrossing goods, nay even the necessaries of life, have oppress'd the people by arbitrary prices, and drove away our trade. Supercargoes, cheating by false invoices. Captains, quitting or losing ships, to defraud insurers and bottomree-lenders: Are not these things written in the books of their chronicles?

But the greatest mischief of all is, that the honesty of the people hath been corrupted, by having pre-

sented

sented to their eyes roguery lightly punished, if not triumphant.

These Companies prevent the increase of our navigation.

By their exclusive charters, debarring us from a free trade to ¾ parts of the known world. The dominions of the *Grand Signior* in *Europe, Asia,* and *Africa,* are confined to the *Turkey* Company. All *South* and part of *North America,* from *Vera Cruz* to *Carthagena,* from *Buenos Ayres* round *Cape Horn* to *California,* that vast extent of coast, is the portion of the *South-Sea* Company. All the coasts of *Africa, Asia,* from the *Cape of Good Hope* to *Japan,* are the lot of the *East-India* Company. And what a small number of ports do they all trade to, and what a trifling navigation do they all maintain? There are a greater number of ship-tonnage employed in the trade to the free port' of *Leghorn* only, than all these three Companies employ in their monopolies to ¾ parts of the world, like the fable of the *Dog in the Manger,* not eating *themselves,* but preventing *those* who would.

Third monopoly. *City and Corporation-Charters.*

Where freemen exclude by charter any of the same trade from settling in their towns, have they not a monopoly against the rest of the inhabitants? Cannot they impose extravagant prices for their goods on their customers, and do they not do it?

Where no journeymen but freemen can work in towns, have they not a monopoly for wages against their masters? Do not both these cases advance the first cost of goods, to the prejudice of their sale abroad, and account for foreigners reckoning our country so dear?

If a journeyman, not being a freeman, gets into work in a city or town-corporate, what an outcry is there not made of a foreigner's being come among them, to eat the bread out of their mouths? How! can a free-born *Briton*

be

be reckoned a foreigner in any part of his own country? What an absurdity is here! yet nevertheless true. Can one man eat the bread out of another's mouth without being more industrious than he? Impossible! it must therefore be idleness and luxury they contend for, not bread.

This is one of the reasons why foreigners flock to our plantations, instead of settling here, and by our decay of trade many of our own people go over to live there yearly; so that many going, and few coming to supply their places, a scarcity of people will hereafter ensue, to the great damage of the mother-country.

Mr. *Stanian* in his excellent *Account of* Switzerland, (p. 140,) observes, *that the tradesmen citizens of* Berne, *are generally esteemed to be proud and lazy; which qualities proceed chiefly from two privileges they enjoy: One is their right of being chosen into the Government by virtue to their burgership, which makes them proud; and the other is, that of hindering any but a citizen from exercising any trade within the cities, which makes them lazy. From whence two inconveniences naturally flow, one that the inhabitants pay very dear for their goods, and the other that the workmen are bad; for where there is no great choice of artificers one must be contented not only with bad work, but to pay such a price for it as they please to impose.*

Mark the dainty effects of monopolising charters, *pride, laziness, dearness of price, and bad work.*

Fourth monopoly. *Laws to prevent the importation of cattle, butter, &c. from* Ireland.

This gives a monopoly to a few breeding counties to impose upon the rest of the people high prices for cattle, &c. to the ruin of our manufactures, forces the labourer to live dear, and of course to raise his wages; is greatly prejudicial also to our navigation, for whatever enhances the expences of a ship, enhances its freight, and gives oppor-

tunity

tunity to foreigners to victual cheaper in *Ireland* than we
can do at home.

But it will be objected to me, that this is done to raise
or keep up the value of our lands?

To which I answer: That there is always a great noise
made about encouraging the home-consumption, by which
is meant making necessaries bear a great price, which can
arise only from an improper knowledge of the true nature
of trade, for this is so far from being beneficial, that
it has just the contrary effect; certainly the less is consumed within, the more will be left to export; the
cheaper things are, the more of them will be exported,
and it is exportation only that makes a nation rich. This
monopoly, with respect to the people, is unjust, and the
benefit of it to the land-holders only imaginary; as for
instance, *A* hath a grazing estate, to raise the value of
which, all cattle from *Ireland* are to be prohibited: *A*
having the sole market, raises the prices of his cattle upon
the rest of the people, *B, C, D*, down to *Z*, twenty-three
in number, and their pockets are to be emptied only to fill
his, a very equitable project indeed! But tho' these people
were as blind as puppies, yet necessity, and the natural
course of things, will force them to retaliate upon him;
for as a monopoly raises the price of cattle, their dearness
raises the price of labour, dear labour makes dear goods;
so that the food, clothing, utensils, labour, every thing *A*
wants, comes dearer to him; an imaginary value is given
to every thing, so that tho' *A* should have more rent for a
time (which yet the decline of foreign trade must bring
down afterwards) the money he receives is of less value,
not going so far, or being able to purchase so much as
when goods bore their natural value only: so that what
he thinks he puts in with one hand, is pulled out by the
other; 'tis all a *deceptio visûs*, setting people together by
the ears to prey upon one another, letting foreigners in
the mean while eat the bread out of their mouths; for a

                                    nation

nation that adds an artificial value to its commodities by monopolies, cannot export them in such quantities to foreign ports, where they are rivalled by those that bear only their natural value; and their home-consumption will likewise sink in price by the nation's having less money brought in by foreign trade; such a two-edged sword are monopolies to lands. Every home-commodity in a free trade will find its natural value; for tho' that fluctuates, as of necessity it must, according to the plentifulness or scarcity of seasons, yet for the home-consumption, every home-commodity must have great advantages over the foreign, as being upon the spot, and free from freight, insurance, commission, and charges, which on the produce of lands, being all bulky commodities, must in the general be about 15 *per cent.* and a greater advantage cannot be given without prejudice; for 15 *per cent.* makes a great difference in the price of necessaries, between the nation selling and the nation buying, and is a great difficulty on the latter, but arising from the natural course of things, cannot be helped; tho' it's a sufficient security to the land-holders, that foreigners can never import more necessaries than are absolutely required, and I presume, in such cases, they have more charity than to starve the people merely for an imaginary profit, which yet would prove their ruin in the end; for it is a fallacy and an absurdity to think to raise or keep up the value of lands by oppressions on the people that cramp their trade; for if trade declines, the common people must either come upon the parish, or fly for business to our neighbours: In the first case, they become a heavy tax upon the rich, and instead of buying the produce of the lands must have it given them: and in the second case, when the consumers are gone, what price will the produce of land bear? A small consumption makes a small demand, and a small demand makes a small price for any commodity; so that when in conversation the wisdom of our laws is magnified to pre-

vent

vent the importation of cattle, &c, from *Ireland*, or corn from any nation, unless it first bears an immoderate price here (as keeping up the value of lands) how would a *Hollander* or *Frenchman* smile when he reflected, that in his country the poor getting provisions from any place where they can be had the cheapest, are thereby enabled to work at prices the *English* can't live on, and by working cheaper work more, that is, run away with their trade, their money, and their working-people, and when these are gone, we may as well give them the land into the bargain, for any value it will be of: Besides, the value of our land is at present but nominal; to prove which,

It won't be suspected to be an under computation to reckon the rental of *England* at	£20,000,000
The exports and freights at	8,000,000
In page 183, the expences of the people of *England* are computed at	64,000,000
The general amount of taxes, and part of their consequences, is	15,289,375
If our exports and freights make $\frac{1}{8}$ of the expences of the people they must be computed to pay $\frac{1}{8}$ of the last article, which makes	1,911,171
Which being deducted, the remainder is what falls on land	13,378,204

Mr. *Locke*, in his *Considerations*, &c., treating of taxes on commodities says, *it is in vain, in a country whose great fund is land, to hope to lay the publick charge of the government on any thing else, there at last it will terminate. The merchant (do what you can) will not bear it, the labourer cannot, and therefore the land-holder must.* If foreign trade will pay but $\frac{1}{8}$, land must pay the remaining $\frac{7}{8}$, which amounting to 13,378,204, and falling on a rental of 20,000,000*l.* is above 13*s.* in the pound tax upon all the lands of *England*; so that land with the present taxes at 20*s. per* acre, or without the present taxes at 7*s. per* acre,

are

are equal, and the land is more reduced by our taxes and monopolies, than by any possible free importation ; and this prohibition, by us called a *remedy*, is only a forwarding our general decay of trade, and consequently our general decay of rents, which actually happened after passing this prohibitory law, as *Roger Coke* informs us in his Treatise, *That the church and state of* England *are in equal danger with the trade*, published in 1671 (p. 64).   His words are, *that the ends designed by the Acts against the importation of* Irish *cattle, of raising the rents of the lands of* England, *are so far from being attained, that the contrary hath ensued.   And here I wish a survey were taken how many thousand farms are thrown up since this Act ; how many thousand farms are abated, some above ¼, others above ⅓, others above ½ ; some I know, which after two years lying waste, are abated one-half.*

Fifth Monopoly.   *Laws to prevent the importation of most sorts of fish by foreigners.*

This gives a monopoly to our few fishermen and fishmongers against our own people, and the consequence is, that fish bears five times the price at *London* that it does at *Amsterdam*, or more, great quantities of fish being thrown away by our dealers to keep up extravagant prices, to the great grievance of our industrious poor.   And it has prevented our gaining the *Scotch* fishery, by banishing from our coasts the *Dutch* fishermen, who would in time have settled with us, our own country being better than *Holland* ; nothing but taxes and monopolies can keep them away ; for who would pay heavy taxes to live in a bad country, when he could live free and untaxed in a good one ? This obstruction hath enabled the *French* to commence fishermen on our coasts, who employ already a great number of vessels ; how dangerous this may in time prove, I leave every honest *Englishman* to judge.   And what a melancholy figure do we make, surrounded by fisheries, yet so bound down by taxes, monopolies, &c. that we can-

not

not undertake them, but sit tamely idle, and see foreigners swarming upon our coasts, and carrying away our riches!

Sixth monopoly. *The Navigation Act.*

Altho' this Act is beneficial to us under our present diseases in trade, but would be needless were they perfectly remedied, yet is it even now not without its inconveniences: For a law that confines, in any degree, our imports or exports to particular ships or men, gives a monopoly to those for whose benefit the restraint is framed, which in this case is either the navigation of the countries whose growths we import, or else our own. And this monopoly is very prejudicial to our manufactures: for 'tis enacting that several necessaries and materials of manufactures shall not be imported by the cheapest navigation, but by a dear one, and of course that they shall pay dear freights, which must raise their price; and if the manufacturer buys his materials dear, he must sell his manufacture in proportion. Besides it is enacted, that these necessaries, &c. shall not be brought from any country but the place of growth, or most convenient usual port of shipping; which gives a monopoly to foreigners, and to our merchants, against our own people; for foreigners will always know our necessity for any sort of goods, and if our sole dependence lies upon any one nation, they will not fail to make us pay for it. Besides, this gives opportunity and security to our merchants for engrossing; because, if they import or buy up large quantities of commodities at the usual times of shipping, they are secured in what extravagant prices they think proper to impose on our people till that time returns, all foreign nations who have laid up stocks being excluded our market, tho' they could afford them ever so cheap. Accordingly, the author of the *Britannia Languens,* informs us, *that the* Danes, *taking the advantage of this Act, raised their prices and customs upon us for pitch, tar, and timber, near double; and the* Leiflanders *the same for hemp and*

flax.

flax. And in page 68 he says, *that the excluding great numbers of foreign ships from our ports, must hinder the vending of great proportions of our beef, pork, corn, beer, clothing, and other necessaries*. And again, *the Dutch allow free commerce to all foreigners and their ships*. Now as this Act makes our navigation dear, it for that reason deprives us of the fishing trade, the great nursery of seamen, which cannot be carried on but by a cheap navigation to vie with the *Dutch* and *French*, in which we make no progress worth speaking of: Therefore, in this case, this Act has deprived us of seamen, instead of increasing them; and the acquisition of foreign seamen, in any degree, being prevented by this Act, gives a monopoly to our own sailors, by which means in war-time, or any spurt of trade, they exact near double the wages that foreign seamen are content with; which oppresses our merchants, brings our goods dear to all markets, giving foreign manufacturers a great advantage against our own, and our sailors lying hid in order to get greater wages by their monopoly in the merchants service, is one, amongst other reasons, of the difficulties we find in manning the King's ships. *Roger Coke*, in his *Discourse on Trade*, published in 1670 (p. 27), says, *that two years after the* Rump *making this law, the building of ships became ¼ penny dearer, and seamen's wages so excessive, that we have wholly lost the trades to* Muscovy *and* Greenland *thereby*.

Seventh monopoly. *Laws to prevent the exporting of woollen manufactures from* Ireland.

After the fear that the value of our lands should be lessened by the improvement of *Ireland*, had produced a destructive prohibition of *Irish* cattle, as has been proved already: The people of that country being necessitated to find out some other employment for their lands, turned their thoughts to the breeding of sheep and raising a growth of wool; no sooner was this effected, but a prohibition ensued on our part to export the manufactures

made

made of that wool. This prohibition on the *Irish* hath ruined the woollen-trade of *Britain*, and raised that of *France*, for unless the *Irish* are suffered to export woollen goods, they must sell their raw wool to the best bidder, and that is *France*; one pack of *Irish* wool works up two packs or more of *French* wool, which is double the damage to *Britain*, that the opening the exports of woollen goods from *Ireland* would be: and *France* by lessening her taxes in times of peace, enabling thereby her people to work cheap, could afford to give large prices for *Irish* wool, and became the chief market for it, having thereby raised for exportation an immense cheap saleable manufacture, which their own wool was not capable of doing: As this increas'd, that of *Britain* declined, and tho' they are now increasing and we declining, yet still this fear, or rather infatuation, about the value of our lands, makes us persist in a prohibition that not only hurts the *Irish*, ruins ourselves, but enriches the *French*: For as the case now stands, either *Ireland* or *France* must have the woollen manufacture; *Britain* by reason of its heavy taxes and monopolies that make labour dear, being out of the question. The *Irish* export clandestinely some camblets to *Lisbon* and undersell the *French*, therefore the *Irish* can recover the woollen-trade out of their hands: And shall we compliment the *French* with a trade that we deny our own subjects? Nay, one third of what *Ireland* gets centers here at last: And shall we refuse such a sum which the *Irish* would snatch from our enemies and present to us?

III. *Of ill-judged Laws.*

The laws which give a bounty on exported corn, fish, and flesh, are very prejudicial to our manufactures.

For wages depending on the high or low price, corn, fish, and flesh bear, the bounties on their exportation serve only to feed foreigners cheaper than our own people to

run

run away with our trade: The pretence of encouraging tillage by a bounty on corn can have no weight now, since our great improvements in husbandry, much less if we erected magazines of corn in every county, against times of scarcity: Foreigners never buy provisions till they want them, and then they must have them whether we give bounties or no. The *British Merchant*, vol. 2. p. 247, says, *if we were to become a province to* France, *we should be obliged to give a bounty on wool as we do on our corn, that* France *might have it cheaper than our people.* And in p. 400, *he computes the value of the manufacture in our woollen-goods in general, at three times the value of the wool.* Now I appeal to all men of sense, whether it be not much more prejudicial in this case, to feed the workman cheaper, than to sell cheaper the material; the manufacture being as three to one in our woollen-trade only, a bounty on exported wool, tho' absurd and destructive, stops there; but bounties on exported corn, fish, and flesh, serve to feed the *French* cheaper than our own people, to run away not only with our woollen, but also our silk, linen, and iron manufactures; every thing we can undertake, all trade, all navigation: Is not this conduct more absurd, more destructive; could we have acted more servilely had we become a province to *France,* or rather is not this the way to make us so? All attempts to confine our wool at home must prove vain until our people are eased of taxes, monopolies, and ill-judged laws, equally with or beyond foreigners; for while the *French* can underwork us so much they can afford to give vast prices for our wool, and what effect any prohibition will have against vast profits, the reader may judge. The penalty of death hinders not bullion from being brought away from *Spain* and *Portugal.* Sir *J. Child* remarks upon this subject of our wool, in his *Tract on Trade* (p. 157), *that they that can give the best price for a commodity shall never fail to have it by one means or other,*

 notwithstanding

notwithstanding the opposition of any laws, or interposition of any power by sea or land; of such force, subtilty, and violence, is the general course of trade. It seems something surprising, that such small countries as the *British Islands* should be ever supposed to grow sufficient quantities of wool, and that of peculiar sorts too, to glut all the world with its manufactures, or that it should be thought a reasonable answer to the question; how comes our woollen-trade to decay? to say, the quantities made are too great for the consumption, did we not frequently meet with it in conversation. These islands are not the 350th part of the computed superficies of the whole earth; to think that one part with only what it can spare from its own consumption, should be able to overstock with a commodity universally necessary 349 other parts, is strange; but the solution of the mystery is this, that we by our taxes and monopolies cannot give the manufacture the vent it formerly had, or is now capable of, for the material is so far from being a drug that foreigners give any price for it, and we are forced to attempt the preventing its exportation by severe penal laws: 'Tis therefore the manufacture, that being raised to an extravagant price by taxes and laws, which make provisions dearer to our own people than to foreigners, we cannot give vent to near home, and are deprived doing of it in the remote trades to $\frac{3}{4}$ parts of the world by our monopolising companies, whereby great quantities of woollen goods being crowded for sale into a few ports, become consequently despis'd and undervalued: whereas, was our trade quite free, we should send but small quantities of woollens to the respective numerous ports we then traded to, which would naturally increase their price, for being the best manufactured, as they grew scarce they would become esteemed and demanded, insomuch that we might be obliged to import wools ourselves to answer the demand: 'Tis our ill management of our trade, and that only, which enables

foreigners

foreigners to deprive us even of our natural advantages, of which our woollen-trade is one.

Our laws relating to our poor are a vast encouragement to idleness.

By obliging parishes to maintain their own poor, we intitle them to a certain maintenance whether they deserve it or no, so that when provisions are cheap they won't work above half the week, but sot or idle away half their time, laying nothing up for sickness or old age, because the parish must provide for them then : This is one of the reasons why the wages of our servants and labourers are so excessive high, because our laws providing for the idle, none will work without being extravagantly paid; whereas had they nothing to depend upon but their industry, or the character of it to recommend them to the charitable in their misfortunes, they would be glad of constant work at moderate prices, to support themselves, be more frugal to make a reserve against times of adversity, and more studious to deserve that relief they might want.

Besides, these laws are vastly unjust, for the poors rates being very high, are a heavy tax on the industrious to maintain the idle, and as every positive tax must raise the prices of labour and goods, the industrious are thereby still more oppress'd, and the sale of our goods hindered abroad, for our labour is grown so excessively dear, that we lose all trades where foreigners come in competition with us.

Idleness is still more encouraged by the defects of our laws against vagabonds, a free people are always brave, and the brave always compassionate, which being a distinguishing character of our people, they are easily imposed on by the least appearance of distress, so that some beggars who can counterfeit misery well, get more money in a day than many diligent labourers, to the great discouragement of the industrious, who see idleness so well rewarded; whereby our roads and streets swarm with

                    beggars,

beggars, all the disturbance they meet with, being now and then turned by a beadle out of his parish into the next, which is only shifting the evil from one door to another, but works no reformation. And if an enquiry could be made into the manner that our poor now spend those alms they receive from their parishes, I believe the greatest part thereof would appear to be squander'd away in drams, and that the bulk of them are maintained only to get drunk.

The suffering people to fine for parish-officers is one of the greatest defects in these laws, for the better sort of housekeepers paying to save themselves the trouble of putting our laws in force, the execution of them is left to the inferior, who have not time to spare from their callings to do it well; who are too often tempted to squander away the money raised for the poor in feasting, or turn it to their profit by furnishing work-houses with necessaries at extravagant prices; whereby the parishioners are high-rated, and the parishes brought into debt.

It is a common saying, that our laws are good, but ill executed: To which I answer, that a law not executed is worse than no law at all, therefore cannot be good; for the weakness of a law appearing by its being evaded, makes the people have a mean opinion of the wisdom of the legislature, and brings a contempt on our laws in general, therefore must be bad. A law that by its rewards or punishments does not enforce obedience to its commands, is in effect no law at all, and what has no effect does no good.

Our laws that create high duties and penalties are extremely cruel.

The humane studiers of the art of government are desired to reflect, how like such laws are to the character the parsons give us of the devil; the high duties make the temptations and the penalties destroy men for falling into them. Besides, the bulk of mankind must live as they

can,

can, not as they will; if some means fail, they must try others; now to make trade criminal, when in the nature of things it is not so, is cutting off the means the people have of living, *i. e.* starving them.

Our laws that fix and settle the proportion between our gold and silver coins, are very prejudicial.

For as the metals themselves vary here in value weekly as the proportion changes abroad, one or other of our coins must be carried away with loss to the nation, as is often the case with our silver coins; as for example: A pound of standard silver is coined into 62*s.* so that one pound and $\frac{1}{62}$ thereof make 63*s.* and exchanges for three guineas. By *Castaing's* paper of *February* 3, 1740, standard silver was 5*s.* 7*d.* $\frac{1}{4}$ *per* ounce, which makes for one pound and $\frac{1}{62}$ 68*s.* 7*d.* $\frac{4}{62}$ being above 5*s.* 7*d.* $\frac{4}{62}$ more than the currency; almost nine *per cent.* loss to us, and gain to foreigners who carry away our silver coin: Can we wonder at the scarcity of it when we make it so profitable an article to be carried away? Mr. *Locke* observes in his *Considerations,* &c. (page 167.) *If your law set it,* i. e. *the proportion of gold to silver at* 15, *when it is at the free market-rate in the neighbouring countries as* 16 *to* 1, *will they not send hither their silver to fetch away your gold at* $\frac{1}{16}$ *loss to you? Or if you will keep its rate to silver as* 15 *to* 1, *when in* Holland, France, *and* Spain, *its market value is but* 14, *Will they not send hither their gold and fetch away your silver at* $\frac{1}{15}$ *loss to you? This is unavoidable if you will make money of both gold and silver at the same time, and set rates upon them by law in respect of one another.*

And here it may not be improper to observe, that our expensive law-suits are destructive to trade, making traders often submit to impositions rather than seek a remedy, that by its expence often proves worse than the disease; or where justice is uncertain to be obtained through the unskilfulness of the courts of law, which

seldom

seldom fully comprehend the intricacy of mercantile disputes and accounts. The counsel confess it in open court, and often perplex a cause by their ignorance, which they should clear up by their knowledge ; and many times the judge in summing up the evidence, will say to the jury that the dispute is a matter of trade which I don't understand and you do; and many causes have by cautious judges been recommended to be left to the reference of some of the jury, ending at a great expence what might have been done without any worth mentioning. It would be just as reasonable for lawyers to consult merchants in points of law, as merchants them in points of trade, cases in which they are equally ignorant : Besides, to what a vast expence are not creditors put in taking out commissions against bankrupts, which of all cases should be attended with the least, and where losses are already but too bad, is it not barbarous to make them worse by a heavy expence? For the rest, the reader is referred to Sir *Josiah Child's Discourse on Trade*, where this subject is finely treated on.

I shall now attempt to shew in some degree, the amount of our monopolies and ill-judged laws.

Though it be above my capacity to point out exactly the advance in the prices of our goods, occasion'd by each separate monopoly or ill-judged law, that ruins our trade, or to fix the utmost degree that our taxes joined to them carry the artificial value to; yet an attempt at some amount, sufficient for our purpose, may be made. As our woollen-trade is our greatest concern, the example shall be drawn from that.

De Wit in his *Memoirs*, (page 57,) says, *that the making a piece of cloth in* Holland *costs* 70 *livres, of which the workmen pay* 20 *for taxes*. That work then untaxed would be only 50 livres, and 20 livres charged on 50, is just 40 *per cent*. tax on labour: The *Dutch* taxes have been considerably raised since *De Wit's* time to support

two

two *French* wars, which may amount to as much again for ought I know; but to make the calculation appear the fairer by being moderate, I shall suppose the increase only at 10 *per cent.* making in all 50 *per cent.* tax on *Dutch* labour.

The war in 1672, created so large a debt, that the province of Holland *only, paid 80 tuns of gold, which is near* 800,000*l.* sterling per annum *interest.* *Vide* The View of the Taxes, &c. during Queen *Anne's* war, reprinted in 1743.

English wool smuggled to foreigners, sells at above 50 *per cent.* advance on the *English* price; they find it answers as well or better than any other foreign wools they import, otherwise they would not covet it so much as they do, or we make so many severe laws in vain, to preventing their having it.

In the *Observations on* British *Wool,* (p. 53,) the author *supposes the value of a pack of* English *combing-wool, at* 6*l.* The weight of a pack of wool being 240 pounds, is just 6*d. per* pound. In p. 23 he says, *The price of* English *and* Irish *combing-wool at* Abbeville *was* (about the year 1738) at 10*d. and* 10½ sterling *the pound*; which last price is 10*l.* 10*s.* a pack, and just 75 *per cent.* advance on the *English* price; which will not be thought extraordinary, when a survey is taken of the penalties the smugglers incur by our laws, if detected, (besides the charges of shipping, &c.) for

By the 9*th and* 10*th of* William III. *wool found carrying towards the sea in* Kent *and* Sussex, *unless entered, and security given, is forfeited, with* 3*s.* per *pound penalty.*

By the 9*th and* 10*th of* William III. *wool laden on any ship for exportation, unless entered, and security given, is forfeited; with* 3*s.* per *pound penalty.*

By the 12*th of* Charles II. *master and mariners knowing thereof, and assisting, to forfeit all their goods and chattels, and suffer three months imprisonment.*

                                                    By

By the 7th and 8th of William III. persons assisting in the exportation, to suffer three months imprisonment, without bail or mainprize.

By ditto, *the inhabitants of a place out of, or through which the wool is carried or exported, are to forfeit 20l. if the goods be under the value of 10l. but if above, treble the value, and treble costs of suit.*

By ditto, *to be recovered by action against the owners and their assistants.*

By the 5th of George II. wool seized on board any vessel without cocket, or warrant, the vessel, her guns, tackle and furniture to be forfeited.

By the 4th of George I. persons not paying the sum recovered in three months, the court may order transportation for seven years, as for felony.

The *Dutch* have intirely beat us out of the trade to *Portugal* in the midling sorts of cloth, between 8 and 11s. *per* yard; and I appeal to our clothiers if the mixt cloths made for exportation, between those prices, are not reduced to a mere trifle in quantity, to what they were formerly; or rather, if hardly any be made. A *Dutch* cloth then may be fairly computed to have 50 *per cent.* advance upon it in the price of its wool and taxes on its labour, and yet comes cheaper to a foreign market than an *English* one; the latter must have a fictitious value of above that sum upon it, and as 1 *per cent.* is sufficient to turn the scale of a trade that is in *æquilibrio*, I shall compute the fictitious value of an *English* cloth but at 51 *per cent.*

In page 183 the amount of our taxes on the expences of our people is above ⎬ 31 *per cent.*

Therefore the monopolies, and ill-judged laws that affect this cloth may be about ⎬ 20 *per cent.*

————

Together 51 *per cent.*

A bale

A bale of *English* cloths now costing	£100
Has included in that price an artificial value arising from taxes, monopolies, and ill-judged laws, with their consequences, as above	51
Which being substracted, the natural value of this bale of cloths, if freed from taxes, &c. would be only	£49

£51 charged by taxes, monopolies, ill-judged laws, with part of their consequences on 49*l.* is above 104 *per cent.* and is so far an artificial value added to our goods, at a low computation.

Besides the prejudice done to trade by this artificial value we give our goods, it likewise weakens and distresses the government, which is forced to raise above double the sums necessary on the people for every piece of service, whereby murmurs and discontents arise, the people grow sooner impoverished and unable to raise the supplies; for above half the value of every thing we want being fictitious, *we are forced to raise the same money to maintain* 112,500 *men, as the* French *do to maintain* 300,000, *as* appears by the *British Merchant*, vol. 1, page 7, and if the same difference of expence holds in the fleets, that single consideration should, I think, open our eyes to make our security greater, by throwing out all fictitious value from our labour and goods, to be able to cope with these our only dangerous enemies on more equal terms.

IV. *Our large national debt.*

This is fraught with many inconveniencies.

First, it has ruined our trade, by serving for a pretence to continue those taxes on commodities, the destructive consequences of which to trade I have before proved.

Secondly, it destroys private credit: The *Annals of Europe* for the year 1739, justly remark, *that these funds first drew out of private hands most of that money which should, and otherwise would have been lent to our merchants*

and

and tradesmen; this made it difficult for such to borrow any money upon personal security, and this difficulty soon made it unsafe to lend money upon such security, which of course destroyed all private credit, and greatly injur'd our trade in general.

Thirdly, it encourages idleness; for several people making from 3 to 4 *per cent.* of their money sleeping, are mere drones in the hive, improving no land, nor extending any trade.

Fourthly, it encourages luxury; idleness is the mother of vice, and a mere stockholder being the idlest person upon earth, has nothing to study but how to kill time by vanities and luxuries, in which this nation has of late days made a great proficiency.

Fifthly, it wastes the body-politick; for a great part of our national debt (computed by some at 20 millions) belonging to foreigners not residing here, but whose interest is remitted abroad, they are in the same state, with respect to the nation as landholders absentees, those cankers to the riches of a country, supposing the interest remitted abroad to foreigners to be only 750,000*l. per annum.*

If our trade prove but a little beneficial, so large a sum going out yearly will certainly keep us poor.

If our trade brings us in neither profit or loss, and the current cash of the nation is 12 millions, the interest paid foreigners in 16 years will run away with it all.

But if the general balance of our trade comes to be against us, the sending abroad yearly money to pay that balance, joined to the above 750,000*l. per annum* interest, must bring destruction upon us like a whirlwind. So fine a situation have our debts brought us to!

Having thus made ourselves tributaries to foreigners, poverty must be our portion, for a foreigner who for fifty years past has received from us for his dividends in our funds 1000*l.* yearly, computing the interest of money at 4 *per cent.* only, has drain'd us of 156,115*l.* having his

64

capital

capital still unsatisfied.   Nay this plunder, tho' monstrous, is much under-rated, for the interest of money at the beginning of this term of years was much greater than 4 *per cent.* but not being able to learn the exact times of the reductions of interest, the reader must content or discontent himself with a modest though shameful account.

That these taxes, monopolies, ill-judged laws and national debts are the true causes of the decline of our foreign trade will appear by demonstrating them to be the causes of the smuggling of our wool to *France*.

It has been proved under this first head that these taxes, &c. cause dear labour, it only now remains to prove that dearness of labour causes the smuggling.

The best bidders for wool are the buyers, and that must be those who work the cheapest.   The value of the labour in the bale of cloth costing 100*l.* mentioned in page 207, according to the *British Merchant,* vol. 2. p. 400. is 75*l.*   In the *Observations on British Wool,* p. 21. the author asserts *French labour to be* ⅓ *cheaper than* English, that is 50*l.* therefore an *Englishman* can afford to give but 25*l.* for the same wool for which a *Frenchman* can afford to give 50*l.* just double the *English* price : which disproportion of price, caused by these taxes, &c. while they continue, will carry away our wool to *France*, in spite of all the penal laws we can make, hanging, that is losing our people to save our wool.

And this wool smuggled to the *French* is by them manufactured and sent to foreign markets, to rival and sink our own manufactures ; so that by the above causes we furnish them with the weapons wherewith they cut our own throats.

To conclude this first head.

The foreign trade of every country must decline, that

Lays unequal taxes and oppressive excises on its people.

                                    Cramps

Cramps its trade, the fountain of riches, by high customs and prohibitions.

Suffers many monopolies.

Oppresses its people by prohibiting the importation of victuals, under the pretence of raising the value of its lands.

Gives bounties to feed foreigners cheaper than its own people.

Encourages idleness by bad laws relating to its poor.

Tempts foreigners to carry away its coin for less than its intrinsic value.

Makes the obtaining justice chargeable.

Suffers a heavy national debt, contracted in time of war, to continue unpaid in time of peace.

These are the causes of the decline of our foreign trade, which having made appear, they naturally lead us to treat of

---

PART II.

THE reasons why the decline of foreign trade *sinks the value of land.*

First, *by sinking the markets at home.*

For the produce of land being rendered excessively dear, by the causes before mentioned, foreigners will not take its superfluities; and labour being by the same causes rendered excessively dear too, we cannot manufacture or improve that produce, nations that can afford cheaper supplying the markets abroad; so that the produce of the lands not being carried off as usual, must become a dead stock on the farmers hands, and cause great quantities to be crowded into the markets, where being encouragement but for few buyers, the price naturally falls: as for in-

stance,

stance, the declining demand for our woollen goods abroad, falls the price of wool at home.

Suppose that in 1699 we exported to *Turkey* 40,000 cloths, the value of raw wool in each being 2*l.* amounts to	£80,000
Suppose that in 1738 we exported to *Turkey* 8,000 cloths, the value of raw wool in each being 1*l.* 10*s.* amounts to	12,000
The difference of the value of wool exported in those two years,	£68,000

Wools of this value lying yearly on hand, must make a glut; the farmers push to sell at market, but in vain, unless at under prices; for the wool-staplers, finding the demand decrease, decrease in number themselves; some break, some leave off trade, some take to other trades; for many sellers with great stocks on hand, and few buyers, naturally fall the markets, and the landlords pressing the tenants for rent, and threatning to seize if payments are not made, the wool must be sold at any rate to raise money; and there being yearly 68,000*l.* less money brought into the nation to be laid out in wool than in former times, the price must be still lower on that account; the lower the produce sells, the less rent the farmer can give for land; the worse the markets, the greater arrears of rent the farmer runs into; and taxes, monopolies, &c. making labour and necessaries grow dearer, and the decay of foreign trade making the wool sell cheaper, must break him in the end, and then the farm is thrown on the landlord's hands, who, unwilling to fall the rent, keeps it in the management of stewards or bailiffs, whose profit and charges seldom make it pay the old rent, but generally ends in mortgaging the land, or selling it; and as these cases grow more frequent, more estates will be at market, and consequently the less prices they will fetch.

Secondly, *by increasing the number of poor to burden the land.*

The poor, wanting employment, must be supported by the land; if foreigners give them work, they give them

bread;

bread; but when trade cannot maintain them, land must. When the poors rates are heavier than the tenant can bear, the landlord must pay them, either by allowance in the rent, or by taking the farm into his own hands; or else by the breaking of his tenant, who has paid that money to the poors rates his landlord should have received.

Suppose in 1699 the labour of the above 40,000 cloths to have given employment to	40,000 people
Suppose in 1738 the labour of the above 8,000 cloths to have given employment to	8,000 people
The difference is	32,000 people
Suppose these 32,000 people to have earned by their labour formerly from foreigners 6l. per annum each, it amounts to	£192,000
But, wanting employment, they come on the parish at 1s. 6d. per week each, which for one year amounts to	124,800
The difference to the landholder in one year is	£316,800

For as the land, by the decay of foreign trade, receives not the first sum, and is by the same cause saddled with the latter, it makes an annual difference of the above two sums to the landholders in this single branch of labour; and is the same in proportion for all other decayed branches of trade.

Thirdly, *by decreasing the stock of people.*

For as employment lessens, the most industrious, rather than starve here, will fly to other countries where trade can maintain them; so the consumption of these being taken away, the demand at market must grow less, and of course rents must fall; yet the farmers charges must grow greater; for the fewer hands, the higher wages are; this must break him in the end, and produce all the consequences following that misfortune, mentioned in the first remark: Besides, 'tis men that trade, and bring in money, therefore the fewer they are, the less money will be brought in; and the less money, the less rent can be given for land.

Fourthly, *by decreasing our riches.*

This is a consequence of the above three remarks; for having fewer goods capable of being exported by reason of their dear price, and our manufactures declining must in time be lost, therefore the importation of foreign goods must naturally increase, and more money go out to pay for them.

I have laid it down as an undoubted truth in page 1, that *nations which have no mines of gold and silver, have no means to get them but by foreign trade, and according to the degree of these metals they possess, the prices of their commodities, and therewith the value of their lands, rise and fall in proportion ;* which I shall now prove.

The *Britannia Languens* says, *if there were but* 500*l. in* England, *an ox could hardly be worth a penny* ; therefore the rent must bear its proportion to the riches. This appears by *Maitland's History of London* ; for he says, that in the year 961 *land sold at* 1*s.* per *acre.* The reason that land then bore so low a price, was, the low price the produce sold at ; for he says that in the year 1000, *an ox sold for* 2*s.* 6*d. a cow for* 2*s. a sheep for* 1*s. and a swine for* 8*d.* This could be only owing to the little foreign trade the nation then had, and consequently to the little quantity of gold and silver trade had then brought in.

But if it should be asked, What is the reason that at present all things are naturally so much advanced in price, to what they were in those days? The answer is, that the quantities of gold and silver brought to *Europe* since the progress made by the *Spaniards* and *Portuguese* in *America,* have made those metals more common and of less value than formerly, so that 20*s.* will hardly purchase what 1*s.* would before the discovery of the *West-Indies.*

The *Spaniards* and *Portuguese* don't throw away their gold and silver for us to pick up; we have no mines of

these

these metals, therefore could not get such quantities as we have but by our trade to *Spain* and *Portugal*, or to those countries that had an over-balance upon them, and were over-balanced by us.

So that the present natural price of land, and its produce, is the proportion of gold and silver that foreign trade hath brought into and left in the nation; If the present quantity was to be doubled by foreign trade, the natural price of land, and its produce, must be so too; for according to the price the farmer can sell his commodity at market, he can pay for the rent of land, and no otherwise. If our foreign trade decays until the present money in the nation be half swept away, the produce of land must sell for half the natural price it does now, and land must let at half the rent it naturally bears now; but if we should go on declining, until we have no more money left in the nation than there was in 961 or 1000, the prices of land, and its produce, can be no more than they bore in those days, taxes, &c. deducted.

Therefore if the landed gentlemen have a mind to raise or sink the value of their lands, the encouraging or discouraging our foreign trade is the only means to do either, so closely united are land and trade; their true interests are the same; they must stand or fall together.

The sum of all is this : That

What foreigners take from others instead of us,
What the poor have given them instead of buying, } Sinks the value
The scarcity of people, of lands.
The scarcity of money,

Taxes, monopolies, ill-judged laws, and national debts, are the causes of the decline of our foreign trade; the decline of foreign trade causes the above four calamities; and they sink the value of lands. The taxes, monopolies, ill-judged laws, and national debts, are the causes of all, therefore they are the causes of the decline of the value of lands.

PART III.

OF *the means to restore the foreign trade of* Britain, *and consequently the value of its lands.*

It is a manifest instance of the great natural advantages in trade this nation enjoys, that it hath not been ruined long ago by the consequences of our own ill-management; as I shall have frequently occasion to mention the former, it will be proper here to shew what they are; and, as the *Dutch* and *French* are our great rivals in trade, to compare our natural advantages with theirs.

First, our situation is the securest of any in *Europe,* not liable to the incursions of our neighbours, as the *Dutch* and *French* are; we have more good harbours than any nation on the Continent, open all the year; whereas the *French* ports for ships of any burden are few, and those far asunder; and the *Dutch* ports few, dangerous, and froze up in the winter. Our country is healthy and pleasant; whereas *Holland* is cold, marshy, and unwholsom.

Secondly, our Government is the most mild and excellent of any in *Europe;* whereas the government in *France* is arbitrary, and in *Holland* very severe.

Thirdly, our plenty of provisions exceeds all *Europe;* no nation having that plenty of corn, flesh-meat, and fish, that we abound in; for *Holland* is deficient in the two first, and buys of us; and *France* cannot well victual ships without *Irish* beef; and its harvests being more precarious than ours, the *French* are forced to make frequent purchases of corn from us. We are surrounded by the greatest fishery in the world, which the *French* and *Dutch* are both deficient in, and seek at great hazard and expence on our coasts.

Fourthly,

Fourthly, our islands abound in excellent wool, coals, lead, tin, leather, butter, and tallow; all of which both *French* and *Dutch* are deficient in, and forced to buy of us.

We have oak for ship-building, which both *Dutch* and *French* want. In our plantations we build vast numbers of ships, which the *French* are deficient in, and forced to buy of us.

As the *Dutch* are forced to purchase every thing, they are out of the question; but the *French* have vast quantities of wines and brandies; they have silk, oil, hemp, and flax; in these, at present, we are deficient; but we have lands in our colonies for a trifle, fit to raise them all cheaper than the *French* can do; besides other commodities which they want, such as rice, tobacco, pitch, tar, and masts.

Fifthly, our sailors are the most expert, and our ships the best-built of any; so that we could have the preference in the carrying trade; no merchant but would ship his goods on an *English* vessel at equal freight preferable to one of any other country; and the former can be insured at the cheapest premium.

To all this may be added, that our people are brave, laborious, and strong; extreme neat workmen, improving to the utmost the inventions of others: And our merchants the most generous and honourable in trade, with whom all nations are fond to deal.

With all these superior natural advantages, we cannot be hurt but by ourselves; 'tis our own covetous folly only that can undo us. Had our trade been suffer'd to take its natural channel, foreigners could not have diverted its course, nor ever can, unless these natural advantages are annihilated; and they may as well attempt to sink our islands in the ocean, as while they remain to deprive us of the benefits resulting from their situation and produce, if we take only a resolution to open our eyes; so that tho'

our

our wounds are deep, and have brought us somewhat low, yet are they not incurable; if they are neglected, the general decay must be compleated in our ruin, but with proper care we may rise to a more flourishing condition than we ever yet knew. And tho' all the means necessary thereto cannot be supposed to fall within the compass of any one man's capacity, yet is it the duty of every man, in time of need, to contribute something, though in part only, and by way of essay. As such, the following proposals are offered.

PROPOSALS.

1. *To lay one tax on the consumers of luxuries, to take off all our other taxes, excises, and customs; and when that is done, to make all our ports free.*

II. *To abolish our monopolies, unite* Ireland, *and put all our fellow subjects on the same footing in trade.*

III. *To withdraw the bounties on exported corn, and erect public magazines in every county.*

IV. *To discourage idleness, by well-regulating our poor.*

V. *To pay off our debts by publick bonds, bearing interest, negotiable by indorsement, and liquidating part of our debts yearly.*

First PROPOSAL.

To lay one tax on the consumers of luxuries, to take off all our other taxes, excises, and customs; and when that is done, to make all our ports free.

The

The plan of a tax on the consumers of luxuries.

It is hereby proposed, that all persons using, wearing, or drinking the following articles of luxury as particularly specified, be obliged to take out a licence yearly, paying each one subsidy for each article of three halfpence in the pound only, on the computed income they should have to support the station of life they voluntarily place them- selves in, by the article of luxury they use, wear or drink, as by the example underneath.

All Persons	Computed Incomes		£.	s.	d.
1. Keeping two coaches and six for their use,	£8000		50	00	0
2. Using dishes or plates of silver at their tables, commonly called services of plate,	4000		25	00	0
3. Keeping a coach and six for their use,	2000		12	10	0
4. Keeping a coach and four for their use,	1000		06	05	0
5. Keeping a coach and pair for their use,	800		05	00	0
Note, *chariots, four-wheel chaises, &c. are included in the term coach.*					
6. Wearing jewels for their dress, besides necklaces, solitaires, rings, or ear-rings,	800		05	00	0
7. Keeping a sedan-chair for their use,	800		05	00	0
8. Wearing gold and silver, men on their coats, and women on their gowns,	500		08	02	6
9. Using silver plate for their sideboards or tables, not having services,	500	Three halfpence in the pound	03	02	6
10. Using china services of dishes and plates at their tables,	500		03	02	6
11. Wearing necklaces or solitaires of jewels for their dress, besides rings or ear-rings,	250		01	11	3
12. Keeping a chair or chaise with one horse for their use,	250		01	11	3
13. Drinking wine in their house, lodging, or service,	100		00	12	6
14. Wearing gold or silver for their dress, except on coats, gowns, hats or shoes,	100		00	12	6
15. Wearing jewels in rings or ear-rings,	100		00	12	6
16. Using no silver plate but spoons,	50		00	06	3
17. Drinking brandy, rum, or any spirits, in house, lodging, or service,	50		00	06	3
18. Drinking tea, coffee, or chocolate, in house, lodging, or service,	25		00	03	1½

All articles of the same degree, or under the article paid for, are included in it.

Husbands to pay for their wives the ¼ of the article they pay for themselves, to intitle them to use the same.

Fathers or mothers (if no father) to pay for each child

under age the ¼ of the article they pay for themselves, to intitle them to use the same.

Bachelors to be double-taxed, if of 21 years of age.

No persons keeping publick-houses to have musick, nine-pins, shuffle-boards, cock-pits, card, dice, draught-playing, or any gaming in their houses, out-houses, sheds, yards, gardens or grounds, for money or liquors, except they pay in the same manner as the persons using article 9.

These people being the great encouragers of idleness, luxury, and gaming, the great corrupters of the common people, servants, labourers, and manufacturers, out of whose industry they idly live, to the ruin of many poor families, and are a great cause of the vast increase of the poors tax.

It is not pretended that every article of luxury necessary to be taxed is here hit on, with the several rates proper to be laid on each : such things are too presumptuous for any private man, and befit only the wisdom of the Legislature: All that is here attempted is only to give a specimen of one tax on the consumers of luxury only, the method of raising it, with some remarks on the benefits arising thereby to the nation.

The Method of raising this Tax.

The receiver-general of every county to keep an open office to receive this tax, during the months of *January* and *February, April* and *May, July* and *August, October* and *November*, in the most convenient town in each county ; and to cause attendance to be given on such days in the week as the commissioners shall judge necessary.

All persons to bring or send their money to the receiver-general's office in their county, with a fair written note, containing the name of the county, town, and parish,

                                        their

their titles or names, places of abode, wives, and number of children under age; with the number, title, and amount of the article they pay for subsidies.

Every receiver-general to deliver to the persons, paying their subsidies, a licence for that year, in which the above descriptions shall be specified.

All persons paying their subsidies in the months of *January* and *February*, to have 3 *per cent.* on their licences allowed them; in the months of *April* and *May*, 2 *per cent.* in the months of *July* and *August*, 1 *per cent.* and no allowance afterwards; whereby it will be the people's interest to raise the subsidies with the greatest expedition.

All persons before the end of the year must register their licences with the church-wardens of the parish they live in; persons living in extra-parochial places, to register their licences in the parish nearest to their dwellings.

Persons having houses of residence in several parishes to register their licences in each parish, lodgers, and servants to register their licences only in one parish.

One or both church-wardens to attend at the vestry every *Wednesday* at ten in the morning, to register the licences of the year, during such a number of hours as the vestry shall judge necessary, whereby needless attendance from their private affairs will be avoided.

Church-wardens not registering licences as before directed, and tendered before witnesses, to pay themselves the penalty incurred by their neglect.

Church-wardens to keep a separate account of all those licences which have not the name of their parish, and are brought to be registered on account of parish-rates, by persons having more than one house of residence.

Church-wardens to deposite in the vestry, on the first day of *January*, the last year's register of licences in their parish, for the inspection of the parishioners, and to form a judgment of the income of the parish.

After

After the first register, as above, is delivered in, the vestry of every parish within fourteen days to compute their rates for the current year, and how much in the pound on the licences computed to be registered in the current year will fully defray them, and order the same to be paid to the church-wardens in the vestry every *Wednesday* by publick notice.

No person to be liable to pay any parish rates whatever, by any other rate.

Church-wardens after the first year not to register any person's licence, until they have received their parish rates, on the penalty of paying themselves the fines of the delinquents.

Persons not registering their licences as aforesaid, before the end of the year, for the highest article of luxury they themselves use, their wives, or children under age, to forfeit on conviction three times the sums not paid for subsidies and parish rates, to be divided as follows; $\frac{2}{3}$ to their parish to ease their rates, and $\frac{1}{3}$ to the receiver-general.

The receiver-general to pay no money but into the exchequer, on the penalty of 500*l.* to the informer.

The receiver-general, or his deputy, not to sue the county for a robbery, unless the persons carrying the money be three in company.

The receiver-general to send up his accounts to the exchequer, of every two months receipts as soon as possible, deducting from the sum received, 100*l.* for his salary for one year, and $\frac{1}{4}$ *per cent.* for his charges.

The commissioners of the land-tax to be the commissioners of this, for each county.

No person after the first year, who does not pay for article nine, capable to be a commissioner.

Vestries may order any in the parishes they suspect of not having registred, or fully paid their last year's subsidies, to be apprehended by their constable or beadle, and

                                         carried

carried before one of the commissioners of the county to be examined, and such persons not producing their last year's licence, and church-warden's receipt or receipts, and not proving that the said licence was for the highest article they used, or else that they had not any article to pay, not having used any; the said persons not clearing themselves to the satisfaction of the commissioner, to be by him committed to the house of correction, to appear at the next commissioners sittings, unless they deposite the penalty in the commissioners hands, or give security to appear at the said sittings.

Persons giving security, or depositing the penalty, to register their names, and the names of their sureties, or the sums deposited, at the receiver-general's office for the county before the first day of the commissioners sittings; otherwise to be proceeded against as guilty.

Keepers of houses of correction to deliver into the receiver-general's office before the first day of the commissioners sittings, a list of the persons names in their custody, committed by the commissioners.

The receiver-general, or his deputy, to make a register of all persons names committed, depositing, or giving security to be laid before the commissioners at their sittings: to attend there as their clerk, and record the proceedings.

Commissioners to sit to hear causes in the town the receiver-general keeps his office in, during the months of *March, June, September*, and *December*.

Every commissioner to take an oath in open court the first day he sits, that he will vote according to justice, without favour or partiality; otherwise to have no vote.

Commissioners every day they meet to choose their president, who shall collect the votes, and order the receiver-general, or his deputy, to record the proceedings.

Three or more commissioners to make a court, and

determine

determine causes by majority of votes, if the votes are equal, the defendant to be dismist.

In all causes determined by a less number than seven commissioners, there may be an appeal to seven or more, whose determination to be final.

No commissioner to have any vote in his own cause.

Persons convicted, not paying the penalty, to be sent to the house of correction, and kept to hard labour during the space of six months.

Persons depositing, or giving security, not appearing, to be proceeded against as guilty, their deposite to be forfeited, and paid as directed, or distress-warrants issued out against them and their securities, to levy the penalty.

Any two or more commissioners to determine differences about distress.

Persons whose causes are delayed by any neglect of the receiver-general, or keeper of a house of correction, to petition the commissioners for satisfaction to be made them by the said persons for what loss they may have sustained thereby, which the commissioners may award at their discretion.

The receiver-general of every county within three months after the end of every year to publish his accounts, shewing the sums received the preceding year from each parish of his county, and how he hath accounted with the exchequer for the same, and to deliver when demanded at the price of 2*s.* and 6*d.* one of the said accounts, to every commissioner and church-warden in the county, on the penalty of 50*l.* for each refusal: And one to be transmitted to the King's remembrancer's office in the exchequer.

The receiver-general not accounting with the exchequer for the whole money he receives, to forfeit on conviction, to every parish whose sums he hath given in short, three times the sum received in that parish and not

                                      accounted

accounted for, to ease their rates.   Church-wardens to prefer their complaints against the receiver-general before the commissioners in open court.

Church-wardens to deposite in the vestry one of the receiver-general's accounts for to examine the register by.

Before making any remarks on the benefits arising by this proposal, the general prejudice against the possibility of carrying into execution, any tax on the consumers of luxuries, arising from the supposed evasion and fraud such a tax is liable to, must be first removed: In order to effect which, I hope to convince the reader by the following considerations, that this tax by its very nature and method of raising, is so far from being liable to the above objection, that it is on the contrary capable of a more exact and equal collection than any tax we have at present.

First, *By its nature:*
For what every person should pay must be publickly known, friends, neighbours, and servants, must see whether we drink wine, tea, brandy, &c. in our houses, lodgings, services, or no; and as to our fineries, 'tis our intent they should be manifest, so that concealments are almost impossible.

Secondly, *By the method of raising.*
Which obliges all parish rates to be raised at the same time and in the same manner, for 'tis very observable that most people are more prying into the proportion they themselves or their neighbours pay for parish rates, than into any taxes raised for the government; therefore, as by this method no persons can pay any parish rates at all, until they have paid their subsidies to the government, nor pay less than their due to the parish without making their neighbours pay more than their dues, and proving besides the disproportion paid to the government, which

must

must appear by a register open to the inspection of all the parish, whereby every one can, and will keep a particular eye upon his neighbours, to see not only that they pay, but that they pay fair; and the vestry can and will keep a general watch on all, in order to ease their rates by the fines of delinquents.

Which allowing no private reward to informers, no scandal can be incurred by any persons moving in the vestry to detect the fraudulent; whereas at present the character of an informer being odious, the taxes grievous, the concern not general, and informations requiring attendance and trouble, there is the greatest remissness possible in bringing to light the frauds in the revenue, no person of credit either out of business, or of a different business, does now inform against any trader for defrauding the customs or excise; people do not care to give themselves the trouble of meddling where they think they have no concern. But by this method of taxing, the trouble of attending the vestry on parish affairs serves for this, and every one is concerned in point of interest and honour to detect frauds; interest with regard to himself, and honour with regard to his neighbours, by taking care that the innocent do not suffer for the guilty.

Which directs the receiver-general's accounts to be published, whereby every vestry will have a check to examine its register by, and detect frauds; for if any person does not pay at all to the government, his name will be wanting both in the receiver-general's account and his parish-register; if he does not pay enough, the deficiency will appear against his name in both; if he pays to the government but not to his parish, his name will appear in the receiver-general's account, but be wanting in his parish register; if a forged licence is register'd, the person's name will be wanting in the receiver-general's account; if the receiver-general conceals any of the money the parish-register detects it, and he incurring a

 penalty

penalty to that parish, it will not fail to proceed against him. The receiver-general's account checks the registers, and they him, both in his receipts and payments. Persons of fortune who will pay the largest sums by having houses of residence in more parishes than one, will have an additional check on them in each parish where their licences must be registered to make them pay fair.

Which giving $\frac{1}{3}$ of the fines of delinquents to the receiver-general, makes it become his interest as well as duty, to make his accounts as publick as possible to detect frauds.

Which laying the *onus probandi* on the suspected person, will make every one endeavour to appear fair, in order to avoid the trouble and expence that suspicion will make him liable to.

Which makes it not worth while for the lower class of people to attempt frauds, a penalty of three times the sums unpaid, is too great a risk to avoid paying a trifle, which likewise subjects them to the jealousy of their comrades, who will look out sharp to prevent others from shifting their burdens to their backs; where money is scarce, the greater care is taken in paying no more than is due : Besides, these people being often quarrelling, will revenge themselves by detecting each other's frauds; so that a few being made examples of at first, will shew the rest the improbability of escaping.

I know of no tax at present having so many checks nor so many persons interested to detect frauds as this, consequently none so capable of an exact and equal collection; for if those who pay fair won't detect the fraudulent, they must pay the deficiency themselves, whereby they punish themselves for their own neglect : Detect or pay is the case.

Remarks on the benefits arising by this proposal.

1. The government by this method of taxing need

                never

never borrow any money, nor have the usual clauses of credit every year, whereby part of the expence of advanced money will be saved, for it being the interest of all to pay as soon as they can, the greatest part would be raised the first four or five months, and by thus giving speedy vigour add weight to our resolutions.

2. All persons tax themselves voluntarily, than which nothing can be easier or more equal, and an easy equal way of raising taxes will always produce the most money and the fewest murmurs.

3. Those that would abate of their taxes may abate of their luxury, as those that won't pay for a licence to keep a coach and six horses, may keep only four, or a pair, and pay for no more, or need not keep any, nor drink wine, tea, brandy, &c. in house, lodging, or service, neither wear on their garments gold or silver, nor wear jewels, nor use plate, and so not pay any thing, consequently no individual can be oppress'd, an advantage that no people in *Europe* have at present.

4. When 'tis propos'd to oblige all persons to take out a licence to drink wine, tea, brandy, &c. in services, as well as houses and lodgings, 'tis done to mend our servants manners, by curing their luxury, or making them pay for it.

5. Few that can afford to live high will retrench; those that cannot afford it should be obliged to it; this will be a sumptuary-law to keep all people in their proper stations, and prevent the ruin of several; it will reform, as well as raise money sufficient.

6. When it is proposed that all bachelors of twenty-one years of age should be double-taxed, it is done as well to proportion all payments as equally as possible to peoples situations in life or circumstances, as also to encourage marriages; for tho' bachelors are double-taxed, yet they will then not pay equal to the married-men, who

pay their wives taxes as well as their own, and may be some childrens, consequently compared with bachelors, are at least double-taxed; for these last may, if they please, always live equal to a married-man with half the expence, and have not that anxious necessary care of saving, to provide for the present as well as future well-being of their families; add to which this political truth, that inhabitants being the riches of a country, and marriage a prevention of debauchery, all wise states have made it their care to discourage celibacy: In particular the *Switzers* will not suffer a bachelor to enjoy any balliage, and the superior rank there being almost all married, makes the inferior be so too; so great is the force of example, and accounts for their country, tho' small, being so very populous. Whereas, one of the reasons why *England* is not so, is the abandoned loose lives our single people lead, whereby they get a disrelish to the married-state, and are enervated by debauchery, which unless remedied must render us a poor despicable depopulated nation; 'tis therefore the highest policy to make marriage fashionable by the example of the rich, since it tends so much to the publick good, and the grandeur of our country.

7. But the greatest benefit of all is, that this proposal hath not those extending, pernicious, trade-destroying consequences of our present taxes; for it will not raise the value of any one commodity, but rather by checking luxury, the bane of virtue and industry, we shall become a rich and flourishing people. In vain would the luxurious tradesman lay the expences of his coach, his wine, his plate, or his laces, on the prices of his goods; his frugal neighbour, who indulged not himself in those vanities, would so much undersell him, that he could have no trade; and while the former declined, the latter would be raising an estate able to afford him all the gaieties of life independent of his business; and tradesmen

                                                    should

should wait for vanities until they have raised estates to support them.

8. The first year or two, perhaps, will not demonstrate the exact produce this tax may give, on account of the receivers not being sufficiently versed in their business; the evasions that wicked people may make to defraud, which seldom can be entirely guarded against until they appear; or the consideration that the first year's tax being the only one that will be felt, will be the shortest; for one subsidy being laid on the first year, nothing can be taken off until that produce appears, which will not be until the second year; but then 6*d.* in the pound may be taken off land, and as many of the other taxes on commodities as that subsidy hath provided for; so that until all our other taxes are supplied by this, in every year following the people will have remitted to them in the taxes on land and necessaries, with their consequences, more than an equivalent for what they paid the foregoing year, whereby they will be enabled yearly to pay more to this tax; so that every year's subsidy must increase.

Whatever appears most burdensom should be the first taken off, such as the duties on sope, candles, salt, coals, or foreign materials of manufacture.

9. This proposal being different from the method of raising taxes now used, and designed to take off our present oppressions, every body will be gainers, the poor manufacturer will not pay any thing, nor should he; but here then will appear a sort of paradox, the rich proportionably are to pay all the taxes, yet each of them to have besides a particular gain by it: To solve this, we may fairly divide the rich into three classes, *viz.* landholders, traders, and stock-holders.

10. *To begin with the landholders:*

Suppose a gentleman to have an estate of 1000*l. per annum*; that the land-tax is 4*s.* in the pound, but he being in an easy-rated county pays but 2*s*. in the pound, which amounts to 100*l*. in lieu of which land-tax, excises, customs, &c. are allowed eight subsidies, presuming they would raise a sum equal to the amount of our present duties :

Suppose then this gentleman to pay by this proposal,

For himself, 8 subsidies for the article 4, is	£50 00 00
For his wife the ¼ of what he pays	12 10 00
For four children ⅛ each of what he pays	25 00 00
	87 10 00
He remains a clear gainer	£12 10 00

By this it appears, that where the land-tax is but half-paid, such a landholder hereby saves 12*l*. 10*s*.

But those gentlemen who have borne the unequal burden of the land-tax for many years, paying from 2*s*. even up to 4*s*. in the pound, will be hereby greatly relieved, enabled to live better, and so add to the amount of this proposal.

The following great advantages arise likewise to the land-holders.

The difference in the price of necessaries, when the taxes on them are taken off, must be much superior to the above subsidies; for the present taxes, and their consequences, affect the landholders above 18*s*. in the pound, *vide* p. 194.

The poors rates, so heavy a burden on the land at present, will be hereby reduced to a mere trifle.

The rents of lands will be better paid when the farmers are eased of their heavy taxes.

The farmers will be likwise more able to improve the lands they rent.

Easy equal taxes increase trade, and trade increases rents.

Well-paid increased rents will augment the capitals of those that have occasion to sell their lands.

                                              Land

Land untaxed must yield a considerable better price than when heavily taxed, as at present.

All which duly considered it may be asserted, that upon this proposal's being pass'd into a law, every landholder will actually find the value of his estate at least doubled.

As the benefits arising to our landholders have not been so fully calculated as they are capable of, the calculation above being only comparative to the land-tax, I shall with pleasure set them forth, by way of answer to the following objection, and to illustrate what has been already advanced on this head.

Some have thought it a fatal objection against this proposal's ever being practicable, that our nobility will think it contrary to their interest and never come into it.

This I own wou'd carry great weight, if it was possible for the publick good not to be proportionably the undoubted good of every individual, or if our nobility were not considerable landholders: Whereas many of them are the most considerable, and as all our misfortunes center on our lands, so must our benefits; the greater the property, the greater of either; therefore as our nobility are the greatest landholders, so by this proposal they should and will receive the greatest benefit; of which I hope to convince them, if ever this humble essay shou'd have the honour of their perusal, by laying before them the state they are now in, and the state they wou'd be in by this proposal, the difference of which they will be pleased to consider.

Suppose a nobleman to have a nominal estate of 8000*l. per annum*, out of which by the various reductions in these wretched times he hardly receives in cash 6000*l.* and I appeal to the whole body of nobility if upon a medium they receive so much.

The expences of a man of quality generally are and

should

shou'd be in the richest and best commodities that can be had, consequently the dearest; and as a common *English* cloth is proved in p. 206 to have a fictitious value superior to a *Dutch* cloth loaded with 50 *per cent.* the latter having beat out the former at the *Portugal* market, and only 1 *per cent.* allowed to turn the scale; I may safely affirm, that the expences of a nobleman have a fictitious value included in them of 51 *per cent.* if not more; there being great difference between a nobleman's buying and a merchant's: However 51 *per cent.* fictitious value included in a nobleman's expences of 6000*l.* amounts to 3060*l.* which being deducted leaves only 2940*l.* and is the only real, true, intrinsic value, that a nobleman receives from a nominal estate of 8000*l. per annum* in the state he is now.

What else can be the reason that our nobility can have no taste but they are ruined, if a nobleman has a *goût* either for building, equipage, or entertainments, we presently hear of mortgages and sales of estates, how few places or pensions come in aid to prevent them? Whilst a foreign nobleman perhaps does all with half the nominal estate, and yet keeps within bounds. Is it not hereby plain that tho' the rental of the *English* nobleman's estate is great, yet the taxes and their consequences are so monstrous, that the intrinsic value is by them reduced to a small pittance?

Whereas by this proposal a nobleman with a nominal estate of 8000*l. per annum* pays

For himself 8 subsidies for the first article, is	£400
For his lady ¼ of what he pays	100
For four children, each ¼ of what he pays	200
	£700

700*l.* being deducted from 8000*l.* leaves 7300*l.* of a real, true, intrinsic value, which will purchase as much, go as far, consequently be equal to 14,897*l.* of our present

fictitious

fictitious value, and if his ordinary expences in the state he is now are but 2940*l.* of real value, he would have by this proposal 4360*l.* of the same real value remaining, for building, equipage, entertainments, &c. equal to 8897*l.* of our present fictitious value.

So that by the state he is now in, he is reduced either to his ordinary expences, or to ruin his estate, if he lanches out in any taste; whereas by the state he wou'd be in by this proposal, he might live equal to what he did before, and yet have remaining for improvements a sum superior in real value to the present nominal value of his whole estate.

And whenever our improving trade shall advance the natural value of our commodities, so that the expences of the nobility will be enhanced, they may rest assured that the natural value of their lands will keep pace with them, and their incomes constantly rise in proportion to bear them. The same in proportion to the value of their estates will be the case of all our landholders.

11. *With respect to the trader.*

The difference in the prices of necessaries, when the taxes on them are taken off, must be much superior to the subsidies he should pay for luxuries; I say should, for he need pay no more than he pleases, or can afford, as appears by the third remark; so he cannot be oppress'd.

This puts him in a better situation than any of our rivals in commerce, who all pay taxes on necessaries, always attended with some oppressions.

When those taxes that are burdens upon our trade are removed, then may we send our manufactures to foreign markets as cheap or cheaper than our neighbours, whereby lost markets may be recovered, and new ones found out.

The demand for our goods must hereby increase at those markets where at present they have some vent.

An increasing demand makes profitable sales and quick returns.

Quick returns are the soul of commerce, and enable the merchant to give constant employment to all our working hands.

Commissions for buying will be always sent by foreigners to the cheapest markets, and the cheaper they are the more commissions they may expect.

A flourishing commerce will enable the trader to live more comfortably for the present, and at the same time lay up a future provision for himself and family.

Our rival neighbours, some of whom are our natural enemies, and the best but self-interested friends, will find the scene shifted upon them from their rising and our sinking, I mean in trade, the greatest blessing that can happen to a people; for, as a late patriot observed, *it brings food and nourishment to a nation, preserves and increases its stock, and distributes a convenient portion of maintenance to every part of it.*

12. *In regard to the stockholder.*

His gain will appear by considering that this proposal being calculated to raise as large or larger fund, in a more easy and equal manner than all our other taxes.

He will be more certain than he is now, in any time of war, of his interest being duly paid.

He will be better secured in the value or reimbursement of his capital.

He will rest assured that the government will never be driven to lay a tax on the funds, which would not only lessen his income, but considerably diminish the price of his capital.

By this proposal he will gain security; no small consideration.

Even the difference in the price of necessaries, when the taxes on them are taken off, must be more advantage than any mere stockholder will or need pay for luxuries.

18. As

13. As by this proposal the rich will pay all with advantage even to themselves, so the poor will receive great benefit.

They will be able to work as cheap as foreigners at least, consequently monopolize the manufacturing of their own wool.

They will have lesser wages, but of more value, 4*d. per* day untaxed being more than 6*d.* charged with 8*d.* for taxes.

They will have more constant employment by working cheaper, consequently a better maintenance.

They will have foreigners settling here continually to teach them new branches of trade.

They will not be drove by necessity to fly their country, to starve, beg, or steal.

They will find better support in their misfortunes, when their superiors are in a more flourishing way.

They will have more opportunities of rising to be masters, or seeing their children become such.

14. If it should be asked, how, by this proposal, a larger fund than our present taxes can be more easily raised?

The answers are, that no extension of subsidies for any sum of money equal to what the Government now annually raises, can be so grievous to the subjects, as the consequential extending burden of our present taxes on commodities only, exclusive of the land-tax.

Therefore, if the subjects can save by raising larger sums for the service of the Government, there can be no doubt of their doing it.

It is remarked, with great humour as well as truth, *that a prince who draws his revenues from the vanities of his subjects, will be richer than another who hath mines of gold, because vanity is an inexhaustible mine;* to which I beg leave to add, that it is work'd much the easiest, and is exactly the affair now offered to the consideration of the publick.

Tho'

Tho' all feel, yet as those who are oppress'd more immediately by our present taxes, *viz.* our people in trade, will be hereby reviv'd; an increasing trade will bring in such a flow of wealth, as will make our lands still more valuable, and our people rich; riches will make them gay, and gaiety will make them pay larger, if equal easy taxes; therefore this proposal must prove a growing fund, and produce every year more and more to support the King and nation in so great a figure, and raise us to such a formidable height of power that we may be the envy or dread of all our rivals, and an overmatch for any one nation in *Europe.*

15. Besides, this tax will lessen the expences of the government by untaxing commodities, which of course makes them cheap, therefore every thing will be to be purchased with less money, all provisions, ammunition, naval stores, &c. come cheaper to the Government; sailors, soldiers, placemen and pensioners, be enabled to live upon less wages yet as well as they now do; so that this method making the money raised go the further, the fewer subsidies will suffice, two or three millions may do as much as four or six millions now; therefore the Government can never be straitned, or the people oppressed.

16. This tax will likewise increase the civil list; for as goods grow cheap, money goes the further; therefore the present civil list of 800,000*l. per annum*, when of real true intrinsic value, may go as far and be as valuable as one of 1,632,658*l.* of the present fictitious value: And the value of the pay of officers and of the salaries of places increase in the same proportion.

17. This tax will serve for a political barometer to know the strength of the people in any time of war, for as long as the last subsidy adds to the produce of the former, so long may they be increased; as for instance, suppose eight subsidies to have produced ten millions, which on an average is 1,250,000*l.* each, tho' on laying on

an

an 11th it should produce but half the last sum, yet a 12th subsidy may without any danger be added, and so on until the last produces but a trifle; and that with advantage to the nation: Because many misfortunes happening in time of war, people should therefore be more frugal in their expences to enable them to bear those the better; to effect which a tax of this sort naturally tends, and they may be taxed in this manner as long as they can or will bear, even for their good: Quite contrary to the method of laying taxes on the necessaries of life, or on trade, practised in all countries, which, in proportion as they are increas'd, constantly bring on decay of trade, poverty and misery, not recoverable in many years, if ever.

18. But it may be objected, that this tax will cause a reduction of the officers of the revenue, diminish the power of a minister, be contrary to his interest, and not being to be carried into execution without his countenance, makes it become impracticable.

Answ. What is the interest of a minister, but the favour of his prince and the love of the people to continue himself in power? neither of these singly will always do, but both united are infallible.

The increase of the civil list, the increase of the revenue, the freedom from oppressive taxes, the increase of riches, are consequences of this tax proved in the above remarks. By all these the favour of the prince and the love of the people are secured to a minister. What more glorious to a prince than a splendid court, powerful revenue, free and rich subjects? What more delightful to a people than the splendour and power of their King, their freedom and their riches. It becomes then the interest of both prince and people to continue that minister in power, who procures such mutual happiness. And what better foundation for the continuance of power can be desired, than that which has the general interest for its support?

                                    How

How does the increase of the officers of the revenue give power to a minister? by influencing elections: But these officers disgust many, who know that they are locusts, consequently they cause and give weight to an opposition. Let the minister gain the love of the people, he influences them himself, with more effect than this partial influence of officers, which then becomes useless, and he likewise destroys the foundation of an opposition.

Besides, an increasing revenue furnishes means for useful publick employments, whereby more officers may be better provided for than at present; and with this difference, that a small number of officers detrimentally employed raise clamours, whereas large numbers beneficially employed will gain the love of the people. Now he must be but a sorry politician who cannot gain a greater interest by the prosperity than by the ruin of his country.

If then we have reasoned rightly, and the favour of the prince with the love of the people, are the foundations of a minister's continuance in power, and are the necessary consequences of the carrying of this tax into execution; it follows, that the doing of it is the true interest of a wise minister, and therefore practicable.

19. *Of the benefits arising by a free-port trade.*

By which I mean, that all sorts of merchandize be imported and exported at all times without paying any customs or fees.

1. *It will increase trade.*

By increasing the number of merchants; for small stocks serve where there are no customs to pay, and there are ten people of small fortunes in trade to one of a great one; the more there are, the less liable are they to combine together to impose on the people extravagant prices for their goods, to support themselves in luxuries.

By increasing the capitals of our merchants; for if they pay $\frac{1}{4}$ or $\frac{1}{3}$ of their capitals for customs, they can

trade

trade but for the ½ or ¼ left; but when they have no customs to pay, they can carry on a greater trade with the same stock, sell their imports cheaper, have more money to buy up the superfluous produce of our lands, and give better encouragement to our manufacturers.

By making our country an universal storehouse; for when our merchants have no customs to advance, they will be importing continually upon speculation for better markets all sorts of goods that were to be sold cheap in all parts of the world, whereby such sortible cargoes as were vendible to advantage, being always ready to seize the favourable opportunity, would be as continually exporting, giving employment to a vast number of watermen, carmen, porters, coopers, packers, &c., besides supplying hereby our own manufacturers with all foreign necessaries and materials in the cheapest manner. To which may be added, that where the best assortments of goods are to be had, there will be the greatest trade, one sort helping off another, consequently vast quantities of our own commodities will be required to assort our imports of foreign goods, and be exported with them. A free port causes the best assortments of goods, consequently a free port causes a great exportation of home-commodities.

By increasing our navigation; this is a consequence of the last observation; for by the vast quantities of goods continually going out and coming in, we must have an immense number of ships constantly employed, and seldom send them out in ballast; and whenever our sailors are eased of their taxes, they will be able to navigate as cheap, or cheaper than any; and being indisputably the most able, and expert in *Europe*, must have a great share in the *Greenland* and herring fishing-trades, and in the navigation of the *Baltick*, with other nations whose navigations are vastly increased by those trades; all which, joined to our *Mediterranean* trade, would make us the chief carriers of *Europe*.

By increasing the vent of our goods abroad; for all foreign necessaries and materials coming a great deal cheaper to our people, who having no taxes they need pay at home (if our monopolies were but once abolished) our labour would be so cheap, that we could send all our goods to foreign markets cheaper than any people, by reason of our superior natural advantages. It is a just observation of Sir *William Temple*, in his account of *Holland, there is no sort of goods but what will find a market at one price or another, and they will be masters of it that can afford it cheapest.* It should therefore be our chief study to make all our goods bear only their natural value, which nothing contributes more to than a free-port trade: Add to which, that our merchants being enabled to barter away our goods for whatever commodities they could find in any country where money was scarce, must increase their sale prodigiously.

By putting all traders on the same fair footing; for where no customs are to be paid, smuggling must cease.

By preventing the smuggling of our wool, without registries, dragoons, or cruizers; for as our taxes, monopolies, &c. have been already proved to be the causes of smuggling, so is the removal of them the certain remedy for this evil; as thus,

English labour in a bale of cloth of 100*l.* price, is computed in page 209 to be 75*l.* having, in page 207, an artificial value arising from taxes, &c. of 51 *per cent.* which being deducted, the natural value of that labour is but 36*l.* 15*s.* *French* labour for the same, in page 209, is estimated at 50*l.* 'Tis plain the *Englishman* can give 63*l.* 5*s.* for the same wool for which a *Frenchman* can only give 50*l.* which is 26½ *per cent.* under the *English* price; consequently our people being able to afford the best prices, smuggling of wool must cease, and the whole manufacture of it be secured to ourselves.

By gaining us the herring-fishery; for the *Dutch*
  having

having liberty to sell their fish on the coasts of *England*, would snap at such a market, and some of them settle with us of necessity, by trading on the best footing; for those who would not settle, must make two expensive hazardous voyages, one back to *Holland* to cure and pack the fish, and the other from thence to the coasts of *Britain* to sell them, especially the west-coasts, which those settled here would be free from, and the *Dutch*, by living among our people, must instruct them in the trade.

By securing to us all growths, fisheries, and manufactures the nation is capable of; for what *French* or *Dutch* growers, fishers, or manufacturers could pay taxes at home, the charges of package, putting on board, freight, insurance, postage of letters, relanding, housing, warehouse-rent, and commission on their goods to sell to our people, being growers, fishers, or manufacturers themselves, untaxed, free from the above charges, and blessed with superior natural advantages? 'tis ridiculous to suppose it; unless that in the beginning of a free-port trade, the demand for our goods should be so great, that we should sell what should be our own supply, and content ourselves with inferior sorts of goods from abroad, as the *Dutch* do.

The farther benefit that trade receives by a free port, the reader will find in the answers to the objections raised by some authors against it, which will be considered hereafter.

2. *It will employ our poor.*

This is a consequence of the last remark; for necessaries and materials being by a free-port trade, and the reduction of taxes rendered cheap, labour must be so too; and by the same causes the vent of our goods be enlarged, the poor find constant employment on the wool we shall keep at home, on the hemp and flax we shall raise, in all manufactures we are capable of, in the herring and *Greenland* fisheries, and in the increase of our navigation by the great demand for sailors, so that none can want employ-

ment

ment that won't be idle. *Holland* is an example of this, whose customs are so low that their trade-is almost free, and there is no country in the world where the poor are so well employed, or in sickness better provided for.

One flourishing manufacture promotes all others; for the better employment the people have, the better they live, and the more they spend for a comfortable subsistence: A manufacturer who earns by his industry enough to purchase warm clothing and hearty food, is a greater encourager of the industry of others than a beggar covered with rags and starving with hunger; therefore it need not seem a wonder, that when our woollen trade flourished, all others prospered, and the poors rates were low; and that the reverse happens by the decline of it. If *English* wool was intirely kept at home, the manufacturing of it must employ at least one million of people, who may be supposed to maintain at least another million of helpless infants, women whose labour *is* in part diverted by the care of their families, sick and aged people; and the same in proportion for *Scotland* and *Ireland*.

The silk manufacture, at least for our consumption, must, by taking off our taxes and making our trade quite free, be intirely secured to us: And supposing the quantities of *India, French*, and foreign wrought silks smuggled in upon us by the temptation of high duties, and consumed here, to amount only to the value of 200,000*l. per annum*, the labour whereof to be $\frac{3}{4}$ of the value, and the medium earned *per* head to be 6*l.* the supplying this consumption by our own people would employ about 25,000 of them, and they maintain an equal number, as was observed of the woollen trade above.

The linen manufacture is of such vast consequence, that the *Dublin* Society, in the first volume of their *Weekly Observations*, No. 7, reckon *the consumption of linen in* England, *at the lowest computation, allowing only* 10*s.* per *head, to amount to four millions, the greatest part of which,*

they

they say, *is imported every year :* But as they take no notice of the vast quantities of linens we import for our plantations, which may over-balance what is made in *England,* yet I shall only compute, that we pay foreigners for this article three millions, the labour at $\frac{1}{4}$ of the value, and the medium earned *per* head 6*l.* which a reduction of taxes, and a free-port gaining, will thereby employ about 370,000 of our people, and they maintain an equal number, as was observed of the woollen trade above.

It is impossible to estimate the numbers of people that a free-port trade would give additional employment to, such as watermen, carmen, porters, coopers, packers, &c. or the additional numbers of sailors employed in the carrying-trade, the amount of all which must be prodigious.

Sir *Walter Raleigh* in his *Observations on Trade,* says, that thirty several trades are set on work by the fishing ships; and as this herring-fishery is on our own coasts, we can carry on this trade that promotes thirty others, cheaper than the *Dutch,* and of course beat them out of it; they must make long voyages out and home for the fishery, and receive their supplies in the same dangerous and expensive manner; whereas we are at home, and can land our fish and receive supplies without almost any charge: We can victual in *Ireland,* and some parts of *Britain,* at half the charge they can do in *Holland :* In blowing weather the *Dutch* must lie still, they cannot take in their casks and stores in a rolling sea; whereas we can run into port, and the unloading, repacking, and dispatching our fish go on in all weathers. All fishing-vessels push to get first to market; so our people, from some parts of our dominions, can be at the markets of *Spain, Portugal,* or *Italy,* almost as soon as the *Dutch* can arrive in *Holland,* whereby we may always forestal them. The *Dutch* have heavy taxes on necessaries, we need not have any. All which duly considered, cannot fail securing us this trade, with the navigation belonging to it. The

Scotch

Scotch Islanders are expert fishermen, necessity forces them to it for their own supply; but their poverty prevents their giving the trade that extent abroad it is capable of, and the present clogs upon our trade cut off the people of *England* from any considerable correspondence with them, so that they are in a manner lost to each other; whereas was our trade free, the *Dutch* by settling with us and trading backwards and forwards, would create an intercourse between the *English* and the *Islanders*, whereby the stocks of the former would aid the industry of the latter, make them outdo all foreigners, and besides expert fishermen render them good sailors, and raise the greatest nursery for seamen in the world.

The importance of this fishery will appear from the following authors. In the *Memoirs* of *De Wit* (p. 24) there is a quotation from *Emanuel de Meteren*, who says, *that in the year* 1610 *there sailed from* Holland *in three days time* 900 *ships and* 1500 *busses for the herring-fishery* : And he quotes *Gerard Malines* and Sir *Walter Raleigh*, who agree *that the* Dutch *sell yearly* 300,000 *tons of herrings and salted fish, and that there went out yearly above* 12000 *men for the north and whale-fisheries* : And *De Wit*, in p. 25, says, *that trade and navigation being increased above* $\frac{1}{4}$ *since that time, it is easy to conceive that the sea produces yearly above* 800,000 *tons of salted fish to the* Dutch. And the author of *Britannia Languens*, informs us, *that according to modern calculations the mere fishing-trade for herring and cod, on the coasts of* England *and* Scotland, *employs above* 8000 Dutch *ships or vessels.* Besides, this fishery will support our manufactures, as appears from *De Wit*, whose words are, *tho' it appears from history that many manufactures were made in the towns of* Holland, *at the time that the trade and navigation of* Europe *were carried on by the Hanse-Towns and the East-Country people, and before the fishing and carrying-trades were established in the country; so that it might be said,*

that

that the navigation has been produced by the manufactures; it is nevertheless very certain, that the fishery and navigation give all the motion to manufactures, for 'tis what brings in all raw materials to be work'd up in the country, and to sell afterwards the stuffs when they are made, by the seas and rivers in all foreign countries.

We see then by these reasons that the Dutch *can make, with the greatest advantage to themselves, sea-salt, manufactures of silk, linen, wool, hemp for cordage, cables, and nets; besides the ship-building trade.*

The reasons whereof are plain:

First, a fishery furnishes a cargo to purchase raw materials with instead of money, and prevents a nation's being impoverished, and its manufactures languishing through a scarcity of money.

Secondly, these raw materials are thereby rendered cheaper; for the better profit the fish give, the cheaper the returns can and will be afforded, the general profit of the voyage being computed on the first disburse and incidental charges.

Thirdly, it affords a cheap sustenance to the poor, whereby wages and labour are kept low, to the encouragement of all trade.

Fourthly, it creates a multitude of seamen, whereby their wages are kept low, and of course freights, consequently a great navigation is maintained, which brings in raw materials cheap, and carries out our manufactures the same, by which means only their vent can be extended abroad; therefore the fishery and the navigation are the causes of manufactures.

Fifthly, it is the sailor who is the life of trade; without him the skill of the merchant, the beauty and cheapness of the manufacture, and the quantity of shipping are useless and vain.   Glover's *Speech.*

It has been already proved that we can outdo the *Dutch*

in

in the herring-fishery, consequently we can employ therein more of our poor than they; let us see how many people the fishery employs in *Holland*. *De Wit* in his *Memoirs,* computes the fishing-trade to give employment to 450,000 people in the province of *Holland* only. The author of *Britannia Languens* divides the employment of the above people thus: 200,000 *seamen and fishers, and* 250,000 *people more employed at home about this particular navigation, making of fishing-nets, and the curing, ordering, and preparing of the fish.* *Zealand* is not included in this account, tho' it be a great province for fishers; nor the *Hamburgers, Lubeckers,* and *Bremers*; nor the *French* fishing-vessels that swarm round our coasts: So that upon the whole, it may be supposed that double the above number of people are employed in this trade by those several nations that fish upon our coasts, besides the *Greenland* fishery. So that was our trade eased according to these proposals, this branch only would maintain most of our present poor; and one trade belonging to the fishery is so easy, *viz.* the making nets, that the most helpless of our people may work at it, such as women, children, cripples, and aged people; and the employment is so great, that Sir *Walter Raleigh,* in his *Observations on Trade,* affirms *that* 300 *persons are not able to make one fleet of nets in four months time for one buss.*

Thirdly, it will increase the stock of people.

By inviting merchants to settle where business can be transacted with so little trouble.

By furnishing employment to our own poor they will be kept from deserting their country, preserved from want and diseases, consequently from death; by their industry they will procure themselves a comfortable maintenance, and thereby be enabled to marry and raise families.

By securing the manufacture of our own wool we shall reduce the woollen-trade of our neighbours, which joined to the extensive vent our natural advantages enable us to

give

give this manufacture, will oblige us either to enlarge our growth of wool, or import foreign, whereby we should have occasion for more hands than we ever yet employed, consequently gain them; for it's a maxim in trade, *that such as your employment is for people, so many will your people be.*

By gaining the silk, linen, and other manufactures we must gain some of the manufacturers, for what *Dutchman* or *Frenchman* would pay taxes at home, and the heavy charges mentioned in page 240, on the goods he sent to *Britain*, when he could remove thither, live untaxed in that plentiful country under an easy government, and add all these savings to his profits? It would not be in the power of any laws to keep him at home, he would remove, nay some must; for as our manufactures increase the foreign will of course decrease, the poor want work, and they must either starve or fly, and where would the fugitives find an asylum so inviting as that of *Britain?* Besides, when we became thorowly versed in the linen and silk trades, our own supply would not confine us, but we should rival other nations at foreign markets,

By gaining the herring-fishery we shall gain some of the *Dutch* fishers, who will find it more convenient and cheap to remain here than to go home; add to which what is observed in page 195, that our own country being better than *Holland,* nothing but our cramping of trade could keep multitudes of its people from us.

By drawing in foreign sailors, which is a consequence of the increase of trade and navigation, for our number of sailors is even now too scanty for our confined trade, as appears by the difficulty of manning our ships of war, and the high wages our merchants give, which latter temptation is defeated by the high price of all necessaries; but were these to bear only their natural price, our pay in our ships of war would be of so great value that we should have the picking of all *Europe,* have no need of that

 arbitrary

arbitrary expedient of pressing, for a free-port furnishing employment for more sailors than we now have, vast numbers would flock here to enjoy our plenty, riches, and easy government.

Fourthly, it will increase our riches.

By giving a greater vent to our manufactures by their cheapness, foreigners will be the more indebted to us, which must be paid in money or in goods; if in the latter, and they are laid by for better markets, must resolve at last into more money: By gaining manufacturers from abroad our wants will grow less, consequently less money need go out to supply them; *a penny saved is so much won. Gee* in his *Discourse on Trade*, computes, *that we have one million of people supposed to be out of work.* I have already proved that a free-port with a reduction of taxes can give employment to all our poor, and the labour of individuals makes the riches of the whole; therefore supposing these people to earn at a medium six pound *per annum* each, it makes six millions, as true as if dug out of a mine in our country, nay better with regard to the peoples healths. That this is not all imagination will appear by viewing what a free-port is capable of gaining us in four branches only, *viz.* the herring fishery, the woollen, linen, and silk manufactures.

It is proved in page 243, that we can out-do the *Dutch* in the herring fishery, the value whereof will appear from Mr. *Smith*, in his book called *England's Improvements Revived*, informs us (p. 249 and 250), *that he was sent in* 1633 *to* Shetland, *to discover the manner and way of trading*, &c. *and the manner of the* Hollanders *fishing with busses and other vessels, for ling and cod:* And in page 270 he says, *that during the war between* Spain *and* Holland, *the fishermen agreed among themselves to pay a dollar on every last of herrings, to maintain ships of war to secure the fishing, that a record was kept, the amount of which was* 300,000 *last of herrings taken in one half year, which*

al

*at a medium of the ordinary prices was worth five millions
sterling; whereunto if we add the cod, ling, and hake, and
the fish taken by the* Hollanders *and our neighbours on our
coasts all the year long, the total will evidently arise to
above ten millions yearly.*

<table>
<tr><td>Now though we may be proved capable of gaining the whole of this, I shall compute our gain to be only of the half, or</td><td>£5,000,000</td></tr>
<tr><td>If 100,000 of the above million of unemployed poor are woollen manufacturers, (though I imagine they must be much more in the present declining condition of that trade) however, that number earning six pound per head, makes 600,000l, and the value of the material being computed at ¼ of that, or 200,000l. makes altogether 800,000l. which as a free-port will gain, we may set down as so much additional profit</td><td>800,000</td></tr>
<tr><td>The linen manufacture that we shall gain, and which we now buy of foreigners, is proved in page 243 to amount to</td><td>3,000,000</td></tr>
<tr><td>The silk is computed at</td><td>200,000</td></tr>
<tr><td>Total value of the four branches of trade gained by a free-port</td><td>£9,000,000</td></tr>
</table>

If ⅔ of this sum are paid to the peoples labour, it
makes exactly six millions, or the employment of one
million of people at six pounds *per* head.

As to the value of the materials above which are included in the profit, I must observe that the abatement
made in the value of the herring-fishery doubly over-
balances their value.

But it will be said, that this proves only the employment of our own people, but does not prove that we shall
draw in foreigners; or if we do, that what foreigners come
over will starve our poor, who will have but just employment to maintain them : To this I answer, that the value
of the herring-fishery is computed only at the half, our
woollen-trade is computed only to recover what we have
lost, our linen and silk manufactures are computed only for
our own consumption, but not for what we shall export
when the manufactures are well established; therefore
double the number computed to be employed in these
several branches of trade may be drawn in, there is no
computation for the improvement a free-port will give our

navigation

navigation and other branches of trade, which will all want hands. In short, there is no computing what numbers a free-port can maintain here, consequently no ascertaining the extent of the riches it will bring in ; only this I must observe, that trade maintains in *Holland* seven times more people than the land deprived of it could subsist.

Besides, 'tis the nature of free-port trades to be hoarding up in cheap times all sorts of goods, to sell again when the markets are advanced, whereby they take advantage of the necessities of all the world, and must amass immense over-balances besides supplying their own wants ; and if the goods are only for foreign account, when one considers what a vast sum the freights, boat-hire, porterage, cartage, warehouse-rent, merchants commission, and often package and cooperage before the goods are sent out again do amount to, it must be concluded, that the universal store-house of a free-port must bring a vast profit to a country.

Fifthly, it will increase the value of our lands.

By increasing trade, which carries off our superfluities, furnishes employment, consequently a livelihood to our poor, and eases the land of the burden of maintaining them ; increases the stock of people, which of course increases the demand for necessaries and materials of manufacture, and the greater the demand, the greater price will the produce of lands bear ; 'tis people that trade and bring in money, and the more people there are in the nation to do it, the more money will be brought in, and the more money the people have, the better price will the produce of lands bear : In all countries the natural price of home commodities is according to their plenty, the demand and the proportion of money that trade circulates, and the more of it is circulating, the better rent can the farmers afford to give for the lands ; add to which, that it is people with plenty of money that improve lands, and

the

the more they are improved the better rents they bear, which in purchase increases the value of lands.

The gradations from the encouragement of trade to the benefit of lands are solid and certain, *viz*, whatever causes trade employs the poor, employment increases the stock of people, the increase of employed people causes an increase of money, the increase of money causes the value of lands to rise.   A free-port is proved to be the cause of trade, which is the cause of all the rest; therefore a free-port is a great increase of the value of lands.

Objections against a free-port here having been made by *Joshua Gee*, an author of good credit, for that reason must not be left unanswer'd, in his *Tract on Trade* (p. 165), he expresses himself thus

But to think it would be an advantage for a trading nation to admit all manner of foreign commodities to be imported free from all duties, is an unaccountable notion, and still less suitable to the circumstances of our island than to the Continent; for we have no inland countries beyond us (as they have) with whom we may carry on trade by land; but what is of the utmost consequence to us, is, that by laying high duties we are always able to check the vanity of our people in their extreme fondness of wearing exotic manufactures: For were it not for this restraint, as our neighbours give much less wages to their workmen than we do, and consequently can sell cheaper, the Italians, *the* French *and the* Dutch, *would have continued to pour upon us their silks, paper, hats, druggets, stuffs, ratteens, and even* Spanish *wool cloths.*

To this the following remarks may serve for answer.

First, but to think it would be an advantage for any trading nation to admit all manner of foreign commodities to be imported free from all duties, is an unaccountable notion.   I shall prove this notion to be highly beneficial even from this same author, who in page 164, says, *the*

Dutch *duties are small, and the nature of their trade abso-*
lutely requires it.   And again, *they know very well, that if*
they should load their imports with duties, other trading
places would undersell them and ruin their traffick that way.
The duties on the imports in *Holland* are a mere trifle,
the nature of all trade absolutely requires it, *viz.* not to
be undersold.   The *Dutch* know it, and by practising what
they know, prevent the ruin of their trade; if this is an
unaccountable notion the reader will judge from this same
author again, who, in page 191, shews the consequence of
their knowledge in the following words.   *As* Holland *is a*
magazine or collection of all the products and manufactures
of the world, which they disperse all over Europe, *the mer-*
chants and shopkeepers are every where their debtors, and
money is brought them from almost all countries.   *Gee* here
confesses that by their universal storehouse, the *Dutch*
have every where a balance in their favour; and the purport of his whole book is to prove how greatly the balance
of trade lies against us : With what consistency then can
he argue against our adopting some of those wise methods
the *Dutch* take to procure themselves such advantages?

Secondly, and still less suitable to the circumstances of
our island than to the Continent; for we have no inland
countries beyond us (as they have) with whom we may carry
on trade by land.   But we have in our three kingdoms a
large populous inland country of our own (which the
Dutch have not) to supply with necessaries and materials
in the cheapest manner, or else we raise the prices of our
manufactures to the prejudice of their sales, besides the
supplying our vast possessions in *America.*   But no inland
trade can be compared to the free-port trade, any more
than an inland country town can be to the sea-ports
of *London* and *Amsterdam,* or the navigation of the
Rhine and *Maes* to that of the *Baltick* or *Mediterranean;*
for a free-port must have a finger in all the trade of the
world, even in all those inland Continent trades that *Gee*

so much prises, *viz.* by trading to and supplying the sea-ports that are the inlets thereof in all countries, and the cheaper we can come to market, and with the best assort-ments, which a free-port trade only can effect; the more of that inland-Continent trade must we have, the more vent for our manufactures, and the greater navigation.

Thirdly, but what is of the utmost consequence to us, is, that by laying high duties, we are always able to check the vanity of our people in their extreme fondness of wearing exotic manufactures.——*Gee* says, *we are always able, by high duties, to check the vanity of our people,* &c. The great *De Wit,*in his *Memoirs,* says just the contray, *for it is generally found, that these great and too excessive customs fall of themselves;* the reason whereof is obvious, the higher the duties, the more profit by smuggling. Extreme fondness checked, naturally breaks out into madness, which appears at court every *gala* day in the number of *French* brocades and trimmings then worn, when that person is thought the happiest who hath the most and dearest *French* fopperies. But what will put this affair quite out of question, will be the consideration of the balance of our trade with *France,* (which shall be hereafter treated on;) if it is more in our favour than formerly, then *Gee's* opinion will triumph, and the efficacy of res-traints and high customs appear; but if the reverse appears, we may safely conclude they have none.

Fourthly, for were it not for this restraint.——In the *Memoirs* of *De Wit,* (p. 34,) it is said, *that restraint is always hurtful to trade;* the reason whereof is plain, for nature has given various products to various countries, and thereby knit mankind in an intercourse to supply each others wants: To attempt to sell our products, but to buy little or none from foreigners, is attempting an impossibility, acting contrary to the intent of nature, cynically and absurdly; and, as ours is a populous manu-facturing country, highly prejudicial to our own interests:

　　　　　　　　　　　　　　　For

For could we raise all necessaries and vanities within our-selves, this intercourse designed by nature would be destroyed; and then, how is a navigation, our only bul-wark, to be maintained? To sell all, and buy none, is to have no back-carriage, no freights home; if so, this will raise the freights outwards; a vessel that makes but one freight out and home, must make that one pay all the wages, wear and tear, charges, and living-profit, consequently makes our goods come dearer to market, and naturally stops their sales, by which in time freights outwards would be as much wanted as freights home, and our trade must be destroyed. But where freights are to be had out and home, they ease each other, consequently bring goods cheaper to market; and the encouraging our people by the utmost freedoms in trade, will enable them, by cheap labour to carry all manufactures we are naturally capable of to the utmost height, and in them foreigners could not hurt us, no restraint being so effectual as cheap prices; and to attempt more is laying our people under difficul-ties by taxes to no purpose; as suppose, for instance, we should take it into our heads, in spite of all taxes and disadvantages, to make all our own linens, and, in order to restrain the importation of foreign linens, put on them all the same duties we lay on the *French*; well now, money is to be saved to be sure! the poor employed, and fine things done; but alas! this restraint won't make our own labour one farthing cheaper, but the dearer; for our own linen manufactures having a monopoly against the rest of the people, and a vast demand, will certainly raise their prices; but not being able to supply quantities sufficient, some foreign may pay the high duties, some will be smuggled and sold cheaper than what pays duties, but still dearer than before the laying on this additional duty, which we will suppose to advance the price of linens to the people only 1*s. per* head. Is not this laying a duty of 1*s. per* head on our woollen, silk, and iron manufacturers,

on

on our sailors, on our labourers of all sorts? Certainly it is. Do the same in favour of iron, it will prove a tax on the rest, and so of any one of them. Do the same by them all, and they all tax one another, all raise each others prices at foreign markets, and stop their sales; foreigners gain upon us; we distress our whole trade upon the pretence of gaining only a single branch, and this single branch will grow still dearer, because it being a burden on the woollen, silk, and iron manufacturers, sailors and labourers, the linen manufacturers will pay dearer for those goods, pay dearer freights, dearer for all necessaries; it will be

> Linen dearer to woollen.
> Woollen dearer to linen.
> Linen, and woollen dearer to silk.
> Silk dearer to woollen and linen.
> Linen, woollen, and silk dearer to iron.
> Iron dearer to silk, woollen and linen.
> Linen, woollen, silk, and iron dearer to sailors.
> Sailors dearer to iron, silk, woollen and linen.
> Linen, woollen, silk, iron, and sailors, dearer to labour.
> Labour dearer to sailors, iron, silk, woollen and linen.

The dearer our linens grow, the more foreigners will smuggle in upon us and stifle our fabrick, all our artifices will prove vain to maintain it, and, after injuring all our other trades, find to our cost, that nothing but freedom can secure trade.

By the above account may be also seen, how prolifick the mischiefs of our restraints by customs are to trade; how our many taxes on commodities are oppressive; how they add an artificial price to goods; how our country has grown universally dearer, without being richer; and how foreigners ruin our trade, who soon seeing through our mean designs of engrossing every thing, grow angry, and stir up their Governments to distress us in their turn by easing their trade, which we shamefully neglect. Has the

linen

linen mannfacture in *England* increased by the prohibition
of *French* linens and high duties on *German, Dutch*, and
Flemish? So far from it, that it is decreased by our dear
labour, taxes, and disadvantages: *Scotland* and *Ireland*
attempt it with some success by their cheap labour, and
when our people are eased of their oppressions, so may we.

Besides, the discouraging to a great degree the use of
foreign products by the restraint of high customs, is prejudicial, tho' the contrary is the common received opinion,
arising from a mean selfishness that would let none live
but itself; as for instance, suppose *Portugal* to take annually to the value of 800,000*l.* of our woollens, and pay
it all in wines, what is the result of this? Why nothing
more but that our rich people drink such an amount of
woollens, which they would not consume otherwise; double
the present duty on that wine, thinking that less would be
drank, and we should drain *Portugal* of her gold; see
what would be the consequence, only that the King of
Portugal would lower the duties on the *French* and *Dutch*
woollens, 800,000*l. per annum* would be uncirculated
amongst us, the price of wool must sink, whereby the
French and *Dutch* would get it easier to ruin the rest of
our trades; about 100,000 of our poor would be deprived
of a diligent subsistence, and come upon their parishes for
an idle maintenance, while perhaps at the same time
Portugal wine, by its dearness, would become more
fashionable, great quantities would be drank and paid for
with our money, and instead of our draining the *Portuguese*, be drained by them.

*Fifthly, as our neighbours give much less wages to their
workmen than we do, and consequently can sell cheaper, the*
Italians, *the* French *and the* Dutch, *would have continued
to pour upon us their silks, paper, hats, druggets, stuffs,
ratteens, and even* Spanish-*wool cloths.*

Gee would have done well to have pointed out the
reasons why our neighbours give less wages, and conse-

quently

quently can sell cheaper, and since he has not done it, I shall attempt it. As the *Italians* are more remote, and pay dearer freights on their goods to *England* than the *French* and *Dutch* our neighbours, I shall confine myself wholly to the latter.

The reason why the *French* work cheaper than we, is the care their Government takes of not taxing many necessaries of life, or materials of manufacture, but that the manufacturers shall be supplied with them in the cheapest manner; whereby necessaries bearing only their natural price, they can afford to work and sell cheaper than we; 'tis the taxes that make the difference. To prove this I shall quote the author of a pamphlet called, *Observations on* British *Wool*, published in 1739, said to be wrote by a person sent abroad by the ministry to inquire into the state of the woollen manufactures among our neighbours, and what wool was smuggled to them; he informs us (p. 8,) *that the* French *send vast quantities of stuffs, stockings,* &c. *to* Spain, Portugal, *and* Italy, *and undersell us* 10 *or* 12 per cent. And in p. 21, *the reason that goods are to be bought cheaper in* France *than in* England *is, because the labour is* ⅓ *cheaper there.* And he accounts for labour's being ⅓ cheaper there in p. 28; *at* Lisle *the magistrates have built a storehouse, in a convenient part of the town, ten stories high; in the upper rooms of it they lay wheat, rye, barley; and in the cellars they lay wine, oil, and brandy: Those goods are bought up when they are cheap, and so soon as the markets are short, and goods begin to rise in the price, then the storehouse is opened to the poor, that they may buy what they have occasion for at the old market-price. This storehouse was built since the woollen manufactory hath so increased in this town, in order to support that fabrick, which is a great encouragement to the manufacturers, and a means to keep labour low. All other things that are needful to the poor are also cheap in proportion, as candles, oil, sope,* &c.

Far

Far from raising their prices with taxes, as we do, their study is to make necessaries cheap; and can we wonder that they beat us by 10 or 12 *per cent.* in the markets of *Spain, Portugal,* and *Italy?*

Having shewn how the *French* run away with our trade by reason of our heavy taxes, I shall examine how the *Dutch,* tho' the most taxed in the necessaries of life of any people, beat us out of our trade too, by stating the disadvantages of an *English* woollen manufacturer, and the advantages of a *Dutch* one.

The disadvantages of an *English* woollen manufacturer are, 1. That he must buy bread made of *English* corn, tho' dearer than foreign, whereby the farmer has a monopoly against the manufacturer, and all monopolies enhance the prices of goods. 2. He has no drawback on his corn. 3. He has no drawback on his malt. 4. He has no drawback on leather. 5. He pays a duty on his coals of 10*s. per* chaldron in *London,* and 5*s.* in the out-ports. 6. He must buy *English* beef, pork, mutton, lamb, and butter, tho' he can have *Irish* cheaper, whereby the grazier has a monopoly against him, to make his meat dear. 7. He must buy fish caught by *British* (except a few sorts) tho' he can have it cheaper from the *Dutch, French,* &c. whereby the fisherman has a monopoly against him to make his fish dear. 8. He must not buy foreign hats, cloths, stuffs, stockings, or any coarse woollens for his use that are cheaper now than *English,* even tho' he could sell his own to greater advantage than wearing them himself, whereby these several branches have a monopoly against each other and the rest of the nation, to make all sorts of clothing dear. 9. He must not buy *French* linens for his use, tho' ever so cheap, whereby the other linen countries have a monopoly against him to make his linen dear. 10. He must not buy for his use foreign shearmens shears, iron, or tin wares, tho' ever so cheap, whereby those manufacturers have a monopoly against him to make

his

his iron or tin wares dear. 11. He may not have several sorts of goods imported for his use bought at the cheapest market, but only at the usual port of shipping (*Vide the Index to the Book of Rates, Goods Inwards*, Article 6.) whereby those countries have a monopoly against him to make those goods dear. 12. He may not have those above goods shipp'd at the cheapest freights, but must be shipp'd on *British* ships, or ships of the country, and at the usual port of shipping, whereby those ships have a monopoly against him to make those goods still dearer. 13. He has heavy customs to pay on the oil and sope he uses in manufacturing his goods, which helps to advance their dearness. 14. And lastly, he has long expensive land-carriages to pay to *London*, the chief market for his goods, the navigation of our rivers not being sufficiently improved.

A *Dutch* woollen manufacturer is in a situation just the reverse of this; his advantages are, 1. That he may buy always the cheapest corn that can be got to make bread, has no corn-monopoly on him. 2. He has 5*s. per* quarter drawback on *English* wheat; computing freight, and charges, at 1*s.* 6*d. per* quarter, he is fed by the *English* cheaper than their own people by 3*s.* 6*d.* in every quarter of wheat. 3. He has 2*s.* 6*d. per* quarter drawback on *English* malt, to make his drink come cheaper to him than to our own people. 4. He has 1*d. per* pound drawback on *English* leather. 5. He has *British* coals at 3*s. per* chaldron duty, which is 2*s.* cheaper than the out-ports, and 7*s.* cheaper than the *Londoners.* 6. He may buy beef, &c. in *Ireland*, or any country where it can be had cheapest, has no monopoly on him in this case. 7. He may buy fish of any that sell cheapest, has no monopoly on him in this case. 8. He may buy and wear the cheapest woollens he can get from any country; and if he can buy cloth for his use at 4*s. per* yard, he will, provided he can sell his own of 5*s. per* yard value with the usual profit, no branch of the trade has a monopoly against the rest of the people.

　　　　9. He

9. He may buy the cheapest linens he can get, no country has a monopoly against him in this case. 10. He may buy the cheapest iron and tin wares he can get, has no monopoly against him in this case. 11. He may have all those goods (specified in the *Index to the Book of Rates* in Article 6. of *Goods Inwards*) bought where cheapest, no country having a monopoly against him. 12. He may have all the above goods shipp'd on the cheapest sailing ships, no shipping having a monopoly against him. 13. He has customs so light, that they are a mere trifle, has not the prices of his goods raised by heavy customs on his oil and sope. 14. He has cheap water-carriage almost every where.

I shall now prove, that was our trade quite free, no nation could hurt our staple, the woollen manufacture, and that if cheapness pours in goods to a country, we should do it on the *French* and *Dutch* instead of they on us; consequently that *Gee*'s objection is void.

By the abovementioned observations on *British* wool, we find that the *French* can send to *Spain*, *Portugal*, or *Italy*, 50 stuffs that shall now cost in *England* 100*l.* cheaper by 10 or 12 *per cent.* say 12 *per cent* cheaper, or at   £88

In page 207, I have proved that above half the present value of our woollen goods is fictitious, that our taxes, monopolies, and ill-judged laws advance the natural value of our woollen goods above 104 *per cent.* and that the true natural value of 100*l.* worth of our woollen goods at present is but 49*l.*

So that were our taxes, monopolies, and ill-judged laws removed, 50 stuffs that now cost 100*l.* might be sent to market at   49

The difference is   £39

39*l.* charged by *French* or *Dutch* taxes and natural disadvantages on 49*l.* is an advance of almost 80 *per cent.* on the *English* price.

Therefore the *French* and *Dutch*, who now beat us by 10 or 12 *per cent.* might be beat by us excessively; they could not sell woollens at any foreign market until all ours were sold, much less pour them in here to ruin our manu-

116   factures,

factures, as *Gee* imagined; but the rest of their trade must decline greatly wherever we came in competition with them, and where would be the nation in *Europe* that could hurt us?

By this it appears, that it is only our ill regulations of our trade that give these nations any advantages against us.

Silks and paper are still poured in upon us, and the boasted benefit to the woollen trade by restraints at present is a farce; for as our foreign demand declines, our people naturally turn all their stocks to supply the home-consumption, until it is so overglutted that great quantities have been sold for less than they cost making, or at *French* prices, which must break an over-taxed *Englishman.* Our people manufacture neater than any in felt and wool, so that foreign hats, cloths, &c. being ill made, suit not the *English* taste; for which reason, if it should take ten years time to break the remainder of our clothiers, their stocks would sell so cheap, that the *French* could do very little during that time; but afterwards, by getting some of our fugitive manufacturers to improve their own people, and underselling us so vastly, they will run woollen goods as much as they do teas, brandies, and rich goods now, and reduce us to the state we were formerly in with respect to *Flanders, viz.* they to buy our raw wool, and return it us in manufactures improved three times its first value.

Two more objections may be made.

First, that it seems contrary to reason to take off the duties or prohibitions on the goods of any nation that will not do the same by ours.

Secondly, that the balance against us with *France* must increase by taking off the duties on *French* goods.

To the first objection I answer, that with regard to
                                    duties,

duties, it is already proved that they destroy trade, and constant experience shews us that free ports increase it. If other nations will destroy their trade, ours must rise upon their ruins; and would it not be absurd for us to refuse, by a contrary conduct, to increase ours? If our enemies will commit such follies, why should we? or rather, could we wish them to do worse?

Nothing makes a country's goods so cheap as a free-port, consequently the fewer foreign goods could be consumed here; more might be imported to lay by for better markets, the profits on which must enrich us; for the cheaper our goods are, the greater vent they will have; and the higher the duties foreigners lay on them, the more will be smuggled upon them.

Besides, those nations that are our rivals, in trade, and persist in keeping high customs on our goods, persist also in refusing to make their country an universal store-house, deny their people the advantage of it, and force their customers to buy at other markets those goods they lay high customs on to prevent their coming in. If a mercer, being a weaver, should refuse to admit into his shop damasks, because he did not make them, and think thereby to improve the vent of his other silks, he would soon find his mistake, for his customers that went to other places for damasks, would be importuned and induced, if only to save themselves trouble, to buy other silks they wanted at the same time. The *British Merchant*, vol. 3. p. 298, remarks, that *it is natural for us to buy every thing we want at the shop where we are obliged to buy any thing*. And would it not be strange if another mercer, being also a weaver, should be angry with such a man, and refuse to admit into his shop the others satins, because he refused to admit his damasks, and thereby drive away his trade to those general traders that were wise enough to improve upon their errors, by admitting every thing that could be sold with profit? The case is the same with nations.

Customs on foreign goods hurt ourselves more than foreigners, tho' our false notions of trade make us think the contrary, by confining our thoughts to the seller, without regarding the buyer, who being our own subject, should be the person most considered: As for example, in the case of *Spanish* oil; we have laid a duty on it, no doubt to retaliate on the *Spaniards* the duties they lay on our woollens; but whom does our duty affect? not the *Spaniard*, it cannot hurt him; for he being paid for his oil, has parted with his property in it, and has nothing more to do with it: But 'tis the *English* merchant whose property on payment this oil becomes, and which might be called *English* oil, for such in reality it then is; he is cramp'd by this duty, part of his capital in trade is taken away to pay it, the interest of which, and officers fees in and out, make the oil too dear to export, he is not allowed that profit, he must sell at home, and must shift the load from his shoulders on the manufacturer who uses it, and he on the consumer, whereby our goods are rendered dearer, and less capable of exportation.

Here is a duty on a foreign commodity indeed, but to be paid by our own people; 'tis their feet are entangled in the net laid for these *Spaniards*.

With regard to a prohibition, this acknowledges the goods it is laid on to be good and cheap, otherwise it were needless; for what trader will buy bad or dear goods if he can get better or cheaper, and they must be necessary, otherwise they would not be demanded, consequently would not be imported; for who will import goods where there is no demand?

A prohibition on the goods of any one nation gives a monopoly to other nations that raise the like growths; thus the prohibition of *Spanish* oil in the late war gave a monopoly to *Galipoly*, all monopolies raise the prices of goods; thus *Galipoly* oil, that before our *Spanish* prohibition was sold for 15 to 16 ducats the salm, was thereby

    raised

raised to 26 and 27 ducats; the same with all other sorts of goods used instead of *Spanish*, whereby the merchants profit on the advanced price, and that of the several tradesmen whose hands these goods passed thro', did further enhance their prices vastly to the consumer; which, since my making this remark, hath been verified by a petition of the clothiers of *Stroud-Water* (and of most of our greatest clothing towns) presented to the House of Commons, *Feb.* 2, 1742, complaining that since the prohibition the price of oil is advanced from less than 26*l.* to 60*l.* a tun.

But it will be objected that on the declaration of war, *Spain* prohibited our goods.

To which I answer, that heavy taxes with many other difficulties are the consequences of war, and in a time of such a general calamity, is it not absurd to distress our trade in making our people buy bad or dear goods of foreigners, by a prohibition against any one nation, which other nations having the like commodities, take the advantage of and raise their prices upon us? Is not this adding an unnecessary tax upon our people, whereby they grow sooner impoverished and unable to support a war? If the *Spaniards* will commit such blunders, why should we imitate them?

Trade cannot, will not be forced, let other nations prohibit by what severities they please, interest will prevail; they may embarrass their own trade, but cannot hurt a nation whose trade is free, so much as themselves. *Spain* has prohibited our woollens, but had a reduction of our taxes brought them to their natural value only, they would be the cheapest in *Europe* of their goodness, consequently must be more demanded by the *Spaniards*, be smuggled into their country in spite of their Government, and sold at better prices; their people would be dearer clothed with duties and prohibitions than without, consequently must sell their oil, wine, and other commodities dearer,

whereby

whereby other nations raising the like growths would gain ground upon them, and their balance of trade grow less and less : But should we for that reason prohibit their commodities? By no means, for the dearer they grow, no more than what are just necessary will be used; their prohibition does their own business, some may be necessary, what are so, we should not make dearer to our own people; some may be proper to assort cargoes for other countries, and why should we prohibit our people that advantage? why hurt ourselves to hurt the *Spaniards?* if we would retaliate effectually upon them for their ill-intent, handsome premiums given to our plantations to raise the same growths as *Spain,* might enable them in time to supply us cheaper than the *Spaniards* could do, and establish a trade they could never recover. Premiums may gain trade, but prohibitions will destroy it; of which let the following example suffice.

Portugal being united to *Spain* in the reign of *Philip* the IId. during the revolt of the *Dutch, Puffendorf* in his *introduction to the History of* Europe tells us, *that* Philip *being intent upon the reducing of the Netherlands, thought that nothing could do it more effectually than to stop their trade and commerce with* Spain *and* Portugal, *for hitherto the* Dutch *had traded no further, being used to fetch away their commodities from thence, and to convey them into the more northern parts of* Europe. *Upon this consideration* Philip *concluded that if this way of getting money were once stopp'd, they would quickly grow poor, and thereby be obliged to submit. But this design had a quite contrary effect, for the* Hollanders *themselves being excluded trade with* Spain *and* Portugal, *tried about the end of the latter age to sail to the East-Indies, and as soon as they had got footing there they greatly impair'd the* Portuguese *trade, who hitherto had been the sole managers of it, and afterwards took from them one fort after another. And the* English, *with the assistance of* Abbas *King of* Persia,

forced

forced from them the famous city of Ormus :   *Nor was this all, for the* Hollanders *took from them a great part of* Brazile *and several places on the coast of* Africa *which the* Hollanders, *in all probability, would have had no reason to attempt, if* Portugal *had remained a kingdom by itself and had not been annexed to* Spain.——*i. e.* If no prohibition had happened.

Second Objection. That the balance against us with *France* must increase by taking off the duties on *French* goods.

Answer : Here experience can decide by comparing the difference of the balance against us when we had a free-trade formerly, and later times, when most sorts of *French* goods are loaded with such high duties as amount to a prohibition.

No person who has read the *British Merchant* will say that he is a partial author in favour of the answer to this objection.

He says, (Vol. III. p. 106,) *the stated maxim among merchants to know whether the trade be for or against us, is to have recourse to the course of exchange, it is a nicety many of our merchants are themselves unacquainted with, yet as the exchange holds the balance of trade, so as that is for us or against us it immediately decides the point.*

If the exchange be above the par of the money of the country we trade with, it is a plain argument that the balance is on their side, for no man will bring silver from a country when the exchange is more favourable than the coin.

The author of the *Political Reflexions on the Commerce and Finances of* France, elegantly calls the Exchange the *Barometer of Commerce.*

In the year 1688, it appears by the *British Merchant,* that tho' there was a prohibition, yet *the Court hindered the execution of it.* Dr. *Tancred Robinson* the physician,

122

favoured

favoured me with the sight of a *memorandum* he made in that year, on his setting out for *Paris, viz.* for 60*l. sterling* paid in *London*, he received a bill of Exchange on *Paris* for 259 crowns 1 livre.

The *British Merchant* (III. p. 118,) informs us, *the par of the exchange was 54d. sterling, for the old* French *crown ;* Therefore he should have paid only 58*l.* 7*s.* for 259 crowns 1 livre, consequently the exchange was in the disfavour of *England*, not quite	3 *per cent.*
In the year 1686, the prohibition being quite taken off, the *British Merchant* (I. p. 318,) informs us, *the exchange was at 56d. per crown*, the par as above being 54*d.* the exchange was in the disfavour of *England* about	3¼ *per cent.*
In the year 1729, the *French* goods having been loaded ever since King *William* the Third's reign, with such high duties on most articles, as amount to a prohibition, by *Castaing's* paper of *March* 28, *the exchange was at 32d.* ¼ *per ecu Tournois.*	
By Sir *Isaac Newton's Table of Assays, Weights, &c. of Foreign Coins*, published by *Willock* in 1740, *the par is 29d.* 149 *dec.* was in the disfavour of *England* above	11 *per cent.*
In the year 1740, by *Castaing's* paper of *Feb.* 3, *the exchange was at 32d.* ¼. The par, as above, was in the disfavour of *England* almost	12 *per cent.*
By the custom house books our imports, from *France* in 1686, exceeded our exports, as by the *British Merchant*, (I. p. 305).	769,190 16 0
He adds for goods clandestinely imported, (p. 306.)	428,139 16 9
Total over-balance that year	£1,197,330 12 9

The *British Merchant* says above, *that the exchange holds the balance of trade ; so as that is for us or against us, it immediately decides the point.* By the *so as* he must mean proportionably, that is, that the exchange is affected by the balance of trade, agreeable to the *French* author above, as the quicksilver in the barometer is by the atmosphere. As no man, that understands trade, can deny this truth, I shall leave it to the curious to determine,

what

what proportion an over-balance that affects the exchange almost 12 *per cent.* must bear to one of 1,197,330*l.* 12*s.* 9*d.* that affected it only about 3 ¼ *per cent.*

France takes from *Britain* wool, corn, dye-stuffs, hard-wares, and tobacco in great quantities, some *India* goods, tin, lead, ships, horses, &c.

But since *France* is increased in the woollen manufacture, in navigation, and in sugar planting, she takes vast quantities of wool and provisions from *Ireland*, to improve her manufactures, victual her ships, and supply her colonies, which amount to vast sums yearly; and tho' these articles are vastly increased, yet still the balance of trade cannot be brought in our favour; prohibitions and high duties have made it vastly more disadvantageous to us than in the times of a free-trade, the difference in the exchanges being almost 12 to 3.

As the general interest of the nation, with respect to our trade, seems to have hitherto been little understood, let us examine this *French* trade a little farther.

Our great dealings with this *French* shop formerly, were occasion'd by its cheapness, (*an excellent cause*) and its being near us occasion'd cheap carriage, (*better and better*) and tho' the *French* had a great balance against us yet other nations had the less; but party-prejudice running high against the *French* King's ambitious designs, in King *Charles* the Second, and King *William* the Third's time; and this balance being considered abstractedly, without any view to our general trade; an inconsiderate zeal hurried our ancestors into the vain scheme of distressing the *French* King by prohibitions and high customs on his goods, not considering the hurt we should thereby do ourselves, and without ever effectually putting in motion those means that were practicable to ease our own trade, so that we only dispers'd, during our last wars, our trade to dearer nations; we bought dearer *German* and *Dutch* linens, dearer *Italian* and *Dutch* silks, paper, &c. as

                                        if

if it was better to pay those nations 15 or 18*d.* for what
the *French* would sell for 1*s.* distressing our people by
dear prices and thereby draining us of our money the
faster; for such large quantities of cheap *French* goods as
were consumed here, being prohibited, made the demand
greater for the *Dutch, German,* and *Italian* dearer goods,
giving them at the same time a monopoly against ourselves, which made them raise their prices on us still
higher.   One would be apt to think that our forefathers
had a mind to drive all the money out of the nation.
For God's sake! let us have wit in our anger, and not
pay dear prices to pretended friends when enemies will
sell us cheaper; let us befriend ourselves a little, by saving
our money, which is the life of trade and the sinews of
war; let us keep this power in our own hands, to command weight and respect from our neighbours, not squander it away to them, and be forced to court the assistance
of those we give power to, and sometimes even court in
vain : So much for times of war.

But in times of peace the smuggling-trade goes on
easier, high duties are temptations that promote it, ministers of state may be bribed to brow-beat or discharge
officers for doing their duty; goods that in a free-trade
cost but 100*l.* being charged with 50 *per cent.* duty, a
smuggler will sell for 120 or 125*l.* for the risk must be
paid for, tho' the duties are saved; so that even the smuggling-trade costs us more than a free-trade, and may
perhaps be one of the reasons that the exchange with
France is so much against us : Whereas, had our country
been made a free-port in King *Charles* the Second's time,
and all taxes laid on the consumers of luxuries, the *French*
themselves during their last wars with *England,* would
have fled from misery at home, to a country that by its
freedom from taxes and ease in trade, seems to invite the
establishment of all manufactures, our balance to *France*
could not have arose to that destructive height it has been

at, nor had the *French* ever made the figure in trade they now do.

The courses of the exchanges are facts notorious to people conversant in trade; upon those facts I rest my arguments, in answer to the above objection: by which it appears plainly, that a free-port trade would lessen the balance against us, even with *France*; agreeable to the author of *Britannia Languens*, who says, *now if we look back to the grounds and reasons of the decay of our* English *trade, we shall find them to be no other than our own ill constitutions in trade, which are not a bit remedied by the* French *prohibition, and therefore will prevent any advantage we might, perhaps, otherwise receive from it.* And in p. 286, *should we suppose that it* (i. e. *the prohibition*) *would restore the balance, nay, that it should render the national trade of* England *somewhat beneficial, yet it must be confess'd, that a compleat regulation of our trade would render it prodigiously more beneficial, (perhaps more than all the trade of* Europe *besides) considering how our advantages in trade would reduce the trade of our neighbour nations, as ours does improve.*

Notwithstanding what has been said in favour of a free-port, such strong prejudices against a free trade with *France*, have been raised by most of our late authors on this subject, that few people have any but frightful ideas of it. The *British Merchant*, a work in great reputation, has brought heavy objections against a trade with *France;* the strength of which, it may not be improper to examine. He says;

I.

Goods imported to be re-exported, is certainly a national advantage; but few or no French *goods are ever exported from* Great-Britain, *except to our plantations, but are all consumed at home, therefore no benefit can be reaped this way by the* French *trade.*

126

II.

II.

Letting ships to freight cannot but be of some profit to a nation; but it is very rare if the French *ever make use of any other ships than their own; they victual and man cheaper than we, therefore nothing is to be got from them by this article.*

III.

Things that are of absolute necessity cannot be reckoned prejudicial to a nation; but France *produces nothing that is necessary, or even convenient, but which we had better be without.*

Each of these objections is introduced with a general maxim which the *French* trade is asserted to be inconsistent with, and if understood according to the present or then state of our trade, are founded in truth; so that I would not be thought by the following remarks to reflect on the authors of the *British Merchant*, for seasonably opposing our engaging in trade with the *French* on unequal terms during our present ill regulations. But these objections are founded only on those ill regulations, for they otherwise have no weight, and will fall to the ground when they are removed; so that they affect not an *English*, untaxed free-port trade with *France*, which I shall endeavour to prove, and shall farther confirm by proving, that had our trade no incumbrance on it, a trade with *France* must be beneficial.

To the first objection, I answer, that it can proceed only from our ill regulations of our trade; for high customs prevent merchants engrossing in cheap times, the duties running away with great part of their capitals, the interest of money lying dead for duties, is such a charge as no trade can bear that is rivalled by people free from such clogs; besides, great part of the duties on *French* goods are not repaid on exportation, so that it is impossible

to

to send them to any market but our plantations; our monopolies and ill-judged laws that make navigation dear, prevent our giving that vent to the *French* goods which the *Dutch* are capable of doing, though they have not the natural advantages that we have, and they cherish this trade that we condemn as one of their best branches, being a great support of their navigation. According to the *Representation* of the body of merchants to the *French* King in 1658, a copy whereof was sent to the *States-General* by their ambassador *Boreel, the exports of* France *to* Holland *and* England (Vide *Memoires de De Wit*, p. 211. the *British Merchant*, IV. p. 232.) *amounted to* 30 *millions of crowns, making—*

	£6,750,000 0 0
The *British Merchant*, (I. p. 306,) *makes our imports from* France *in* 1686, *by the custom house accounts, amount to*	£1,284,419 10 03
To which he adds of himself, *for goods clandestinely imported,*	428,139 16 09
	£1,712,559 07 00
But to leave no room for cavil, he publishes *an account of Mr.* Fortrey's, *which made our imports from* France *amount yearly to*	2,600,000 00 00
	£4,312,559 07 00
The medium of which two accounts is	2,156,279 13 06
Which being deducted, the remainder must be the *Dutch* imports, amounting to	£4,593,720 06 06

De Wit, in his *Memoirs*, says, *the greatest part of the* French *exports are for* Holland; the above account verifies it; and he farther says, *that the* Dutch *consume and sell almost all the wines and salt that go out of* France; and in page 213, he says, *it is certain that the* French *gain every year upon the* Dutch *above* 30 *millions of money, besides the goods they send to* France; these I take to be livres, making 10 millions of crowns at 54*d.* is 2,250,000*l.*

The *Dutch* cannot consume that quantity of *French* goods, for if they did, they could not have a shilling left in the country with such an immense yearly over-balance

for

for near a century; therefore the bulk of these imports must be for re-exportation, which the Objection says is certainly a national advantage; this the *Dutch* know, and feel the sweets of, for they were so far from being, like us, frightened at the amount of the imports, or the over-balance above, tho' vastly superior to ours, that neither the *French* war in Queen *Anne's* reign, nor the intreaties of their allies, could persuade them to prohibit that trade; nay, they are grown excessively rich with double the importation that we thought would beggar us. Such clear perceptions have the *Dutch* of trade, and that true foundation of it, *freedom*: Such enemies are they to prohibitions, or to give any foreigners monopolies against them, or to pay dearer to friends for what enemies will sell them cheaper. Therefore as the *Dutch* reap a benefit by this trade, much more may the *English*, whose natural advantages, if disencumbered, are greater than theirs.

To the second I answer, it is notorious that foreign ships frequent the *French* ports and take in ladings, some of which I presume are for *French* accompt; but that we can get nothing from them by freight, because they victual and man cheaper than we, can arise only from our ill regulations in trade, for our natural advantages are superior to theirs in navigation.

In the shipping-article the *French* are deficient, and forced to buy of us to a large amount yearly.

In the victualling-article the *French* are deficient, and forced to buy in *Ireland* to a large amount yearly.

These articles bring some profit to our own people, and are attended with some charges in their transportation to the *French*, consequently are enhanced in price to them.

By our bounties we furnish the *French* with wheat for biscuit at 3*s.* 6*d. per* quarter cheaper than our own people, *Vide* p. 259.

That the *French* man cheaper than we, I doubt, though they pay less wages; for not being so expert as we, they

are

are forced to put more hands on board their ships, whereby their expences are enhanced by additional wages and consumption of stores; to which add the advance of insurance they are forced to pay, no insurer in general will underwrite on *French* ships for so low premiums as on *English.*

Before the prohibition of *Irish* provisions we victualled cheaper than any people, and sold to both *French* and *Dutch*; and was that monopoly, with our taxes and bounties, taken of, we should be in the same state as before, consequently victual cheaper than either.

As customs and excises enhance the prices of necessaries, they make all victualling and stores come dearer to our owners of ships.

As customs and excises enhance the prices of necessaries, they oblige the sailor to demand high wages to support himself and family.

We have more sailors than the *French,* as appears by the lists of ships at foreign ports, consequently should navigate cheaper; for it is a maxim in trade, *the greater plenty of hands, the lower the wages.*

But this benefit we defeat by our Navigation Act, which gives the sailors a monopoly against our merchants, so that on the least spurt of trade they extort excessive wages.

Let these ill regulations be removed, and will any one say that the people who are buyers of ships, and victuals for them, can navigate cheaper than the sellers? that the people who put the most hands on board, and pay a high insurance, can navigate cheaper than those that put few hands on board, and can be insured the cheapest of any people? that a nation that has a less number of sailors can navigate cheaper than another that has a greater? that a people that pay arbitrary taxes can navigate cheaper than those that pay voluntary taxes? It cannot be.

As no people by their natural advantages can navigate so cheap as we, so no people are enabled to give such a vent to their growths, manufactures and imports as we,

　　　　　　　　　　　　　　　　and

and those nations that would give theirs the same vent must employ our shipping, or trade to disadvantage; therefore we can force the *French* either to give us freights, or ruin their trade, either of which must lessen their navigation, riches and power, and increase ours.

To the third I answer, these very authors reckon, *that had the duties on* French *goods been lowered according to the stipulations in the treaty of commerce made at* Utrecht, *our annual consumption of* French *linens would have been* 600,000*l.* being the greatest amount of any one article: This objection therefore is a mistake, occasioned by an over zeal; for it appears by the same authors (i, p. 283), *that we used to import from* France *several necessary articles, such as prunes, salt, sope, thread,* &c.

I believe I need not prove linens to be either necessary or convenient, since no body can deny it, therefore *France* produces something that we want, and until we can gain the manufacture of it ourselves (which the removing the clogs on our trade only can effect) highly necessary to be bought where cheapest, which I presume by the quantities imported, and the prohibition, to have been in *France*, otherwise the prohibition had been needless; and if we raise the price of *French* linens by customs to exceed other foreign that are dearer, I have proved in page 254, that we distress our whole trade; and in p. 243, that by a free-port trade we must gain that manufacture, at least for our own consumption.

I come now to a bold attempt, and what at first view will startle most people, and that is to prove, that were all our taxes, monopolies, and ill-judged laws removed, or, in other words, if our trade had no incumbrance on it, but was quite free, that then our trade to *France* must be beneficial.

The authors of the *British Merchant*, writing against the treaty of commerce made with *France* at *Utrecht*, compute, *that had the duties on* French *goods been lowered according*

according to those stipulations, we should have paid to
France yearly for

Wine	.	.	.	.	£450,000
Brandy					70,000
Linen					600,000
Paper					30,000
Silks	.	.	.	.	500,000
					£1,650,000

Let us examine how much of this sum we should pay if our trade was quite free.

As to the wine-article, I agree, that being the most esteemed of any in *Europe*, our importation might even exceed that sum, but great part of it would be reduced by our re-exportation; for our natural advantages being greater than the *Dutch*, we should give those wines a greater vent than they were yet ever able to do, and be the common carriers of them, by which means our profits and freights would make our own consumption come very easy, easier than ever it was to *Holland*; but to avoid all objection, I will allow for that expence the above sum of 450,000*l.*

As to the brandy-article, that could not cost us any thing; for as our rum can be imported cheaper, and is more wholsom, our consumption would be chiefly that, so the brandies imported would be chiefly for re-exportation; for which reason I can't help thinking but the profits and freights must greatly exceed our consumption in value.

But there is one consideration that will reduce this wine-article, and that is, that as it is not a perishable commodity, we should hoard up in cheap times vast quantities, and when the markets were advanced by bad seasons, or other accidents, make extraordinary profits by the stocks we had by us, which besides would be a great benefit to our navigation.

As

As to the linen, paper, and silk-articles, them I strike out entirely, for by the encouragement of our trade we must gain those manufactures, as is proved in p. 242;

Therefore all these mighty consumptive importations are reduced only to the wine-article above of £450,000

The authors of the *British Merchant* compute (i, p. 15), *our yearly exports to* France *on the peace at only*   .   .   200,000

Whereas, by a custom-house accompt, they publish (p. 305), *viz., from* Mich. 1685 *to* Mich. 1686, (in which are wanting the *Michaelmas* quarter for *Deal, Dartmouth, Whitby* and *Milford*) *our exports amounted to*   .   .   .   515,228

Note, In this account there is no mention either of the wool or ship-articles; the corn-article amounts but to 14285*l.* 8*s.* the hard-ware, under the heads of wrought-iron, clock-work, and nails, amounts but to 1646*l.* 12*s.* 6*d.* and the tobacco but to 2793*l.* 9*s.* 2*d.*

They also quote Mr. *Fortrey,* who makes our annual exports amount to   1,000,000

£1,715,228

The medium whereof is £571,742

The *Dutch* can't be supposed to export less of their *French* imports than the amount of what *De Wit* says the over-balance of *France* is on them viz., 2,250,000*l.* which is a very moderate computation, for it makes their annual consumption far superior to whatever *England's* was proved to be, and must be a great deal too much for that frugal people; now the freights, charges, and profits paid the *Dutch* on that re-exportation cannot be less than 10 *per cent.* amounting to 225,000*l.* clear gain to *Holland* by that trade.

As the natural advantages of *Britain* are shown (p. 215) greatly to exceed those of *Holland,* so by a free-port trade we cannot be supposed to give a less vent to our *French* imports than the *Dutch* did, or with less profit, therefore we may safely add to our exports the gain *Holland* received by re-exporting *French* goods amounting annually to   .   225,000

£796,742

From that must be deducted the wine-article above, amounting to   450,000

Therefore the annual benefit to *Britain* from *France* by a free-port trade must be at least £346,742

Our goods are so well manufactured that their neatness recommends them every where, nothing obstructs

them

them but their dear price; but was their fictitious value once taken off, they would come cheaper than ever they yet were, so that our exports to *France* would naturally increase, and might exceed even Mr. *Fortrey's* computation of 1 million *per annum.*

The letter in defence of the *East India* Company, printed in 1677, informs us, *that there was formerly vended in* France, *annually*, English *drapery to the amount* of 600,000*l.* As we beat the *French* out of foreign markets their manufactures must decay, and of course they will want the greater supply from us; if they prohibit them by high duties they put themselves in the case of the *Spaniards.*

Here is, I think, demonstration to those that will open their eyes, that *Great-Britain*, by disencumbring and making its trade quite free, cannot be hurt by *France*, much less by any other power in *Europe*, but must of necessity hold the first rank in trade.

But now perhaps it will be said, this savours of *French* designs, this author is a concealed *Frenchman*, the *French* are already too powerful, we must take care.

To this I answer, that *Britain* should be always vigilant over the designs of *France*, but need not be afraid of her power; her wise regulations in trade should be the objects we should keep our eyes upon, and out-do her if possible, or else as she rises we must sink; but it is our comfort that our remedy is always in our own hands; nor can there be any solid reason for the nation's paying dearer to other countries for goods we could buy cheaper in *France :* Would any wise dealer in *London* buy goods of a *Dutch* shopkeeper for 15 or 18*d.* when he could have the same from a *French* shopkeeper for 1*s.*? Would he not consider that by so doing he should empty his own pockets the sooner, and that in the end he would greatly injure his family by such whims? And shall this nation commit an absurdity that stares every private man in the face? Do

our

our good friends, the *Dutch*, commit such a blunder in favour of us? They know their own interest too well, and have too good notions of trade to do it. The present power of *France* is indeed great, her dominions in *Europe* are bigger and more populous by at least $\frac{1}{4}$ than ours; but as her naval force cannot match the half of what we have, our situation makes us the only one of her neighbours that need not fear her; besides, her people are not in proportion so rich, her colonies not so populous as ours: but the certain way to be secure is to be more powerful, that is, to extend our trade as far as it is capable of; and as restraints have proved its ruin, to reject them, and depend on freedom for security, bidding defiance to the *French* or any nation in *Europe* that took umbrage at our exerting our natural advantages. Before these taxes we were more powerful, why not so again? 'Tis our own fault if we are not.

The exports of France *in* 1658, according to *De Wit, were*	£6,750,000
And *the exports of* England *in* 1699 *were* . . .	6,788,000
To which we may add the value of the four branches of trade gained by a free-port (*vide* p. 249), besides the other benefits not enumerated	9,000,000
	£15,788,000

Suppose the *French* to have now doubled their trade of 1658, we can not only double the value of ours of 1699, but more, as appears above: Besides, the progress we should make in *Europe* and in the *East-Indies* by a free trade, and the vast improvements our colonies in *America* are capable of, must increase the demand for our manufactures beyond what was ever known. Let all these be duly considered, with the vast strength of our navy, and the fear of the *French* power must vanish like a phantom. *Imperator maris terræ Dominus*, is a proverb applied by *De Wit* in his *Memoires*, to a king of *England*; let us examine whether this remark on our power will hold good at this time. If *France* can give laws by land, *Britain* can do it by sea; and in a little time the sea will command the land, for our men of war can destroy their ships, ravage their coasts, batter down their forts, and burn their sea-port towns: this must ruin their trade, as trade goes so must their money, and when the money is gone the armies cannot be supported, they must be drawn from the countries they invade, or they will desert rather than perish with hunger for want of pay. Had we push'd on the war in Queen *Anne's* reign only by our fleets, we should have given quicker relief to our allies, saved our money, prevented a load of debts, and soon brought the war to a conclusion; for the strong towns which we took in *Flanders* with so much expense of blood and treasure, must have been abandoned by the *French* troops for want of pay, want of ammunition and provision, and have fallen into our allies hands without striking a stroke, or making only such a faint resistance as the Queen of *Hungary's* unpaid troops and unprovided towns did lately. We have never yet exerted our natural naval force; had the *French* ever felt the full weight of it they would be more humble, they would not dare so wantonly to invade our allies on the continent, for fear of drawing down our vengance upon them.

If any *Englishman* should be so vapourish as to doubt whether trade and navigation can effect this, I desire him only to consider what a few *Dutch* fishing-towns were enabled thereby to do in their revolt from *Spain*, whose power was then the dread of *Europe*; the mighty wars they maintained by sea and land for fifty-seven years against that crown, which at last gave such a shock and reduction to the power of *Spain* as it hath not been since able to recover. The extending at the same time their trade all over the world, and making vast conquests in both *East* and *West-Indies*, until they arose to such a prodigy of riches and power, that they became the envy

and

and terror of all their neighbours; and that from so low a condition, that at the union of *Utrecht, Puffendorf,* in his *Introduction to the History of* Europe, says, *They coined a medal, wherein their state was represented by a ship without sails or rudder, left to the mercy of the waves, with this inscription,* Incertum quò fata ferant.

And will not trade and navigation have greater effects in these three kingdoms, whose natural advantages exceed any in *Europe?* and had two years ago a greater naval force in commission than all *Europe* could oppose against it in a twelvemonth, and would we but exert it, should hardly suffer our enemies to have a fishing-boat at sea, or to gain a penny thereon to pay armies to invade their neighbours: This is the shortest, cheapest, and best way to reduce the exorbitant power of *France,* which, when distress'd on the sea-coasts, like a human body that has one part diseased, will languish throughout, and afford an opportunity to its neighbours to make easy conquests upon it in their turn.

There are two farther considerations in favour of carrying on a *French* war by sea only, and ruining their trade.

First, What trade they lose we shall get, for by harassing their coasts, their merchantmen could not, without great risk, get out or in; the *Turkey, East-India,* fishing and sugar-trades would be rendered impracticable to them, and the bulk of them fall into our hands again: Every 100*l.* that we get by supplanting them in trade, or taking their ships, makes them so much weaker to defend themselves, and we so much stronger to attack them, which is a double damage to them and a double benefit to us; now the stronger our attacks are, and the weaker our enemy's defence, the sooner must a war terminate to our honour: And the *Spaniards,* whom we are uncapable of attacking in any other manner with success, have a proverb, *Paz con Ingalaterra y con todo el Mundo Guerra,*

Peace

Peace with England *and war with all the world;* so severely did they formerly feel the effects of our naval force.

Secondly, Money is the sinews of trade as well as war. The bulk of our expences in a sea war, being laid out at home or with our colonies, circulates back again among our people, and prevents our trade from languishing by a scarcity of money : Whereas the bulk of our expences in a land war being laid out abroad, circulates among foreigners, to the enriching of them, and the encouragement of their trade, but to the impoverishing of us, and the discouragement of our trade.

A sea war is our natural strength, and can preserve our riches, our trade, and our power. A land war is our unnatural strength, and always has proved and always must prove destructive to us.

But because the incumbrances on our trade at present have given the *French* so much the start of us in times of peace, that war seemes absolutely necessary to obstruct their growing power : Might not a compleat easing of our trade, put us in such a situation as to be above fear, consequently unconcerned at *French* quarrels, and make it contrary to our interest to be constantly embarking in them ?

To this I answer, That such a situation is one of the many happy effects of freedom in trade : For turbulent Ambition defeats itself; to what a low condition has not a set of war-delighting kings reduced the kingdom of *Sweden?* War is so far from increasing the strength of any country that it really weakens it, by cutting off several channels of trade, by oppressing the people with grievous taxes, by wasting their numbers, by lessening their riches, dragging away the laborious who bring them in, to recruit armies which dissipate them : What person that can fly from such calamities will stay to take part in them ? What nation that can avoid them would wantonly

bring

bring them on ? Countries are powerful by their numbers of people, not by their extent: *Spain* tho' larger than *France*, having ⅔ less people is ⅓ less powerful; but *France* by the calamities of war may reduce its people and power to the standard of *Spain*; and tho' it should thereby equal the latter in extent, yet would that make it still weaker, for the greater the extent of any country, the fewer the number of people to defend it, the more easy it is to be attacked with success. The *United Provinces* tho' not much above ⅓ part of the extent of *Portugal*, yet being 4 times as populous are 4 times as powerful. Where trade is most free thither people flock, as may be seen in the *United Provinces*, therefore freedom in trade may make these kingdoms more populous, consequently more powerful than *France*, and that sooner and the more so, the oftener the latter embarks in destructive wars, which if sufficiently attended to, or if our own interest only was consulted, would make us sit down quiet and easy, without frightening ourselves at every motion made by *French* armies on the continent, being assur'd that the more employment they have from their other neighbours, the weaker they grow, consequently have the less inclination and ability to hurt us: 'Tis their cultivating the arts of peace that makes them truly formidable, and which we should dread; not their losing the substance by catching at the shadow, in attempting to extend their frontiers with the loss of their trade and people; for then is our time by preserving a strict neutrality, to have the trade and navigation of *Europe* left free and unrivalled to our share, to increase our people, and therewith our power; the happiest situation we ever can be in: A situation the *Dutch* so hugged themselves in lately, that even the repeated most humble entreaties of our ministers cou'd not prevail with them to quit, by declaring war against *France*. And tho' it is a hellish policy to set other people together by the ears for our own advantage, yet if of themselves they will commit such follies, it is the height of madness in us to distress ourselves by entering into destructive land wars to prevent the *French* from doing, what we should most wish they would do.

But now methinks I see some politicians who would be thought to understand foreign affairs, shrugging up their shoulders and asking, whether we shall not be the last devoured, when our allies are swallowed up?

To such timorous gentlemen I answer, that foreign affairs, in the literal acceptation of the terms, have been shewn above to be affairs quite foreign to us; that when our allies find that we are not so weak as to take their loads on our shoulders, or pay them for doing their own business, they would exert themselves in a different manner to what they have done of late years, that they are not so easily destroyed as is imagined, that the *French* have no reason to boast of their late campaigns in *Germany;* that supposing they should destroy these dear allies, they must by so doing in some degree destroy themselves, that peace will increase our riches, and the calamities of war on the continent increase our people, and both increase our power: Now I would ask these politicians, these men of foreign affairs, what probability there is of a weakened nation's devouring a strengthened one, how by understanding our own affairs and pursuing them only, *viz.* in reviving our militia, easing our trade and promoting good officers in our navy, the mercenary slaves of an absolute monarch could devour freemen in arms, superior in numbers, fighting *pro Aris & Focis,* and what instances there are in history to warrant such a prodigy?

But to return, our prohibitions and high duties have not ruined the *French*, who make a greater figure in trade, and empty our pockets more than ever, so that unless we have thereby improved our trades to other countries, we are in a fine condition.

The authors of the *British Merchant* (ii, p. 4), writing against the shameful treaty of commerce made with *France* at *Utrecht*, in the year 1713, say, *We gain a million every year by the balance of our trade with* Portugal *and* Italy, *and near twice as much as that with* Flanders, Germany, *and* Holland, *and shall we venture the losing the gain of three millions every year from those countries, not for the sake of gaining, but of losing a fourth million every year to* France?

Let us see now how these advantageous balances have been secured to us by high customs and prohibitions.

By *Castaing's* paper of *Feb.* 3, 1740,

London gave to *Genoa*   for the dollar   54d.¼
  „   to *Venice*   for the ducat banco 51d.¼
  „   to *Leghorn* for the dollar   50d.¼

By Sir *Isaac Newton's* tables,

Genoa, the par is 54d.
    Loss to *England* about 1 *per cent.*

Venice, the par is 49d. 492 *dec.*
    Loss to *England*, about 3¼ *per cent.*

Leghorn, the par is 51d. 69 *dec.*
    Gain to *England* about 2 *per cent.*

To *Genoa* and *Venice* the balance is against us, and favourable only a small matter to *Leghorn*.

Feb. 3, 1740.

London gave to *Lisbon* for the millree 65d.
The par is 67d. 166 *dec.*
    Gain to *England* about 3¼ *per cent.*

The *British Merchant* informs us that *in some years, when corn was cheap here and dear in* Portugal (he means during Queen *Ann's war*) *our balance was so very great, that notwithstanding we paid subsidies to the King of* Por*tugal, and paid for troops, there were also vast sums for supplies of our armies in* Valentia *and* Catalonia, *yet still the over-balance lay so much against them, that the exchange has been at* 5s. 2d. *and* 5s. *a millree.*

                                Portugal

Portugal is a constant market for corn, either from *Britain* or its *American* colonies; the latter, together with *Ireland*, supply it with vast quantities of provisions, great part of the payments of which ceuters in *London* : And tho' we have no subsidies or armies to pay, as in the last war, yet the *Lisbon* exchange is so far from falling to 5*s.* or 5*s.* and 2*d. per millree*, that it has not for many years been under 5*s.* 3*d.* which can be only owing to the decline of the *Portugal* market for our manufactures, particularly the woollen. Foreigners working cheaper steal it away by degrees : Cloths between 8 and 11*s. per* yard the *Dutch* supply them with; and have beat out ours about that price entirely, as has been observed before. *France* begins to supply them with some woollens, but to *Italy* she sends vast quantities. So that it appears by the exchanges now, that not much of the supposed annual gain of a million from *Portugal* or *Italy* can now remain, great part of the *Portugal* gold brought here, being for *Dutch* account; and the moidores circulated for 2*d.*$\frac{1}{10}$ more than they are worth, by which the nation is cheated about $\frac{3}{4}$ *per cent.*

Feb. 3, 1740.

London gave the pound *sterling* to *Antwerp* for 35*s.* 10*d.*
The par is 35*s.* 17 *dec.*
Gain to *England* about 2 *per cent.*
London gave the pound *sterling* to *Amsterdam* for 34*s.* 11*d.*
The par is 36*s.* 59 *dec.*
Loss to *England* about 4$\frac{1}{4}$ *per cent.*
London gave the pound *sterling* to *Hamburgh* for 33*s.* 11*d.*
The par is 35*s.* 17 *dec.*
Loss to *England* about 3$\frac{1}{4}$ *per cent.*

London exchanges with *Norway*, *Sweden*, and *Russia*, by the way of *Hamburgh* and *Amsterdam*. *Joshua Gee*, who was also a writer in the *British Merchant*, as appears by the preface; in his *Treatise on Trade*, published several years after, supposes (p. 178), the balance we pay to *Norway* to be

the balance we pay to *Norway* to be	£130,000
Sweden	240,000
Russia	400,000
	£770,000

He

Brought over	£770,000
He supposes that we pay a balance to *Flanders* of 250,000*l.* but as the exchange to *Antwerp* appears to be advantageous, to avoid all exceptions I shall suppose we gain as much.	250,000
The interest paid to foreigners, proprietors in our funds in 1740, being chiefly *Dutch.*	400,000
Neat annual balance due to *England* from *Germany* and *Holland*, to make the *British Merchant's* calculation. .	580,000
	£2,000,000

Such a formidable sum due to us yearly, as 580,000*l.* must make the *Hamburgh* and *Amsterdam* exchanges something at least in our favour. But is it so? Alas! it appears by the course and par of the exchanges above, that this balance in our favour is not only all gone, but that we have a balance to pay ourselves, to both *Germany* and *Holland;* and it cannot be a small one neither, since it makes the exchange to both so much in our disfavour.

We are going headlong to destruction with carrying on losing trades with our neighbours; and what has brought us to this low ebb? certainly our excises, customs, prohibitions, ill-judged laws, monopolies, and national debts; these are the causes; the effects are lost trades, and decaying rents; no quacking with the effects will restore us to a sound constitution, the causes must be removed or it is all lost labour.

Before unloading our manufacturers of the above-mentioned grievances, it would be an unaccountable notion (agreeable to *Gee's* opinion) to make our ports free, but after those political fetters are taken off, having so many superior advantages, nothing could be feared but by those who envy our success: Our natural advantages are so great that they are the foundation of great part of the riches of our rivals, and that they may make the greater impression on the reader's memory, page 215,

where

where they are enumerated, should be here turned to:
And after that view will any one doubt whether any
foreign manufacturers can underwork a people untaxed,
free from oppressions, and with such advantages; 'tis an
affront to the *British* nation to suppose it.   We may
rather suppose, that by such blessings, upon every war or
calamity on the continent, the declining manufacturers
would fly to this asylum with their arts, adding wealth
and strength yearly to the nation.   We have acted upon
narrow principles, as if the trade of the world could
be made subservient to our restrictions, which are inconsistent with its very nature, and always throw it into a
new channel.   Customs have been compared to a tradesman's setting up a turnpike at his door to raise money on
his customers, and would it be a wonder if they contracted
their dealings with so wrong-headed a man?   Sir *Walter
Raleigh's Remark on the Fate of* Genoa, fully proves this,
which being formerly a free-port, was the storehouse of
Italy, *but setting a custom of* 16 per cent. *on goods imported, they lost their trade of foreign merchandize to* Leghorn, *made a free-port by the Duke of* Tuscany, *which continuing still free, retains its flourishing condition.*   If such
a duty ruined the trade of *Genoa,* what will become of
ours that is loaded on some articles from 50 to 100 *per
cent. ?*

Monsieur *Colbert* made *Lewis* the XIVth so sensible
of the advantages accruing by easing the trade of *France,*
that after declaring in the introduction to the *Tariff* of
1664, *that a large bounty should be given to encourage
manufactures and navigation,* yet he lays not such a stress
upon the bounties *as the lessening the duties on the exports and imports,* which he calls *the most effectual means
for the restoring of trade :* What effect they have had, the
ruin of our sugar, *Turkey,* woollen, and home-fishing
trades declare.

The *French* now permit the landing the sugars and

indico

indico of their colonies, at *Havre* and *Bourdeaux* for re-exportation, duty free.

To conclude the remarks on this first article. Whatever is necessary for life or manufactures, we should study to let our people have in the cheapest manner, that the poor may maintain themselves by their labour without burdening the rich, and raise taxes only on the luxurious; and, if low prices rather prevent than encourage the consumption of foreign vanities, why should we recommend them by raising an esteem for them with high customs? Let us politically, like the wise *Dutch*, tempt foreigners to encourage our manufacturers, pay our ships freights, and to our merchants commission, and warehouse-rent for the goods they lodge here upon speculation; no concern of ours what they are, we must get by them, so shall our poor have full employment, our country become the store-house, and our sailors the carriers of the world.

Second PROPOSAL.

To abolish our monopolies, unite Ireland, *and put all our fellow-subjects on the same footing in trade.*

By abolishing monopolies, I only mean all exclusive trades, not to prevent any from trading with a large joint stock who choose it, but that every one should trade in the manner he found most beneficial.

Of the Benefits arising by abolishing Monopolies, &c.

First, *It will increase trade.*

By restoring our people to their natural rights, and

allowing

allowing them to gain, by their industry, an honest livelihood, wherever they can find it.

By preventing any set of people from combining
together to raise extravagant wages for labour, or prices
for goods.

By furnishing us with the cheapest necessaries and at
the cheapest freights, the market being open for all.

By taking away from our goods all their present fictitious value, whereby their cheapness must prodigiously
increase their vent; especially the woollens, whereby the
price of wool will be raised, and its smuggling prevented.

By lessening the *French* and *Dutch* woollen-trades, in
depriving their people of our wool to assort their goods.

By extending our commerce to three-quarter parts of
the globe, where it now languishes.

By ruining all foreign *East-India* Companies, who
could not support themselves against our free-traders.

By increasing the number of buyers at home for our
goods, consequently raise their value; a company being
but one buyer.

By increasing the number of buyers abroad; private
dealers trade at a less expence than companies, and pushing against one another, must sell for reasonable profits,
whereby a greater vent is given to our goods.

By gaining us the herring-fishery, for the reasons
mentioned in page 240.

By increasing our navigation vastly; for by the fishery,
and by opening the *East-India* and *Turkey* trades, twenty
ships would be employed where one is now. There go
above twenty private ships to *Africa*, to one the company
sends.

By opening the woollen-trade of *Ireland*, that of
Britain will receive benefit (tho' the contrary is the com-
mon opinion) which I prove thus: Suppose one pack of
Irish wool of 6*l.* value, to make four cloths, that pack of

wool

wool being smuggled to *France* works up two packs of *French* wool, making altogether twelve cloths.

A pack of *Irish* wool smuggled to *France*, hinders the sale of twelve *English* cloths, supposing them of 6*l.* value each, prevents the circulating of £72

A pack of wool manufactured in *Ireland*, can hinder the sale but of four *English* cloths at 6*l.* each; can prevent the circulating but of 24

The difference is £48

It is computed that one third of what *Ireland* gets centers here at last, which on the four cloths at 6*l.* each, making 24*l.* is . 8

The benefit that *England* receives by every pack of wool manufactured in *Ireland*, instead of being run to *France*, is . . £56

The wool of *France* is too coarse to manufacture for exportation, but being mixt with one third *Irish*, makes saleable cloth; every four cloths exported from *Ireland* as above, stops the exportation of twelve *French* cloths; the foreign consumption is still the same, let who will supply the market: *Ireland* can export no more manufactures of our sorts than it grows wool, for were the *English* untaxed, and unmonopolized, they would manufacture all their own wool; if twelve cloths are wanted at any market, and *Ireland* can supply but four, and *France* for want of *Irish* wool, not any, *Britain* must supply the remaining eight.

Our colonies in *America* extend as far north, and farther south than the latitudes of *Europe*, and seem capable of raising all *European* growths; they have a more convenient navigation to the *Baltick* and *Mediterranean* than they have to each other: They build ships cheap, have land for a trifle, therefore can supply the *Baltick* with the southern growths, and the *Mediterranean* with the northern growths, cheaper than they can each other, therefore our ships with plantation cargoes, must swarm in those seas, by low freights beat out other nations, and

be

be the common carriers of *Europe*. The *British Islands*, when free-ports, by their natural advantages must be the center of the trade of *Europe*, therefore cargoes home will present themselves in abundance; and our manufactures, when reduced to their natural prices, becoming the cheapest in *Europe*, the supply for the colonies must of course be here: The labour of their white people being at present very dear, our manufactures would come cheaper to them than they could make them, and a free trade causing a prodigious demand for their growths, these would give better profit than manufactures, consequently cause them to be neglected. Besides there must be a large importation of negroes to raise these growths in our colonies, which must increase the demand for our manufactures; and as the northern colonies supply the *French* and *Spanish* plantations with great quantities of provisions, our people would have thereby opportunities to introduce the cheap manufactures of *Britain*, to which the saving the high *European* duties would be vastly conducive.

By this proposal the taxes on *Britain* will be lessened, suppose our numbers of people as follows,

In *England* . . .	8 millions
Scotland . . .	2 ditto
Ireland . . .	2 ditto
America . . .	1 ditto
Total .	13 millions

The general amount of our. taxes and part of their consequences, in p. 188, is 15,289,375*l.*

If part of the people, the 8 millions, in *England*, pay this, it amounts to 1*l.* 18*s.* 2*d.*¼ *per head.*

But suppose the tax on the consumers of luxuries to take place, adding no artificial prices to goods, but diminishing the expences of the government, yet that by

paying

paying off our debts and carrying on public works, 8 millions of money are wanted, to which the whole 13 millions
of subjects contribute, it amounts but to 12*s*. 3*d*.¼ *per*
head, not the one third of the above.

Thus by putting all our fellow-subjects on the same
happy footing, no discontents could arise, but a general
improvement spread over our whole dominions.

Secondly, *It will employ our poor*.

This is a consequence of the last remark, for the more
manufactures, navigation, and fisheries flourish, the greater
employment they provide for the poor.

Thirdly, *It will increase the stock of people*.

This is a consequence of the first remark, for wherever
trade is most free, thither people flock : If the door be
opened to receive, whatever sailors, fishermen, and manufacturers we want, will be drawn in.

Fourthly, *It will increase our riches*.

This is a consequence of the foregoing remarks, for
the abolishing monopolies making our goods cheaper, and
at the same time opening the trade of the whole world to
vend them in ; foreigners must be more indebted to us,
and the people that flock here teaching us new manufactures, or improving some of those we already have, our
wants must grow less, and the general balance of trade be
brought more in our favour.

By opening the trade of *Ireland* and the colonies,
which countries being too poor to give it the extent it is
capable of, must therefore be carried on for years to come
by *English* stocks, consequently a great part of the profit
fall into the hands of the *English* merchants : Add to
which, that about one third of what *Ireland* and the colonies get, is sent here for goods, or spent by absentees,
therefore the richer they grow, the richer must *Britain*
become.

Fifthly, *It will increase the value of our lands*.

This is a consequence of all the above remarks ; for

whatever

whatever causes trade, employs our poor, increases the stock of people, and increases our riches, must increase the value of our lands ; for the proofs of which the reader is referred to p. 250.

The abolishing of monopolies is proved to be the cause of trade, which is the cause of all the other remarks; therefore the abolishing of monopolies is a great increaser of the value of lands.

Third PROPOSAL.

To withdraw the bounties on exported corn, and to erect publick magazines of corn in every county.

Having shewn in p. 192 the prejudice we do our trade in feeding foreigners cheaper by bounties than our own people, and that the pretence of keeping up the value of lands by any method that hurts trade must prove fallacious, I shall now shew how their value may be kept up without any bounties, *viz.*

By permitting each county to form a company at 100*l.* each share, to erect magazines of corn, to be managed by twelve or more directors, one sixth part of whom to go out yearly, uncapable ever to be elected again, their shares to remain one year unsold after they go out, as a security for their past conduct.

No person capable of being chose a director who is not possess'd of ten shares.

Every share to have a vote for directors.

That the stock be not less than one quarter of wheat for each head in the county, after the computation of 5 persons to each house.

That

That they never buy but at 20*s. per* quarter of wheat precisely.

- That they never sell but at 40*s. per* quarter of wheat precisely.

Except that to prevent its spoiling, with the consent of a general court, they may sell the old corn, and replace the same quantity of new.

That they never sell but to the millers of the county, who shall give security to grind the wheat and not export the flour.

That they never sell more *per* week than the 52nd part of the corn they have in the magazines at the time of opening.

That their general-courts be impowered to enact by-laws.

Of the Benefits arising by erecting publick Magazines of Corn.

1. *It will increase trade.*

By creating this new branch which we never yet had, and by which the *Dutch* reap great advantage, and it cannot fail answering the same to us; for with regard to the proprietors it may be observed, that this is a solid trade, not liable to seizures at the caprice of foreign princes, to captures by privateers, to storms and shipwrecks at sea, or to the frauds of officers in remote countries; here the provident, who store up the excess of the bounties of nature against the unavoidable calamities of bad seasons, besides the pleasure of seeing our own people fully supplied, whilst our neighbours are complaining, will be benefited in their incomes, not by grinding the faces of the poor, but by preventing their miseries; and as corn is seldom many years together under 40*s.* the magazines may pay better interest than any of our present funds.

By rendering all our other laws relating to the importing, engrossing, exporting, &c. of corn, needless; for

when

when the fictitious value of our goods is taken away, we
can raise corn as cheap or cheaper than our neighbours,
therefore none can be imported for our own consumption
to sink the value of our lands, but only upon speculation
for better markets abroad, which a free-port trade giving
encouragement to, we should have thereby more corn in
more hands in the nation than at present, consequently
be less liable to be imposed on by engrossers, who even
could afford to sell to our own people 10 or 15 *per cent.*
cheaper than to foreigners by the freight, charges, and
risk being saved? and when any foreign demand happens,
having not only our own publick magazines for our own
supply, but also more private granaries, the exportation of
corn, so far from being dangerous, must create a trade
vastly beneficial.

By encouraging manufactures, as being a means to
keep labour low; for as the income must bear its proportion to the necessary expence, when corn in bad years is
dear with our neighbours, their labour, and consequently
their manufactures, must grow dear in proportion; whilst
our own people being supplied cheap from the magazines,
are able by cheap labour to bring their manufactures cheap
to market, whereby they make their way against foreigners,
and establish a reputation difficult to be removed.

By encouraging our navigation; for as freights must
bear a proportion to the ship's expence, so by this method
our ship-owners in general will be furnished with biscuit
cheaper than either *French* or *Dutch*, and the cheaper our
freights the more of the carrying-trade must we get;
besides, the importation of corn upon speculation for
better markets, and its re-exportation when the markets
are advanced, must give constant employment to a vast
number of ships.

2. *It will employ our poor.*

This is a consequence of the last remark, for the
cheaper labour can be performed, the more constant em-

ployment

ployment will be found; and this being a means to feed the poor cheaper in times of scarcity than foreigners, can give no pretence of raising their wages above them, but the miseries the poor now suffer in hard winters be in a great measure prevented, and the granaries and corn-trade will furnish employment to great numbers of sailors, watermen, carmen, &c. &c.

8. *It will increase the stock of people.*

This is a consequence of the encouraging trade and employing the poor, as has been before proved; to which may be added, that all times of scarcity produce distempers which carry off great numbers of people, whereas this will prevent that calamity, consequently preserve many lives; and the better the means of living are in any country, the more people will be drawn in to partake of them.

4. *It will increase our riches.*

By bringing in vast sums of money in scarce years from foreigners.   Sir *Walter Raleigh*, in his *Observations on Trade*, presented to King *James* I. says, *that* Amsterdam *is never without* 700,000 *quarters of corn; a dearth in* England, France, Italy, *or* Portugal, *is truly observed to enrich* Holland *for seven years after; that in a scarcity of corn in his time, the* Hamburghers, Embdeners, *and* Dutch, *out of their storehouses furnished this kingdom, and from* Southampton, Exeter, *and* Bristol, *in a year and a half carried away near* 200,000*l.* and he computes *their supply then for the whole kingdom carried away two millions.* Had magazines of corn been erected some years ago, what immense sums might we not have brought into the nation in the year 1740?

5. *It will increase the value of our lands.*

This is a consequence of all the above remarks; for whatever causes trade, employs our poor, increases the stock of people, and increases our riches, must increase the value of our lands, for the proof of which the reader is referred to page 250.

The erecting publick magazines of corn is proved to be the cause of trade, which is the cause of all the other remarks: therefore the erecting of publick magazines of corn is a great increaser of the value of lauds.

This proposal will prevent the price of wheat from ever sinking so low as to ruin the farmer, but on the contrary keep up a good price that must even increase the present natural value of our lands; 20*s.* of real, true, intrinsick value *per* quarter of wheat, taxes, *&c.* taken off, being as good a price as 40*s.* 9*d.* $\frac{7}{8}$ of the present fictitious value; at which last price if wheat could be kept now, the value of our lands would rise considerably, consequently must do the same when a price equivalent to it is constantly preserved.

Fourth PROPOSAL.

To discourage idleness by well regulating our poor.

Sir *Josiah Child's* scheme in his *Discourse on Trade,* chap. 2, seems very conducive to this, with some few additions.

That there be a Corporation established in every county for regulating the poor, to consist of fifty persons with perpetual succession, to be stiled Fathers of the Poor.

That the said number of fifty be constantly filled up by election of the freeholders once a year.

That all the parish-officers within each county be subordinate and accountable to their respective Corporations.

That the said Corporations have power to assess and compel the payment from every parish in their county of the medium of the poors rates raised in the three years preceding.

That

That one tenth part of the said sum be abated yearly, until the whole in ten years time be done away, and the poor maintained by the donations of the charitable only.

That each Corporation do appoint a treasurer to receive the alms of all charitably disposed persons.

That the said Corporations have power to erect workhouses, hospitals, working-schools, houses of correction, and to exercise all other powers relating to the poor, that any number of justices of the peace may now do in their quartersessions, or otherwise.

That they receive none but infants, and persons wellrecommended for their diligence and sobriety, as proper objects.

That each of the said fathers of the poor have power to commit any vagrant, or person not having a visible estate or trade, and their own disorderly poor, to the county goal.

That the said commitments be bailable.

That at the assizes for the counties the persons names so committed be called over, and those who cannot give a good account of themselves be transported for three years.

That the said Corporations have power to admit as members, having equal power with those elected, every person paying in 100*l. to the poors use.*

That seven or more fathers of the poor do make a court.

That every minister and church-warden go together once a year to every house in their parish to collect the alms of charitably disposed persons, entering the same in a book.

That the whole collection being made, the money be remitted to the Corporation the parish belongs to, with the said book signed by the said minister and church-wardens.

That all money given for the poor be accounted sacred, and that it be felony to misapply, conceal, lend, or convert it to any other use or purpose whatsoever.

                    That

That every Corporation do publish its accounts yearly.

That whatever the said Corporations want, be publickly bought of the lowest contractor.

That whatever the said Corporations dispose of, be advertised to be sold by publick auction to the best bidder.

That whenever they want money, or whenever a time of general calamity brings on an extraordinary charge, they take care to give publick notice thereof, to stir up the charity of all good people to relieve their distressed and starving brethren.

Of the Benefits arising by well regulating our Poor.

1. *It will increase trade.*

For our poor seeing that no idle vagrants can live here, but must be transported, and that none but those well recommended for their diligence and sobriety can be maintained by the fathers of the poor in sickness or old age, they must of necessity become frugal, industrious, and work at such prices as trade will afford ; not spend half of their wages in drink (as the *British Merchant,* Vol. 1, p. 7, asserts it to be *well known that ours do*) whereby no nation can out-rival us on account of the plenty of provisions of all sorts that our country abounds with, and its natural advantages for trade superior to 'any nation, the exemption from oppression by taxes, the advantage of a free-port, and other good regulations offered by these proposals ; so that our poor, by abating their luxury and idleness, will be able to work as cheap as any people, the consequence of which is a certain increase of trade.

By taking off our burdensome and unjust poors rates on the industrious, who now maintain the idle, our goods will become cheaper, consequently more vendible.

2. *It will employ our poor.*

This is a consequence of the last remark ; for as 'tis certain that they who bring their goods the cheapest to

market

market will have the most trade, so those that work the cheapest must have the most employment; for 1. It will be more constant by being cheaper. 2. Though they receive a less number of pence for wages, yet they will be more valuable by the prices of necessaries being freed from taxes with their consequences. 3. The poor being by this proposal inured to labour and restrained from idleness, they will work more and spend less, therefore be enabled to lay up a better provision for their families than they now do.

3. *It will increase the stock of people.*

Though this has been proved before to be a certain consequence of the two former remarks, yet as some people, out of a false tenderness, may think that the transporting of many vagrants may depopulate the nation, I shall endeavour to show the contrary.

1. Idleness is the root of all evil, and two of the punishments of evil-doers with us are hanging and transportation, so that idleness deprives us of many people; but this proposal tending in its nature to make our people frugal and industrious, will preserve and save many from those two calamities.

2. Idleness brings on want, diseases, death, and thins a nation; but frugality and industry cause plenty, health, long-life, and people a country.

3. Idleness disables men from supporting a family, therefore prevents marriage; frugality and industry enable men to marry and stock a country with people.

4. If this proposal drives away the idle so much the better, they are a burden instead of a benefit to the community; it will supply their places by increasing trade with more deserving people from our neighbours, agreeable to this maxim, *such as your employment is for people, so many will your people be.*

5. When our people see that idleness is deemed a crime, and punished accordingly, but that frugality and

                                              industry

industry are virtues, rewarded with good wages and a comfortable subsistence, a thorough reformation must ensue among them, the idle be few, and this objection vanish.

4. *It will increase our riches.*

This is a consequence of the other remarks, and of the proposal itself, which tends to make our people industrious; *the hand of the diligent maketh rich*, and the greater number of diligent hands we have, the more riches we shall get.

5. *It will increase the value of our lands.*

This is a consequence of all the above remarks; for whatever causes trade, employs the poor, increases the stock of people, and increases our riches, must increase the value of our lands; for the proofs of which the reader is referred to p. 250.

The well regulating our poor is proved to be the cause of trade, which is the cause of all the other remarks, therefore the well regulating our poor is a great increaser of the value of lands.

Objection. But perhaps it will be said, that the poor being left to subsist on charity only, will be starved.

To this I answer, that the great number of idle beggars we now voluntarily maintain proves the contrary; that in all times of general calamities our charity is eminent, as Sir *Josiah Child* says it was after the fire of *London*, and was again proved in the hard winter in 1789; besides, the fathers of the poor hereby proposed being persons of character and fortune, will for their own honour, by their delicate sense of publick good, and their love for true charity, take care to distinguish between the real and pretended objects of want, by which the numbers of the former will appear to be but few, and they by good management maintained at a small expence, whereby the encouragement to charity will be vastly increas'd by people's knowing certainly where to give their money to do good,

    the

the want of which certain knowledge is a great damp to our charity at present.

Therefore as we now maintain voluntarily more idle people than really want, there can be no doubt but they will, when reduced to proper objects only, be sufficiently provided for.

Fifth PROPOSAL.

To pay off our debts by publick bonds, bearing interest, negotiable by indorsement, and liquidating part of our debts yearly.

That books be opened at the exchequer for receiving money from any person or persons desiring publick bonds, which money to be applied immediately to pay off our national redeemable debts; those that bear the highest rate of interest and are of the longest standing to be first paid off.

That the said bonds, for the conveniency of trade, be for any sums not lower than 5*l.* nor exceeding 1000*l.*

That they be divided into classes according to their rates of interest.

That the 1*st* class do not exceed 3 millions *sterling,* at 3 *per cent.*
   2   6   at 2$\frac{1}{4}$ *per cent.*
   3   9   at 2 *per cent.*
   4   12   at 1$\frac{1}{2}$ *per cent.*
   5   15   at 1 *per cent.*
   6 for the remainder of the debt at $\frac{1}{4}$ *per cent.*

That the bonds of every class be numbered, and the numbers never altered.

That the interest be payable at an office to be erected

for that purpose, whenever it be called for, and a new bond given in the name of the person receiving it, with its original number, and the date the interest is paid to.

That the bonds be negotiable by indorsement to any creditor, and for any tax to the Government.

That the bonds for the amount of both principal and interest, be a legal tender for any tax, bill of exchange, note, or any debt whatsoever.

That a sum equal to the amount of one subsidy be granted yearly by Parliament, to pay off our redeemable debts and publick bonds, those that bear the highest rate of interest, and are of the longest standing to be the first paid off.

That publick notice be given in the *Gazette* monthly, by the commissioners of the office, how far they can pay off the bonds, specifying the number of the class, and number of the bond they pay to; the interest on all the included numbers to cease and determine at the expiration of three months after such notice.

That accounts be delivered yearly to Parliament by the commissioners.

That a curious stamp be added to the bonds; for though their being negotiable by indorsement only to creditors, may make forgery difficult, yet too much caution cannot be used to prevent it intirely, and give the bonds the greater credit.

Of the Benefits arising by paying off our Debts by publick Bonds.

1. *It will increase trade.*

By putting our debts that have almost ruin'd us, on a footing of being speedily paid off with honour.

By creating a currency more valuable than our coin, money lying by brings in nothing, but all these bonds pay something for keeping, and I presume that no persons

(much

(much less the bank or the bankers) would keep money by them lying dead, when they could have current bonds that bore only a half *per cent.* interest; would the bank, who are computed to have always a dead cash of above one million by them, refuse making 5000*l. per annum* profit of it at a half *per cent.* in bonds? could the directors answer to the proprietors the neglect of not adding such a sum yearly to their usual profits? would any person take out a bank-note that bore no interest, when he could have a bond carrying a half *per cent.* and equally convenient, for any trader would as soon give change for it, as for a bank-note?

By increasing the currency of the nation; for as trade always languishes where money is scarce, so the benefit by taking off all monopolies might be defeated, for want of a proper currency to carry on the flow of trade thereby caused: whereas, adding an increase of currency to an increase of trade, must carry it to a greater height than we ever yet knew.

By reducing the interest of money, which is a great encouragement to trade, by forcing people to industry, who would otherwise live idle on the high interest of their money; whereas the interest of these bonds sinking gently to a degree too low to indulge people in idleness, the possessors of them who have not lands to improve, must either find out new branches of trade, or study to improve the old; enter into partnership with traders of experience, or lend them their money to trade with, whereby private credit will be increased, and our traders enabled to buy at home with ready money, and sell at long credit abroad, which will make them steal away the trade of all those nations whose high interest will not enable them to do the same, and the lower the interest the more moderate profits our traders can content themselves with, whereby the vent of our goods must be increased; for was the natural rate of interest at 2 *per cent.* a trader who borrowed

money

money would think 4 *per cent.* good profit; whereas he who borrows at 4 *per cent.* cannot be satisfied with less than 6 or 7, and must neglect all trades that will not give that profit, which the *Dutch* by their low interest are glad to undertake, and when our case is the same, so shall we.

By making our people frugal; for a low rate of interest forcing a low profit in trade, people's expences must grow more moderate, and the less we consume the more we shall have to sell, which is the most solid way to make a nation rich.

By gaining more experience; for low profits raising estates slowly, men cannot quit business so soon for idle country lives as they do now, but must bring up their children to their business, in order to assist them in their old age, which may go on to the fourth or fifth generation, before an estate is raised to turn country esquires upon, whereby a foreign correspondency with the best houses, the knowledge of proper workmen, and the characters of masters of ships, are secured to the son by the father's experience, consequently from such a foundation the utmost skill in trade must be attained.

2. *It will employ our poor.*

3. *It will increase the stock of people.*

These having been already proved to be the consequences of the increase of trade, the reader is referred back to these heads in the remarks on the foregoing proposals.

4. *It will increase our riches.*

Not only as a consequence of the above remarks, but also by reducing those vast dividends the foreign proprietors of stocks have now remitted to them, whereby more money will be kept in the nation.

5. *It will increase the value of our lands.*

This is the consequence of all the above remarks, for whatever causes trade, employs our poor, increases the stock of people, and increases our riches, must increase

the

the value of our lands; for the proofs of which the reader is referred to p. 250.

The paying off our debts by publick bonds is proved to be the cause of trade, which is the cause of all the other remarks; therefore the paying off our debts by publick bonds is a great increaser of the value of lands.

Besides, where plenty of currency is to be had, there it will be borrowed by the land-holders, and employed in different manures, cultures, plantations, new products, whereby yearly improvements will be made, and when the corn magazines are compleated, there being no other employment for money but in trade or lands, those who did not understand trade, or care to trust their money to those who did, or who had raised sufficient estates by it, must become purchasers of land, which number by increasing, must increase their value.

Having thus attempted to shew that our natural advantages in trade are undoubtedly superior to any nation's whatsoever; that if properly cultivated they would render us more formidable than *France*; consequently than any country in *Europe*; that if we had no taxes but on the voluntary consumers of luxuries, and if our trade was quite free, all fictitious value wou'd be taken from our goods, whereby they might be afforded cheaper than any in *Europe*, and if those vast sums that now lie dead in our funds were circulating in bonds, we should raise an immense trade all over the world, a vast navigation for our protection, increase the number of our people, give employment to all our poor, accumulate riches yearly, and that all this cannot be done without vastly increasing the value of lands, which in the remarks on the several proposals I have endeavoured fully to prove, to the conviction, I hope, of those gentlemen for whose benefit this *Essay* chiefly was intended, *viz.* our country-gentlemen the landholders of these three kingdoms. Before concluding I

must

must repeat, that my chief intent herein was to remove that destructive prejudice arising from the false distinction of *landed* and *trading interests*, by shewing, that there neither is or can be any difference of interest between them; for whatever clogs trade must sink the value of lands, and that any benefit to trade, how remote soever it may seem from land, will at last terminate in increasing its value; therefore I dare boldly affirm, that the giving trade the utmost freedoms and encouragements is the greatest and most solid improvement of the value of lands. *It must be evident,* says the author of *Britannia Languens, that were our trade eased as our neighbour nations,* England *would have the superiority, since the same causes must produce greater effects* in England, *being invigorated with these our national advantages which no other nation doth or can enjoy.*

Was our trade eased and encouraged by the foregoing proposals beyond that of our neighbours, to what a height of riches and power would not our national advantages carry us? The consideration of which is hereby submitted to the legislature, which can whenever it pleases make us the most flourishing people in the world.

FINIS.

A

BRIEF ESSAY

ON THE

ADVANTAGES and DISADVANTAGES
Which respectively attend
FRANCE and GREAT BRITAIN,

With regard to

TRADE.

WITH SOME

PROPOSALS

For Removing the

Principal DISADVANTAGES of
GREAT BRITAIN.

IN A NEW METHOD.

By *JOSIAH TUCKER, M.A.*

Rector of St *Stephens* in *Bristol,* and Chaplain to the Right Reverend
the Lord Bishop of *Bristol.*

The THIRD EDITION Corrected,
With ADDITIONS.

LONDON:

Printed for T. TRYE, near *Grays-Inn* Gate, *Holborn,*
MDCCLIII.

To the Right Honourable

THE

EARL of HALIFAX,

First Lord Commissioner

For *Trade* and *Plantations*.

My LORD,

PERMIT me once more to wait upon your Lordship with a new Edition of the ensuing
Treatise, now greatly enlarged, and, I hope, in
some respects, made less unworthy of your Lordship's protection. A Treatise relating to the Interests and Commerce of *Great Britain*, naturally
seeks to shelter itself under the patronage of an
Earl of Halifax.

But there is still a more particular motive for
this address. His Majesty, ever studious of the

　　　　　　　　　good

good of his people, in appointing your Lordship First Commissioner of Trade and Plantations, hath shewn the most vigilant regard to the welfare of both, by committing this important superintendency to hands universally allowed the most able, and the most inclined to execute so great a trust with increasing success. Your Lordship, in a very short space of time, has confirmed our warmest hopes. And *Great Britain*, with its dependent colonies, form to themselves the most pleasing prospects on this occasion.

Were not your Lordship's candour great as your abilities, this inconsiderable performance would never have appear'd before so skilful a judge, nor the author have presumed to profess himself in so publick a manner, what in great truth he is, with the utmost respect and esteem,

My Lord,

Your Lordship's most Obedient,

And most Devoted

Humble Servant,

JOSIAH TUCKER.

THE
INTRODUCTION.

ALL *commerce* is founded upon the wants, *natural* or *artificial*, *real* or *imaginary*, which the people of different countries, or the different classes of inhabitants of the same country, are desirous, in defect of their own single abilities, to supply by *mutual* intercourse. If this commerce be carried on between the inhabitants of the same country, with the growth or manufacture of that country only, it is called home consumption: Which is so far serviceable, as it preserves the several professions and stations of life in their *due order*, as it promotes arts and sciences, with a rotation of industry, wealth, and mutual good offices between the members of any community. For these reasons, traffick, merely of this kind, is of great importance, though it neither *increases* nor *diminishes* the publick stock of gold and silver.

But Providence having intended that there should be a mutual dependance and connection between mankind in general, we find it almost impossible for any particular people to live, with tolerable comfort, and in a *civilized* state, independant of *all* their neighbours. Besides, it is natural for men to extend their views, and their wishes,

5

beyond

beyond the limits of a single community, and to be desirous of enjoying the produce or manufactures of other countries, which they must purchase by some exchange. Now this intercourse with other nations is called Foreign Trade. And in the exchange of commodities, if one nation pays the other a quantity of *gold* or *silver* over and above its property of other kinds, this is called a Balance *against* that nation in *favour* of the other. *And the science of gainful commerce principally consists in the bringing this single point to bear.**   Now there can be but one *general* method for putting it in practice; and that is, since gold and silver are become the *common measure* for computing the *value*, and *regulating* the *price* of the commodities or manufactures of both countries, to export larger *quantities of our own*, and import less of *theirs*, so that what is *wanting* in the *value* of their merchandise, *compared* with *ours*, may be paid in gold and silver. The consequence of which will be, that these metals will be continually *increasing* with us, as far as relates to that *particular* trade and nation, and *decreasing* with them.   And in what proportion soever their money comes into our country, in that proportion it may truly be affirmed, that our *sailors*,

6

freighters,

---

* This is spoken with respect to the *ultimate* balance of trade. For in reference to the *intermediate* balance, it doth not *always* hold true.   A trade may be *beneficial* to the nation, where the *imports* exceed the *exports*, and consequently the balance paid in *specie*, if that trade, directly or indirectly, is *necessary* for the *carrying* on of another *more profitable* and *advantageous*.   But then it is to be observed, this trade is not beneficial considered in *itself*, but only as it is *relative* and *subservient* to the carrying on of another.   This is the case, with respect to the greatest part of our trade to the *Baltick*, and the *East-Indies*:   They are *instrumental* in procuring a balance *elsewhere*, though, properly speaking, *disadvantageous* in *themselves*.   Which brings the matter to the point from whence we set out; *viz.* "That " the science of gainful commerce consists, *ultimately*, in procuring a " balance of gold or silver to ourselves from other nations."

freighters, merchants, tradesmen, manufacturers, tenants, landlords, duties, taxes, excises, &c. &c. are paid at *their expence.*

Or to put the matter in another light; when two countries are exchanging their produce or manufactures with each other, that nation which has the greatest number employed in this *reciprocal* trade, is said to receive a balance from the other ; because the price of the *overplus* labour must be paid in gold and silver. For example; if there are only *ten thousand* persons employed in *England* in making goods or raising some kind of produce for the market of *France* ; and *forty thousand* in *France* for the market of *England.*—Then we must pay these additional 30,000 *Frenchmen* in gold and silver; that is, be at the charge of maintaining them. This is the clearest and justest method of determining the balance between nation and nation : For though a difference in the value of the respective commodities may make some difference in the sum actually paid to balance accounts, yet the general principle, that labour (not money) is the riches of a people, will always prove, that the advantage is on the side of that nation, which has most hands employed in labour.

The principles of trade therefore being so *clear* and *certain* in themselves, and withal so *obvious* to any man of common *capacity* and *application,* it is a very surprizing matter how it comes to pass, that both men of good understanding are many times totally *ignorant* of them, and merchants themselves so *divided* in their sentiments about them.

As to the *first* case, perhaps it may be accounted for, if we consider what *disadvantageous* notions men of a *liberal* and *learned* education have *imbibed* of this noble and *interesting* science ; on which the *riches,* the *strength,* the *glory,* and I may add, the *morals* and *freedom* of our country, so essentially depend. Yet it has been represented as a dry unentertaining subject, dark and crabbed,

 perplexed

perplexed with endless difficulties, not reducible to any
fixed and certain principles ; and therefore fit for none,
but the *mercantile* part of the world, to give themselves
any trouble concerning it.   But upon a fair examination
it will perhaps appear, that this representation is very *false*
and *injurious*.

As to the *second*, it must be indeed confessed, that *merchants* themselves are very often *divided* in their sentiments
concerning trade.   Sir * *Josiah Child*, Mr *Gee*, Mr *Cary* of
Bristol, and almost all commercial writers, have long ago
taken notice of this difference of opinions.   But however
strange and *unaccountable* it may appear to persons not
conversant in these matters, there is a very strong and
convincing reason, when the affair is searched to the bottom, for the *disagreeing* opinions of different merchants
pursuing their *respective* interests.   The *leading* idea, or
the point aimed at by *every* merchant must be, in the
nature of things, and in *every* country, a balance in favour
of *himself*.   But it doth not always follow, that this
                          8
                                              balance

---

* The words of Sir *Josiah Child* strongly corroborate what is here
alleged.   " Merchants, says he, while they are in the busy and eager
" prosecution of their particular trades, although they be very wise
" and good men, are not always the best judges of trade, *as it relates*
" *to the power and profit of a kingdom.*   The reason may be, because
" their eyes are so continually fixed upon what makes for their pecu-
" liar gain or loss, that they have no leisure to expatiate or turn
" their thoughts to what is most advantageous to the *kingdom in*
" *general.*"—

" The like may be said of all *shop-keepers, artificers, clothiers,* and
" other *manufacturers,* until they have left off their trades, and being
" rich, become by the purchase of lands of the same *common interest*
" with most of their countrymen."

This justly celebrated writer was himself an instance of the truth
of this observation.   For, if I am not greatly mistaken, he did not
write this very treatise, *till he had left off trade, and being rich,
became by the purchase of lands of the same common interest with the
rest of his countrymen.*

balance is likewise in favour of the *nation*; much less of *other* merchants, whose interests may be *opposite* to his own. While therefore each person sees in a favourable light his *own branch* of commerce, and desires to procure all *possible advantages* to that traffick, on which the *prosperity* of himself and his family, perhaps *totally, depends*, it is but reasonable to expect their sentiments should *clash*.

Hence therefore some have thought, that a person of a *liberal* and *learned* education, *not concerned* in trade, is *better qualified* to engage in the study of it as a science, than a *merchant* himself: Because, say they, his mind is *freer* from the prejudice of *self-interest*, and therefore more open to *conviction* in things relating to the *general good*. They add, that though he may not understand the *buying* and *selling* of particular commodities, or the fittest *time* to bring them to a *profitable* market, (which is the *proper province* of a merchant) yet he may understand, in *what respects* the *nature* of *that* trade contributes to the *loss* or *gain* of the *publick*, with a degree of evidence, which perhaps the merchant never thought of: As being indeed not concerned, *merely as a merchant*, in *such kinds* of disquisitions.

But without pretending to determine *who* are the best *qualified* to engage in the study of this most useful and extensive science, let us rather humbly recommend it to the *attention* of them *both*. For undoubtedly both have their advantages; and perhaps the application of both together, might be more successful than either of them separately. If the one should happen to be *less* self-interested, by means of his situation in life, and more *open* to conviction in cases relating to the *general* good; the other, for the very same reason, is more *skilful* in the *practice* of *trade*, and a *better judge*, whether the project, perhaps so fair in *theory*, is *feasible* in *fact*.

As to the *private interest* of *merchants*, which is here

supposed to be a *biass* upon their minds, this, most certainly, coincides, *for the most part*, with the *general* interest of their country : And *so far* it can be no argument in their *disfavour*. But nevertheless, truth obliges us to acknowledge, that in *certain cases*, * "a merchant may " have a *distinct* interest from that of his country. He " may thrive by a trade which may prove her ruin." Nay more, he may be *impoverished* by a trade that is *beneficial* to her. But undoubtedly, the moment he perceives he is carrying on a *losing* trade, he will quit it, and employ his thoughts and his substance in the prosecution of some other. Moreover, as it is a *balance* in *favour* of *himself*, which is the *principal* object of his aims and endeavours, it cannot be expected, but of two trades, both advantageous to the community, he will embrace *that* which is most profitable to himself, though it should happen to be less gainful to the publick. It is a maxim with traders, and a justifiable one, *to get all that can be got in a legal and honest way*. And if the laws of their country do give them the *permission* of carrying on any particular *gainful* trade, it is their business, as *merchants*, to *engage* in the prosecution of it.—As to the great point of *national* advantage, or disadvantage, this is properly the concern of others, who sit at the *helm* of *Government*, and consequently whose province it is, *to frame the laws and regulations relating to trade in such a manner, as may cause the private interests of the merchant to fall in with the general good of his country.*

For these reasons therefore the *appointment* of the Board of Trade, must certainly appear a very *wise* and *necessary* institution. The intent and design being, as I humbly conceive, to answer this *very end*. And the

10

honourable

---

* *British Merchant*, vol. II. page 141. 8vo. Edition, 1721. See likewise the instances there given to confirm this observation.

honourable members of it may be looked upon in this light, as the guardians of the publick welfare. In *presiding* over the *general* commercial interests of the kingdom, they are to *inspect* the several branches of traffick, that are carried on, and to *give notice* to the *legislature*, whether the *profit* of the *kingdom*, or of the *merchant*, is most *promoted*; that the proper *remedies*, or *encouragements* may be applied, according as the case requires, by *stopping* up the *former* channels of a *disadvantageous* trade, *opening new* ones, which may enrich the *publick* and the *adventurer* together; *encouraging* him to *persevere*, and to *enlarge* his dealings in every branch, which is *beneficial* to the community; and in one word, by *enabling* the merchant to find his own *private advantage in labouring* for the *good* of his *country*. *Self* and *social* happiness, in this case, must be made to unite: Otherwise it will happen in this, as in most other affairs, that *social* happiness will *not* be promoted at all.

And as the affairs of commerce must for these reasons ultimately come under the *cognizance* of the *legislature*, it were greatly to be wished, that men of *eminence* and *distinction*, whose *birth* and *fortunes* procure them an admission into the *British Senate*, would employ a little more of their time in the cultivation of a science, so *worthy* of their *greatest* regard and attention. The interest of their country, and their own, do both concur in requiring such a conduct from them. I beg leave to mention not only the interest of their country, but *their own*: For it is a most certain fact, though not sufficiently attended to, that the *landed gentleman* is more *deeply* concerned in the *national effects* of an *advantageous or disadvantageous* commerce, than the *merchant* himself. If this assertion should appear a *paradox* to any one, I hope a few lines will convince him of the truth of it.

Suppose then some *general* calamity to befal the trade of the kingdom:—Or, to put a more *striking* case, suppose

pose

pose the *mouth* of the *Thames* to be *choked* up with *sands* and *marshes*, (as that fine river in *France*, the *Rhone*, really is) so as to afford no port worth mentioning for the purposes of commerce: In such a melancholy case, the *merchants, manufacturers, owners* of *ships, sailors*, and all the *multitudes* of tradesmen *dependant* upon this commerce, would indeed be the *first* affected ; but they would not be the greatest losers. For after the *first shock*, they would *easily* remove with the best of their effects, and try their fortunes elsewhere. But the *landed gentleman*, what must he do? he is *bound down* to the soil, and *cannot* remove his estate, though the persons are gone, who used to *consume* the *product* of it. Thus the evil becomes *incurable*, and *perpetual* with regard to him, and every day *increasing :* Whereas with respect to the merchant, it was only a shock at first, which he has the chance of getting the better of, by removing to a more advantageous situation.

It is fervently to be wished, that Providence may never visit us with so terrible a judgment, as the choking up the mouth of our *principal* river leading to the *metropolis* of the kingdom. But the bare supposal of such a case is sufficient to prove, I humbly presume, with irresistible evidence, that the *landed* gentlemen in the counties *adjacent* to *London*, are more *deeply interested* in the consequences of the trade of *London*, than the *merchants* themselves : And therefore, that those *supposed* distinctions of *landed* interest, and *trading* interest, in the sense they are commonly used, are the most *idle* and *silly*, as well as *false* and *injurious*, that ever *divided* mankind.

But above all, we must beg leave to observe, by way of *inducement* to the *landed gentleman* to turn his thoughts to this study, that his *very private interest* is rather a *help*, than a *detriment* to him in the *prosecution* of it. It puts no *wrong bias* upon his mind, but directs him to the *true point* of light, from whence to see, and to judge of these

affairs :

affairs: Which is a circumstance in some respect *peculiar* to his situation.

For, if we suppose the scene still to continue in and about *London*, (though the same would hold true of any other part of the kingdom) as the *private interest* of the *landed* gentleman arises from the *general commerce* of the place, he can have no *partial* views in relation to trade, nor can reap any advantage from *monopolies, exclusive* companies, or such like destructive *artifices.* The *more* persons there are employed in *every* branch of business, the *more* there will be to *consume* the *produce* of his *estate :* so that he will have no temptations to complain, that the trade is over *stocked*, or wish the *promotion* of *this* trade, in order to the *declension* of that. In short, his *own interest* is *connected* with the *good* of the *whole ;* so that he cannot but be extremely *well qualified* to *understand*, and to *promote* it, if he will please to make use of the advantages he is happily possessed of.

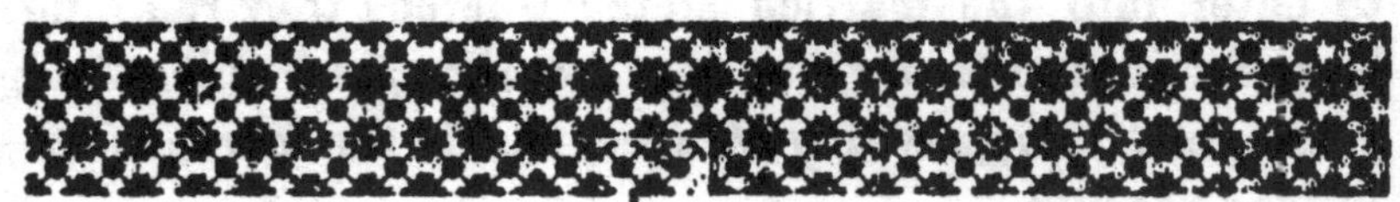

A BRIEF
ESSAY on TRADE.

The principal ADVANTAGES *of* FRANCE *with respect to* TRADE.

I. THE *Natural Produce and Commodities of the Country.*—These are *chiefly* wines, brandies, silk, linen, hemp, and oil. I do not mention *corn*, for though they raise a great deal, yet, as they are great *bread-eaters*, they *consume* a great deal, and have little to spare for *exportation.* Their harvests also are more *precarious* than ours, and often *fail.*

II. The *Subordination of the Common People is an unspeakable Advantage to them in respect to Trade.*—By this means, the manufacturers are always kept industrious: They dare not run into shocking lewdness and debauchery; to drunkenness they are not inclined. They * are obliged

15

to

---

* The law of *France*, obliges all *unmarried* men to serve as *common soldiers* in the militia and the army, unless they have *particular* exemptions on account of their *stations* and *professions.*

to enter into the married state; whereby they raise up large families to *labour*, and *keep down* the *price* of it: And consequently, by *working cheaper*, enable the merchant to *sell* the *cheaper*.

III. The *rules and regulations they are obliged to observe in manufacturing their goods, and exposing them to sale*, is a great advantage to the credit of their manufactures, and consequently to trade. All sorts of goods for exportation, must undergo an inspection of the proper officer in the publick hall: There they are compared with the *patterns* or *samples* delivered in before. The *bad*, and such as do *not answer* to their samples, are *confiscated*, with a *fine* levied upon the *offender*. By these means, the *fraudulent* designs of *private* traders, who would get *rich* at the *publick expence*, are *prevented*, and the *national* manufactury constantly kept up in *high credit*.

IV. *Their excellent Roads, their navigable Rivers and Canals, are of singular Advantage to their Trade.*—Their great roads are always in *good order*, and always carried on in a *straight* line, where the nature of the ground will permit; and made at a most prodigious expence; each province being obliged to make and repair their own roads. And yet there is no expence for *turnpikes* from one end of the kingdom to the other.

Their *rivers* are indeed, for the most part, the work of Nature: The *Seine*, the *Loire*, the *Garonne*, and the *Rhone*, with all the rivers which fall into them, help to carry on a communication with most of the great cities of the kingdom.

But their *canals* are their own proper praise; and equally deserving admiration on account of their *grandeur* and *contrivance*, as for their *usefulness* to trade, in *lowering* the *price* of *carriage*. Among these, that of *Languedoc*, and the two canals of *Orleans* and *Briare*, are worthy to be particularly mentioned. By means of the former, a communication is opened between *Bourdeaux* and *Mar-*

seilles,

seilles, between the *ocean* and the *Mediterranean*, without passing through the Streights of *Gibraltar*, and surrounding all the coasts of *Portugal* and *Spain*: And by virtue of the two latter, an easy intercourse is maintained between all the great towns situated on the *Seine* and the *Loire*. Many other canals there are, and more still *intended* to be *made*, greatly *advantageous* to their commerce.

V. *The* French *enjoy a great Advantage in the Goodness of their Sugar Colonies.*—It is not owing to any *superior* skill in *them*, or *wrong conduct* in *us*, nor yet any greater *oeconomy* in their planters, or *profuseness* in ours, (for upon the strictest enquiry, *both* will be found to be very culpable) that they *exceed* us in the *cheapness* or *goodness* of their commodities: but because our *leeward islands* are *worn out*, being originally of *no depth* of soil; and the ground is more upon a *level*, consequently more subject to be *burnt* up; whereas their islands are still very good. In *Martinico* particularly the ground is *rich*, the soil *deep*, diversified with *high hills*, affording *copious streams* of water, and refreshing *shades*. Another great advantage which the *French* have over the *English* in their sugar colonies, is their *Agrarian Law*, whereby monopolists are prevented from engrossing too much land. So that the number of whites are greatly encreased, the lands improved, more commodities raised, the planters *obliged* to a more frugal manner of living, and all things rendred cheaper. By these means *Martinico* can muster 16,000 fighting men; but *Jamaica*, which is near three times as as large, only 4,000. Add to this, that the inhabitants of *old France* do not use the *tenth* part of the sugars for *home consumption*, which the *English* do; and therefore have that commodity to *export* again to *foreign* markets, and with it to *encrease* the *national* wealth.

VI. *The* French *Colonies receive all their Luxuries and Refinements of Living from their Mother Country;* which is a very great Advantage to it.—They are not *suffered*, nor

indeed

indeed doth it appear, that they are much *inclined* to go to any other *shop* or *market* for *these things*. Neither have they set up any *manufactures* of their own, to the *prejudice* of their mother country. Indeed, as to the *necessaries* of life, they supply themselves with *them* where they *can*; and frequently buy of the *English*. But this is a case of *necessity*, which *cannot* be subject to *restraints*. As to articles of *luxury, parade*, and *pleasure*, we very seldom hear that they buy any of *them* from us.

VII. *The Manner of Collecting their Duties on several Sorts of Goods imported*, is of greater Advantage to Trade, than can easily be imagined.—In the port of *Bourdeaux* (and I take it for granted so good a regulation obtains in *other* places) there are publick warehouses, very *proper* and *convenient*, adjoining to the custom-house. And all provisions and goods necessary for the use of their sugar colonies, are there deposited by the merchant, till the ship sails, *duty-free* paying only a moderate price for cellerage. When she returns, the sugars, &c. are landed in the King's warehouses, where they remain, till the importer has found a purchaser for a proper quantity: Then he pays the duty for *that*, and has it taken away, letting the rest continue. Or if he intends these goods for *exportation*, there they lie ready and convenient. By this means he is never driven to *streights* on account of the King's duty; and is enabled to carry on a very *extensive* trade with a *small* stock. The consequence of which is, that many persons are hereby capacitated to enter *considerably* into commerce, who could not otherwise have done it. For one thousand pounds sterling in *France*, will go near as far as two thousand pounds in *England*.—Not to mention, that as there is no money immediately advanced on account of the King's duty, the whole gains of the merchant will arise only from the money *actually* in trade: Now as this is less by near *one half* to what it would have been, had the duty been all paid *at once*; consequently he

can

can afford to sell *one half* less than he must have demanded in the other case.

VIII. *Their Neighbourhood to* Spain, *and present Connection with it,* is of so great Advantage, as to be worth all their Trade besides.—For it is certain, they get *more* from the *Spaniards* than all the trading nations in *Europe.* Their *poor* from *Perigord, Limosin,* and other places, come *yearly* into *Spain* to *reap* their corn, and *gather* in their vintage; and *carry back* what they have earned to *spend* in *France.* The *fishermen* from *Bayonne,* and the neighbouring places, supply them with great quantities both of *fresh* and *salt* fish to eat on *fast-days,* and to keep *Lent.* The *pedlars* and *shop-keepers* in *Spain* are mostly *French,* who retire into their *own country* when they have made their *fortunes.* The towns in *Languedoc* supply them with cloth, silks, and stockings, *Roüen* with hats, and coarse linen stuffs; *Abbeville* with superfine cloths : *Amiens* and *Arras,* with worsted and camblet stuffs; and *Lions,* with all sorts of rich silks, gold and silver lace, &c. for their consumption both in *Europe* and *America.* In short, the greatest part of the produce of the mines of *Potosi* is brought into *France.* Hence it is, that their payments are all in *silver;* and *gold* is more scarce in *France,* in the currency of coin, than silver is in *England.* A plain proof, that *they* have the great trade to *Spain,* as *we* have to *Portugal.*

IX. *Their Address in drawing raw Materials from other Countries to work up in their own,* serves greatly to enlarge and extend their Trade.—*France* produces some *wool* and *silk;* but not a *fourth part* of what they *manufacture.* Wool they import from *Barbary,* the *Levant* and *Spain.* They also bring wool from *Switzerland.* Some little perhaps is run from *England;* but, I have good reason to believe, not much. The quantity from *Ireland* is very *considerable;* which is owing to our own wrong policy. The best of their raw silk they draw from *Piemont,* the

19

Levant,

Levant, Italy, and *Spain.* Their cotton is brought from the *Levant*, and from their sugar colonies. And the *ashes* for making *soap* at *Marseilles*, are chiefly imported from *Egypt.*

X. *They reap unspeakable Advantage, by the Permission and Encouragement given to Foreign Merchants and Manufacturers to settle among them.*—By this *good policy* the price of labour is always kept *sufficiently* low. A *competition* and *emulation* are raised, *who* shall work, and sell the *cheapest*; which must turn out greatly to the *national* advantage, though it may not be so favourable to the *private interest* of *individuals.* For these reasons, the Government is particularly *gentle* and *indulgent* to *foreigners.* And the situation of the country is greatly assistant to this disposition of the Government.—*France* is surrounded with populous, that is, *prolifick* nations, who have no trade and manufactures of their own to employ their poor. *Flanders*, all *Germany* on the side of the *Rhine, Switzerland, Savoy,* and some parts of *Italy*, pour their supernumerary hands *every year* into *France*; where they are *caressed*, and received into the army, or the manufacture, according to their inclinations. The *Rhone* is so easy and cheap a conveyance, for the swarms of inhabitants bordering on the lake of *Geneva*, that so small a sum as one shilling, or eighteen pence each person, will bring them to the chief manufacturing town in the kingdom, *viz. Lions.* And there are said to be no less than ten thousand *Swiss* and *Germans* employed in that city. The numbers also in all the other commercial towns are very great, and daily increasing.

XI. *The* English *Monopolies, which are so destructive to the Interests of* Great Britain, *become, for the very same Reason, of the greatest Benefit and Advantage to* France.—*Marseilles* is a flagrant, and a melancholy proof of this assertion. For the trade of this place hath *flourished* and *increased* just in the same proportion, as that of our *Turky*

Company

Company *sunk* and *declined*. All the fine streets and new buildings of the city, date their original from *this period*. So that we may truly say, they were *built*, and are now *supported*, by the *exclusive Turky* Company of *England*. Moreover, the *English Hudson's Bay* Company is the only cause, which can make the *French* settlements in so wretched a country as the northern parts of *Canada*, to flourish; with so difficult and dangerous a navigation, as that up the Bay of St *Lawrence*. It is this, and *no other*, is the cause that enables them to *extend* their colonies, and to *undersell* the *English* in all the articles of furr; which they apparently do in times of peace.

XII. *The publick Stock of Wealth is greatly encreased, by Foreigners of all Countries travelling among them.*—— The advantages from hence accruing have not been so much attended to, as, I humbly think, they justly *deserve*. For while these foreigners reside in the country, they not only pay for their *food* and *board* at an *high rate*, but they also *cloath* themselves with the *manufactures* of it, and *buy* many *curiosities*. But this is not all: For having contracted a *liking* to the *produce* and *manufactures* of the country they travelled in, they *continue* to use them when they are returned to their own; and so *introduce* them to the *knowledge, esteem* and *approbation* of others: This begets a *demand*; and a demand for them draws on a *correspondence*, and a *settled* commerce. These are the advantages which the *French* enjoy by such *numbers* of foreigners *travelling* among them; whereas they scarce ever travel themselves; and by that means circulate the money in their own country.

XIII. France *enjoys no small Advantage, as it doth not lose much by the Article of Smuggling*, in comparison to what *England* doth.—This is owing to the strictness of their government, the many spies they have upon every man's actions, and being able to punish the slightest offence more severely, and in a more summary way than we can, or is consistent with a free constitution to do.

The Principal Disadvantages of France *with regard to* Trade.

I. **T**HE *first Disadvantage to a free Trade is the Government, which is arbitrary and despotick* ; and therefore such as a merchant would not chuse to live under, if he knows the Sweets of Liberty in another Country, and has no attachment of Family, or Interest, to keep him still in *France.*—It must be acknowledged, his *property*, generally speaking, is *secure* enough, but his *person* is not so.   To explain this, we must beg leave to observe, that though there are *fixed* and *stated* laws in *France* to decide all cases of *property*, and *criminal* causes, as here in *England*; so that a man may know the rules he is to be governed by in those respects, and can have an *open* trial for his life and fortune : Yet there are no laws to ascertain the nature of *political* offences, or to *circumscribe* the power of the judge : So that he must be *entirely* at the *mercy* of the *Lieutenant de Police*, and his deputies ; who can *imprison* him at *will*, without assigning *any* reason, or bringing any evidence to confront him.   And therefore his *only* security consists, in being continually *lavish* in the *praise* of the *King* and the *Ministry*, and in saying nothing which may afford the least pretence to the *spies*, who *swarm* all over the kingdom, to *inform* against him.

II. *The second Disadvantage to the Freedom of Trade, is the* Romish *Religion*, which has added to its many other Absurdities, a spirit of *cruelty* and *persecution, so repugnant* to the *Scope* and *Tendency* of the *Gospel.*—Therefore a Protestant merchant, if at the same time a *conscientious*

man,

man, will find himself very often reduced to great difficulties, in order to *avoid* on the one hand the *sin* of *hypocrisy*, by *compliances* against his *conscience*, or on the other, the *danger* attending the *exercise* of his *religion*, and the *educating* of his children in the *Protestant* way. This, I say, will often happen, even at *present*; though the *bigotry* of the court of *France* is not near so great, as it was in *former* times.

III. Another great *Burden*, and consequently a *Disadvantage* to the *Trade* of *France*, is, *the great Number of Religious of both Sexes.*—The lowest computation of these amounts to near three hundred thousand persons: A great part of which number might, and would be employed in *trade* and *manufactures*; and the rest might be useful to society in other spheres. But that is not all; they are a very heavy weight upon the publick. *Vast* estates are *appropriated* for the *support* of *some* of these religious orders, whose fund is continually *accumulating*, not only by *legacies* and *donations*, but also by whatever fortune *each* person is *possessed* of, at the time of *taking* the *vow*. And others, who are of the *mendicant* orders, and are allowed to have *no property*, become a continual *tax* upon the *industry* and *charity* of the people; and these mostly of the *middling* and *lower* sort. Not to mention the increasing riches and *dead* wealth in *all* their churches.

IV. A fourth great *Disadvantage* to the Trade of *France, is their numerous and poor Nobility.*—The *nature* and constitution of that government require the notion of *birth* and *family* to be kept up *very high*, as it will always create an *indigent* nobility, and consequently *dependant* upon the court for *such* preferments as may not *deroge*; or bring a *stain* upon their family. Moreover, the same *refined* policy induces the court to make the *military* service be esteemed the most *honourable*; as it must render the whole body of the nobility *soldiers to fight their battles*; the *richer* serving for *glory*, and the *poorer* for an *honour*

able

able support. The consequence of all this is, that they heartily *despise* the *Bourgeois**, that is, the *merchant* and *tradesman* : and he, when he gets rich, is as desirous of quitting so *dishonourable* an employ, wherein his riches cannot secure him from *insult* and *contempt*. Being therefore ambitious of raising his own family to be of the *noblesse,* he leaves off trade as soon as he can, and breeds up his sons to the *military* profession, or purchases some office in the law on civil government, which may *ennoble* them.

V. The Trade of *France* suffers another Inconveniency by the *Nature of its Taxes.*—Some of these, in *certain* provinces, are very *arbitrary*; as the *taille,* which is levied mostly upon the poor *peasants* and *manufacturers* in the country villages. Others are very *heavy*; as the duty upon *salt,* which is *shockingly* oppressive. Others again, though not quite so oppressive, are yet equally *improperly* laid; because they are upon the *necessaries* of

24

life,

---

* In *France,* the inhabitants are usually *distinguished* by three ranks, or orders; the *Noblesse,* the *Bourgeois,* and the *Paisans.* Each of these are totally distinct from the other. The *posterity* of the *Noblesse* are *all* Noblesse, though ever so *poor,* and though not *honoured* with the titles of *count, marquis, &c.* as *noblemen* are here in *England.* The *posterity* of a *bourgeois,* though ever so *rich,* and though the family have *left off* trade a hundred years ago, are still *but bourgeois,* until they are *ennobled* by *patent,* or have wiped off the disgrace of having been merchants, by some *signal military* service, or have *purchased* some *honourable* employ. Therefore when the *noblesse* call the *merchants bourgeois,* burgesses, they mean it as a term of *infamy* and *reproach,* answering to that of *pitiful low mechanick* in *English.* Indeed, by some ordinances, the noblesse are permitted to engage in certain branches of *foreign* and *wholesale* trade, *without* bringing any *stain* upon their family. But these permissions will have very little efficacy to induce the nobility to turn merchants, as long as the military service is so *highly exalted* in credit and reputation *above* merchandize. The very *genius* of the government, makes it a scandal not to be a *soldier*: Laws will have little force against this.

life, which are to feed the *tradesman,* and to *victual* the *shipping.* Thus, for example, all sorts of *provisions,* corn, wine, butchers meat, poultry, eggs, fish, garden-stuff, and fruit, pay a *duty* at the *entrance* of some of their great cities. There are duties also lately laid upon *soap* and *candles.* And in the *Païs des Etats,* where the *most grievous* of these imposts are not levied, they lay a *provincial* duty upon all things going *in* or *out* of that *province,* which makes the merchandise so *passing* through, become the *dearer* at a *foreign* market.

VI. The *Maitrises,* which so generally prevail in *France,* is a *Clog to the Trade of the Country.*—These maitrises are much the same as our *companies* in *towns corporate;* only we have this advantage, that in *England* their pernicious effects can be more easily eluded by having shops, &c. within glass windows. Besides, our *best* manufacturing towns, such as *Birmingham, Manchester, Leeds,* and even four-fifths of *London* itself, viz. *Westminster, Southwark,* and all the suburbs, have no companies at all. Whereas in *France* all tradesmen are obliged to be free of their proper maitrise, before they can set up. The fine for this, in some trades, is very considerable. And there is also in time of war, an *annual* demand of a certain proportion of men out of each maitrise; which is understood to imply a *sum* of *money* by way of *equivalent.* Thus, the more these maitrises become useful to supply the exigencies of the government at a pinch, the more privileges they will acquire; and the greater the privilege is of any *particular* company, the less will be the *general* trade of the country.

VII. The *French* sustain some Disadvantage by their *Monopolies and exclusive Charters.*—They have an *East-India* Company at *Port l'Orient : Marseilles* is a free port for the *Levant* and *Barbary* trade; whereas there is a duty of 20 *per cent.* upon all merchandize of those countries, if imported into any *other* port of *France* in the *Mediter-*

ranean.

ranean. And even at *Marseilles*, there is a particular exclusive company for importing corn and wool from *Africa*. *Lions* is free for all silk entering, or going out; whereas there is an heavy duty in the neighbouring towns; by which means, *Lions* may be said to have an exclusive charter. And there is good reason to conclude, there is something of the same nature for the *Turky* cloth at *Carcassonne*, the silk and worsted stockings at *Nismes*, the clothing for the soldiery at *Lodeve*, the superfine cloth at *Abbeville*, the stuffs at *Amiens*, the camblets at *Arras*, the painted linens and cottons at *Roüen*, &c.

VIII. The *French* labour under no small disadvantage on Account of the *Expence they are at in the Article of Shipping*.—They have more men to navigate their ships than the *English*, because they are not so *expert* sailors. They must carry some *supernumerary* landmen, by the King's orders: They must have many officers to govern these men, because the merchant is to be *responsible* for them when the ship returns. These officers will have a grand table, a cook, and new bread *every* day. The ship lies long in port, if sent to the *West-Indies* to dispose of the cargo: Because their *Creolians* are said to be so *dishonest*, that they do not care to trust them with commissions. And so the expences of the officers and of the crew run very high. Add to this, that the officer belonging to the *marine* in *France*, will find ways and means to give great trouble to the merchant, both as to the choice of sailors, and of officers, unless he is *properly considered:* Which is generally done by buying some ship stores of himself, or friends, at an *exorbitant* price.

IX. The two *National* Vices of the *French*, *Gaming* and *Fine Clothes*, is a great Hurt to their Trade.—These expences cannot be supported but by a *large profit*; and *that* will always *lessen* the demand at a *foreign* market, if their *neighbours* can afford to sell *cheaper*. Not to mention

the

the *swift* ruin which *gaming* sometimes brings on, and the loss of time occasioned by it.

X. The *situation* of the *French* ports, are a great disadvantage to them, with respect to the *Hamburg* and *Northern* trade: And in regard to the *Southern* and *West-Indies*, they are not better situated; and are not near so *many*, nor so *good* as *ours*, especially if we take *Ireland* into the account. They have only an advantage with respect to the *Mediterranean*.

XI. The *Farming* of the Revenue is another great Disadvantage to the Commerce of *France*. For these Farmers have most immoderate Profits, and live in all the Splendour and Expence of the first Princes of the Blood. And as they act by the King's Authority, they tyrannise over the Subjects with Impunity.—Yet I cannot see how the *French* Government can be without such a set of people. For when money is wanted, they are ready to lend, while the subject is afraid: Therefore they borrow of the subject, giving their own securities, and then lend to the government at an advanced price, paying themselves, as the duties are collected.

To these disadvantages, it has been intimated, I ought to have mentioned their *many holidays*, on which they *must not work*, and their *pompous processions*, which draw the people a *gazing* after them.—The thought did occur to me before, at the time of writing the *first* edition: But *I suppressed* it then, and now beg leave to assign the reasons; *viz.* In the first place, these things are greatly *wearing off* in *France* every day; so that the loss of time is not so *considerable*, as one may imagine. Secondly, allowing that *some* time is *idled* away during these holidays, and in seeing processions, &c. still, if we cast up the account of the *time* and *money* which are spent here in *England* by *all* sorts of *manufacturers* in *horse-races, cock-fightings, cricket-matches, bull-baitings*, but more especially in *mobbing* and *electioneering*, (all which are not in *France*) I am per-

27

swaded,

swaded, we shall find the advantage gained over them, on the score of their holidays and processions, to be none at all; and that upon comparing both articles together, the amount of the disadvantages will be found to be greater on our side, than on theirs.*

The principal Advantages *of* Great Britain *with respect to* Trade.

I. THE *natural Produce and Commodities of the Country*; Corn, Wool, Lead, Tin, Copper, Coal, Butter, Cheese, Tallow, Leather.—All which are not to be found in *France*, in that *plenty* and *abundance* they are in *England*.

II. *The Number, Goodness, and Situation of our Ports.* —Those on the *western* side of *Great Britain* (especially if we reckon *Ireland* a *part* of *ourselves*, and include both islands under one general interest, as in *reason* and *policy* we ought to do) are almost as well *situated* for the *southern* trade, as the *French*; They are *four* times as many in number, and much better for *safety*, and *depth* of *water*. And as to the *north* and *Baltick* trade, the *French* can come into no comparison with ours.

III. *Nature has been very bountiful, in bestowing on us such excellent Fisheries*; particularly the *Herring-Fishery,* on the *Northern* coasts of *Scotland*, and the *Cod* on the *South West* of *Ireland*.—These great advantages are *always* in our power to *cultivate* and *improve*; and it is our *fault*, and our *reproach*, that we *do not*.

IV. England enjoys another Advantage by means of its *free Government*.—A merchant can go to law with the *Crown*, as easily as with a *private* subject. The *judges* are

　for

---

* Some statements supplementary to this chapter, are given in the Appendix.

for the *life* of the *Prince* on the *throne*, and consequently *not under* the *immediate* influence of the court. No man's person can be detained, but a *reason* must be given, and the matter brought to an *open* trial, where his *equals* are to be his *judges*, and to decide *between* him and the Crown, *whether* he hath committed an offence against the *State*, or not.

V. Another *inestimable* Blessing, and a great Advantage, considered merely in a *Commercial* View, *is the Liberty of Conscience we enjoy in these Kingdoms.*—Every man is permitted to worship God in the way he thinks the *right* and *true*, without *fear* or *reserve*; and may *educate* his children in his *own religion*. The *Roman Catholicks* indeed are under some *legal* discouragements: But it is plain, the legislature considered them rather as a *political*, than a *religious* sect, when those laws were *enacted*. And the *present* government, by its conduct towards them, has given them sufficiently to understand, that they shall *not* be disturbed in the free exercise of their religion, *provided they will give no disturbance to the state in civil affairs, by siding with its enemies.* This, surely, is but a *reasonable* demand: And here the matter seems to rest.

VI. England has always enjoy'd an Advantage in Trade, *as its Manufacturers have ever been in high Repute for their Skill and Ingenuity.*—Our locks, chains, clockwork, mathematical instruments, and all sorts of cutlery ware, far exceed all others at this day, and are *deservedly* preferred by *foreign* nations. And our sailors are considerably superior to the *French*, in their art and dexterity.

VII. England enjoys a very visible Advantage over *France, as the whole Bulk of our People may be concerned in Trade, if they please, without any Disreputation to their Families.*—The profession of a *merchant* is esteemed full as *honourable* as that of an *officer*. And no man need leave off trade, when he finds himself rich, in order to be respected as a gentleman. It is likewise *no scandal* for

younger

younger brothers of the most antient families to be *bred*
up to *trade* and *business*.

VIII. We enjoy a singular Advantage *by our vast
Colonies on the Continent of* America.—From *Newfound-
land* to *Georgia*, is an immense country; where all the
inhabitants do use more or less of the growth of their
mother country; and *England* again receives the produce
and growth of theirs. This is a mutual benefit, and still
improveable.

IX. The *island of Jamaica* has some advantages over
any of the *French* islands, on account of its situation, to
carry on a beneficial trade with the *Spanish* main; the
sweets of which have been so sufficiently felt during the
late war, as to need no further illustration. And this
island is capable of great improvements in many other
respects.

X. The very *Wants of Great Britain*, in *one* Respect,
might be turned into a singular Advantage *over* the *French*
in *another*.—It is certain, France *cannot carry on a trade
to most countries with that advantage to the country it
trades with, as the* English *can*.—For example; the *English* can trade with the *Spaniards* to mutual advantage:
If the *English* export cloth and stuffs to *Spain*, they can
take off fruits, oil and wine, by way of barter. Whereas
the *French* can make no use of these commodities, having
so much of their *own growth* both to *use*, and to *spare*.—
A consideration of this nature, *well timed*, and *strongly*
urged, might have a good effect upon the *Spanish* court, to
induce them to favour the *English* commerce, and discountenance the *French*. It is owing to the *successful*
application of Sir *Paul Methuen* on this very head, when
envoy to the court of *Portugal*, that the *English* at this
day enjoy the whole trade of *Portugal*, and that the *French*,
in a manner, are *excluded*.

XI. The *low interest* of money, and the *easy* and
expeditious transfers in the funds, give to *Great Britain* a

manifest

manifest advantage in the affairs of commerce. For were the interest as high as in *France*, the exportation of our manufactures would be much dearer, as every exporter would expect to get a profit superior to the interest of money; the sure consequence of which would be, a lessening of the quantity exported.—Besides, the merchants of *London*, by means of *East-India* bonds, and the quick transfers of stocks, are enabled to make a profit of their money, when not employed in trade; by which means they can afford to buy and sell for less gains.

The principal Disadvantages *of* Great Britain *with regard to* Trade.

I. **T**HE first and capital Disadvantage, is the *Want of Subordination in the lower Class of People.*—This is attended with *dreadful* consequences, both in a *commercial* and a *moral* view. If they are *subject* to little or no *controll*, they will run into *vice:* Vice is attended with *expence*, which must be *supported* either by an *high price* for their *labour*, or by methods *still* more *destructive.* The *end* of all is *poverty* and *disease*; and so they become a *loathsome burden* to the *publick. Nothing is more visible, than the great difference between the morals and industry of the manufacturing poor in* France, *and in* England. In the former, they are *sober, frugal,* and *laborious :* They *marry*, and have *flocks* of *children*, whom they bring up to *labour.* In the latter, they are given up to *drunkenness* and *debauchery :* The streets swarm with *prostitutes*, who spread the *infection*, till they are carried to an *hospital*, or their *grave.* The *men* are as bad as can be described; who become more

vitious,

vitious, more *indigent* and *idle*, in proportion to the *advance* of *wages*, and the *cheapness* of *provisions*: Great numbers of both sexes never working at all, while they have any thing to spend upon their vices.

II. The *prodigious Expence of Electioneering, is another fatal Stab to Trade and Industry.*—It is not only so much money *spent*, but it is spent mostly upon *manufacturers*; and so it gives them a *taste* for *idleness*, and brings on an *habit* of *drunkenness*, and *extravagance*. The *want* also of *subordination*, just now complained of, is mostly to be *imputed* to the same cause, as it sets them *above* controll, *frees* them from all *restraint*, and brings down the *rich* to pay their *court* to *them*, contrary to the *just* and *proper* order of society.

III. Another *very great Burden* on the *English* Commerce, *is the vast Numbers of Poor; and those every Day increasing.*—If we trace the matter to its *fountain-head*, we shall find it to be owing principally to the same causes, viz. *electioneering*, and the *want* of *subordination*. And if a *calculation* was made of the *expences* of *electioneering*, and the *ruinous* consequences of it, together with the *annual* poor tax, I am very sure it would exceed, in the proportion, what *France* expends in maintaining three hundred thousand *religious* of both sexes: So that we gain *no* advantage over *France* in this respect, through our own *dissoluteness* and *ill management.*

IV. Our Trade is greatly burthened by the *Nature* of *most of our Taxes, and the Manner of Collecting them.*—The *customs* on the goods *imported*, make those goods come much *dearer* to the *consumer*, than they would do, if the consumer *himself* was to pay the *duty*: And this becomes a strong *temptation* to our people to *smuggle*. The taxes upon the *necessaries* of *life*, are in fact so many *taxes* upon *trade* and *industry*: And such must be accounted the duties upon *soap, coal, candles, salt* and *leather*. Likewise the duties upon the importation of foreign *raw* materials,

to

to be employed in our own manufactures, are so many fetters and chains to prevent the progress of labour, and circulation of wealth. These imposts were first laid on, under a notion of promoting the *landed interest*; but happy would it have been for these kingdoms, if the *landed* gentlemen had *understood* their interest, before they attempted to shew their zeal in promoting it.

Moreover, the expensive manner of collecting all our customs, is still an *additional* disadvantage; such as the *multiplication* and *splitting* of *offices, patent-places, fees, sinecures, pensions,* &c. &c. These things indeed create a dependance upon the court, and are said to strengthen the hands of the government; but if they do so in *one* respect, they *weaken* it much more in *another.* They give too *just* cause for *complaint*; the *best* friends of the present establishment are *grieved* to see *any* measures which they *cannot vindicate.* *Repeated* murmurs, where there is a *real* foundation for them, naturally tend to *alienate* the *affections* of the bulk of the *people,* which *above all* things should be *guarded* against; because in times of *actual* danger, it is the *people,* and not *place-men* and *pensioners,* who can *save* the government, and *oppose* themselves against the *invasions* of *foreign,* or the *insurrections* of *domestick* enemies: As was *plainly* seen in the case of the *late rebellion.*

V. The *great Number of Smugglers in* England, *are of infinite Detriment to Trade.*—They carry nothing but *bullion,* or *wool* out of the kingdom, and return mostly with the *commodities* of *France.* They are the *necessary* cause of creating many offices, maintaining sloops, smacks, &c. to guard against them; and they furnish a *pretence* for adding many more. Thus they become *doubly* mischievous. They *tempt* others to do the *like,* for fear of being *ruined* in their lawful trades by being *undersold.* The practice of smuggling debauches the *morals* of the common people, it *leads* them into *perjury,* and *tutors* them up

in

in all vice and extravagance. So many *expences* incurred, so many *deficiencies* in the *revenue*, must be made up some other way; that is, by duties not so liable to be *embezzled*. And therefore fact it is, that every man in paying taxes for *land*, &c. pays for the damage *done*, or *caused* by *smuggling*. And yet *till* there is a proper subordination introduced, and the *qualification* for *voting* something altered from what it is at *present*, it is easy to see, there never can be any *effectual* cure for this *growing* evil. Smugglers are, for the most part, inhabitants of *boroughs* and *towns corporate*: They, or their relations, friends, dealers, acquaintance, &c. are voters, And——*verbum sat sapienti.*

VI. Our *Monopolies, publick Companies, and Corporate Charters, are the Bane and Destruction of a free Trade.*—By the charter of the *East-India* Company, at least *nine thousand nine hundred and ninety nine British* subjects, out of *ten thousand, without having committed any fault to deserve such a punishment,* are *excluded* from trading any where *beyond* the Cape of *Good Hope.* By the charter of the *Turky Company* a *like,* or a *greater* number, are *excluded* from having any commerce with the whole *Turkish* empire. The *Hudson's* Bay Company *engrosses* all the furr trade with the *Indians,* in an extent of country almost as *large* as half *Europe.* Thus the interest of nine thousand nine hundred and ninety nine fellow-subjects, is *sacrificed,* in so many respects, for the sake of a single *one.* The *whole* nation suffers in its commerce, and is debarred trading to more than *three fourths* of the globe, to enrich a few *rapacious* directors. *They* get *wealthy* the very same way by which the *publick* becomes *poor, viz. First,* by exporting *small quantities* of our *own manufactures,* in order to have an *exorbitant profit*; and 2dly, by importing but a few of the *raw materials* of *foreign* countries, that they may have the *higher price* for what they bring home, ——A double mischief! equally fatal to the community, both by the smallness of their *exports* and *imports.*

And as to *corporate* Charters, and *Companies* of Trades, they are likewise so many *Monopolies* in the *Places* to which they *belong*, to the great Detriment of *National* Commerce.—To convince any one of this, let him but suppose a set of *town* and *country* butchers frequenting the same market; and that the country butchers were *excluded* for a market or two; would not the town butchers raise their price? *i. e.* put all their fellow citizens under *contribution*, by means of this *privilege?*   And doth not every *other* company the same in all things they sell?   And what is the consequence?—A general dearness among one another, which must light at *last* upon the *foreign* trade, and therefore *diminish* the *quantity* to be *exported*.

VII. Our *Imprudence and Narrow-spiritedness in not inviting Foreigners to settle among Us*, is another *material* Disadvantage to the *English* Trade.—Foreigners can never get rich in a strange country, but by working *cheaper* or *better* than the *natives*.   And if they do so, though *individuals* may *suffer*, the *publick* is certainly a *gainer*; as there is so much merchandize to be exported upon *cheaper* terms, or so much *saved* to the merchant, whereby he may *afford* to export the cheaper.   Not to mention, that by this means the price of labour is continually *beat down, combinations* of *journeymen* against their *masters* are prevented, *industry* is encouraged, and an *emulation* excited.   All which are greatly for the *publick* good.

Besides, a foreigner just escaped from *slavery* and *oppression*, when he gets rich in a land of *liberty* and *plenty*, is not likely to return home, but will settle among us, and become one of ourselves, with his whole family.   And what are all *Englishmen* but the *descendants* of *foreigners?* In short, it is the same weak policy to prevent foreigners settling among us, as it is in the poor about *London*, to oppose the *Welsh* and *Irish* coming up to work in the *gardens*, and carry in the *harvest*: not considering, that if the gardener or farmer cannot have his work done cheap,

he *cannot afford* to sell the garden-stuff, bread, *&c.* cheap
to them.　So that they themselves find their account in
the cheapness of the labour of these persons.　Indeed the
English should give more encouragement, if possible, to
strangers than *France* doth; as for many other reasons, so
particularly for this, that the *Flemish, Germans, Swiss,
Piedmontise, Italians,* &c. can arrive at most of the manufacturing towns in *France* at a *trifling* expence; whereas
the *long* journey from their own country, and the *passage*
over into *England,* are a very great discouragement to
foreign manufacturers to come to settle here.

VIII. Our *ill judged Policy, and unnatural Jealousy in
cramping the Commerce and Manufactures of* Ireland, is
another very great Bar against extending our Trade.—
This is a most unaccountable *infatuation,* which has not
the *shadow* of a *publick* and *national* reason to defend it.
For if *Ireland* gets rich, what is the consequence? *England* will be *rich too,* and *France* will be the *poorer.*　The
wool which is now smuggled from * *Ireland* into *France,*
and manufactured there, and *from thence* sent to *oppose*
our own commodities at *foreign* markets, would be manufactured in *Ireland*; the *French* would *lose* the benefit of
it, the *Irish* would *get* it:—The rents of the estates in
Ireland would rise; and then the money would soon find
its way into *England.*　Besides, the *Irish* might be *incorporated* into the *English* parliament, and make *one nation*
with ourselves, bearing an equal share of taxes, and so
86
easing

---

* A clergyman, whose living is in the *West of Ireland,* assured
me, that just after the peace, the *wool smugglers* of his parish, got
upwards of 50 *per cent.* by the wool they sold to the *French.*—As long
as this is the case, *laws* and *restrictions* will signify *nothing.*　If we
have a mind to *prevent* the *Irish* sending their wool to *France,* we
must make it their interest to keep it *at home*; which can never be
done, but by *permitting* them to *manufacture* it *themselves,* and *export*
it to any market *they can.*

easing *England*, at the same time that *Ireland* is enriched.
—But more of this hereafter.

IX. Want *of a less expensive Way of Repairing our Roads*; *Want of more Navigable Rivers and Canals*; are a very great Disadvantage to *England*, in Comparison of *France*.—Every one must be sensible of the heavy tax, which so many turnpikes lay upon trade, and how bad even the turnpike roads are in many parts of the country, distant from *London*. We have no canals to open a communication between city and city, river and river, though *our* country is much better adapted for them than *France*.

X. We labour under a very great disadvantage, *as most of our Leeward Islands are now worn out*, and indeed were *never* so fertile, or of so *lasting* a soil as the *French*; therefore they require a *greater* expence to cultivate them: So that our sugars must come the dearer to *Europe*. Besides, as we use so much for home consumption, we have the less to spare for foreign markets. But the greatest misfortune is, that the planters in these small islands are suffered to monopolize as much land as they please; by which means the plantations are engrossed in a few hands, and the number of whites is daily decreasing; so that the sugar colonies now consume much less of the produce of the mother country; and yet in time of danger, *England* is obliged to be at the expence of a greater force to protect them, as they are less able to defend themselves.

XI. England labours under a peculiar Disadvantage in Comparison to *France, as its Colonies are not so much under the Command of their Mother Country, nor so studious of her Welfare*.—In many of these colonies *several* manufactures are set up, and *more* intended to be erected, which will greately *interfere* with the trade of *England*. And we must expect that this evil will not *decrease*, but *increase* by time, unless an effectual method can speedily

 be

be put in practice, to *divert* the thoughts of our *American* colonies *from* these pursuits, *to* some others, equally *serviceable* to *them*, and less *detrimental* to *us*. Besides, they not only set up manufactures of their own in opposition to ours, but they purchase those luxuries and refinements of living from *foreigners*, which *we* could *furnish* them with. It is computed, that they are supplied with at least *one third* of these articles from foreign nations; amongst whom the *French* come in for the *greatest* share.

XII. We also suffer a further Inconvenience *in not inviting Foreigners to travel into* England, and spend their Money among Us; and in *being too fond of travelling ourselves.*—It is certain, *England* has as many curiosities for a foreigner to observe, as any country in the world: The whole island, and every thing belonging to it, being in many respects *different* from the *Continent*, and worthy the attention of a stranger. And even as to fine *paintings*; original *statues*, and *antiques*, we have *prodigious* collections of them in private hands, though little known even to our own countrymen, for want of a *publick* and *general* catalogue. Moreover, our *English* travellers in *France* and *Italy*, are continually making new collections in order to carry home, and embellish their own country. And yet our gentry are so *shy* to strangers, the servants expect so much *vails*, and the common people are so *rude* and *affronting*, that very few care to travel in such a country.

XIII. The *high Price of Labour is another insuperable Bar to a large Trade.*—The causes of which are such as have been assigned already, viz. *electioneering*—the *corrupt morals* of the *people*—*taxes* on the *necessaries* of life—*monopolies*, publick *companies*, and corporate *charters* of *trades*.

XIV. We suffer a very great detriment through the *want* of *publick inspectors*, to see that our manufacturers produce every thing *good* in its *kind*: that they give good *weight* and *measure*, and fold the *worst side outermost*.

And

And what is still worse, where such have been appointed, they have degenerated, through some unhappy abuse, so far as to *increase* the evil they were intended to *correct*.

XV. Add to all these, the *discouragements* and *oppositions* which the most *generous* scheme will too often meet with from *self-interested* and *designing* men, who *pervert* the invaluable blessing of *liberty* and a *free constitution* to some of the *worst* of *purposes*. In a *despotick* kingdom, the ministry have none to *oppose* them in their *good designs*: But among us, let their plan be ever so well calculated for the *publick good*, yet if it clashes with the *private* interest of any *particular* persons, trading *companies*, or *boroughs*, (as it necessarily *must do*) then it is opposed, under various pretences, by the united force of *false patriots*, who *inflame* the *populace* with *words* and *names*, and *blacken* and *misrepresent* the *best* designs in the most *malevolent* manner.

Besides, in an absolute government, there is no possibility of gaining preferment by making one's self formidable to the ministry. Whereas in *England*, it is the *sure road* to it. A bold plausible speaker in the House embarrasses the schemes of the ministry, not because he thinks them *wrong*, but because he expects to be bought off by a *place*, or a *pension*. A news-writer, or a pamphleteer, puts every measure of the Court in the most *odious* light, in order to make his paper *sell* the *better*, or to be thought considerable enough to be *retained* on their *side*.

On the other hand, the ministry are too apt to endeavour to *quash* a motion, *not* because it was a *bad* one, but because it came from the *party* in the *opposition*. A good motion, a publick-spirited and generous proposal, would raise the *credit* of the *authors* of them too high with the *people*, were they carried into *execution*, to the *detriment* of the *ministry*. Therefore *salus* sui, not *salus* populi, *suprema lex esto*.

Thus it is on *both* sides: And an honest well-meaning

person,

person, whose views are *single*, and who is conscious to himself of no *other* attachment but the *good* of his *country*, cannot but *lament* these *pernicious* evils. And the more so, as he must *despair* of seeing them effectually *removed* or *cured*, without introducing *worse evils* in their stead,—unless men were much *honester*, and more *upright* than they are ; which, it is to be feared, is not likely to be *soon* the *case*.

                              CERTAIN

CERTAIN
PROPOSALS

For remedying many of the above-mentioned INCONVENIENCIES; *and encreasing the* TRADE *and* CREDIT *of* GREAT BRITAIN.

I. PROPOSAL.

*T*O *alter the Qualification of Voting, and to introduce a just Subordination among the People.*—When * *forty shillings* a year was fixed upon as a *standard* for a voting freeholder, it was certainly more than an equivalent to

41

twenty

---

* The very recital of the statute, which ascertained the qualification of voting freeholders, is the best proof of the reasonableness and necessity of what is here proposed.

" *Anno octavo Henrici VI. cap. 7.*
What Sorts of Men shall be Choosers, and who shall be chosen Knights of the Parliament.

' Whereas the elections of knights of shires, to come to the par-
' liament of our Lord the King, in many countries of the realme of
' *England,* have *now of late* been made by *very great outrageous and*

twenty pounds per ann. of *modern* rent. Suppose, now, that *twenty pounds per ann.* was the requisite sum for a freeholder and *two hundred pounds* stock in trade for a tradesman, to *qualify* them to vote ; the immediate consequence would necessarily be, that the manufacturing part of our nation would not be called from their work, to run *roving* after every electioneering : A proper *subordination* would be effectually introduced : The laws against idleness

42 and

' *excessive number* of people, dwelling within the same counties of the
' realme of *England*, of the which most part was of people of *small*
' *substance, and of no value*, whereof every of them pretended a voice
' equivalent as to such elections to be made, with the most worthy
' knights and esquires dwelling within the said counties ; whereby
' *manslaughter, riots, batteries, and divisions* among the gentlemen and
' other people of the same counties shall very likely rise and be,
' unless convenient and due remedy be provided in this behalf :
' Our Lord the King considering the premises, hath provided, or-
' dained and established, by authority of this present parliament,
' that the knights of the shires to be chosen within the same realme
' of *England*, to come to the parliaments of our Lord the King,
' hereafter to be holden, shall be chosen in every county of the
' realme of *England*, by people dwelling and resident in the same
' counties, whereof every one of them shall have land or tenement,
' to the value of *forty shillings by the year at least, above all charges* ;
' and that they which shall be so chosen, shall be dwelling and
' resident within the same counties. . . . . Provided al-
' ways, that he which cannot expend *forty shillings by the year as*
' *afore is said*, shall in *no wise be chooser* of the knights for the par-
' liament.'

Here we find the same cause tending to produce the same effect in former times, as in the present. Only there is this difference, that the evil could not be near so great then, as now ; because the common people were used to much greater subordination, and the trade of the kingdom was very inconsiderable, consequently could not have suffered by it in any degree to what it doth at present. And yet, if such were the reasons which induced the legislature to pass the above-recited Act at that time, how much more reason have we to follow their example now ?—The present value of *forty shillings*, is not a tenth part of what they intended : Therefore, if we would keep up to the *spirit* and *meaning* of this law, we should at least fix the qualification at *twenty pounds per annum.*

and debauchery might be *executed*; and smuggling in a great measure *suppressed* : And all this without running the *risk* of *disobliging* such voters, and *losing* their votes. Moreover, when things were put upon such a footing, it would be a matter of *honour* and reputation to have a vote ; and consequently the voter would pique himself more upon his *integrity* and *uncorruptness*, than he now doth. He would be above that *bribery* and *corruption*, which appear so openly and avowedly *on all sides*, at present, throughout the kingdom. Likewise a spirit of *emulation* and *industry* would be excited ; and the *privilege* of voting would become a laudable inducement to every *artificer*, (not to get *drunk*, or to take a paltry *bribe*, as at present is the case) but to be *frugal* and *saving*, in order to raise himself to the degree of a *voter*. And many artificers might accomplish this by a *few years* industry after they are set up. The number also of the poor would consequently be *lessened*; the price of labour *reduced*; and the persons themselves, who would be debarred of voting by such a supposed Bill, much *happier*, much *richer*, and *quieter* than they now are. Add to this, that a *militia* for land service, and a *register* for the sea service, might then be introduced, if it was judged expedient ; whereas at present it is *impracticable*; because such a power wherever lodged, would infallibly be applied to the bad purposes of *influencing* votes at the time of elections.

II. PROPOSAL.

To erect certain courts in all manufacturing places of the kingdom, where the chief dealers themselves shall petition for them, with the title of * guardians of the

43

morale

---

* The complaints against the morals of the manufacturing poor become louder every day, and certainly demand, if any thing doth, the *serious* attention of the *legislature*. *Combinations* of journeymen

morals of the manufacturing poor. Perhaps something to the following effect, might suggest *hints* to be *improved* upon.

44

The

---

to extort *exorbitant* wages.—This money spent in *drunkenness* and *debauchery*, so that they are the *poorer* rather than the *richer* at the *week's* end, by the *advanced* price,—their *unfaithfulness* to their *trust* —the *badness* of their work, whenever their masters have a great *demand*, and dare not *turn* them *off*,—the *increasing* number of the poor ; these, and many other articles of the like nature, are the complaints *justly* made on this head.

A certain very *ingenious* gentleman, and himself a *great* manufacturer in the clothing way, has attended to them with great assiduity; and is engaged in a scheme which he intends to exhibit to the publick, of a *very singular* nature, for the reformation of these abuses. He has carefully observed, that in *exceeding dear* years, when corn and provisions are at an *extravagant* price, then the work is *best* and *cheapest* done :—but that in *cheap* years, the manufacturers are *idle*, wages *high*, and work *ill done*. He has carried these observations through many years back ; and confirmed them by the testimony of several great writers upon trade.

Therefore he infers, that the high duties, taxes, and excises upon the necessaries of life, are *so far* from being a *disadvantage* to trade, as things are circumstanced among us, that they are *eventually* the chief support of it :—and ought to be *higher still*, in order to oblige the poor either to work or starve.

Some things may certainly be said in favour of this scheme. But an humane and compassionate man cannot but be *sorry*, to see the morals of the poor so *very corrupt*, as to oblige any one to think of *such* an *expedient*. In the mean time, as much may be said against it ; and as it would involve the *innocent* as well as the *guilty* in the same punishment ; perhaps some *other* expedients would better answer the good end proposed, and not be liable to the same objections. If the qualification for voting was settled as in the *first* proposal, and court guardians erected, as proposed in this ; and foreign manufacturers naturalized, in order to keep down the price of labour, and prevent any combinations among our own people, (as shall be mentioned in a succeeding proposal) perhaps the morals of our poor would be as unexceptionable, and the price of labour as cheap as in any other trading country.

But which ever scheme is right, or if neither are, the affair itself deserves the most serious regard of every one, who wishes well both to the *souls* and *bodies* of his fellow creatures, and the *good* of his *country.*

The *qualifications* of each member of this court to be as follows; 1*st*, That he employs not less than twenty manufacturers on his *own account*, the greater part of the year? By this regulation, the most *eminent*, as well as the most *concerned*, will be the only persons admitted. 2*dly*, That each member subscribes a certain sum, suppose two guineas at least, every year, towards the good purposes hereafter to be mentioned; but that they be admitted to receive the legacies and donations of others. 3*dly*, That each member be a *married* man, in order to set the good example here recommended.

The aim of this court to be to *discourage* vice, idleness and debauchery,—and to *encourage* industry, probity and fidelity, in the lower class of people.

The means to effectuate these good designs, with great submission, perhaps may be as follows;

1*st*, By *removing all temptation*, as much as possible, out of the way; to which end, this court guardian shall have the *sole power* of *judging*, how *many ale-houses*, &c. are necessary to be *licensed* in their respective districts: That is, they shall *not* have a power to *exceed* the number allowed by the justices, but to *lessen* them as much as they *please*. Neither shall they have the power to *nominate* the persons to be *licensed*; but after they have delivered in their lists, the justices shall nominate,—unless the justices delay to do it for a month after delivery: In such case, they shall be impowered to nominate themselves. They shall likewise have the power of levying a *certain* fine by distress of goods, or in default of that shall inflict corporal punishment, on all persons who keep *cock-pits*, *skittle-allies*, and all such places for the resort of the common people, within their district, also those who set up *stages* for *cudgel-playing*, &c. or *booths* for *horse-races*, or bring liquors, cakes, fruit, or any like temptations, to draw people together. They shall also be impowered to *expel* out of their district, all such common people as cannot give a good account of themselves by what means they subsist; and shall particularly be enabled to remove such *women,* as are *suspected* to have a *bad character,* unless they can clear themselves from the imputation, by the oaths of three, at least, of their neighbours of good *substance* and *repute,* that they believe them to be *innocent* of the charge, and esteem them to be *honest, chaste,* and *sober* persons.

2dly, These court guardians shall endeavour to *encourage* industry, probity, and practical religion, by the following methods; *viz.* By allowing forty shillings apiece to any young couple going to be married, that can make it appear by the testimony of their masters, that they have *saved* three pounds and upwards, by *working* in their service; and have *behaved well.* If *each* of these can produce such a character, then this forty shillings to be made four pounds. But not to be paid till a year and a day after marriage, during which time they are still to behave well. By allowing also something *discretionally* to those, who are over-burdened with large families, or are sick, whose characters are known to be good: By presenting also a few good books, to the *remarkably* diligent and industrious. Suppose these were the *Bible,* and *Gastrel's Christian Institutes;* which are books that no persons of ever so different religious perswasions can object to. If these were neatly bound, gilt on the back and leaves, with a cloth case, and had stampt on one side in gold letters,

The Hand of the Diligent maketh Rich;

And on the other,

To the Praise of them that do well;

they would be kept as *family pieces,* and *trophies;* and might *excite* the same laudable *emulation* in their *posterity,* which it had done in *themselves.*

N. B. The district here so often mentioned, is supposed to be *ten miles* round from the town or place appointed for

46

keeping

keeping this court. The court to sit every month, at least, for the dispatch of business, wherein the attendance of *three* members will be sufficient: And every quarter a general meeting, which must be composed of seven.

These are only offered, with great submission, to the publick, as *hints* to be improved upon. The *importance* of the affair requires that *some* expedients should be *tried* without *delay*. If these are judged improper, the author would exceedingly rejoice to see better in their room; and those effectually carried into execution.

III. PROPOSAL.

To *incorporate both the* British *isles together, and to make* one kingdom *in all respects, as to parliament, trade and taxes.*

This proposal of *incorporation* has long been the wish of every generous *disinterested patriot* of both kingdoms. And indeed, inexpressibly great would be the benefit on *both sides*. The *Irish* would share in the advantage of *our trade*, and *we* in *theirs*. By permitting them to *get rich* at the *expence* of the *French*, they would be *enabled* to *ease* us of the *burden* of the *worst* and heaviest of our *taxes*: Whereas at present, the *French*, thro' our own *unaccountable* infatuation, *get rich* at *their expence*. By this *mutual* benefit, neither kingdom would be looked upon as *foreign* to the other: But the goods of both would be imported *duty-free*, or perhaps be considered only as coming *coastwise*. The *hostile* prohibition against *wearing*, or *using* the produce of either kingdom, would be *repealed*; and all that *unnatural war* between the commerce of the two nations, would be *at an end:*—which would be attended with these further happy consequences, that many of the *necessaries* of life would be imported *cheaper* into *England*,

than

than they now can be purchased; a great *advantage* this to the *merchant* and *manufacturer*:—and many more of the *luxuries, ornaments,* and *delicacies* of living, would be *exported* from hence into *Ireland.* For most certain it is, that in proportion as *Ireland* grew *rich*, they would take the *lead* for the *richest* of their *cloaths, furniture, plate, jewels, equipages,* &c. &c. from *England.* Likewise the inducements of being near the *Parliament,* the *Court,* the *Publick Funds,* &c. would bring many more *Irish* families to *reside,* and *spend* their fortunes here, than now do. In short, whatever wealth *Ireland* would draw from other countries by its produce, manufactures, and happy situation; all that would continually *center* in *England.*

But here, methinks, I hear self-interest making an outcry, "*They would* run away *with our trade.*" But pray let me calmly ask, *who* would run away with it? or *where* would they run to? Why truly *our own people,* our *own countrymen,* (who may as justly be *called* so, as the inhabitants of any *neighbouring* county,—and are some of the *best,* and most *faithful* subjects the government has) would perhaps carry *some part* of a manufacture *from* us *to* themselves. But what *detriment* would this be to the publick? The people of *Yorkshire* have done the very same thing by *Glocestershire* and *Wiltshire.* Let us therefore have a meeting of the clothiers of these two counties to petition the parliament, that the *Yorkshire looms and mills* may be all *broke* and *destroyed: For they have run away with our trade.* This is so *ridiculous* and *absurd* a proposal, that I believe there is no person living, but must *see* and feel it to *be so.* And yet let me ask, is not this the *very case* with respect to the objection against incorporating with *Ireland?* Or if there be a *difference* between the two cases, I should be glad to know *wherein* it consists? Is *Ireland* to be looked upon as a distinct kingdom?—more is the pity: For as the two kingdoms have but one *common head,*—one *common interest* both in *Church* and

State,—the *same* friends,—and the *same* enemies; they ought to have been long since *consolidated* together. But allowing it to be *called* a distinct kingdom at present, *till it is united:*—so is *Yorkshire* a *distinct* county, and was formerly, in the times of the Heptarchy, a *kingdom* likewise *distinct* from the two counties above mentioned. Is *Ireland* a great way *distant* from *England?* *Yorkshire* is at a greater distance still from the counties above mentioned. And the *communication* between them is not *so easy* by *land*, for the *purposes* of *commerce*, as the *other* is by *sea*.

 " But Ireland *is more advantageously situated for the* " *trade to the* West-Indies; *therefore—*" Therefore we must deny our *own people* the *benefit* of *trading*, because they are *advantageously* situated for *carrying it on.* This is a *weighty argument*; *Bristol*, for instance, is *better situated* for the *Irish* trade than *London*; therefore let us *Londoners* petition, that the port of *Bristol may be locked up.*

It would be an endless, and a tedious piece of work, to wade through such *gross* and *palpable* absurdities. One thing is plain and obvious, that *self-interest*, the *bane* of all publick good, is *driven* to *hard shifts*, in order to *cover* such *views* as she dare not *openly avow.* If *England* itself was divided into *two* kingdoms, one comprehending all the south, the other all the north side of the *Thames*, and there were *hostile* prohibitions against *importing* certain sorts of goods from *London* to *Southwark*, and *vice versa*, and *high duties* upon all the rest: Many individuals on both sides, would find their own *private interest* in upholding the division, and would cry out, upon any proposal being made for an *union—these foreigners will run away with our trade—they are better situated than us—our trade is in danger.* But would this cry weigh with upright men on both sides, who had the welfare of the community *truly at heart?*—If it *would not*, what shall we think of the *same*

same argument, when urged *against Great Britain's* incorporating with *Ireland.*

IV. PROPOSAL.

After such an union of the two kingdoms, as above proposed, *to lay by degrees the* English *taxes upon* Ireland; *and to ease the* English *of the most burdensome of theirs in the same gradual manner.* Suppose, therefore, the first year, that the *English* laws of *excise,* and the duties upon *French wines and brandies,* are extended to *Ireland;* then *England* might be *eased* of the *salt tax,* the *same* year, or the *following* one. If in the second year *Ireland* were charged with the *stamp* and *paper duties, England* might be *discharged* of the tax upon *soap* and *candles.* If in the third, a tax was laid upon the *window-lights* in *Ireland,* the *coal duties* might be *taken off* from *England.* If in the fourth, the tax was laid upon *coaches,* this would enable the parliament to *discontinue* the duty upon *leather.* Lastly, If in the fifth year, *Ireland* was subjected to a *land-tax,* this would ease the *lands* and *houses* of *England* of at least *one third* of their *burden.*

V. PROPOSAL.

To *set up woollen and silk manufactures in the west of* England, *and south-west of* Ireland, (supposing the former proposals to take place) *in order to rival the* French.

The price * of labour is as cheap in *those parts,* as any

50

where

---

* The price of labour at the places under mentioned was given me, as follows:

At *Lisle,* the wages of journeymen stocking and camblet weavers, where in *France*.   And when a proper *subordination* is introduced, the temptation of *electioneering* removed, the most grievous of our taxes *abolished,* and a trade set open ; it is probable, that labour might be still *much cheaper* : By which means, the *French* might be cut out of a great deal of their *Levant,* and *Spanish* trade.

Moreover, when the woollen manufactures come to be effectually established in those parts, it will be next to impossible to *run* the wool to *France :* For both the wool itself will bear a *better* price, so as not to make it worth their while ; and each *manufacturer* will be a kind of *centinel,* to prevent its being exported *unmanufactured.*   This therefore I humbly conceive, is a much better scheme of prevention, than that of the Reverend Mr *Smith,* in his

51   *Memoirs*

---

about 24 *sous per* day, *i. e.* about 13 pence *English* ; a *sous* being a little more than an halfpenny.

Abbeville and *Amiens :* Journeymen weavers, and cloth-workers, according to the nature of the work, and their dexterity, from 20 to 50 *sous per* day.

Ditto : To women employ'd in the manufacture, not more than 12 *sous per* day.

Hedgers and ditchers in the country, about 10 *sous per* day.

Nantes : Journeymen ship-carpenters, about 30 *sous per* day.

Castelnaudary : Labourers mending the canal of *Languedoc,* by the jobb, earn about 12 *sous per* day.

Nismes : Journeymen weavers in the silk and stocking trade, from 30 to 35 *sous per* day.

Marseilles : Journeymen taylors 30 *sous* per day.—Ditto carpenters, 30.—Ditto silk-weavers, from 30 to 35 *sous per* day.

Toulon : Journeymen carpenters in the King's yards, 30 *sous per* day.

Lions : Journeymen workmen have several prices, according to the silks, velvets, gold stuffs, lace, &c. &c. from 50 to 100 *sous per* day.

Land-carriage of goods from *Marseilles* to *Lions,* and *vice versa,* (230 *English* miles) which is often done either for speed, or safety ; the *Rhone* being difficult to mount, and fine goods may take damage in going down, *per* hundred, (108 *lb. English*) from 6 to 7 *livres. N.B.* A *livre* is 10 pence halfpenny *English.*

Memoirs of * *Wool*; for it answers *all* the *ends* proposed by him in that scheme, and is subject to *none* of those inconveniencies which his is *generally supposed* to be attended with. This gentleman,—for his *indefatigable* labours in collecting *all* that has been ever said upon the subject, and presenting it to the reader in *one view*,—for his *judicious* remarks, and the pains he has taken in correcting many *popular* errors, which had too generally prevailed,—most justly deserves the *universal* thanks and applause of his country.

But among the several requisites necessary to enable us to rival the *French* in the *Levant* and *Spanish* trade, one, and which ought principally to be regarded, is, *to lay the trade open.* Wherefore I now proceed to the

VI. PROPOSAL.

Viz. To *lay open and extend our narrow and restrained companies*; beginning with the *Turky* and *Hudson*'s Bay Companies, which hurt the trade of *Great Britain* more essentially with respect to *France*, than any other company can do.

<table><tr><td>52</td><td align="right">Here,</td></tr></table>

---

* The scheme of prevention proposed by the reverend and ingenious author of the Memoirs of Wool, is to this effect ; " That the ports be opened for exportation, but that such a duty be laid upon the wool, as shall greatly *discourage*, or rather *absolutely prevent* the exportation of it ; unless the markets in *England* happen to be so low, and those abroad so high, that the difference in the price would countervail the expence of carriage, freight, and the duty paid at exportation." This is his scheme fairly stated : Upon which I shall only make this brief remark, that the quantity of wool run from *England* is *extremely inconsiderable*; the difficulty, danger and expence of smuggling, together with the *hush-money*, necessary on such occasions, being already almost a sufficient bar : But if his scheme took place, the quantity exported of long *combing* wool to make *stuffs*, which the *French* chiefly want, would sometimes be much greater, and the price at home always *dearer* than it is at present.

Here, again, that *watchful dragon*, self-interest, *will be apt to take the alarm*; and I do not expect any thing I can say will have charm enough to lay him asleep. Many specious reasons have been offered in favour of *exclusive companies*; which, though they convinced none but those that were *interested* in them, yet they served to perplex a debate, by drawing off mens attention from the true merits of the cause.

I shall endeavour therefore, for the sake of such as have *honest* intentions and a *publick spirit*, to give an *impartial* state of the case, with as much clearness and conciseness as I can.

First then, I will *allow*, that in *certain* cases, and at *certain* junctures, exclusive companies might have been a *prudent* institution, *calculated* for the *publick good*; as,

1*st*, In order to introduce arts, sciences, and manufactures among a *barbarous* and *savage* people: Which was the case with the late *Czar* of *Muscovy*. It was necessary for him, in his *circumstances*, to give such *extensive* privileges to merchants and tradesmen to come and settle in his country, as would *over-balance* the temptation of *self-interest* for *residing* any where else.

2*dly*, In order to induce *skilful* artificers to come and instruct an *ignorant* people; which undoubtedly they will *not do*, unless upon a *valuable* consideration. This was the case with our *English* princes about two hundred years ago, in granting so many privileges and exemptions to the *Flemish*, and other *foreign* manufacturers.

3*dly*, In order to conquer the deep-rooted habitual *laziness* of a people, by bringing examples of industry and the good effects of it, before their eyes. This, among other reasons, is much the case with the *Spanish* Court at present, in being so desirous of introducing foreign manufacturers into *Spain*.

4*thly*, In order to have a *large capital*, sufficient to embark in any hazardous undertaking, which may call for

great

great sums to be expended, before the *project* can be brought to bear, and the *trade* to answer.   And whereas no *private persons* by themselves, or *voluntary associations*, can be supposed equal to such an undertaking ; therefore when individuals *refuse* or *decline*, it is but reasonable that those who adventure in a joint stock should be incorporated, and have a privilege excluding all others from interfering in this new branch of commerce, * till the adventurers are *sufficiently paid* for the *risks* they ran, and the *expences* they were at.

Now all these are very good and sufficient reasons, *where they hold*, for the establishing of *exclusive* companies. For it is better to have the trade of an exclusive company, than *no trade at all*.   And in *process of time*, according as the reasons for *continuing* them *do cease*, the trade should be laid open.

5*thly*, There is also another reason in certain governments, whose *credit* is not esteemed *good* with the *people*, for the erecting of such publick bodies.   And that is, for the sake of *borrowing money* at an *exigence*, when individuals will *not trust* them.   This, I believe, *was* the case with our *own government* in *former* times.

But 6*thly*, There is still a further motive remaining, which, though a very *bad* and *scandalous* one, yet it is to be feared, hath had the *greatest* share in erecting *monopolies* of all the rest.   And that is, in plain, but very expressive *English*, jobbing.   And most of the charters for monopolies, which were so *plentifully* granted in the time of King *Charles* the Second, whose *pleasures* made himself and his

54

courtiers

---

* If private persons will not associate voluntarily to embark in some hazardous undertaking, the better way would be, to allow a sufficient premium or bounty to encourage *all* adventurers, rather than to grant exclusive privileges to a *few*.   For both the one and the other are a *charge* on the publick ; but the monopoly is by much the worse, the dearest, and the most difficult to be broken through.

courtiers very *needy* of money, *betray* the *original* from which they were derived. Particularly that *famous* one for the *Hudson's* Bay Company, which is a grant without any *bounds* or *limits* of *seas, mountains, rivers, degrees* of *latitude* or *longitude*; and therefore, *if valid*, might *impower* the company to *challenge* all the lands of *America*, which were *not disposed* of by *prior grants*, as well as the coasts on *Hudson's Bay*.

But enough, I hope, hath been said, as to the reasons for the institution of exclusive companies.

My second attempt therefore, will be to shew, that *none* of *these reasons* do *hold* in *our* present circumstances. For *if* any of them do, let me ask *which?* Is it the first, second, or third? I believe the most sanguine advocate for exclusive companies, will not insist upon either of these. Is it then the fourth?—This, I am aware, will be *chiefly* insisted on.—Not that it can be pretended at this day, that private adventurers are either *unable*, or *unwilling* to engage in *any trade* carried on by a company, were it *laid open*; but the pretence is, that a *recompence* should be made them, *before* they are *dissolved*, for the *expences* they have been at. And doubtless, if the *original* adventurers, or their *representatives*, can make it appear, that they have not yet received a *reasonable* profit for the money *advanced* by them to make a *capital stock*, the publick will consider them *so far*, as to make good the *deficiency*. They have a plea of *right* and *equity* for this. But they have no colour of right for any *imaginary* value, which they may put upon their stocks. Nor is the publick concerned to regard it: Nay, the very plea defeats itself: For if their stocks have been really sold in the market greatly *above par*, this is a plain proof, that they have received a *reasonable* profit *already*, for the money advanced to make a capital. And therefore *ought not* to have any *farther compensation*.

To proceed: As to the fifth reason for exclusive companies, there can be no pretence for it any longer in our times.

times. For it is well known, the credit of our government
is so good, that individuals rather *chuse* to lend their money
upon *publick*, than *private* securities. And that they do
it even on *cheaper* terms.

Wherefore, lastly, if these *nusances* to a *free trade*, and
the *publick good*, shall *still continue*, it is too plain, that
they will owe their *preservation* to the *same cause* that gave
them *birth*, viz. A job. But that I may express my utter
dislike against them, in common with *every* other disinterested man, who *wishes well* to the good of the *whole community*, I shall go on,

Thirdly, To point out a few of the *principal* evils, and
destructive consequences attending them.

In the 1*st* place, These *exclusive* companies *cannot*
trade, *if they were inclined*, upon so *easy* terms, as *private*
adventurers *would do*, were the trade *laid open*. So many
*directors, supercargoes, storehouse-keepers, factors, agents,
clerks*;—and all the *pickings* of their *several dependants*:
—So many *fees, sweetnings*, &c. from the *manufacturer*, or
under merchant, that *his goods* may have *the preference* to
others,—and the *expences* of *carrying* many sorts of goods
from *distant* parts of the country, *where* they are *manufactured*, up to the *metropolis, there* to be *shipped* off, instead
of being exported from the *next convenient* port:—*Expences* of *warehouses*, &c. &c. make it *impossible* for any
corporate company to trade upon an *equal footing* with
private adventurers:—And consequently of *extending* their
dealings so far as if the trade was open. ☞ For this
reason it has been *always* found, that if *private* adventurers shall be *permitted* to *engage* in the *same* trade, they
will infallibly carry it away from the company.* And

56

upon

---

* We have a *convincing* proof of the truth of both those observations, 1*st*, in the case of the *African* Company, and the *Bristol* and
Liverpoole traders: 2*dly*, we have another, and a *woful one*, in that
of our *English* Company trading to *Turky*, and the *French* trading

upon the same principle, if there are two nations, *rivals* in the *same trade*, that nation which permits a *free* and
57
open

---

thither also from *Marseilles*. Our *English* Company had formerly *all* the trade for cloth to the *Levant* : Which being observed by the *French*, ever *jealous* of the *English* commerce, they set up manufactures of their own in *imitation* of them. These manufactures still bear the *name* from whence they were derived, viz. *Londrins premiers—Londrins seconds.—Londrins larges.—*But they have so *supplanted* the trade of *London*, because it is in the hands of an *exclusive* company, that the *English* have *little* or *nothing* of a trade, *comparatively* speaking, in those parts. Whereas the *French* shipped off to the *Levant*, the very day the seas were free, after the peace, *July* 1⅔, 1748, four thousand bales of the above-said cloth : Each bale, one with another, worth about 1200 livres. That is about 210,000*l.* sterling in all.

If it should be said, that the *French* have gotten this trade from us, *not* so much on the account of the *disadvantage* we *labour* under from an *exclusive* company, as the *advantageousness* of their *situation*. I have this further remark to offer ; *viz.* That if the trade was *open, we* have many advantages which they have not, to *counterbalance* the inconvenience of our situation.—They are obliged to *import* most of their wool from *Turky, Spain*, or *Africa*, into *Marseilles* ; and to carry it *chiefly* by *land-carriage* from thence to *Carcassone*, about 130 miles.—Then to carry the cloth back to *Marseilles* which cannot be done at a *small expence.* They are also obliged to fetch *tin, lead,* and *shot* from *England*, and *spices* from *Holland*, for the *Turky* markets ; in *all* which we have most certainly the *advantage* over them. And therefore, if we had *woollen* manufactures erected in the west of *England*, and the south-west of *Ireland*, (according to Proposal V.) where *labour* is as *cheap* as in *any* part of *France*, where we have *wool* on the spot,—and when manufactured, might be *immediately exported*, without being carried up to *London* ;—where *tin, lead,* and *spices*, may be had upon much *easier terms* than they can at *Marseilles* : I say, with *all these* advantages, and an *open trade*, we could more than *counterbalance* any advantage that the *French* can draw from the *situation* of *Marseilles* : And then we might *import* the *raw* materials of *silk, camels hair, skins,* &c. much *cheaper* than at present, to the emolument of *thousands* of families. But for a more particular detail of the nature of the *Turky* Company, see a little tract just published, entitled, *Reflections on the Expediency of opening the Trade to Turky*, printed for *T. Trye, Holborne.*

open trade, will *always* be *superior* to the other, which *confines* it to a company : *Other* circumstances supposed to be *equal*, or *nearly so.*

2*dly,* As they cannot trade so cheap as private adventurers, *even were they inclined,* ☞ They must therefore *necessarily omit* many *lesser branches,* as *not answering* their *expense,* which in the hands of *individuals* would turn to good *account,* and perhaps give *bread* to *thousands* of families. These articles are called *lesser,* not because they are *less extensive,* for perhaps in *that respect* they may be the *greatest,* but because they are *less gainful;* which therefore a company must leave *untouched,* unless they will trade to their *own loss.*

But, 3*dly,* It must be observed, That the views of *every exclusive* company are quite of a *different* nature from what was *supposed above.* ☞ For they *do not,* and *never did,* desire to trade *as cheap* as *others,* but as much *dearer* as *they can.* The *charter* itself *secures* them from any *competitors*; and therefore they have *no need* to seek to get the trade to themselves by *selling cheap.* But on the contrary, *wherever* they have the *market* to *themselves,* they will *both sell* and *buy* at their *own price.*

This is the *greatest* and most *intolerable* of *all* the *evils* of *monopolies.* It is a *prostitution* of the *trade* and *welfare* of the *publick,* to the *merciless ravages* of *greedy* individuals. ☞ We may the better judge of the *mischievous* effects of *all monopolies,* by *attentively observing* the *indefatigable* pains, and *great* expence, which every *self-interested* person *chearfully* submits to, in order to *acquire* it, even in a *free trade.* For if he has a *large capital,* he will *sink* some part to *undersell* another *adventurer,* who has *less,* in order to break him : And then, when he has done that, he will *raise* the *price* of his commodities again, so as to make himself soon *whole* for the *losses* he had *incurred.* Now if a *private* merchant can find *his account* in *losing* so much *money,* in order to *get at* a *monopoly* in a *free trade*, what *exorbitant* gains must an *exclusive* company make, who are *fenced* in by *law*, and have none to *rival* them?

☞ Nay the evil becomes *without remedy* in this *latter* case. For whereas in the former, either the *engrosser* himself, or his family, will *retire* from business, after they have amassed great riches; by which means the trade will again be *opened*. In the latter case, *viz.* that of a company, *one succeeds another upon the same plan of preying upon the publick, without intermission.* So that neither the *death*, nor *exorbitant wealth* of *one set* of *proprietors*, give us any prospect of being *delivered* from the *power* and *oppression* of the *next*.

But the affair of a publick company (viz. the *Hudson's Bay*) was,* *last sessions*, brought upon the carpet before the *British Parliament*,—let us see, therefore, what they had to *say for themselves*, when called upon by *their superiors*, —and when, doubtless, they said *all they could*,—and gave every thing the *best colouring*.

It appears, therefore, from the papers, which the honourable committee, appointed to examine into the state of their affairs, were pleased to make publick, for the general *information* of the kingdom, that the following particulars were *proved* to the *satisfaction* of the *committee*,—and even were *not contradicted* by the *agents* for the *company*.

1st, That the Company always have *discouraged* the *settling a colony* in *any part* of their *vast* and *boundless* empire.

2dly, That they *discouraged* the Company's servants from *conversing* with the *Indians*,—whereas the *French* *promoted* an intercourse with each other *as much as possible.*

3dly, That the climate is much *warmer*, and the soil

59

better

---

* *Viz.* In the year 1748.

better, higher up the country, than towards the sea-side. Yet *no settlements attempted.*

4thly, That the *French* have *extended* their settlements *more and more :* And *wherever* they have come near the *English,* they have carried most of the trade *from the* English,—not *vice versa.*

5thly, That the *forts* * pretended to be erected and
60 garrisoned,

---

* A great stress is laid by the advocates for exclusive companies, on the *necessity* of erecting *forts* in certain distant countries, for securing the trade to ourselves ;—Therefore they infer companies ought to be established in order to support this expence. A strange argument this ! And a stranger inference ! For if forts are necessary to be erected ; against *whom* are they necessary ? Not against the people of the country who are to trade with us. That is too absurd. We are to *cultivate* their *friendship,* and ought to *ingratiate* ourselves by all due acts of kindness, into their favour. But if these forts are necessary to be erected, in order to keep the *whole* trade to ourselves, and prevent other *European* nations from *interfering* with us ; how came it then to pass, that we were some years ago so alarmed at the *Ostend* Company, who had *no* forts, and no design of attacking ours ? Yet it is very plain, they could carry on a trade, and even *undersell* the *English East-India* Company, notwithstanding their forts. And the same fears are again revived with regard to the *Embden* Company established by the King of *Prussia.* If the trade was now to be *laid open,* subject only to the single restriction, that the private traders should *not* come into the *same* ports or harbours, where the companies have forts : What would be the consequence ? Plainly this ; that the companies would be ruined : And the private adventurers, though destitute of forts, would get all the trade from them.—If it is said, that these forts are necessary to guard and defend their magazines against *thieves* and *robbers* ; How then comes it to pass, that the *East-India* Company themselves have none on the coast of *China,* were the people are said to be as *thievish* and *dishonest* as in any place in the world ? —And how did the *Bristol* and *Liverpoole* traders maintain their ground along the coast of *Guinea,* without forts, where the natives are much more *warlike* than in any part of *India.* Besides, the affair of *Madrass* has sufficiently opened our eyes, as to the *use* and *importance* of these pretended forts,—and the *national* advantage arising from them. And as to the forts in *Hudson's Bay,* Father

garrisoned, are of *no strength*, were they *attacked* by an *European enemy*; and only serve to subject the *Indians* to the *command* of the Company.

6thly, That many *other branches*, besides the staple trade of the *Company*, might be attempted, were the *trade open*, with the *greatest probability* of *success*. Particularly the several *branches* of the *fisheries:* Whereas the Company, *who know when they are well*, as one of their witnesses expressed himself, or in words to that effect, give themselves no concern about the matter.

7thly, That the *Indians* do actually take a *great many more beaver*, than they carry to the factories. Not finding it *worth their while* to bring more to trade with.

8thly, That the *Indians* cannot carry *large* quantities, not any thing *so large* as they take in *hunting, were* they *desirous*,—because their canoes, *deeply loaden*, are *not able* to *withstand* the *waves* and *storms* they may meet with upon the *lakes*;—because they are forced to *unload* very often, and carry the skins upon their *backs*, on account of the *falls* and *currents;* which create much *fatigue* and *labour*, and *loss* of *time:* Because also they are obliged to *hunt* as they travel, for their *daily* sustenance; which article alone causes a *delay of* a *fortnight*, and longer, in going the space which might be gone in *three days.*

But, *9thly*, all these *inconveniencies* might be *easily remedied,—*

Charlevoix observes in his history of *Canada*, that when a *French* vessel with about fifty hands, appeared before the best of these forts, the brave *English* governor surrendered without firing a gun! Thus it is, that forts, in the hands of exclusive companies, have defended the honour, and preserved the commerce of *Great Britain!*

But even allowing, that they are necessary and advantageous to the *general* trade of the nation; what need then of a *company?* Is it not a *national* concern? If so, why should they not be erected and supported at a *national* expence? Take the argument therefore either way, what reason is there for an *exclusive* company?

remedied,—by *erecting* a *fort* about sixty leagues above *York* Fort upon *Nelson* River, upon a fork, where the river divides,—by *making a settlement* about eighty or ninty leagues above that, upon the lake of *Pachegoia,*—and by introducing our *European* conveniencies of *magazines* and *carriages*. By these *means, all* the beaver would be bought, which the *Indians* now make use of *otherways,* as *not answering* to bring it to the forts,—the *time* might be *saved,*—and the *French* driven to relinquish all that trade. In short, both our *exports,* and our *imports* would be *prodigiously* increased; and many tribes of *Indians* would, in that large tract of country, be brought to trade with the *English,* who have yet *scarcely heard* of the *English* name.

So many *important* particulars *alleged,*—*proved,*—and even *not contradicted,* one would think, would have been sufficient to have carried any national cause, against the *private interest* of a *few individuals*.

But—Let us in the next place see, what they and their friends had to offer in *justification* of their conduct,—*pretending*, that they carried on a trade *equally beneficial* to the nation, as if the trade *was open*.

The 1*st* thing alleged, was, that they *buy all the beaver which is brought them ;*—and if more was offered, *more they would buy*.

This may be very *true* ; and yet no ways inconsistent with the charge summed up in the above-recited particulars, against them. The *Indians,* as *savage* as they are, have the natural logick of *feeling* when they are *well* or *ill used,* as well as other people : And if they find *better* treatment in *one* place than *another,* will go to the *best,* and have as *little* dealings with the *worst,* as *they can.* Nothing but *absolute* necessity will oblige *them* (or *any people*) to bring their goods to a market, where they *expect beforehand* to be *ill used.* And for that reason, they will bring as *little* as *they can.* But when they have brought them, *necessity* obliges them to *sell* for what the purchasers *will give*. It may therefore be very true, that the Company *buy* all the furs that are *offered* them.—If they did not give *half as much* in barter as *they do*, they would *buy all*; because it would not be worth the *Indians* while to carry them back; and because they greatly wanted *European* goods. But these *Indians* would seek *another* market against the *next time*, if they could; and would bring *no more* goods to the *Company*, than *absolute* necessity obliged them.

But, *2dly*, It was alleged, that if *more* goods were given to the *Indians* in exchange, they would not bring *more* beavers; because they are an *idle, lazy* race of people; and, having no *artificial* wants to gratify, have no *ambition* to spur them on to take more pains. It is true, they have not *such* artificial wants as we have; they do not want *sumptuous* houses and gardens, *rich* furniture, or *coaches* and *chairs*: But they want *beads*, *bells*, little *looking-glasses*, *rings*, and such trinkets; (besides many articles of their cloathing, bedding, hunting, fishing, and fowling) and are as *impatient* to be *gratified* in these respects, as *we* can be in *ours*. In these things, therefore, they are as *covetous* and ambitious as the *rest* of *mankind*,—take as much *pains* to *acquire* them,—and *repine* and *murmur* at the factories, when they have not *as much* for their commodities as they *think* they *deserve*. Besides, it should be remembered, that *hunting* is rather a *diversion* with them, than a *toil*; and that, in fact, they do take a great *deal more* than they bring down to the forts. What they consider as a *toil*, is not the *hunting part*, but the being obliged to be the *porters* of what they have taken in hunting, down to the factories; and yet be paid *so little* for their trouble.

But, *3dly*, As to the charge against them, of *exporting so little* of our *own manufactures*; it was said by their *advocates*, that if *five thousand* pounds worth of goods

bought

bought all the furrs the *Indians* had to *sell*, *that* * sum was *as good* as *ten thousand* pounds : Nay, it was *better ;* because thereby *five thousand* pounds were *saved* to the nation.

This is a reason, which is *specious* enough at first view, but will not bear the *examining*.　First, therefore, we *deny the fact;* and insist upon it, that the *Indians* had *more* furrs to *sell*, if the Company would have given a *sufficient* price to the *Indians*, to have made it worth their while to have *brought* them *down;* or rather, if the Company had built settlements and magazines higher up, so as to have *superseded* the necessity of the *Indians* coming down.

But 2d, We will *allow the fact*, and argue with them upon their *own state* of the case.　Now if *five thousand* pounds worth of manufactures, in this respect, is as *good*, nay *better* than *ten thousand* pounds worth ; for the same

64

reason

---

* There was an egregious *fallacy* used in this argument.　If the barter or exchange with the *Indians* had been in *bullion*, the argument would have held *good ;* and so much *money* would have been saved to the nation.　But as it was all in our *own manufactures*, *i. e.* the *labour* of our own people, the diminishing of *such* exports, is in fact the *diminishing* of our own *manufactures*, and *defrauding* the nation of so much *labour*, whereby the hands employed in those manufactures must become a *rent-charge* upon the publick,—or *steal*, —or *starve*, or *fly* their country.　☞ The *only* limitation which *ought* to be put upon the *quantity* of our own manufactures, to be *exported*, is what the nature of the thing will of *itself* put upon them ; *viz.* To export *no more* than is consistent with the *reasonable* gains and profit of the *exporter*.　If he can afford to export *ten thousand* pounds worth of *English* manufactures, where an exclusive company would export but *five thousand;* it is for the *general* good of the country, that he *should do* it.　And all trade ought to be laid *free* and *open*, in order to *induce* the exporters to *rival* each other ; that the publick may obtain this general good by their *competitorship*.　But if they cannot afford to export so much, there is no need to *restrain* them by *laws* and *penalties*, from doing *that* which their own *private* interest will suggest to them soon enough.　And it is really astonishing, that such a fallacy, so gross in itself, so destructive in its consequences, could have escaped the notice of a *British* Senate, and could have passed not only without censure, but with some degree of applause.

reason, *one thousand* pounds worth is *better still,* because *more* would be *saved* to the nation. Suppose therefore, that the *Company,* and every other *exporter* in the kingdom, (for every other has the *same right* of arguing in this manner) suppose, I say, that *all exporters* could *lessen* the *exportations* of our own manufactures by *nine tenths,* and yet could get *as much* money, or effects in *return,* as they had *before*; what would be the *consequence?* Why, only this, that *these exporters,* would become princes; and the *rest* of the kingdom beggars. They would be like a *Spanish Don* in *Mexico,* or *Peru,* who has a prodigious rich mine, which required but *few hands* to work it. And therefore he indeed would be a *great lord*; but all his wealth would *not enrich* the *neighbourhood,* so much as a *single manufacture* here in *England,* which being *branched* out into *various* hands, gives a *comfortable* subsistence to *many* families, causing a general circulation of labour.

It is not therefore *gold and silver,* considered *merely in themselves,* that can make a kingdom *flourish,* but the *parceling* them out into *proper shares,* by means of the *divisions* and *subdivisions* of *different* trades. Without this the *more riches* in a *few* hands,—the *greater* would be the *poverty* of the *rest,* and the more *abject* and *dependent* their state would be. And if *all merchants* were no *better* commonwealths men than *these,* the *interior* of a kingdom would be very *little profited* by *foreign merchandize,*—nay, in *some* respects would be *much the worse.*

In short, *such* an *argument* as this, *viz.* to *decrease* our *exports,* and *increase* their *price* abroad, beyond what is *necessary* for the *comfortable subsistence* of the *merchant* and *manufacturer, is only worthy of such a cause.* Were it put in *practice,* it would get all the *wealth* of the *nation* into a *few hands,*—it would turn *nine tenths* of our manufacturers a *begging,*—and *reduce* them to the *necessity* of becoming *lacqueys* and *footmen* to *such exporters,*—or starving,—or flying the country. It would *sink the value*

of

of our *lands*, and bring *swift* destruction on the *manufacturer, farmer, gentleman*, and *all stations,—except* the *exporter*. He indeed would be great,—and *he alone*. One may therefore the better judge of the *goodness of such a cause*, which required *such kind* of arguments to *support it*. And so much for *exclusive Companies*.

VII. PROPOSAL.

To *encourage foreign merchants and tradesmen to settle among us, by a general naturalization Act for all Protestants*. And if it be judged improper to admit them into *offices* of *trust* or *power*, it is easy to add a clause, that *these privileges* shall still be *confined* to the *natural-born* subjects.

Here again the *baleful* spirit of *self-interest* exerts all its powers to *oppose* so *publick* and *general* a benefit,— *" What! must foreigners, and we know not who, come and take the bread out of our mouths?* An honest *Cambro-Briton* would have called *all Englishmen* foreigners, *and he knows not who*. But waving that,—let me calmly ask, *what bread* do they eat?—and *out* of *whose mouths?* It must be *English* bread: The corn *grew* here,—was *manufactured, was sold* here. And the foreigners, who eat it, *earn* it by their *labour*, and *pay* for it. So far then, we hope, there is *no offence*. The *more inhabitants* there are to *consume* the *produce* of our lands, the *better* can the *farmer* and the *gentleman* pay their *shopkeepers* and *tradesmen*, and the *more manufactures* will they consume in *every respect*. Let us see therefore, in the next place, *out of whose mouths do they take this bread?* If they introduce *new* manufactures, or carry those already established to *greater* perfection, in that case the publick is greatly benefited, and no individual can be injured. If they employ themselves only in such as are already *settled* and *perfected*, they will not defraud the mouths of *sober, frugal*, and

industrious

industrious persons, who may work *as cheap,* and can work as well as *foreigners.* And therefore should be obliged to do both. It can be, therefore, none but the *abandoned, debauched,* and *dissolute,* who would chuse to be *idle three* or *four* days in the week, and want to have their wages so *high* as to *support* this *extravagance,* that can make such a *complaint?* And shall *they* be heard? Shall we *continue* the exclusion of all sober and industrious foreigners, so much to the *national disadvantage,* merely to gratify the *extravagant* and *unreasonable* humours of such wretches as *these?* Surely, it is to be hoped, we shall pursue more prudent measures, both for *our sakes,* and *their own.*

But we are told farther, " *That* English *tradesmen, of* " *every denomination, are* used *to live better than foreigners;* " *and therefore* cannot *afford to work or sell so cheap as* " *they.*" Be it so: Carry then this argument to a *foreign market,* and see whether it will *perswade* the *inhabitants* of *that country to trade* with you. A *French,* and an *English merchant,* are *competitors* with, and *rivals* to each other in the markets of *Spain, Portugal, Italy, Turky,* and in short all over the world. The *French* man offers his goods at 20, 15, 10, or 5 *per cent.* cheaper than the *English.* Our countryman is demanded, *why* he will not sell his goods *as cheap* as *others?* His answer is, " *that* " *the manufacturers and merchants live better in* England " *than foreigners do, and therefore he cannot afford it.*" This is a most *perswasive* argument. Undoubtedly he will *sell* much cloth by *alledging* it. He is asked again, why they will not in his country *admit* foreigners, who work *cheaper,* to *settle* among them, that so they may be able to trade upon an *equal footing* with their neighbours? To this he replies, " *that foreigners, and he knows not* " *who, ought not to come and take the bread out of the* " *mouths of the natives.*" Such *kind* of *reasoning* must give them an high idea of the *sense* and *discernment* of our *countryman.* Let us therefore apply the case to our-

selves,

selves, and not argue in that *absurd* and *ridiculous* manner at *home*, which he is represented as doing *abroad*.

The admission then of foreigners to settle in our country, is so far from taking the bread *out* of the mouths of the natives, that it is putting bread *into* the mouths of those, who, *otherwise*, in a short time must have *none*. For the *English* must trade, at least, upon an *equal* footing with other nations, or not trade *at all*. And then, when the *not trading* at all is the consequence, we shall indeed have *no foreigners* to complain of, but we shall have a much *sorer* evil :—and then, perhaps when it is too late, the most *self-interested* among us will be sorry, that we had not admitted the frugal and industrious from all parts of the world, to share the gains of trade with them, rather than to have none at all.

But let us try all this reasoning by plain matters of fact. The town of *Birmingham*, for example, admits all persons to come and settle among them ; whom, though they are *Englishmen*, the *original natives* of the place may as justly term *foreigners* with regard to *them*, as we stile other nations by that name. " *Foreigners*, therefore, and " *I know not who*, came from *all* parts, and settled at *Bir-* " *mingham* ; and—took the bread *out* of the mouths of the " *original* natives." What then was the consequence of this great wickedness? Why, within these few years, the trade and buildings of the town have been prodigiously increased, and all the estates for a great many miles round, have felt the benefit of this *great accession* of trade and inhabitants. *Birmingham*, from being a place of *little consequence*, is now become one of the most *flourishing* and *considerable* in the kingdom. And there is no town, with its *exclusive* charters, that can boast of so many *skilful* artists, as this which *admits all comers*.

Moreover, there are *fewer beggars* in this town, *Manchester* and *Leeds*, where all are *free*, than in any which has *companies* of trades, and *exclusive* charters. ☞ So

true

true and certain it is, that these *rights* and *privileges*, as they are *called*, do *multiply* the numbers of the *poor*, instead of diminishing them; because they *damp* the spirit of industry, frugality, and emulation. A manufacturer, who knows, that no foreigner *dares* come in to be a *competitor* against him, thinks himself privileged to be *idle*. And all such privileges are just so many combinations to *sink* the *value* of lands, and prevent the *extension* of commerce.

The other instance I shall mention, is the case of the *French Hugonots*, who fled from the persecution of *Lewis* XIV, and took refuge in *England*. But great was the outcry against them, at their first coming. "Poor *England* would be *ruined*! Foreigners *encouraged*! And "our own people *starving*!" This was the popular cry of those times. But the *looms* in *Spittle-Fields*, and the *shops* on *Ludgate-Hill*, have at last sufficiently taught us another lesson. And now, it is hoped, we may say without offence, these *Hugonots* have been so far from being of *disservice* to the *nation*, that they have partly *got*, and partly *saved*, in the space of fifty years, a balance in our favour of, at least, fifty millions sterling.

In short, self-interest apart, what *good* reason can be assigned, why we should not admit foreigners among us? Our country is but *thinly* inhabited, in comparison to what it *might* be : And many hundred thousands of acres of *good* land, in *England* and *Wales*, not to mention *Scotland* and *Ireland*, lie either entirely waste, or are not sufficiently cultivated, for want of hands, and persons to consume the product. Our vast *commons*, all over the kingdom, and many of the *forests* and *chaces*, might be parcelled out in lots, to such of the foreigners as chuse a country life; and the rest might find employment, in some shape or other, in the different manufactures. The natives of *England* likewise do not *increase* so fast, as those of other countries; our common people being much more

　　　　　　　abandoned

abandoned and *debauched*.　The *marriage state* also is not sufficieutly encouraged among us：And ten thousand *common whores* are not so fruitful (setting aside the *sin* of the *parents*, the *diseases* of the *few* children that are *born*, and their want of a *proper* and *virtuous* education) I say, 10,000 eommon whores are not so fruitful as *fifty* healthy young married women, that are *honest* and *virtuous*：By which means, the State is defrauded of the increase of upwards of 199 subjects out of 200, every year.　Add to all this, that it has been long observed by men of thought and speculation, that more *young children* die in *England* from the *birth* to *two years* old, than in any other country. The sea likewise, and our extensive plantations, are a continual drain upon us.　And the manufacturing poor at home are *killing themselves*, and, if I may be allowed the expression, their *posterity* likewise, as fast as they can, by those sure *instruments* of *death*, *gin* and *spirituous* liquors. For all these reasons, therefore, as well as on account of *lowering* the price of labour, and preventing the *combinations* of journeymen, so *loudly* complained of, and *severely* felt throughout the kingdom, it is humbly hoped, that those persons who have hitherto opposed the *Naturalization* Bill, will see cause to change their sentiments; and will look upon it as highly *useful* and *expedient*, and productive of the greatest *national* advantages.　There are many thousands of manufacturers, both in silk and woollen, in the south of *France*, all *zealous Protestants*, who would gladly come over, if they could learn that they should meet with a kind reception.　As to the difficulty of making their escape out of the *French* King's dominions, they would find ways and means to deceive even the *vigilance* of *their* governors, by retiring, as it were one by one, and removing under various pretences, towards the manufacturing towns in *Picardy* and *French-Flanders*, (from whence they could so easily pass over to us) were they sure of finding protection and reasonable encouragement.

And

And as *England* and *France* are *rivals* to each other, and *competitors* in almost all branches of commerce, every *single* manufacturer so coming over, would be our gain, and a double loss to *France*.

Upon a review of this proposal, as it stood in the second edition, the author cannot see any cause for that fury and resentment, so liberally bestowed upon him, for offering his thoughts, he hopes in no improper manner, to publick consideration. If his arguments were *inconclusive*, why were they not answered? If *absurd*, they ought to have been despised: But since they were thought worthy of so much notice, why doth not some person undertake to *confute* a late treatise, *viz. Reflections on the Expediency of naturalizing foreign Protestants*, wrote expressly to vindicate this proposal? Such a method would have been fair and ingenuous, deserving the regard of the publick, and the thanks of the writer of this treatise, who would have thought it *no disgrace* to have acknowledged his error in the most open manner. But it *ever was* the hard fate of those who have laboured to promote the *true interests* of their country, and to establish a general system for the propagation of *national virtue and good morals*, to be vilified and insulted, while *living*, and never to have real justice done to their characters, till they are *dead*. A man may write pieces of *entertainment*, and be *applauded*: Or he may dip his pen in *gall* for the use of a *party*, and be *adored*; But he must not bend his studies for the *general good*, with a dependence on any other reward, than that which arises in his own breast for having done his duty.

VIII. PROPOSAL.

To encourage a trade with our own plantations, in *all such articles as shall make for the mutual benefit of the mother country, and her colonies.*

The

The reasons for this proposal are very obvious and convincing : And yet, as *self-interested* persons will be apt to start objections, and raise difficulties, it may be proper to expatiate upon these reasons a little.

1st, Therefore, it is necessary that we should encourage a trade to our own plantations for all sorts of *naval stores*, in order that we may not be too *dependent* upon the *will* and *pleasure* of *foreign* courts, with regard to these necessary things. Many, if not most of the *implements* for *navigation*, and consequently for a *sea war*, are purchased from the several nations bordering upon the *Baltick.* Suppose then that *Sweden, Russia*, or *Denmark*, should, for certain reasons of State, or by the *intrigues* of the *French*, lay an embargo on these commodities, at a *crisis* when we greatly wanted them ;—or should *refuse* them to us, and *sell* them to our enemies ; to what a *distressed* situation would this reduce us ? and who can tell what might be the consequences of it ? And as the politicks of princes are ever *fluctuating* and *changing*, why should we put it in the power of any potentate to have such a *command* over us ?

2dly, As the balance in regard to all these countries is considerably *against us*, common *prudence* will suggest, that we ought to *turn* it in *our favour*, if we *can.* Now this we shall be *able* to do (or at the worst, bring it to an *equilibrium*, which in itself is *no disadvantageous* kind of commerce) if we can purchase the same commodities in our own plantations, which we used to import from these countries. Besides, the balance is not only against us with regard to *Sweden*, but also the very money which is drawn from us by means of this *losing* trade, is converted to *support* a *French* interest, in *opposition* to ours. But

3dly, Were the case *indifferent, where* we traded, (which it *is not*) the natural affection, which the mother country should have for her colonies, where we have so many friends, relations, and acquaintance, should deter-

mine

mine us to give *them* the *preference.* But indeed our own interest is *nearly* and *essentially* concerned in this affair: For,

4thly, Unless we *promote* a trade with *them,* and take off the *growth* and *commodities* of their *plantations,* they will be reduced to the *necessity* of *offering* them to sale at *other markets,* or *permitting* other nations to *come* and *trade* with them: The consequence of which will be, that they will take the product and manufactures of these nations in *return.* And indeed this is too much the case at present: For *one third,* at least, of the luxuries and elegancies of life, brought into our colonies (as was observed * before) is the growth and manufacture of other countries, and principally of *France.* And as our trade, particularly to some of the northern colonies, is growing less and less, this evil must daily increase in the same proportion. Moreover,

5thly, Unless we can supply our colonies with such commodities and manufactures as they *want,* by way of *barter* for some of theirs which they can spare,—they will be *obliged* to raise those things themselves. And seeing that many of the *new* settlements on the continent of *America,* are several hundred miles up the country, *between,* and *beyond* the mountains; this distance of situation will *increase* the necessity they are already under of manufacturing for themselves,—unless we can *divert* their thoughts to some other *projects.* Nay more, when once a manufacture is set up in those distant regions, it will extend itself downwards; and the inhabitants on the sea-coast will be supplied by their neighbours in the up-lands, upon cheaper and easier terms than we can supply them. It is a just complaint, that many of the provinces have set up several species of manufactures, which greatly interfere

---

* See the XIth disadvantage of Great Britain. Page 345.

with the trade and prosperity of their mother country. Yet how shall we prevent them? There is but one way to do it, that is either *just*, or *practicable*: And that is, by an *exchange* of commodities to mutual benefit. A mutual benefit is a mutual dependence. And this principle alone will contribute more to the preserving of the dependency of our colonies upon their mother country, than any other refinement or invention. For if we are afraid, that one day or other they will revolt, and set up for themselves, as some seem to apprehend; let us not *drive* them to a necessity to *feel* themselves *independent* of us: As they *will* do, the moment they perceive, that they can be supplied with all things from *within* themselves, and do not *need* our assistance. If we would keep them still dependent upon their mother country, and in some respects *subservient* to her *views*, and *welfare*;—let us make it their interest always so to be.

For these reasons therefore, it is humbly apprehended, that the trade to our *colonies* and *plantations*, must appear to be of the utmost consequence to the power, strength, and prosperity of *Great Britain*. But to effectuate this good end, an important question comes next to be decided; *viz.* " What produce should our colonies be most encour- " aged to raise and cultivate? And what sort of manu- " factures shall they be allowed to barter in return for " ours?" It is easy to see, that they cannot make large payments in gold and silver; and it is also equally plain and certain, that we *will* not, *cannot*, indeed allow them to introduce such things among us, as will prevent the consumption of *our own* commodities, to such a *degree*, as to be *upon the whole*, of *national* disadvantage.

Wherefore, with great submission, I will beg leave to offer some few plain *observations*, which perhaps might not be altogether unserviceable as to the regulation of such a trade.

First then, it seems chiefly requisite, that due *encour-*

agement

agement should be given to our colonies, to apply their thoughts towards the raising of *such* commodities, as do *not* interfere with those of the mother country.

Secondly, They should also not only be allowed, but be *particularly incouraged* to *import* all such raw materials as are to be *manufactured* here in *England* ;—even though we raise the same sort ourselves: Because the *more* we have of these, the *better ;* since the *cheaper* they are *purchased*, the more of them can be *worked* up, and the more there are worked up, the *greater* number of hands are *employed ;* and consequently, the more labour, or employment is procured to the nation. Moreover, this argument becomes so much the stronger, if the *raw materials* we have of our own, are by no means *sufficient* for the demand of the manufacture, either as to *quantity,* or *goodness ;* which is the case with the *bar-iron* here made in *England ;* so that we are obliged to have recourse to foreign countries for a supply ; as in the case of bar-iron we do to *Sweden,* to the amount of near 200,000*l.* sterling a year.

Thirdly, we ought to permit our colonies to supply us upon easy terms with all such articles of luxury as we are *wedded* to, and *will* have either from *them,* or *others.* Consequently, in reason and good policy, *they* ought to have the preference, by being *indulged* to import these articles under the advantage of an *easy* and *reasonable* duty ; whilst the commodities of *foreign* nations are charged with *higher* imposts and customs. In such a case, the mutual *exchange* of commodities between us and the colonies would become a *mutual advantage :* But that is not all ; for as the duties would be *moderate,* the temptations to smuggling would be *small ;* the consumption of the commodities of our own colonies *greater,* and that of other nations *less :* By which means, the revenue itself would rise much higher than it doth, when there are large and heavy duties : For these will ever be attended with one or other of the following effects, either the preventing

the

the *importation* of the commodity, or its *entrance* at the custom-house.

Fourthly, In the regulation of a trade with our colonies, some regard should be had to those distant parts of the country, which lie remotest from the sea; that even the farthest inhabitants may likewise find employment in the raising of such commodities as are fittest for their situation, and are light of carriage. And if their thoughts are properly taken up in the cultivation of these things, they will have neither time, nor inclination to pursue other *projects*, which might prove detrimental to the mother country.

From these principles therefore it seems clearly to follow, that the culture of *coffee, cocoa nut, cochineal, indico*, and *pimento*, ought especially to be encouraged in the *mountainous, inland part* of *Jamaica*. And that of *bar-iron, hemp, flax, indico*, and *raw silk*, in the countries between, and beyond the mountains, on the back of *Carolina, Virginia, Pensylvania*, &c.

Some of these indeed are *heavy* goods; and therefore seem not so proper to be raised in a country so far distant from any *sea-port :* But on the other hand, when it is considered how particularly rich the soil in those parts is, and how well adapted the country for the raising such articles, and how conveniently the inhabitants could load the cattle they bring down every market day, with these commodities, the difficulty, I hope, in great part vanishes, and the propriety of assigning these tracts of land for the culture of them, evidently appears.

Enough therefore has been said, to evince beyond all contradiction, that it is the interest of the kingdom, that such a trade as here described, should be carried on : But whether it is the *interest* of the *merchant* to embark in it, is another question : And yet, till he can find his own *private* account in the affair, it is too clear a point, that whatever has been said as to the *publick* and *national* ad-

vantage,

vantage, will pass for *nothing*. A merchant will not engage in a *losing* trade, and *ruin* himself to *benefit* his country. Indeed it is unreasonable to expect he should. And the great complaint against the trade to some of our *northern* colonies long has been, that there is *nothing* to be *got by it*; that is, that the merchant can get nothing, or next to nothing, if compared to his gains to and from other places. The trade to *Denmark*, *Sweden*, or *Russia*, is more *advantageous* to *him*, though very *detrimental* to his *country*; and therefore, if we would expect the merchant to turn his thoughts wholly to the plantation-trade, we must cause him to find his *chief* interest in the pursuit of it.

Now there are *four* ways or methods for *turning* a trade into a *new* channel, and *stopping* up the *old* one.

The *first* is, by laying *additional* duties upon the commodities of *one* country, but not on those of *another*. By this means, if the commodities are in any degree *equal* to each other in *goodness* and *value*, the former will be prevented from being imported, on account of their *dearness* to the consumer; and the latter will have the preference, by reason of their *cheapness*. But this method, however expedient at particular junctures, is to be used with great wariness and caution. For every such additional duty put upon the commodities of a foreign country, will be looked upon by that country, as an act of *hostility* committed upon its trade and commerce; which they will be sure to revenge upon the commodities and manufactures of the country that was the *aggressor*. Besides, high additional duties are too *violent* and *precipitate* a method of turning a trade into a *new* channel,—especially where the manufacture is yet in its *infancy*, and cannot *answer* the *demand* for it. It is therefore much more safe and prudent, to incline the scale *gently* and *gradually* on the side you would favour; that so the inhabitants of that country may have *time* to raise the proper *quantity* of the commodities

dities

dities that are wanted, and may *increase* and *perfect* their manufactures, by due *application* and *experience*. And also, that we ourselves may not be distressed on account of the *scarceness*, or the *badness* of the commodity; or be forced to pay an exorbitant price, by means of the *monopoly* which the inhabitants of the *favoured* country will have against us.

Wherefore, *secondly*, another more *commodious*, and less *exceptionable* way, is, to grant certain *privileges* and *exemptions*;—which shall *continue* till the trade is sufficiently *established*, and needs *no support*; that is, till the merchant can find it *worth* his *while* to *engage* in it, without being paid at the *publick* expence. Suppose therefore, that at the *beginning* of such a trade, certain commodities were permitted to be imported upon *easy terms*; —or rather duty free, which is better still: Then our colonies would turn their thoughts to the *raising* them; and the merchant would find his own private account in *importing* them. But if any thing obstructed, so that this did not prove sufficient to engage them in the prosecution of such designs; or that the demand *still* ran in favour of the goods of *another* nation; then,

Thirdly, The scale must be turned by the addition of a bounty upon importation: And to quicken their *diligence*, and excite a spirit of *emulation*, to these encouragements may still be added,

Fourthly, A personal premium to such merchants, as shall import the *most* of these commodities, and the *best* in their kind. *Prizes* of this nature, are observed to do wonderful things in the *raising* and *perfecting* of a manufacture. We have seen their good effects in *Ireland*; and it were greatly to be wished we had the same laudable institution here in *England*. If certain sums were vested in the *Board of Trade* for this purpose, we might not despair of seeing the mother country in a *few* years supplied

plied

plied with *pot-ashes, bar-iron,*[*] *flax, hemp, indico, cochineal, coffee, cocoa nut, pitch and tar, all sorts of naval stores, and raw silk*, chiefly from her own colonies. The fact is undeniable, that all these things *can* be raised in our plantations either on the *Continent*, or in the *islands*. And though some difficulties would attend the enterprize at first setting out, yet industry and application, together with the inducements of *bounties* and *personal premiums*, would surmount them all. If *prizes* were fixed, *viz.* So much to the *first*, the *second*, and the *third* importer of the *most* in quantity, and *best* in kind; and notice given thereof in the Gazette by *publick authority;* what an *emulation* would it excite amongst all the merchants of the kingdom? How gladly would our colonies *embrace* such proposals, and *quit* the pursuit of the manufactures they are now engaged in? It is certain, these manufactures, tho' *highly* detrimental to *us*, are not *so* advantageous to *them*, as the raising the above mentioned commodities *would be* because they could employ their *negroes* in such work; whereas the negroes are found to be not so proper to engage in a manufacture, which has a *long* course and *different* parts before it is compleated; and the labour of the white people is dear and expensive.

As to the article of *raw silk*, the importance of it, I

79

hope,

---

[*] The great clamour lately raised against the introduction of bar-iron is an astonishing instance of the ignorance and infatuation of the *English* in regard to their own interest. For let us ask even an iron-master, if the *Americans* shall not be permitted to import iron duty free, what course will they, nay *must* they take, but to manufacture it themselves? For how shall they be able to pay for *English* goods, unless they can make proper returns? And if you will not admit their bar-iron, you drive them to the *necessity* of manufacturing it: Nay more, you give them a *bounty*: For as the bar-iron will be cheaper in *America*, if there is no *English* market; this difference in the price is in fact a bounty given by yourselves for the encouragement of iron-manufactures in *America*.

hope, will justify the recommending of the culture of it in a very *particular* manner. The *excessive* price it now bears, and the great difficulties to which the manufacturers are driven, in order to get it at *any rate*, require that something should be attempted without delay. Every nation now begins to perceive, that it is *imprudent* and *impolitick* to suffer such *precious* materials to be exported *unmanufactured* out of their country. They have therefore prohibited the doing it under the severest penalties: And we cannot blame them. But for that very reason we ought to endeavour to raise the commodity ourselves. And, with humble submission, no time ever seemed so favourable for the doing it, as the present. For as the *price* is *high*, this is not only an *inducement* to set about it: But also as we have now a *different* sort of inhabitants in our colonies to engage in it, than we had before, we have therefore the greater prospect of success. The complaint formerly was, that the cultivation of it would *not answer* on account of the *dearness* of labour. The inhabitants towards the *sea-coasts* could employ their time to greater advantage in the culture of *tobacco, rice,* &c. therefore the scheme for raw silk must fail. But at present we have several thousands of *Palatines* and *Moravians*, settled in the vallies between the mountains, in a country much like *Piemont*, where the best silk grows: Now as they *cannot* cultivate rice or tobacco for *exportation;* and as they are far removed from the center of trade, and are also a *parsimonious, abstemious* people, they will certainly work much *cheaper* than the *English* heretofore towards the sea-side, who were ever noted for the contrary qualities. So that upon the whole, the *time* and the *occasion* invite; the *necessities* of the manufacture, and the *interest* of our country, require that some attempt should be speedily made for the raising of *raw silk* in our colonies.

　　　IX. PROPOSAL.

IX. PROPOSAL.

To establish a police for the prevention of smuggling.

* " It may indeed be too difficult for a private person
" to find out a remedy equal to a disease so universal, and
" of so long a continuance : But yet as every well-meant
" endeavour for the publick service is candidly accepted,
" when offered with modesty and submission, it is to be
" hoped the following thoughts, which proceed no farther
" than by way of *query,* will be favourably received.

" Query I. If the privileges and exemptions of the
" islands of *Guernsey* and *Jersey,* &c. were abolished, and
" those remains of the dukedom of *Normandy* perfectly
" united to the *British* Crown, could the same frauds be
" then practised, as to the running of goods which have
" a drawback granted them, smuggling of *French* wines,
" brandies, teas, coffee, chocolate, silk, lace, and all other
" commodities, as are at present ? Could the *French* wines
" be mixt with *port,* and then entered as if they were all
" the growth of *Portugal,* to the great detriment of the
" revenue, the manifest injury of the *Portugal* trade, the
" certain irreparable loss to the nation, and the open
" avowed encouragement to perjury ? Could the smacks
" and cruisers, which were designed to guard the coast,
" have the same pretence to enter the ports of *France,*
" which they have now to step into *Guernsey* and *Jersey,*
" viz. to see what vessels were lading ; and *sometimes* take
" in a lading for themselves?—*Et quis custodes custodiat*
" *ipsos ?*

" Query II. If the jurisdiction of the *Isle of Man*
" was annexed to the Crown, in the same manner as the
" hereditable jurisdictions in *Scotland* lately were, could

81

France

---

* This quotation is taken out of my *Inquiry concerning the Use of
low priced Spirituous Liquors* ; printed for *T. Trye, Holborn.*

" *France, Holland, Denmark,* &c. find any place in *our own*
" seas, as a *storehouse* or *magazine* for depositing their
" several contraband goods, in order to run them on the
" coasts of *England, Wales, Scotland,* and *Ireland?* If
" the collectors of the customs of the present noble pro-
" prietor of this island, were obliged to lay before the
" parliament their books of entries for the last seven
" years, and such entries compared with the accounts that
" might be transmitted from *France, Holland, Denmark,*
" &c. would it not appear, that the respective *India* com-
" panies of those countries had imported vast quantities of
" teas, and other *India* goods, principally with a view to
" smuggle them into *Great Britain* and *Ireland?* And
" ought not that circumstance alone be an alarming con-
" sideration to the *English East-India* Company, to the
" Government, and the whole *British* nation?—Do the
" *French, Dutch, Danes,* &c. permit the *English* to use any
" port of their dominions for the like purposes? And
" would it not be more advantageous to the *British* nation,
" as *to the mere article of profit and loss,* to pay subsidies
" to these countries of 200,000*l. per annum,* than to let
" matters continue on the present footing? Lastly, with
" regard to our own subjects, if this island were annexed
" to the Crown, could the *corrupt* part of the commanders
" of the smacks and cruisers receive any emolument for
" *conniving* at the evils here complained of? Or the
" *honest* part be insulted, and even imprisoned by the
" deputy governors or their agents, for discharging faith-
" fully their duty? And would the necessary expences
" for the prevention of smuggling be a *fourth part* the
" sum, to which they now amount?

Query III. Whether the present methods of collecting
" the duties on *French* brandies, and other foreign goods,
" are not found to be *eventually* productive of great temp-
" tations to smuggle them? Whether such temptations
" could possibly be so strong, if there was a *permission*

" somewhat

" somewhat of a like nature granted to the importers of
" these commodities, as there is now granted to the im-
" porters of rum, *viz. To put them in the King's warehouse,*
" *paying the duties only for the quantities they take out,*
" *when they meet with a purchaser, and leaving the rest to*
" *continue?* Whether a smuggler with one hundred
" pounds stock, would run the risque of his life and for-
" tune, which the present laws subject him to, if he could
" commence a fair trader, to sufficient advantage, with so
" small a capital? And whether, in case of such a per-
" mission, a man would not carry on a more extensive
" trade with one hundred pounds, in certain sorts of
" goods, than he can do now with six times the sum?

" ☞ Whether the great frauds, lately complained of
" in the tobacco trade, to the prodigious detriment of the
" revenue, and the national interest, cannot likewise be
" accounted for, upon the principle here suggested? And
" if the importers of tobacco were allowed to lodge their
" cargoes in the King's warehouse (or in their own, under
" the lock and key of the *custom-house* officer) and from
" thence to take it away in small quantities, *viz.* a hogs-
" head or two at a time, suitable to their convenience,
" would not this circumstance alone cause the *Virginia*
" trade to flourish, prevent smuggling, and supersede the
" necessity of all other devices?

" Query IV. If all seizures were absolutely prohibited
" to be sold for home consumption, could they then *cover*
" the vending any considerable parcels of *un-customed*
" goods, which are now vended in large quantities by this
" means? And if the seizures were *not* to be used at
" home, would the purchasers give an *higher price* for such
" goods, than they do for others of like intrinsick value?
" And is not the *advanced* price now given, a plain indica-
" tion of the uses to which they are applied?

" Query V. If the commanders and officers of the
" smacks and cruisers were to be paid only one half of

" their

" their salaries of *course*, and the other half by way of
" *gratuity*, when it appeared that they had been vigilant
" and active to an *high degree*, would not this quicken
" their motions, and add new life and vigour to their
" endeavours? If those who could give no proof of an
" *extraordinary* vigilance were to lose such gratuities, and
" others to receive them, as an *additional* reward, who had
" distinguished themselves the most eminently, would not
" this be a means of raising a spirit of emulation among
" them, and making the *active* principles of interest,
" shame, fear, honour, disgrace, all unite and operate for
" the publick good.

" Query VI. If a few independent companies of light
" horse were raised, in the nature of *hussars*, would not
" such kind of cavalry, (viz. *English hunters*) be much
" more proper to scour the coast, and pursue smugglers,
" than heavy horse and dragoons, and regular forces?
" And if their officers were paid in the same manner, as
" is proposed for the officers of smacks and cruisers, would
" it not be an additional security for their integrity, and
" an incentive to their vigilance?

Query VII. If the *whole* seizures were given to the
" captors, would it not be a greater encouragement than
" giving them a part? And if the fees and expences of
" the Court of *Exchequer* for condemnation did not rise
" so high, would not this enhance the value of the prize,
" and consequently make the captors more active and vigi-
" lant? Whether there have not been instances of cus-
" tom-house officers *compounding* with the delinquents for
" *petty* seizures, rather than be at the expence of con-
" demning them in the *Exchequer*, as that would swallow
" up the profit?

" These queries the author would humbly offer to
" publick consideration; not doubting but many other
" methods might be found out, greatly conducive to the
" same good end. As to the difficulties against putting

" this

" this scheme in immediate execution, he is not aware of
" any, but is far from presuming to determine that there
" are none."

X. PROPOSAL.

To *invite foreigners of distinction to travel among us*,
that so we may have something in return for the vast
sums which we yearly send abroad. To this end there is
wanting a concise treatise in *French* and *English*, setting
forth the advantages which persons of different tastes and
inclinations may enjoy by such a tour : The man of pleasure and diversion—the virtuoso—the scholar and man of
letters—the lawyer—physician—divine—merchant, *&c.*
with directions how to perform a regular tour—a shorter
or a longer—what things are most remarkable to be seen :
—Churches—seats—gardens—pictures—manufactures—
ports, *&c.*—what books or treatises are necessary to be
consulted—how to learn the language—with the proper
stages marked out—and a calculation of the expence in
the moderate way of travelling.

It has been observed before, under the XIIth Advantage of *France*, page 329, that travelling into a country is
of greater consequence to the trade and manufactures of
that country, than is usually apprehended. And as *England* is as deserving the notice of *curious* and *inquisitive*
foreigners, as any country on the globe, it is a great pity,
that some ingenious hand hath not yet lent them his
friendly assistance, by an express treatise on the subject.
It would be a great pleasure to the author to contribute
what he can, only as an *inferior workman*, in the accomp-
lishing such a design. And therefore if he could *fungi
vice cotis*, as *Horace* expresses it, and be considered only
as a *whet-stone* to give an *edge* to the inclinations of

                                                    others,

others, who have *abilities* to execute such a scheme, he would gladly offer his assistance.

With these sentiments therefore he begs leave to propose the following *rough sketch*, only as general hints to be *improved* upon, *viz.*

Suppose a modest treatise was wrote, without puffing, or too much extolling ourselves, or our country, containing a plan for a foreigner to travel in *England* a year, or longer, with pleasure and advantage:

Chap. I. Setting forth the situation of the country, the air and climate, nature of the soil, and its general productions.

Chap. II. The present inhabitants, principles of their government, their virtues and vices, humours, diversions, the manner of conversing agreeably with them, and accommodating one's self to the general taste and genius of the country, method of learning the language—and pronounciation—method and expence of travelling—manner of obtaining recommendations from abroad to *London*, and from *London* to the other parts of the kingdom.

Chap. III. Containing the plan for a foreigner to make the tour of *England* in eight stages, within the compass of a year, each stage illustrated by a *Map*, containing *les environs*, or the district of ten miles round the place of residence: in which district the principal seats—towns—manufactures—curiosities, *&c.* should be briefly described: *viz.* Supposing the stranger landed the beginning of *April*; then the

1*st* stage, *London* and *les environs*, in the month of *April*.

N. B. It might be improper a foreigner should stay longer in the capital, upon first coming over, than to settle his correspondences, and get recommendations to other places; lest, whilst he is a *stranger* to the *language*, he should associate too much with his own countrymen, and be little benefited by his travelling.

                                   2*d* stage,

2d stage, *Cambridge* and *les environs*, in *May*. Here he should begin in earnest to learn the language by the help of some good grammar, and to learn the pronounciation by coming to church with his *French* and *English* Common Prayer, and listening to the clergyman's slow and deliberate reading. If this method was duly practised, foreigners would not find that difficulty in learning the pronounciation of our language, as they are apt to imagine. And this is an advantage of teaching it, in some respect peculiar to us.

3d stage, *Oxford* and *les environs*, in *June*. Note, in laying out the route between place and place, it would be proper to contrive it so, as the traveller might see as many things worthy of notice in his passage, as he could.

4th stage, *Birmingham* and *les environs*, in *July*.

5th stage, *Bristol* and *les environs*, in *August*.

6th stage, a tour from *Bristol* to *Portsmouth*, through *Wilton, Salisbury,* &c. and then return to *Bath* at the end of *September*.

7th stage, *Bath* and *les environs*, during *October* and *November*.

8th stage, *London*, during the months of *December, January, February* and *March*, which complete the year.

If after this the foreigner chooses to reside longer in *England*, and to see other parts of the kingdom, then he might take a tour of six months in the following manner; *viz.*

1. *York* and *les environs*, in the month of *April*.

2. *Leeds* and *Manchester*, in *May*.

3. *Liverpoole* and *Chester*, in *June*.

4. *Chatsworth* and *Derby*, in *July*.

5. *Nottingham* and *Northampton*, in *August*.

6. From thence through *London* to the place of embarkation, in *September;* visiting the principal seats,

towns,

towns, &c. of *Kent* or *Essex*, in the way to *Dover* or *Harwich.*

Chap. IV. Containing observations on the literature and learning of the *English*; and the advantages which persons of different tastes may reap from being acquainted with them.—Concluding with a small catalogue of the *choicest* authors in polite literature, and the several sciences;—with a list of our best plays, as to *morals, language,* and *design;* that so a foreigner may know, when it shall be worth his while to go to our theatres.

XI. PROPOSAL.

To *cut some canals between our great towns of trade, for the conveniency and cheapness of carriage.*—Canals are much preferable to the making rivers navigable, even where both might be done. For in the first place, the *expence* is not greater, except perhaps the purchase of the ground. In the next place, they are kept and repaired at a much easier rate. They are not subject to inundations, or the shifting of the sand and gravel, and are generally much *shorter* and *streighter.* But what is above every other consideration, a boat laden with merchandize in a canal, may be drawn by a *single* horse, on a full *trot,* as in *Holland, up* or *down* the stream, whether there be a *flood* or *not;* and requires but *two* men to guide it.

If a canal was dug between *Reading* and *Bath,* then there would be an easy and cheap communication between the two principal cities of the kingdom, *London* and *Bristol:* Goods and passengers might be carried at *one quarter* of the present expence: And surely 75*l. per cent.* saved in *freight,* deserves consideration. The River *Kennet* from *Reading* to *Silbury-Hill,* is a plain illustration how practicable *so far* such a scheme might be. And from thence

to

to the descent towards *Caln*, on the *Bath* side, is the only difficulty. But such who have seen the great canal of *Languedoc*, are very well assured it might easily be performed, and at a fortieth part of the expence which the other was. Nay, on the flat grounds near *Yatesbury* Church, water is so plenty in the winter time, that it lies upon the surface for weeks together. And as there are rising grounds on both sides, reservoirs might be made to receive the land-floods, and supply the canal with water, during the dry season. But if the canal itself was only sunk ten or twelve feet *deeper than ordinary*, for two or three furlongs, it is very probable, that natural springs would be met with between those hills. For the wells at *Yatesbury*, as I remember, are not twenty feet deep. What a pity is it therefore, that so many advantages are *neglected?* If the like situation had been in *France*, a canal had been made long ago. Indeed something might have been alleged in our excuse, had we the same difficulties to encounter with, which the *French* surmounted in making the canal of *Languedoc*, and are again to surmount in making the new canal, from the *Durance* to *Marseilles*. But there are no obstructions of rivers and rivulets in our way; no need of making arches, and troughs of stone to carry the canal over them;—no steep hills to ascend, or mountains to pierce through : And yet the thing is not so much as attempted, though the common interest, and the situation of the country, so strongly invite us to perform it.

A canal also ought to be dug between *Glascow* and the shoar opposite to *Alloway;* which would open a communication between *Glascow*, and *Leith* the port of *Edinburgh*. The situation in these parts is extremely inviting, even more so than the former; as the passage is much shorter. And our soldiers in times of peace might be employed in the publick works, alternately with performing their exercise, receiving a suitable addition to their pay, when they are at work.

89 XII. PROPOSAL.

XII. PROPOSAL.

To *raise a fishery on the northern coast of* Scotland, by giving a double premium for some years, till the trade is sufficiently established, for all herrings caught and cured by persons *residing* within certain districts, and *exported* to *foreign* markets.

Several other schemes have been lately offered to the publick in relation to this matter; and all of them, undoubtedly, good in *some* respects. Every thing of this nature hath its respective convenience and inconvenience. And if the scheme for carrying on the fisheries by means of a *joint stock*, and a *company*, impower'd to make *bylaws*, and prescribe *rules* and *regulations*, can stand clear of the imminent hazard of degenerating into a jobb, through the corrupt influence and sinister views of the *managers* and *directors* of such a Company;—I say, if the scheme is freed from all reasonable suspicion of tending to such a point, I should much rather prefer it to that which is here, with great submission, offered in its stead. It is certain, that a joint stock is a *quicker* and more *expeditious* way;—but the encouragement of a *double bounty* appears to me more *sure*, and *less liable* to be corrupted. For in this latter case, there are no sums advanced till the work is done, and the herrings publickly examined, whether they are marketable or not: There is no *fingering* of the money in the mean time by *managers* and *directors;* nor can there be any *items* of *expences* and *disbursements, fees* and *salaries*, brought to account: Things which are the *bane* of all publick societies, and the great cause of their corruption, and degenerating from their original institution.

Besides, if a *double bounty*, or perhaps *five shillings per* barrel, were given for all herrings so *cured* and *exported*, it seems to me, that the *Dutch* themselves would be

tempted

tempted by the *lucre* of such a *bounty*, to settle on the northern coasts of *Scotland*, and make one people with the inhabitants of the country;—which would be the greatest advantage that part of the kingdom could possibly receive.

XIII. PROPOSAL.

To *establish Civil Governments at* Gibraltar *and* Port-Mahone, *and make them free ports.*—The situation of *Gibraltar* is extremely commodious for vending several sorts of commodities in *Spain* and *Barbary:* And the island of *Minorca* is not less happily situated for carrying on an advantageous commerce with some parts of *France* and *Italy*, and, by means of the neighbouring island of *Majorca*, with *Spain* also. Several sorts of coarse woollen stuffs, and *Manchester* goods, would be acceptable in *Barbary*, provided they could be had reasonably cheap: Which can never be till there is a *free port*. Several sorts of the manufactures of *Manchester* and *Spittle-Fields*, would be very agreeable to the taste of the *Spaniards, French*, and *Italians*. But above all, our *Birmingham* ware, our cutlery, razors and scissars, watches and chains, locks, metal buttons, snuff boxes, toys, and all the sorts of *Bijoux d'Angleterre*, as the *French* call them, which they are inexpressibly fond of, would find a prodigious vent in all these countries. The least amount of the whole trade, that might be carried on by means of these two ports, were they made *free*, would be 100,000*l.* a year. And surely such a sum is worth the *getting;*—especially by a nation 80,000,000*l.* in *debt*.

If a scheme of this kind was to take place in the island of *Minorca*, it would then also stand a fair chance of being peopled by *English* families, or by such as are *well-affected*

to

to the *English* Government. Whereas at present there
are scarce any, except the garrison, but *bigoted Spaniards*,
who at the first taking of the place, would have been glad
to have parted with their possessions for a trifle, and to
have retired into *Spain*. But now they are got immensely
rich; their lands are said to be more than *five times* their
former value; and yet their *bigotry* and *aversion* continue
as strong as ever.

XIV. PROPOSAL.

To have *publick inspectors* into all our manufactures;
and to oblige *all exporters* to deliver in *samples* of the
commodities they intend to export, in order that they may
be *compared together*, before the goods are suffered to be
put on *ship-board*. This, if faithfully and honestly executed, would always keep up the credit of our manufactures at home and abroad, on which the spirit and life of
trade principally depends. All possible means should be
taken to prevent private frauds in packing—deficiencies
in weight and measure—undue stretching of cloths upon
the rack, which alone hath occasioned *irreparable* loss to
this nation. The fraudulent and deceitful should be prevented, as *much* as it is *possible*, from getting rich at the
expence of their honest neighbours, and the welfare of
their country, which is too often *sacrificed* to their
knavery.

In short, in all kinds of manufactures, the worst part
of it should be put *outermost* for a *sample*, not the best;
that so the buyer, in seeing the *mark* and *seal* of the *office*,
may *confide* in *that*, and be assured, that he is *not deceived*
by what is *out* of *sight*.

XV. PROPOSAL.

To *alter the method of collecting our duties upon parti-cular sorts of goods imported, viz.* By lodging them in warehouses erected at the publick expence, till the importer fetches them away, according as he wants them, and pays the duty, or causes it to be paid by the person who purchases of him. This scheme, I am sensible, would raise a great clamour, if enforced by any *compulsive* law; but if left to each person's *free choice*, there is the highest probability, that it would universally obtain. Suppose therefore, that the laws relating to the customs in general should continue as they are; but that *permission* should be granted to such persons as are *desirous* of using it, to land their goods in the *publick* magazines, there to remain at the usual moderate rent for cellerage, till such time as they find it their interest to remove them, and then to pay the duty. If such a permission was granted to the importers of *sugars, rum, wines, brandies, tobacco, raisins, prunes,* and *currants,* it is easy to foresee, that almost every one concerned would embrace it. For, in the first place, the † expence of warehouse-room would be just the same; but the difference between paying the duty *all at once* upon importation, and paying it *by degrees*, would be very great, and much to the advantage both of the importer, and the publick. The importer would be a gainer,

98   a a

---

* Something hath been already said on this subject, page 389. Where a police was proposed to prevent smuggling: But as truth is uniform throughout, and is attended with all possible advantages, the proposal is now considered under another view.

† If no publick magazines were erected, the merchant might put the goods in his own warehouse, having one key himself, and the King's officer another.

as he would not be streightened for money to pay the duties every time his ship arrives; and might keep his goods till he saw a promising market, or might export them to some foreign country, if they bore there a better price.   And this itself would be a great advantage to the publick, as it would render *our* country a kind of common magazine for *others*, and as we should get by it all the profits of freight and commission: And persons of *intelligence* and *speculation* would then engage in the speculative part of trade; that is, they would buy up all commodities that were cheap in foreign countries, lodge them in their own, or the King's warehouses, and then re-export them to those countries where the demand ran highest.   But this cannot be done upon the present system of paying duties.   Moreover, the publick would be more especially beuefited, as the trade would be increased, and the goods afforded much the cheaper.   When a trade can be carried on with a *small* stock, the more persons are capable of embarking in it: And when the duties are not paid all at once, but by degrees, as the goods can be sold, the *home-consumer* will buy so much the cheaper.   For he will only pay the king's simple duty,—the expences of the adventure,—and the merchant's single gains upon that adventure: Whereas, according to the present way of collecting the revenue, every consumer pays *another* considerable article, viz. *the gains of the merchant on the sums advanced to pay the King's duty.*   And if the goods have passed from the merchant *importer* to the last *retailer*, through two or three hands, before they come to the consumer, then he pays *two* or *three* advances the more.[*]   So that in fact, he not only pays the *first* duty to the King, but perhaps twice as much again to others, by means of these

94

advances

---

[*] See this affair set in a *true* and *strong* light in a Treatise entitled, *An Essay on the Causes of the Decline of the Foreign Trade,* *London,* 1744.   Printed for *J. Brotherton.*

advances upon *advances.* The consequence of all which is, that trade becomes monopolized by a few rich persons, because there is a greater stock required to carry it on: And *smugylers* will be the *more numerous*, and the more audacious, because the *temptations* to, and the *gains* of *smuggling*, become so much the greater. Whereas by the method now proposed, both these mischiefs would be prevented to a great degree. ☞ Observe, 1*st*, the proposal here made, *compels* no persons to submit to these regulations, but only *permits* them to make use of them, if they are *disposed* to do it. ☞ Observe, 2*dly*, that this scheme requires no *new officers*, even at the commencement of it: And when it has been thoroughly tried and known, it would certainly greatly *lessen the number* of them. A set of publick magazines (which, by the by, might be so contrived, as to be *ornamental* as well as *useful*) built uniformly, and in a quadrangular figure, might easily be taken care of and inspected by a very few officers, who might well be spared from the numbers now employed as *land-waiters, tide-waiters, searchers, deputies, extraordinary men,* &c. &c. ☞ Observe 3*dly*, that with respect to any *embezzlement*, which these magazine-keepers might be suspected of, this might be prevented, as much as any thing of such a nature can possibly be (not only by weighing the goods, gauging them, and taking samples before they are delivered into the officers care) but also by making it necessary, that these officers should be engaged with two sufficient bondsmen in two sorts of securities, *one* to the King, to enforce their fidelity to him, and *another* to the mayor or chief magistrate of the town, and his successors, where the magazine is kept, in trust for the merchants, to ensure their honesty to them: And that when any of these officers are suspected of embezzling the merchants property, the party aggrieved may be at liberty to bring an action in the name of the mayor, or chief magistrate for the time being, and recover *treble* damages, with

costs

costs of suit, on proof of such embezzlemeut. Now in *all* these respects the *present* proposal differs entirely from the *late famous excise scheme;* and *every* objection made against *that,* is obviated *here.*

As this last proposal, and one or two more, would be attended with some expence, were they carried into execution;—and as the nation, in its present circumstances, might be supposed incapable of bearing a farther load; I shall therefore endeavour to point out a method how certain taxes might be raised, without *burdening* any of the *necessaries* of life,—and yet *sufficient* to answer *all* these expences,—and be moreover highly conducive to the reformation of the morals of the people, and the general welfare of the kingdom, *viz.*

XVI. PROPOSAL.

To lay certain taxes on the following articles of *luxury, vice,* or *extravagance;* which taxes shall be applied to the general improvement of commerce; by maintaining consuls, and erecting forts, according to Proposal VI. Building of magazines and warehouses, as specified in Proposal XV. Giving bounties and personal premiums to the *greatest exporters* of our *own* manufactures,—the like to the *greatest importers* of *raw materials* from *foreign* countries,—especially from our *own plantations,* according to Proposal VIII. And in short, by pursuing all such ways and means, as serve to *excite* the merchant and manufacturer to promote the interest of their country, and their own together. Wherefore, the

　1st tax proposed is, that upon *batchelors* and *widowers,* of a certain age, without children.

The manifold ill consequences that flow from the

modish

modish practice of mens living batchelors, are too glaring and evident. For we may venture to pronounce, without any degree of uncharitableness, that it is *one* great cause of all the lewdness and debauchery of this age. Some *few* indeed undoubtedly there are, who no ways contribute to these immoralties by their single life. But they are too inconsiderable in number to deserve to have particular exemptions, even were it possible to *distinguish* them from others, which it is not possible to do in a *legal* way. In all things calculated for the *general* good, some *individuals* must suffer; and it cannot be avoided. Now (to consider this matter merely in a *commercial* light) as there are at least ninety-nine in an hundred, who gratify their desires, but *so as to add* no *proper* increase to the *publick* stock of inhabitants, in which the *riches* and *strength* of a nation do consist, one may easily judge of the evil of such a practice, by its bad consequences. And in *London* particularly, where this vice of living batchelors *mostly prevails*, there it is observable, by the *bills of* * *mortality*, that

97

more

---

* To this paragraph it has been objected, that the yearly bills of mortality, which make the burials more than the births, are not to be *relied* upon, as to this point: " Because there are no births registered, " but the births of those who are baptized according to the form of " the *Established* Church; whereas *Dissenters* of most denominations " are *buried* in the Church, and consequently *registered* there."

Now as it is a very material article to know, with some degree of *certainty*, whether more persons *die* in *London*, than are *born*;—and consequently, whether the whole city would not be *depopulated* in a century or two, if the inhabitants followed the *same courses* they *now* do, were it not for the influx of *strangers*, to supply these *deficiencies*; I shall therefore beg leave to offer the following considerations, in reply to the above objection.

I. Some children are *begot* in the country, yet *born* in *London*; such, for instance, whose mothers come up to town for the convenience of *skilful* attendance : And as this is the case with *many* families of distinction, consequently, the *number of births* is so much *increased*.

II. Many persons contract their *death-sickness* in *London*, yet are *more* persons *die* than are *born*, every year.　So that were it not for the continual supplies from the country, where the marriage state is not yet quite so *unfashionable*, that great metropolis would be *depopulated* in a course of years. And yet there is no place, in which there are so great numbers of the female sex, in the proportion, as in *London*. Can it be credited, though perhaps it is too true, that in this city alone there are upwards of *ten thousand loose women*, from sixteen years old to forty, who have not *fifty* children in a year?　And the few they have, are *born* with all *sorts* of *disorders*, and *educated*, if they chance to live, in all *kinds* of *vice* and *wickedness?*　In short, it has been often remarked, that the greatest *rakes*, that all *Europe*

98

can

---

carried out of it for the benefit of the air, and *die* in the country; there they are *buried*, and *no notice* taken of them in the *registers* within the bills of mortality.

III. Just the same is the case of those, who *die* in *London*, yet are *carried* to their *burial-places* in the country : The number of these is considerable in the year ; whereas there are few instances of persons being carried out of the country, to be interred in *London*.

IV. Many Dissenters of different denominations have *burial-places* of *their own* ; and consequently, the numbers of their dead do not *swell* the registers of the Established Church *so much* as might be imagined.

But allowing, that the numbers of Dissenters buried in the Established Church, may make *some* difference in the account, still this difference cannot amount to any thing *near* the sum which is found to be the difference between *births* and *burials* in the compass of a year ; *viz.* about seven thousand souls. The numbers of births, generally speaking, amount to 14, or 16000 in a year ; and the burials from 21, to 24,000 in the same time : A difference of *three* to *two*. How soon would this depopulate any country, were it not for foreign supplies !　And how terrible do the effects of *vice, lewdness* and *debauchery*, appear to the general interests of a kingdom, when seen from this point of view !　What an absurdity, therefore, was it in the author of *The Fable of the Bees*, to say, *that private vices are publick benefits !* It is *virtue* alone, which can make a nation *flourish*. And vice of every kind is, either *immediately*, or in its *consequences*, injurious to commerce.

can produce, when they arrive in *England*, and come to *London*, are quite *shocked* and *scandalized* at the *unparalleled* lewdness and debauchery reigning among *us*, so far beyond any thing they could have imagined. Now if these 10,000 *loose* women had not been *debauched* and *corrupted*, and were married to persons of their own rank and condition, they might have had at least *one thousand* healthy children every year; and these in a fair way to be bred to *honest* trades and callings. Besides, upon the present footing, the *injustice* done to the *married* tradesman, and landed gentleman, is most grievous and intolerable. * For *they* pay the excise, and several other duties, in proportion to the consumption of their families; but the *batchelor* pays only for his *single* self; *i. e.* Those who are *most beneficial* to the publick, are *doubly*, *trebly* or *quadruply* taxed, *in proportion* as *they are beneficial;* and others who are a *nusance* to it, are *therefore* exempted. Is there any justice or equity in this? I add, men may understand these things as *patriots* and *politicians*, who would turn a deaf ear to lectures in *morality* and *divinity*. Nay more, such *abounding of lewdness*, and *surfeiting of prostitution*, doth in fact tend to *increase* the more *unnatural vices*, instead of preventing them, as it is vulgarly, though erroneously, supposed. And the history of *all* nations, from the former times down to the present, confirms this assertion. Antient *Greece* and *Rome*, and modern *England*, to mention no more, have furnished *too many* examples in proof of this point. And reason itself should tell us, that it is with *this*, as with all other *depraved* appetites, where *surfeiting* and *satiety* are inducements to seek out *less natural* ways of gratification.

Wherefore the *proposal* here is, that all *batchelors*, after they have attained to the age of *twenty-five* years, shall pay treble King's tax,—poor tax,—window tax,—and the taxes

99

upon

---

upon coaches, till they *marry:* And that all *widowers,* between *thirty* and *fifty, if they have no children,* shall pay double. Thus the *greatest, i. e.* the *wealthiest* offenders, are properly mulcted. For undoubtedly *they* have it in their power to settle in the world, if they will. They are the people who set bad examples; and by their station, riches, intrigues, and address, debauch those young women at first, who afterwards become the *common prostitutes* of the town. But as this only reaches the *wealthiest* of them; and as there are *vast numbers* of single men, whom this scheme would not affect, therefore there should be added to it a *general capitation* tax for *all batchelors,* of whatsoever degree, above twenty five years of age. And if this was fixed at *twenty shillings* a head *per ann.* for all above the condition of day-labourers, and at *ten shillings* for them (with an exemption only for common soldiers and sailors) it would be a very just and equitable law, and would certainly be attended with many good consequences, both as to the *morals* and the *commerce* of the nation. The

2*d* tax proposed, is, that upon *menial* men-servants, *i. e.* such who are *not* employed either for the purposes of *husbandry* or *commerce,* but for *state* and *grandeur.*

It was the great principle, which run through the whole plan of *The Essay on the Causes of the Decline of Foreign Trade,* before quoted, that each person should tax himself according to the figure and station of life he *chose* to appear in;—but that all the *necessaries* of life should be *duty free.* Now in the case before us, livery servants, footmen, valets, men cooks, &c. &c. certainly *cannot* be ranked among the *necessaries* of life, and therefore are the *proper* subjects for such a tax. If any one *chooses* to have them, he himself chooses to *appear* in an *elevated* condition, and therefore is the *fittest* to *pay* towards *improving* the commerce, and *extending* the general interest of the kingdom.

But

But that is not all: For these men-servants, generally speaking, are by nature *fitter* for *other* employments, had they not taken up with this *idle* one; and might have been *useful* to their country, by *sea* or *land*, either in the several parts of *husbandry*, or in *laborious* trades; whereas by their present way of living they render themselves *useless* in *all* respects; and not only so, but keep thousands of the other sex out of an *honest* employment, which by *nature* they are *fittest* for; and very often are *tempted* for the want of it to take to *vicious* courses. I believe it will hardly be denied, but that women servants *might* perform all the functions, which men servants do, in respect to *waiting* at *table*, *tending* the *tea-kettle*, &c. and equally as well. They *might* walk behind their ladies, and *carry* their books to church, as well as any footman, and *why* they are not permitted to do it, is matter of some *astonishment* to a thinking mind. In short, the *poorer* and the *middling* part of the female sex, are *deprived* of those employments which properly *belong* to them, very often to their own *utter ruin*, and the *detriment* of society. If a young woman has a *genteelish* education, and a *small* fortune, she stands upon the *brink* of *destruction*; and even if she is desirous, she scarcely knows, *what trade* to put herself to, in order to be out of the way of *temptation*. For, excepting two or three trades, which women still retain, all the rest are *engrossed* by *men*. We have *men-mantua-makers*, *men-milliners*, *men-staymakers*, *men-shoemakers for womens shoes*, *men-hair-cutters for womens hair*, &c. and very likely in time we shall have *sempstresses*, *laundresses*, and *clear-starchers*, of the same sex.

Such perversions as these, of the order of society, are not of *small* ill consequence, either to the welfare of *individuals*, or the good of the *State*. And therefore to *discourage* such practices as *much* as may be, in the affair of men-servants, the proposal is, that each of them shall be taxed *two-shillings and sixpence* in the pound, according to their wages, to be paid by their masters and mistresses, and to be collected by the officers of the window tax. If a scheme of this nature were effectually put in practice, the consequence would be, either, that women-servants would be employed, *rather* than men, which would answer a good end in that respect;—or else, that these men-servants tho' idle and useless in themselves, would contribute to the promoting of commerce and extending our trade, by means of the tax they pay for this end;—though sorely *against* their *will.*

The 3*d* tax proposed, is, that upon saddle-horses.

The tax upon coaches, as far as it went, was an *excellent* and *publick-spirited* Act of the Legislature. It was laying the burden, where it ought *always* to be laid, *viz,* upon the *luxuries,* the *ornaments* and *refinements* of living. But undoubtedly it was *defective* as to its *extent;* Many gentlemen of fortune, especially if they are single, do not *choose* to keep coaches; and others may live in such parts of the country, where the situation is not *convenient* for their so doing. Yet they all keep *saddle* horses in abundance,—*hunters,*—and perhaps *racers,*—without paying any tax: though these things are articles of mere luxury, parade and pleasure, as much as coaches. Is there now any equity or justice in this? And are not such persons the properest subjects to pay towards the support of our manufactures, and extending our commerce? Undoubtedly they are: And therefore the proposal is this, that all owners of *saddle horses,* young horses under *five years* old excepted, be *taxed* at the rate of *five shillings* per horse *every* year;—saving only *one horse,* which shall be admitted to be kept *free* of all *tax* by each owner, on the supposition, that *riding* may be *necessary* for his *health,* or on account of *business.* If *greater* allowances than this were made, it would be opening a door for *fraud* and *collusion:* And if *less,* it might bear hard upon the *real* wants and necessities of many people. Perhaps even this in-

dulgence

dulgence of one horse, *tax-free*, to each proprietor, might seem too rigorous a restraint; and might actually be so in *certain* circumstances; but in all cases of *publick* concern, it is impossible to adjust things in such a manner, as that *every* person can be *pleased*,—or even that the interest of *every* individual may be so *particularly* taken care of, according to the nature of his *peculiar* circumstances, as that he can have no just reason to *complain*. To proceed therefore, the

4th tax proposed to be levied is on *dogs* of *every* sort and kind, except *shepherds* dogs, and *house* dogs. For every thing beyond this, is most undoubtedly an article of *luxury*, and *diversion*; and as *such*, justly liable to be taxed.

Wherefore the proposal is, that the owners of all dogs shall pay *one shilling* for each dog every year. And as there are such prodigious numbers of hounds, greyhounds, pointers, setters, spaniels, beagles, lap-dogs, and turnspits all over the kingdom, this would bring in a very considerable revenue, which might be employed to the greatest national advantage, in supporting and extending our trade and commerce. If this tax should cause a *diminution* of the species, there would be no *harm* in *that*; nay, it would be attended with a great deal of *good*; as for many *other* reasons, so particularly for this, that the *dreadful* and *shocking* calamities attending the *bite* of *mad dogs*, would be less frequent than they now are. If any one should object, that *turn-spits* ought to be considered as *necessary implements* for dressing of *victuals*, and therefore ought to be excepted out of this regulation. The answer is obvious and easy; *viz.* That *jacks*, and *smoke-jacks* are preferable to *turn-spits* in every respect: They are cheaper, all things considered; and a species of manufacture, which ought to be encouraged. But above all, there is no danger from them of those shocking consequences aforementioned, which every year have occasioned the deaths of many people, in the most dreadful manner.

Add to this, that no other method, than what is here proposed, can be effectual for the preservation of the game. For as long as poachers of all kinds are allowed to keep dogs, free of any tax, it will be impossible for penal laws, in such a constitution as *England* is under, to prevent their using them to the destruction of the game. But the laying a tax upon dogs strikes at the principal root of the evil complained of.

The 5*th* tax proposed, is a *double* turnpike tax on all persons who *travel* on *Sundays*. A *modish* and *reigning* vice this! which ought to receive some *check* and *discountenance* from the Legislature. Not once in a thousand times can there be a just and reasonable excuse for this practice; and therefore it becomes a proper and fit subject for a tax, according to the principles before laid down.

In short, we submit it with great deference to the judgment of the intelligent reader, whether there is not ample provision made in this proposal, for all the expences which might be incurred by the execution of any of the rest;—and that without burdening *any one* article of the *real* necessaries of life. Were the taxes to be laid, as here recommended, they would indeed very probably cause a *considerable* diminution of the articles which were to pay these taxes: But even that circumstance would prove, in many respects, a very great national advantage. And were the monies raised by these taxes, properly, judiciously, and faithfully applied to the good uses and purposes before mentioned, perhaps there would not be a nation in the world, which could vie with us in uumber of inhabitants, extent of commerce, and the flourishing state of our colonies and factories in both the *Indies*.

Taxes, in their own nature, if they are properly and judiciously laid on, are so far from causing commerce to stagnate, that they quicken and enliven it: And therefore may be compared to the *pruning* of a tree by a *skilful* hand, by which means the tree is preserved in health, and

lasts

lasts the longer. The fruit (upon the whole) is more in quantity and better in quality, and a vigorous circulation, and equal nourishment are maintained throughout. Whereas, on the other hand, one single tax, though small in its amount, if injudiciously laid on, so as to stop the progress or circulation of labour, is in fact the *heaviest* and most *insupportable* of all others. This is a doctrine little understood, especially by the *landed* interest, who of all persons ought to study it the most, as it never can be their interest to act upon a contrary principle.

CON-

CONCLUSION.

AND thus have I ventured to give my sentiments, with that *freedom* and *unreservedness*, which is natural to men who mean well, and whose *sole aim* is the good and prosperity of their country. As I have no *private ends* of my own to serve, either the one way or the other, I have had no biass of self-interest upon my mind.

It is true, I confess, that *many* of the proposals here made, are subjects very *unpopular* in the present times: Neither would I willingly have advanced any thing *harsh* or *disagreeable*, even to *prejudiced* minds, *were it possible* to have made *truth* and *popularity*, in this case, consist together. But since that cannot be, what must be done? Must we still go on, increasing in our *disorders*, and beholding our *rivals* taking their advantage of these misfortunes, merely because some people do not *choose* to be told where the *core* of the evil lies, and how it may be *taken out?* If the alterations here proposed, are *necessary* or *advantageous* to the publick, *that* alone should be *sufficient* to recommend them to the esteem of *all* persons of *worth* and *character;* but if they are not, I put in no plea or apology for them:—Only I will add, on behalf of the author, that his *intentions* were *good*, though he was mistaken.

I am also well aware, that there is a customary prepossession entertained against projects of all kinds; and that projectors are looked upon as a race of beings who have something very singular and whimsical in their composition. And yet I think it must be allowed, that, notwithstanding all the prejudice which some chimerical gentlemen of this stamp have drawn upon themselves, there must be both *projects* and *projectors*, when things are *bad*, and

want

want *mending* ; otherwise they never could be *better*, nor the faults *corrected*.

With respect to the case before us, there are two *general objections*, as far as I am able to perceive, which may be made against what has been advanced.

The *first* is, that many of the *proposals*, though they may be *right* in *theory*, are *impracticable* in *fact*.

The *second* is, that the schemes here laid down, are attended with their inconveniences as well as others.

To the first of these I reply; that no one can be *certain* of this, till an attempt has been made to put them in practice : And we may be very sure, every one of them might be easily put in execution, were persons as really animated with the love of their country, and as truly concerned for its welfare and prosperity, as they *pretend* to be ; and had some among us, in *their opposition* to every measure of the government, no *dark, latent* scheme at heart, which they *cover* over with *specious* names.

Besides, none of these schemes, no, not all of them together, are so difficult in themselves to be carried into execution, as that *single* one which has been so happily *perfected* in our own days, the union with *Scotland*. In that case, inveterate *national* prejudices,—*national* pride, —*family*-interest, — *self*-interest, —*jacobitical* interest,— *pretences* of *conscience*,—*fears* of *religion*, and the respective *Churches* of *both* kingdoms : All these conspired to heap up difficulties in the way. And yet all were surmounted by the firmness and address of those *true* patriots of both kingdoms, to their immortal honour, who had the management of that affair. Whereas in the present case, there can be no *pretences* of *conscience*, no *fears* of the *Church*'s being in *danger*, to encounter with : There are no *national* animosities, or *national* pride, or the *interest* of great families, to obstruct us ; and very little of *party spirit* can mingle in any of these affairs : *Self-interest* is the chief obstacle to be surmounted. This is indeed a

great

great one, which will draw every thing that it can to its assistance.　But it is not insuperable, if withstood by men who have a *true* love for their country, and prudence and discretion to *time* their endeavours, and *guide* them aright.

Moreover : Supposing *none* of these *proposals* are such as will go down at present, while men are full of their prejudices, and fond of their own opinions : Yet, even in that case, it may not be amiss to lay before them the things *that are right* ; which they may consider of at their leisure.　When men come to *reason* and *reflect*, their prejudices will begin to *soften* ; and time will *reconcile* them to those expedients, which they had *inveighed* bitterly against before ; perhaps for *want* of *understanding* and *knowing* them better.　Thus it often happens, that proposals deemed impracticable at *one* season, on account of the *popular outcry* against them, may be called for at *another*, with equal vehemence and impatience.　And therefore, with humble submission, it may not be amiss to leave these proposals upon record for future *examination*, though none of them should be judged *feasible* at the present.

But besides the former *objection*, a second is, that this scheme itself is attended with *inconveniencies*, as well as others.

I grant it is : And surely no man in his senses could ever suppose, that there could be any scheme calculated for the *general* good, which would not bear hard upon the interests of some *particular* people,—the true way of estimating any proposal is, to consider, whether it doth remedy more *old* inconveniencies than it introduces *new* ones ; and whether, upon the *whole*, it is *beneficial* or not, and its benefits of such *importance* as deserve to be regarded?　Lastly, whether likewise some of these very inconveniencies which are supposed to attend it, may not be *prevented* or *amended* by further experience and obser-

vation.

vation. This is the true way for estimating any proposal: And by this rule I would choose that my own should be tried; and then let them stand or fall.

We are always complaining of the bad morals of our people; of a general corruption; and the being out-rivalled in trade. Nevertheless, it is very certain, that the present system of things greatly contributes to the increase of each of these evils. My meaning is, that it lays powerful temptations in peoples way. And then, what can be expected? Some *few* perhaps will prove their virtue to be superior; but the *great majority* will certainly be corrupted. For evident it is, that the *innocence* of the bulk of mankind, is best preserved by their being kept *ignorant* of the temptation, or at a great distance from it. Now what is the natural tendency of *customhouse oaths, election oaths, freedom oaths,* &c. &c. but to entice and encourage mankind to be guilty of the foul sin of *wilful* and *deliberate* perjury? What are the *heavy* taxes upon the *married* state, and *exemptions* for *batchelors,* but the like inducements to men to remain *single,* and to gratify their desires in an *unlawful* way? What are all the *exclusive* Companies, all the heavy duties upon importation, and the many statutes for *cramping* the trade of *Ireland,* but so many continued attempts to *drive away* the trade from ourselves to the *French,* who are not only our *rivals,* but the most *dangerous* ones we can have? And truly we have greatly succeeded in all these: Yet who can we blame but ourselves: It may be pleaded indeed in excuse for these laws and establishments, that they were not originally intended to produce those *bad* effects. I allow they were not; nor are they charged with any such design. But the question here is, not what was the view of the makers of these laws, or what was the end proposed by such establishments, but what is the *tendency* of them, as verified by *experience,* and how they do *operate* in fact? And if it is made to appear that they are so destructive in their consequences, and subversive of our *morals, liberties,* and *commerce,* it is but of little consolation to know, that they were established with a better view; as we are now considering the things themselves, with their natural consequences, not the characters or design of their authors and projectors.

I will only add one reflection more to what has been said; *viz.* that if we would still keep on our trade at a *foreign* market, we must, at least, be upon an *equal* footing with *other* nations, as to the *goodness* and *cheapness* of what we have to sell; otherwise we cannot expect, that foreigners should give us the preference to their own loss. This then being the state of the case, it necessarily follows, that we must always have an eye upon the practices and proceedings of our *rivals,* and take our measures accordingly, as far as regards this mutual emulation. If *they* contrive ways and means to render their *manufactures* cheaper or better than they did before, so as to outvie us, *we* must strive to outvie them in cheapness and goodness, or be deprived of that part of commerce by them: If *they* invite foreigners to settle among them, in order to have the more hands, and to keep down the price of labour; *we* must do the same, or take the consequence to ourselves: If *they* allow of no exclusive companies in a branch of trade which *interferes* with our trade; *we* must put down our companies, or lose *that* trade: If *their* manufacturers are sober and industrious, and work for low wages, and seldom become a burden upon their parishes; *we* must endeavour to put *ours* upon the same footing, or be content with the poverty which will be brought upon us: If *their* government requires little or no duties upon importation, in order to encourage the greater numbers to engage in trade, and that all merchandize may come the cheaper to the consumer; *we* must *imitate* them in that respect, and change our customs into in-land duties; or administer continual temptation to the needy and fraudu-

lent

lent to turn smugglers, and suffer ourselves to sink under these evils, together with the burden and weight of our customs. These are the alternatives which are set before us; and one would think, that if mankind were not greatly blinded with their prejudices, and biassed by private interests and sinister views, they need not be long in deliberating which to choose. Not to 'mention, that as every country in *Europe* now begins to understand the maxims of trade, and apply themselves to commerce, and are actually raising *all sorts* of manufactures of their own, and have laid *new* duties upon ours;—for these reasons, *we* ought to be *more* intent than *ever* to contrive all ways and means possible to *lower* the price of every thing we *export*, in order to *overbalance* these additional duties by dint of *cheapness* of labour, and to outvie these *new rivals* by the *goodness* of our manufactures.

APPENDIX.

THE author has annexed an Appendix to his Tract, containing some extracts from the " Essay on the " Causes of the Decline of Foreign Trade," with comments thereon. But as this Essay, has already been laid before the reader, and the comments are of little value, we have not thought it worth while to re-print them. We believe, however, we shall do an acceptable service to the reader by substituting in their stead an extract from the travels of the celebrated Dr. Smollett, which embodies some striking statements with respect to the condition of France in 1765. They may be regarded as supplementary to those of Tucker (*ante* pp. 330-336); and they are especially interesting from their fore-shadowing that tremendous convulsion which, at no very distant period, overwhelmed the government, the church, the aristocracy, and all that was established in France.

" You ask whether I think the French people are more taxed than the English; but I apprehend, the question would be more apropos if you asked whether the French taxes are more insupportable than the English: for, in comparing burthens, we ought always to consider the strength of the shoulders that bear them. I know no better way of estimating the strength, than by examining the face of the country, and observing the appearance of the common people, who constitute the bulk of every nation. When I, therefore, see the country of England smiling with cultivation; the grounds exhibiting all the perfection of agriculture, parcelled out into beautiful in-

        closures,

closures, cornfields, hay and pasture, woodland and common; when I see her meadows well stocked with black cattle; her downs covered with sheep; when I view her teams of horses and oxen, large and strong, fat and sleek; when I see her farm-houses the habitations of plenty, cleanliness, and convenience; and her peasants well fed, well lodged, well clothed, tall and stout, and hale and jolly; I cannot help concluding that the people are well able to bear those impositions which the public necessities have rendered necessary. On the other hand, when I perceive such signs of poverty, misery, and dirt, among the commonality of France, their unfenced fields dug up in despair, without the intervention of meadow or fallow ground, without cattle to furnish manure, without horses to execute the plans of agriculture; their farm-houses mean, their furniture wretched, their apparel beggarly; themselves and their beasts the images of famine; I cannot help thinking they groan under oppression, either from their landlords, or their government; probably from both.

"The principal impositions of the French government are these: First, the taille, payed by all the commons, except those that are privileged: Secondly, the capitation, from which no persons, (not even the nobles) are excepted: Thirdly, the tenths and twentieths, called dixièmes and vingtièmes, which every body pays. This tax was originally levied as an occasional aid in times of war, and other emergencies; but by degrees is become a standing revenue even in time of peace. All the money arising from these impositions goes directly to the king's treasury; and must undoubtedly amount to a very great sum. Besides these, he has the revenue of the farms, consisting of the droits d'aydes, or excise on wine, brandy, &c. of the custom-house duties; of the gabelle, comprehending that most oppressive obligation on individuals to take a certain quantity of salt at the price which the farmers shall please to fix; of the exclusive privilege to sell tobacco; of the droits de controlle, insinuation, centième denier, franchiefs, aubeine, echange et contre echange arising from the acts of voluntary jurisdiction, as well as certain lawsuits. These farms are said to bring into the king's coffers above one hundred and twenty millions of livres yearly, amounting to near five millions sterling: But the poor people are said to pay about a third more than this sum, which the farmers retain to enrich themselves, and bribe the great for their protection; which protection of the great is the true reason why this most iniquitous, oppressive, and absurd method of levying money is not laid aside. Over and above those articles I have mentioned, the French king draws considerable sums from his clergy, under the denomination of dons gratuits, or free-gifts; as well as from the subsidies given by the pays d'etats, such as Provence, Languedoc, and Bretagne, which are exempted from the taille. The whole revenue of the French king amounts to between twelve and thirteen millions sterling. These are great resources for the king: But they will always keep the people miserable, and effectually prevent them from making such improvements as might turn their lands to the best advantage. But besides being eased in the article of taxes, there is something else required to make them exert themselves for the benefit of their country. They must be free in their persons, secure in their property, indulged with reasonable leases, and effectually protected by law from the insolence and oppression of their superiors.

"Great as the French king's resources may appear, they are hardly sufficient to defray the enormous expence of his government. About two millions sterling per annum of his revenue are said to be anticipated for paying the interest of the public debts: and the rest is found inadequate to the charge of a prodigious standing army, a double frontier of fortified towns, and the extravagant appoint-

ment

ments of ambassadors, generals, governors, intendants, commandants, and other officers of the crown, all of whom affect a pomp, which is equally ridiculous and prodigal. A French general in the field is always attended by thirty or forty cooks; and thinks it is incumbent upon him, for the glory of France, to give a hundred dishes every day at his table. When don Philip, and the marechal duke de Belleisle, had their quarters at Nice, there were fifty scullions constantly employed in the great square in plucking poultry. This absurd luxury infects their whole army. Even the commissaries keep open table; and nothing is seen but prodigality and profusion. The king of Sardinia proceeds upon another plan. His troops are better cloathed, better payed, and better fed than those of France. The commandant of Nice has about four hundred a year of appointments, which enable him to live decently, and even to entertain strangers. On the other hand, the commandant of Antibes, which is in all respects more inconsiderable than Nice, has from the French king above five times the sum to support the glory of his monarch, which all the sensible part of mankind treat with ridicule and contempt. But the finances of France are so ill managed, that many of their commandants, and other officers, have not been able to draw their appointments these two years. In vain they complain and remonstrate. When they grow troublesome they are removed. How then must they support the glory of France? how, but by oppressing the poor people. The treasurer makes use of their money for his own benefit. The king knows it; he knows his officers thus defrauded, fleece and oppress his people: But he thinks proper to wink at these abuses. That government may be said to be weak and tottering which finds itself obliged to connive at such proceedings. The king of France, in order to give strength and stability to his administration, ought to have sense to adopt a sage plan of œconomy, and vigour of mind sufficient to execute it in all

 its

its parts, with the most rigorous exactness.   He ought to
have courage enough to find fault, and even to punish the
delinquents, of what quality soever they may be: And the
first act of reformation ought to be a total abolition of all
the farms.   There are, undoubtedly, many marks of re-
laxation in the reins of the French government, and, in all
probability, the subjects of France will be the first to take
the advantage of it.   There is at present a violent fermen-
tation of different principles among them, which under the
reign of a very weak prince, or during a long minority,
may produce a great change in the constitution.   In proportion to the progress of reason and philosophy, which
have made great advances in this kingdom, superstition
loses ground; antient prejudices give way; a spirit of
freedom takes the ascendant.   All the learned laity of
France detest the hierarchy as a plan of despotism,
founded on imposture and usurpation.   The protestants,
who are very numerous in the southern parts, abhor it
with all the rancour of religious fanaticism.   Many of the
commons, enriched by commerce and manufacture, grow
impatient of those odious distinctions, which exclude them
from the honours and privileges due to their importance
in the commonwealth; and all the parliaments, or tribu-
nals of justice in the kingdom, seem bent upon asserting
their rights and independence in the face of the king's
prerogative, and even at the expence of his power and
authority.   Should any prince therefore be seduced by
evil counsellers, or misled by his own bigotry, to take some
arbitrary step, that may be extremely disagreeable to all
those communities, without having spirit to exert the violence of his power for the support of his measures, he will
become equally detested and despised; and the influence
of the commons will insensibly encroach upon the pretensions of the crown.   But if in the time of a minority,
the power of the government should be divided among
different competitors for the regency, the parliaments and

people

people will find it still more easy to acquire and ascertain the liberty at which they aspire, because they will have the balance of power in their hands, and be able to make either scale preponderate. I could say a great deal more upon this subject; and I have some remarks to make relating to the methods which might be taken in case of a fresh rupture with France, for making a vigorous impression on that kingdom. But these I must defer till another occasion, having neither room nor leisure at present to add any thing."—Travels through France and Italy, vol. ii, p. 196, 2nd Ed.

PROPOSALS

Made by His late HIGHNESS the

PRINCE of ORANGE,

To their HIGH MIGHTINESSES the

STATES-GENERAL,

AND TO THE

STATES of HOLLAND

AND

WEST FRIEZLAND,

For redressing and amending the Trade of the REPUBLICK.

Translated out of *Low Dutch*, from the Original, printed at the *Hague*, by Authority.

LONDON:

Printed and sold by H. KENT, at the Printing-Office in *Finch-lane*, near the *Royal Exchange*; and by the Booksellers, and Pamphlet Shops of *London* and *Westminster*,

MDCCLI.

EXTRACT

FROM THE

Register of Resolutions of their High Mightinesses the STATES-GENERAL of the UNITED NETHER-LANDS.

Friday, 27 August 1751.

HIS Highness having represented to the Assembly, that ever since his accession to the stadtholdership of these countries, he has had nothing more at heart, than (under the blessing of Almighty God) to assist, in restoring to the republick, its former flourishing condition; delivered it as his opinion, that the most effectual means hereto, was to put trade, which is one of the principal supports thereof, upon a better footing.

That, as nothing had given his Highness more anxiety, on the one hand, than to hear the daily complaints of a decay of trade in these countries, and the considerable progress and advance which others make therein; so, on the other, he desired nothing more than to contribute something, that might tend to retrieve the commerce of the republick.

That his Highness had already, to that end, for a considerable time past, left no stone unturn'd, in his inqui-

ries

ries after the most skilful and experienced merchants;
who might properly inform him, as well, in what condition,
trade is at present, as suggest to him the best means, for
re-establishing the same.

That he had happily succeeded in this attempt, and
those gentlemen had, with great assiduity, applied themselves to the management of this momentous trust: But
that the difficulties arising from a due discharge of so
arduous and extensive a province, had prevented its being
so soon executed as the importance of the affair required.

That his Highness now had the satisfaction, to deliver
to their High Mightiness, the annexed dissertation, on
the trade of the republick of the *United Netherlands*,
which had been previously put into his hands: wherein
he found such reflections and ideas, as well on the present
situation of the trade of this State, as on the means that
ought especially to be made use of to redress the same,
that his Highness thought proper to present it to their
High Mightinesses.

That his Highness, in the said dissertation, had met
with a proposal for a free port, in regard to such goods and
merchandizes, as are the source of trade in general; and
also for a considerable diminution of the duties on every
branch of commerce, which his Highness considered, as
the only means to revive trade in these countries, and put
the merchants in a condition to deal with others, at least,
on an equal footing, and draw the same into these parts.

That the same appearing to his Highness, to be no less
desirable and advantageous for the trade of the republick,
than useful and necessary for the support of the State,
and having found the said plan or dissertation so well calculated and adapted to the present crisis of affairs, he
could no longer defer the recommending it to their joint
deliberations, in the most pressing and pathetick terms;
and at the same time earnestly desire them with a spirit of

4   unanimity,

unanimity, and all possible dispatch, to give such a due attention to, and draw such salutary reflections from the whole, as the importance of the subject, and a necessity for redressing and amending so general a decay of trade, calls for and requires.

That in confidence of the confederate States being fully persuaded of the same, his Highness doubts not but they will speedily conform thereto; and, by setting aside all sinister and private views, from a sole regard to the publick interest, take such wholesome resolutions, as may give his Highness the desired proofs, that his zeal and application herein, tending to the good of the whole community, has not been disagreeable to their High Mightinesses.

That his Highness wishing these deliberations may be brought to a happy issue, from considering this affair to be of such weighty consequence, that the safety and well-being of the State, under God, depends on the preservation and recovery of trade, has the greatest reason to expect and hope, that, agreeably to his request, not only all prejudices should be removed, and all inconveniences and difficulties still subsisting, set aside; but also, that some speedy resolution should be entered into, for the good of the republick, in order to put in execution the new concerted measures, in the commencement of the succeeding year.

On which, having deliberated, their High Mightinesses return his Highness their sincere and hearty thanks, for his care and particular attention, to the welfare of this state, and the trading inhabitants thereof; and his unwearied zeal and application, in tracing the causes of the decay, and proposing the means of a redress, and recovering the trade thereof.

And further, it is ordered, that copies of the abovementioned proposal, and of the dissertation thereto annexed, be sent to the respective colleges of the admiralty; and it be signified to them in writing, at the same time,

 that

that under the direction of his Highness, as admiral-general of these countries, they do narrowly examine the said dissertation, and maturely weigh the articles therein proposed, for a redress and amendment of trade, carefully collating each article; in order to frame from thence, such drafts of placarts, rules and lists, as they shall judge will be most conducive to the aforesaid salutary design of his Highness; and, in an after conference, with the deputies of their High Mightinesses, acquaint them with the result of their consultations; that on report being made thereof, their High Mightinesses may make such orders relating thereto, as shall be found most for the service of the country, and the benefit of the trading inhabitants of the same.

That, previous to the result of the said consultations so expected, the said proposal of his Highness, and the dissertation thereto annexed, shall be printed; and some copies thereof sent to the States of the respective provinces; earnestly recommending such attention to be given, and such reflections to be made by them on the same, as the importance of the subject, and the necessity of the said amendment, and redress of trade, brought to so low an ebb, require; to the end, that when the deliberations thereon, are brought to maturity, a speedy resolution may be taken on the same, with that mutual harmony and condecension, as shall evidence them to be divested of all prejudices and partial prepossessions arising from personal concerns and self-interested views.

The said proposal was likewise made the same day, by his Highness, in the assembly of their High Mightinesses, the States of *Holland* and *West Friezland*, and a like resolution taken thereupon.

          DISSER-

DISSERTATION

ON THE

Trade of the United Netherlands.

HIS Highness having nothing more at heart, than the preservation and welfare of the trade of this republick, hath thought proper to order, that some eminent and experienced merchants should be consulted on this affair; in order to enable His Highness, as far as in him lay, to contribute towards this fountain of the prosperity and riches of the *United Netherlands*, whose considerations and advice should chiefly turn on the following questions.

1. What is the actual state of the trade? and if the same should be found to be diminished and fallen to decay; then,

2. To inquire by what methods the same may be supported and advanced; or, if possible, be restored to it's former lustre, repute and dignity?

In obedience to these respectable orders of His Highness, some merchants have been accordingly consulted; and tho' in some particular instances, they have not been of the same joint opinion, and have sometimes disagreed in their respective difinitions, yet an entire concurrence has been found in the general, as to their sentiments and argumentations upon the first question.

7

1. What

1. What is the state of our trade?

That for the term of twenty-five years and upwards, the same is remarkably diminished, and in many branches lost. As to the second question,

2. By what methods the same may be supported and promoted?

That the same, in the present circumstances, could only be effected with any tolerable hopes of success, by a diminution of the duties on goods imported and exported, particularly the latter, and the impost on them; which renders the transporting of foreign goods and merchandize through this country difficult and expensive; whereby such merchandizes being conveyed through another channel, must consequently put our neighbours in a condition to undersell our merchants at foreign markets.

It is acknowledged, that the bare allegation of the merchants consisting in this, *that the trade of the republick is diminished*, is no sufficient proof of the argument, tho' back'd with an appeal to their own experience.

But when we examine this affair to the bottom, and attentively reflect on all the circumstarces, which in former times had, and still have relation to trade; and endeavour, more particularly, to discover the means, whereby the trade and commerce of the republick was then established, and afterwards became flourishing; as also, how remarkably the whole system of trade in *Europe* has been since altered; we are well assured, that this representation will not only add a great weight to the said allegation of the merchants, but will be judged equivalent to an ample demonstration.

In order, therefore, methodically to discuss the state of the first question, we shall begin with inquiring into, and pointing out the causes, whereby trade was settled and established in the republick.

Which, it is thought, may be reduced to these three points.

8

I. To

 I. To natural and physical
 II. To moral   } Causes.
 III. To adventitious and external

I. The natural and physical causes, are the advantageous situation of the country, on the sea, and at the mouth of considerable rivers.

Its situation between the northern and southern parts, which, being in a manner the center of all *Europe*, made the republick become the general market, where the merchants, on both sides, used to bring their superfluous commodities, in order to barter and exchange the same for other goods they wanted.

Nor have the barrenness of the country, and the necessities of the natives, arising from that cause, less contributed, to set them upon exerting all their application, industry, and utmost stretch of genius, to fetch from foreign countries what they stand in need of in their own, and to support themselves by trade.

The abundance of fish in the neighbouring seas, put them in a condition, not only to supply their own occasions, but with the overplus, to carry on a trade with foreigners; and out of the produce of the fishery, to find an equivalent for what they so wanted, through the sterility and narrow boundaries and extent of their own country.

II. Amongst the moral and political causes, are to be placed: The unalterable maxim and fundamental law, relating to the free exercise of different religions; and always to consider this toleration and connivance, as the most effectual means to draw foreigners from adjacent countries to settle and reside here, and so become instrumental to the peopling of these provinces.

The constant policy of the republick, to make this country a perpetual, safe, and secure asylum, for all persecuted and oppressed strangers; no alliance, no treaty,

no

no regard for, or solicitation from any potentate whatever
has at any time been able to weaken or destroy; or make
the State recede from protecting those who have fled to it
for their own security and self-preservation.

Throughout the whole course of all the persecutions
and oppressions, that have occurr'd in other countries, the
steady adherence of the republick to this fundamental
law, has been the cause, that many people have not only
fled hither for refuge, with their whole stock in ready
cash, and their most valuable effects, but have also settled
and established many trades, fabricks, manufactures, arts
and sciences in this country; notwithstanding the first
materials for the said fabricks and manufactures were
almost wholly wanting in it, and not to be procured but at
a great expence from foreign parts.

The constitution of our form of government, and the
liberty from thence accruing to the citizens, are further
reasons, to which the growth of trade, and its establishment in the republick, may fairly be attributed: And all
her policy and laws are put on such an equitable footing,
that neither life, estates, or dignities depend on the caprice, or arbitrary power of any single individual; nor
is there room for any person, who by care, frugality, and
diligence, has once acquired an affluent fortune, or estate,
to fear a deprivation of them, by any act of violence, oppression, or injustice.

The administration of justice in this country, has in
like manner always been clear and impartial, and without
distinction of superior or inferior rank; whether the parties have been rich or poor, or even this a foreigner, and
that a native: And it were greatly to be wished, we could
at this day boast of such impartial quickness and dispatch
in all our legal processes, considering how great an influence it hath on trade.

To sum up all, amongst the moral and political causes
of the former flourishing state of trade, may be likewise

10

placed:

placed: The wisdom and prudence of the administration; the intrepid firmness of the councils; the faithfulness with which treaties and engagements were wont to be fulfilled and ratified; and particularly the care and caution practised to preserve tranquility and peace, and to decline, instead of entering on a scene of war, merely to gratify the ambitious views of gaining fruitless or imaginary conquests.

By these moral and political maxims, was the glory and reputation of the republick so far spread; and foreigners animated to place so great a confidence on the steady determinations of a State so wisely and so prudently conducted; that a concourse of them stock'd this country with an augmentation of inhabitants, and useful hands; whereby its trade and opulence were constantly from time to time increased.

Amongst the adventitious and external causes of the rise and flourishing state of our trade, may be reckoned:

That at the time, when the best and wisest maxims were adopted in the republick, to be the means of making trade to flourish, they were neglected in almost all other countries: and any one, on reading the history of those times, may easily discover, that the persecutions on account of religion, throughout *Spain*, *Brabant*, *Flanders*, and many other states and kingdoms, have given rise to the establishment of trade in the republick.

To this happy event, and the settling of manufactures in our country; the long continuance of the civil wars in *France*, which were afterwards carried on in *Germany* and *England*, and divers other parts, have also very much contributed.

It must be added, in the last place, that, during our most burthensome and heavy wars with *Spain* and *Portugal* (however ruinous that period was for commerce otherways) these powers had both neglected their navy; whilst the republick, by a conduct, directly the reverse, was at the

11

same time formidable, and in a capacity, not only to protect the trade of their own subjects, but to annoy and crush that of their enemies in all quarters.

Having recited the principal causes of the rise, and flourishing state of the republick ; it will be proper, antecedent to the treating of the first question : *What the actual state of commerce is ?* To examine which of these causes, relating to the settlement of trade in the republick, do still subsist, and which do not, in order to draw a conclusion on the question proposed : By what means, under the present circumstances, the trade, in all its branches, may be promoted ?

I. As to the natural and physical causes, which chiefly consist in the happy situation of our country, no detrimental change or revolution can be supposed to have happened since the establishment of the republick ; and no other, but these, can be supposed to have occurred, *viz.* That the entrance of our rivers being choaked up, renders the sailing in and out of vessels more difficult and hazardous ; and that the seas, which we alone formerly navigated and fished in, are still in the same situation : But we have at present only a share in the fisheries, from whence the decay of our herring, cod, and whale fisheries, must necessarily proceed.

But as, in this dissertation, our design is to confine ourselves to trade only, we shall drop the fishery, with this short digression, and only mention, in regard

II. To the moral causes of the rise and flourishing state of our trade, that they are still subsisting in an equal force and vigour. But as to

III. The adventitious and external causes of the former prosperity of our trade, we must, with a very sensible concern, acknowledge, that they have, from time, undergone

                              very

very remarkable and detrimental changes and revolutions, partly owing to the persecutions of the times, the remissness and neglect, and partly, to the despicable opinions, that people in foreign countries then had, both of trade and merchants; which prejudices have not only been corrected and abated since, but the policy of the republick, in promoting trade, substituted and adopted: And it has ever since become the standing rule, with all foreign princes and States; to begin, with endeavouring to cause trade to be settled and flourish in their countries, to encourage manufactures, and to animate their subjects to apply themselves to the fisheries; by all which methods, the prosperity of our trade and commerce must have been affected.

The *English* were the first, in whom we raised an emulation: And it is now a full century from the time of their beginning to make new laws and regulations, tending to the drawing off the trade of the republick to themselves; in opposition to a contrary policy, practised not half a century before, in suffering the wool to be exported raw into this country, but since prohibited under the severest penalties. We might here add the latter examples of almost all other countries, whose general views, with regard to trade and commerce, and all the dependencies thereof, have tended to the very same practice.

And if the question, whether the trade of the republick is diminished or not? must remain undecided, for want of sufficient proof; it is, however, certainly notorious, that all these circumstances; such as, the adopting of our political maxims in trade by foreign powers, and the pains they all take, to draw the same to themselves, ought to stir us up likewise, on our parts, to put in execution, all suitable methods for that purpose: unless we have a mind to see the trade of the republick entirely sink and run to ruin.

Having thus briefly pointed out, what were the causes

and the means of establishing the trade in this republick;
of promoting and raising it heretofore to so high a pitch
of grandeur; and having also shewn which of these
causes have since ceased, and brought about the diminution and falling off of our trade; we shall, in order
to come nearer the point, proceed to examine its present
state: And the conclusion that may be drawn from thence,
is; that the promoting the same, can only be effected by a
lowering of the duties, on a well-concerted plan, supported
by reason and experience.

In order to come at the extent of the present state of
our commerce, with some degree of certainty, we ought,
principally, to examine each branch in particular, as it
now stands, and compare it with the condition, in which
the same branch has continued from the time of its greatest
prosperity, to its present diminution and decay.

A great insight into these matters might be had, from
the registers of the admiralties, in case proper entries had
been made, of what goods were entered, and what part
thereof was again exported, from and to all places, and of
all species.

By such registers, might be discovered, the decrease of
trade in the general, and of each branch in particular:
And these would shew its falling off, as well in its beginning as in its progress; but for want of such direct proof,
which our neighbours have, and we have not, we are
obliged to make use of indirect ones. As these are numerous, we shall, for the sake of brevity, be satisfied with
producing a few; tho' the concession made by the several
colleges of admiralty, by their letters to their High Mightinesses, of the 1st of *June*, 1745, ought to determine the
question, without any further contest in favour of the
merchants complaints; since their Noble Mightinesses
themselves admit, that they have, for several years past,
perceived a diminution in the trade and commerce of this
country, and have spoke of it, as a thing generally known:

Herein also, do all merchants and brokers, and even every person, whose dependance is on trade, agree.

This decay is visible in the chief trading cities of the republick, from the considerable number of shops, that are empty and untenanted : To be convinced hereof, we need but appeal to those who knew *Amsterdam* five and twenty years ago; and the decrease and scarcity of sea-faring people, is another indisputable testimony of the same.

Our merchants set forth in their complaints, that they formerly furnished the northern and eastern parts with the products of *France, Spain, Portugal,* and *Italy,* and these last again with those of the former; but that now they pass by this country, in order to save our duties on imports and exports, together with other charges.

It is but a few years since, that the city of *Amsterdam* was the magazine or storehouse, amongst other goods, of indico and other materials used in dying; but, at present, scarce any traces of the same are to be found.

Germany has begun, for some years, to order the goods directly from *France, Spain, Portugal,* and *Italy,* and receive them by way of *Altena* and *Hamburgh.*

By the last register of the exports of sugar, coffee, and indico from *Bourdeaux,* from the 1st of *June,* 1750, to the last of *May,* 1751, and on comparing the same commodities from *Nantz* to *Amsterdam, Rotterdam,* and *Hamburgh,* from the 1st of *October,* 1750, to the 1st of *August,* 1751; it appears, that no more than one fourth part thereof was shipt for this country, and three fourths for *Hamburgh ;* a disproportion, which but a little while before was exactly the reverse.

Where does one now see the hemp, flax, and other eastern commodities shipt off from hence to *Spain, Portugal,* and *France,* as formerly? One need only consult the *Sound* list, to see that all these nations carry them directly forward, and beside this country,

There are no *Dutch* houses any longer now in *Spain ;*

15

and

and the small share the republick has at present in the galleons, is a matter of surprize; and no less so, is the prodigious decrease of the *Dutch* trade to the *Levant*.

The great number of callico-printers, sugar-houses, and other fabricks, that within a few years have been erected and set up in *Hamburgh*, and *Bremen*, and not long since, in *Brabant*, and *Flanders*, are likewise all proofs of our decaying trade: And to what can this decline be attributed, but to the exhorbitant and heavy duties.

Notwithstanding all that has been said of the decrease of our commerce, there are still those who insist, *that our trade is on the same footing now as heretofore*: And the grounds, on which they build this opinion, are

1. That the imposts on goods imported and exported, the weigh-money, and duties on shipping, and on the consumption, &c. are not diminished.

2. That the complaints of the merchants prove nothing, since the profits on trade are still much the same, but divided amongst a greater number of persons.

3. That the present grand way of living, leads the merchants into greater expences than our forefathers, and gives reason for these complaints.

However, without entering minutely into all that is here advanced, or shifting it off by saying, that none of these allegations are proved; we shall content ourselves with replying to the substance of them: And as to the first allegation of those, who argue as above, from the several imposts on goods imported and exported; and pretend to evince, that because these are not diminished, the commerce of the republick is therefore not decreased; we cannot but remark, that they must have very imperfect ideas of trade itself, or they would have entirely waved speaking of the duties on the imports, as having nothing to do in the case. For that the duties on imports are no proofs of a flourishing trade, will appear from considering;

What

What causes are frequently introductive of an increase of the duties on goods imported?

What does the present elegant way of living produce, but the bringing in more high-rated foreign commodities, and consequently an increase of the duties on importation?

What other causes were to be assign'd for the increase of the revenues of the State, after the fatal winter in 1740? but that in proportion, as the produce in this country of most of the necessaries of life was almost entirely ruin'd by the hard frost; that want was to be remedied no other way, than by importations from abroad, to supply our own consumptions? Yet the republick would be scarce able to sustain many such flourishing years.

Lastly, what, besides the calamitous sickness amongst the cattle, has increas'd the revenues of the country, on the importation of foreign butter, cheese, and cattle? But whoever should impute this to an increasing trade, would grossly deceive himself.

And who sees not, that if the trade of the republick once came to consist only in the importation of foreign goods; instead of being advantageous, how destructive it would be, and more and more consume the substance of the State. Thus by not examining the affair to the bottom, one might imagine, we had a flourishing trade; whilst we were, at the same time, running on to ruin. We apprehend therefore, as a refutation of the first argument, *that our trade is not diminished, because the duties on goods imported are not decreas'd*, that it cannot be apply'd here with any propriety, as it is nothing to the purpose, and rather proves trade to be in a ruinous than in an advantageous situation. And one need only read the Act of Navigation in *England*, and their policy by means of the drawbacks, to find, that for above a hundred years past, they have considered the exportation and sale of goods and merchandizes abroad, as the only profitable and advantageous trade of that kingdom; and, on the contrary, left it very doubtful, whether the importation of goods be prejudicial or beneficial.

But the consideration of the sundry duties on goods exported, is widely different : And we make no scruple to determine, in regard to these, that in case it can be made appear they are not diminished, we will, in consequence thereof, agree, that the trade of the republick is still on the same footing. But in examining these registers of the duties on exportation, regard must be had to such years, as were subject to *circumstances arising accidentally from foreign causes* : As for example, we must except the years of the last war, declared by *England*, with *Spain*, in the year 1739; and by *France*, with *England*, in the year 1743; for as these three nations could not have any direct dealings with each other at that time, it being prohibited on all sides, their trade was carried on through this republick; which not only occasioned an increase in the export duties, but also such a diffusive spread of commerce, as had a happy influence on every branch of trade, and produced a general welfare and advantage to the Provinces: Such years must therefore be excepted, as they prove nothing, and have no relation to the question in debate.

It may not be amiss, however, to remark, how much the welfare and prosperity of the republick is advanced; and to what a flourishing and happy crisis the means for the support of her inhabitants are brought, from an encouragement given to the transporting of foreign goods and merchandize through these Provinces, as was the case during those wars. And in short, if one would define the trade, which is advantageous to the republick, so far as relates to navigation, he might, with strict justice, affirm, that the same consists alone in the buying, and afterwards exporting, of imported foreign goods and merchandize.

It is this trade, therefore, which must be always had in view; countenanced, facilitated, and promoted, by all methods of relief, favour, and encouragement.

For what advantage occurs to the republick, from a merchant, who lets his goods directly pass from one foreign country to another, without coming through their provinces?

What profit arises to this country, when a merchant sends the products of the north and east seas, directly from thence to *French*, *Spanish*, *Portuguese*, and *Italian* ports; and from thence back again to the same places? Hardly any: Nay, none at all, if he embarks them in a foreign ship, which depends upon a circumstance merely casual. And when one further considers, that, to carry on such a trade, there is no necessity for his living at *Amsterdam*, or *Rotterdam*, where the taxes are heaviest, or even in these provinces; and that this trade and navigation, beside our country, is promoted by nothing more than the duties laid on transportation; it is beyond all dispute, that the transporting of goods through this country, which is so visibly disused, is not to be revived otherwise, than by a lowering and reduction of the duties on the same.

Such reasonings might, perhaps, give room for a supposal, that what we hint at, is a general free passage, which would have the desired effect, in making trade to flourish; but as some further speculations and fresh difficulties may be started, and arise on this point; at least, a narrow inquiry into its influence on all branches of trade, our fabricks and manufactures; which, of itself alone, would require an extensive dissertation; and as such a digression would lead us too far from the point in hand, we shall refer the treating hereof, to a place in the sequel, where it will be more suitable.

It has been further alleged, that so far as the produce of the tax, entitled Last-Money, is not diminished, the same is an additional proof, that the trade of the repub-

lick

lick stands upon an equal footing: Yet, not only as the exception already made, touching the years of the last wars between *France, Spain*, and *England*, may be applied to this circumstance; but over and above, as these three nations could in those times navigate with our ships at less risque and expence than with their own; besides making use of our ships to transport their products, they were even obliged to sell theirs to the *Dutch*; whereby it was easily perceived, that our shipping increased in those years, at least one third: and has again decreased in near the same proportion, since the conclusion of the peace.

The shipping has undoubtedly a great connection with trade; but in order to form proper ideas of the same, it will be necessary to consider it in all its branches, in this republick: However, as this is not the proper place to treat of the same, we shall observe thus far by the bye, *as some have endeavoured, from the last-money tax, to shew, that the trade is not decreased*, that a country may have, or be concerned in a good deal of shipping, without having any trade; when it is considered, that many of the ships made use of for transporting of goods and merchandizes from one foreign place to another, and beside our country, are not *Dutch*.

There is no province of our country, where more owners of smacks, sloops, galleots, and other such like vessels reside, than in that of *Friezland*, without having any trade: And therefore, it is reasonably to be concluded, that this objection against a decrease of trade in the republick, may be rejected, and esteemed of as little weight, as the duties on the consumptions, which only affect the manufactures, fabricks, &c. and for that reason is here entirely out of the question.

Having thus shewn what is the state of our trade, drawn a conclusion from thence, that the same is diminished, and also refuted the grounds, on which a contrary

opinion

opinion was founded, namely, that the trade continues much on the same footing; we may next proceed to examine the causes of its decay; as one may best judge from the source of the whole, what remedies should be applied in order to stop its progress.

We have already taken notice of, and placed at the head of all the causes, that have co-operated to the prejudice and discouragement of trade, the oppressive taxes, which have, under divers denominations, been imposed on trade; such as those called convoy and licent, additional last and sale money, the premium, duties, weighing-money, &c. and it may justly be said, that it can be only attributed to these taxes, that the trade of this country has been diverted out of its channel, and transferred to our neighbours, and must daily be still more and more alienated and shut out from us, unless the progress thereof be stopt by some quick and effectual remedy : Nor is it difficult to see, from these contemplations on the state of our trade, that the same can be effected by no other means than a diminution of all duties.

In former times, this was reckoned the only trading republick in *Europe*; and foreigners were content to pay the taxes, as well on the goods they brought thither, as on those they came there to buy; without examining, whether they could evade or save them, by fetching the goods from the places where they were produced, and carrying others to the places were they were consumed: In short, they paid the *Dutch* their taxes with pleasure, without any further inquiry.

But since the last century, the system of trade is altered all over *Europe* : Foreign nations seeing the wonderful effect of our trade, and to what an eminence the *Dutch* had rose, only by means thereof; they did likewise apply themselves to it; and to save our duties, sent their superfluous products beside our country, to the places where they are most consumed; and in return for the

same.

same, furnished themselves, from the first hand, with what
they wanted.

The question then at last turns upon this: By what
methods, and by what regulations, we may best contribute to, facilitate, and advance these desired encouragements and benefits of trade, which the present circumstances of affairs seem to require.

If but one point was herein to be considered, namely,
what are the most proper methods to re-establish trade in
general, without having regard, at the same time, to other
concerns; the remedy would be soon found, by only introducing a general free port, and reducing as many taxes
as possible, whereby this affair would be effectually compleated.

But there seems to be a condition, over and above, not
to be gainsayed or withstood; which is, that the usual
revenue to the colleges of the admiralty, whereof they
stand so much in need to defray their charges, must be
preserved at all events. And, on the other hand, it is
incumbent on us to prevent the lowering of the duties on
the importation of goods, from becoming any prejudice to
the products, manufactures, and fabricks of the country,
our *East* and *West India* colonies, fisheries, &c.

Although it is an opinion deeply rooted, that all these
matters can never be reconciled, and that it is impossible
to promote trade in general, without prejudicing the interests above specified: Yet we trust, that upon an impartial and minute examination, it will not be found so
difficult and impracticable a thing, as is usually imagined,
to unite all these jarring interests ; nay, we even flatter
ourselves, that when the difficulties of finding an equivalent fund of revenues for the admiralties, preventing the
frauds, and bringing the publick taxes to be raised on an
equal footing, throughout all the provinces, were once surmounted : the obstacle thrown in the way by these repugnant and clashing interests, would shortly be removed.

22

There

There will certainly some circumstances intervene, that may give room for a disagreement in opinion: But even in such cases, which we hope, however, will not occur so often as is apprehended; reason dictates, that, in these particular instances, we should set it down as an invariable and standing rule, *of two evils to chuse the least :* That the concerns of the whole republick must be preferred to those of one province, as well as those of one province to those of a city: And in such case, but not otherwise, the small damages that any single province, city, corporation, or private person might sustain, must be overlook'd.

This must, however, be understood, with this restriction, that it is not hereby intended to set up a new republick, or to make any alteration in the interior constitution of our country; far from it, for it is certainly best, and most advantageous for the country, that the reformations in trade should be made, as far as possible, according to the actual situation and state of its affairs; nor could any thing be conceived more dangerous, than to attempt innovations of this nature.

From what has been premised on the subject of our general trade, we take it for granted, that we may lay it down as an indisputable truth, that the duties and imposts must be lowered and abated.

From whence the two following questions will naturally arise.

1. What goods ought principally to have the benefit of such a diminution; and what rules, in relation thereto, will be proper to be observed.

2. Wherein it must consist, and in what proportion it must be settled.

As to the first question, on what goods, the lowering and abatement of publick duties should principally fall; it has been observed, that principally, all foreign goods, which are not only brought and consumed in our country, but also taken off our hands by foreigners, should enjoy

this

this benefit : For, to put our merchants in a condition, to trade on an equal footing with their neighbours, at foreign markets; the carrying of goods through, and trafficking in this country, should be made as cheap and easy, as can possibly be contrived.

Of these goods, a preference should be given to all the prime materials, that are serviceable in our fabricks, manufactures, handicrafts, &c. as also the ingredients necessary in the said handicrafts, manufactures, and fabricks. By such measures, our fabricks, manufactures, and handicrafts, would be encouraged on the same footing as our general trade, and no cause of dispute given between those pretended jarring interests.

All foreign goods and merchandizes, that come here to be sifted and assorted, and afterwards again exported, ought likewise to enjoy the benefit of this diminution and abatement ; for these are an inducement to the industrious trader to exercise his talents, in setting them to work : And were it requisite to enumerate in this article, all the advantages that trade reaps from those assortments, even under the present heavy taxes; we should find, that the falling off of our trade, has thereby, in some measure, been stopt.　But when people in foreign parts set about the same, as it is already perceiv'd they do, it will be then too late to guard against, or to prevent it.

Neither can such goods, as are not work'd, manufactured, or sorted here ; but re-exported in the same condition, as they were imported, be excluded from this advantage, without prejudice to trade in general ; for these goods, when there is a superfluity of them, furnish the merchants with an opportunity to make magazines of them in this country.

The advantages arising from hence, and which have only relation to trade, are these,

That whenever afterwards a scarcity happens, foreigners can buy these goods of us, at a lower price, than at the

places

places where they are produced; not to mention many other advantages accruing therefrom to this country; and considering, that the plenty of money to be found here above other places, and the low interest it bears in comparison to other countries, contribute to this sort of trade, one may promise one's self great success from the diminution so desired.

Finally, we should reflect on such foreign goods, which being admitted not prejudicial to our fabricks, yet, as they are principally consumed in the country, should on importation pay some duties, in order to make the loss of the admiralties, as small as possible.

As to the second question, how far the same ought to take place on such goods, a few words will suffice to shew; and we need only remark, the more these are relieved, the greater will be the success of the diminution.

Having thus established some principles concerning what goods should enjoy the benefit of a free port coming in and going out; we may now proceed to such, as, by their importation, are prejudicial to our said fabricks, manufactures, and handicrafts; and to the products of our country, colonies, and fisheries.

As to all these last mentioned goods, it is agreed, that they ought, on importation, not only to remain taxed; but so far as they tend to luxury, to superfluities, and to use, are thereby prejudicial to our said fabricks, manufactures, &c. therefore should be as heavily charged as possible; with proper regard, however, to our treaties; as also, that by too heavy imposts, we do not involve ourselves in those difficulties, of which the list of the year 1725 produces many instances, which have had this effect, that the colleges of the admiralties would have raised and received more, had they asked less; a consideration, which ought to be well remembered, when we set about a reformation of their revenues.

Being now come to the means of redress, that are pro-

posed

posed as most proper to restore the trade of the republick
to its former lustre, dignity, and credit, if possible; three
different plans shall be mentioned, each of which, separately considered, will remedy several of the causes of decay
above specified.

These have been the occasion, that most of the merchants proper to be consulted, and whose advices might be
relied on, after many discussions and debates, have approved of a fourth plan of redress, composed out of the
three former; selecting out of each, that which was found
to be of the greatest use, and most applicable to the actual
situation of affairs; and which, it is thought, will be liable
to the fewest difficulties in the execution.

The three first plans we shall here briefly specify.

The first plan consists in a *free passage* for all foreign
goods and merchandize appertaining to trade in general;
subject, notwithstanding, to this precaution, that the goods,
upon their first landing, shall be immediately sealed, and
remain inclosed in the same chests, packs, and bales, until
they are again sent out of the republick.

The second proposes *a considerable alteration and diminution in the placart and list of* 1725: This diminution
to take place on most articles, but especially on such goods
as have most influence on the general trade and navigation.

According to the third plan, *a general free port would
answer the end*; in which case, it would be proper for the
duty on lastage or tonnage, to be so far increased, that the
deficiency to the colleges of the admiralty might be
thereby supplied.

Were we to give these three plans their full scope and
due extent, by describing them with all their limitations
and restrictions, as they were delivered by those who
patronized them; and to annex the advantages that might
be expected from, and the inconveniences and difficulties
that would attend each in the execution of them, it would

lay

lay us under a necessity, to enter upon a long detail of particulars, and very much swell this dissertation; which we think more proper to decline, especially, as we have been obliged to expatiate on some articles, whereby this treatise is already become longer than was at first proposed.

The fourth method therefore here proposed, as an expedient plan, not only to preserve the trade of the republick from a further decrease, but also to revive and render it still more extensive, is *a limited free port.*

It consists in dividing the goods and merchandizes into certain lists or classes; according to which, some goods shall enjoy the benefit of a free port, others to be excepted, and to pay certain duties on importation; but, when some of these last are designed to be again exported out of the country, they to have a drawback, or in lieu thereof a free passage.

Upon a close examination of this plan, it will be found best adapted to the present state of the republick, the actual constitution of our trade, the nature and property of our commerce, the real situation and traffick all over *Europe,* and those general grounds and principles above set forth; over and above all this, some special considerations have been had on some particular species of goods.

According to this plan, it is proposed, in the first place, that all the goods mentioned in the list marked A, shall enjoy the benefit of a free port, and be exempted from all duties on importation; of what denomination, or how inconsiderable soever, the same may be.

With this restriction, notwithstanding, that all the goods, when imported, shall be subject to the visitation of the commissaries, and others appointed for that purpose, and be liable to a seizure and confiscation; in case, under this colour and pretext, an attempt should be made to enter other goods that are not free, thereby fraudulently to diminish the revenues of the country: On a discovery

whereof,

whereof, the goods, both free and not free, shall be forfeited.

Whoever shall be pleased, attentively, to examine this first list, will find, that regard has commonly been had, in making the same, to the grounds herein before laid down : But to prove this of every particular, to point out the application of each single article to the said principles, and to add all the reasons pro and con, would spin out this treatise to a tiresome length, which we think ought to be avoided, in a proposal of this nature.

In the second place, all the goods specified in the list marked B, are brought under a second class, and the same should be obliged to pay certain duties on their importation into the republick.

On this second list, a large commentary might be required, to set forth, for what reasons and causes the different goods therein mentioned, are neither rated higher or lower: But, not to swell this dissertation beyond its proper bounds, we shall in general observe, without dwelling on a subject so copious and extensive, that in drawing up this list, besides the interest of the admiralties, we have kept this in view, that by the importation of some goods, our manufactures, handicrafts, and products of our own country might not sustain any damage, whose interest herein would be opposite to what the general trade requires.

We were, therefore, of opinion, that all those goods, on their importation into the republick, ought to stand charged, in such a manner, as not to cause any prejudice to the sale of our own, within the limits of the republick.

All these duties to be collected in the same way and manner, and by the same persons, as they have been received by heretofore, with this only difference, that they shall be hereafter raised on an equal footing, and that all fraudulent receivers be proceeded against with the utmost severity.

But

But here arises a difficulty, that merits the utmost attention, and must, one way or other, necessarily be removed.

The goods, which, for the reasons aforesaid, ought not to be brought into the republick, without paying certain duties, will therefore not be imported in larger quantities, than what may be required for the use and consumption of the inhabitants of the republick; and consequently, the general market and magazine for those goods will not fix itself here, according to these proposals; nor will they be sent through this country; which is, however, so very desirable, that it ought to be our principle and chief aim.

For a removal of this difficulty, to the utmost of our power, two different methods have been thought on, which we shall set forth as briefly as possible.

The first method should consist in a drawback on some of the goods, enumerated in the list marked B, which are the cause of this objection.

This method must be understood as follows.

The importer of these goods by sea, on paying the duties at the entry, to have a receipt; by which receipt, the possessor thereof shall be entitled to be reimbursed, the duty paid at such entry, on making it appear, by certificates from the commissaries, that the said goods, or other inland goods of the same sort, in lieu thereof, were exported.

The consequence whereof would be, that on one side, the importation of those foreign goods might be free and open, the merchant be always master of his goods, have a right to open the chests, packs, and cases, and might put in practice his skill and industry in sorting the same, without thereby prejudicing the inland sale of our own goods; that, on the other hand, our own goods, merchandize, and manufactures would, whenever they should be

sent

sent out of the republick, reap the benefit and indulgence of the said receipts, and of the duties paid thereon; and that the foreign goods which had laid here some time, might, by means of the said receipts, be exported again free, and without any duty charged on them; since by this way of drawback, the duties they had paid would be fully reimbursed.

This proposal, how ingenious and plausible soever it may seem, is subject to a variety of difficulties; to prevent which, without taking notice of them here, we should find ourselves very much embarrassed; and a door might, perhaps, be thereby opened to a great number of frauds, extremely pernicious to our manufactures, handicrafts, colonies, &c. at least, it is certain, that nothing is more apt to make us apprehensive of this, than to consider the immense sums expended in *England*, to prevent frauds, in regard to such goods as are entitled to a drawback, and which would be still more difficult in a country so constituted as this republick.

This, however, is no reason why the same deserves not to be more amply considered.

The second proposal is, to grant a free passage for such goods, the transportation whereof, through this country, ought to be encouraged, without thereby prejudicing our own goods and manufactures; which free passage should take place under such precautions, as are prescribed by former ordinances and placarts, and such amendments as shall be found necessary, according to the state of things.

By these precautions it is presumed, that the frauds might be prevented; and that such goods might be imported without paying any duties inwards, and pass through our country without suspicion of any frauds, or becoming any way a prejudice to our fabricks, handicrafts, colonies, companies, fisheries, &c.

Be

Be this as it will, it were highly to be wished, that one of the two proposals aforegoing could be rendred practicable, to preserve the passage of the goods, already referred to,

According to this plan of redress, it must absolutely be determined, that all the goods, which by former ordinances and placarts, were prohibited to be either imported or exported, still continue to be prohibited in the same manner; for as the causes, that gave room for the issuing out such prohibitions, still subsist, there cannot be a cause assigned for any change or alteration to be made therein.

Thus, in as concise a method as possible, you may see the whole plan of redress; which, it is thought, might be brought to a successful issue, and happily effected; and whereby, it is believed, the whole trade of the republick might not only be preserved from a total ruin, but also be retrieved, re-animated, and invigorated with new life and spirits, in case it was supported by other particular amendments, which we shall not insist on here; as the proper occasion for it, will be only, when a limited free port shall be approved of, as the general means of a redress.

In the contriving of this plan, it has been more than once discovered, as has been already several times remarked before, that in this affair, a variety of jarring interests did frequently occur.

And hence has sprung the cause, why the goods and merchandize could not be reduced under some certain general rules, and that obliged us to consider and weigh almost every article apart; and after examining what could be alledged for and against each article, we have determined on that which appeared liable to the least difficulties.

Not that we look on the lists, as they are drawn out, as absolutely perfect and compleat, nor do we flatter ourselves that they are not capable of amendment. This was neither intended, nor indeed possible, for although the

most

most eminent and experienced merchants were consulted, yet their extensive knowledge, in regard to trade in general, would not enable them to attain to an equal penetration and insight into all the various particulars, and different species of goods, with their several uses in our fabricks and manufactures. However, it has been thought proper to put the goods and merchandize to that list to which they reported them to belong, according to the best of their judgment and experience: Which was done with this view, that whenever the plan, in general, shall be properly examined by those in the republick, who are always consulted about mercantile affairs, and the lists likewise shall be examined, with such reflections made on each article, abstracted from the rest, as they shall think fitting; then those merchants, who trade in each species of goods, may be heard against it; whereby one will be enabled, on comparing the reasons and arguments on both sides, to chuse that which shall be found to be most for the advantage of the trade.

From what has been hitherto said, with regard to the duties that must remain, according to this proposal, on some goods and merchandize; it evidently appears, that all methods, means, and regulations which can be made use of on the head of trade, will be invalid and to no purpose; as long as no effectual remedies are taken against the unequal levying of the duties by water, and the frauds and malpractices crept in: The importance of this affair requires, that it be canvassed and examined to the bottom.

To treat of this subject in a regular order, it may possibly be required of us, to shew, that various frauds, in different shapes, have been committed since the list or regulation in the year 1725, and that the precautions then taken, are insufficient.

To attempt the proving this by particular instances and circumstantial cases, would appear extremely ridiculous:

The

The affair is too notorious to need our spending any longer time about it.

It is as undeniable, that in case the running of goods is tolerated more, or less severely punished in one province or city only than in another, it will be absolutely impracticable, in the other provinces or cities, to prevent the same.

Every one who shall consider this evil impartially, and without prejudice, must be self-convinced of the necessity there is immediately to remedy the same, in the most effectual manner, and by such means, that all the provinces and cities may be thoroughly satisfied, that there is no connivance more allowed of in one place, than in another.

But the necessity of such redress, will more evidently appear, when we consider the effect which this remissness, in receiving the duties, produces in those cities and provinces which are otherwise inclinable enough to levy the taxes, according to the placarts and ordinances; but on account of what is practised in other provinces and cities, either cannot, or dare not, use greater severity; from whence it is, that every one connives at daily smuggling, to keep the trade amongst themselves.

These precautions against all frauds become now the more requisite, by the proposed diminution of the revenues from a free port.

In regard to which, however, the redress is not more necessary than it is difficult: Let us but consider, what precautions, pains, and expences, are to this end bestowed in *France*, in *England*, and in other places, and all incessantly without effect; how much more difficult it must be in such a country as ours, where the constitution of the land, the different interests and jurisdictions of the provinces and cities, render our care and precautions exceedingly more irksome.

The tricks and inventions from time to time made use

of

of to carry on this practice, are so manifold, so private, and so artfully contrived; that, were a person to devise new methods that should be valid and sufficient to prevent all smuggling, he would at once throw up his project in despair; especially, as such means must be fit to be reduced to practice, not clogg'd with too many obstacles, and at the same time effective of producing the end aimed at.

These difficulties are not here started with an intent to give up all hopes, to look upon it as an impracticable scheme, or to deter us from pursuing the same; but only to shew, that it is of such a nature, that it requires the use of such means, as in the ordinary course of things ought not to be made use of; since allowance must be sometimes made for the common frailty and depravity of the multitude: But, as the preservation and prosperity of the country and its inhabitants depend on this particular, the means ought not to be rejected, because they seem to be attended with an unusual hardship and severity.

How strongly were it to be wished, that the respective provinces and cities might be so thoroughly convinced, by what has been advanced on this subject; that for the welfare and the preservation of the State, they would lay aside at once all views and pretexts, as might seem to be repugnant to it.

And now proceeding to the methods, which we presume, might be successfully made use of, to prevent these frauds, we shall lay it down as the basis and foundation of the whole fabrick,

That the fines, penalties, and punishments must be enlarged; and sometimes, if the nature of the case shall so require, extended to infamy and banishment, or even death itself; and that these laws be strictly put in execution without the least connivance. Were this but done, what honest man would run the risque of being infamous, or accounted a plunderer or robber of his country, or of being liable to suffer banishment or death.

That

That the searching after goods must be more extensive, especially, when there is any suspicion or proof of fraud.

That new regulations be made concerning watermen, porters, carmen, and all others that are employed in unloading of goods.

The informations and proof of smuggling, ought to be left free and open to every individual; even to the accomplices, under promise of indemnity; allowing to the informer the whole or the greatest part of the fines and penalties.

That the pass-ports of the goods, which come down by the rivers, do for the future remain along with them, the searching such goods again chiefly depending thereon; and which, at different times, has been earnestly requested by the colleges of the admiralty residing in *Holland.*

To consider, for the future, the duties upon all goods imported, as revenues belonging to the State in general, and not to any one province in particular.

Consequently, the management and direction of these publick revenues of the country, ought to be taken away from particular provinces and cities, and such power and authority invested in the generality, to put the laws in execution, relating to levying the duties on goods imported by sea, in all the provinces and cities, as the nature of the case may require; it being notorious, that the best laws are mere cyphers, if not duly executed : For it is otherwise very much to be feared, that all regulations will be of no effect, be they ever so useful and necessary, or ever so well calculated for the common benefit.

In order to effect this, the jurisdiction and authority of the colleges of admiralty ought to be maintained and strengthened against all those that are guilty of any frauds; and all offences against the said jurisdiction and authority, ought to be speedily and effectually decided and prevented.

The

The magistrates and civil officers ought to bind themselves by oath, to promise and agree, that they will assist the collectors of the customs and licences, in all things relating to their duty, nor hinder, oppose, or resist, directly or indirectly, the colleges of the admiralty, in the execution of their commission; nor their officers in things relating to the collecting of the publick revenues, and executing the placarts, nor suffer the same to be done, as far as in them lies.

Consequently, the cases of such who are guilty of any frauds, must for the future, not be removable from the jurisdiction of the colleges, to the sheriffs courts of the cities.

Above all, the respective colleges of admiralty ought solemnly to oblige themselves to collect the duties every where alike, and on the same footing, without respect to persons or places, and strictly to execute this trust without the least connivance: For as soon as it is but surmised, that any thing is wrong managed, in regard to the collection of the duties, in any one place; that bad example, whether the supposition be well or ill-grounded, will be immediately espoused and practised, as it were, by way of retortion, in other places: And therefore such proceedings should be the more cautiously avoided.

For the strictest laws, without an universal obedience to them, are only ties on the most scrupulous, and consequently the best part of mankind; when at the same time, they are sensibly hurt, by having their trade and navigation withdrawn from them.

For this purpose, it might be also requisite, that some new orders and regulations be made concerning the officers employed by the colleges of admiralty, in the collecting and receiving the duties on goods coming by water.

It may be necessary here to take some notice of the duties, which, according to this proposal, the colleges of

the

the admiralty will be entitled to; and iu what manner, it is judged, that the deficiency which will be occasioned in the ordinary revenues, by these regulations, may be supplied.

The admiralties will continue to receive all the duties, which the goods mentioned in the abovesaid list marked B, remain charged with, and to collect, as usual, the last-money, pass-ports and stamps.

And as this new plan lays it down for a fundamental maxim, that it must go hand in hand with the most strict and effectual precautions, against all frauds and male-practices, particularly, against any partial or unequal collection of the duties; we therefore doubt not, but that the general produce of the duties, on those goods which remain liable to part thereof, will be considerably in-creased: For we think we may with reason assert, that above half the goods now imported into this republick, pay little or no duties; for the truth whereof, we appeal to the experience of the admiralty colleges themselves; whereto other proofs might be added, did not the thing speak for itself.

We shall now briefly examine the consequential ad-vantages of this proposed project of redress; which, it is not doubted, will be found of that nature and importance, as not to suffer a few difficulties that may be foreseen to attend the execution of it, to intimidate or deter us from putting it in practice, but rather put us upon using our utmost endeavours to conquer and remove them.

The effect of this plan will be, that by thus disbur-thening trade in general, and some branches of it in par-ticular; the commerce of the republick will be preserved from a further decay, and give room to hope for its increase daily; whereby, probably, this republick may in time become once again, as it was heretofore, the general mart of *Europe*; at least, there is a great likelihood thereof, in regard to some particular goods and commo-dities.

This

This first advantage will be attended with a second, namely, a proportional augmentation of shipping and navigation.

Again, the increase of trade has a great influence upon navigation, that of navigation alternately the same on trade; and they reciprocally enlarge each other.

The bringing in and carrying out again of such goods as enjoy the benefit of a free port, will occasion the continual flux and reflux of ships and goods coming in and going out; which, tho' they pay not any duties to the State, leave always more or less benefit and advantage behind them in the country.

This plan is further look'd on as the means for getting again possession of the trade from the *North* to *Portugal, Spain, Italy*, &c. and back again in the same manner; the advantages whereof are vastly great, and very much contribute to the increase of navigation.

By these general amendments, we shall put ourselves in a condition to reduce the trade of *Hamburgh, Bremen, Lubeck, Denmark*, and other places; at least, to prevent their doing us a further prejudice. At the same time, it will be an efficacious remedy, to smother in its infancy the trade, which is endeavoured to be settled and established in some other parts.

This proposal would have as favourable an effect on the inland trade of the country; But without mentioning the concourse of all sorts of people that would again resort hither, especially of merchants flocking in to such a general mart, and the consumption of necessaries arising from the same motive, we shall only take notice of the great vent which will thereby likewise be occasioned, of such goods, merchandizes, and manufactures, and among handicrafts, as might be had cheaper elsewhere; and yet the merchant will chuse rather to buy them in this country; because he finds his advantage in sending them again, forward from hence with more ease, expedition, and

less

less expence, and along with other goods, which he may have bought at other places : Besides, it is well known, that the sale of one article often introduces the disposing of another.

There are several particular advantages besides of a different kind : The merchant gains, at least, something by forwarding of goods, which business will, in all probability, increase greatly : If he advance money on these goods ; he has interest for his money : Insurances will also be considerably augmented : Exchanging and remitting of money will be again drawn into this country ; and by that means the circulation of it, with foreign nations ; which always brings more or less advantage to a country, and must necessarily tend to an increase of the inland circulation.

The augmenting the circulation of money in trade, will prevent our inhabitants from placing out their money in the funds abroad, because they can employ it to advantage at home. If this plan could have such a salutary effect as to fix the general magazine of goods, and merchandizes here, we should then run no risque of ever having a scarcity or dearth of such goods in this country.

As the navigation increases, so must the seamen likewise, and consequently the number of sailors to mann our fleet in time of war : During the late troubles, the republick too well knew the want of seafaring people.

We shall conclude with this remark, that we are verily persuaded, the plan, as here laid down, is the most proper of any thing that can be proposed for that purpose, being free from a multiplicity of laws, cautions, and restrictions, which generally create so much trouble and perplexity in trade. This plan of redress also has the nearest affinity to the actual situation and constitution of our commerce, and has finally this advantage, that the practice of running goods, will thereby be very much diminished.

We shall pass by in silence here, what further advan-

tageous

tageous consequences may be expected from these proposals: What has already been advanced, will be abundantly sufficient to make us sensible, that nothing ought to be neglected or omitted for the surmounting and removing every obstacle, which may be possibly thrown in by way of opposition to the plan before us; and not to spare our pains and application to cultivate, improve, and bring the same to that perfection, as will reduce it into practice.

There will possibly be several objections started against this proposal: And it is not to be dissembled, that in a matter of so copious an extent, and of such weighty consequence, there must some difficulties still subsist; which cannot well be otherwise, in a country, where the abuses have insinuated themselves, and crept in by slow degrees, and therefore must, of course, make it the interest of many persons now, that every thing should rest upon its ancient footing. Hence it is our opinion, that in an affair of this nature, where it is morally impossible fully to satisfy each individual, and, at the same time, to secure the publick interest, the best way is, amongst a number of difficulties, to obviate those that are the most essential: To this end, we have throughout this whole design, and all the circumstances attending it, always kept close to the concerns and advantages of the admiralties, the colonies, fabricks, and handicrafts, as well as of the fisheries and products of the country; at least, so far as they were reconcilable with the general commerce, which has been the principal aim we had in view; and therefore flatter ourselves, that no material scruples will arise from these colleges and corporations. Besides, having at present only regard to commerce in general; the inquiry in what manner best to favour the different branches of our trade by particular regulations and dispositions, will more properly fall in hereafter.

As the plan now stands, that every branch of our trade will receive a benefit by it, infinitely greater, than by the

present

present actual state of commerce, will not admit of the least doubt: We shall therefore, for the present, setting aside all particular objections, content ourselves with a few of those general ones which regard the whole plan.

In the *first* place, it may be objected, that the means herein proposed for a redress, will not prove so advantageous to trade, as is pretended, inasmuch as the frauds, which have been hitherto practised, have as much disburthened trade, as is attempted to be done by these new regulations.

Secondly, an appeal may be made to what happened at the alteration of the list in the year 1725, made with a view, at that time, to increase the revenues on imports by sea, by lessening the duties, by levying the same in a more impartial manner, and under a pretext, that the diminution thence arising, could only be overbalanced, and again made good by the more frequent entries of goods, which were all expected from it: But the event has made it appear, how much those who depended on an increase of the revenues of the colleges, by a strict and punctual execution of the aforesaid list and placart, were out in their calculation.

To which may be added, *thirdly*, to give it still more weight, that the bad state of our treasury, together with the precarious and uncertain issue of this proposal, might prove of the most ruinous consequence to the republick, that at all events, it would be a work of time to bring these alterations to operate with effect, and therefore best to leave things on their old footing; that even admitting, some abuses had crept in, they were of an ancient standing, the circumstances of the republick had been accommodated and conformed thereto, and it might prove dangerous to attempt a redressing of the same at one stroke, and in an instant, which might introduce a scene of confusion; and, in a word, we should run a greater hazard in applying the remedy, than in enduring the evil.

As

As to the *first*, we shall remark, that it may appear a very plausible objection, to such as have never once considered the intrinsic nature of the thing: For, upon a supposition, that the burthen remains the same on commerce in general, yet the manner in which that burthen is divided among the several branches of trade, makes a wide difference; since it must needs become extremely pernicious, when the highest duties are levied on such goods, as are the objects of trade in general; and, on the contrary, those which only serve for a home consumption, and administer to luxury and pride, are lowest rated.

It is equally detrimental to our trade, when the same sorts of goods pay more duties in one part of the republick than in another; as when some merchants continue to pay them, whilst others, by frauds and male-practices, screen themselves, and elude the payment of them: To which may be added, that those, who by smuggling, evade the duties, are generally obliged to be at great expences to compass or effect it: All which reflections might have been more enlarged upon, and set in a clearer light, had it been judged necessary. We shall therefore conclude with remarking on this head, that the load, which by these proposals is still left on the trade of the republick, is too heavy to be supported, and it were highly to be wished, a further ease could be administered; but, as this is not practicable, there remains no other remedy, than to impose and divide this burthen, in such a manner, on and amongst the sundry branches of commerce, goods and merchandize, as may be least hurtful to, and least sensibly felt in trade.

2. In regard to the *second* objection, that the expectations from the placart and lists of the year 1725, were the same, as are now conceived from this plan; an answer here above has been already given, that the reduction was, at that time, not sufficient; that the duties which remained, were very unequally divided; and that there is

reason

reason to doubt, whether the chief aim, in the transactions of that year, was to increase the revenues of the colleges of admiralty, or to favour trade and make it flourish.

Frauds are rather more numerous, than at all lessened since that period, and the partiality used in collecting the duties, has contributed not a little, towards frustrating the effect of those alterations.

3. What is advanced, *thirdly*, on the uncertainty of its success, and the danger which might result to the republick, were this proposal to miscarry; is an allegation, which has no probability, no foundation to support it.

The nature of the thing implies, that the large advantages granted by this plan, to particular goods and merchandize, must necessarily have a powerful effect, on the trade of those commodities; which leads us to entertain a contrary opinion, that the appearance of the success is so clear and evident, that nothing but absolute certainty, could be more so; and that without some such redress, the trade of the republick, and consequently the republick itself, must entirely sink.

The conclusion endeavoured to be drawn from thence, rather to leave every thing on the old footing, through fear of introducing a confusion and disturbance; has as little foundation, and by proving too much, proves nothing, the consequence of this argument would be.; that nothing ought to be redressed in any state or large œconomy, because every such redress is liable to the same objection.

Who would venture to assert of a private œconomy, that the whole family would run into confusion, upon an attempt to discountenance and prevent pilfering, waste, sluttishness, neglects, extravagance in house-keeping, with other indiscretions and bad management? From whence we would infer, that the business ought not to be undertaken without mature consideration, well weighing the consequences to be expected from it, preventing as much as possible, whatever difficulties can be foreseen; and then resting assured, that no assistance can be given to our trade, without some very effectual remedy, which ought to have a very speedy operation: And as for any private inconveniences which might arise from it, they would amply be compensated, by the benefit, the publick would reap from it.

A *second* sort of objections may be deduced from the effect, which these dispositions in our commerce will have among our neighbours: It will be alledged, that they will all look with an evil eye upon a limited free port; that such sudden alterations will awaken the jealousy, and excite the envy of all trading nations, and instigate them, by all possible means, to thwart our trade; either by granting the same priviledges and emoluments, as we are about doing to our merchants; or to follow the example of the *English*, and other nations, by prohibiting the importation of any goods or merchandize, except in such ships only, as belong to those nations and places, where the goods are produced or made, &c.

To which we answer;

First, that as to the jealousy of our neighbours, we need be under no apprehensions about it, whilst the republick tenaciously adheres to this fixed maxim, not to give any well-grounded cause of offence, by those dispositions and measures which are proposed to be made in our trade: On the contrary, most of the neighbouring nations will be more or less concerned, in the conservation of our trade, as their commerce chiefly consists in the vending of their own products: and will therefore rather protect than obstruct ours, which has such a connection with their own, that it may not improperly be called a part: It is easily perceived, that we would be understood here to speak only of those nations which employ our merchants and shipping to dispose of and transport their goods: As to others, they have, at all times, endeavoured to thwart our trade, continue to do so daily, and are not likely to recede for

the

the future, from such a practice : These will, doubtless, be chagrined, on seeing the regulations we may make for the benefit of our commerce : However, as their endeavours are not wanting, to do us all the prejudice they can, even now, whilst our trade is on the decline, we shall be able to frustrate their attempts with more success, when the same shall be put under better regulations. And in regard to this objection, the following reflection occurs, that when this republick was formerly in possession of an universal commerce, it was at the same time in a condition also to defend and protect that commerce against any, that endeavoured to disturb it.

Secondly, if we once come to a resolution, to ease and promote our foreign trade as much as possible, then our neighbours will never be in a condition, to put themselves in all respect, on an equal footing with the *Dutch*. The republick possesses within herself such advantages as are not to be found any where besides, in the like quantity, or to the same degree, which sets her in a point of eminence, above all other nations of *Europe*; in reference whereto, we need only remember what has been mentioned above, concerning the increase and growth of our trade.

The whole republick seems to be formed and designed for carrying on of trade : And as the goods may be transported from one place to another, in such an easy, cheap, and expeditious manner, by means of our canals and inland roads, it may be looked upon as one compact city.

The situation, in regard to all *Europe*, is extremely advantageous.

No nation in *Europe*, is so happily situated for promoting of fisheries.

No nation has a greater or more extensive knowledge of trade and navigation.

All the capacity and qualifications essential to, or requisite in trade, are found among the *Dutch*, to a greater degree than any where besides.

                                            Their

Their frugality and saving disposition exceeds that of all other seafaring people, since they can mann a ship with eighteen or twenty men, where other nations require near a third number of additional hands.

Whereunto may be added, their management in providing for the crews, in building their ships, and in knowing how to make a much longer use of them than others. All which taken together, are a reason, why no other nation can carry goods by sea, on the same terms as the *Dutch*.

A great plenty of money is another advantage which the *Dutch* have above their neighbours; the benefit whereof in trade, as well by buying goods cheap, as accumulating magazines in proper time, is largely and curiously discussed and set forth, throughout the 2d Chapter of *Law's* Treatise, entituled, *Considérations sur le Commerce, & sur l'Argent*.

No other nation is satisfied with such a small profit as ours, or waits for favourable opportunities with an equal degree of patience; insomuch that with us, it is become a common proverb; light gains make heavy purses.

In *Holland*, there is no impressing into military service, but the inhabitants enjoy full liberty; and being for the most part Protestants, have but few holy-days of course: Nor is there any country that is a more commodious nursery for sailors or seamen, when the proper means are used for that purpose.

The veuding of our *East* and *West India* commodities, especially of the former, is another peculiar advantage we enjoy, and which gives our trade a preference to that of other nations.

The spices, in particular, in some places do, in many instances, stand us in stead of, and are equivalent to, ready cash.

Other reflections might here be added, of a like nature; but what has been already said, may be sufficient for us

safely

safely to conclude, that no neighbours or foreigners, by any domestick regulations they may make within themselves, or by any accessions of advantage, how great soever to their trade, will ever be in a capacity, to prejudice the commerce of this republick, at least they never will be able to prevent its more diffusive spread; provided always, that the State knows how to take the proper advantages, and shall, above all things, resolve to lessen the imposts and duties, or at least to divide such as shall remain, with deliberation and precaution, upon and amongst those goods, which can best bear the burthen.

Thirdly, it is not to be denied, that nothing could be thought of more dangerous, or even fatal to our commerce, than for our neighbours to prohibit the importation of all goods and merchandize, except in such ships only which belong to the place where the goods are fabricated, or are the produce of that country; but then, such a prohibition is, on the other hand, very little to be apprehended by this republick, since the circumstances of most countries will not admit thereof, as it would necessarily prove a very great detriment to those nations, which have a superfluity of their own products and fabricks. Besides all this, such a prohibition would be equally dangerous to the republick, even upon a supposition, that things were to be left on the old footing.

We have, *lastly,* reserved to this place, an objection, which is the usual refuge of those, who find their account in the old abuses, and has several times been made use of with success, in these countries, against all reformations, namely, that a limited free port is a novelty.

It must indeed be owned, that this remedy of redress is new, and that there never was a limited free port in this republick; but it is as expressly denied, that the grounds and principles are new, on which the same is founded, or that they recede from those fundamental maxims, which the republick has at all times pursued. Yet, as these

fundamental

fundamental principles may be susceptible of different appellations, according to the different circumstances of the republick and its trade, whether internal or external; alterations or novelties must some time or other take place in the regulations of trade, whenever there is a revolution in our own country, or in the trading nations about us, agreeably to the proverb, *when rivers alter their course, the beacons needs must be removed.*

To illustrate this with an example; it has always been an universal maxim in this republick, to charge trade only in a certain proportion with other nations, and by those means to influence foreign merchants to come to us, rather than go to them.

If therefore the outward circumstances of trade are so altered, that neighbouring countries lay less impositions on trade, and grant it more immunities, encouragement, and favour; or, in a word, if foreign merchants finds it turn out more to their advantage, to go to those adjacent nations; then the old principles and maxims of our State require, that we should also mutually combine, to ease our trade, by granting it some fresh accessions of advantage, in order for it to remain much in the same proportion with other trading nations.

In that sense therefore, and no other, the present scheme of redress may be called a novelty; and to show this yet further, let us only reflect, what alterations have been made, and in what different shapes trade has, in general, appeared throughout all *Europe.*

In earlier times, the *Dutch* were the sole possessors of commerce, and the only people who visited all quarters of the globe, to fetch commodities from such countries, where there was any superfluity, in order to furnish others with them; while other nations were content to supply themselves with what they wanted, in this republick, without going for them to the places where they had been made: Now there is not a nation, but what, more or less, apply

themselves

themselves to trade, and use their utmost endeavours to draw it into, and promote it in their native soil; nor is there one, but has in a greater or a less degree herein succeeded, to the manifest disadvantage of this republick.

This, therefore, obliges us to alter our measures, conformably to the state and circumstances, in which we find ourselves; for nothing requires a more close attention than trade, it being subject to continual fluxes and variations; and in consequence hereof, to frequent, if not daily, alterations and amendments.

Let us but attentively reflect on the history of the trade in *England* and *France*, since the establishment of this republick; what measures, both these nations have concerted to make trade flourish amongst them; what progress they have made therein; and of what prejudice, the same have been to our commerce, more especially in *England*, which has given us the deepest and most fatal wound; we shall then be obliged to confess, that were we only to sit still, and neglect the making some regulations for the benefit of our trade, we should be in great danger of perishing.

To which we shall add, the measures lately taken in the *Netherlands*, to draw the trade thither; and the almost incredible expences they are at, only with a view to make commerce flourish amongst them; and considering the number of ships which daily arrive at, and go out from *Ostend*, to and from all parts of *Europe*, it will be astonishing to observe the sudden progress trade has made there since the peace.

These are novelties, which tend to the manifest detriment of the republick, and therefore require new regulations. Whoever reflects on these consequences, must be obliged to confess, that there ought to be no hindrance or obstacle in the way, but what should be endeavoured, to be removed and overcome, with an united strength and vigour.

The

The same remarks hold good of *Dunkirk, Hamburgh, Bremen, Lubeck, Altona,* all *Denmark,* and several other cities, as well as countries, contiguous to the Eastern Sea, which all apply themselves with great success to trade, and omit nothing to allure it to them, by granting, to that end, all possible advantages thereto; that a foreign merchant may find a greater profit, by fetching the commodities he wants from thence, than from *Holland,* where there are generally such heavy duties payable thereon.

Particularly remarkable has been the progress of the trade of the city of *Hamburgh*; nor less observable, that of the kingdom of *Denmark,* for some years past.

It is computed, that the ships which sailed for *Cadiz* in the last year 1750, were thirty-six and upwards; and that whereas in former times, very few ships came to *Copenhagen,* no less than six hundred trading vessels arrived there, in the course of that year; which, in its consequences, needs must be extremely dangerous to us and exceedingly alarm us: For should the *Danes* go on in such a manner, they will make themselves entire masters of the *East Sea* trade.

These again are novelties that challenge our most serious attention, and ought to render us regardless of encountering those lesser difficulties, which will be the spring of mischief infinitely greater to us, if they should prevent the proposed redress from taking place.

When trade has once absolutely altered its course, it would be fruitless labour to endeavour the bringing it to flow in the same current back again upon us: The fate of the Hanse Towns, and other trading nations, may convince us of the impossibility to recover trade, being established in some other place.

The dismal consequences which would attend a further decline of trade, are the more to be apprehended in a country, constituted like ours; where the decay of it must needs occasion a sudden and immediate wreck of the

whole

whole structure tumbling into ruins: For, if we consider, that the major part, and principal inhabitants of this republick, consist of merchants, artizans, mechanicks, fishermen, owners of shipping, and of such whose whole dependance doth arise from thence; it inevitably follows, that when the general ruin of a country happens, these men can easily remove their 'goods, ships, arts, and handicrafts, to other places, and there occupy the same professions. The principal, at least, if not the only knot, that binds and fastens these inhabitants to this country and republick, is interest, ard the means to get a good subsistance, and an affluent fortune, which here they have in more abundance, than any where besides: These ties once loosened or dissolved, there will no remedy be left, for the retaining them in this republick, but they will be forced to quit it, and to settle themselves in other countries; where, over and above, they would not fail of meeting with all suitable encouragement from neighbouring princes.

But in this respect, it is quite otherwise circumstanced in those countries, where the chief riches of the inhabitants consist in landed and immovable estates : When any misfortune befalls such a country, the carrying off their effects is a thing impracticable; and therefore they are not so easily reduced to the extremity of leaving the country, especially, as they would find no way to subsist, on their arrival in strange places. The heart of a true *Dutchman* must be pierced with horrour, perplexity, and anguish, and he must shudder at the prospect, when he seriously considers and reflects on those impending dangers that threaten the republick; if no considerable and effectual relief be given (and that too, with the utmost expedition and dispatch) to our trade, which is the main support of the greatest part of our inhabitants: For when the evil once is epidemical, and so far spread, that the merchants gradually retire into foreign countries, the putting then a stop to it will be entirely ineffectual. In short, trade is

to

to the republick, what the first link is to a chain; which breaking, the whole chain, with all its appendages, must fall to the ground at once.

Nothing remains then to be done, for the preserving this republick, but to make use of some new means that shall be clear, explicit, speedy, and effectual, for the redressing of trade; and a limited free port alone is such a remedy.

We are now drove to the last extremity, and the waters risen to such a heighth, as to touch our very lips: And whatever obstacles and difficulties may possibly occur, in the plan proposed, surely they would not prove of such a dangerous consequence in the execution, as would be equal to the sad dilemma and distress, in which the whole republick must be plunged, if it continues any longer in a state of inactivity.

From whence we would conclude, that, readily admitting the proposals to be in some degree perplexed and intricate; yet, as the question turns not upon this concession, but whether they are requisite for the redress of trade; if they shall be found necessary to that end, then to prefer what is most eligible, either by making use of our utmost efforts, to carry a difficult scheme into execution; or to leave the situation of our trade unremedied, to fall without redress, into a more visible decay; the consequences whereof, to expatiate upon further, is entirely needless.

Our intention in this dissertation was, only to point out the means by which our trade in general might be relieved and restored to its former flourishing condition; without entering, at present, into a discussion of every branch thereof, in particular, such as the commerce with *France, England, Spain, Portugal, Italy,* and the *Levant;* including, over and above, the trade in the *North, Sweden, Muscovy, Denmark, Norway,* the *East Sea,* and *Germany,* to the *East* and *West-Indies,* and on the coast of *Africa.*

All

All these different branches ought to be separately treated of, and inquired into, in what condition they formerly stood, how situated now, and what is to be done, to support and recover such of them, as are any ways already fallen to decay; and to prevent the others, which remain in a thriving state, from suffering any prejudice.

Our fabricks likewise will require a more narrow scrutiny and close inspections; in order, as attentively as possible, to trace the sources from whence the general decay, in the several branches thereof, arises.

The surest way to come at the most proper means of redress, for amending, increasing, recovering, and extending the former flourishing state of our manufactures, will be, to enquire severally into them, with a minute nicety and exactness, and to examine those who are therein employed; in order to put our merchants into a condition to make their appearance again, at all the marts of *Europe,* and to dispute their ground with every other nation.

We have, in this proposal, insisted only, in general, on an indulgence towards navigation, and those concerned in shipping, without entering here into the particulars, how the same should be effected.

All these matters will make the subject of a separate essay, abstracted from the present Dissertation, which only considers trade, with all its different branches, summarily, and under one general head. When once this plan shall be approved, the further dispositions may be attempted in their course, and will then meet with no obstruction.

Then too will be the time for a considering in what manner to increase and to extend our general commerce throughout all the parts of *Europe,* by an application to foreign courts out of the republick, and to chuse those remedies, that are most likely to succeed.

We have omitted likewise, to enlarge on some grievances which were mentioned in the beginning of this Dissertation, as the cause of our declining trade; not that

we

we esteem them of small importance, but as they are no proper subjects of deliberation, until the most essential parts of this plan shall have been approved.

We have also declined the mentioning a better protection of our trade, since such protection cannot be expected, till the affairs of the admiralty are put on a better footing; and this it would be fruitless to attempt, till proper regulations shall be made, tending to redress its present situation.

In short, these proposals are only to be looked upon as the first and most perplexing step, in order to advance some further steps hereafter, and at last attain to the main point in view, of rendering this country again rich, happy, flourishing, and powerful, as heretofore it has been seen.

A VINDICATION

OF

COMMERCE

AND THE

ARTS;

Proving that they are the SOURCE of the Greatness, Power, Riches and Populousness of a State.

BEING

An Examination of Mr. BELL's *Dissertation* upon Populousness, read in the Schools, and honoured with the Lord Viscount *Townshend*'s PRIZE, by the UNIVERSITY of CAMBRIDGE.

Wherein Mr. *Bell*'s Calumnies on TRADE are answered, his Arguments refuted, his System exploded, and the principal causes of *Populosity* assigned.

By I——— B———, M. D.

Æquè pauperibus prodest, locupletibus æquè. HOR. Ep.

LONDON:

Printed for J. NOURSE at the *Lamb* opposite *Katherine-Street* in the *Strand*. MDCCLVIII.

TO THE

RIGHT HONOURABLE

THE

Lord Viscount *Townſhend*.

My LORD

YOUR extensive knowledge of commerce, your generous attempts to introduce the study of it into one of our universities, and your glorious efforts in the senate to establish laws for its enlargement, not only render you the object of the esteem of every wise and good man; but also seem to constitute you the patron of all commercial essays, which shall be written with the same public-spirited views by which you are actuated. You are well-apprized that numbers of people are the strength of a State, and you have bravely dared to encounter common prejudices, by standing up as an advocate for a general naturalization of all foreign Protestants; and by attempting to abolish all corporation-exclusions in trade.

It appears likewise, from your assignment of prizes for the purpose, you are oesirous, that one of our universities should instruct the people in the advantages resulting from commerce and populosity. How far your expectations have been answered, I shall not pretend to determine; but I flatter myself, that the following essay is as worthy of your patronage, as the Dissertation, which oc-

casioned

casioned it, was of your money; and this vanity has emboldened me to inscribe it to your Lordship.

Though your Lordship's generous endeavours have been opposed by ignorance, maligned by self-interest, exclaimed against by malice, traduced by faction, and defeated by a combination of all these foes to virtue; yet your noble struggles for the public welfare must render you for ever the object of the esteem and approbation of every good patriot, and your memory dear to posterity. It is true, the opposition to your scheme, from the enemies of our happiness, has robbed you of the glory of doing a signal piece of service to your country, but they cannot deprive you of the satisfaction of having designed nobly, nor of the honour all wise and good men will pay to your virtues and merit. The attempt was glorious, though it failed.

I doubt not but some judicious *historian* in futurity will record in our annals a paragraph to this purpose. " The *English* had, from time immemorial, laboured under " a ridiculous prejudice against foreigners, according to " the observation of *Horace, Britannos hospitibus feros,* " and carried it so far as even to refuse to receive their " persecuted protestant brethren: But this year* a noble- " man of eminent parts, and of distinguished zeal for the " public welfare; a statesman profoundly skilled in the " interests of commerce, and the most refined politics, " animated with a patriotal fervour and zeal for the glory " of his country, and to advance its riches, power, and " splendour, as well as out of humanity and compassion to " the persecuted and oppressed for the sake of their " religion; by name Lord Townshend, appeared an ad- " vocate for a general naturalization of all foreign pro- " testants, and forwarded a bill in the house of lords to " abolish all corporation-exclusions, &c. which he sup-

4

" ported

---

* 1752

" ported with a masterly eloquence, that worked conviction
" and conversion in that house; but which, notwithstand-
" ing, had the misfortune to be rejected afterwards in the
" h--se of c-mm-ns by a faction which laboured to raise
" a clamour without doors against it; by appealing to the
" passions of the rabble, and deceiving them with specious
" arguments calculated to affect them in point of private
" interest, through which that noble design was rendered
" abortive!"   Thus I *augur* the Lord Viscount *Townshend*
will stand characterized to future ages.

When I reflect on your generous endeavours to serve
your country, I find myself brimfull of admiration, gratitude, esteem, and reverence.   I have no other way of
making it known publicly, but by offering to your lordship
this small present, which I consider as a tribute I owe to
your merits.   If my talents were equal to your virtues,
the offering should be more worthy of the shrine; but
such as it is, I trust your candor will accept it.

The French use every art to rob us of our trade in
order to rob us of our liberty. Their great men encourage
its study as a science, and its practice as an honour; but
who, saving your lordship, has prompted to its study, or
given it any public marks of favour among us.

In regard to myself, I am conscious of the purity of
my intentions, and the uprightness of my views; and as
to what *ignorance*, *faction*, or *malice*, may say of the sheets
which I inscribe to your Lordship, I value not, provided
they meet with your approbation; for I shall receive more
satisfaction from thence, than from the loud huzzas of the
rabble, or from the *eulogiums* of the *great* vulgar and the
small combined.

I am, my Lord,
Your Lordship's most humble servant
The Author.

PREFACE.

THE *religion and liberty of this nation have such an intimate connection with the flourishing state of its trade and navigation, that every true lover of his country cannot help considering an Essay artfully calculated to depreciate commerce and the arts, as a premeditated design and attempt to undermine and destroy those most invaluable blessings which we enjoy. Whoever considers the present state of Europe, the manners and customs which prevail, and the state of this island, will clearly perceive that agriculture is not so necessary for the nourishment of our bodies, as commerce and navigation is to the protection of our liberties, the defence of our properties, and the security and preservation of our religious institutions.*

The author we have examined in the subsequent pages, represents agriculture and a beastly rusticity, as the most effectual means of rendering a State free, independent, populous, virtuous and happy ; while he reviles the cultivation of commerce and the arts, as having an immediate tendency to depopulate a nation, and as the inlets to all manner of vice and debauchery, which will terminate in its destruction. To avoid those evils, he proposes an equal division of lands, and a retirement into the country. The purport of his doctrine seems to be contained in the following speech.

Gentlemen and Countrymen,

The only way to become free, virtuous and happy, is to renounce commerce and the arts, and to stick only to tillage and husbandry. I would advise you therefore to leave your smoaky cities, your trades and manufactures, and to build

you

you huts in the country, and apply to the plough and the spade. To be sober and temperate, you must leave off the consumption of exoticks; and in order to have a proper support for yourselves, you must restrain and prohibit the exportation of all native commodities. It will be proper therefore, to burn all your ships, that you may be under no temptations to the use of foreign luxury, or to the practice of navigation, an employment destructive of health, and the populousness of a State. By the practice of this advice, your numbers will so increase, that at last your lands will be unable to furnish nourishment sufficient for them. When you have brought this to pass I would advise you to adopt commerce and the arts, in order to lessen your numbers; which they will effectually do, and at last bring you to certain destruction. A very pretty scheme truly! which one should have rather expected from* Pere Ḥardouin *and* St. Omers, *than from a protestant university.*

But our Author in order to induce us to follow his instructions, tells us that the Jews became a very populous State, by neglecting commerce and the arts, and addicting themselves to husbandry. This example seems a little unfortunate, for we find by this conduct, that they were almost in perpetual servitude to one or other of the neighbouring states; one while to the king of Mesopotamia, *then under the* Moabites, Canaanites, Midianites, Ammonites and Philistines, *to this last, for forty years together. But at length emerging from barbarity and this rustick life, they chose a king, under* Solomon *adopted commerce and the arts, asserted their liberty, and figured as high as the neighbouring states. Here one might ask, what is there in this account that can induce a wise people to renounce the arts, and apply solely to husbandry and tillage according to the advice of this politician?*

8

If

---

* His system amounts to this, though in the beginning he says otherwise, and contradicts himself at last.

If this scheme were to be put in practise we should soon become tributary slaves to France; and make a very pretty exchange of liberty for the phantom of populosity. But we hope, that we have fully proved, in the following pages, that however favourable a rustick life may be to fecundity and health, yet that it cannot be reckoned among the principal causes which contribute to render a nation populous.

We are informed in the title page, that the Dissertation examined, was read in the publick schools in the university of Cambridge, on Friday July 26, 1756, and that my Lord Townshend's prize was adjudged to it.

As a thorough knowledge of the interests of commerce is necessary to a profound skill in politicks; and as our noblemen and gentlemen receive the first rudiments and principles of the political science in the schools; what politicians are they like to turn out when the first university in Europe can give the stamp of approbation to such a crude and superficial performance?

But this gentleman is not the only one of his university, who has been liberal of his invectives against trade and commerce; for his predecessor Mr. Baker, in his reflections upon learning, after shewing the insignificancy of it, the imperfection of human knowledge, and the vanity of the sciences; and after labouring obliquely to introduce universal scepticism, could not quit his subject without speaking of commerce with contempt, though it is a matter of the greatest consequence to the state, and of the highest importance to his country. But by his treatise, he has recorded his knowledge of trifles, and his ignorance of the most useful politicks. The sciences are of no manner of service, but so far as they aid and assist commerce and the arts, which contribute to the increase of general happiness, and to the relief of the miseries to which human nature is incident. The settling the text of an author, and whether an ac or an et be the right reading; whether an Etruscan letter was ever written this way or that; what is the true

reading

reading of an inscription upon an antient coin; how the Romans made their fibula, and what was the usual form of it; what sort of pans they used in their close-stools, &c. are matters of no manner of consequence to society: and yet what volumes have been written upon these subjects, and with what importance and solemnity have they been treated? Are the poor creatures in the hospitals in Moorfields *who assume airs of dignity when straw crown'd monarchs in mock majesty, so ridiculous as multitudes of those who are called* learned, *that spend their whole lives in unravelling trifles, clearing up frivolous mysteries, and in discovering things which if they had continued profound secrets to all eternity, would have been no injury to mankind? The noble architecture of card-houses and dirt-pies among children is of a piece with such learning.*

In Spain *a jesuit has lately recommended commerce to his countrymen in order to pull down heresy.* In France *it was the study of the great* Huetius; *and a canon of* St. Maur *wrote its panegyric in* Savary's *dictionary.* In England *Lord* Castlemain, *a papist, a hundred years ago, traduced it. He tells us foreigners carried on our traffick formerly, yet then we conquered* France. *We know his lordship's design, but our university's Mr.* Bell's *and Mr.* Brown's *we can only guess at.*

But let this be as it will; 'tis commerce and the arts alone which humanize mankind, make the difference between the Moors *on the* Niger, *and* Britons *on the banks of the* Thames; *and which lift brute nature to contemplations of Deity.*

INTRODUCTION.

AS the strength of a nation, all other things being the same, is in proportion to the number of its inhabitants, it behoves every prince, practical statesman, senator, and legislator to be thoroughly acquainted with the causes, which principally contribute to render a nation populous. It is likewise the duty of the rulers of every commercial state, carefully to consider what effect the populousness of a nation may have on its trade. The noble lord who proposed this subject, and allotted a prize or prizes to the authors of the best dissertations on it, is a *senator, legislator, statesman* and *patriot;* no doubt, but his zeal for the public welfare prompted him to instigate by rewards one of the great luminaries of this nation, to throw its light upon it, and to thoroughly canvass an affair of so great importance, so highly interesting. I presume his lordship and the public have received as little satisfaction and instruction from the dissertation which has been published as myself.

But if the increasing the populousness of a state by certain measures would render it more powerful in one respect, and yet reduce its strength, and make it more feeble in proportion in another, the populosity of the state ought to be sacrificed to its political strength and general

safety,

safety : For people alone are not the strength of a state, or, it does not consist only in its numbers. If this kingdom were a nation of husbandmen without navigation and commerce, without arts and manufactures, whose wealth consisted only in corn and cattle, there is little reason to believe it would preserve its independence long; but on the contrary would soon become a prey to a neighbouring ambitious state. It is therefore weak to recommend a system of police, which is not in the least adapted to the present state of things, or manners and customs, which now prevail in *Europe:* And to enlarge on speculations which are not adapted to practice, and omit those that are, is no more at best than ingenious trifling.

The learned author of the Dissertation seems to have set out in a most unfortunate manner by mistaking the question, or wilfully deviating from it. And therefore the bestowing the prize upon him was a misapplication of his lordship's generosity, and an abuse of his bounty, which demands correction or reparation. Instead of expatiating upon the causes which principally contribute to render a nation populous, the learned writer has rather given us a dissertation on this question, viz. *What causes principally contribute to promote propagation, and render a nation prolifick?* And in, *what respects does commerce tend to render a people less prolific, and diminish their numbers?* But as he has treated the subject, his Dissertation is a satire upon commerce, and a panegyric upon agriculture and a rustic life; but explains none of the principal causes which render a nation populous; nor clearly traces the effects, which the populousness of a nation has on its trade.

In order that we may not fall into the same mistakes, we shall endeavour to explain the question, and to learn the noble lord's intention in proposing it.

In the first place it is necessary to enquire, what is meant by the populousness of a nation?

12

2dly,

2dly, What are the principal causes which contribute to render a nation populous in the sense of the definition. The word populous is in itself vague and equivocal. Without defining it, and shewing what is meant by it, all that is said may be either true or false, as people shall please to accept the word. We must therefore suggest what idea the noble lord had of the word populous, when he proposed the question; and this we conceive to be what is commonly formed and entertained, when people talk of the populousness of a country.

First then, we understand by the word populousness, an abundance of people crowded into a small territory or compass of land; so that the towns and villages stand thick and near together, and are full of inhabitants. When a country is thus inhabited, we say the country is populous.

But on the other hand, where there are large tracts of land with few towns and villages scattered here and there with few people residing in them, we say such a country is not at all populous; or that it is thinly inhabited, and has but few people.

Having acquired some clear idea of the word populous, it will be necessary to have an adequate idea of what is meant in the question by the *principal* causes which contribute to render a nation populous?

There is reason to believe that the noble lord who propounded the question perceived that there were a few *principal* causes which contributed to render a state populous; and that there were a multitude of subordinate causes; to specify and treat of all which, would be tedious and irksome; and therefore that he designed the declaimers on the *thesis* should omit the minor causes, and confine themselves to the *principal*. Our learned author seems so little to have regarded the instruction and limitation in the question, that he has left untouched the *principal* causes of the populousness of a nation, and has

expatiated

expatiated largely on some of the lesser causes which promote propagation, and tend to render a people prolific; and assigned them as the *principal* causes of the populousness of a state; not considering that the politician who takes no other method to people a state thinly inhabited, besides what arises from enforcing the practice of temperance, and the affording all possible encouragement to propagation, is a bungler in his profession; since other methods may be pursued a thousand times more certain and expeditious.

In a country without an extensive commerce, two or three bad harvests would go near to depopulate it by starving the people, and causing migrations. But in a country, where great stocks of money and commodities are heaped up by the industry produced by commerce, there in such case, a state may subsist, and keep its people together, partly by the credit it has among neighbouring states, and partly by the money and superfluities it has accumulated, by practising the arts and encouraging commerce among its people.

The causes of the populousness of a state may be divided into *natural, political, commercial, religious* and *moral.* The most expeditious means of making a country populous is conquest. If a prince possess a large tract of country thinly inhabited, the quickest means of peopling such a country is by transplanting and bringing conquered multitudes from other countries, and assigning them lands in his own.

2dly, Another *principal* means of rendering a nation populous, is the establishing the best laws, forming the most just and equitable government, and the rendering the person and property of every individual safe and secure. This will tempt and invite people into such a state.

3dly, Another *principal* means of rendering a nation populous, is an universal toleration of all religions; so that no one be disturbed in the exercise of his own particular ceremonies, which are innocent in themselves; and that every one be indulged in the profession of his own particular principles or opinions, provided he is guilty of no breach of the peace of the state, but demeans himself soberly and quietly in the community.

4thly, The fourth *principal* cause of the populousness of a state, is the encouragement given to foreign commerce; the honouring industry, the enforcing labour; the preventing idleness by good laws; and the taking due care to administer all manner of necessaries to the poor, who cannot provide such for themselves.

5thly, After establishing a good police at home, such as is recommended above, the *principal* and most expeditious means of rendering a state populous is a general naturalization act, inviting all foreigners to reside in it; and as to *England*, to tempt all protestants to come and settle amongst us, affording to them all the privileges of citizens as to person, property, and trade.

6thly, Another cause of the populousness of a state, is the healthiness of the climate; and the people's not being afflicted with wars.

7thly, Another cause of the populousness of a state, is the hiring mercenary troops from other nations to fight its battles, and encouraging some few persons to serve in foreign wars, to learn the art and to officer its own people, and discipline them at home when necessity requires.

8thly, And finally, another means of increasing the numbers of the people, is the keeping as small a standing army as is consistent with the peace and safety of a state, and permitting soldiers to labour and marry.

These are the *principal* ways of rendering a state populous in an expeditious manner: not one of which the learned writer has taken notice of: Or if he have, it is with such limitations and restrictions, as destroys in some measure, the force and efficacy of the means he proposes.

From

From whence it follows, that his Dissertation is foreign to the question proposed, and the adjudging the prize to him, is an abuse and misapplication of the public spirit and generosity of the noble lord, who bestowed the reward for a discourse on the subject.

But the learned author's mistaking the question, or deviating from it, by treating of the minute concurring causes of populousness, instead of the *principal*, is not the only fault and defect in his treatise; for he has also been guilty of many gross errors, false representations, and injudicious remarks; and has advanced many inconsistencies, puerilities and absurdities, in his animadversions upon, the causes of depopulation and the effects of arts, the refinements of civil life, and the commerce at present carried on among mankind.

To say that agriculture, or that ploughing and sowing wheat is a principal cause of the populousness of a nation, is as dry and as little to the purpose, as if any one were to assert that

Eating was a principal cause of the populousness of a nation.

It is true that in most countries, agriculture is necessary to the sustenance of a people. But as a nation may, by sundry other causes, be rendered so populous that the produce of its lands will not feed half its inhabitants, it is manifest, that agriculture cannot be one of the principal causes of the populousness of a nation. The internal police, or political institutions of such a state, if any such there be, or ever were, must of course furnish us with some of the causes which principally contribute to render a nation populous.

But were there no such state, reason itself dictates the causes which we have enumerated above.

Though by agriculture wholesome food be produced, yet poisons may be raised by the same industry; or wholesome foods and grain be converted into poison by the

intemperance,

intemperance, wickedness and luxury of mankind. And thus our learned author proposes to cultivate the earth, and establish such a police, as will tend to destroy all order, industry, and sobriety, and to depopulate a state, though he weakly pretends and imagines, that the practice of his rules will render a nation populous.

Agriculture is a healthy exercise, but it does not furnish out employment for one fourth of the people of a state; and therefore if the arts were wanting, the people would be idle, debauched, and luxurious in a low mean way, or starve. If a whole people could be employed in agriculture, and kept from debauchery, to be sure (*cæteris paribus*) such a life would be most favourable to propagation. But this cannot be; and therefore the arts must be introduced to prevent the evils of sloth and debauchery. But if a country life and husbandry be most favourable to propagation, this does not argue, that it is therefore one of the causes which contribute principally to render a nation populous, because other causes may be assigned which will contribute more expeditiously to the peopling a state, as will be shewn in the sequel.

In the introduction to his discourse, he complains that there are but few inhabitants upon the earth in proportion to what it can nourish: And attributes this thinness of people to the badness of the political institutions among mankind.

But it may be replied, that wars, famines, pestilence, and contagious distempers, make great havock among mankind. What political institutions can guard against these calamities? The more populous the world is, the more those two great destroyers of mankind, *war* and *famine,* are likely to prevail. Great crowds of people bordering on each other under different princes, frequently occasion wars and famines: A mutual interest arising from commerce, is most likely to prevent and relieve the pernicious effects of both. To say, that if all the world conformed

to

to the rules of virtue, and lived according to the precepts of religion, the earth would be more populous, is a mighty important discovery truly! To remark to us, that temperance and sobriety, and following the dictates of nature, conduce to the peopling a state, is a trite observation for which no one owes the learned author any thanks.

SECT. I.

One of the great obstacles to the natural increase of mankind; our author says, * *is the great difficulty men experience in procuring support for themselves and their families; and 2dly, from hence that people avoid marriage.*

1. Of what use is this observation to us, where all the necessaries of life are attainable by common industry; and its common calamities to be guarded against by a little foresight and œconomy? Seven parts in eight of the people are labourers, and are guided in their pursuits by hunger and lust. The consideration of the cares of a family does not prevent one in a thousand from marrying. When does the fear of hunger extinguish the incitements and allurements of lust? It is no easy matter to find a young couple in high health, who having an affection for each other, are kept from marrying through the fear of the cares of a family, and the dread of hunger. The man who imagines that this is ever the case, knows little of human nature, and has attended very little to the manners of men. If among the rich now and then a monster of this kind is seen, it is very seldom.

We find that the *Hebrews* lived under a hard slavery in *Egypt*, and were rewarded for all their toil with only

18

onions

---

* Page 3.

onions and garlick. And yet those hardships did not destroy their fecundity or prevent marriages, for they grew and multiplied exceedingly, and became so formidable to the *Egyptians,* that *Pharaoh* commanded all the *Hebrew* midwives to strangle every male child at his birth. And though they lived under the dread of this cruel law, this did not prevent either marriages, or prompt to the using any arts to prevent fecundity or propagation. They continued to marry and beget children, though they were conscious that half their innocent babes would be strangled as soon as they saw the light. This is a strong proof of the weakness and inconclusiveness of our author's argument, " that the difficulty of acquiring sustenance for a family " in nations which cultivate the ornaments of civil life, " prevents propagation." This shews too, that the strong inclination and propensity to a union between the sexes, is not to be extinguished by the most severe hardships and distressed circumstances. The same may be said with regard to the *Helotes* among the cruel *Spartans,* and to the multitude of slaves among the *Athenians* who were twenty times as many as the citizens : As likewise of the vast numbers among the *Romans,* who increased to such a degree, as to wage war with their masters with great success. But if a simplicity of manners tend to render a country populous, why are not the vast tracts of fertile lands from the *Apulacian* hills to the *South Seas,* and from the lakes of *Canada* to the gulph of *Mexico,* the most populous countries in the world? If we examine the various scenes of the globe we shall find those countries the most populous, where the arts, commerce, and the ornaments and refinements of civil life prevail : That is all other things being equal. It is true, if a particular country through its natural poverty and barrenness and advantageous situation, has been so happy for a long course of years, as to avert war from its territories ; and through its good police to prevent famines, such a country probably may grow more populous than its neighbours, who have been plagued with wars and domestic feuds. We learn from the first book of *Thucydides*, that the poverty and barrenness of *Attica* secured it from wars and invasions, and rendered it a sort of asylum to those who loved ease and a quiet life, which made it populous.

2. *Our learned author says,* * *whatever serves to create or improve labour and industry in a state, tends to promote the speedy and great increase of a people.*

The industry recommended here, appears repugnant to the ease of acquiring the support of a family represented before as necessary to render a nation populous. In a country where all the arts, ornaments and refinements of civil life take place, or are introduced and prevail, as in *England;* it is computed that near seven eights of the people labour for their bread. Here a labourer may acquire all the necessaries of a family by his constant work. His ambition never rises above coarse food and rayment and the means of a low debauch. If the lower class of people can acquire these necessaries by labouring three days in a week, they will not work four. Necessity must therefore be created before industry can be introduced and excited.

3. A plenty of provisions and a general industry are incompatible. In order that this may appear more clearly, it may be necessary to observe what is generally understood by a plenty of provisions. If we have not clear and distinct ideas of the terms we use, our reasonings may be both true and false, according as the terms we make use of, shall be accepted and defined.

By a plenty of provisions, we mean such a small price for them, that a common family may acquire all the necessaries and luxuries that the poor usually consume by the

20

family's

---

* Page 6.

family's labouring three or four days in a week, or only a part of the time usually allotted to labour. When this is the case we say that the price of provisions is low, and that they are in plenty.

Again, on the other hand, when the price of provisions is so high, that though a man and his family labour six days in a week, the usual time each day, yet such family cannot purchase the necessaries and superfluities it used to consume in common, then we say, there is a scarcity.

To suppose then provisions to be at a low price and plentiful, that is, the support of a family to be obtained by working three or four days in a week, and at the same time to suppose, that a general industry may be practised, and that the mass or bulk of labourers will work full six days in a week, is to suppose a moral impossibility, what is contrary to common experience, what never was, nor ever will be, and shews a great ignorance of human nature, and little attention to the manners of the populace, as well as little acquaintance with the observations of the judicious.

On the contrary, Sir *William Temple* observes, that the poverty and laziness of the *Irish*, are owing to their great plenty of provisions; and their being able to procure all the necessaries they want with labouring two or three days in a week. Sir *William Petty* makes the same observation, and says, they can subsist by working only two or three hours in a day from their great plenty, and to this ascribes their great poverty and laziness. To suppose then a great plenty and great industry to exist together, is absurd and repugnant to the very nature of things. In truth they are moral contradictions. The great plenty of provisions in *Ireland* and the cheapness of land, seem to place the country in the state of an infant colony, and yet we do not find that mankind multiply in that nation, faster than in *England*; nor have they half the industry. The people live in a mean, nasty, lazy manner, and content themselves with coarse necessaries which may be easily acquired.

Land is cheap and provisions plentiful enough in *Wales*; but the people do not multiply faster than in *England*, neither are they so industrious.

4. Our learned author from page the 1st to page the 8th, seems under a pannic, lest people should neglect to marry; which in page the 8th, rises to a sort of enthusiasm, and occasions him to talk of *the prevalence of a corrupted taste, which may put a stop to marriage among the bulk of the people.*

The desire of union between the sexes, is so strongly implanted in mankind by the wise Author of nature, that a man may with as much reason expect to see the laws of vegetation suspended, as marriages *to stop among the bulk of the people.* If through a dissoluteness of manners, some few in high life shun the marriage state, such conduct cannot, nay has not, much influence among their own class; this daily experience testifies. The *rich* are not one in a thousand, and not one in a hundred of them lives unmarried: And of those who do, perhaps not one in a hundred but has offspring. But that sobriety and temperance should render a people prolific, is such a common, trite, and puerile observation, that we presume the noble lord who propounded the question at the head of our remarks, never dreamt that he should see the prize adjudged to a writer, who could rank temperance and sobriety among the principal causes which contribute to render a nation populous.

SECT. II.

1. Page 8, our learned author recapitulates, and gives us a summary of the principal causes which contribute to render a nation populous. And says,

22

These

These therefore appear to be certain and effectual methods of rendering a nation populous.

" 1. The procuring a great plenty of every thing " necessary to their support.

" 2. The diminishing the number of their imaginary " wants.

" 3. The universal encouragement and increase of " industry.

" 4. And the restraining debauchery, &c."

But surely though it should be allowed that these may conduce to increase mankind, yet they are not the *principal causes*, which *contribute to render a nation populous.* This learned author must think mankind very weak and ignorant, if he conceived he could palm such trifling remarks on them for the *principal* causes, which contribute to render a nation populous.

The three first of these observations are repugnant among themselves, and militate with each other; and the last with the first and third.

2. If the diminishing the number of the imaginary wants of mankind tend to render the support of a family more easy, to promote marriage and increase the numbers of a people; certainly it must tend still more to promote the same great and beneficial ends, if all the imaginary wants of mankind were cut off and extirpated from society; and the greatest simplicity and frugality of manners were restored. If such frugality and simplicity were revived or established, and nothing but what was absolutely necessary to life, was manufactured and cultivated, there could not possibly be any room for exerting general industry. If mankind confined themselves to the use of the bare necessaries of life, labouring one hour in a day in each family would procure them all: Where then, and how could universal industry be exerted? It is manifest that a simplicity of living and universal industry are incompatible

 and

and repugnant to each other ; and what the learned author has advanced, is very crude and superficial.

Further, if men were to labour no more than what is sufficient to procure them bare simple necessaries, this would be so little, that they would soon contract a habit of sloth, and from an idle life and a habit of sloth sink into barbarism. Nothing can preserve a disposition for labour, but the daily and constant practice of it. The more a man labours, the less irksome it becomes ; the less he works, the more burdensome the task. Sir *William Temple* thinks the change from constant labour to constant ease, as difficult and disagreeable as from constant ease to constant labour ; of such force and prevalency are use and habit.

3. Nay he observes farther, that in *Holland*, labour by practice, becomes not only necessary to the health of the people, but to their entertainment. And though such bread as our poor eat in *England*, is commonly at three-pence *per* pound, flesh at nine-pence, and wages only one shilling and two-pence *per* day, I could never find, that it was any obstruction to their marrying. It is certain it does not hinder them from being populous, nor from receiving a constant accretion of strangers. And all this must be ascribed to their good police, their toleration in religion, and their attention to commerce. From whence it follows, that a cheapness of provisions and a want of the ornaments and refinements of civil life, are not any of the principal causes, which contribute to render a country populous. And consequently that what our author has said on these topics, is not to the purpose, but quite beside the question.

4. It would be difficult to account for the barbarism of the *Africans* upon any other principles. The tropical fruits which are the spontaneous production of nature, are delicious, cooling and nourishing. Little or no raiment is there wanting, and houses are almost unnecessary, the

climate

climate is so warm. From hence the inhabitants are under little necessity of labouring, or of any regular police for their support. This first produced idleness, which degenerated into sloth and terminated in barbarism and a savage life. But should two or three great geniuses arise among their princes, succeed each other, and incline to refine the people, and bring them under a good police, it would be absolutely necessary to introduce a great number of imaginary wants among them, in order to establish the arts, and bring them under a regular government. If you would introduce any innocent gratifications and pleasures above what brutes enjoy, you must first create and introduce imaginary wants.

5. If you find in a country, treatises upon metaphysics, geometry, astronomy, policy and rational discourses, upon the being and attributes of a God, you will certainly in such a country, find the ornaments and refinements of life and a thousand imaginary wants, which in general are of great use to society, by keeping mankind employed. It is a general observation among moralists, *that the next step to having nothing to do, is to do ill.* The arts and sciences likewise yield innocent amusement, pleasure, and entertainment to those who labour in them ; as well as to those who possess the works of great masters, and have cultivated a taste.

6. We learn from history, that *Phœnicia* was happy in a fruitful soil, but commerce drew vast multitudes of people into the country, encouraged the arts, ornaments and refinements of civil life ; and at last filled the country so full of inhabitants, that they were in want of corn, as appears from the letter of *Hiram* king of *Tyre* to be seen in *Josephus*. They carried navigation, traffic, manufacture, dying, architecture, and all the elegancy of life, to the highest pitch of perfection. At the same time philosophy was cultivated among them, as appears from the doctrine of *Moschus* the famous writer, who was a *Phœnician,*

cian, and the founder of the atomical philosophy*. But it was not agriculture that made the country populous, but commerce and the arts, which filled the country so full of people, that a rich soil and the powers of agriculture were insufficient to support them.

7. Imaginary wants are therefore so far from being injurious to mankind, that they are highly useful for the reasons just assigned. If there were no other advantages and pleasures *innocent and rational*, which arose from the arts and refinements of civil life, but that they employed the attention of mankind, and kept them out of idleness and mischief, this alone would render them highly eligible.

8. To want nothing is the existence of a post, or a God. One wants nothing because it perceives nothing. The other because it perceives, and commands all things. To want what may be innocently acquired is no crime. To be in pursuit of what is innocent, to strongly desire it, and to have a moral certainty of attaining it, is one of the highest degrees of human felicity. It is no hurt to have wants and desires, but to indulge and gratify irregular and vicious ones, at the expence of our own real happiness, and that of others.

9. The *Chinese* have carried the ornaments and refinements of civil life to the highest degree, are the most luxurious people upon the face of the earth; provisions are often very scarce there, and yet they are the most populous nation in the world. We do not find these circumstances obstruct marriage, though it is said they are often obliged to expose their children because they cannot provide for them. If they planted colonies and carried on a large foreign commerce, they would be under no necessity of practising such inhumanities. But though

26

they

---

* See *Cudworth's* Intellectual System,

they labour under such disadvantages, it does not prevent marriages and propagation. From hence it is manifest, that our author needs not entertain any chimerical notions, that fear of want is an obstacle to marriage and propagation in *England*. From what has been offered, it appears to every unprejudiced reasoner, that banishing imaginary wants from society, would be an injury to it, and is more likely to depopulate a nation than fill it with people.

II. That the diminishing the imaginary wants of mankind, creating a great plenty of provisions, and at the same time enforcing a general industry are morally impossible; are incongruous, repugnant and militate with each other.

1. After our author has contended for the banishing all imaginary wants, and stinted us to the use of bare necessaries, he proceeds to treat of agriculture and the arts necessary to life. We cannot help observing here, that this term *necessaries* is of very equivocal, vague and uncertain signification. If we apply to a prince of the *Hottentots*, a chief of the *Laplanders*, a king of the *Negroes*, or a Sachem of the *Canadese Indians* for a catalogue of their necessaries, we shall find it very short. On the other hand, if to a citizen of *London*, or even a porter, we should have a long list of particulars that the others would laugh at as ridiculous superfluities. As this gentleman deals only in generals, we cannot therefore divine what he means, by such a plenty of the necessaries of life as is requisite to promote marriage and increase mankind, so as to render a nation populous, or be a *cause which principally contributes to it.*

2. Agriculture is justly in esteem among all civilized nations in the world, and in every place where the spontaneous productions of nature are not sufficient for the nourishment of the people, it is considered as a necessary means of their support and preservation, not as a

cause

cause which *principally contributes to make a country populous.*

3. But in order to render the necessaries of life cheap, and thereby promote marriage and increase mankind with greater expedition, this learned author proposes to banish imaginary wants and commerce. But if commerce and the ornaments and refinements of civil life render the necessaries of families dear and difficult to be come at, how comes it about, that people fly from countries where there is little commerce, little refinement, few arts, and a simple way of living prevails, to settle in a country where commerce and arts are practised? It is clear this could not be, if people did not find it easier to support themselves in such countries, than in states where there is little commerce, few arts, few refinements, and where husbandry is the principal employment. People migrate to mend their condition. It is not therefore at all likely, that mankind find themselves so much at ease where husbandry prevails, and there is little commerce, as where the arts, ornaments and refinements of civil life are in esteem, and commerce is cultivated and honoured.

4. Besides where commerce prevails most, and is in highest esteem, the lands are always well cultivated, and their produce becomes an object of commerce.

SECT. III.

Our learned author says, page the 10th, *that the state of agriculture in a nation, prescribes limits to its populousness.*

1. It may be observed too, that the consumption of a people, where there is no commerce, prescribes limits to its agriculture. Don *Jeronymo Ustaritz* informs us, that a plentiful year in *Spain* reduces the price of corn so low,

that

that it ruins the farmer, and produces the succeeding year a famine. From whence it is plain, that there must be a certain proportion between the quantity grown and the consumption, otherwise a plenty destroys itself, if we banish commerce. There is nothing but great riches or great exportation can prevent this evil. Thus a plenty destroys itself, and produces a scarcity: And thus the cheapness our author dreams of in page 11, appears a chimera; and when a crop fails a dreadful famine ensues, which starves the people and depopulates a state. Our *histories* shew this to have been our case formerly, once in about twenty years; and sometimes it continued for two or three years together, and made great havock among the people*.

2. Page 10. Our learned author remarks, *that a general application to agriculture, &c. that is a general industry, must evidently produce a vast plenty of all the necessaries of life, so that every single person will* be able fully to supply his wants *with the utmost ease.*

1. The author of these remarks apprehends that the learned writer of the Dissertation had no clear, determinate, precise, and distinct ideas of a general application, or industry. If he had, we must confess ourselves so dull as not to be able to perceive it; and so ignorant and stupid as not to be able to understand or comprehend his meaning. If he mean by a general industry, that all in a society shall work, it will be necessary immediately, that all the lands and property of the kingdom should be equally divided. This would be a pretty scheme truly, but is as impracticable as *Plato's* republick.

2. Besides there is a manifest repugnancy and contradiction in what our author proposes. By a general industry, is commonly understood, every man's labouring
29
in

---

* See *Stow*, and Bishop *Fleetwood.*

in his particular craft as much time as his health, spirits
and strength will permit. And yet he proposes and declares, that by this industry every man shall be able fully
to supply his wants *with the utmost ease.* This is a palpable contradiction in terms.

8. If he had said, " in case every one in the com-
" munity laboured equally, and all imaginary wants were
" abolished, then each individual might procure all the
" simple and coarse necessaries of life in plenty, by
" labouring a small part of his time," there would have
been some sense in it; but to talk of the practice of
general industry in a country, and yet at the same time
propose *the acquisition of all the necessaries of life with
the utmost ease,* is rank nonsense. It is likewise absurd
and nonsense, to talk of banishing all imaginary wants out
of a community, and yet at the same time propose the
universal practice of industry. When all these wants are
expelled from society, what are the people to be employed
about? It is proposed to prohibit the practice of commerce, so no foreign consumption could engage and employ their industry. Truly when this fine scheme and
these political *Lycurgic* institutions are reduced to practice, you will have little or nothing to do, but to follow the
example of the disciples of the *Spartan* legislator, that is,
to sing, dance, fiddle, wrestle, run, eat black broth, live in
huts, and wear sheep-skins, and in the issue, be extinguished or made slaves of by your invading neighbours.
But there can be no place for the practice of general
industry.

4. The institutions of *Lycurgus* were far from being
favourable to populosity, though he enjoined an equal
division of the lands. In the time of *Agis* king of *Sparta,*
we find there were but seven hundred *Spartan* families
left out of thirty nine thousand, among whom their great
founder or legislator had divided the lands, and not above
a hundred of these possessed estates. So little favourable

was his system to populosity. War destroyed the original *Spartans*, they were too proud and vain to admit of naturalizations, disdained strangers, puffed up with a conceit of themselves; and thus in the issue, spilled their blood to defend a state for the posterity of their slaves to inherit*.

5. But if property be equally divided, how is each individual to be made perform his share of the general fund of labour necessary to support the community in the simple way proposed? Where one man is idle or impotent, and another is industrious and vigorous, and the first has an inclination to alienate his property, and the other to purchase it; what is to be done in this case? How is this to be prevented? Here is an end of your political institutions at once.

6. If general industry and œconomy, if prudence and frugality, could be enforced among our labourers, they might all, as things stand at present, be furnished not only with all manner of necessaries, but also with superfluities, and the means of gratifying their fantastical and imaginary wants. But if this conduct cannot be enforced as things stand at present; what reason have we to expect it when property has been put on a level? In short, our author's scheme tends to destroy all industry and to lessen labour instead of increasing it.

7. The best spur to industry is necessity. The mass of labourers work only to relieve the present want, and are such votaries to indolence, ease and voluptuousness, that they sacrifice all considerations to the pleasures of the present moment, regardless of sickness and old age. Nay some declare it a crime to provide for either and rely on the parish. Mr. *Locke* observes, that they live only from hand to mouth. To this purpose Sir *William Temple* remarks, *all men prefer ease to labour, and will not take*

31

pains

---

* *Vide Plut. in vita Agis.*

pains if they can be idle : That is, unless by practice and habit their disposition be altered. The author of *the causes of the decline of our foreign trade*, Sir *Josiah Child* and others observe, " that in cheap times of provision our " poor do not work half their time; that they are paid " extravagant wages at all times," &c. If this be the case, as most certainly it is, what other reason but the want of industry and œconomy can be assigned, why all the labourers in the kingdom have not a full supply of all their wants? And that too at all times; in both good and bad seasons? But our author's scheme is impracticable, as well as absurd and contradictory.

8. Nothing but necessity can enforce industry. We must take human nature as it is : But what is necessary to make one family industrious would starve another. And what wages would be sufficient to supply a family with all the necessaries of life after a common harvest, and with many of the luxuries after a plentiful, would not afford him a living support after a bad one. There is no making provision for numerous families, sickness, old age, frosts, floods, rains, wars, want of employment, fires, dearths and other distressing accidents, but by œconomy. But not one in a thousand is possessed of this œconomy, but live as Mr. *Locke* observes *in diem*, from hand to mouth.

9. It has been observed that those nations have excelled most in industry and commerce, which have laboured under the greatest disadvantages from soil and scantiness of territory; and that their necessities from those inconveniences have whetted their invention and spurred their industry. As for example, *Phœnicia, Athens, Tyre, Carthage, Venice, Marseilles*, and *Holland.* Why may not then wants created by the arts of the politician, if judiciously introduced, produce the same effects as those arising from nature? But it requires great dexterity and finesse in governours to conduct such matters so as to attain the end desired; and whenever it is carried into

execution,

execution, its progress must be gentle, and its approaches almost imperceptible, and especially in a popular state. It is as unnatural to expect men should labour, when they have no real nor imaginary wants, as it would be to expect matter to act contrary to the laws of gravitation and attraction. The greater the weight to be moved, the less the velocity in mechanicks, when the moving power is feeble. It is the same in morals and politicks as in physicks.

10. As this is the general disposition of human nature, no wages, not if the present were trebled, would keep the bulk of labourers, or at least a great part of them from want: because they never provide against the times of calamity specified above, which they might all do, if they were as industrious as our author proposes they should be, and banished the imaginary wants be explodes. For this reason his chimerical scheme would be of no use, if it could be reduced to practice, so far as to level all the property of the kingdom; alienations would soon be made, and the old system of things restored or revived.

SECT. IV.

1. But as our maxim is, that nothing but necessity produces industry; and nothing but an œconomy which the mass of mankind will never practice, can prevent poverty, want, and distress: We will propose by a political institution to obtain all the good consequences of œconomy among the people without the actual or direct practice of it. This institution is much more practicable, than the visionary scheme of our author; and with a little management and address, such as beginning to put it in practice in a dearth might be easily established.

1. The institution we mean is to lay a tax on the first

necessaries

necessaries of life when cheap, as well as on the objects of imaginary wants, form a fund of its produce, and pay a certain sum *per* head out of it in a time of sickness, dearth, want of work, or in any other distress. This would prevent the labourers from being lazy in times of high wages and great plenty; and from suffering want in times of scarcity and adversity. A proper workhouse added to this institution, would prevent vagrancy, idleness and beggary.

2. Upon the footing of this scheme, the more a man spent the more he would pay, and the more children he got the more he would receive back again in times of calamity. The poor practice this among themselves in some places, but there are only a few so prudent. The pleasures of the present moment, and the gratification of the present appetite are what govern ninety-nine out of a hundred. Next to hunger and lust, the love of ease is the predominent passion; and in some this governs, and they become beggars. This scheme would certainly and assuredly supply every family's wants, and relieve every ones necessities and distresses, and is practicable; whereas what our author suggests is not. But though this scheme be favourable to propagation by preserving the lives of poor persons, who would sacrifice them to sloth, indolence, and voluptuousness: and though it would tend more to promote those good purposes than our author's unnatural, visionary, and enthusiastical scheme, yet we are far from thinking that it would be a *cause which would principally contribute to render a nation populous*.

8. But the inconsistency there is between banishing imaginary wants, and the means of general industry, and between a great plenty or cheapness of provisions, and the practice of general industry, are not the only absurdities and contradictions in this learned author's *theory:* There is also another manifest repugnancy, *viz.* between a plenty of provisions, a cheapness of necessaries, or high wages

(which

(which are all one and the same thing) and a temperate and sober life, which he so highly recommends as absolutely necessary to render a nation populous. To suppose a general sobriety and temperance to prevail either in town or country, where high wages, or great plenty, are found is absurd. If a labourer can procure by his high wages or plenty, all the necessaries of life; and have afterwards a *residuum*, he would expend the same, either in gin, rum, brandy or strong beer; luxurize on great heaps of fat beef or bacon, and eat perhaps till he spewed; and having gorged and gotten dead drunk, lie down like a pig, and snore till he was fresh. This is the common consequence of high wages and plenty. From whence it follows, that our author's scheme would manifestly encourage idleness and debauchery, and furnish the means of practising of both those vices.

4. We do not say these are the necessary consequences of a plentiful supply of provisions or high wages, but we assert that where a populace have the means of sloth and debauchery, that there it is morally impossible that they should be industrious, sober and temperate. Our author is for banishing commerce, which he argues furnishes the means of luxury; and where they are, it will be practised. But our author should distinguish, there is a vicious luxury, and an innocent luxury: Such authors are apt to confound a vicious luxury with a great expence. A porter may be viciously luxurious on fat bacon, tobacco, red herrings, gin, malt-spirits, and with a nasty bunter, or stinking dirty fish drab; whilst a nobleman may be innocently luxurious on ortelans, pine-apples, Tokay and the richest wines, and foods accompanied with a fine lady flaunting in jewels and brocade, and " fragant as *Chloe* issuing to an " evening mask."

5. To suppose that by industry the people have the means of acquiring, and that they enjoy the liberty of spending, and at the same time to suggest, that they shall

not use what they acquire, but in a temperate manner as
becomes philosophers, is ridiculous, and only worthy of a
monk who lives in a cell. The only way to keep a populace temperate, is to deprive them of the means of debauchery by paying them low wages; and to increase their
numbers by propagation, to administer all necessaries to
them in their distresses, from want of employment, dearth
of provisions, numerous families, or accidental sickness,
impotence, &c. But where the lands are fertile, it would
*be worth while to buy people from foreign states, to plant
on them if they are not cultivated.*

Thus we have proved that the cutting off all imaginary
wants, such as the ornaments and refinements of civil life
and the use of exoticks would

1. Deprive the people of the means of practising
industry.

2. That a plenty of provisions, or a capacity of procuring them with little labour, would take away the obligation and motives to industry.

3. That a plenty of provisions would introduce among
the common people voluptuousness and a pernicious debauchery.

4. That the way to render a people sober, temperate
and industrious, is to render provisions so dear, as to
deprive them of an opportunity to be either idle or
debauched.

5. And lastly, to secure them from distress, the best
way is to raise a fund by a tax on necessaries in a time of
plenty, to bestow on them in a time of dearth and scarcity.
But perhaps our author will say, he intends no strong beer
shall be brewed, no spirits distilled, no exoticks, such as
silk, tobacco, sugar, rum, &c. shall be imported; and that
by this means luxury shall be banished, and that
we shall become *Mahometans* as to fermented liquors.
But if this be the case, how will he prevent gluttony,
unless he makes the people all *Pythagoreans* too, and

renders

renders flesh odious and abominable? Or if he prohibits
the use of spirits and fermented liquors, &c. from being
manufactured at home, how without navigation, commerce
and a great naval force, will he prevent these from being
smuggled in upon us, and the country from being debauched and robbed of its money and the medium of its
domestic trade? These reflections shew the ridiculous-
ness of his system.

SECT. V.

In page the 10th, *our author proposes to keep our money,
and banish commerce, or to prohibit the practice of foreign
trade.   He then observes the price of all necessaries must
principally depend upon the proportion which the quantity of
current money in a nation bears to the quantity of necessaries produced in it.   If money increases fastest, these will
become proportionably dearer ; but cheaper, if it does not.*

1. This is a maxim adopted by some political and
commercial writers; and it is commonly said that the
increase of money is the sole cause of the increase of the
price of commodities in general; and that where money
increases, the price of commodities rises in proportion.
We shall offer a few reasons to prove this doctrine false.

When queen *Mary* died, there is reason to believe,
there were above four millions of money in the nation.
Though queen *Elizabeth* recoined all the old money in
1561, yet we find that there were not above six millions
coined during her reign. And there is reason to believe
all the gold she coined was transported, so that all the
current money at her death seems not to have much exceeded what Henry VII. left in the nation at his death.
And yet provisions were near eight times as dear, or at
least wheat, at the end of *Elizabeth's* reign, as the beginning of the reign of *Henry* VIII. or at any time of his
                                                    reign,

reign, or of his successors to 1601. At the end of the reign of *James* I. there was not above 5,500,000*l*. of cash in the kingdom, yet wheat was in general at eight shillings or ten shillings a bushel, labour as dear as at present, and other commodities for the mouth very dear. Here provisions, &c. were advanced to six or eight times their former price, and yet money not increased above a third.

3. On the other hand, the coin and paper money of this kingdom is increased to above forty millions, or eight times as much; and yet the average price of wheat is not above half so much, many commodities and manufactures thirty *per cent*. cheaper, and labour no higher if so high as in those days.

4. Again in the year 1715. *Dutot* says, there were about 44,700,000*l*. sterling in *France*. Since 1727, *Debonaire* says, about 52,500,000*l*. have been coined, all which money is in the kingdom, as might be shewn by irrefragable reasons, and yet *Dutot* says the price of corn, provisions, labour, salaries and commodities, are not risen; and this might be made appear from the writings of their authors, but the detail is too long to insert here.

5. Here we have proofs on both sides of the question, to demonstrate the falsehood of the maxim, *viz*. of a vast rise of commodities without an increase of money; and of a vast increase of money without a rise of commodities. We may add farther, that *Spain* had imported 700 millions sterling of money into *Europe* before there was any material rise on commodities in *England*. We might here shew the true causes of the rise of commodities, but it is foreign to our present design.

SECT. VI.

Page the 11th, our author advances another false maxim, *viz. Necessaries can no sooner grow cheap, but labour will be so likewise.*

38

1. Here

1. Here it will be necessary to make a few observations on the relative terms *dear* and *cheap*. When a man can purchase all his necessaries with a little labour, we say they are *cheap*. When it requires a great deal of labour to purchase or provide them, we say they are *dear*. Now if we look back to our histories of antient times, when wheat was in common at about two shillings a quarter, we find labour so high, that two days work would purchase a bushel of wheat in common. When wheat is at ten shillings a bushel, labour is no dearer in *England* than when it is at two shillings and six-pence. Nay when it is so cheap labour generally rises; the poor not being necessitated to work so much as when dear. Sir *Josiah Child*, Sir *William Petty*, Sir *William Temple* and many others remark this. Such bread as our people eat in *England*, is in *Holland* commonly at three-pence a pound, flesh at nine-pence; but a day's labour is not above one shilling and two-pence sterling. Wheat sometimes pays a tax there, of near a crown a bushel to the state, and flesh is high taxed likewise. From whence it is manifest the maxim is false.

2. If labourers could purchase the common necessaries of life for half the money they usually do, théy would work but half the time they do now. Sir *Josiah Child* * observes in such times they play and get drunk half their time. Sir *Matthew Decker* † observes that wages are so high, they spend half their time, and spend their money in luxury. Cheap necessaries must then raise the price of labour, till it destroys itself. Therefore our author's scheme is impracticable, and absurd.

---

* See his Discourse on Trade.
† See the Causes of the Decline of Foreign Trade.

SECT. VII.

In pages the 11th and 12th, our author advances some absurd reasonings concerning the reduction of the price of provisions, without reducing the price of labour in a proportion equivalent. He concludes his absurd account with this remark.

" *The advantage gained by the great cheapness of all necessaries is equivalent to the decrease of the price of all put together; while the inconvenience resulting from the low price of labour is equal only to the reduction of that one in which each man is employed.*"

1. This seems a most strange account of the formation of the price of commodities. If the value of each man's labour be abated one eighth, and the value of labour in all commodities be four eighths; all commodities through the abatement of labour will fall only one sixteenth. In this case the labourer will receive the abatement only of one eighth of labour on four shillings worth of labour, which is six-pence; and consequently will not be able to purchase so many commodities with his labour, as he did before the abatement by one sixteenth or the value of six-pence.

2. But if the value of the land which produced the raw materials of those commodities, and the value of the art, labour and industry, which provide them and bring them to market, be the other half or four eighths of the value of the necessaries the labour consumes; in this case if the value of land and the brokerage of those necessaries be abated one eighth as well as labour, then the labourer will purchase his commodities two sixteenths cheaper than he did before; and consequently will provide as many necessaries by his labour as he could before the abatement. In both these cases the labourer has no advantage from the abatement of labour.

There

There remains a third case, *viz.* If the value of the land and brokerage of commodities fall four eighths or one half, and the price of labour remains the same; this will sink the price of the labourer's necessaries only two eighths or one fourth, which is 25 *per cent*. And from hence a labourer who earns at present eight shillings *per* week, on such a fall of the value of lands and brokerage, will be able to purchase as many commodities with six shillings, as he could before with eight shillings, and consequently will be capable to furnish himself with more necessaries by the same quantity of labour. But that man who imagines he would in such case work so much as he did before, knows nothing of the manners of a labouring populace, nor is any more qualified to reason on the subject, than a blind man is to write a treatise on colours. All our histories prove that the lower the price of provisions has been, the higher the price of labour: And that when land was let at a low rate, labour was at a high price, and so high, that two days labour would purchase the annual rent of an acre of land, and a bushel of wheat: And yet this high price of labour did not prevent poverty and distress among the poor, nor the low price of land avert the evils of famine.

4. The common conduct of the labouring populace in times of plenty proves, that the easier the means of acquiring necessaries, the less work is generally done: And the dearer necessaries are, the more they labour, if full employment can be procured. Therefore the best charity is that which provides them work, by which they may be capable of relieving their distresses by their own honest industry. If wheat be eight shillings a bushel instead of four shillings, provide the poor with employment to the value of two shillings *per* week more, and they will live as well as they did before. Repairing roads, grubbing commons, draining fens, cutting canals, and making rivers navigable at such times, would be of great use to the com-

munity.

munity. The labouring hours of the fathers of families, might then be increased, and all the young sent to those public works. At such times, the working hours of single men, and fathers of small families should be lessened by law; and those of the heads of numerous families be increased. But we shall leave this digression, and return to our author.

SECT. VIII.

1. It seems from our author's reasoning in page 11, and 12. that he fancies, if the price of a man's labour be reduced one eighth, or we will say a shilling a week, and he consumes part of the labour of a hundred persons, that he shall save a hundred shillings in his expences by it. This is absurd; but if this be not his meaning, I confess myself so dull as to be unable to fathom it. But as I cannot with all my attention apprehend his reasoning, or fix any clear ideas to his words, I am inclined to conceive he had no distinct ideas of what he has said, and of the arguments he has advanced in those pages.

2. I can most clearly perceive that the value of all commodities or the price, is a compound of the value of the land necessary to raise them, the value of the labour exerted in producing and manufacturing them, and of the value of the brokerage which provides and circulates them.

3. Now vary or alter these a thousand ways, the labourer can receive no advantage, unless it be at the expence of one or both the other two. That is, it must be taken out of the value of the land, or the value of the brokerage. But if the broker's gains do not please him, he will withhold his sales. The farmer will not sow, the manufacturers will leave off their trades, if their employ-

ments

ments and occupations produce a loss instead of a profit. When a glut of commodities has produced by their cheapness a stop of trade, how are labourers to procure necessaries? This shews, that a student in a college is not a very proper person to settle the political œconomy of a state.

4. Let us suppose the value of the lands of the kingdom fifteen millions, houses five millions, brokerage twelve millions, labour thirty-two millions, and consequently the whole consumption sixty-four millions. Now supposing all the arable, pasture and other lands of the kingdom were to be sunk half in price, or let at half their present annual value, this amounts to but seven million and a half, and if this sum were abated in the price of all commodities, it would diminish that price, but in the proportion of seven and a half to sixty-four, or less than one eighth of the value of a poor man's consumption.

5. But our learned author premises, that all people of property, will go on raising and producing commodities with a view to lose by the sale of them, and from this continued and constant loss, that they shall become cheap; a presumption unnatural and absurd; for which reason no consequences can be considered as arising from it.

SECT IX.

1. *From page the 12th, to page 13th, he talks of obstacles to marriage arising from the refinements of civil life;* which exist no where but in the author's fancy; or at least the obstructions which arise from the refinements are a small dust, that weighs little in the balance; the rich whom it affects being very few; in proportion to the multitude, and few of them under the pernicious influence he represents.

2. It

2. It is false that poverty and want are the concomitants of arts, and the ornaments and refinements of civil life. Poverty and want generally prevail where they are not adopted. And where they are, if poverty and want ever appear, they are the consequences of sloth, imprudence, extravagance and folly; not of the arts, for these provide the means of a comfortable support, excite emulation, furnish employment and provoke industry. It is the abuse of these advantages, arising from the refinements of life, which causes poverty. Baron *Montesquieu* observes " a man is not poor because he has *nothing, but because he* " *does not work :* And he that has an employment, is in a " better condition than he that has ten acres of land " without one*." But if all the lands in the kingdom were to be divided among the people, they would not amount to four acres a-piece. A man is not poor because the refinements of the arts, policy and manners have left him without lands, or rather the folly, luxury and sloth of his predecessors; but he is poor because he spends what he acquires from the arts of refinement in a foolish manner; or neglects from sloth to make so proper and prudent advantage of those arts as he might. If the arts were banished, and the lands let for one tenth of their present annual rent, such persons would be more miserable than at present, and much poorer. Every one who has closely attended to human nature, knows this to be true. This is so just a remark, that there are few politicians who have reflected on this subjeet, but what have joined in the sentiment. The arts and the ornaments of civil life furnish labour, that is food. It is notoriously false to say, where the arts of refinement prevail, that there succeeds a scarcity of all things, necessary to the sustenance of the people. The reverse is true; and this makes people crowd

44

in

---

* See L'Esprit des Loix.

in flocks to those countries. It is the greater certainty and ease of procuring sustenance which make people leave the mountains of *Scotland* and *Switzerland*, the woods of *Germany* and the barren rocks of *Auvergne*, to settle at *London, Amsterdam, Paris,* and *Hamborough.*

SECT. X.

In page the 14th, our learned author observes, *that the populousness of Egypt, Palestine, the Græcian states, and Roman republick was owing to the plenty of things requisite for their sustenance.*

1. We would remark here, that *Diodorus Siculus* informs us, that when *Egypt* was in its most flourishing condition, it had but seven millions of people, and in the reign of *Ptolemy Lagus,* but three millions; so that it appears, it was never half so populous as *England* is at this present time. And yet in this nation all the arts, ornaments, refinements of civil life, commerce, the consumption of exoticks, and the imaginary wants of mankind prevail: the pernicious luxury our author complains of, and contends ought to be banished out of the state. But in truth, as plenty or agriculture did not render it more populous than *England,* neither did commerce or the arts depopulate it. Nor is there any conclusion to be drawn from the history of that state, which tends to support our author's system or our own. All we can remark from the accounts we have of *Egpyt* is, that the arguments our author has drawn from its history, are not founded on facts, and that it was not such a country as he represents it to be. Besides, if *Egypt* had been crowded with people so full as *Holland* has been by commerce, it would .have been no wonder, when we consider the conquests of its

 monarchs,

monarchs, the transplantation of captives, the purchases of slaves that were made there, and that the country was the center of commerce between the *East Indies* and *Europe*.

2. It is recorded of *Sesostris*, that to leave eternal monuments of his memory, he erected a temple in every city in *Egypt*, and other expensive and admirable works, all which were built by the prisoners he took in war, for which reason he caused the following inscription to be made upon all the temples. *None of the natives laboured here.*

3. It is said that *Cephres*, &c. erected one of the pyramids, and fed the people who laboured at it with herbs, onions, garlick, and that others did the same, &c. that the labour was so hard, and the pay so little, (that is, only a support from the above herbs,) that the people being highly incensed by reason of their cruel labour and toil, threatened to pull them out of their graves, tear them to pieces, and cast their carcasses to dogs; upon which account they directed their servants to bury them privately, and not in the sepulchres they had built. And *Diodorus* informs us, that the people in *Egypt* generally subsisted on herbs, the *lotos*, *papyrus*, kidney beans, &c. He says, they bring up their children with very little cost, and are sparing upon that account to admiration. For they provide for them broth made of any mean poor stuff that may be easily had; and feed those who are of strength able to eat it, with the pith of bulrushes roasted in the embers, and with roots and herbs got in the fens; sometimes raw, and sometimes boiled, and at other times fried and boiled.

4. Notwithstanding the labour and toils of the *Egyptians* were so great, and their sustenance so poor and mean, and their condition so wretched, we have our learned dissertator's word for it, that the country was extremely populous, and that this miserable supply of food did not prove any obstruction to marriages and propagation.

46

2. Our

2. Our learned author is equally unfortunate in what he says of *Greece* and *Rome*. *Attica* was a barren country. *Thucydides* observes, that the sterility of its soil screened it from foreign wars, and intestine broils; that it was an *asylum* for the exiles of other states, and a refuge to those who loved repose. That the *Athenians* allowed of a sort of general naturalization, and gave the freedom of the city to all refugees, which at last rendered it so populous, that it was obliged to ease itself by sending colonies into *Ionia*. We find afterwards, by its conquests, its traffick, and the purchase of slaves, it became exceeding powerful, vastly rich and extremely populous.

3. As to the other *Græcian* states, he informs us, that their fertility was their ruin; for it either rendered them obnoxious to conquests from abroad, or seditions at home: And that they had no incitements to the acquisition of riches, being exposed to the depredations of every invader; and therefore cultivated no more ground than what was barely necessary for their support for the present, confiding that they should find in all places sustenance sufficient to serve them from day to day. Thus we find for want of great walled cities to secure them, commerce and the arts to enrich them, the people of those states wandered from one place to another, neglecting agriculture, poor, impotent, in a word, exposed to the insolence of every one who should think it proper to assail them, either from caprice or avarice.

4. Some of the first paragraphs of the first book of *Thucydides* seem to be a full confutation of our author's account of the *Græcian* states; and in every respect a perfect and compleat contradiction of his whole system.

As to *Palestine* it never contained so many fighting men as *Great Britain:* After *David* had added large territories to his dominions by conquest, upon *Joab's* numbering the people, he found but one million of fighting men; which perhaps is not half what is in *England*.

And

And we learn from holy writ, that the arts and luxury were carried to a very high pitch among the *Jews*. But they owed the acmé of their power, riches, and influence to the commerce under their great and wise prince, king *Solomon*.

Rome was at first a sanctuary afterwards increased by the conquest and incorporation of the *Albans*, &c. At last to increase their numbers, they granted the freedom of the city and a general naturalization to all the world. My lord *Bacon* says, that all states which are liberal of naturalization are fit for empire, and that the *Romans* granted it to whole cities and nations; so that it was not the *Romans* spread upon the whole world; but the whole world upon the *Romans**.

Upon the whole it appears, that the *Egyptians, Jews, Græcians* and *Romans*, did not owe their populosity, power and riches to agriculture, but to strong cities, good laws, navigation, commerce, conquest and transplanting and purchasing people from other states, to increase the inhabitants of their own. So far are the examples brought from history, from corroborating our author's hypothesis. It is no wonder *Swisserland* should grow populous, since it has been so long free from wars, and is secured by its barren rocks and poverty from the invasions of its neighbours, and is also an asylum for the distressed. But is it either so populous as *England* or *Holland*, which have been both drained by large colonies and long wars by sea and land?

SECT. XI.

In page the 14th, our learned author says, *the second foundation of populousness is the diminution of imaginary*
48
wants.

---

* See Parag. the 5th of the XIth Section.

wants. That they require the labour of great multitudes and procure them great wages.

1. Here is a manifest absurdity, that great multitudes acquire great wages by the exercise of the arts, and yet that they introduce a scarcity and penury. Great wages is the same thing virtually as a great plenty of provisions; for great wages, which will not purchase a great quantity of provisions, cease to be *great wages;* such wages are in fact small wages. This every one must see, who does not confound a low value of money with great wages. But did the miserable sustenance arising from radishes, onions, garlick and other herbs, prevent the kingdom of *Egypt* from growing populous, or destroy the fecundity of the *Hebrews,* though both natives and slaves were condemned to cruel labours and toils under such wretched support* ? Which are most populous, *England, France,* and *Holland,* where the arts, the ornaments and refinements of civil life prevail, and where large and populous cities and towns are frequent: or the states of the *Caffers, Hottentots,* and the republicks in *North America,* where there are no large stinking cities, and where a simplicity of manners obtains, and the objects of curiosity and expence, art and elegance are unknown?

2. But there may be nasty luxury even among these, as we find from Dr. *Douglas's* account of *North America:* for he says, that after success in hunting, they gorge and gluttonnize like dogs, fall a-sleep and wake to repeat the debauch, and seek no farther till hunger excites them again to the chace. And *Wafer* informs us, that on the isthmus of *Darien,* the *Indians* set their old women to chew mace, which they throw into a tub of water to ferment; and that this slovenly brewing produces a heady spirituous liquor, with which they get as drunk as *David's*

 sow.

---

* According to our author it did not.

sow. From hence we see it is not abolishing the ornaments and refinements of civil life, that will preserve temperance and sobriety, since there may be a beastly luxury in poverty, or at least where none of the elegancies of life prevail, which may be more abominable, and more destructive of health, than the more refined luxury among polite nations.

3. A clean shirt and a laced hat are not inconsistent with piety and virtue, nor ortolans and Burgundy with temperance, nor a feather-bed with fortitude, nor a pinch of snuff with sobriety, nor a handsome woman with chastity. A man may enjoy them all, and yet act up to the dignity of his nature, and conformably to the precepts of religion and morality.

Neither on the other hand, does a man's confining himself to the use of fat bacon, *Lacedæmonian* broth, muddy beer, coarse woollens, a leather doublet, a canvass shirt and a thatched hovel upon a common, render him the more pious, temperate, sober, chaster, religious and virtuous; for he may confine himself to the use of all these, and yet be a most slovenly sinner and beastly profligate. And it seems, that the refined debauchee is the most eligible character of the two.

Drunkenness was a very fashionable vice among the *Scythians*; nay the *Persians* gave them from that vice, the name of *Sacæ*, or *Sakai*, which in *Persick* signified a glutton and a drunkard. And yet these people lived a very simple life, subsisting mostly on horse-flesh, mare's milk, roots, &c. without towns or even houses. See *Universal History*, Vol. XX. page 15.

4. Our author in page 16. *inveighs bitterly against great cities as being injurious to health.* This is true; but great cities are not necessary to commerce and the practice of the arts. All the ornaments, elegancies and refinements of civil life may be obtained without such large congregations of people. Neither is debauchery and in-

temperance

temperance a necessary effect or consequence of commerce alone. If a country or nation had not two houses standing together; and there were no more than a hundred houses in every town, the people might be luxurious and debauched. And if we had no commerce, spirituous liquors, gin and strong beer might do as much mischief to health as *Burgundy, Arrack, rum, citron-waters* and *French brandy*. The refinements, elegancies and ornaments of civil life, do not make intemperance and debauchery necessary; neither will the exclusion of them make a people abstemious, chaste, virtuous and sober. A people may be all that is bad without commerce and the refinements of civil life, and all that is good with them. A simple life does not extinguish the force of the selfish and cruel passions; but on the contrary, they appear in more horrible shapes among the *North Americans*, than among the nations which practise refined luxury and cultivate the arts and ornaments of civil life; which certainly restrain in a great measure their ferocity.

5. But it appears from the history of the *Romans* and *Italians*, that they had many large cities, and that arts, trades and manufactures were practised at *Rome*, as well as in the great city of *London*, in the infancy of the state. *Numa* divided all the inhabitants into distinct societies, according to their several trades and occupations, appointing to each their respective courts and privileges; such as the goldsmiths, carpenters, curriers, dyers, taylors, &c. *Tarquinius Priscus* built the common sewers at *Rome*, which were the wonder of the world. The stately and magnificent temples they built, the ornaments they wore, and the trades they employed, shew that they were no more strangers to the refinements of civil life than the *Londoners* are now. These transactions seem to imply, that husbandry was no more in esteem at *Rome*, and in the *Roman* states than it is now in *England*. The same may be said as to the *Grecian* states and the *Hebrew* com-

monwealth

monwealth. And yet our author absurdly speaks of them as if they were a nation of husbandmen. But if *Rome* in her infancy had cultivated commerce she would not have been so often reduced to straits by famine.

6. But as a plenty of provisions and simple necessaries is but another name *for great or high wages*, it seems that our author's scheme tends more to debauch and corrupt the lower class of people, than to render them sober and temperate; and from hence to introduce all the evils he exclaims against and pretends to redress. And we think it would rather depopulate the state, than increase and promote propagation. In short if people will be debauched, there is no preventing of it, but by cutting off the means. One of the best and surest steps towards it, is to enforce industry by necessity, so as deprive the lower class of both time and wages which may admit of luxury, intemperance, and debauchery. But this is the very reverse of what our author proposes.

7. Wages in *Holland* are low in proportion to the price of necessaries, every thing being excessively taxed; the people from hence are exceedingly industrious. And whether from want of the means of debauchery and being constantly obliged to labour, they are more virtuous and sober; or whether their laws are better, or the people more religious, or whatever be the cause, there are not above four malefactors capitally convicted in a year in the great city of *Amsterdam*. This seems to argue that their police is much better than ours at *London*.

8. Here we would ask this author, whether if his scheme is to be put in practice, we must not set *London* and all our other great towns and cities on fire? Whether strong *beer, malt, brandy* and *gin,* together with eating animal flesh must not be prohibited? And how he proposes to keep luxury from being run in upon us from our neighbours? And if we can do all this, how we are to prevent invasions and a conquest from abroad? Alas

what

what is it this gentleman means by the publication of such a whimsical scheme?

S E C T. XII.

In page the 16th and 17th, our learned author talks of the virtues of the *Græcian* and *Roman commonwealths*, and their sumptuary laws. But had not the *Romans* in the early times of the commonwealth, their *Appius Claudius's, C. Marcius's, Coriolanus's, A. Virginius's, &c.* and a proud, avaricious, and tyrannical senate, that were always struggling to enslave the Plebeians, and aiming to abolish their liberties and privileges? And in regard to the common people, they were much the same as they are now in *England*, as we find from their riots, insurrections and secessions. Here this author is fallen into the fashion of applauding the past times we know little of, and of condemning the present unmercifully, because we see all its vices and imperfections: though it is certain human nature has at all times been pretty uniform; and especially among the common people who have enjoyed liberty.

We may learn also from *Plutarch*, &c. that in the time of *Numa* they had all manner of trades practised among them, that contribute to ornament, magnificence, sumptuosity and luxury*.

As to the *Græcian* states, the *Athenians, Corinthians*, &c. they cultivated arts, practised commerce, and carried all the ornaments and refinements of civil life to the greatest perfection and excess; and yet they sent out colonies to *Ionia*, to all the islands of the *Ægean* sea, to *Sicily*. *Italy*, &c. and dispersed themselves all over the world. This does not seem to imply, that commerce and the arts

53

depopulated

---

* See above.

depopulated the country, or prevented fecundity and propagation. The *Phœnicians* did the same, and planted *Carthage*, and many other colonies. The people grew too numerous by commerce for their countries to contain them, which necessitated them to lessen the burden and reduce the overstocked hive by planting colonies in other countries. So far are these states, their manners, customs and occurrences from supporting our author's visionary and chimerical system. Commerce drew multitudes to them ; colonies eased them of their burthens. In short, our author's discourse serves every where to shew his great ignorance of antiquity, and little knowledge of mankind at present.

2. Page 17th our author says, that a *third cause of populousness is industry; and that no greater encouragement can be given to universal industry than every one's having a certain prospect of obtaining by it a comfortable subsistence for himself and his family: That a moderate proportion of their time and pains may furnish an ample provision for all their demands.*

This is the state of our poor at present, and therefore we cannot conceive why such useless instruction is given here. But our poor cannot only acquire a comfortable support by working only a small part of their time, but also the means of debauchery; and this is the reason why our common people both in town and country are so wicked, debauched and profligate. The only way to make them temperate and industrious, is to lay them under a necessity of labouring all the time they can spare from meals and sleep, in order to procure the common necessaries of life. That is, to reduce them to a state the very reverse of what this author proposes; as his system tends to nothing but the promotion of luxury, insolence, profligacy and debauchery, by furnishing the poor with the means and temptations to these, *viz.* high wages, a plenty of every thing, and spare time. Besides, how is this con-

sistent

sistent with the populousness of *Egypt*, which our author speaks of, and which we have shewn was the consequence of being obliged to subsist on *radishes, onions* and *garlick?*

8. The reason why the populace in cities are so profligate, is the high wages they receive; the chief reason of the greater sobriety among husbandmen is their low wages. For in the country where manufactures are carried on, and wages are high, the people are as profligate and debauched as in towns and cities. When provisions are dear, so that virtually wages are less, industry and sobriety assume their seat among the manufacturers; and if they have employment they live better than in times of plenty. All our author's reasoning on those matters arises from his unacquaintance with mankind: And what he advances in the contrast, he has drawn between the city and country, he ascribes to wrong causes. Great wages and certainty of employment render the inhabitants of cities insolent and debauched. Low wages and uncertainty of employment near at hand, if discharged, make the husbandman temperate and humble. Yet this gentleman proposes by cheapness of provisions and spare time, to make this insolence and debauchery general. And if his principle that temperance increases propagation be true, the cheapness of provisions he proposes, tends to depopulate a state.

From what has been offered it appears clearly, that there is a manifest absurdity in all our author's principles, and that they are repugnant to each other.

1. A plenty or cheapness of provisions is manifestly incompatible with general industry.

2. That the diminishing, or abolishing imaginary wants and the consumption of exoticks, takes away the very object and means of industry.

3. A great plenty or cheapness of provisions, and the abolishing the consumption of exoticks, and diminishing or excluding imaginary wants, would introduce an univer-

 sal

sal sloth and insolence among the mass of the people, which might end in barbarism.

4. That a great plenty of provisions, or high wages, with a diminution of the consumption of exoticks and imaginary wants would make way for universal luxury and debauchery, and furnish the mass of the people with the means of it, and temptations to it; *viz.* high wages and spare time, by which profligacy, intemperance, insolence, contempt of order, and all manner of debauchery, like a flood, would overspread the state, and end in depopulation.

S E C T. XIII.

In page the 19th and 20th, our author has advanced the same false principle but inverted, which he had in page 11. and 12; *viz. that as commerce increases money, it increases the price of commodities to the disadvantage of the labourer: Because it augments the price of his necessaries in a greater proportion than it increases the price of labour.*

Our author says page the 20th, *when by an increase of money things grow dearer, it is obvious the whole increase of the price of any one's labour can be no greater, than the advance upon that particular commodity in which every man is employed. But the additional expence of living incurred unavoidably by the same means, must be equivalent to the whole advance upon the price of all the necessaries of life put together.*

1. We have proved above, that the increase of money in a state does not necessarily augment the price of commodities, to which we refer the reader. And we shall here endeavour to demonstrate, that if it does, it will not augment the price of living in a greater proportion, than

it

it augments the price of labour, in the manner which our author contends for.

2. Let us suppose that by the increase of money, the price of any one man's labour is increased fifty *per cent:* That he used to earn twenty pounds a year, and that half of his earnings was paid to land and brokerage of commodities, and the other half to labour bestowed on them, that is ten pounds to labour and ten pounds to the other two. If then labour be raised fifty *per cent.* he will receive thirty pounds for his year's labour, instead of twenty pounds: If likewise a hundred persons labour to provide his necessaries, their labour will amount on fifty *per cent.* advance, to fifteen pounds, which cost before but ten pounds. And if the value of the land and brokerage which produces and circulates them, remains as before: in this case the labourer will be able to purchase as many necessaries as he did before the advance, for twenty-five pounds; by which he will be a gainer of five pounds. But if land and brokerage advance fifty *per cent.* likewise, then he must give thirty pounds for the same necessaries he purchased before for twenty pounds; and in this case he will be no loser. If he spent eight shillings a week in the first case, he paid no more than four shillings to labour, though a thousand trades received a part of it. If he spend twelve shillings in the second case, he pays but six shillings a week to labour, though a thousand trades more divide it among them. Nay often, if he spend exoticks, he purchases them cheaper, than he can native commodities of the same kind, *viz.* linen cloth, grain, &c. It is from hence demonstratively plain, that all our author has said on this head is absolutely false.

3. Besides since our commerce has been increased to eight times what it was, and our treasure in the same proportion, the price of all our native commodities on the average is sunk not less than thirty *per cent.* An increase of money lowers interest, and falls the price of brokerage

in

in proportion. If money were as scarce as in queen *Elizabeth's* reign when it yielded ten *per cent.* the price of brokerage would be now three times as high as it is. Suppose the interest of money was ten *per cent.* and a commodity passes through three hands, and that at the same time the amount of brokerage is double the value of the annual interest of money. In this case the amount of commodities to the value of a hundred pounds in the first hand, will be raised in the third hand from the maker or importer, to a hundred and seventy-four pounds: Whereas if the interest of money be but five *per cent.* the amount of such commodities would be but a hundred and thirty-three pounds, which makes a difference of forty-one pounds on a hundred pounds laid out by the merchant. But if we may believe many accounts given of the profits of trade when money was ten and twelve *per cent.* there is reason to believe that the price of foreign commodities and home manufactures were advanced three hundred *per cent.* higher than at present. Likewise when the interest of money is high from its scarcity, people can make a greater advantage of it by putting it into trade, or out on securities, than by employing it in agriculture, from whence the lands are neglected and in a greater degree. Hence it follows, that where there is a great plenty of money brought in by commerce, and more than the trade of a state can employ, there the lands will soon be improved to the highest degree possible considering the quantity of people. This is the case in *Holland* where their lands have been raised to fifteen pounds *per ann. per acre.* Where the improvement of lands takes place, provision must grow cheap. It is then more likely, that the increase of money should introduce intemperance and sloth among the bulk of the people, than obstruct marriage and propagation, by rendering the necessaries of life dear and its common supports difficult to be acquired. The great exportations of grain shew that this is the case

in

in *England,* and that the lands produce more than we can consume, though we eat great quantities of flesh, butter and cheese, and though the poor consume such vast sums in gin, which require immense heaps of grain for its manufacture.

4. But this author says page 21, *that when money becomes plentiful, necessaries will be more scarce; for the numbers which would otherwise be employed in their production, must be unavoidably diminished by as many as are engaged in commerce and the arts of ornament alone.*

To this it may be answered, that if mankind employed themselves in nothing but the productions absolutely necessary to life, seven in eight must be idle, or all be idle seven eighths of their time. And yet they might indulge intemperance, and sink in the beastly vices of slovenly gluttony and drunkenness. And this we find to be actually the case among the *Hottentots, North Americans* and the *Mosquetoes* on the *Isthmus* of *Darien.*

5. If arts, commerce and elegancies were to be banished out of this nation, sloth, intemperance and gluttony, would become universal: that is if commerce be prohibited and all the lands as well cultivated as at present, which our author proposes. But we think the consequence at first would be great poverty and distress among the poor for want of employment, and therefore this argument must be considered only *ad hominem;* or what would arise from our author's own principles, supposing the plenty he contends for would ensue from the practice of his own system: For we do not think such consequences would actually arise, as the price of lands and labour are settled at present. Provisions are so low and wages so high at present, that is in plentiful seasons, or on the average, that these vices have spread themselves through all the lower ranks of people. The excise books will convince any reasonable man, that a dearness of provisions and little employment, are the best curbs to those

                    vices.

vices. Whilst through a cheapness of necessaries, high wages and a plenitude of employment, the instruments of excess, intemperance and debauchery are to be procured, the lower class of people will gratify their appetites. To extirpate vice is impossible; all the ruler can do is to cramp it by obliging the lower class of people to labour constantly to acquire necessaries, which cuts off the sources of intemperance and debauchery. But so little acquainted is our author with mankind, that he proposes to open the sluices of excess, and depopulation, *viz.* high wages and a plenty of provisions, in order to render a people prolifick and sober.

6. When we had but little commerce we had but few people. The lands were in an over proportion to the number of inhabitants, and so of little value. From hence the price of labour and brokerage was high, and the price of provisions low; so low, that a man might purchase a bushel of wheat by two days labour. In *Edward* III's time, wheat was cheap and not above one eighth of the relative value as at present. This made the people very idle and debauched as we find from the statutes of the 23d and 25th of his reign. In his reign for want of commerce there was a most grievous famine, so that the price of wheat was thirteen times as high as in common, through poverty and a want of foreign trade. And though the exportation of wheat was prohibited once in about twenty years, thousands generally perished of famine.

It must be observed, that we premise in case the arts and refinements of civil life were banished out of society, that letting the lands at a high price would be of no use to their possessors: And therefore that they would be reduced to one eighth of their present value. For if the lands were to be let at the price they fetch now; and the arts were to be banished out of society, three fourths of the people would be starved for want of employment.

7. Our

7. Our author complains *that the farmers cultivate their lands only in such a manner, that the staple commodities of life may not fail of a high price and quick demand.*

But if we banish commerce upon a bad crop from unseasonable weather, the farmers will have a monopoly against the people, and may make what price they please of their grain. Nay they will have this monopoly against the people at all times. Nothing contributes more to the increase of mankind than the relief commerce affords in times of a dearth of wheat. High wages and a plenty of provisions which admit debauchery, are as fatal to the increase of mankind, as bad harvests and a want of commerce to supply the defect. When we had no commerce and this nation was thinly peopled, one scanty crop destroyed more people in one year, than the practice of all the virtues recruited in a hundred.

Upon the whole, this author proposes to banish commerce in order to procure a plenty of provisions, and with a plenty of provisions to preserve ebriety and industry; things the most repugnant to each other in nature. No political dreamer ever stumbled upon a more inconsistent project.

On the contrary we have fully proved, that by abolishing commerce, by excluding all imaginary wants, by banishing the arts, ornaments, refinements and elegancies of civil life, and as a consequence by rendering all necessaries extreamly cheap.

1. All industry will be destroyed, and sloth be introduced, which are likely to end in barbarism.

2. Debauchery, slovenly luxury, and coarse intemperance and insolence will prevail; and sometimes desolating famines ensue; all which are destructive of the increase of mankind, and tend to depopulate a nation.

SECT. XIV.

In page 22. our author says, *when commerce has thrown wealth into the hands of many, expensive enjoyments will extend to each inferior order, and introduce an extravagant manner of living in all.*

A few pages back, this author represents commerce as rendering all the necessaries of life scarce, but here he says, it will introduce an extravagant manner of living in each inferior order and among all. But how is this possible? There is nothing but high wages and a plenty of provisions can support an extravagant way of living. As necessity is the parent of industry, so it obliges to œconomy and frugality. But our author is so unfortunate as to be always joining repugnancies in friendly concert, and uniting contradictions and inconsistencies.

2. As to celibacy occasioned by employing servants, in the more simple times, as our author calls them, it may be replied, the retainers and servants in great men's families in those times were much more numerous than at present. But the celibacy of the priesthood, which in *France* deprives the state of three or four hundred thousand souls *per annum*, and depopulates *Europe* more than all its wars, and the luxury practised in it, this gentleman has slipped over unnoticed. The removal of this cause of depopulation would prove one of the principal causes of rendering many nations populous. Why he has left this ridiculous superstition unattacked we cannot divine, but he best knows himself.

3. In page 22. he likewise at last confesses, that the commercial arts promote industry and allure foreigners into a country: And that they may make it flourish for a long period of time, but at last will destroy it.

4. Here he has given up his whole system. As to the

destruction

destruction it produces, he may be asked how comes the republick of *Venice* to have subsisted for one thousand three hundred years, which was the greatest commercial state in *Europe* for many ages? The diminution of its glory has been owing to the diminution of its commerce, which by various accidents has been diverted to other states. *Holland* has maintained its power and influence for near two hundred years, and is now the richest and most populous state in *Europe*, and the center of all its exchanges. It is true, its prodigious struggles for freedom and the wars it has carried on to vindicate its liberty and establish its independency, have involved it in debt, and loaded it heavily with taxes: But yet the people are very rich, very frugal, and their country a magazine of all the commodities of the universe.

5. But how does the ruin he speaks of agree with what he has laid down in page the 85th, *viz.* That when a country is grown so populous, that its products will scarcely maintain them, its end being to procure the very requisites of life, trade will ever be accompanied with a general industry and a national frugality. In one place he says the arts and commerce will destroy themselves, and in the other, that they will produce universal industry and national frugality. Here he avers two opposite effects will spring from the same cause, a manifest contradiction. But it is no strange thing to see an author whose system is not founded in truth, to oppose in one place the arguments he has offered in another.

6. The populousness of *Holland* was owing to its freedom, its good government, and its commerce. This populousness has rendered its lands unable to support their inhabitants, and has been a capital cause of the extension of its commerce still farther, by making the superfluities of other nations necessary to their own subsistence. Thus other nations give them their superfluous provisions in exchange for the necessary manufactures of *Holland*. If

the

the *Dutch* could not take off their raw materials and provisions, those nations could not purchase *Dutch* fish, spices and manufactures.

7. The reason why commerce seldom flourishes in a fertile country thinly peopled, is because land being there of small value from the scarcity of inhabitants, provisions are cheap and plentiful, and labour dear. *Edward* III. tried to remedy this evil in order to extend commerce, as we find by the statutes of the 23d and 25th of his reign; but his remedy was unequal to the evil, he could not sink the price of labour so low as he intended, and as was necessary to establish a foreign trade; so that for many years after, the *Flemings* bought our wool, paid high custom *out*, manufactured it and paid custom in, and yet sold cheaper than the natives.

8. But if a state thinly peopled, by a good internal police can keep down the price of labour, and thereby establish a large foreign commerce; if its political institutions do not prove obstacles, it will soon be full of people, and have all its lands fully improved. These arguments prove the very reverse of what our author advances to be true; for here a plenty appears an impediment to an increase of people. Our author always presumes, that a nation can never increase in people, but by rendering the inhabitants prolifick. This assumption and error tacitly run almost through all his discourse. But it is evident to any man of common sense, that a police which will allure and induce foreigners to reside in a country, may render it more populous in a year's time, than the practice of all our author's maxims would in a thousand years. Therefore agriculture is not the *principal cause of the populousness of nations, as our author suggests*: nay, nor would be, though it was combined with the practice of all the virtues and political institutions he recommends.

The frugality in *Holland* is the consequence of their great taxes; and the dearness of provisions arise from the

                                              same

same source; to which may be added, that the product of
their lands must be necessarily dear from the great expence they are at in keeping up their dikes and draining
off the waters with which they are flooded. This in some
places amounts to near seven eighths of their value, in
others to three fourths: And their taxes on grain at the
mills to the value of the wheat ground. This of course
makes the people laborious and frugal.

9. But according to our author's reasonings in page
the 23d, commerce and the arts ought to have introduced
luxury, and to have brought on their ruin instead of
having introduced *universal industry and national* frugality,
which he declares to be the consequence of a people's
growing by commerce too numerous for its lands to support.

But those who have closely attended to human nature
and to the progress of human affairs, know that commerce
naturally leads to justice, temperance, industry and frugality; and if it does not encourage a profuse generosity,
at least it cultivates an amiable benevolence and humanity.
On the other hand, war and conquest naturally lead to
injustice, murder and rapine. Ambition excited by pride
and vain glory, avarice prompted by luxury and profusion,
insolence swelled by dominion and authority, create a
passion for slaughter and plunder. And when men have
been used to the exercise of those diabolical arts among
their neighbours, it is no wonder if they turn to the practice of the same among themselves. This was the case
among the *Romans,* who were a nation of soldiers, not a
republick of merchants, as *Venice* and *Holland* are. The
empire of the *Romans* founded and established by conquest, did not last much above half the time which the
republick of *Venice* has subsisted by commerce.

History does not furnish accounts of any state rendered so populous by agriculture, as *Holland* has been by
commerce. Besides the populousness of *Holland* did not
 take

take its rise from agriculture, but its improvements in agriculture were the effect of its commerce and populosity. No states were ever rendered so populous by agriculture as *Tyre, Carthage, Venice* and *Holland* have been by commerce. The lands have never been so well cultivated in any states, as in those where commerce and the arts have been cherished and have flourished. Commerce allures people, people must be fed, necessity of food prompts invention, and carries the arts of agriculture to the highest pitch of perfection.

To say that agriculture must first fill a state with people, before commerce should be cherished and encouraged, seems ridiculous. What reason can be assigned why the lands should not be cultivated, if the inhabitants are constantly increased by an influx of people from abroad, as well as if there were no such accretion? Nay, is it not a glaring absurdity to suppose a superfluity of lands should be as soon and as well cultivated by the natural increase of mankind, as by the rapid multiplication and increase produced by the allurements of commerce? And yet this absurdity is the very essence of this gentleman's system.

SECT. XV.

In Sect. IV. p. 23. our author inveighs against great cities as prejudicial to health and morals.

1. Why should this be a disparagement to commerce, since great cities are neither necessary to commerce nor peculiar to a commercial state? There is a district in *England*, where the houses stand a furlong apart, and yet the people are as debauched as in the city of *London.* But this is owing to high wages, or a plentiful supply of provisions, which our author contends ought to be the lot

of

of every labourer. When a dearth of grain happens, these labourers are as sober, humble and temperate, as any thresher in *England*, whose acquaintance is confined to the ploughman and his helper.

Page 24. our author says, dissolute and debauched habits owe their influence to luxury and idleness. And yet he contends for a plenty of provisions. Where wages are low, there it is impossible luxury and idleness should exist. But where they are high, labourers will indulge themselves in both. But when did we ever find celibacy in fashion among the common people, who are the mass of mankind? The bulk of the people want no incitement to the union of the marriage state, Providence has taken great care of that matter. Every wise state will promote marriage and punish bachelors, but no state can prevent monsters. The laws for promoting marriages were original laws among the *Greeks* and *Romans*, and not institutions consequent to luxury and commerce, and so they prove nothing to our author's purpose. They were made to influence the conduct of the rich and great men, not the poor. For they were suffered to expose their infants in order to limit populosity, and restrain the natural increase of mankind.

3. It is acknowledged, that commerce is in some degree prejudicial to health, and that navigation destroys many sailors. But the relief it brings to a country in case of failure of crops from unseasonable weather, there is reason to believe, saves a thousand times more lives than it destroys. The histories of the dreadful famines in this kingdom formerly as well as in other inland states prove this most clearly.

The *Longobardi* left their country by lot, compelled by famine. The migrations from the north were generally occasioned by famines; but as in our days, commerce alleviates or redresses those evils, there is no reason for such fatal expeditions, which generally produced the de-

struction

struction either of the emigrants, or the invaded; and must have been extremely mortal to both the assailants *and the assailed.*

4. But whether this be true or false is not to the purpose, for the question is, *what causes principally contribute to render a nation populous;* not whether or no navigation destroys many of the species. This may be the case, and yet commerce and the arts for every one that is lost, may allure twenty more in its room from other states, which do not favour them. And this is actually the case. Cherishing commerce and a peculiar regard to the arts, is therefore one of the causes which principally contribute to render a nation populous, and not a peculiar regard and attention to agriculture; which is diametrically opposite to what our author has advanced.

SECT. XVI.

Page 26. *This gentleman says, that commerce and the arts assuredly beget licentious and vitiated inclinations, and a contempt for institutions the most sacred and necessary to society.*

It has been observed that commerce and travelling soften mens manners, and rub off the rudeness and brutality natural to a rustick life: And that it is a means of banishing bigotry and superstition; and calming the animosity, which people who do not converse with mankind, often entertain against those who differ from them in sentiments of religion and other customs and usages. But that commerce, the arts and ornaments of life tend to beget a contempt for the most sacred institutions, is certainly a falsehood and a calumny that cannot be supported by facts or experience.

But

But though this gentleman entertains such a great opinion of the temperance, sobriety and purity of manners, which prevail in the country, we fancy if he were to attend to the manners, behaviour and conversation of a crowd of hay-makers, reapers, &c. but one summer, he would be thoroughly convinced that luxury, voluptuousness, sensuality, debauchery, prophaneness, filthy discourse, &c. are no strangers to the country : And that the sobriety and simplicity of manners he talks of, are no where to be found but in the kingdom of *Utopia*.

2. History informs us, that wars, animosities, the passions of pride, lust, avarice, revenge, cruelty, &c. appear as strongly in *North-America* and among the *Negroes* of *Africa*, as among the *Europeans*, where the ornaments of civil life are cultivated. Nay we may aver, that they appear in more horrible and dreadful shapes. If we lived the simple lives of horses, cocks and bulls, we might still suffer all the evils arising from the violence of the passions and selfish affections.

8. In page 26. *our author says, that a nation which is not fully peopled, will certainly become at length more populous by agriculture, than by commerce.*

We can only say to this, that we believe, that this sentiment never entered into the heart of any other man besides our author, and that this has been sufficiently demonstrated in the preceding pages.

4. But before we leave this subject, we would take the freedom to ask this learned gentleman, whether he thinks, that if the *Dutch* from the year 1567, to the present time had renounced the arts of commerce and addicted themselves to agriculture only, their country would have been so populous, and so fertile as it is at present? It is certain its commerce drew people, and its people increased its commerce, and improved its lands. It is the best cultivated of any country in the world, and the most populous: But its agriculture was not the cause

of its populosity, but its populosity the cause of its agriculture, and the arts and commerce the cause of both. *De Wit* and Sir *William Temple* both agree, that the lands of *Holland* were in themselves poor and sterile, and that the present fertility of the soil, is not owing to its natural richness, but to the industry of its inhabitants, and their attention to agriculture. From whence it appears that it is the populousness of a country enriches the lands, and not the richness of the lands renders a country populous. *England* has increased more in people the last hundred years, than ever it did in any two hundred years before, though we have been drained by long wars, have excluded foreigners by severe laws, and have been very frugal of naturalizations; a conduct full of absurdity, whilst we have so many large tracts of land that lie waste.

5. The antients pursued a different policy often, *Diodorus Siculus* informs us, that the *Trachineans*, having lost great numbers of their people, applied to *Sparta* for a new stock of inhabitants. The *Spartans* sent them ten thousand men, among whom they divided the lands of those who perished.

6. *Timoleon* finding *Syracuse*, &c. depopulated by war, tyranny and faction, invited new inhabitants from *Greece* to people the cities. *Plutarch* says, sixty thousand men immediately offered themselves, among whom he distributed as many lots of lands to the great satisfaction of the antient inhabitants.

7. Our political maxims are the very reverse: There are people would bring wealth, arts and industry among us, instead of desiring lands as a reward or allurement to reside with us, and yet we most impolitickly refuse to admit them. Is not this madness?

8. In page 26. our learned author says, *that commerce and the arts should not be admitted, till a people are become so exceeding numerous, that the whole produce of the country will feed no more.*

We

We believe, that without the aid and succour of commerce and the arts, that there never was such a country in the world, nor ever will be. If the absence or want of commerce and the arts is so favourable to propagation and populosity, how comes it about, that *Russia, Tartary, Arabia, Africa* and *North-America* are not the most populous countries upon the face of the globe? If the arts, ornaments, refinements of civil life, and the most elegant luxury tend to curb the increase of mankind, how comes it that the *Chinese* are the most populous nation in the world? All agree, that they are as luxurious as populous; and that provisions are very dear throughout the country, for the whole subsistence of the lower class of people is only a little rice.

9. A country without commerce and the arts will very difficultly subsist. Famines must often happen in such a state: We find this was the case of the inhabitants of *Palestine.* It seems from holy writ by the charity to the poor so often recommended, that the state was very poor and wretched, till *Solomon* introduced and improved commerce and the arts. Without commerce and the arts, it will be difficult likewise to support their liberty; thus the *Jews* were often carried away captives and made slaves to other nations. The reason now subsists much stronger, as the art of war is much altered.

10. In a state where there is great luxury and refinements, there must be great labour and riches among individuals. This luxury and these refinements furnish the labourers with the means of their support. The rents of the lands must furnish the rich with the means of this luxury; without which it cannot subsist: The lands must then be well cultivated. An extensive luxury then implies a large production of all the necessaries of life, and great employment of the people. So that where such luxury reigns among the rich, a full supply of necessaries must attend it among the poor, because it creates great employ-

 ment,

ment. Yet it is true the support a man may receive from his labour, depends on the compound relation between the price of land, labour and money, in a state, which often arises from accident.

11. If so great a number of people be employed in the arts, that the price of labour is raised in husbandry, and necessaries thereby become dearer; this high price of labour in husbandry will draw the manufacturers from arts to husbandry, and occasion more labour in husbandry, by which the equilibrium will be restored, and the price of provisions reduced to their former state. This is easily done, because bare labour in husbandry requires little dexterity, genius and skill. It is not so in the arts; from whence there is no reason to suspect, there will ever be a want of hands in husbandry; or that the price of labour in it will ever advance high. If provisions in general rise much in price whilst there are waste lands, more will be converted to tillage, and what are in use will be farther improved, so that all these inequalities tend to correct themselves.

This will more especially obtain in a country where money is plenty, because there its interest and brokerage being low, a man will not be able to turn it to any use, so profitable and advantageous as to the culture of lands, if provisions bear but a tolerable price. Thus it appears that the very reverse to what our author suggests, will be the consequence of a great plenty of money, namely a low price for provisions instead of a high one: This theory is confirmed by experience, and by the present price of provisions on the average, compared with what it was a hundred years ago; notwithstanding we sometimes export grain to the value of three millions in one year.

Therefore a great home consumption or luxury in native commodities cannot render them dear. The poor can spend no more than they earn, or is given them by the rich; the farmers and traders save, and the rich can-

not

not spend more than their incomes without becoming poor, upon which the trader and farmer will divide his estate amongst them. The stock of commodities in the nation, which is still increasing, the great national debt, and the increase of plate and jewels, shews that if the publick spend, individuals in the state save. From these reasonings it is manifest, that a great home consumption does not tend to produce a scarcity of commodities. That is where the lands are not cultivated to the highest degree of perfection. It is only foreign luxury which ruins a state, that is, such a consumption of exoticks as drains us of our cash, turns the poor out of employment, and robs the lands of consumptioners of their product.

. 12. There are two circumstances in which there may be a scarcity; these are when bad crops of grain happen from unseasonable weather, and when the farmers from their great riches are enabled to withhold a supply from the market, and advance its price. There is nothing but granaries or commerce which can produce a cure for these evils. But in a country where a failure of the crops seldom happens, it would be difficult to manage granaries to any great advantage, for the stock of grain in them would be liable to corrupt and must be sold often. We will not say such an expedient for preventing scarcities is impracticable, but there is reason to think so many difficulties attend it, that such a scheme will never be carried into execution.

The admission of the exportation of grain and the rendering it an object of commerce, is the best method which can be pursued to prevent scarcities from bad crops. If one third of the lands employed in tillage be cultivated for the use of foreigners, and at the same time one third of the crop should fail; by a prohibition of the exportation of grain, the price would be kept down, and there would be enough left for our own use and consumption. In case there should not be enough to suffice the inhabi-

tants,

tants, a supply might be brought from our *American* colonies. These two circumstances shew the great use of commerce, and how much it conduces to the preventing depopulation in a state; and at the same time they prove the weakness of our author's principles and the absurdity of his system.

SECT. XVII.

In page 27, Our author says, *an equal division of the lands is necessary to carry his system into execution, and raise it to perfection.* We will cite the passage at large *which runs as* follows.

1. *" Of all political institutions, none seems more immediately requisite (to promote agriculture) than an equal division of lands. For as soon as the wants of each are satisfied,* which in times of simplicity a very small possession will be sufficient for, there can be no farther inducement to cultivate more land. In this case therefore, if the property of numbers is much larger than their wants require, *great quantities of land must remain uncultivated,* and a country be deprived of a proportionable number of inhabitants." Then he says; " whenever this inequality obtains, the *introduction of commerce and elegance is the only remedy for its pernicious effects.* These (that is commerce and elegance) by multiplying the desires of men, will induce such as have large possessions to cultivate them for the purchase of superfluities, and *thus create employment and subsistence for greater numbers than before.* But from what has already been proved at large, they can never increase by these means, as where property is equally divided, and the necessary arts principally attended to. There every one will possess and cultivate enough to satisfy his demands, and the same provision will remain

for

for the increase of each succeeding generation, till the country is stocked with as many inhabitants as its produce can support."

2. This is a strange jumble of reasoning, the first part damns his whole system; the last clause recalls and revokes the sentence again. We will examine it in a particular manner.

Our author in the first place, proposes an *Agrarian*, but in consequence allows, that great quantities of land must remaiu uncultivated, and a country be deprived of a proportionable number of inhabitants.

3. Then he proposes the introduction of commerce, and all that he had exploded before, in order to remedy *its pernicious effects*. That is, depopulation or want of people, and the lands lying without cultivation. And yet he retracts immediately, and denies that this will remedy the pernicious effects he had acknowledged just before would flow from an *Agrarian;* and in contradiction to the remedy proposed to the pernicious effects, he declares that he has proved at large, that a people can never increase by commerce and elegance, *so much as they may where the necessary arts are principally attended to.*

4. Or thus the argument stands. An *Agrarian* restrains the increase of people and the cultivation of the lands. 2. The *only* remedy for these pernicious effects is the introduction of commerce and elegance. 3. But though the introduction of commerce and elegance be the *only* remedy to the pernicious effects flowing from the *Agrarian*, yet, 4. it has been proved at large, there is a better remedy than the *only remedy*, viz. a principal attention to the necessary arts; though he has declared, that an inattention to the necessary arts will be the consequence of an *Agrarian*.

Good Gods! what a heap of absurdity, contradiction and nonsense! Reason what art thou! Where art thou!

5. An

5. An *Agrarian*, or equal division of the lands, is not adapted to the genius of mankind. Neither among the *Jews* or *Romans* did it produce any advantageous effects, nor was the continuance of it practicable. *Licinius Stolo* established an *Agrarian* at *Rome*, that no person should possess above five hundred acres of land for himself, and half as much for every child; and yet broke through it himself, and suffered the penalty. And though at first the citizens had two acres a-piece, they soon transferred their property to the industrious and frugal. This *Agrarian* neither remained long, produced universal industry, nor prevented poverty, either in *Jewry*, *Greece*, or *Rome*, as most flagrantly appears from their histories. No wise people upon these accounts ought to adopt any such ridiculous institutions. Nay our *Janus faced* author says, page 28. "that where it prevails, great quantities of "land must remain uncultivated, and a country be de- "prived of a proportionable number of its inhabitants." And yet proposes it immediately in the next paragraph as a *cause which principally contributes to render a nation populous;* amazing!

In page 30. our learned author observes, *that the very being of republicks is founded upon a general equality of possessions.*

6. But we would ask whether there was ever any republick or state in the world where there was such an equality prevailed? There was no such equality either at *Rome*, in the *Grecian* commonwealths, or in *Jewry*. The history of our country shews, that the power of alienation of lands and the cultivation of commerce and the arts, is the best way to diffuse possessions, and distribute property in the most equable manner; as well as to promote industry and frugality among the mass of the people. The laws of *Moses* and the institutions of *Lycurgus* were far from answering this valuable end. *Moses*'s prohibition of usury was by no means favourable to industry, or to a

large

large consumption, and a terrible hardship upon orphans and widows.

7. In page 30. paragraph the second, our learned author says, *the cultivation of agriculture and the necessary arts alone founded on an equal division of property, &c. is the only means capable of increasing a small people to the full extent of those numbers which their country can conveniently support.*

8. And yet in the last paragraph of page 27, &c. he tells us, " that if the lands be divided in this manner, " great quantities must remain uncultivated, and the " country be deprived of a proportionable number of in- " habitants." Strange! how do those things agree?

9. *Holland* is the most populous state in the world*; but *Holland* did not owe its populosity to an equal division of the lands, nor to the cultivation of them : But it owed its people to its commerce, and its agriculture to its fulness of people. The badness of its air would soon depopulate *Holland*, if it were not for a constant influx of strangers. But its government which secures liberty and property equally to every man, its strict justice and equality in taxations, its toleration in matters of religion, its free naturalisation, and its great commerce constantly allure people from all parts, to settle in the country, though wages are low and provisions exceeding high. It was these arts raised a few fishermen seated among unhealthy morasses in small villages, to be the *high and mighty states of Holland.* This drew crowds of people to them from all parts, and raised insignificant hamlets into great cities. By this they took pastures out of the sea, and fattened the dry land. *Neptune* stood amazed, beheld the daring robbery, but connived at the theft, struck with the wonderful industry of the people.

SECT. XVIII.

In page 31. our author comes to consider the principal effects of the populousness of a nation on its trade. He seems as unfortunate in his reflections upon this part of his question as he was upon the first.

His first remark is, that while the numbers of a people are small in comparison to the extent of country they are possessed of, it has always been found that their employments and inventions continue limited to the satisfying a few natural wants and the acquiring such conveniencies only as are common among themselves.

This is not true; *Spain, Portugal,* and *Italy* are but thinly inhabited, and especially the dominions of the church in the last; and yet they consume a vast quantity of exoticks.

Page 34. our author says, the productions of art have been discoveries of the finest geniuses, and such as do honour to human nature. And again, the contrivances which increase their real usefulness and value, &c.

This writer deals excessively in contradictions. The arts which a few pages back obliterated virtue, ruined society, and destroyed mankind, consequently most pernicious inventions, and one should think begotten in hell, and dictated by Satan, now are represented as doing honour to human nature. The refinements and ornaments of civil life, that were but just now so ruinous and destructive to mankind, are become useful and valuable. Strange inconsistency!

And though our author has throughout his essay suggested and declared, that commerce and the arts tend to depopulate a state, and in the issue will ruin it, yet in page 35. he presumes, that there are means where trade exists, though the country be not full of people, to render it so populous, that the lands may not be capable of main-
78
taining

taining them. This is again a contradiction to the tenor of his whole discourse. Like a *Proteus* or *Camelion* he is always changing shape and colour, and shifting his principles just as the last train of ideas influences, without ever considering whether what he lays down is consistent with his first principles, and what he advanced in the beginning of his discourse.

If after a nation be full of people, and commodities are become so scarce and dear, as to enforce general industry and national frugality ; in case a plenty be necessary to render a state populous, how comes it to pass, that a nation under the disadvantages of a scarcity can increase farther ? If this be possible, as our author confesses it is, there must be some strong attractive cause to produce this effect; an effect so contrary to his premises, *viz. that a plenty is necessary to populosity*. This cause is the attractions of commerce, which draw a people into a nation under all his pretended oppositions to multiplication arising from scarcity ; and which increase a people vastly more expeditiously, than they can in the natural way, tho' they pursued every means, that art, nature, and virtue combined can suggest. Though our author is silent as to the causes, yet he himself allows the effects.

But if this attraction operate in this manner where commerce is, though the country be full of people, and they labour under a scarcity of every thing necessary to life ; why may it not operate still stronger where commerce is in a country not fully peopled, and where every thing is in great plenty? It certainly must, upon our author's own principles. If after *Holland* were full, and provisions scarce, people continued still to flock thither, what was it drew them? Not plenty according to this author. It must then be commerce. If so, how much more readily will commerce draw them into a plentiful nation? From hence it is manifest, that our author admits of other causes of populosity which act more powerfully

 than

than *plenty, temperance, sobriety, banishing imaginary wants, agriculture and a country life,* all put together.

The principal of those causes is commerce, supported by an equitable government, an equal taxation, a general toleration in religion, and a full security of person and property. These allure people, and naturalization with open arms receives them. When he presents these blessings, the industrious, the indigent, the distressed, the persecuted fly to her for relief. They do not ask whether laughing *Ceres* pours her bounties over the fertile plains, or *Flora* decks the enamelled meads, but whether they can be assured of the enjoyment of the civil advantages specified above. If so, thither people will flock, and soon convert the standing pool and lake into fat meadows, cover the barren rock with verdure, and make the desert smile with flowers. Such O liberty! O commerce! are thy blessings.

The arts and sciences, O commerce! follow in thy train, attended by politeness and humanity; whilst superstition, bigotry, and fiery zeal, fallen from their throne, lie under thy feet chained and gnashing their teeth.

Upon the whole, it is clear from experience, as well as from our author's concessions, that nothing tends to render a nation populous, and to fill it so soon with a multitude of people as commerce supported as above.

Page 35. He falls into a common mistake, that populousness produces cheapness of labour and commodities. In the first place people create employment for each other: But cheapness depends chiefly on the high value of money. This is the case in *France.*

Page 86. Our author says, that a concurrence of circumstances flocked *Holland* with a people too numerous for the country to maintain; that their trade sprung from necessity and indigence, not choice, and was nursed in want.

If this gentleman had vouchsafed to have specified to

                                                                    us,

us, what the concurrence of circumstances was, which stocked *Holland* with people, and to have entered into a particular detail, he would have given us a just account *of the causes which principally contribute to render a nation populous*. Their commerce and naturalization of strangers, and the open arms with which they receive all comers, were not only the first sources of their populosity, but *De Wit* informs us is still the cause of the populousness of the country, which he says, from the badness of its air, would soon be but thinly peopled, were it not for the constant influx of strangers.

As our author began and went on in paradox and contradiction, so he continues to deal in this sort of traffick to the last, and finds out a perfect harmony in destroying commerce to support it, and to advance it to the highest pitch of greatness.

We presume we have fully proved that the means our author proposes to render a nation populous are not at all adapted to promote such an end; and that the banishing commerce and refinement, instead of tending to render a state populous, would depopulate and ruin it: As there are sundry principal causes, which in a state not half peopled, may concur to render it very populous in a small space of time; and as from the common multiplication of mankind, it must require a great length of years to fill such a state with people; it is a little surprizing that our author should never animadvert upon one of those principal causes, but should confine his reasonings only to what is relative to the promotion of propagation, and rendering a people prolifick.

After we have so clearly demonstrated the repugnancies in our author's discourse, it is merry to see him go off triumphing in the harmony of the several parts of his system. Though in truth it is a chaos, and

Non bene junctarum discordia semina rerum;

a Tohu and Bohu of jarring elements, and warring matter.

NEW AND OLD

PRINCIPLES of TRADE

COMPARED;

OR A

TREATISE

ON THE PRINCIPLES

OF

Commerce between Nations.

Et penitus toto divisos orbe Britannos.
Virg. Ecl.

LONDON:

Printed for J. JOHNSON, No. 72, ST. PAUL's CHURCHYARD,
and J. DEBRETT, PICADILLY.

M DCCLXXXVIII.

PREFACE.

IT is proper to notice a few detached circumstances by way of preface.

The following treatise was written not so much to prove, as to defend opinions. I therefore consulted in it the works of the opponents, rather than of the friends of the free system of trade. The notes since added will not diminish the pleasure to arise from a complete perusal of the performances from which they are borrowed.

With respect to the writers on these subjects, I know of none who have treated of commercial liberty in express detail and with a view to remove objections, before the French. I do not refer to particular passages in Fenelon* and others; but to the works of the *œconomistes*, who first reduced the free system to elements, and gave to it its modern precision and extent. The French writings (and since we owe them the praise, let us chearfully give

3

it)

---

* Much is said of the beauties of Fenelon's Telemachus and little of its precepts, which contain the seeds of all the sentiments, if not of all the doctrines of modern political œconomy. The temple of Gnidus of Montesquieu, seems to rival Telemachus in points of taste and description, but Montesquieu in his writings on the subject of political prosperity, has scarcely made nearer approaches to the truth, than Fenelon; and he certainly fell short of him in courage in declaring it.

it) have long abounded in eloquent lessons of philanthropy, which have sensibly affected the way of thinking of European authors, and consequently must sooner or later influence the manners of the western world, and thence of all the earth. With the exception of a few enlightened persons, especially in Scotland, the free system of commerce has been little patronized by the writers of our own island; and indeed unless in Flanders, which is deeply interested in a transit trade, we have seen it favoured in its full extent by few European traders in modern times.

The pages here presented to the public are silent as to mercantile companies; for the public has objects more important even than its commerce. The question respecting the British East India Company in particular, stands involved in deep considerations of domestic and foreign politics; and there are many monopolies which must subsist, till indemnity shall be given to the holders. Happy would it be for Europe and for India, could India become self-governed, under the auspices of her ancient freedom of trade and her sober system of morals; from which principally her arts and wealth seem to have arisen. Our Chinese trade is embarrassed neither with wars, forts, nor expensive establishments, compared with the burthen of which, the commercial impositions we suffer in China, deserve no mention; which is solely owing to China being an independent power. It is not indeed meant to commend a trade which consists of an exchange of useful articles on our side, for agreeable articles on theirs; but our East India trade in this respect can claim no preference over that to China.

I have no where employed the terms of *active* and *passive* commerce. If by active commerce is meant, diligence in the production of commodities, I accede to the distinction; but by no means so, if it is merely in question, whether commodities shall be exchanged at home or abroad. It may be convenient to some nations to be active abroad in search of foreign markets; but others may find no detriment in waiting for the appearance of foreign traders at home. For example, I have just shewn the possibility of navigating many thousand miles to pursue a losing eastern commerce, in a case too where the advantage falls to the less civilized over the more civilized people.

The new governments of North-America may offer another instructive instance in this particular. If these governments pursue their advantages for agriculture; if they admit the manufactures of Europe, rendered cheap by bounties and by the real advantages attending the arts in rich and populous countries, without regard to their own manufactures, (which will always be established with ease, when their establishment is beneficial;) and if they avoid politics; they may outwit, by a natural conduct, a multitude of nations who think themselves wise because their plans are intricate. It cannot be useful for America to be noticed at present in Europe, otherwise than by her good sense: she should grow to greatness, like the trees of her wildernesses, in the midst of silence and retreat. Nothing can check her population depending upon a facility of subsistence; or oppress her strength springing from numbers, situation, and knowledge. If Europe does not treat America with wisdom, America would do ill to copy the weak example of those whom the discipline of experience has not yet been able to instruct. She has the peculiar happiness of being able to shape her course free from the influence of her *own* errors and those of *others*; beginning where all nations may be happy to end.

The protest which I shall be found to have entered, against rash changes in the regulations of commerce, cannot

not

not be renewed too often. In a work dedicated to the pursuit of principles, a detail of the necessary exceptions, which must be different in different countries, cannot be expected; especially as those they interest, will not be wanting in suggesting them. I shall rather make the following observation.—In tracing original principles, we must contemplate the *natural* circumstances of man; but in applying these principles to practice, we must consider his *actual* situation. In modern commerce, we have to allow not only for the pardonable errors of traders themselves, but for the faulty establishments they have made under the sanction of laws or long continued systems of administration. If we attempt violent and sudden alterations, we may be disappointed even in our pursuit of wealth, and we shall certainly injure the more weighty concern of justice. To attain therefore the knowledge of sound principles, is but a part of our object; we must know when and how to introduce them into action. Almost every Scylla in politics has a Charybdis in its neighbourhood; and we must remember that *in vitium ducit culpæ fuga, si caret arte.*

This caution is not designed to counteract the original view, with which this treatise was written. The public must steadily pursue its interest; but not *per fas & nefas.* It must sometimes purchase a liberty to use its original powers, by making compensations for the result of its own intervening laws; it must avoid adding new errors to old ones; it must reform its national foreign politics; it must pave the way for happier times; and it must execute some of those many measures, which are for the benefit of all and injurious to none. Though I have intimated in what follows, that there is a *speculative* limit to prosperity in politics, a statesman must adopt for his constant motto that of Charles V. *plus outre.*

I shall be ready to acknowledge any mistakes into which I may find I have fallen, but I shall unwillingly mix in disputes which time alone shall seem likely to dissipate.

Conceiving peace to be the best friend both of commerce and of mankind, I think it proper to intimate, that I meditate the publication of another short treatise under the title of Pacific Principles.

TABLE

TABLE

OF

CONTENTS.

OF THE

PRINCIPLES

OF

Commerce between Nations.

CHAPTER I.

INDIVIDUALS, who depend upon themselves for their support, naturally apply their labour to such objects as they can best accomplish, and purchase from their neighbours such articles of use or consumption as it would be difficult for themselves to produce. Are the interests of political societies, in this respect, different from those of individuals? Two systems have been maintained, upon this subject, in modern times by European writers, of which, unfortunately, only the worst has of late been reduced to practice.

It has been the general object of one of these systems to seek a great *variety* in the species of its productions: to procure sundry preferences for its favorites, either in buying or selling; and to employ bribes and penal laws (in some cases supported by expensive treaties) to remove the competition of foreigners. This system, it is to be observed, has been particularly adhered to in the home-

11

market

market in the case of subject against subject, (the legislature, upon the principle that its duty is to subdue difficulties, usually taking part here with the few subjects against the many.) This system may be called the system of *monopoly*; and it has lately been common to all European nations. The system of *free trade*, on the other hand, preferring abundance to ostentation, would force nothing but a disposition to industry; concluding, that if one nation raises flax with most success, and another wool, the sum of these commodities must be augmented in the world, when each nation devotes itself to its separate talent; and that, upon exchanging the two commodities, each nation will have a greater share of the two conjunctively, than if each had attempted to raise them both at home. But, besides thus multiplying the mass, and circulating the exchange of products throughout the universe, it is affirmed, by the favorers of this system, that the animosity and bloodshed, supposed to be generated by the other system*, would be abated, together with its prodigality, favoritism, and necessary mistakes.

12

Though

---

* Though I do not state it as the declared, or necessary, yet it has certainly been the *actual*, property of the narrow system, to be devoted to wars of conquest and offence: while one of the chief professed objects of the free-trade system (as stated above) is to extinguish such wars, and to encourage such principles in our neighbours and in mankind generally, as shall lessen the frequency of the occasions even for wars of self-defence. There is scarcely one writer on *free-trade*, at the present day, who does not make this pacific turn more of a primary, than of a secondary, consideration. On the other hand, there has been scarcely one of our latter ruptures with France, or other nations, which has not, directly or indirectly, originated from systems of trade or colonization founded in *monopoly*. In short, estrangement and jealousy, violence and revenge, by whatever cause they are set in motion, tend to war; while liberal intercourse and exchanges seem to make the corner-stones of peace and concord.

Though the controversy respecting these systems is of recent date, yet a just decision in it is doubtless as important an object in politics, as any that can engage us. Voluminous works have indeed lately appeared on this subject; but, since many, whose only object is truth, still seem either to adhere to the false, or to want a practical persuasion of the true, doctrine; I conclude, notwithstanding the ability of the authors of these works, that nature and common sense have not been enough trusted to in the dispute. I shall, therefore, simply state what to me appears the only just opinion; and, after drawing a few inferences out of it, principally employ myself in removing the difficulties of different natures to which it may seem liable.

CHAPTER II.

BY commerce, I presume, is meant, that mode of acquiring the property of our neighbours, which depends upon a voluntary interchange with them of supposed equivalents. Pursuant to this definition, the true theory of this interchange, I think, may be comprised in the following sentence: *Climates, soils, and circumstances, being differently distributed, and each contributing to man's accommodation, if every nation cultivates what is to itself easy or peculiar, all products will not only thus be most abundant, but, likewise, most various and most perfect; and, in order completely to diffuse them among industrious nations, nothing more seems requisite than the*

18   *quicksighted*

quicksighted interest of the trader, favored by facility of transport, by peace, and by commercial freedom.

I shall, for a moment, consider this as a self-evident proposition, in order to draw certain clear and natural corollaries from it, which seem to confirm its truth. The first of these corollaries is, that nations should seek to augment the *total* mass and value of their commodities, rather than attempt to rival each other in any *particular* articles; or, in other words, should consult more to improve their own circumstances than how to oppose their neighbours. A second inference, from this theory is, that statesmen should principally befriend commerce by cherishing the *means* of production; and endeavour to fertilize the soil of commerce, instead of regulating the species and the form of what it produces. A free trade, sooner or later, will unerringly direct the faculties of a country; and knowledge, joined to wise manners and customs, good morals, and public spirit, (if favored by easy communications, under the safeguard of fixed justice and religious liberty,) will, in general, sufficiently stimulate it to enterprise; particularly where the state provides for it those aids, which, though of general use, are not likely to be established by mere individuals. A third conclusion is, that the position, that nations flourish in proportion as their exports are many and their imports are few, is inconsistent with the institution of commerce; commerce not only being meant to procure us enjoyments, but naturally consisting in that complete interchange of commodities which is thus objected to.* A fourth deduction from the above fundamental principle is, that if commerce implies exchange, an attempt to

14

open

---

* This alludes to the mistaken conclusions generally made on the topic of the balance of trade.

open or to seize fugitive channels for commerce by the aid
of expensive wars, before industry is ripe on *both sides* with
articles to be exchanged through the medium in question,
is a measure that is premature and improvident; and
that must often be the parent of useless strife*.   In the
fifth place, though industry is best employed upon home
objects, yet it seems wisdom of a partial nature to force
one set of subjects in a state to give much of their property to another set, in return for little, by allowing them
to buy and to sell only between each other; particularly
as the export of what is *superabundant* in one country, in
order to be exchanged for what is superabundant in
another, must produce a *double* gain to the public, (to wit,
in the sale and in the purchase.)   Sixthly, the dismay of
certain patriot minds, lest other countries should prosper
besides their own, is a proof that the competition of
passions, in trade, is far more fatal than the competition
of commodities; facts discovering that productions both
of nature and of art always vary sufficiently in every
nation to promise advantageous exchanges; and, whenever
the mart for these exchanges widens, the accommodation
to follow from it to each nation ought to increase in proportion.   A seventh and concluding hint is, that, distorted
as is the actual state of our commerce in consequence of
impolitic laws, domestic and foreign, it is never too late
for us to attempt a gradual and prudent return to common

15

sense;

---

* Hence the present maritime aims of Austria and Russia, who
may each rely on visitants spontaneously frequenting their ports for
such trade as they have yet prepared, seem impolitic; and the more
so, exactly in proportion as their situation renders maritime defence
superfluous.   Not less impolitic was our own bigotry at the peace of
1782, respecting the distant American waste forest-lands; as these
lands cannot, for ages, become serviceable to any, and least of all to
ourselves, provided it should continue our system either to bribe or
to force obedience from their growing, but remote, dispersed, and
naturally self-willed, inhabitants.

sense; for, notwithstanding individual traders may profit by a continuance in the present errors, yet a persistance in monopoly-systems must necessarily injure the class of *traders themselves at large*, since nothing can be more clear, as a general maxim, than that traders must flourish with trade.

Such seems to be the *theory* of commerce, viewed in a general light, and abstracted from the interference of any particular set of circumstances; and such seem to be the *inferences* fairly arising out of this theory. I shall not attempt any positive proof of this theory. I think it best to leave it to the test of past experience, of common sense, and just sentiments. Much less shall I defend it as founded on *right*, notwithstanding it respects, in its consequences, all the inhabitants of the globe. I cannot indeed avoid secretly giving ear to the generous theorists, who assert that governments have no title to control mankind in the conduct of their private property; yet the cause of liberality, in the present moment, seems likely to be most solidly advanced by referring for support here to the topics of expediency and of good politics, instead of founding it upon a positive claim.

As to *authority* and *example* (which have often been appealed to on the present occasion) they appear to be less in favor of the modern monopoly-system, than is perhaps suspected. Among the elder (herein including the Eastern) nations of the world, no distinguishing traces appear of a general deliberate system of trading prohibitions and permanent bounties, established for a nation's internal benefit. Whether this has arisen from a practical sense, that societies increase in wealth by vending dear and purchasing cheap; or whether it has arisen from a system of tribute (rather than of trade) being connected with the ancient system of conquest; or from a preference to the pursuit of agriculture; or from other causes pre-

16

vailing

vailing among these nations; the fact itself appears incontrovertible, that favorable precedents in this quarter are deficient to the monopolist. And if we are forbid to cite the general example of *ruder* nations to the same effect, it is fair to exclude, on the other hand, such cases of constrained trade, as appear to have originated from motives of jealousy, from domestic or from foreign tyranny, from sumptuary laws, or from other causes that were merely local or occasional*. Though monopolies in favour of particular individuals, and high taxes upon foreign articles, often had place in early feudal times†; yet the true æra, when a general systematic restraint was imposed upon European commerce, seems to have been when petty states (as well as individuals) in Italy and the Low Countries, as likewise in other parts, rose into wealth and importance by the apparent medium of a trade of manufacture and of agency. Neighbouring sovereigns, who were of themselves too prone to jealousy and avidity, to impatience and the use of force; when they became urged by particular traders and interested grandees, seem to have thought of no other mode of rivalship in this situation, but such as was founded on violent laws for regulating trade; which laws being retaliated from abroad and growing habitual at home, gradually and unfortunately became, with few exceptions, universal in the western empires of the world. I must not allow myself to wonder at an error, which it was then natural to adopt and perhaps somewhat difficult to combat; but the several pleas for it may, it is to be hoped, by the aid of subsequent experience, be at present readily con-

17

futed

---

* See Montesquieu's Spirit of Laws, Book 21, ch. ii. for examples of this.

† This arose rather from political motives, or motives of revenue, than from mercantile theories.

futed.   I shall now, therefore, proceed to consider the various arguments adduced either in favour of the narrow, or in opposition to the liberal, system.

CHAPTER III.

IN the following chapter I have undertaken to discuss the principal of the various motives which have operated in regulating the commerce, and consequently the colonization, and in a great measure the manners and politics of Europe, during several centuries, down to the present moment. Were the object of my task less interesting from its different connections and aspects, it would at least remain curious in point of speculation. I trust therefore that proper allowance will be made for the variety of considerations, which it has been necessary to assemble here in a small space.

1st. *To employ, and thereby to enrich, subjects, preferably to strangers,* was, doubtless, one prevailing motive for the monopoly system.   The motive was proper, but it was palpably misapplied; for the capital and the skill of an unimproved country, not being equal to the sudden supply of *all* its wants, those occupations ought to have been first selected of which the pursuit would have been *most* profitable, and the omission *most* detrimental.   Trade then was neither the sole nor yet the first object, corresponding to this description.   When it is considered that the earth, in all populous and civilized countries is a *subject of monopoly*, it will soon appear that a preference is necessarily due in the first instance to agriculture, and to those arts which give the largest vent for agricultural products; for if other advantages in agriculture are supposed to be counterbalanced by equivalent advantages existing in trade, nevertheless, so much of the landlord's *rent* as is founded upon his mere ownership of the soil is a gain in agriculture, which has no real parallel* in trade. Other things therefore being equal, the more pure and simple are the earth's productions from being *rude* or *little* manufactured, the nearer must the purchase or the sale of them in foreign trade, approach to the difference of paying or of receiving the value of this immense monopoly. And if such is the superiority of agriculture, the supply of all the wants† of those who labour in it on the one hand, as well as the vent of all their commodities on the other, should be facilitated as anxiously as possible, as the means of laying foreigners under the heaviest contributions; or in other words, a free trade should at all times *second* agriculture. Every other advantageous employment in a state should be treated on similar principles with agriculture, and the parties concerned in it be aided in their purchases and in their sales, by means of freedom given to trade; and for similar reasons. By thus assisting each leading occupation in the state, there would gradually

19

supervene

---

* The land of the farmer and the raw materials of the artist, each call for labour to make them useful; and each require the assistance of various persons for bringing to market what is produced from each. So far the two agree. They differ in the particular named in the text. As to fair and natural *monopolies* derived from peculiar *inventions*, or from peculiar public or private good regulations of any kind; they are not confined solely to products of the arts; but occur also in the case of landed products, (where the total amount of their effect will be found to compensate for any supposed want of variety in the instances.)

† Viz. of food, clothing, tools, materials for habitations, &c.

supervene capital and population; and with these would succeed the several finer arts, whose appearance can never be precipitated, but with an immense expence that is too often abortive.

2. *To prevent the export of the precious metals* in exchange for foreign products, was formerly considered as a second political duty, almost superior to the preceding. But modern discussions have at last taught us that property may assume various useful shapes; and that, after having collected a proper stock of the precious metals for preventing the inconveniences usually attending the necessity of barter and for other direct uses, it is an extravagant folly to let any lie dead at home in hoards and treasures[*]. Besides, if England obtains silver from Portugal by means of goods, and then buys goods from China with silver, this is ultimately a trade of goods for goods, the silver only intervening: in which case, if the silver were more wanted here than the China goods, it is reasonable to think it would be detained here.

3. Another pretence for the narrow system was, that *foreign articles afforded laudable objects for taxation :*—But if taxing was thus in view, it should at the same time have been recollected, that, whatever *collateral* effects may attend a tax laid on a foreign article, the amount paid under it commonly falls upon the country imposing the tax, when consuming the article. We may add, that if revenue is here the only object, taxes that are moderate are confessedly the most productive. Taxes also being easily retaliated, it will soon be found that the tendency

of

---

[*] It has become almost a trite remark, that the coin of a nation is dead stock, and ought to be dispensed with, if its uses to the general circulation of commodities could be safely supplied by cheaper means. These uses however are too considerable to be foregone; and consequently every society acts wisely that makes coin a part of its capital.

of these taxes is to produce animosity rather than income; and animosity again is found to produce mutual injuries in trade, and a mutual propensity to war (which is the certain devourer of revenue and the natural enemy to civil prosperity.)

4. Some, in defence of the contracted system, have held the ingenious persuasion, that *provided trade can be kept at home, it matters not whether subjects obtain for their money, good or bad, many or few articles;* the loss of one subject constituting the gain of another. But this doctrine (which comes with an ill grace from any who descant on the *blessings* of commerce) proceeds with the most evident contradiction from all who advise cruel and ruinous wars for obtaining *trivial* trading benefits and commodities. It forms also a reverse to the taxing system just noticed, as the *difference* in every extra-payment or under-purchase, made in the home-market, might have been saved by means of an open trade, and have been applied by law as a substitute to taxes vexing the poor. But the position teems with other errors: For example, many of the foreign articles which it is proposed to exclude in favour of a few subjects, are not luxuries, but *necessaries* of the first order, and useful to every subject. And, with respect to luxuries, if our only objection to these is, that they are foreign, is it not evident that foreigners will refuse the purchase of our exported luxuries as being foreign to them? In the last place, if we determined to be content with scanty, high-priced, and inferior, productions at home, (the certain result of the policy in question,) it will naturally tend to introduce such neglects into the whole system of our trading operations (the arts being all related,) that we can have little prospect of surpassing foreigners, who shall proceed on different principles, in a general trade abroad.

5. *The confinement at home of useful articles for the benefit of subjects* was another specious allegation used in

21

favour

favour of the bigotted system; the miserly eye of monopoly not being able to discern, that when men have enough of a necessary, the surplus is no longer to be called a necessary; and that, without a vent for it is regularly allowed, the very surplus in question would never be produced.   By the same sort of timid avarice, exports of commodities seem at certain moments to have been viewed as absolute gifts to foreigners, instead of exchanges with them.   But time has at length taught, that every nation has various wants; and that it is fortunate to be possessed of a necessary as a staple, to use in barter for the supply of these wants: Not only as a necessary is an article of steady sale; but as foreign demand, by multiplying the production of it, insures a supply at home in case of accidents; " *Enough*" (according to the adage) " *being enough and a little to spare.*"   But in foreign commerce, not only are many of the foreign articles that are imported, real necessaries, but many of our own that are exported are real frivolities; and, to prevent distinctions on either side in a scheme of exchange, the good and the bad of the system must be taken together.   Besides, as most *necessaries* spring from the earth, those who would forcibly lessen the export of such products, would injure agriculture the most profitable employment, for the sake of manufactures the least profitable; to say nothing of the superior qualities of farmers over manufacturers, as subjects.   It is another material consideration, that (as price will always direct the course and supply of every article) whenever so much of any article is exported as to make it rise to a certain value at home, the exportation of it will thence naturally diminish, or totally cease.   We may add, that the various circumstances and charges which tend to embarrass exportation and importation, of themselves operate as a considerable bounty here in favour of the home consumer.   Lastly it is almost superfluous to repeat, that, when the beneficial export of a native article to

22

foreign

foreign markets is impeded, the producer of it suffers materially in his profits*.

6. That the monopoly system *renders a nation invulnerable, and independent of its neighbours*, by creating supplies and markets for it *within its own bosom*, is another plausible argument in favour of the monopoly system; but an argument contrary to truth and examples. Small territories are incapable of furnishing the proposed variety of productions†; and the same incapacity may be affirmed of the *vents* which small territories afford for those articles in which they really excel. And with respect to the English monopolist in particular, we may remark that home commerce so little corresponds to his wants and his capacious views, that two of his daily repasts, and certain approved ingredients, or accompaniments of the rest, are brought from across the ocean; nay his very iron and timber, his flax and his hemp, and a thousand of the

23   necessaries

---

* Happily the rage for encouraging exports prevents the prejudice, alluded to in the text, from being carried into practice in any great number of instances, though some of the instances it must be confessed are very important.

† France (that large and most happily situated territory) has as many staple *commodities* as any European kingdom whatever : viz. corn, wine, brandy, oil, and silk. That other commodities however are still acceptable to them, is plain from an examination of the objects of their import trade. They can even in foreign parts find varieties of their own articles, (pulse, wine, oil, and silk) worth making an exchange for.

The same thing may be said of *talents*, even of the same species: Thus, for example, the weavers of one country might advantageously supply and be supplied in many instances by the weavers of another ; so much does the single manufacture of weaving differ every where in its materials, texture, patterns, or dyes. In a scene of open traffic, superior talents need not fear a competition at home ; and inferior talents evidently require the aid of examples to excite domestic emulation and improve practice, in those cases where success is possible.

necessaries which he requires, or of the luxuries which he covets, are principally imported from strangers ; and it is his usual prayer, that his exports to foreign parts may yet exceed these imports. It is not then for one who sells his blood for subjects, for colonies, and for connections in distant seas, and who supports with bribes a foreign trade which is every where liable to derangement and attack ; it is not I say for *him* to boast, that monopolies, prohibitions, and bounties render his country safe, and place its industry under a domestic shelter. A defender of free trade, it must be observed at the same time, is not less disposed to allow of a beneficial intercourse with foreign countries than is the monopolist ; he differs only in the single desire that the *species* of goods circulating between them should be left to nature and not to laws. Exterior trade under such an easy system one may hope, would not only become more extended and leave room for fewer wars ; but good sense might at last induce European states reciprocally to allow a mutual freedom to commerce during the very period of hostility. And let it be added, that it is a mistake to think that retaliation, of one kind or other*, is not a resource open to the *free trader* against any act of commercial injustice, as well as to the monopolist.

7. Another supposed advantage of the narrow system has been that of *depressing rival nations*, by excluding such from commercial advantages, wherever practicable. The

24

obviousness

---

* Those who do not possess the means of retaliation in the first instance might apply to some of those political *allies*, (who are usually sought after for more unworthy purposes,) to retort their commercial wrongs for them at second hand. Our own country however, according to the opinion of its wisest statesmen, has always this power residing in itself ; and may still do, what Montesquieu says it has formerly done, " sacrifice its politics to its commerce, " while other nations must sacrifice their commerce to their politics."

obviousness of retaliation, I may observe, and the probability consequently of wars accompanying such unsocial
principles, seem strong objections to them. But, besides
this, we may ask, if foreigners are thus to be made poor,
to whom shall the monopolist sell? And if foreigners are
to be rendered universally destitute, where shall many
foreign articles, requisite for the use or accommodation of
the monopolist, be obtained, and sometimes too in moments of urgent want? But many are the cases in which
a state of advancement in our neighbours may be conceived
of positive benefit. For instance: the foreign trade and
the internal circumstances of various commercial nations
have been improved, in different ways, by the inventions
and discoveries of foreigners, (which the contracted policy
in question would necessarily have prevented.) The stimulus of rivalship has frequently afforded another capital
advantage; this stimulus often becoming the means of
raising a nation not only above others, but above itself.
A familiarity with the arts also increases the disposition
of a foreign nation to admit and to consume various arti-.
cles from other nations. And if *commercial* ideas of a
proper kind could by any means be introduced among turbulent and martial neighbours, they would clearly contribute to soften and dispose them to tranquillity. Without
looking however for farther arguments, it seems sufficient
to say, that all the trading distresses which nations in
general have it in their *power* to impose upon their neighbours, without proceeding to dangerous or expensive extremities, are comparatively so trivial, that the project of
imposing them ought without hesitation to be abandoned
on account of its mischiefs, both direct and indirect. It
is thus then that a manly policy may reconcile the trader
to the prospect of happiness existing out of the pale of his
own petty native nation; and lead him to view in the
civilization and in the industry of his surrounding neighbours, ready, cheap, and ample supplies for his own

 wants;

wants; and extensive and liberal vents for his own productions.

8. As to the *fear of other commercial nations depressing us, unless we employ forced exertions to counteract them*, (which is only another branch of the foregoing consideration;)—mutual fears of superiority we may remark are frequent in commerce, but cannot easily be founded on both sides. While the gifts of nature are local and human talents various, no nation refined by commerce, will find its own resources sufficient for gratifying all its own demands; and large exports cannot long exist without occasioning large returns. Other replies to this apprehension occur in the preceding paragraph and in the general theory we have given of commerce; and it would be easy to enumerate better modes of exertion than any of those which monopolists have proposed. But above all let me add, that there is one peculiar means of self-defence belonging to an unimproved nation, which is; that of its importing skilful cultivators, artists, merchants, and other useful citizens, from countries that are more advanced than itself; for, where a community is *fit* for a stranger's residence, thither strangers will eagerly flock*.

9. It is proper here to treat the *expence of carriage* as an objection to the liberal system of commerce, in order to shew more and more the merits of that system. And for this end in the first place we may state, not only that this expence of carriage belongs to every system of trade; but that wherever this expence exists, it is plain from its

26

existing,

---

* No nation indeed can be said to do itself justice till the adoption of strangers is permitted, and till every unnecessary *corporate right* that fetters the free exercise of labor and of talent, and the free circulation of capital, is removed. If strangers avoid any country, there needs little proof that the government of that country is such, as requires alterations, before trade of *any* kind can originate or subsist to advantage even among the natives.

existing, that the difference saved in the price or quality of the commodity, is deemed to compensate for the amount of this expence. Secondly, carriage is peculiarly favorable to navigation, which is the fashionable object of modern European nations. Lastly, transit charges, whatever may be their amount, are exceeded (not only by the increased prices of goods whenever the transit is forbidden, as above mentioned, but also) by the losses sustained by the smuggler on the one side in supporting contraband, and by government on the other side in endeavouring to suppress it.

10. The injuries or neglects which agriculture has experienced from modern legislators, when standing in competition with manufactures, have not prevented the favorers of the monopoly system from considering the *promotion of agriculture,* as one of the merits of that system. And certain it is that agriculture has a tendency to prosper in the neighbourhood of commerce and of all the arts; as well on account of the market which merchants and traders afford for its products, &c. as of the capital and information usually introduced by them whereever they reside. But to render this concession of any weight in favour of the monopoly system, two very material assumptions under the head we are considering must be made good: First, that trade is the most eligible means of forwarding agriculture; and next, that monopoly is the most eligible means of forwarding trade. Now, as to the preferable means of encouraging *agriculture,* I presume none can doubt that the direct, are better than the circuitous means; and that if the same attention had been given to agriculture, that has been bestowed upon manufactures or upon commerce, agriculture would have boasted a far earlier and far greater perfection, than it has yet attained in any European country. Next, as to what are the preferable means of encouraging *trade;* to investigate these being the object of the present treatise, I

might

might rest on the whole of this treatise for my answer;
but I shall rather select three remarks, viz. I. That it
is an assertion equally allowable (as such) with the contrary one, that free principles form the *best* basis of trade;
and whoever shall doubt this must yet allow that a free-
trade cannot be supposed to mean *no trade at all*; since
every country that pursues its own talent (of which manufactures will soon make a part) and at the same time
avails itself of the excellencies of other countries by means
of interchanges, must necessarily secure to itself a trade
that is comparatively respectable.   2. I may next observe,
that agriculture has higher pretensions to be considered
as productive of trade, than trade has to reverse that pre-
tension : and consequently that trade and agriculture will
be made to exist together with most certainty if we commence with agriculture; agriculture not only implying
the existence of many arts, but exciting an attention to
many other arts : as well by the easy subsistence it offers
to artisans, as by the raw materials it provides.   And it
would certainly be singular to suppose that any citizens in
a state are to refrain from the exercise of trading occupations, when those of agriculture shall prove insufficient to employ them*.   3. and lastly, Since pacific
principles are of the utmost importance to every pacific
occupation, they necessarily give to free-trade (to which
they seem congenial) a decisive preference with respect to
agriculture, the monopoly system being the perpetual parent of wars and taxes.   Thus it seems clear that *free*
principles of trade contribute as much, and we may venture to say more, to the promotion of agriculture than
those of monopoly; though *no trade* we may repeat, can

28

be

---

* We may add too, that the very pretext we are contending
against supposes trade and agriculture to be blessings that are fully
consistent one with the other.

be at all depended upon for advancing agriculture, equally with that direct encouragement, which it is the duty of every territorial state to afford to its pursuit. It is an unanswerable proof in favour of this, that many of the antients as well as the Chinese, though each so little noted for *foreign* trade, (the great favourite of the monopolist,) have particularly excelled in agriculture, though unprovided with many of our modern European helps for pursuing agriculture to advantage.

11. An equal prejudice with the preceding has prevailed as to the supposed tendency of monopolies to favour *population.* The arts however, I must observe, are much oftener the result than the cause of population; and in many cases where they seem to promote population, a great part of their effect is to assemble in one spot, and not to create a people. Population also, I must add, is the consequence of enjoying means of procuring subsistence, as marriages in such situations naturally become more general, and are contracted at an earlier period of life; and the children also that are born, as well as the adult persons among the lower ranks, are in such case better provided for than is elsewhere usually their lot. And in this view, every agricultural country has a peculiar advantage in its very nature; not only as being saved the expensive carriage of its subsistence : but as possessing the remnants* (or offals) attending its principal products, which remnants, though they will not bear exporting, yet lessen the expences of its natives. And indeed as the healthfulness of agricultural pursuits renders the inhabitants of such countries more capable of vigorous and continued exertions, than where manufactures prevail which are so often the causes of sickness, this of

itself

---

* Straw and other articles are the offals of corn; milk and manure of cattle; meat of wool and leather; or vice versa, &c. &c.

itself is to be considered as equivalent to an increase of people, since it implies an increase of labour at the same expence of subsistence, (aids of machinery and inventions being open to both situations.) Should it be urged that it is important not only to population, but also to œconomy, where a trader shall have his residence; that is, whether he shall stay at home and pay his taxes and rent, and render his personal services there; or whether he shall do this abroad, (perhaps for an hostile government) and moreover impose upon his customers the additional expences of carrying his subsistence outwards, and his manufactures, &c. back again; should this advantage of residence be urged, I say, it is easy to remark, that the position however true, ends in nothing favorable to the system of monopoly. We may reply, for instance, as in the preceding paragraph, that to prove the usefulness of *some* sort of trade to population, does not prove any superiority in a trade founded in monopoly in particular; and much less does it prove any inferiority of landed occupations respecting population. And with respect to pacific principles, as they are more naturally allied to agriculture than to monopoly, they naturally increase the favour due to agriculture; since war (which is the usual associate of monopoly) has not only a direct tendency to lessen numbers, but (which is if possible still more important), interrupts the progress of that subsistence, which makes the basis of numbers both with men and with animals.

12. There is another prejudice respecting the narrow system, namely, that *commerce must be aided*, as deep rooted and in certain respects not less erroneous than the foregoing. That permanent prohibitions and bounties indeed used internally, and that the force of arms acting externally should often aggrandize particular traders, is little wonderful; but when the traders in question attempt to betray their country into any *general system* of trading laws, by

                                        the

the display of their pampered commodity, it should be remembered that other commodities and the public revenue
have each languished to feed its growth, and that to this
principally are to be attributed our frequent wars and enormous debts. The particularly depressed state of Ireland
proves in a more comprehensive sense, that monopolies have
only partial advantages ; and even England itself after ab-
sorbing so much of the nutriment of its connected kingdoms cannot be compared, (its territory considered) either
in wealth or in numbers of people, with a certain neighbouring republican province. It is therefore to the real prolific principles of liberty, and to certain internal advantages,
joined to the bad conduct of our neighbours and to other
incidental causes, that England may attribute its chief
successes, whether in war or in trade ; and not to selfish or
to peevish trade-laws. Every legislative favour to trade,
that is *particular* and at the same time *permanent*, (whether
positive or negative,) proves either the branch receiving it
to be unnatural, or the favour granted to it to be a job :
it is in short a larger kind of letters patent, of which the
mischief is aggravated as well by the duration, as by the
extent of the grant. Even feeble beginnings in trade
should be protected by bounties only ; and those also be
temporary ; and if possible, consisting rather of countenance and of honours, than of money or even immunities.

13. But permanent *bounties* it may next be pretended
are free from those *irritations* towards foreigners, complained of in prohibitions : and it may also be added
that wherever there are branches of trade composed of
various operations, the artificial aid given to a few of these
operations may be the cause of a spontaneous movement
as to the rest of them. But it may be urged in reply to
this, that as bounties are provided by means of taxes,
bounties amount to a premium given to one subject out

of

of the property of another. We may even go farther, and affirm that the state contributes on these occasions to the trader, much more than its ostensible gift; not only because the yielding of every tax is burthened. with charges of management; but because almost every tax in it itself forges a new fetter for commerce, the very controul arising from which will frequently prove the balance of the public benefit proposed by the bounty. Bounties also are generally bestowed with little discernment; as for instance, to forward at home what is singular to *ourselves*, instead of what is singular to foreigners; to excite arduous, instead of easy attempts; or what is precarious, instead of what is certain. And with respect to the influence of such conduct upon foreigners, as no state can boast of a monopoly of its folly, the examples of such folly migrate abroad and stimulate kindred folly there; and bounties abroad contending with bounties at home, scarcely any other effect arises from them, than that of their mutual burthen or perversion. These arguments alone are sufficient to overbalance any pretended benefit from the permanency of bounties (their permanency it is to be observed, being the single point against which we are in *this* place contending.) But we may add, that allowing *such* bounties when joined to permanent prohibitions, to effect the end of keeping up none but *useful* articles, this would only be rendering one useful article tributary to another; or making weighty objects depend for their support upon each other, without giving them the benefit of a solid general base.

14. While the free trader conceives ' that the welfare ' of the state at large results from the *particular* welfare ' attending its several parts ;' the monopolist affirms that individuals, if *released from controul, may frequently pursue their private interest in modes detrimental to the public.* If the monopoly system, we might first reply to this were

itself

itself free from all the jobs and the folly with which it notoriously abounds under legislative sanction, there might be some colour for this insinuation. But (not to be content with a mere answer of recrimination) we may obviate the present difficulty in another way, by allowing at once the propriety of the public interposition, whenever, *after duly weighing circumstances*, the public interposition shall be found requisite. Without however referring here to the danger of foreign retaliation, of wars and of expence, where government pretends to restrain commerce ; and without adverting to the frequent failure of the most plausible measures of government on these occasions (which are considerations that appear to meet us every where ;) there remains a new topic which militates against any use of discretionary powers in the case in question, which is as follows. Where a restraint is imposed to favour the class of *producers*, its direct operation is to injure the class of *consumers*, whereas these two classes ought to flourish conjunctively* ; and what makes this case still more unfortunate and unequal is, that the class of consumers in each instance is usually the most numerous, and that the loss sustained by the consumers generally *far exceeds* the gain secured to the producers. We may even go farther with respect to the class of consumers, and say that this class

38

is

---

* " Modern states appear seldom to think of more than one class " of their subjects at a time, and generally of the wrong class ; for " in prohibiting an *export*, they think only of the buyers at home, " whereas they ought then to think of the sellers there ; and in pro-" hibiting an *import*, they think only of the sellers at home, and " forget the buyers: the very reverse of which, ought to happen, " because when the private sagacity of the subject has taught him " that he can make a gain in any sale, or a saving in any purchase, " the state ought in general to facilitate his operations ; which in " large concerns would produce an immense balance to the country." *Anonym.*

is rarely found patronized by the state since the restraints on importation are not only far more frequent than those on exportation; but even where restraints on exportation have been admitted, it has usually been with the idea of providing an abundance of raw materials to certain *secondary producers*, (without attention either to the interests of those who originally produce these materials, or of those who are to consume the ultimate compound production). This neglect of the consumers is more remarkable, as consumers are often at once both consumers and producers. Let us conclude then, that none will carry into execution the commercial rule of selling for much and buying for little, better than individuals; and that a free trade, sooner or later, will naturally produce such an arrangement of markets and of productive employments, as that each individual, while he is thus pursuing his own interest, shall in so doing be found to benefit the whole without producing permanent injury to any.

15. There is another plea which it may here be useful to discuss, merely to give an instance of the universality of the liberal principles of trade: It is that *a poor country will find it requisite to resort to bounties and to restrictions in absolute self-defence on account of the competition of other superior countries.* But where poverty is fundamental, the preferable object to such a system certainly is, to improve the manners and talents of the natives; not only that the natives may push such powers as the country has to their greatest extent, but that they may obtain the lucrative confidence and employ of their less enterprising neighbours. Those articles also here, as well as in a richer country, seem naturally to ask for attention, which (cæteris paribus) are in most demand and are of easiest production: and whenever the motives to exchange any of these articles with foreigners shall exceed the expence attending such exchange, the poorer country would aug-

ment

ment by such exchange the value of what it had to consume*. These seem natural and obvious principles. If a jealousy should however arise in the poorer country on account of a balance of *necessaries*† being exported, the intercourse should not be checked here upon trading, but upon œconomical principles: that is, not by means of mercantile, but of sumptuary laws; trade in every other respect being left entirely free. This last concession however is made rather for the purpose of distinction in theory, than with a view to practice; as less danger seems likely to follow from the absence of all restraints, than from a power of imposing them at discretion residing in legislatures notoriously subject to passion and delusion. If after all, a poor country under the liberal system should still be said to be poor, compared with its more fortunate neighbours, it should be remembered that *this* mode of comparison is a false one; and that the only just comparison is, when such a country is compared with *itself* while it was governed under the narrow system. I may add that no objection can arise to a system of exchanges, from a supposition that a country may be so utterly destitute, as to have *nothing* to offer in the way of exchange with foreigners;

35

---

* " Each merchant is a gainer, if his returns, after paying all the " expences of the voyage, are worth more at home (or will purchase " a greater quantity of goods) than he had exported : This overplus is " the merchant's profit, without which he would no longer trade." *Harris's Essay on Money and Coins.* Part I. chap. 2, §. 16. note.— " A nation's situation becomes *bounded* as soon as its powers are " confined at home ; and it is only by interchanging with *foreigners* " and by foreign connections, that its prosperity can be increased." *Anonym.*

† An objection to a wrong balance of *necessaries*, is much better founded than the ideas respecting a wrong balance of *trade:* It prevails with a sensible nation, the Chinese, very strongly. Yet even this objection may be carried much too far.

reigners ; since I believe there is no country that does not
naturally produce more of some things than it wants, and
less of others, (which is precisely the situation in which
our system may be useful :) and it is needless to apprehend
danger from exchanges in a country where no exchanges
are supposed capable of taking place.

16. Notwithstanding all that has been said above, it
may be conceived that *when a nation under the free system
has attained its* apparent ne plus ultra *of prosperity, the
application of bounties and restraints becomes indispensible
for exciting* extraordinary *domestic exertions.* But this
seems a position admitting of easy confutation. For,
first, we find no reason why those modes of encouragement that appear improper in an early stage of a society,
should be thought eligible in a more advanced state of
it ; there being if possible more cause than ever in an
advanced state of society to trust to general (rather than
to particular) sources of improvement, as improvements
are then accomplished with most facility. Secondly,
it appears undoubted, that there is not only an apparent
but a real *ne plus ultra* in the affairs of nations, which it
is in vain to think of exceeding ; every nation either
internally or externally, having natural limits occurring
to its progress. The wealth of a state therefore consisting
only of its given sum of *commodities* added to its
faculties ; and the pacific improvements of either with
respect to neighbours depending upon their mutual
exchange or intermixture; when this is perfected (which
has never been seen perfected) a state stands at its summit
as to commerce ; and has nothing to do but to be happy,
to œconomize, and to avoid decline. It can never be
richer without more rudiments from riches, (wealth, like
population, having perpetual relation to its sources ;) and
the application of the monopoly system to its situation,
would apparently only be weaving the web of Penelope ;
or in other words be found a mode of enriching the pro-

36

ducer

ducer by depressing the consumer, or vice versa; that is, of losing with one hand what it gained with the other, established at a known cost, and with a certainty sooner or later of foreign opposition.

17. There is yet another (which may be considered as the last) plea of the monopolist; for he may contend that notwithstanding a free-trade is proper for the world generally, yet, that *single states may find their advantage in monopolies, and be justified in pursuing them.* As I professe not to touch here upon topics of justice, and much less upon those of benevolence, I will not observe upon the liberality of such a position; especially as it is to be attacked in other modes. But I shall notice here (once for all) the oversight of those monopolists who pronounce monopoly *to be the plainest of all policies* and yet think that it will *escape the vigilance of their neighbours,* after the practice has been suggested by their own example and rendered contagious by revenge or the study of redress. So slight has been the attention paid either to events or to principles upon this occasion, that after foreigners have actually been seen imitating our national partialities on the one hand and resenting the injuries received from us on the other, the error in question has still survived. When nations have proved too wary to be pilfered by art, they have next been thought likely to be tamely submissive to force: And numerous parties are yet to be found, even in this improving age and country, who would commence or continue *wars for promoting trade;* although experience has shewn that enemies however ignorant are at least jealous, and that wars are often as fruitless to the particular traders for whom they are undertaken, as they are certainly onerous and devastating to other traders, and to the public that has to support them. Let me add in the next place, that when an exception from general rules is left in the power of each individual state, the peculiar benefits to be expected from such exception by any particular

nation

nation must naturally diminish; not only as exceptions assumed on one side, would then be balanced by the exceptions to be assumed on another; but as *all* would lose the advantages arising from liberal systems being pursued by *all*[*]; and the present unhappy system of selfishness and of hostility, would in consequence soon be revived. And when commercial wars either exist or are apprehended, the tranquillity of neighbouring countries is seldom to be deemed secure. In short, since states (like individuals) are too improvident, too intemperate, and too ambitious, to be freed from the rule of equal laws; and since monopolising systems are injurious, as well on account of their odiousness and their bad example to other countries, as of their domestic evil consequences; it is wise for all countries to submit in commerce to an universal system, which is not only incapable of perversion either by friends or enemies; but whenever it is once established, requires so little effort and intelligence to carry it on, that it may be said to be self-moving and self-conducted.

88   **CHAPTER IV.**

---

[*] See the statement of the general theory of commerce Chap. II. of this treatise and passim. There is indeed no European nation that has any pretensions to form the exception to general rules here alluded, if we are to judge from their past conduct; since they have not only each frequently yielded to evident misinformation on commercial subjects, but have each plunged themselves, in supporting monopolies, into expensive projects or cruel wars.

If it were here made a general question whether it would be for the happiness of the human race that *all* should seek to live upon their neighbours, or *all* should depend upon themselves and live fairly by their own endeavours; whether all should attempt to over-reach, or all endeavour to be equitable? The answer would be easy. Nor is it less easy to decide whether a system of commercial exceptions made in favour of all or a few, would not quickly terminate in a total abolition of commercial system, and introduce a lawless state?

CHAPTER IV.

IN the preceding chapter we have seen what are the pretences of a general nature in favor of restrictions in trade, which it has occurred to notice; and we have seen the replies. Our immediate fore-fathers therefore have been unhappily self-deluded respecting trade as well as respecting other particulars: and state-counsels (usually alas without system !) in this case going upon wrong systems, were obstinate and vindictive in the usual proportions. But to apply a fine expression here, "We "have lived upon the credit of those times too long." Our predecessors by their immense exertions have wrought indeed some benefit for their posterity, though comparatively but little, and that little inferior in kind and alloyed with serious evil. Right in attributing riches to industry, they were nevertheless wrong in fostering industry by force. Properly awake to their own interests, they were to blame to expect that other nations would be provoked, and yet remain asleep to theirs. Instead of attempting what was serviceable and within their reach, they sought chiefly what was novel and artificial. And their policy, which was in itself adverse to internal prosperity, became still more ruinous by the intervention of rivals; for when their administration was at any time supine, contraband undermined their unnatural system; and if over-active, this system generated foreign contests. Thus their love of commerce stifled commerce, as their love of lucre always betrayed them into profuse expences: and had it not been for vigorous principles of a totally different complexion*, conspiring to arrest or repair these mischiefs,

39

it

---

* Such as civilization, long and extensive experience, philosophical and chemical knowledge, the invention of printing, liberty in the middling and lower orders of people, the countenance of government,

it is difficult to say to what excesses they would not have extended.   In short, to interdict beneficial purchases and sales to subjects ; to excite similar interdictions on the parts of foreigners ; to keep up a chargeable apparatus for enforcing these purposes ; and to go to war for these preposterous objects ; bespeaks defects in our system of such a *magnitude*, that we may demonstrate the error of the principle from the nature of these results.   If other proof were wanting, we have only to inspect those kingdoms where monopoly has most raged, and we shall find agriculture every where still imperfect in them : though it is the pursuit of all others that is the least injured by arbitrary power, and that would have flourished with half the encouragement lavished on the frippery of trade. In some of these ill-fated kingdoms, their arts are infinitely more wretched than their agriculture ; and even in

40

England

---

the decline of monopoly-grants and also of corporation and feudal privileges, trading occupations being less reproachful than formerly, increasing religious toleration, commercial and maritime law, accumulated capitals of money and lowered interest, astonishing machinery, more perfect arts and in many cases better raw materials, various important advantages respecting fuel, buildings and other useful establishments provided at the cost of former ages, improved agriculture, known and extended markets, increased motives and opportunities of intercourse, regulated posts, established connections, bills and courses of exchange, bankers and banks, policies of insurance, with quays, known harbors, canals, superior roads, sea-charts, the mariner's compass and quadrant, and various astronomical inventions, &c. &c. all of which are articles that in their nature are independent of the monopoly-system of commerce.   When a monopolist therefore attributes to himself alone the modern improvement of European commerce, he becomes the boastful fly upon the chariot-wheel ; or rather, when he sets aside or disparages the influence of such benign causes as the above, and wishes us to trust to artifice and empiricism, he resembles the conceited cultivator, who should dream that by waterings, by hot-beds, and nostrums, he could be enabled to reject and supersede the light, the warmth, the air, the rains, and the dews of heaven.

England (in defiance of invigorating liberty, of favoring nature, successful wars, imperial rights, and dominions that are sufficiently expansive to embrace a variety of products*) many arts are still infant, many lands are still waste, more are ill-husbanded, and the *interest of money* attending our debts contracted in pursuit of monopolies, amounts to near *two thirds of the annual value of our favourite exports* (and certainly infinitely exceeds the *profits* upon those exports;) and if the constant public and individual loss sustained *internally* under the system of bounties and prohibitions, does not equal the other third of this amount, we seem to have enmities, jealousies, and projects enough still on foot, sooner or later to complete the afflicting total, unless we reform our system.

I shall only add, that if commercial freedom is advantageous for a nation's *own* concerns, it is if possible still more proper for qualifying it to conduct the concerns of *other nations.* Not only can those serve others on the *cheapest* terms, who have placed their own affairs to the best advantage; but a free trade must necessarily lend help to a trade of agency, by the supply it offers of wide correspondencies, ready markets, extensive assortments of goods, freights, experience, and various other facilities; as also by relieving it from the curb of every odious trade-law, not called for by retaliation. So that (military means out of the question) the only methods in which a nation can gain adventitious wealth, being first, by pushing its *natural* articles to the utmost, and then *exchanging* them with other nations who have done the like with theirs; or else secondly, by becoming *an agent* for other nations, (as their

41

artificer,

---

* " England has had so many connections in the four quarters of " the earth, as in effect to have enjoyed a *free* trade in a little world " of its own." *Anonym.*

artificer, carrier, factor, or accomptant;) it follows that the only two civil means of adding to the native stock of national wealth, require a free trade as their assistant. And with respect to *peace* (that still greater source of national œconomy and wealth) the preference of a free trade may be proved from history to be indispensible both to its real, as well as to its assured duration.

CHAPTER V.

Conclusion.

SUCH seems the general theory of what is eligible and what is injurious for trade. The application of this theory to old mis-shapen practice, fortified by prejudices, and in part deemed necessary for retaliation, is certainly an attempt at once delicate and arduous. Yet the rule of Montesquieu is still irrefragably true, "That "one nation should never exclude another from trading "with it, except for *very great reasons.*" And there can be no harm in proposing it as a problem to a minister, that he should endeavour to promote trade, without calling to his aid either restrictions, permanent bounties, or wars. If a virtuous glow should grandly seize his mind for amending the manners of his nation, not only the production and the exchange of commodities (which after all are the *two only constituents* of trade) would instantly increase, but other secret blessings would attend this reform to console his cares. But if, like other minions of fortune, he should slumber over the nobler duties of his situation, his country would still benefit by its being left

alone

alone to nature and itself; free from the chimeras of a court, the plausibilities of traders*, and the aversion to reforming errors so inveterate and notorious in persons in office. It can be no objection to a free trade, that it leaves room for inaction and for want of instruction in ministers; and ministers themselves will probably scarcely object to it on this account. Infinite however must be the discretion requisite in the interim, for changing that system externally and internally which now oppresses us; and those only ought to be intrusted with direction in it, who have been used to study the parts and the movements of a great society; a revolution in which, being little short of a new formation of it, as much requires a master's hand to lead it to a safe conclusion. *Justice*, I will only say, must form an indelible part of the plan, and justice includes not only authentic and timely warning, (whenever needful) of every change; but also public relief†, where no warning can remedy the positive ills which former laws

43   shall

---

* It is remarkable that England and Holland, though each the seat of so much trade, have produced few eminent writers on commercial subjects, except for particular branches, (such as fisheries, low interest of money, banks, commercial law, &c.) The original writers on trade of most esteem from having gone upon *general principles*, have chiefly been found in France and Scotland, where trade has formerly flourished but little, notwithstanding the laws always favored monopolies. The known influence of traders in commercial countries and the application often made of that influence, sufficiently elucidate the caution given in the text; for though Holland for example, has been more liberal in her home-market than England, yet even Holland has been equally bigotted with ourselves in her external systems.

† " Men in their innovations should follow the example of time " which innovateth but quietly, and by degrees scarce to be " perceived; for otherwise what is new and unlooked for, ever mends " some and improves others: and he that is holpen takes it for a " fortune and thanks the time, and he that is hurt for a wrong " and imputeth it to the author." *Lord Bacon's Essay.*

shall have imposed or invited. The subjects, trade, or commodities, that shall specially benefit by the meditated change, offer the first resource for supplying the indemnity in question; but if this resource fails, and if the public at large also refuses the burthen, the change proposed should itself be foregone; since a *few* persons should never be made to sustain that loss, which is thus held too grievous for the *many*. Happily there is nothing requisite, for which a willing administration and a confiding people cannot easily provide; and *half* the expence of *one* of those many commercial campaigns, which must otherwise be certainly repeated, would furnish a fund (with due time and management) adequate to relieve us from our complicated errors, if accompanied with patient address, and with that sort of contriving œconomy which is a most important state-accomplishment. I do not make myself too full of hopes on this subject, but I do not abandon myself to despair. Knowledge is increasing and truth daily approving itself: and as there are many vibrations in public concerns, in one of these we shall perhaps see the accomplishment of the wish here alluded to, distinctly pointed out, and happily effected. In the mean time, if truth is frequently obliged to give way to prejudices and to necessity, it will not be without its receiving manifold confirmations of its existence, as well as of the degree of its salutary tendency.

With respect to particular countries, there is scarcely any one in the universe which appears more fitted to profit by the system of free-trade than Great Britain; especially as a system of interchanges must favor her navigation. · Blessed with a happy climate, surrounded by seas from which she is in no part distant, placed between the old and new world, between northern and southern regions, possessing connections in various quarters of the globe; and boasting considerable liberality in her civil and religious government, considerable activity, consider-

able

able character, correspondencies, skill, capital, and shipping; she has the strongest grounds for confiding that
the same causes that have produced her present commercial
superiority, in defiance of her narrow politics, will attend
her more and more where favoured by liberal systems, the
folly of our neighbours especially considered. As fashions
prevail among courts and nations, as well as among
individuals, her new example would probably soon be
pursued spontaneously abroad, and more products in
consequence be brought into circulation through the
earth; and those nations in such case, who were most
active, most wise, and most rich, would derive most
profit from the revolution. To accelerate this happy
moment, she would naturally in many particulars, make
the extinction of her own prejudices a condition with
other nations, for the extinction of theirs; and if other
nations neglected to adopt her instructive lesson and
example, her benefit from her new line of conduct would
at least be peculiar and unrivalled. Should Great Britain
however from indolence or timidity decline to reform her
old established errors at present*, she may to a certainty
avoid all preposterous adherence to them in critical cases,
as well as all unnecessary violation of the true system in

45

new

---

* Many who would act wisely in new affairs, feel terrified at the
correction of antient errors. They are patients who would shun the
operation that is to restore their health, and as such, are treated
with some asperity by the moralist:

> " Unhappy race ! who never yet could tell
> " How near their good and happiness they dwell:
> " Fetter'd in faults, they seek not to be free,
> " But stupid, to their own sad fate agree;
> " Like pond'rous rolling-stones, oppress'd with ill,
> " *The weight that loads them makes them roll on still.*"
>
> Rowe's Translation of the Golden
Pythagorean Verses.

new and future occurrences; and time will gradually, it
is to be hoped, render easier the accomplishment of the
rest.

Every improvement that takes place, however slender
and retarded, is still a blessing; and let me here be
allowed to add, that it is the more to be prayed for on account of the benefit that may result to humanity at large,
were free-trade and pacific systems more generally prevailing. Nations might then no longer view each other
as strangers and as rivals; and individuals, learning more
and more their real public interests, might consider themselves not merely as the members of separate nations (a
sentiment which has hitherto seldom been the companion of
general liberality * or general justice,) but likewise as members

46

---

* Dr. Price has the following remarkable passage respecting the
love of one's country. " Foreign trade has in some respects the most
" useful tendency. By creating an intercourse between distant king-
" doms, it extends benevolence, removes local prejudices, leads every
" man to consider himself more as a citizen of the world than of any
" particular state, and consequently checks the excesses of that *Love*
" *of our Country* which has been applauded as one of the noblest,
" but which *really* is one of the most destructive principles in human
" nature." He then adds the following observations in a note. "The
" love of our country is then only a noble passion, when it engages
" us to promote the internal happiness of our country and to defend
" its rights and liberties against domestic and foreign invasion, main-
" taining at the same time an equal regard to the rights and liberties
" of other countries. But this has not been its most common effect :
" On the contrary, it has been nothing but a spirit of rivalship
" between different communities, producing contention and a thirst
" for conquest and dominion. What is *his country* to a Russian, a
" Turk, a Spaniard, &c. but a spot where he enjoys no right, and is
" disposed of by owners as if he was a beast ? And what is his *love*
" to his country, but an attachment to degradation and slavery ?
" What was the love of their country among the Jews, but a wretched
" partiality for themselves and a proud contempt for other nations ?
" Among the Romans also what was it, however great in many of
" its exertions, but a principle holding together a band of robbers

bers of the universe, and as the common children of a common father. That common Father cannot be pleased that the pretended interests of *artificial* commodities should be made a motive for disturbing either the good order which is said to be the basis of their own institution, or the peace of the general community of nature; nor can it be acceptable that his partial gifts, which (as having a local distribution accompanied with a general use) appear given in shares to each nation in trust for every other, should wantonly or maliciously be frustrated in their circulation, and even be made the cause of mutual devastation and bloodshed over the globe. Mr. Hume who considerably favors the liberal system, and considers the other as founded in "narrow and malignant politics," concludes his short Essay on the Jealousy of Trade with a declaration, which I shall not be afraid of making the conclusion of the present:—" I shall therefore venture to " acknowledge that not only as a *man,* but as a *British* " subject, I pray for the flourishing commerce of Ger- " many, Spain, Italy, and even *France* itself * * *."

47

" in their attempts to crush all liberty but their own ? Christianity " has wisely omitted to recommend this principle. Had it done " this, it would have countenanced a vice among mankind. It has " done what is infinitely better. It has recommended *Universal* " *Benevolence.*" See p. 74-5 of that edition of his *Observations on the Importance of the American Revolution,* &c. to which is annexed a *translation of the Will of M. Fortuné Ricard,* 1785.

If this very amiable and respectable author when speaking of trade, had limited his praises to a free-trade, they would have been better merited. But how unfortunate is it that his sentiments respecting patriotism, as it is commonly called, should appear singular, when they contain nothing but the language of sense and nature confirmed by every page in the history of nations.

INDEX.

C.

R.

S.

X.

THE END.

CL Press

A Fraser Institute Project

https://clpress.net/

Professor Daniel Klein (George Mason University, Economics and Mercatus Center) and Dr. Erik Matson (Mercatus Center), directors of the Adam Smith Program at George Mason University, are the editors and directors of CL Press. CL stands at once for classical liberal and conservative liberal.

CL Press is a project of the Fraser Institute (Vancouver, Canada).

CL Press includes a series called CL Reprints. CL Reprints was undertaken to make selected older works—no longer under copyright, chiefly—more available.

People:

Dan Klein and Erik Matson are the co-editors and executives of the imprint.

Jane Shaw Stroup is Editorial Advisor, doing especially copy-editing and text preparation.

Zachary Yost is Production Manager for CL Reprints.

An Advisory Board:

Jordan Ballor, *Center for Religion, Culture, and Democracy*

Caroline Breashears, *St. Lawrence Univ.*

Donald Boudreaux, *George Mason Univ.*

Ross Emmett, *Arizona State Univ.*

Knud Haakonssen, *Univ. of St. Andrews*

Björn Hasselgren, *Timbro, Uppsala Univ.*

Karen Horn, *Univ. of Erfurt*

Jimena Hurtado, *Univ. de los Andes*

Nelson Lund, *George Mason Univ.*

Daniel Mahoney, *Assumption Univ.*

Deirdre N. McCloskey, *Univ. of Illinois–Chicago*

Thomas W. Merrill, *American Univ.*

James Otteson, *Univ. of Notre Dame*

Catherine R. Pakaluk, *Catholic Univ. of America*

Sandra Peart, *Univ. of Richmond*

Mario Rizzo, *New York Univ.*

Loren Rotner, *Univ. of Austin*

Marc Sidwell, *New Culture Forum*

Craig Smith, *Univ. of Glasgow*

Emily Skarbek, *Brown Univ.*

David Walsh, *Catholic Univ. of America*

Richard Whatmore, *Univ. of St. Andrews*

Barry Weingast, *Stanford Univ.*

Lawrence H. White, *George Mason Univ.*

Amy Willis, *Liberty Fund*

Bart Wilson, *Chapman Univ.*

Todd Zywicki, *George Mason Univ.*

Why start CL Press?

CL Press publishes good, low-priced work in intellectual history, political theory, political economy, and moral philosophy. More specifically, CL Press explores and advance discourse in the following areas:

- The intellectual history and meaning of liberalism.
- The relationship between liberalism and conservatism.
- The role of religion in disseminating liberal understandings and institutions including: humankind's ethical universalism, the moral equality of souls, the rule of law, religious liberty, the meaning and virtues of economic life.
- The relationship between religion and economic philosophy.
- The political, social, and economic philosophy of the Scottish Enlightenment, especially Adam Smith.

www.ingramcontent.com/pod-product-compliance
Lightning Source LLC
Chambersburg PA
CBHW011922050726

47591CB00009B/2304